AF758544

A POLITICAL AND ECONOMIC DICTIONARY OF AFRICA

A POLITICAL AND ECONOMIC DICTIONARY OF AFRICA

FIRST EDITION

David Seddon

with Daniel Seddon-Daines

Routledge
Taylor & Francis Group
LONDON AND NEW YORK

First Edition 2005
Routledge
Haines House, 21 John Street, London WC1N 2BP, United Kingdom
(A member of the Taylor & Francis Group)

© Routledge 2005

All rights reserved. No part of this publication may be photocopied, recorded, or otherwise reproduced, stored in a retrieval system or transmitted in any form or by any electronic or mechanical means without the prior permission of the copyright owner.

ISBN 1 85743 213 4 24109045

Development Editor: Cathy Hartley
Copy Editor and Proof-reader: Simon Chapman

Typeset in Times New Roman 10/12

The publishers make no representation, express or implied, with regard to the accuracy of the information contained in this book and cannot accept any legal responsibility for any errors or omissions that may take place.

Typeset by AJS Solutions, Huddersfield – Dundee
Printed and bound by MPG Books, Ltd, Bodmin, Cornwall

UNIVERSITY OF BIRMINGHAM LIBRARY

FOREWORD

This **POLITICAL AND ECONOMIC DICTIONARY OF AFRICA** considers the whole of the continent. It is common to make a distinction between North Africa and Africa south of the Sahara, or sub-Saharan Africa, on the grounds that economically, politically and culturally, the countries and peoples of North Africa are more closely related to and involved with those of the Middle East than those of sub-Saharan Africa. But North Africa has always been linked to the rest of Africa, by the trans-Saharan trade and by cultural, social and political relationships of various kinds. Even today, when state borders are generally better defined, there are vast areas of the Saharan region across which flow people, funds and commodities in a wide variety of different transactions, both legal and illegal, linking the north with the rest of Africa. Also, there have been many initiatives over the last few decades to create pan-African institutions, most of which involve the governments and states of North Africa as well as those of sub-Saharan African, including the Organization of African Unity and its successor the African Union. One of the most recent initiatives for the development of the African continent, the New Partnership for Africa's Development (NEPAD), includes countries of north and south, east and west, across the continent.

There are, nevertheless, important regional groupings within the continent into which the numerous individual states are often divided: North Africa and sub-Saharan Africa are the two most 'inclusive'. Others are: West Africa, the Horn of Africa, East Africa, Central Africa and Southern Africa. But in addition to these quasi-geographical groupings are numerous associations and institutions established to promote close economic, social, cultural and/or political ties and linkages. Some of these have a real vitality and have become more or less effective associations; others exist for the most part as bureaucracies or even 'paper' institutions with little real effective capacity or significant activity.

In addition to the independent states of Africa there are also several territories whose status is more complicated, such as the Spanish praesidios of Ceuta and Melilla, the British Indian Ocean Territory, Mayotte (Mahore), which remains under French authority, 'Somaliland', which declared its independence of Somalia in 1991, Western Sahara, whose status is disputed and which remains the one major piece of unfinished post-colonial business, and Zanzibar, now part of the United Republic of Tanzania.

Some entries, notably those relating to the North African countries and Western Sahara, overlap with those in the companion volume, *A Political and Economic Dictionary of the Middle East*, which includes North Africa as part of the Middle East.

Entries are arranged alphabetically, and cross-referencing between entries is indicated by the simple and widely familiar device of using a bold typeface for those words or entities which have their own coverage.

David Seddon, October 2005

ACKNOWLEDGEMENTS

The compilation of this dictionary was achieved during 2004 and 2005, with the very considerable assistance of my son, Daniel Seddon-Daines, who managed to find time during a very busy first year as an undergraduate reading Geography at the University of Cambridge to provide a significant additional input. Earlier assistance was provided by Leo Zeilig, now of Brunel University, who provided a preliminary entry for each of the Francophone countries of sub-Saharan Africa, and by Tom Skinner, a graduate of the School of Development Studies at the University of East Anglia.

I am also grateful to Cathy Hartley of Routledge, who, as commissioning editor of the Europa Political and Economic Dictionaries series, initiated the process and saw it through to publication, and to Simon Chapman, who acted as copy editor and read the proofs. Omissions and other inadequacies are my responsibility, but readers are invited to make constructive suggestions for future editions.

ABBREVIATIONS

Adm.	Admiral
BCE	Before the Common Era
b/d	barrels per day
Capt.	Captain
Co	Company
Col	Colonel
Corpn	Corporation
DC	District of Columbia
e.g.	exempli gratia (for example)
FAO	Food and Agriculture Organization
GDP	Gross Domestic Product
Gen.	General
GNI	Gross National Income
Gov.	Governor
km	kilometre(s)
Lt	Lieutenant
Ltd	Limited
m	metre(s)
m.	million
Maj.	Major
MP(s)	Member(s) of Parliament
NGO	Non-Governmental Organization
Pres.	President
rtd	retired
Sgt	Sergeant
UK	United Kingdom
UN	United Nations
UNDP	United Nations Development Programme
UNESCO	United Nations Educational, Scientific and Cultural Organization
UNICEF	United Nations Children's Fund
US	United States
USA	United States of America
USS	United States Ship
USSR	Union of Soviet Socialist Republics
WHO	World Health Organization

TRANSCRIPTION OF ARABIC NAMES

Arabic names occurring in the entries of this book have been rendered in the system most commonly used by British and American Orientalists, but with the omission of the diacritical signs. The system used is a transliteration—i.e. it is based on the writing, which is standard throughout the Arab world, and not on the pronunciation, which varies from place to place. In a few cases consistency has been sacrificed in order to avoid replacing a familiar and accepted form by another which, although more accurate, would be unrecognizable.

Sun- and Moon-Letters

In Arabic pronunciation, when the word to which the definite article, *al*, is attached begins with one of certain letters called 'Sun-letters', the *l* of the article changes to the initial letter in question, e.g. *al-shamsu* (the sun) is pronounced *ash-shamsu*; *al-rajulu* (the man) is pronounced *ar-rajulu*. Accordingly, in this book, where the article is attached to a word beginning with a Sun-letter, it has been rendered phonetically.

There are 14 Sun-letters in the Arabic alphabet, which are transcribed as: d, dh, n, r, s, sh, t, th, z, zh (d, s, t and z and their emphatic forms are not differentiated in this book). The remaining 15 letters in the Arabic alphabet are known as 'Moon-letters'.

A

Abacha, Gen. Sani

Gen. Sani Abacha took power in Nigeria through a military coup. His regime was characterized by serious human rights abuses, the most notorious being the execution of **Ken Saro-Wiwa**, the leader of the **Ogoni** human rights movement, and eight associates in 1995. Abacha's death in May 1998 and the elevation of **Gen. Abdulsalami Abubakir** to Head of State led to immediate changes, such as the release of political prisoners, a commitment to hand over power to an elected civilian government and the repeal of many restrictions, including those on freedom of expression. The inauguration of **Olusegun Obasanjo** as President of Nigeria on 29 May 1999, following elections, and the swearing in of a new National Assembly, marked the beginning of a new era and the longest period of civilian rule that Nigeria has enjoyed since **independence**.

Abbas, Ferhat

Ferhat Abbas and his followers initially developed a form of anti-colonial politics, which accepted the constitutional framework of French rule but sought equal civil and political rights for Muslim Algerians. First President (ceremonial) of Algeria, when the country achieved **independence** in 1962.

Abboud, Gen. Ibrahim

Gen. Ibrahim Abboud led a military coup to take power in Sudan in 1958. Under his regime the situation in the southern provinces of Sudan deteriorated drastically. In October 1964 Abboud's regime was itself overthrown. Having shared power for a few weeks with a civilian administration, Abboud resigned in favour of a transitional coalition of intellectuals and re-emergent politicians, which was itself replaced in early 1965 by a coalition of political groupings dominated by the **Umma Party**—which consolidated its position at elections held in April. This government was, in turn, overthrown in 1969 by **Gaafar Muhammad Nimeri**.

Abdel Aziz, Muhammad

President of the **Sahrawi Arab Democratic Republic** and secretary-general of the **Frente Popular para la Liberación de Saguia el-Hamra y Río de Oro (Frente POLISARIO—Popular Front for the Liberation of Saguia el-Hamra and Río de Oro)**. Abdel Aziz has led the Front since the mid-1970s and has been President of the Republic since it was proclaimed in February 1976.

Abubakir, Gen. Abdulsalami

The death of **Gen. Sani Abacha** of Nigeria in May 1998 led to the elevation of Gen. Abdulsalami Abubakir to Head of State. Gen. Abubakir played a crucial role in the restoration of civilian rule and the establishment of a less oppressive regime. The inauguration of **Olusegun Obasanjo** as President of Nigeria on 29 May 1999, following elections, and the swearing in of a new National Assembly, marked the beginning of a new era and the longest period of civilian rule that Nigeria has enjoyed since **independence**.

Abyssinia

Old name for Ethiopia. Used by the Italians during their occupation of the country.

Acção Democrática Independente (ADI—Independent Democratic Action)

Political party in São Tomé and Príncipe.

Acción Democrática y Progresista (ADP—Democratic and Progressive Action)

Political party in Equatorial Guinea.

Acheampong, Col I. K.

Prime Minister of Ghana in 1972–78. Col Acheampong was the chairman of the army committee (the National Redemption Council) that overthrew the long-time leader of the **United Party** and Prime Minister of Ghana in 1969–72, **Dr Kofi A. Busia**. This well-intentioned group struggled with economic problems that were aggravated by steep rises in the price of **oil** and other essential imports, and by consequent rises in the cost of living. By 1978 Acheampong's regime had become corrupt and ineffective. He was ousted by **Gen. F. W. K. Akuffo**, who held power for less than a year himself.

ACP – *see* African, Caribbean and Pacific countries

Action for Meritocracy and Equal Opportunity Party (AMEC)

Political party in Cameroon, led by Joachim Tabi Owono.

Action tchadienne pour l'unité et le socialisme (ACTUS—Chadian Action for Unity and Socialism)

Political party in Chad, led by Fidel Moungar.

Adja

An ethnic group which, together with the **Fon**, constitutes 40% of the population of Benin.

Afewerki, Issaias

President of Eritrea. Born in 1945, Issaias Afewerki joined the Eritrean Liberation Front in 1966. He received military training in China in the same year, then went on to be deputy divisional commander. In 1970 he co-founded the Eritrean People's Liberation Forces (EPLF, Eritrean People's Liberation Front from 1977) and in 1987 he was elected as secretary-general of the EPLF. In 1993 he was elected as President of independent Eritrea. Once an ally of the Ethiopian Prime Minister, **Meles Zenawi**, Issaias purports to favour economic integration with Ethiopia. Under Afewerki, Eritrea is, in effect, a military dictatorship. His government argues that the suppression of freedoms is necessary in a country 'at an early stage of development'.

Africa

Originally a term used by the Greeks to refer generally to the land mass south of the Mediterranean. Subsequently used by the Romans to refer particularly to that part of **North Africa** that is today Tunisia (as opposed to Numidia, roughly present-day Algeria, and Libya), but also more generally to refer to northern Africa. Used today broadly of the continent that lies south of the Mediterranean. It is often roughly divided into regions—e.g. **North Africa**, the Horn of Africa, **East Africa**, West Africa, Central Africa and **Southern Africa**. The major conventional division is between North Africa and **sub-Saharan Africa**, although a number of countries incorporate areas of the Sahara within their boundaries. Those countries lying immediately to the south of the Sahara, but which include areas of desert, are often referred to as the Sahel ('desert fringe') or the Sahelian countries. Sudan (which means 'the south') is sometimes included as part of the Sahel although more usually this term is used for the former French territories of Senegal, Burkina Faso, Mali, Niger and Chad. Africa extends for approximately 8,000 km from the **Maghreb** to South Africa (north to south) and for some 10,300 miles across from Senegal to Somalia—with a population in sub-Saharan Africa of some 700m. and a further 250m. or so in North Africa, so that the total amounts to close to1,000m. people. However, the continent is relatively poor in global terms, with a total annual gross domestic product (GDP) of less than US $500,000m. A typical African country has a GDP of $2,000m.–3,000m., equivalent to that of a medium-sized town in a rich country. Moreover, average per caput incomes are now lower than in South Asia, which some 20–30 years ago was equally poor. One of Africa's disadvantages is the relatively large number of states—more than 50, the precise number depending on what is counted as an independent state. This has made it difficult to develop even regional international trade, let alone a pan-African economic system. Trade barriers have been dismantled: the unweighted tariff is now 16%, compared with about 30% in 1990. However, those states that have reduced or removed tariffs have often also erected other barriers, such as discriminatory taxes on imported products that provide nearly the same degree of protection. Not all trade barriers are of the legal kind. Bad roads and poor communications; bureaucratic red tape, both official and unofficial; and other impediments to the easy movement of goods and services all restrict economic exchanges between African countries. Furthermore, African goods sold in countries that are members of the Organization of Economic Co-operation and Development (OECD) face tariffs that are roughly 10 times greater than those levied on goods traded within the OECD. Barriers are greatest in areas where Africa, with its vast land area and relatively cheap workers, has a comparative advantage, namely agricultural goods and textiles. Rich countries subsidize their farmers by some $320,000m. annually. Combined with high tariffs and small quotas for many farm products, this makes it extremely difficult for African farmers to export to rich countries. Heavy reliance on the export of primary goods, notably minerals, has tied many African economies to the fluctuations and generally downward trend of prices for such goods on world markets. Broadly, the terms of trade have not helped African economies generate from their exports the foreign exchange badly needed for investment and growth.

Foreign direct investment (FDI) in Africa is low in comparison with investment in other parts of the developing world. Political instability, bureaucratic red tape and **corruption**, limited domestic markets and the absence of large regional markets all contribute to a landscape that is generally inimical to private FDI. This may, however, be starting to change. One important source of FDI is South Africa. With sanctions gone, South African firms now invest more in the rest of Africa than elsewhere—about $1,000m. annually since 1994. Pepkor, South Africa's largest retailer, for example, has expanded recently into Zambia and Mozambique; while South African Brewery, which bought a controlling share in the state-owned Tanzanian Brewery in 1993, managed to triple its output in five years and, moreover, make a healthy profit. Another new source of investment is the People's Republic of China—described by Global Witness, a United Kingdom-based campaigning group, as 'the new resource colonialists in Africa'—which is investing heavily in mining, in Angola and Liberia for example, and in **oil**, in Sudan.

Malaysian textile enterprise Ramatex has invested in Namibia, from where it plans to serve the world's garment market. Prospects for the future may prove better than the experience of the past.

Africa has suffered in recent decades from considerable political instability. In the early period after **independence**, **changes of government** by *coups d'état* were significantly more frequent than by any other means. During the 1980s and 1990s border conflicts and civil wars—often referred to as 'complex political emergencies'—involved and affected numerous African states and their peoples, undermining development policies and programmes, reducing rates of growth and deterring FDI.

In the past few years, however, several of the longer-running conflicts have apparently ended and some of the most extensive seem to have been reduced in scale. Angola and Sierre Leone are at peace. The border war between Ethiopia and Eritrea has ceased. The war in the Democratic Republic of the Congo, the worst anywhere since the end of the Second World War, is formally over. Liberia's warlord, **Charles Taylor**, has been driven into exile. In Sudan, despite the conflict in **Darfur**, the overall situation has been improved by the conclusion of a peace accord between the government and the rebel Sudan People's Liberation Army. On the other hand, sporadic but brutal conflict continues in Burundi, Côte d'Ivoire and eastern Congo. There is still a risk that new wars may begin, or old ones reignite, for many of the causes of Africa's political instability have yet to be resolved.

Also, one of the scourges of contemporary Africa—**HIV/AIDS**—continues to affect morbidity and mortality rates across the sub-continent, in central, eastern and southern Africa in particular. Current UN estimates suggest that there is a total of about 26.6m. HIV-infected people in sub-Saharan Africa and a number not far short of 30m. in the whole of Africa. However, recent studies suggest that these figures may over-estimate the prevalence of HIV/AIDS in Africa, and that the real figure (bad enough!) for sub-Saharan Africa is closer to 21m. Models based on testing pregnant women and then extrapolating (so-called 'sentinel' models) may suffer from inherent upward bias, compared with those based on samples drawn from the whole population. Refined models using sentinel studies have also begun to suggest that estimates of prevalence made in the late 1990s may have been too high. Even the more conservative figures, however, imply a major epidemic and substantial social and economic consequences. In most of the heavily-affected countries, life expectancy has fallen dramatically over the last two decades as the impact of HIV/AIDS has been felt. HIV infection increases vulnerability to other diseases and so raises morbidity. Given the poor state of the health services and support services in most African countries, the negative effect on the health status of the population is significant. The fact that young adults are the majority of those infected has also had negative repercussions across the economy, in **agriculture** and other production and service sectors, and in terms of aggregate demand for goods and services.

Africa Reinsurance Corporation (ARC)

Known as Africa-Re, the ARC started operations in 1978. Its purpose is to foster the development of the insurance and reinsurance industry in Africa and to promote the growth of national and regional underwriting capacities. It has an authorized capital of US $50m., of which the **African Development Bank (ADB)** holds 10%. It has 12 directors, one of whom is appointed by the ADB. Its members include 41 African countries, the ADB and some 90 insurance and reinsurance companies.

African Action Plan

At its summit in Kananaskis, Canada, in June 2002, the **G8** released details of its Africa Action Plan, in response to the **New Partnership for Africa's Development** initiative.

African, Caribbean and Pacific countries (ACP)

From 1976 until 2000 the principal means of co-operation between the **European Union (EU)** and developing countries were the successive Lomé conventions, concluded by the EU and the group of African, Caribbean and Pacific (ACP) states. A total of 44 African states are members: Angola, Benin, Botswana, Burkina Faso, Burundi, Cameroon, Cape Verde, Central African Republic, Chad, Comoros, the Democratic Republic of the Congo, the Republic of the Congo, Côte d'Ivoire, Djibouti, Eritrea, Ethiopia, Gabon, Gambia, Ghana, Guinea, Guinea-Bissau, Lesotho, Liberia, Madagascar, Malawi, Mali, Mauritania, Mauritius, Mozambique, Namibia, Niger, Nigeria, Rwanda, São Tomé and Príncipe, Senegal, Sierra Leone, Somalia, Sudan, Swaziland, Tanzania, Togo, Uganda, Zambia and Zimbabwe. The First **Lomé Convention** (Lomé I) that came into force in April 1976 replaced the last of the **Yaoundé Conventions** and the Arusha Agreement, and was designed to provide a new framework of co-operation, taking into account the varying needs of developing countries. Lomé II was concluded at Lomé, Togo, in October 1979, and came into force in January 1981. Lomé III was signed in December 1984 and came into force in March 1985 (trade provisions) and May 1985 (aid). The Fourth Lomé Convention, which had a 10-year commitment period, was signed in December 1989; its trade provisions entered into force in March 1990, and the remainder followed in November 1991. In February 2000 negotiations on a successor arrangement to the Lomé Convention were concluded. The new partnership accord was signed by ACP and EU Heads of State or government in Cotonou, Benin, in June 2000, and was to enter into force following ratification by the European Parliament and ACP national legislatures. Pending the entry into force of the **Cotonou Agreement** and the conclusion of the new economic and trade arrangements, existing EU-ACP preferential trade agreements remained in effect. The ACP-EU institutions include the Council of Ministers (one member from each signatory state), the Committee of Ambassadors, the Joint Assembly, the Secretariat, the

Centre for the Development of Enterprise and the Technical Centre for Agricultural and Rural Co-operation.

African Christian Democratic Party

A conservative, largely white political party in South Africa, which gained one seat in the National Assembly in the 1999 elections.

African crisis

By the 1970s it had become clear that African economies in general were performing less well than economies in other regions, and during the 1980s, when the global economy was gradually recovering from the recession of the late 1970s and early 1980s, it became apparent that Africa's recovery was not taking place as anticipated. Many began to speak of a distinctively 'African' crisis and to seek explanations for this supposed distinctiveness. For some, the emphasis was on the international economy and the ways in which African economies were integrated at a disadvantage within that system, given their heavy reliance on primary products; for others, the 'crisis' was more centrally related to structural problems—economic and political—within Africa, and within most of the African countries. The language of 'crisis' was resisted by some, but images of **drought**, floods, **HIV/AIDS** and conflict, combined with the statistics of population growth, slow and even negative economic growth and increasing inequalities, continued to be pervasive throughout the 1990s and into the 21st century. One of the major disadvantages of the language of 'crisis' is that it not only underestimates the progress achieved in the last few decades, but also presents a homogenous vision of 'Africa', and fails to recognize the enormous heterogeneity of African economies and societies.

African Development Bank (ADB)

Established in 1964, the African Development Bank (ADB) began operations in 1966, with the aim of financing economic and social development in African countries. African members (from **North Africa** and **sub-Saharan Africa**) total 53 in number and non-African members 24. The ADB's primary goal is currently to reduce **poverty** and improve living standards by mobilizing resources both in and outside of Africa, and by providing financial and technical assistance for development projects and programmes in Africa. At the continental level, its vision focuses on economic integration, while at the country level, three broad policy priority themes are predominant: agricultural and rural development, human resources development, and private-sector development. The highest policy-making body of the Bank is the Board of Governors—each member country nominates a governor and an alternate governor. The Board meets once a year and elects its Board of Directors and president. The Board of Directors consists of 18 members (of whom six are non-African) whose term of service is three years. This Board meets once a week. The ADB group of development financing institutions comprises the **African Development Fund (ADF)** and the Nigeria Trust Fund (NTF), which provide concessionary loans, and the ADB itself. The group uses a unit of account worth slightly more than US $1. Initially the capital stock was exclusively open for subscription by African countries, but in 1978 the governors agreed to open the stock to subscription by non-regional states on the basis of nine principles aimed at maintaining the African character of the institution. This decision was finally ratified in May 1982 and the participation of non-African states became effective in December. African countries still held two-thirds of the share capital and loan operations were limited to African members. The Bank's president is always an African national. In May 1998 the Board of Governors approved an increase in capital of 35% and resolved that the non-African members' share be increased from 33.3% to 40%. A new credit policy, adopted in May 1995, effectively disqualified 39 low-income African states deemed to be non-creditworthy from receiving non-concessional ADB funding, in an attempt to reduce the accumulation of arrears. In 1997 it adopted a Supplementary Financing Mechanism (which became effective in March 1998) to provide countries eligible for ADF funds with quick-disbursing resources to meet interest payments on outstanding Bank debt. Sectors receiving the greater proportion of loans from the ADB are **agriculture**, transport, multi-sector activities and finance. By 2000 the ADB group had disbursed a total of 27,592.59m. units of account in loans and grants since operations began in 1967.

African Development Fund (ADF)

The African Development Fund (ADF), part of the **African Development Bank (ADB)** group, began operations in 1974. It grants interest-free loans to low-income African countries for projects with repayment over 50 years (including a 10-year grace period) and with an annual service charge of 0.75%. Grants for project feasibility studies are made to the poorest countries. In May 1994 donor countries withheld any new funds, owing to dissatisfaction with the ADB's governance. In May 1996, following institutional reforms to strengthen the Bank's financial management and decision-making capacity and to reduce its administrative costs, an agreement was concluded on the seventh replenishment. The ADF aimed to provide concessional assistance to 42 African countries during 1996–98 and the seventh replenishment provided for an ADF Microfinance Initiative, initially for a two-year period, to support small-scale capacity-building projects.

African Export-Import Bank

Established in 1993 and known as Afreximbank, the African Export-Import Bank aims to increase the volume of African exports and to expand intra-African trade by financing exporters and importers directly and indirectly through trade finance institutions, such as commercial banks.

African Growth and Opportunity Act

The primary instrument of US policy towards Africa, a law which provides a 'preferential' framework designed to encourage greater trade between the USA and Africa, largely by opening African markets to US foreign direct investment and allowing 'preferential treatment' in return. To become eligible for help African countries must bring about 'a market-based economy that protects private property rights', 'the elimination of trade barriers to US trade and investment', and 'a conducive environment for US foreign policy interests'. In return they will be allowed preferential treatment for some of their products in US markets. The emphasis is on 'some'. Clothing factories in Africa, for example, will be allowed to sell their products to the USA as long as they use fabrics 'wholly formed and cut in the United States', or if they avoid direct competition with US products. The Act is very specific. For example, garments containing elastic strips are eligible only if the elastic is 'less than 1 inch in width and used in the production of brassieres'. Even with these restrictions, African countries will no longer be afforded preferential treatment if it results in 'a surge in imports'. The arrangements are classified as part of US aid to Africa. The Act instructs the USAID to help develop 'a receptive environment for trade and investment' and its implementation has been confided to the Corporate Council on Africa, a lobby group representing the interests of large US corporations.

African Institute for Economic Development and Planning (AIEDP)

Established in 1963 by the **Economic Commission for Africa** in collaboration with UNESCO, FAO, WHO and the UNDP, the AIEDP had its headquarters in Dakar, Senegal. The centre exists for the study of African development problems and for the training of specialists and government personnel involved in planning and development.

African Mission in Burundi (AMIB)

The **African Union**'s peace-keeping operation in Burundi, undertaken during 2003 and 2004 and transferred to the UN's ONUB in 2004–05.

African Muslims

Millions of Africans are Muslims. The vast majority are in the North African countries, but a sizeable proportion are to be found in countries south of the Sahara. In West Africa, nearly half of the total population of Nigeria (around 115m. people) are Muslims. In Niger Muslims account for about 85% of the total population (11m.). In Senegal more than 30% of a total of 16m. are Muslims. In Ethiopia about

30% of the total population of 63m. are Muslims, and in Sudan about 70% out of a total of 31m.

African National Congress (ANC)

The African National Congress (ANC) of South Africa was founded in 1912, when Pixley ka Seme summoned 'African leaders' of all kinds to fight the iniquitous Land Act, from the small, educated élite of the day to an array of tribal chiefs and elders. It has always been an alliance of disparate elements brought together for the common purpose of fighting racial oppression. When later it drew in white, coloured and Indian leftists and formed an alliance with trade unionists and communists, it became even more eclectic and necessarily developed a tradition of robust internal debate. It was an organization that the young **Nelson Mandela** aptly described as 'an African parliament'. In exile, the range of ideological elements widened still further, as members became scattered across the global diaspora and subject to a variety of local influences. Overall, the centre of gravity was firmly to the left, but on many crucial issues—for example, economic policy—there was no clear, consistent and coherent position. Only on fighting racialism and repression—the struggle against **apartheid**—was there clear agreement and commitment. When the ANC came to power in 1990, the **Freedom Charter** of 35 years earlier was still the only major official statement of overall intent, including economic policy. Only in the mid-1980s, when the great uprising in the black townships began to attract international attention and visibly threaten the apartheid regime, did the exiled leadership begin to focus more on policy issues inside the country and for the future.

African Peer Review Mechanism (APRM)

The APRM is a voluntary appraisal mechanism of national governments' economic and political performance by fellow Africans. The assembly of the **Pan-African Parliament**, which was launched in 2004 when African leaders vowed to improve governance and alleviate **poverty** in Africa, passed a resolution at its session in March 2005, calling on national parliaments to urge their governments to accede to APRM as a demonstration of their commitment to **democracy** and good governance in Africa. The APRM requires that each country's review report and recommended plan of action be publicly tabled in the Parliament. At every successive sitting, the assembly should compel MPs from APRM countries to report on their governments' progress in implementing the national action plan in the five-year period between the reviews.

African socialism

African socialism, like **Arab socialism**, has emphasized the possibility of radical economic and social reform and change, and above all, modernization. It has drawn heavily on both European traditions of national socialism and conceptions of 'traditional' pre-colonial African society as founded on various forms of collective and community-based interaction, without clear-cut and antagonistic 'class divisions'. Regimes which have espoused the notion of African socialism have tended to emphasize the importance of national unity, strictly limiting and controlling the extent to which different interests may be expressed (through trades unions, political parties, etc.), often banning such organizations entirely in favour of a 'national front' or single party supposedly representing 'the people' as a whole. A classic example is that of Tanzania under President **Julius Nyerere**, whose concept of *ujamaa* was an expression of a form of African socialism.

African stock exchange(s)

The establishment of a pan-African stock exchange in the long term is being brought closer by efforts by the Johannesburg Securities Exchange in South Africa to create a virtual regional exchange in the near future. The South African stock exchange has shared a trading system with neighbouring Namibia since 1997. Now Ghana, Zambia and Zimbabwe, are also considering listing their companies on a separate African segment in Johannesburg. Many of the existing stock exchanges in African countries are tiny, listing only a handful of companies and operating for just a few minutes a week. But, despite their small size and vulnerability to exchange rate difficulties, they are attracting outside attention, especially from African-American investors. In all, some 2,200 African companies are listed on the African continent's various exchanges. Half of the continent's 21 exchanges have been opened in the last dozen years. In Accra, a local company, Databank, invests in stock markets in Ghana itself, Nigeria, Botswana and Kenya that consistently rank among the world's top growth markets. Botswana, with its A-plus credit rating, boast one of the highest per caput government savings rates in the world, surpassed only by Singapore and a handful of other fiscally prudent nations. Ghana's stock exchange also regularly tops the list of the world's highest performing stock markets; in 2003 it was the fastest-growing in the world. A joint bourse already exists for eight mainly Francophone countries of West Africa—Benin, Burkina Faso, Côte d'Ivoire, Guinea-Bissau, Mali, Niger, Senegal and Togo. So far, 10 exchanges have agreed to find ways of co-operating more closely with Johannesburg. A regional exchange would create greater liquidity by making stocks available to a wider range of investors. Given the right technology and co-ordinated trading regulations, one bourse might suffice for all transactions. Already a close link is being developed between the Johannesburg stock exchange and the London Stock Exchange (LSE), whose electronic trading system the South African bourse already shares. The LSE also already carries the primary listings of several major South African companies.

African Union (AU)

Successor to the **Organization of African Unity (OAU)**. An extraordinary summit meeting, convened in September 1999 in Sirte, Libya, at the request of the Libyan leader **Col Muammar al-Qaddafi**, determined to establish an African Union (AU), based on the principles and objectives of the OAU and the African Economic Community (AEC), but furthering African co-operation, development and integration. Heads of State declared their positive commitment, and in July 2000, at the annual summit meeting of the OAU, 27 Heads of State and Government signed the draft Constitutive Act of the African Union, which was to enter into force one month after ratification by two-thirds of member states' legislatures. In May 2001 the Constitutive Act of the AU duly entered into force, and in July 2002 the Union became fully operational, replacing the OAU, which had been founded in 1963. The AU operates on the basis of both the Constitutive Act and the Abuja treaty of May 1994 establishing the AEC. The AU aims to support unity, solidarity and peace among African states, to promote and defend African common positions on issues of shared interest, to encourage human rights, democratic principles and good governance, to advance the development of member states by promoting research and by working to eradicate preventable diseases, and to promote sustainable development and political and socio-economic integration, including co-ordinating and harmonizing policies between the continent's various regional economic communities. In July 2001 the OAU adopted a New African Initiative, which was subsequently renamed the **New Partnership for Africa's Development (NEPAD)** and launched in October 2001. NEPAD is ultimately answerable to the AU Assembly. The first Assembly of Heads of State of the African Union was held in July 2002. One of its first acts was to suspend Madagascar from meetings of the Union, despite growing international recognition of the new **Ravalomanana** administration. In March 2004 the AU announced a plan to establish its own Security Council, with a standing army, to prevent or resolve civil conflicts in the African continent.

Afrikaans

The language, related to Dutch, spoken by the **Afrikaners** of South Africa.

Afrikaanse Weerstandsbeweging (AWB—Afrikaner Resistance Movement)

Right-wing Afrikaner extremist movement, led by **Eugene Terre'Blanche**, which for many years attempted to oppose the black African resistance movement and then, after the political transition in 1994, continued to try to obstruct the new government and its agenda.

Afrikaners

Term used for the descendants of the Dutch settlers in South Africa, who speak **Afrikaans** and consider themselves a distinct people of South Africa. Represented very largely during the period 1948–94 by the **National Party** of South Africa.

Sometimes called 'the white tribe of Africa'. The Afrikaners represent some 60% of the white population of South Africa, while the remaining 40% are English speakers.

Afrique équatoriale française (French Equatorial Africa)

Former French colonial territory, established in 1910, comprising Gabon, **Middle Congo** (now the Republic of the Congo),**Oubangui Chari** (now the Central African Republic) and Chad.

Afrique occidentale française – *see* French West Africa

Agence française de développement (AFD—French Development Agency)

Established in 1941, the Agence française de développement (AFD) was formerly the Caisse française de développement (CFD—French Development Fund). It is a French development bank which lends to member states and former member states of the **Franc Zone** and several other states, and executes the financial operations of the Fonds d'aide et de coopération (Aid and Co-operation Fund). Following the devaluation of the **Communauté financière africaine (African Financial Community)** franc in January 1994, the French government cancelled some 25,000m. French francs in **debt** arrears owed by member states to the CFD. The CFD established a Special Fund for Development and the Exceptional Facility for Short-Term Financing to help alleviate the immediate difficulties resulting from the devaluation. In early 1994 the CFD made available substantial funds to assist in the establishment of the **Communauté économique et monétaire de l'Afrique centrale (Economic and Monetary Community of Central Africa)**. It serves as the secretariat for the Fonds français pour l'environnement mondial (French Fund for the World Environment), created in 1994. Since 2000 the AFD has been implementing France's support for the **World Bank**'s **Heavily Indebted Poor Countries initiative**.

Agriculture

Most of the African economies remain heavily dependent on their agricultural sectors for the subsistence needs of their populations—particularly on dryland farming and pastoralism. In Mauritania, for example, the agricultural sector contributes more than 20% of the gross domestic product. Some (Mauritania, for example) are unable, however, to provide sufficient food for their populations and are obliged to import supplies. There has been increasing pressure on African economies since **independence** to develop cash cropping for export (as well as for growing urban domestic markets), but often they have relied very heavily on particular single crops for foreign exchange (e.g. **cotton**, **cocoa**, **coffee**, tea and tobacco) making them vulnerable to fluctuations in the prices of those commodities, many of which are produced by a wide range of competitors, in Africa and elsewhere. North African economies, which tended to concentrate on producing vegetables and fruit for the European market, have experienced intense competition in the last decades, not only from other non-European Mediterranean countries but also from countries joining the European Community. Despite investment in irrigation in several African countries, particularly in the 1960s and 1970s, the bulk of the sector remains heavily dependent on rainfall. Only in the central, tropical regions of Africa is there reliably sufficient rainfall for agriculture to be a major contributor to the wealth of countries; in the northern regions (including the Sahel and Horn of Africa), and in much of **southern Africa**, **drought**, combined with poor soils, affects agricultural yields and output.

Aguiyi-Aronsi, Gen. Johnson

A senior army officer, Maj.-Gen. Johnson Aguiyi-Aronsi took power in Nigeria in 1966, after a rebellion by young **Ibo** army officers, with the mission of preventing the country from disintegrating and providing competent and honest administration. Aguiyi-Aronsi was well intentioned, but as a senior army officer he was not well equipped for the delicate political task of holding the country together. When he incautiously suggested that a unitary constitution might be better for Nigeria than a federal one, northern fears that he intended to unify Nigeria under Ibo rule precipitated another coup, and he was murdered, to be replaced by **Col Yakubu Gowon**, a northern Christian.

Ahidjo, Ahmadou

President of Cameroon until 1982, when he suddenly resigned, to be succeeded by **Paul Biya**, who had been Prime Minister since 1975. Biya set about replacing Ahidjo's northern allies with southerners like himself. In 1983 he accused Ahidjo of organizing a coup against him, forcing the former President to flee the country.

Ahmed, Hocine Aït

Born in 1919. A key Algerian nationalist leader, who founded the **Front de libération nationale (FLN—National Liberation Front)** and began the eight-year war of independence against France. After Algeria achieved **independence** in 1962, he strongly opposed the ruling faction of **Ahmed Ben Bella**. Having been sentenced to death for opposition activities, Ahmed was subsequently pardoned and escaped to France. In 1999 he stood as a presidential candidate in Algeria, but later withdrew his candidacy in opposition to political fraud.

Aid and development

Since the 1960s large quantities of development assistance—financial, technical and advisory—have been provided to Africa. All too often it has proved ineffective in promoting development, for reasons associated both with the 'aid' agencies themselves and programme and project design, and also with the governments, which have tended to spend the resources unwisely and selfishly. Studies by the **World Bank** in the 1990s suggested that countries with 'sound' economies—characterized by low inflation, budget surplus and relatively free trade—and good institutions (characterized by rule of law, limited **corruption** and effective bureaucracy) benefited from aid, while those with 'bad' economies and institutions failed to develop, even with large hand-outs. Since then it has been conventional wisdom that development aid should favour those governments that conformed to the World Bank's idea of well-governed poor countries. This is the logic behind US President Bush's promise of a 50% increase in US development aid by 2006 and behind the **New Partnership for Africa's Development**. But some economists believe that the evidence for the conventional wisdom—that aid promotes growth in good policy environments—no longer obtains. National government policies are not sufficient on their own, if the global economic climate and institutional structures are unfavourable. African economies struggle to make headway in the harsh world of the 21st century, in which the most powerful economies still maintain their own advantages, despite the rhetoric of 'free markets' and '**globalization**' and the best efforts of the **World Trade Organization** and other international regulatory institutions. Aid is a poor alternative to an enabling global economic environment in which African economies have a reasonable chance of access to markets for capital, commodities and labour—*see also* **development aid**.

Aideed, Gen.

A US-led coalition force **(UNITAF)** began humanitarian relief operations in Somalia in December 1992. The main relief centres in the starvation area had been secured by January 1993. Following the success of this exercise, UN Security Council Resolution 814 was adopted, providing for the deployment of 28,000 UN troops and 2,800 civilians, to take over from UNITAF for six months from 1 May. This operation was called **UNOSOM** II. In June 1993 UN forces were attacked by militia belonging to the **United Somali Congress (USC)/Somali National Alliance (SNA)**, led by Gen. Aideed. Twenty-four Pakistani UN troops were killed. Subsequently UN Security Council Resolution 837 was adopted, authorizing all necessary measures against those responsible, including their arrest and detention for trial. The UN Secretary-General's Special Representative, Adm. Howe, ordered the arrest of Gen. Aideed. Between June and October 1993 70 UN troops were killed in total. UN Security Council Resolution 865 was adopted on 22 September supporting UNOSOM's efforts, but calling for greater emphasis on the political front. However, Somali deaths totalled several hundreds in clashes, as UN troops hunted unsuccessfully for Aideed in Mogadishu. Following the death of 12 US troops in early October, US President Clinton announced that US armed forces would be withdrawn by March 1994. Subsequently, UN Security Council Resolution 885 was adopted, suspending the arrest actions against Gen. Aideed.

Aix-les-Bains Conference

Took place in August 1955 to discuss the future of Morocco. The French delegation of five ministers was led by Prime Minister Edgar Faure. A key issue was the future role of the Sultan **Mohammed V**, exiled in Madagascar. **Ben Barka**, for the **Istiqlal** party, favoured a solution that avoided the return of the sultan—a position that angered the resistance movement, which aimed at the restoration of the sultan.

Akan

A major ethno-linguistic grouping in São Tomé and Príncipe, accounting for some 42% of the population, with its **Baoule** sub-group in the south.

Akintola, Chief

When Nigeria became independent in 1960, with a federal constitution based on three major regions, the north, the east and the west, **Sir Abubakar Tafawa Balewa** became federal Premier, while the eastern leader, Namdi Azikiwe, became President. The political parties of both leaders co-operated in government. The opposition was formed by the followers of **Chief Obafemi Awololo**, the western leader. This basic arrangement did not, however, last very long. The accord between east and north broke down and divisions grew in the west, as Chief Awololo was challenged by Chief Akintola, who succeeded in having his rival and other leaders tried and imprisoned. Akintola was not satisfied with Awololo's policy of forming an opposition at federal level and preferred an alliance with the north, displacing the eastern **Ibos** and obtaining for his own people a share in the power, perquisites and finances of central government. In 1963 a fourth, mid-western region was formed. Elections in the western region in 1965 prompted allegations of flagrant malpractice and fighting. In the next year more serious fighting began in the north. In January 1966 a group of young Ibo officers rebelled, partly in protest against bad government and partly as a demonstration against the north and its Western allies. The federal and northern Prime Ministers, Sir Abubakar Tafawa Balewa and the Sardauna of Sokoto, were murdered, together with Akintola and many others. Senior military officers quickly intervened to suppress the rebellion. Within a year, however, the eastern region, and the Ibos, had broken away to establish an independent state, **Biafra**.

Akuffo, Gen. F. W. K.

By 1978 **Col I. K. Acheampong**'s regime in Ghana had become corrupt and ineffective. He was ousted by Gen. F. W. K. Akuffo, who held power for less than a year himself, against a rising tide of popular unrest. He too was removed and, together with Acheampong and six others, executed after a coup led by **Flight-Lt Jerry Rawlings**, who promised to end **corruption**, reverse economic decline and restore civilian rule.

Alawite dynasty

The present King of Morocco, **Mohammed VI**, is the most recent ruler of the Moroccan Alawite dynasty, which claims to be descended from Ali and the Prophet Muhammad, via the holy lineage of the Filali *shorafa* (holy men), who established themselves in the oases of Sijilmassa in the 15th century. The first Alawite Sultan of Morocco was Moulay Isma'il, who came to power in the middle of the 17th century. Sultan Mohammed V of Morocco, who was the first king of Morocco after **independence**, was the grandson of Moulay Hassan (d. 1894). King Mohammed's father, Moulay Yussef (d. 1927), was the brother of both Moulay Abd al-Aziz and Moulay Hafidh, the last two sultans before the establishment of the **French Protectorate of Morocco**.

Alexandria

City in northern Egypt with a population of 3.9m. Founded by Alexander the Great in 332 BCE, Alexandria is a large tourist resort, as well as a commercial and economic centre, with 80% of all Egypt's imports and exports passing through the city's harbours.

Algeria, People's Democratic Republic of

Lying between Morocco and Tunisia along the Mediterranean coast and down into the Sahara, Algeria's southern **borders** are with Mauritania, Mali and Niger. Algeria is the second largest country in Africa after Sudan, with an area of 2,381,740 sq km, only 3% of which, however, is arable. The capital is Algiers. Algeria is divided into 48 provinces: Adrar, Aïn Defla, Aïn Témouchent, Algiers, Annaba, Batna, Béchar, Béjaïa, Biskra, Blida, Borj Bou Arreridj, Bouira, Boumerdes, Chlef, Constantine, Djelfa, El Bayadh, El Oued, El Tarf, Ghardaïa, Guelma, Illizi, Jijel, Khenchela, Laghouat, Mascara, Médéa, Mila, Mostaganem, M'Sila, Naâma, Oran, Ouargla, Oum el Bouaghi, Relizane, Saïda, Sétif, Sidi-bel-Abbès, Skikda, Souk Ahras, Tamanrasset, Tébessa, Tiaret, Tindouf, Tipaza, Tissemsilt, Tizi Ouzou, and Tlemcen. The population was estimated at 32,277,942 in July 2002, of which 75% were **Arabs**, 24% **Berbers**, and 1% others (mostly Europeans). The overwhelming majority of the population are **Sunni** Muslims, with about 1% belonging to other sects or faiths. The official state language is **Arabic**, with French and Berber dialects also recognized.

Political profile

Algeria is a republic, of which the President (**Abdelaziz Bouteflika** since April 1999) is Head of State. The Council of Ministers is appointed by the President, as is the Prime Minister (**Ali Benflis** from August 2000 until April 2003, when he was dismissed by President Bouteflika). The President is elected by popular vote for a five-year term. The legislature includes the Majlis ech-Chaabi al-Watani (National People's Assembly) and the Council of the Nation. The members of the Assembly (whose number was raised from 380 to 389 in the 2002 elections) are elected by popular vote to serve five-year terms. Elections to the National People's Assembly were last held on 30 May 2002, and are next scheduled to be held in 2007. The Council has 144 members, one-third of whom are appointed by the President, the remainder being elected by indirect vote. Members serve six-year terms and the Constitution requires one-half of the Council to be renewed every three years. Elections to the Council of the Nation were last held on 30 December 2000, and were due to be held in 2003. The legal system is based on French law and Islamic Law; judicial review of legislative acts takes place in an *ad hoc* Constitutional Council composed of various public officials, including several Supreme Court justices. Algeria has not accepted compulsory International Court of Justice jurisdiction.

Until 1988 Algeria was a single party regime, with the **Front de libération nationale (FLN—National Liberation Front)** in power. During 1988–90, following economic liberalization and large-scale anti-government demonstrations, which were brutally suppressed, the government allowed a degree of political liberalization. Other political parties, including Islamist groups, were recognized. In 1991 the **Front islamique du salut (FIS—Islamic Salvation Front)** was poised to win the second round of the national elections, but the army intervened to prevent the party from taking power, plunging Algeria into civil unrest, violence and a state of emergency from 1992 onwards. The **military** plays a major role in Algerian politics. A law specifically banning political parties based on religion was enacted in March 1997.

The major political groupings are:

- Algerian National Front; Leader Moussa Touati
- Democratic National Rally; Chair. Ahmed Ouyahia
- Front islamique du salut; Leaders **Ali Belhadj**, Dr **Abbasi Madani** (imprisoned), Rabeh Kebir (self-exiled in Germany); the Front was outlawed in April 1992
- Movement of a Peaceful Society; Chair. Mahfoud Nahnah
- National Entente Movement; Leader Ali Boukhazna
- Front de libération nationale; Sec.-Gen. Boualem Benhamouda
- National Reform Movement; Leader Abdallah Djaballah

- National Renewal Party
- Progressive Republican Party; Leader Khadir Driss
- Rally for Culture and Democracy; Sec.-Gen. Said Saadi
- Renaissance Movement (En Nahda Movement); Leader Lahbib Adami
- Social Liberal Party; Leader Ahmed Khelil
- Socialist Forces Front; Sec.-Gen. **Hocine Aït Ahmed** (self-exiled in Switzerland)
- Union for Democracy and Liberty; Leader Moulay Boukhalafa
- Workers Party; Leader Louisa Hanoune
- National Liberation Army
- **Groupe islamique armé**

History

Algeria was occupied by French forces in 1830. Despite continuing local resistance for several decades, by the 1870s Algeria was a French colony characterized by a substantial French settler population. The nationalist movement began to take shape after the Second World War and in 1945 fighting broke out. The nationalists were ruthlessly suppressed and some 15,000 killed. All they demanded at this stage was autonomy in a federation with France. In 1947 France made a number of concessions and constitutional reforms, not wishing to abandon the white settlers (***colons***). In 1952 **Ahmed Ben Bella** formed the Algerian Revolutionary Committee in Cairo, Egypt. In 1954 the nationalists formed the FLN and the Armée de libération nationale (ALN—National Liberation Army). In 1956 France, Great Britain and Israel collaborated to invade Egypt when **Gamal Abdel Nasser** nationalized the **Suez Canal**. After the failure of the old European imperial powers to gain control of Suez, the FLN gained support from the governments of the newly independent non-aligned countries. The war of liberation in Algeria, which resulted in the deployment of some 500,000 French troops there, contributed to the collapse of the Fourth Republic in France. Gen. Charles de Gaulle was recalled. In January 1960 the *colons* rebelled against de Gaulle. He began secret negotiations with the FLN provisional government in Cairo. **Oil** was discovered in the Sahara, leading France to consider retaining control of the oil-rich desert region while granting **independence** to the rest of Algeria. In 1962 Algeria became independent, with a government under the control of the FLN. For the next 27 years, until 1989, the FLN was the only political party in Algeria. The February 1989 amendments to the Constitution permitted the formation of other political associations, with some restrictions; the right to establish political parties was not guaranteed by the Constitution until November 1996. This political 'opening' in the late 1980s, however, enabled several new groupings to contest elections. The surprising success of the FIS, first in municipal elections and then, in December 1991, in the first round of the general election, led the army to intervene, cancel the subsequent elections and ban the FIS. The response from the Islamists, who established a number of militant armed groups to oppose the government and fight for an Islamic state, resulted in a continuing civil conflict with the secular state apparatus, which nevertheless allowed legislative elections featuring pro-government and moderate religious parties in June 1997 and elections to the Council of the Nation in December 1997 and again in December 2000. The FIS's armed wing, the **Armée islamique du salut (AIS—Islamic Salvation Army)**, disbanded itself in January 2000 and many armed militants surrendered under an amnesty programme designed to promote national reconciliation. Nevertheless, the conflict continued well into 2004, albeit on a reduced scale, with groups such as the **Groupe islamique armé (GIA—Armed Islamic Group)** and the **Groupe salafiste pour la prédication et le combat (GSPC—Salafist Group for Call and Combat)** remaining active. General elections to the National People's Assembly were held in May 2002 and presidential elections in April 2004. The first produced a majority for the FLN, and the second secured the re-election of President Bouteflika. In the previous presidential election, held on 15 April 1999, Bouteflika had received more than 70% of the vote. The six candidates who opposed him withdrew on the eve of the election, having alleged electoral fraud. In the elections of April 2004 Bouteflika was the army's candidate and favourite to win; his main rival was Ali Benflis, Bouteflika's campaign manager in the previous elections and Prime Minister until dismissed in 2003. Bouteflika won with an overwhelming majority, gaining some 87% of the vote in a poll in which nearly 60% of registered voters participated. Benflis secured only 8% of the vote. A 'moderate' Islamist candidate, Abdallah Djaballah, came third with 5% of the vote, and a left-wing woman candidate (and leader of the **Workers Party**), Louisa Hanoune, also stood. Major outstanding political concerns include Berber unrest in Kabylia—clashes during the April 2004 elections between Berbers and members of the security forces disrupted voting in Tizi Ouzou, Béjaïa and Bouira provinces.

Algeria, economy

Gross domestic product (GDP) totals 4,222,000m. dinars (US $54,700m., equivalent to per caput GDP of $1,770). Average annual growth in GDP in 1991–2001 was only 1.7%. Industry and manufacturing account for more than one-half of GDP, **agriculture** for 10.5% and services for 38%. The hydrocarbons sector is the backbone of the economy, accounting for approximately 60% of budget revenues, 30% of GDP, and more than 95% of export earnings. Algeria's principal exports are petroleum and **natural gas**, together generating some $11,600m. f.o.b., with other **energy** products accounting for $9,400m. Algeria has the fifth largest reserves of natural gas in the world and is the second largest gas exporter; it ranks 14th in the world in respect of **oil** reserves. Algeria's financial and economic indicators improved during the mid-1990s, in part because of policy reforms supported by the **International Monetary Fund** and **debt** rescheduling by the Paris Club. Algeria's finances in 2000 and 2001 benefited from the temporary spike in oil prices and the government's tight fiscal policy, leading to a large increase in the trade surplus, record highs in foreign exchange reserves, and reduction in foreign debt. Economic growth, which was slow in the 1990s, is now a brisk 7%, boosted by oil and gas exports. In 2001 the government signed an Association Treaty with the **European Union** that will eventually lower tariffs and should increase trade. Political instability in the 1990s threatened many projects and led to an exodus of skilled, mostly expatriate, workers. The situation is improving, however, and although the security and human rights situation remains repressive, there are signs that the long **civil war** is coming to an end. The government's continued efforts to diversify the economy by attracting foreign and domestic investment outside the energy sector have, however, had little success in reducing **poverty** or high (nearly 30%) unemployment or in improving the availability of housing and living standards. Agriculture remains under-funded and poorly-performing; there are often shortages in basic foodstuffs. There is a large black market. The bureaucracy remains cumbersome, inefficient and corrupt.

Aliança Democrática de Angola (Democratic Alliance of Angola)

Political party in Angola, led by Simba da Costa.

Aliança Democrática para a Mudança (ADM—Democratic Alliance for Change)

A political coalition in Cape Verde, formed in October 2000 by the **Partido da Convergência Democrática (Party of Democratic Convergence)**, the **Partido de Trabalho e Solidariedade (Party of Labour and Solidarity)** and the **União Caboverdiana Independente e Democrática (Independent and Democratic Union of Cape Verde)**.

Alliance burundaise-africaine pour le salut (ABASA—Burundi-African Alliance for Salvation)

Political party in Burundi, established in 1993 and with predominantly **Tutsi** membership. Its leader is Serge Mukumarakiza.

Alliance pour le Congo (AC—Alliance for the Congo)

Political party in the Republic of the Congo. A member of the **Forces démocratiques unies**. Its leader is Justin Coumba.

Alliance congolaise pour l'ouverture, le salut et la solidarité (ACOSS—Congolese Alliance for Openness, Salvation and Solidarity)

Political party in the Republic of the Congo. A member of the **Forces démocratiques unies**. Its president is Léon-Alfred Opimbat.

Alliance pour la démocratie et le développement (ADD—Alliance for Democracy and Development)

Political party in Cameroon. Its secretary-general is Garga Haman Adji.

Alliance pour la démocratie et la fédération-Rassemblement démocratique africain (ADF-RDA—Alliance for Democracy and Federation-African Democratic Rally)

Political grouping in Burkina Faso. Founded in 1990 as the Alliance pour la démocratie et la fédération, it absorbed a faction of the Rassemblement démocratique africain in 1998. Several factions broke away in mid-2000. The second largest party in the Assemblée nationale after winning 13% of the vote and gaining 17 seats in the general election of May 2002.

Alliance pour la démocratie et le progrès (Alliance for Democracy and Progress)

Political party in the Central African Republic, established in 1991. Its national secretary is Tchapka Brédé.

Alliance démocratique pour le progrès du Cameroun (ADPC—Cameroon Democratic Alliance for Progress)

Political party in Cameroon, established in 1991.

Alliance étoile (AE—Star Alliance)

An alliance of six social democratic parties in Benin, established in 1999.

Alliance des forces progressistes (AFP—Alliance of Progressive Forces)

Political party in Cameroon, established in 2002. Its leader is Maidadi Saidou Yaya.

Alliance impulsion pour le progrès et la démocratie (AIPD—Impulse for Progress and Democracy Alliance)

Alliance of political groupings in Benin, founded in 1999. Its leaders are Bertin Borna and Théophile Nata.

Alliance pour la justice and la démocratie (AJD—Alliance for Justice and Democracy)

Political party in Mauritania, led by Kabeh Abdoulaye.

Alliance pour une Mauritanie démocratique (AMD—Alliance for a Democratic Mauritania)

Established by a group of conservative businessmen and members of the banned Mauritanian People's Party, the Alliance pour une Mauritanie démocratique (AMD) was the vehicle by which **Mokhtar Ould Daddah** (overthrown in a coup in July 1978) hoped to return to power. Based in Paris, France, but with support from Morocco and Senegal, the AMD sponsored the unsuccessful coup attempt against **Ould Haidalla** in March 1981. Thereafter, it suffered serious reversals. Senegal expelled known AMD activists, the major AMD military leaders captured in Mauritania were executed, and Ould Daddah apparently renounced the leadership. After Haidalla's removal from power, the AMD declined and most prominent members, apart from Ould Daddah himself, returned home from exile.

Alliance nationale pour la démocratie et le développement (ANDD—National Alliance for Democracy and Development)

Political party in Chad, established in 1992. Its leader is Salibou Garba.

Alliance nationale pour les droits et le développement économique (ANADDE—National Alliance for Rights and Economic Development)

Political party in Burundi, established in 1992, with predominantly **Tutsi** membership. Its leader is Patrice Nsababaganwa.

Alliance nationale républicaine (ANR—National Republican Alliance)

Algerian political grouping, founded in 1995. An anti-Islamist party, it is led by Redha Malek.

Alliance nigérienne pour la démocratie et le progrès (ANDP—Nigerien Alliance for Democracy and Progress)

Political party in Niger, with four members in the Assemblée nationale.

Alliance pour le progrès et l'émancipation des dépossédés (APED—Alliance for Progress and the Emancipation of the Dispossessed)

Political party in Cameroon, founded in 1991. Its leader is Bohin Bohin.

Alliance pour le progrès et la liberté (APL—Alliance for Progress and Freedom)

Political party in Burkina Faso. Its secretary-general is Joséphine Tamboura-Sama.

Alliance pour le redressement du Cameroun (ARC—Alliance for the Recovery of Cameroon)

Political grouping in Cameroon, established in 1992 by a number of opposition movements.

Alliance suru (Suru Alliance)

Alliance of four political parties in Benin, founded in 1999.

Alliance tchadienne pour la démocratie et le développement (ATDD—Chadian Alliance for Democracy and Development)

Political party in Chad, led by Abderrahman Djasnabaille.

De Almeida, Damião Vaz

Prime Minister of São Tomé and Príncipe since 17 September 2004.

Aluminium and bauxite

Aluminium is the most abundant metallic element in the earth's crust, comprising about 8% of the total. The major markets for aluminium are in transportation, building and construction, electrical machinery and equipment, consumer durables and the packaging industry. Bauxite is the principal aluminium ore although there are several other sources of alumina that are currently not economic to process. Of all bauxite mined, roughly 85% is converted to alumina for the production of aluminium. Total world output of aluminium in 2000 was around 24m. metric tons, of which African producers accounted for almost 1.2m. tons. Guinea, the leading African producer, possesses more than one-quarter of the world's known bauxite reserves and is the world's leading exporter, ranking second only to Australia in terms of ore production. Alumina, aluminium and bauxite account for almost 60% of Guinea's external revenue. Cameroon has extensive bauxite deposits, estimated at some 1,200m. tons, but these await commercial exploitation. In Nigeria, the Ikot Abasi primary aluminium smelter, with an annual capacity of 193,000 tons, entered into production in late 1997, but, after operating at only 20% of its capacity, was forced to suspend its activities temporarily in June 1999 for lack of working capital—total output in that year was only 16,000 tons. Ghana has reserves estimated at 780m. tons and is the second largest African producer of bauxite and aluminium. Ghana has a substantial aluminium smelter facility at Tema, which processes imported alumina. The smelter is operated by the Volta Aluminium Company (VALCO), which is 90% owned by Kaiser of the USA. Sierra Leone has estimated bauxite reserves of 100m. tons, but production has been adversely affected in recent years by internal conflict. Malawi has an estimated 29m. tons in reserves, but these have hardly begun to be exploited, despite interest on the part of neighbouring Mozambique. A major aluminium smelter project was formally inaugurated in Mozambique in 1998, although the country is not itself a major producer of bauxite. The Mozal smelter, located near Maputo and owned by a consortium that includes the mining group BHP Billiton, represents the largest single investment project in Mozambique, with an estimated cost of about US $1,300m. The smelter reached annual operational capacity of 250,000 tons in 2001. In mid-2001 plans to expand the facility were announced. In 1992 the South African aluminium producer Alusaf announced plans to construct the largest smelter complex in the Western world at Richards Bay, with an annual capacity of well over 600,000 tons. This complex started production in 1995 and by the end of the 1990s annual output was around 670,000 tons. This has substantially increased Africa's overall output. During the 1990s there was a substantial increase in production of bauxite and aluminium world-wide, creating conditions of over-supply. In 1993 the market fell to an 11-year 'low'. However, international negotiations among the world's largest producers led to reductions in output and a recovery took place in 1994 and 1995. By May 1996 stocks had declined to their lowest level since 1993 and in the mean time demand grew appreciably and remained strong throughout the rest of the decade. Even by 2001, however, the export price index for aluminium was 82 (base 1980 = 100) and there was a further decline over the next few years.

Amharic

Language spoken widely in Ethiopia and also in Eritrea.

Amin, Idi

Army chief in Uganda under the regime of **Milton Obote**, but succeeded Obote after a military coup in January 1971. He presided over what rapidly became a reign of terror in Uganda, unleashing the army and allowing paramilitary forces to terrorize the Ugandan population. He evicted the British High Commissioner and military mission, accusing them of complicity in Obote's attempt to return to power in September 1972. He also gave notice to Uganda's approximately 70,000 Asians (most of whom were British citizens) to leave the country within three months, though he later exempted those who were Ugandan citizens. He then initiated the take-over and 'Africanization' of hundreds of foreign businesses. At the same time, his repression of the Ugandan population increased and by the time he was overthrown, in 1979, it is estimated that some 500,000 people had 'disappeared'. Amin's fall was effected by an invasion from Tanzania when Tanzanian forces accompanied by a Ugandan National Liberation Army seized the capital, Kampala, meeting little resistance, and installed a provisional government. Amin left the country for exile in Saudi Arabia, where he died in 2003.

de Andrade, Mário

First leader of the **Movimento Popular de Libertação de Angola (MPLA—Popular Liberation Movement of Angola)**. The MPLA, a successor to the oldest Angolan anti-colonial movement, the Partido da Luta Unida dos Africanos de Angola (Party of the United Struggle of the Africans of Angola), was considered to be dominated by the Mbundu people, who inhabit the area around the capital, Luanda, and by the views of urban intellectuals, mostly *assimilados* (Europeanized Africans granted Portuguese citzenship) and *mesticos* (people of mixed European and African descent), personified by de Andrade himself.

Anglo-American Corporation

South African mining enterprise – *see also* **De Beers**.

AngloGold Ashanti

Part of the international mining conglomerate **Anglo-American**. According to a report published in June 2005 by the human rights organization Human Rights Watch, AngloGold Ashanti developed links with the Front pour les nationalistes et intégrationistes (FNI—Nationalist and Integrationist Front) near the town of Mongbwalu in Ituri District in the Democratic Republic of the Congo, and provided 'meaningful financial and logistic support' which led to substantial political benefits for the FNI, a group responsible for some of the worst atrocities. The company responded to the report by denying that it gave support to militia groups, but admitted that company employees had yielded to extortion by the FNI in an incident that would not recur. AngloGold Ashanti drew a distinction between 'support' for a group like the FNI and 'some level of unavoidable contact', given the proximity of some of its mining operations to the local communities where the FNI was present. Human Rights Watch stated that fighting between armed groups for control of the gold-mining town of Mongbwalu cost the lives of at least 2,000 civilians between June 2002 and September 2004.

Angola, Republic of

Angola is located in **Southern Africa**. It is bounded to the west by the Atlantic Ocean and shares **borders** with the Democratic Republic of the Congo (DRC), Zambia and Namibia. The enclave of Cabinda in the north, adjacent to the DRC and the Republic of the Congo, is also part of Angola. Angola is 1,246,700 sq km in area and its population was estimated at some 12m. in 2001. The capital is Luanda, whose population was estimated at 2.8m. in 2001). The majority of Angola's people are of Bantu origin—the largest groups are the Ovimbundu, Mbundu, Bakongo, Tchokwe and Nyaneka. There is also a small *mestizo* (mixed-race) community. Languages spoken include Portuguese (the official language of the country) and many local African languages. There is a wide range of religions but Christianity, of which Roman Catholicism is the largest single denomination, is dominant. There are also Protestants, Methodists, Baptists, the United Church of Christ and Congregationalists, as well as a number of indigenous African and Brazilian Christian denominations and a small Muslim community.

Political profile

Angola is a republic based on a multi-party political system and the government is the transitional government of national unity and reconciliation (GNUR). The Head of State and of the government is President **José Eduardo dos Santos**, who has held office since 21 September 1979. (The President is elected by universal suffrage. Dos Santos was first elected, unopposed, under a one-party political system in 1979. He was re-elected in 1992, having contested Angola's first multi-party presidential election—see below.) The President appoints the Council of Ministers. Since 6 December 2002 the Prime Minister has been **Fernando da Piedade Dias dos Santos**, and the foreign minister Dr João Bernardo Miranda. Each of the 18 provinces of the country is run by a governor appointed by the President. The major political parties are: the **Movimento Popular de Libertação de Angola (MPLA—Popular Movement for the Liberation of Angola)**, which occupied 129 seats in the country's unicameral, 220-seat Assembléia Nacional, having won some 54% of the vote in the most recent legislative elections that were held in September 1992; and the **União Nacional para a Independência Total de Angola (UNITA—National Union for the Total Independence of Angola)**, which occupied 70 seats in the Assembléia, having won about 34% of the vote. Seven minor parties—the **Frente Nacional de Libertação de Angola (FNLA—National Liberation Front of Angola)** with five seats, the **Partido Liberal Democrático (PLD—Liberal Democratic Party)** with three seats, the **Partido Renovador Social (PRS—Social Renewal Party)** with six seats, the **Partido Renovador Democrático (PRD—Democratic Renewal Party)**, the **Angolan Democratic Coalition (AD Coalition)**, the **Partido Social Democrata (PSD—Social Democrat Party)**, the **Partido de Aliança de Juventude, Operários e Camponêses de Angola (PAJOCA—Angolan Youth, Workers' and Peasants' Alliance Party)**, the Fórum Democrático Angolano (FDA—Angolan Democratic Forum), the **Partido Democrático para o Progresso—Aliança Nacional de Angola (PDPANA, Democratic Party for Progress—National Alliance of Angola)** and the **Partido Nacional Democrata de Angola (PNDA—National Democrat Party of Angola)**—share the balance of 21 seats in the Assembléia, whose deputies are elected by proportional representation for a four-year term of office.

In June 2003, during UNITA's Ninth Congress, Isaías Samakuva was elected as president of UNITA after defeating two other candidates in a secret ballot of members. In December the MPLA held its Fifth Congress, at which Julião Mateus Paulo was appointed as secretary-general. José Eduardo dos Santos remains chairman of the MPLA.

History

Angola was formerly a Portuguese colony. The main groups which fought for independence were the MPLA, UNITA and the FNLA. The MPLA received substantial backing from the Soviet Union and Cuba, UNITA from South Africa and the USA, and the FNLA from **Zaire** and the USA. The conflict had become a **civil war** by the time that Angola gained **independence** on 11 November 1975. The MPLA was able to gain the military advantage and formed a government that did not include UNITA and the FNLA. UNITA regrouped and commenced a guerrilla war against the MPLA. Until the late 1980s the MPLA had the assistance of 60,000 Cuban troops to help it to contain the UNITA insurgency. Until 1989 Angola suffered from frequent attacks by South African forces, both air and ground, from bases in **South West Africa** (now Namibia), acting both in support of UNITA and in hot pursuit of **South West Africa People's Organisation (SWAPO)** guerrillas. In a complicated deal engineered by the USA in 1989, South African forces left South West Africa and Cuban forces left Angola, thereby paving the way for Namibia's independence and for an internal settlement in Angola. Peace talks between the MPLA and UNITA took place between April 1990 and May 1991, leading to a cease-fire and the signing of a peace agreement known as the Bicesse Accords in May 1991. The cease-fire was monitored by a UN mission, known as **United Nations Angola Verification Mission (UNAVEM)**.

Angola's first multi-party presidential and legislative elections were held in September 1992 and resulted in victory for the MPLA (dos Santos won 49.6% of the vote in the presidential election, **Dr Jonas Savimbi**, the UNITA candidate, 40.1%). The run-off election for the presidency, which was to be contested by the two leading candidates, did not take place as UNITA rejected the result and returned to war. In September 1993 the UN Security Council imposed sanctions on UNITA (an embargo on arms and related material and on all petroleum products). (Additional sanctions, including a travel ban, an assets 'freeze', and a ban on illegal sales of **diamonds**, *inter alia*, were imposed on UNITA in 1997 and 1998.) UNITA's subsequent acceptance of the outcome of the 1992 elections led to renewed talks between the government and UNITA in Lusaka, Zambia, in October 1993. This resulted in the signature of a second peace agreement, known as the **Lusaka Protocol**, on 20 November 1994. A formal cease-fire took effect two days later. **UN Security Council Resolution 976** of 8 February 1995 authorized the deployment of a 7,000-strong peace-keeping force particularly to oversee the demobilization of troops on both sides. The United Kingdom provided a 600-strong logistics battalion for a three-month period. The UN declared that all military tasks had been officially completed on 13 December 1996. This prepared the way for UNITA deputies (elected in 1992) to the Assembléia Nacional in Luanda to take their seats.

A GNUR, including four UNITA ministers and seven vice-ministers, was inaugurated on 11 April 1997. On 1 July 1997 **UN Security Council Resolution 1118** reconfigured UNAVEM as the UN Observer Mission in Angola (MONUA). As well as deploying military and police observers, MONUA also focused on human rights issues. Although both sides were publicly committed to the peace process, progress in implementing the provisions of the Lusaka Protocol was slow. On 1 September 1998 the government of Angola suspended all UNITA ministers and deputy ministers in the GNUR and it created a movement called UNITA Renovada from among those in UNITA who no longer supported Savimbi's military strategy. The security situation throughout Angola continued to deteriorate. UNITA retook many areas originally handed over to state administration and heavy clashes took place. Against this background, the UN Secretary-General recommended the withdrawal of the military elements of MONUA. The UN Security Council accepted this recommendation.

At the end of 1998 the MPLA, at its party congress, changed its strategy and decided to achieve 'peace through war'. A full-scale return to war was agreed. In the course of its military offensive the government all but destroyed UNITA's conventional military capability, forcing it to revert to guerrilla tactics. On 26 February 1999 **UN Security Council Resolution 1229** was adopted, which terminated MONUA's mandate but allowed the human rights element to continue functioning. The chairman of the UN Angola Sanctions Committee visited Angola and the region in May 1999 and produced a list of recommendations on ways to make the implementation of sanctions against UNITA more effective. These were examined by two panels of experts. **UN Security Council Resolution 1295** was adopted, which focused on the panels' key recommendations, and proposed a monitoring mechanism to follow on from the work of the panels. A UN Office was re-established in Angola in October 2000. In the mean time, over the next year or so, government troops managed to regain notional control of almost 95% of the areas previously under UNITA's control, including their main strongholds in the Central Highlands. In February 2002 UNITA president Savimbi was killed by government forces. His successor, António Dembo, also died soon afterwards. In March it was announced that the national army of Angola had halted all military operations against UNITA. UNITA rebel forces subsequently declared a cease-fire, and an official agreement was ratified on 4 April 2002.

This presented a unique opportunity for the MPLA and UNITA to pursue peace talks once again. On 13 March 2002 the government instructed the General Staff of the Angolan Armed Forces (FAA) to end offensive movements 'in order to permit the establishment of '*in situ*' contacts between military commands of the FAA and of UNITA military forces'. This was followed by a Memorandum of Understanding (MOU), establishing a formal cease-fire and a joint military commission, signed in Luanda on 4 April. The UN Secretary-General's Special Adviser on Africa visited Angola during April to assess the situation on the ground with a view to future UN involvement, not least with regard to the 85,000 UNITA ex-combatants, and their family members, totalling around 300,000, who were quartered under the terms of the 4 April MOU. On 31 July 2002 a formal ceremony for the induction of some 5,000 former UNITA combatants into the FAA took place in Luanda. A ceremony on 2 August formally marked the end of UNITA as a military entity, after the successful completion of the disarmament and demobilization of its troops. A mandate was agreed in the UN Security Council on 16 August for the establishment of a new United Nations Mission in Angola (UNMA), headed by Dr Gambari as Special Representative of the Secretary-General. In this capacity Dr Gambari chaired the reconstituted Joint Commission that was charged with completing the remaining tasks under the Lusaka Protocol. On 21 November a ceremony in the Assembléia Nacional declared the Lusaka Process, and with it the role of the Joint Commission, to have ended. On 9 December 2002 the UN Security Council unanimously voted to lift all remaining sanctions against UNITA, as UNITA had met all of the conditions necessary for it to do so.

Angola was now in a 'post-conflict' situation. The UN estimated that there were some 4.5m war-affected people, one-third of the population, who required humanitarian assistance. In addition, more than 400,000 had fled to neighbouring countries to escape the conflict. The suspension of hostilities opened up access to areas previously beyond the reach of humanitarian agencies. Including former UNITA fighters and their families, it was estimated that there might be as many as a further 500,000 people in urgent need of assistance. It was reported that a total of 400,000 soldiers and their dependants had been moved to family reception areas by November 2002, and, according to a report by Human Rights Watch in August 2003, 'a year after the signing of the peace accord, more than two million internally displaced persons and approximately 25 percent of refugees living abroad have already returned to their places of origin'.

International relations

The government of Angola, having initially intervened in the war in the Democratic Republic of the Congo (DRC), subsequently worked to try to bring various factions involved in the hostilities to an agreement. In August 2002, having withdrawn its own troops, Angola brokered an agreement between the DRC and Uganda on the withdrawal of Ugandan troops. Beyond the immediate region, Angola now has good relations with a wide range of commercially interested countries, such as the USA, Portugal, Spain, Norway, France and Brazil.

Angola, economy

In 2002 Angola's gross domestic product (GDP) was US $10,200m., equivalent to $700 per head. GDP increased by 9% in that year. The rate of inflation was forecast at more than 100% in 2002. Angola's major industries are the production of **oil** and **natural gas**, and the mining of **diamonds**. The main destinations of Angola's exports are the USA, Belgium, the People's Republic of China, France and Spain, while the principal suppliers of imports are Portugal, the USA, South Africa, Brazil and France. The national currency is the kwanza. In March 2005 the exchange rate was US $1 = 86.9130 kwanza.

Before **independence**, Angola's economy was already diversified; **coffee**, sisal and **cotton** were the main agricultural exports; diamonds and iron were mined; oil production had reached 170,000 barrels per day (b/d); and import-substituting light manufacturing was fairly successful. Angola is potentially a wealthy country, with a population of more than 13m. and substantial natural resources. The country has enormous reserves of petroleum (8,000m. barrels), natural gas, iron, manganese and diamonds as well as considerable hydroelectric potential, varied agricultural land, and adequate rainfall. However, its economy is one of the most distorted and inefficient in Africa, having suffered from chronic mismanagement since independence. Combined with the long-running **civil war** this resulted in the virtual collapse of the non-oil sectors.

In 1999 UNICEF described Angola as 'the worst place in the world to be a child', based on rates of under-five mortality, malnutrition, school non-attendance and **HIV/AIDS**. The UNICEF 2000 Appeal for Angola stated that Angola ranked third world-wide in under-five mortality and that Angolan children are the most at risk in the world. Since then the prospects have improved only a little, and still one in every three children dies before reaching the age of five. Only half of the children of primary school age are enrolled at school, and of those that are only 35% ever reach the fifth grade, with the majority of the drop-outs being girls. In total Angola's children spend an average of only two years at school. One mother in every 50 dies during childbirth. Nation-wide, 50% of men and 70% of women are illiterate. Only 34% of households in Angola have ready access to potable water and only 44 % to basic sanitation. Extreme **poverty** means that school fees are unaffordable for most, and children are expected to start earning a wage, or helping in the home while other family members go out to work, as soon as possible.

At the end of 2002 Angola's total external **debt** was $9,900m. War, together with vastly increased oil production, has radically changed the country's economic profile. Oil now accounts for more than 60% of GDP and for 85% of government revenue—**agriculture** contributes 8% and manufacturing 4%. Offshore oil now dominates the economy. Angola, which is not a member of the **Organization of Petroleum Exporting Countries**, is Africa's second largest exporter of oil (after Nigeria) and oil production was expected to rise from about 900,000 b/d in 2003 to 1.4m. b/d by 2005 and to almost 2m. b/d by 2007.

Angolan Democratic Coalition

Angolan political party. Its acting president is Evidor Quiela.

AngloGold

The world's biggest mining company, located in South Africa.

Anjouan – *see* Nzwani

Ankrah, Col Joseph

Leader of the first of four Ghanaian military governments that succeeded President **Kwame Nkrumah** after he had been overthrown in a *coup d'état* in 1966. On coming to power the Ankrah regime found that Ghana's reserves had been reduced by Nkrumah's extravagances to only £4m., while the country's external **debt** had risen to £279m. Ghana also had a deficit on its external account of £53m. The Ankrah regime made some improvements to the situation before relinquishing power to **Dr Kofi A. Busia** in 1969, but annual economic growth remained below 1%, while the population was growing at a rate of 3.5%–4%.

Annan, Kofi

Kofi Annan is the seventh Secretary-General of the United Nations and the first from a sub-Saharan African nation, Ghana. He is also the first Secretary-General to have been elected from the ranks of United Nations staff. Born in Kumasi on 8 April 1938, he studied at the University of Science and Technology in Kumasi and completed his undergraduate work in economics at Macalester College in St Paul, Minnesota, USA, in 1961. From 1961 until 1962 he undertook graduate studies in economics at the Institut universitaire des hautes études internationales in Geneva, Switzerland. In 1971–72 he was a Sloan Fellow at the Massachusetts Institute of Technology. Annan joined the United Nations system in 1962 as an administrative and budget officer with the WHO in Geneva. Since then he has served with the UN Economic Commission for Africa, the UN Emergency Force, the Office of the **UN High Commissioner for Refugees (UNHCR)** in Geneva; and, at UN Headquarters in New York, as assistant secretary-general for human resources management and security co-ordinator for the UN System (1987–90) and, subsequently, as assistant secretary-general for programme planning, budget and finance, and control (1990–92). In 1990, following the invasion of Kuwait by Iraq, Annan organized the repatriation of more than 900 international staff and citizens of Western countries from Iraq. He was also directly involved in leading the first UN team negotiating with Iraq on the 'oil-for-food programme'. On 13 December 1996 Annan was selected by the UN Security Council to be Secretary-General and was confirmed four days later by the General Assembly. Starting his first term on 1 January 1997, Annan replaced **Boutros Boutros-Ghali**. Annan's first major initiative was a plan for reform, 'Renewing the United Nations'. His report to the Security Council in April 1998 on 'The Causes of Conflict and the Promotion of Durable Peace and Sustainable Development in Africa' is an example of the efforts Annan has made to maintain the international community's commitment to Africa, the most disadvantaged of the world's regions. During his time in office he has mediated many delicate political situations. These have included: an attempt in 1998 to gain Iraq's compliance with Security Council resolutions; encouraging a peaceful transfer of power in Nigeria during 1998; producing an agreement in 1999 to resolve the long-running stalemate between Libya and the Security Council over the 1988 **Lockerbie** bombing; and encouraging Israel's withdrawal from Lebanon in September 2000. Continuing efforts are being made to encourage Israelis and Palestinians to resolve their differences through peaceful negotiations based on Security Council resolutions.

In April 2001 Annan issued a five-point 'Call to Action' to address the **HIV/AIDS** epidemic—which he described as his 'personal priority'—and proposed the establishment of a Global AIDS and Health Fund to serve as a mechanism for some of the increased spending needed to help developing countries confront the crisis, not only in Africa, which suffers most acutely, but across the world.

On 29 June 2001, on the recommendation by the Security Council, Annan was granted a second term of office, which began on 1 January 2002 and will end on 31 December 2006. On 10 December 2001 Annan received as the head of the UN the Nobel Peace Prize for his ambitious reforms that 'had been pre-eminent in bringing new life to the Organization'. Controversy has surrounded the 'oil-for-food programme', with which Annan was involved and in connection with which his son, Kojo Annan has been implicated in influencing the award of contracts to companies with which he worked. Annan called for an investigation into the programme and the commission that was charged with that task made no specific allegations against the Secretary-General himself in its report in March 2005, stating only that an investigation should have been initiated earlier. Outside of the USA Annan has few opponents and has enjoyed the unanimous support of the UN Security Council.

Ansarollah Group

Libyan opposition group, founded in 1996.

Apartheid

Doctrine of 'separate development' espoused in particular by the **National Party (NP)** in South Africa from the late 1940s and elaborated during the 1950s and 1960s by a succession of NP governments. Eventually, in 1994, the release of **Nelson Mandela** from prison and the acceptance by the government of **F. W. de Klerk** of the need to establish a broader base for democratic politics in South Africa, the components of the apartheid regime began to be dismantled. The legacy of apartheid remains strong. In the fields of **education** and professional development in particular, the black population is clearly at a major disadvantage. In 2002, for example, only 1% of black high school students passed higher-grade mathematics and in the same year only 246 of South Africa's 19,000 chartered accountants were black.

Aptidon, Hassan Gouled

Born in 1916. First President of Djibouti, from 27 June 1977 until 8 May 1999, when he was succeeded by **Ismael Omar Gelleh**, his nephew. Prime Minister of Djibouti from 18 May 1977 until 12 July 1977.

Arab African International Bank

Founded in 1964 as the Arab African Bank, renamed in 1978. Its shareholders are the governments of Kuwait, Egypt, Algeria, Jordan and Qatar, Bank al-Jazira (Saudi Arabia), Rafidain Bank (Iraq) and Arab individuals and institutions. Based in Cairo, Egypt.

Arab Bank for Economic Development in Africa (ABEDA)

Initiated in November 1973 at the sixth summit meeting of the **Arab League** in Algiers, Algeria, established 18 February 1974 (effective from 16 September 1974) and began operations in 1975. Its headquarters are in Khartoum, Sudan. It is funded by the governments of the member states of the Arab League and serves to channel funds from members of the **Organization of Arab Petroleum Exporting Countries** to promote, in particular, development. The Bank's purpose is to strengthen economic, financial and technical links, to increase solidarity between Arab and African countries and to promote economic development, especially in the latter. Its subscribing members are Algeria, Bahrain, Egypt, Iraq, Jordan, Kuwait, Lebanon, Libya, Mauritania, Morocco, Oman, Qatar, Saudi Arabia, Sudan, Syria, Tunisia, the United Arab Emirates and the Palestine Liberation Organization; that is, all of the members of the Arab League except Comoros, Djibouti, Somalia and Yemen. It provides loans and grants to African countries to finance development projects. By the end of 2001, the total value of loans and grants approved since the start of funding activities in 1975 was US $2.2m. Recipient countries: all members of the **African Union**, except those which also belong to the Arab League.

Arab Common Market

The implementation of an Arab Common Market by the **Council of Arab Economic Unity (CAEU)** was proposed in August 1964. This was eventually to involve all of the members of the CAEU. A meeting of the ministers of the Council in Baghdad, Iraq, in June 2001 issued 'the Baghdad Declaration' proposing a four-economy free-trade area to begin with, involving Egypt, Iraq, Syria and Libya. Palestine expressed interest in joining, which delayed implementation. This initiative was regarded as a cornerstone for a **(Greater) Arab Free Trade Area** being implemented by the **Arab League**.

Arab Economic Unity Council

Arab organization established in June 1957 by a resolution of the Arab Economic Council of the **Arab League**, consisting of Egypt, Iraq, Jordan, Kuwait, Libya, Mauritania, the Palestine Liberation Organization (now Palestine), Somalia, Sudan, Syria, the United Arab Emirates and Yemen. The Council's focus is regional, devoted to achieving economic integration through the framework of economic and social development.

Arab Free Trade Zone (AFTZ)

An association established in May 2003 to promote economic co-operation and trade between its members, when Egypt, Jordan, Tunisia and Morocco signed a declaration—the Arab Free Trade Agreement—to this effect. Officials expressed the hope that four countries would operate the zone by the end of 2004 and that other Arab countries would also join over the next 10 years. Yemen was expected to become a full member of the AFTZ in 2005. The AFTZ is regarded by some as the last means to preserve a significant role for the **Arab League**, whose reputation and effectiveness has been severely limited over the past decade. Advocates point out that external pressures and the structures afforded by the **World Trade Organization** are propelling this initiative forwards. Others, however, are sceptical. They point out that the region as a whole lacks a significant intra-regional trade base, apart from **energy** products and some agricultural commodities; that intra-Arab commerce accounts for only 8% of the overall foreign trade of the countries involved and that many Arab countries compete to sell similar goods in global markets; that any potential for regional economic co-operation will be hampered by significant territorial disputes; and that smaller-scale initiatives (the **Arab Maghreb Union** and the Gulf Co-operation Council) have had limited success. Finally, it is remarked that the **Euro-Mediterranean Partnership** is progressing rapidly, with the objective of creating a Euro-Med Free Trade Zone by 2010 that incorporates 27 countries, including 20 (not all Arab) that directly border the Mediterranean. The scale of this initiative will possibly obviate a regional AFTZ.

Arab Fund for Economic and Social Development (AFESD)

Established on 16 May 1968 by the Economic Council of the **Arab League**, although it did not begin operations until 1974. Its aim is to promote economic and social development in the Arab World. Its member states are Algeria, Bahrain, Djibouti, Egypt (suspended 1979, but subsequently allowed to re-enter), Iraq (suspended 1993), Jordan, Kuwait, Lebanon, Libya, Mauritania, Morocco, Oman, Qatar, Saudi Arabia, Somalia (suspended 1993), Sudan, Syria, Tunisia, the United Arab Emirates, Yemen and the Palestine Liberation Organization. AFESD makes loans and grants for economic and social development projects in Arab (and some other) countries. It co-operates with other Arab agencies, such as the **Organization of Arab Petroleum Exporting Countries**.

Arab International Bank

Founded in 1971 as the Egyptian International Bank for Foreign Trade and Investment, renamed in 1974. Owned by Egypt, Libya, the United Arab Emirates, Oman, Qatar and private Arab shareholders. Offshore bank which aims to promote trade and investment in shareholders' countries and other Arab states.

Arab League (League of Arab States)

The League of Arab States was created on 22 March 1945, in **Alexandria**, Egypt. Its founding members were Egypt, Iraq, Lebanon, Saudi Arabia, Syria, Transjordan and Yemen (North). As other Arab states gained **independence**, the League was enlarged and now numbers 22 members. African members, in addition to Egypt, are Algeria, Comoros, Djibouti, Libya, Mauritania, Morocco, Somalia and Sudan. The League's headquarters is located in Cairo, Egypt. Its aim is to promote economic, social, political, and military co-operation among Arab states.

Arab Maghreb Union (AMU)

Established on 17 February 1989, the Arab Maghreb Union (AMU) aims to promote co-operation and integration among the Arab states of northern Africa. Its member states are Algeria, Libya, Mauritania, Morocco and Tunisia. The AMU was envisaged initially by **Col Muammar al-Qaddafi** as an Arab super-state. It was expected to eventually function as a North African common market, although domestic economic problems and civil unrest (especially in Algeria), divisions between the member states, and external events (e.g. the sanctions applied against Libya after **Lockerbie**, and the **Euro-Mediterranean Partnership** process) have hindered and even undermined progress on the Union's joint goals. The AMU has not held a meeting since 1994, despite several attempts to convene one. A summit meeting of Heads of State, intended to create a free-trade zone and planned for December 2003, was postponed, largely because of the continuing dispute between Morocco and Algeria over the **Western Sahara** 'peace process'. On this occasion, King **Mohammed VI** of Morocco refused to attend, calling for direct talks with Algeria before participating in an AMU meeting. Moreover, the Mauritanian authorities accused Libya of funding a plot to overthrow the government of Mauritania. The failure to meet was a set-back for President **Bouteflika** of Algeria, who was committed to improving Algeria's image and revitalizing the ***maghreb***.

Arab Monetary Fund (AMF)

Established on 27 April 1976 by the Economic Council of Arab States, the Fund commenced operations in the following year. Its member states are Algeria,

Bahrain, Djibouti, Egypt, Iraq, Jordan, Kuwait, Lebanon, Libya, Mauritania, Morocco, Oman, Palestine, Qatar, Saudi Arabia, Somalia, Sudan, Syria, Tunisia, the United Arab Emirates and Yemen. Egypt was temporarily suspended from the Fund in 1979, but was subsequently readmitted. From July 1993 loans to Iraq were suspended as a result of that country's failure to repay debts. The offices of the AMF are the board of governors, the board of executive directors and the president. Its finances are computed in the Arab accounting dinar, worth three **International Monetary Fund (IMF)** Special Drawing Rights. Its objective is to assist Arab co-operation, development and economic integration in monetary and economic affairs. It makes available technical and financial assistance to client states, with particular reference to balance-of-payments problems. It supports the Arab Trade Financing Programme. It is, in effect, a regional IMF.

Arab socialism

Arab socialism has tended to be, ideologically and in political practice, a form of radical authoritarian populism. It has little to do with the classic Marxist notion of **socialism** and has shown itself to be hostile to the various 'communist' parties and groupings which derive their political theory and practice from the Marxist-Leninist tradition. Arab socialism has emphasized above all the importance of Arab nationalism and of the Arab people. It has stood for radical economic and social change, and above all for 'modernization'. It has drawn heavily on the European 'national socialist' tradition and emphasized the importance of national unity, strictly controlling the extent to which different interests may be expressed (through trades unions, political parties, etc.) and often banning such organizations entirely, in favour of the 'national front' or single party representing 'the people' as a whole. Arab socialism has been predominantly secular in outlook, particularly in the Middle East (the ***mashreq***) although attempts have been made in some cases (e.g. Mauritania and Libya) to combine it with '**Islam**'. The Arab socialist movements of the Middle East have been led generally by men from the 'new middle classes' (army officers, civil servants, school teachers, etc.) opposed to the old ruling élites, but firmly believing in the possibility of radical reform and modernization by suitably educated and/or trained cadres, rather than in Marxist-style revolution from below. The most important of these movements was the Arab Socialist Party, usually called the Ba'ath Party. In later years, President **Nasser** of Egypt regarded himself as espousing a form of Arab socialism, **Nasserism**. His efforts to create a **United Arab Republic** were linked to his vision of Arab socialism.

Arab West

The Arab West (***maghreb***) refers to the Arab countries of **North Africa**: Libya, Algeria, Tunisia, Morocco and Mauritania, which all belong to the **Arab Maghreb Union**. It includes by implication the **Western Sahara**, whose status remains undetermined.

Arabic

The language of the Arabs that originated among the indigenous peoples of the Arabian Peninsula. The language of the Koran and therefore the language of **Islam**. It is spoken today by 250m. people in Arab countries, and by many of the world's approximately 1,000m. Muslims. Arabic is divided into three groups: Classical written Arabic; written Modern Standard Arabic; and spoken Arabic. Classical written Arabic is principally defined as the Arabic used in the Koran and in the earliest literature from the Arabian Peninsula. Modern Standard Arabic is a modernization of the structures of classical Arabic, and includes words for modern phenomena as well as many additions from dialects across the Arab World. Spoken Arabic is a mixed form, usually with a dominating influence from local languages, and it is correct to refer to different versions of Arabic as separate languages. Classical Arabic usually refers to the formal language of poetry, prose, oratory and sermons, and to the language of the Koran. The Koran is expressed in Arabic and traditionally Muslims deemed it untranslatable. Arabic is, therefore, a sacred language—it is the only language in which the Koran is believed to be fully understood, with all translations reducing the quality of the revelations of God. Arabic is the language of Islam, but is also spoken by Arab Christians, Arabs of other faiths and so-called Oriental Jews. Arabic is a Semitic language, closely related to the Hebrew language. Standard Arabic usually refers to the language as used by the press, radio and television across **North Africa** and the Middle East (from Mauritania and the **Western Sahara** to Iraq). Arabic in a wider sense—colloquial Arabic—can also refer to one of the many national or regional so-called dialects spoken across North Africa and the Middle East, which can sometimes differ enough to be mutually incomprehensible. These dialects are frequently not written.

Arab(s)

The birthplace of the Arabs was the Arabian Peninsula. After the advent of **Islam** on the Peninsula Arab armies embarked on a conquest of the world in the name of **Islam**. Gradually they assimilated, or were assimilated into, the populations they dominated—large numbers of whom converted to Islam. The term 'Arab' is used to designate a people made up of individuals who speak one of the variations of the Arabic language, possess an Arab identity, and consider themselves a part of the history and culture that has developed in the Middle East and northern Africa since the establishment of Islam in the 7th century AD. Though there are close links between the Arabs and Islam they are not synonymous; there are many Christian Arabs as well as many non-Arab Muslims. Today what is known as the Arab World corresponds approximately with the membership of the **Arab League**. However, there are Arab minorities on the fringes of this area in Turkey, Africa and Israel.

Armée islamique du salut (AIS—Islamic Salvation Army)

The Armée islamique du salut (AIS) was established in Algeria in mid-1994 as the armed wing of the banned **Front islamique du salut (FIS—Islamic Salvation Front)**. Its precise numerical strength is unknown, but in 1995 it was estimated at approximately 6,000. The exact relationship with the FIS was not always clear, but AIS leaders evidently acted with a degree of autonomy and were not directly controlled by the FIS. The AIS merged with the Armed Islamic Movement. Its main leader was Medani Mezrag. Following a cease-fire in October 1997, the AIS declared a definitive end to its guerrilla operations and armed struggle against the state on 6 June 1999. The AIS took advantage of the amnesty provided by the Civil Concord Law and disbanded in January 2000. Some of its members were integrated into the army in operations against the **Groupe islamique armé (GIA—Armed Islamic Group)**. In February 1998 four other armed Islamist groups—the Ansar Battalion, the Mawt Battalion, the ar-Rahman Battalion and the **Ligue islamique de la daawa et le djihad (Islamic League for Call and Jihad)**, joined the truce announced by the AIS in October 1997.

Arusha Declaration

A major policy statement (speech and document) produced by **Julius Nyerere**, President of Tanzania, in February 1967, announcing a new form of **African socialism** and socialist construction—*ujamaa*—involving decentralization in **agriculture** and the nationalization of manufacturing industry. Most commentators now agree that *ujamaa* failed tragically and was associated with a significant per caput decline during the 1970s. Even Nyerere himself, prime architect of the *ujamaa* policy, admitted in 1984 that 'there are certain things I would not do if I were to start again'.

Nyerere was correct, however, to insist in the Declaration that development aid ought only to be used as a catalyst, while the main thrust of development should come from within. Once a **Third World** country turns to the international aid agencies, he suggested, it surrenders control over part of its development. The 'donors' decide what is needed, how much they will provide, on what terms, and when they will come and go.

Asari, Mujahid Dokubo

In September 2004 Asari, the son of a judge and a member of the Ijaw ethnic group, which inhabits the Niger Delta, who had been fighting with a rival local warlord and political leader, Tom Ateke, since 2003, threatened 'all-out war' on the Nigerian state if the Ijaws were not given more of the profits from the **oil** that is being exploited in their homeland. Allegedly having first risen to prominence as an enforcer for a state governor, Asari draws his support from the Ijaws, many of whom are extremely poor. Indeed, the villagers of the Delta are among the poorest in Nigeria, even though its governors are among the wealthiest. President **Obasanjo** has tried to defuse the situation. In October 2004 he brokered a cease-fire between Asari and Ateke, and their respective supporters have now surrendered their weapons in return for generous compensation.

Asante – *see* Ashanti

Ascension Island

The island of Ascension lies in the South Atlantic Ocean. It was uninhabited until a small British garrison was placed there at the time of the arrival, in 1815, of Napoléon Bonaparte in **Saint Helena**, some 1,131 km to the south-east. It remained under the supervision of the British Admiralty until 1922, when it was made a dependency of Saint Helena. In 1942 the US government, by arrangement with its British counterpart, established an airbase ('Wideawake') on the island, which it subsequently reoccupied and extended in 1956, in connection with the extension of a long-range proving ground for guided missiles, centred in Florida, USA. A further agreement in 1965 allowed the US government to develop tracking facilities on the island in support of the NASA 'Apollo' space programme. This operation was terminated in 1990. Facilities underwent rapid development in 1982 to enable the island to serve as a major staging post for British vessels and aircraft *en route* to the Falkland Islands. Today the island is an important communications centre. The government is provided by the resident Administrator, aided by two advisory groups—one comprising senior managers of resident organizations and one comprising their employees' representatives. The Administrator answers to the Governor of Saint Helena, who is also Governor of Ascension Island. The population in March 2001 was 982 (excluding British military personnel), of whom 760 were Saint Helenians and the remainder (215—150 UK nationals, 65 US nationals) were expatriate civilian personnel of Merlin Communications International, which operates the BBC Overseas World Service Atlantic relay station, of Cable & Wireless PLC, which provides international communications services and operates the 'Ariane' satellite tracking station of the European Space Agency, and of the US military base. On 31 March 2001the joint venture between the BBC and Cable & Wireless, dating from 1984, to provide public services to the island, was dissolved. The Ascension Island government took over responsibility for health and **education**, the Ascension Island Works and Services Agency, a statutory body, was established to maintain transport and infrastructure, and any remaining services were taken over by the new Ascension Island Commercial Services Ltd. This company was jointly owned by the Ascension Island government, the BBC and Cable & Wireless and had the declared aim of privatizing the new enterprises by 2002. Dissent developed among the resident population in June 2002, when the British Foreign and Commonwealth Office decided to impose taxes for the first time. Residents claimed that this was taxation without representation. The Governor responded with plans to introduce a democratically elected council with a purely advisory function. In August 95% of those who voted in a national referendum favoured the establishment of an elected Island Council, to comprise seven elected members, the Attorney General, the Director of Finance and one or two appointed members. A joint consultative council was also to be established, with representatives from both Ascension and Saint Helena, to develop policy relating to economic development and tourism common to both islands.

Ashanti (Asante)

Today an ethnic group in Ghana. In pre-colonial times a kingdom of some complexity, with a tradition of sculpture and manufacture of bronze figurines and heads. Resisted the British intervention in a series of wars known as the Ashanti Wars.

Ashigga Party

Political party formed in the 1940s by **Ismail al-Azhari**, which aimed at the union of the Sudan with Egypt.

Association of African Development Finance Institutions (AADFI)

Founded in 1975, the Association of African Development Finance Institutions (AADFI) aims to promote co-operation among financial institutions in the region in matters relating to economic and social development, research, project design, funding and the exchange of information. It has more than 90 members in 43 African and non-African countries.

Association sociale-démocrate du Cameroun (ASDC—Social Democrat Association of Cameroon)

Political party in Cameroon, established in 1991.

Assoumani, Col Azali

President of the Union of the Comoros. Born in the island of Grande-Comore (now Ngazidja) in 1959, Col Azali Assoumani assumed power in a coup in April 1999 in the wake of a violent backlash against people originating from the breakaway island of Anjouan (now **Nzwani**). A former chief of staff, he pledged to eradicate political **corruption** and resolve the secessionist crisis. A bloodless military coup was attempted on 24 September 2001 on the island of Nzwani; the coup was suppressed on the following day. In early November there was another attempted coup, which was again suppressed. Later in that month 76% of the electorate in the Comoros voted in favour of a new constitution, which provided for a greater devolution of power to the separate islands. The country, henceforth to be known as the Union of the Comoros, was to be led by the President of the Union, a post that was to be rotated between the islands. A transitional government of national unity was established on 20 January 2002, but collapsed on the following day after the withdrawal of opposition representatives. It was reorganized in February. In April Azali was elected unopposed as Federal President of the Union of the Comoros. The title was confirmed by an international committee overseeing the islands' transition to the Union of the Comoros, although rejected by his rivals. A new, five-member government was formed at the beginning of June 2002.

AV-Intware (Alliance of the Brave)

A political party in Burundi, established in 1993, with predominantly **Tutsi** membership. Its leader is André Nkundikije.

Awololo, Chief Obafemi

When Nigeria became independent in 1960, with a federal constitution based on three major regions, the north, the east and the west, **Sir Abubakar Tafawa Balewa** became federal Premier, while the eastern leader, Namdi Azikiwe, became President. The political parties of both leaders co-operated in government. The opposition was formed by the followers of Chief Obafemi Awololo, the western leader. This basic arrangement did not, however, last very long. The accord between east and north broke down and divisions grew in the west, as Chief Awololo was challenged by **Chief Akintola**, who succeeded in having his rival and other leaders tried and imprisoned. Akintola was not satisfied with Awololo's policy of forming an opposition at federal level and preferred an alliance with the north, displacing the eastern **Ibos** and obtaining for his own people a share in the power, perquisites and finances of central government. In 1963 a fourth, mid-western region was formed. Elections held in the western region in 1965 were characterized by violence and, allegedly, flagrant malpractice. In the following year more serious fighting erupted in the north. In January 1966 a group of young Ibo officers rebelled, partly in protest against bad government and partly as a demonstration against the north and its Western allies. The federal and northern Prime Ministers, Balewa and the Sardauna of Sokoto, were murdered, together with Chief Akintola, Awololo's rival in the west, and many others. Senior officers quickly suppressed the rebellion. Within a year, however, the eastern region, and the Ibos, had broken away to establish an independent state, **Biafra**.

Azanian People's Organization (AZAPO)

Radical popular movement in South Africa, which gained a seat in the National Assembly at the 1999 elections.

Al-Azhari, Ismail

Sudanese nationalism gathered strength in the1930s under the leadership of Ismail al-Azhari who became secretary of the Graduates General Congress, formed in 1938. He formed the **Ashigga Party** in the 1940s, which aimed to achieve a union between the Sudan and Egypt. He was arrested in the late 1940s after anti-British demonstrations. After his release he re-formed his party, as the National Unionist Party, and when elections were held in Sudan at the end of 1953, he and the party won an overwhelming victory. Al-Azhari became Prime Minister at the beginning of 1954 and called for **independence** for the Sudan. This was achieved on the first day of 1956. Subsequently, however, al-Azhari's party disintegrated. He formed a coalition and then was ousted, in 1956, by Abdullah Khalil. Khalil feared an alliance between al-Azhari and **Nasser** and he was suspected of having been involved in a coup which swept away al-Azhari's government, and the Constitution, and brought to power a supreme council of army officers, with **Gen. Ibrahim Abboud** at their head.

B

Ba'athism

Ba'athism, the basis of the Ba'ath(ist) movement, was conceived as an ideology of renaissance and reform for the Arab World (in **Arabic** *ba'ath* means 'renaissance') around the notion of Arab unity and the Arab nation. According to its creators, the Arabs form a single nation aspiring to form an Arab state and play a unique role in the world. Ba'athism was developed in Damascus in the 1940s by the Orthodox Christian, Michel Aflaq, and the **Sunni** Muslim, Salah ad-Din Bitar. The Ba'ath(ist) movement established the (Arab) Ba'ath Party at its first congress in 1947.

Ba'athists (Mauritania)

The largest and most active Arab nationalist faction in Mauritania, this group has maintained close ties with the Iraqi Ba'ath(ist) Socialist Party. It favours the full Arabization of Mauritania. Its extreme views have been considered racist by the government, and by many other political groupings, in view of the ethnic diversity of the country and the risk that ethnic divisions may be expressed violently as they sometimes have been (particularly during 1989). Scores of Ba'athist activists were arrested by security forces during **Ould Haidalla**'s presidency. The Ba'athists have also been under constant scrutiny during the long period of **Ould Taya**'s presidency. On the other hand, the government of Mauritania was broadly sympathetic during the Gulf War (1991) towards Iraq, and there were even rumours that members of Saddam Hussain's family took refuge in Mauritania. More recently, however, in 2003, Ba'athists in Mauritania have been arrested on suspicion of plotting against the government.

Babangida, Gen. Ibrahim

A recurrent figure in Nigeria's political leadership during the 1980s and 1990s, Babangida was a member of the ruling council of **Maj.-Gen. Muhammadu Buhari**, who had seized power in Nigeria at the end of 1983 but presided over a disastrous regime. Babangida replaced Buhari as Head of State in 1985. One of the new regime's most notable acts was to restrict the repayment of foreign **debt** to a fixed proportion of the national product.

Bakassi Peninsula

Area between Nigeria and Cameroon. These two countries have long disputed their border, including the **oil**-rich Bakassi Peninsula. In December 2003 the Nigerian government ceded control of 32 villages on its north-eastern border to Cameroon, but sovereignty over the disputed territory where petroleum resources are located remained under discussion. In January 2004 Presidents **Biya** and **Obasanjo**, meeting in Geneva, Switzerland, with UN mediation, agreed to exchange consular envoys, and to establish joint security patrols in the disputed region; the signing of a 'non-aggression' treaty was also envisaged.

Balewa, Sir Abubakar Tafawa

When Nigeria became independent in 1960, with a federal constitution based on three major regions, the north, the east and the west, Sir Abubakar Tafawa Balewa became federal Premier, while the eastern leader, Namdi Azikiwe, became President. The political parties of both leaders co-operated in government. The opposition was formed by the followers of **Chief Obafemi Awololo**, the western leader. In January 1966 a group of young **Ibo** officers rebelled, partly in protest against bad government and partly as a demonstration against the north and its Western allies. The federal and northern Prime Ministers, Sir Abubakar Tafawa Balewa and the Sardauna of Sokoto, were murdered, together with **Chief Akintola**, a rival of Awololo's in the west, and many others. Senior officers quickly intervened to suppress the rebellion. Within one year, however, the eastern region had seceded, declaring itself the independent state of **Biafra**.

Baluba

Major ethno-linguistic group in the southern part of the Democratic Republic of the Congo. Gave its name to a political party in the Belgian Congo, led by Jason Sendwe—**Balubakat**. Whereas **Moïse Tshombe** was interested in promoting **Conakat** with the aim of enhancing the ability of the Balundaba to exercise power in **Katanga**, either through a federal state or **independence**, Sendwe viewed the Balunda to the south with suspicion and prevented Conakat from speaking for the whole of Katanga, gaining his support from the Baluba.

Balubakat

A political party in the Belgian Congo, led by Jason Sendwe, and supported mainly by the **Baluba** people as a counter to **Moïse Tshombe**'s **Conakat**, through which the Balunda hoped to exercise power in **Katanga**, either through a federal state or **independence**.

Bambara

One of the major groups within the **Mande** peoples who constitute about one-half of the population of Mali. The Bambara language is spoken by some 80% of the inhabitants of Mali.

Banana, Rev. Canaan

Zimbabwe's first President and the country's non-executive Head of State from 1980 until 1987. He died in November 2003.

Banda, Dr Hastings Kamuzu

Prime Minister and then President of Malawi after **independence**, Dr Hastings Banda ruled Malawi as Life President and personal dictator until the country's first multi-party elections, forced upon it by its external creditors, in 1994. At an early age Banda left **Nyasaland** for neighbouring **Rhodesia**, and then South Africa. By 1925 he had saved enough money—reputedly by working in **gold** mines—to buy a ticket to the USA to take up a medical scholarship at the Wilberforce Institute, Ohio. From there he went to Chicago University and then to a medical college in Nashville, Tennessee, where he qualified as a doctor in 1937. He acquired further qualifications in the United Kingdom where he practised until 1953; he subsequently established a medical practice on the **Gold Coast** (now Ghana). In 1958 he returned to his native country, and in the following year founded the Malawi Congress Party (MCP) to lead the fight for independence. The MCP was to become his personal political machine. He was arrested in Rhodesia for subversion and imprisoned for nearly one year before being deported to Nyasaland. In 1961 Banda's MCP won an overwhelming electoral victory. Nyasaland, which he led as Prime Minister, became independent from Britain as Malawi in 1964. Under a new constitution, Banda became Malawi's first President in 1966. He appointed himself Life President in 1971. In that year he also became the first African leader to visit South Africa, with whose **apartheid** government he literally came to terms. His regime was deeply conservative and became increasingly autocratic; opponents were routinely jailed and some were killed. Eventually bowing to opposition pressure, anti-government riots and the suspension of Western aid in 1992, he was obliged to abandon his one-man, one-party rule and Life Presidency, opening the way for a pluralist system. In October 1993 he underwent brain surgery, temporarily handing power to a presidential council and allowing democratic elections to take place. In 1994 Dr Banda was a candidate in the first free presidential election to be held for 30 years, but was defeated by **Bakili Muluzi**. His ill health forced him to announce his retirement from active politics in August 1994, and he died in South Africa in 1997. Banda's funeral was attended by **Nelson Mandela**, **Robert Mugabe**, **Kenneth Kaunda**, and Joaquim Chissano, who all came to pay their respects to a fellow liberator and the father of the Malawian nation. After his death the MCP remained a major force in Malawi politics, and most of those who hold power in the party are former associates of Banda.

Bandung Conference (1955)

The Afro-Asian Conference held in 1955 in Bandung, an hour's flight from Jakarta in Indonesia, led to the establishment of the **Non-aligned Movement** in 1961 and the emergence of the **Third World**. More than 1,000 representatives of 29 African and Asian nations and 30 anti-colonial resistance and liberation movements, including the Algerian **Front de libération nationale (FLN—National Liberation Front)**, the Tunisian **Neo-Destour Party** and the Moroccan **Istiqlal**, participated in the Conference. Apart from these three **independence** movements, Africa was also represented by **Gamal Abdel Nasser** of Egypt, who was subsequently to become a major figure in the Arab World. South Africa was not invited to attend the Conference. The aim was to promote economic and cultural co-operation and to oppose **colonialism**.

Banque Centrale des Comores

Founded in 1981, this is the central issuing bank of the Comoros.

Banque centrale des états de l'Afrique de l'ouest (BCEAO—Central Bank of West African States)

Founded in 1962, the Banque centrale des états de l'Afrique de l'ouest (BCEAO) is the central bank of issue for the members of the **Union économique et monétaire ouest-africaine (UEMOA—West African Economic and Monetary Union)**—Benin, Burkina Faso, Côte d'Ivoire, Guinea-Bissau, Mali, Niger, Senegal and Togo.

Banque Centrale Populaire (Crédit Populaire du Maroc)

Leading Moroccan public-sector bank, whose internal management problems delayed privatization.

Banque Commerciale du Maroc SA (BCM)

Morocco's leading private bank. In 1987 Omnium Nord-Africain, a leading industrial corporation, acquired a major stake in the BCM, as well as in other banks.

Banque de développement des états de l'Afrique centrale (BDEAC—Development Bank of Central African States)

Established in 1975 to promote the economic development and integration of the countries of central Africa, its members and shareholders are: Cameroon, Central African Republic, Chad, the Republic of the Congo, Gabon, Equatorial Guinea, the

African Development Bank, the **Banque des états de l'Afrique centrale**, France, Germany and Kuwait.

Banque des états de l'Afrique centrale (BEAC—Bank of the Central African States)

Established in 1973 as the central bank of issue of Cameroon, the Central African Republic, Chad, the Republic of the Congo, Equatorial Guinea and Gabon. A monetary market, incorporating all national financial institutions of the member countries, came into effect in July 1994.

Banque Marocaine du Commerce Extérieur (BMCE)

Morocco's leading private export bank. In 1995 Othman Benjelloun, a leading member of the wealthy Benjelloun family from Fez, acquired a core stake in this bank, which was previously a public-sector organization. It was reported that his winning offer for the BMCE was so high that it indicated royal patronage.

Banque Misr

Egypt's first national bank, established in May 1920, inspired by Talaat Harb, the nationalist industrialist, who published a book calling for the foundation of a national bank. The shares of the Bank were nominal and exclusively held by Egyptians, all of the Bank's dealings were in **Arabic**, and it was operated by Egyptian employees. The foremost aim of Banque Misr was to serve national economic interests.

Banque Ouest-Africaine de Développement (BOAD)

Established in 1973 to promote the balanced development of member states and the economic integration of West Africa. A Guarantee Fund for Private Investment in West Africa, established jointly by BOAD and the European Investment Bank, was inaugurated in December 1994. The Fund aims to guarantee medium- and long-term credit to private-sector businesses in the region.

Banyamulenge

Ethnic group in the eastern region of the Democratic Republic of the Congo (DRC). Their nationality status is disputed and there is considerable hostility between the Banyamulenge, considered to be of Rwandan origin, and local Congolese. The Banyamulenge are members of a group of diverse origins, many of whom came from Rwanda and Burundi but settled in the hill areas of Uvira in what is now the DRC before 1885. There are, broadly, four different groups who constitute the present-day Banyamulenge (literally: 'people of the hills'): an original group which fled from oppression under the regime of the Mwami of the kingdom of Rwanda; a group originating from Burundi; a group from Tanzania; and a group comprising slaves from local tribes (Bashi, Bafuliro and Batetela) who have been progressively incorporated into the Banyamulenge. Over the last 100 years these diverse groups have gradually established an authentic social and cultural identity, in part by virtue of lengthy cohabitation, social interaction and a degree of intermarriage. The majority of the Banyamulenge are of **Tutsi** origin, while a minority are of mixed ancestry.

Baoule

An ethno-linguistic group in São Tomé and Príncipe. The **Akan**, with their Baoule sub-group in the south, are the largest single ethnic constituent of the grouping.

Al-Baraka

International Islamic banking group. Established a joint venture with a public-sector bank in Algeria in 1988, and paved the way for other private-sector Islamic banks to gain permission to operate in Algeria after 1992. In Morocco it was able only to establish a leasing company.

Al-Barakaat

Informal Somali money transfer organization. It was the major mechanism for the transfer to Somalia of remittances by expatriate **Somalis** and virtually the sole source of funding for the Somali economy. It had offices in the USA and 40 other countries, but was closed following the events of 11 September 2001, as it was suspected, chiefly by the US Federal Bureau of Investigation and the US Foreign Terrorist Asset Tracking Centre (FTAT), to have been involved in financing **terrorism**—channelling US $15m.–$20m. to al-Qa'ida annually. On 7 November 2001 FTAT designated al-Barakaat as a terrorist-related financial entity and co-ordinated efforts were begun to block assets and to assist other law enforcement agencies to take actions against al-Barakaat. On the same day US federal agents executed search warrants in three cities (Boston, Columbus, and Alexandria) across the country and closed eight al-Barakaat offices across the USA, including those in Boston, Seattle and Minneapolis. As part of that action, $1.9m. of assets were 'frozen', and, in addition, al-Barakaat's Middle Eastern assets in Dubai, United Arab Emirates, were blocked. Disruptions to al-Barakaat's world-wide cash flows were estimated to be as high as $300m.–$400m. per year. Al-Barakaat was in fact just one of thousands of informal businesses and money transfer companies that transfer funds through the informal Hawala money transfer system. The Hawala system is especially important for Somalia, which has a huge diaspora that has fled from the country during the years of conflict and internal turmoil. This diaspora is estimated to have provided as much as 23% of Somalia's income annually. The majority of remittances are sent through the informal money transfer businesses that charge a lower rate of commission than bigger corporations, such as Western Union or Moneygram, and are more widely accessible to recipients in Somalia, a state with no central bank. Further investigation has apparently revealed that al-Barakaat was not obviously involved in funding terrorism; conversely, direct funding of the 11 September 2001 attacks appears to have taken place via money transfers through conventional commercial banking systems. The US Treasury Department has subsequently removed some Somali individuals and three other money transfer companies from a list of alleged supporters of terrorism and dropped all charges against them. Despite no evidence having been produced by the Bush administration to substantiate its claim that the Somali company gave direct financial support to al-Qa'ida, the US Treasury Department has not shifted its position on al-Barakaat specifically.

Bardo Treaty

Treaty of 1881 that established a French protectorate in Tunisia.

al-Bashir, Lt-Gen. Omar Hassan Ahmad

President of Sudan. Lt-Gen. Omar Hassan Ahmad al-Bashir came to power in 1989 after a military coup that was backed by the **National Islamic Front**. He was appointed as President in 1993 by the Revolution Command Council. In 1996 he was elected to a five-year term of office as President. He was re-elected, having obtained more than 80% of the vote in the absence of any significant opposition, in December 2000. He has the power to appoint the council of ministers. The legislative body is the National Assembly, which has 400 seats, but this is generally subordinate to the President. After 20 years of conflict between the north and south of the country, of which the government of al-Bashir has undoubtedly contributed to the failure to achieve any settlement, a peace agreement seemed finally to have been concluded in 2004–05. However, the sudden death in a helicopter crash of **John Garang**, leader of the rebel Sudan People's Liberation Movement in the south, has jeopardized the realization of that peace agreement in a process which gives autonomy to the south for six years, with the option thereafter of secession. In the mean time the conflict in **Darfur**, which many regard as having been of a kind and on a scale, which demands the term **genocide**, continues.

Basutoland

The land of the Ba-sotho people. Britain obtained control of Basutoland, later, after **independence**, called Lesotho, in 1968.

Bechuanaland

In 1885 Britain declared a protectorate over Bechuanaland, a huge and largely desert area to the north of the **Cape Colony**, at the request of local **Tswana** rulers who wished to deter **Boer** encroachment from the Transvaal in the east. In 1895 the southern portion of the Bechuanaland protectorate was incorporated into the Cape Colony, and the northern portion, which continued to be ruled by Britain through the High Commissioner, was then known as Bechuanaland. **Cecil Rhodes** was instrumental in Britain's acquisition of Bechuanaland as a protectorate, to safeguard the land route from the Cape into the interior, which had been threatened earlier by German activity in **South West Africa**. His company, the British South Africa Company, was chartered by the British government in 1899—the year when the **Boer War**, in which Britain fought the South African settlers of Dutch origin, known as the Boers, commenced—to administer the territory. There was some expectation that Bechuanaland would join the new **Union of South Africa** after 1910, but the Tswana made clear their opposition to this, and the territory remained under British rule until it gained **independence,** as Botswana, in 1966.

Bechuanaland Democratic Party (BDP – *see also* Botswana Democratic Party)

Political party formed in 1962 by Seretse Khama, former heir to the chieftainship of the Bamangwato, who had been forced to renounce his chieftainship in 1956 under pressure from the British, South African and Southern Rhodesian governments, after he married a white woman. Many white settlers gave their support to the BDP in preference to the more radical **Bechuanaland People's Party (BPP)**. In the territory's first direct legislative elections under universal adult suffrage, held in 1965, the BDP won 28 out of a total of 31 seats and Seretse Khama became Prime Minister. **Independence** followed in September 1966, when Bechuanaland became the Republic of Botswana, with Khama as President. In the years following independence, the BDP, now renamed the Botswana Democratic Party, was challenged by the BPP (particularly in urban areas) and by a new 'socialist' party, the **Botswana National Front**. The BDP has, however, retained power over the last 40 years.

Bechuanaland People's Party (BPP)

The first nationalist party in **Bechuanaland**, founded in 1960. It had close links with the **African National Congress** in South Africa. The BPP soon split in two, with one section becoming the **Botswana Independence Party** and the other the more important **Botswana People's Party**.

Bedouin(s)

Literally, people of the countryside (**Arabic**: *bedu*). Widely used to refer to tribal populations still living in the desert regions of **North Africa** and the Middle East, including the Sahara (Libya and Egypt).

Belhadj, Ali (Sheikh)

Born 1954. Deputy leader of the **Front islamique du salut (FIS—Islamic Salvation Front)**, an Algerian political party. A high school teacher and the imam of the al-Sunna mosque in the popular quarter of Bab el-Oued in Algiers, he, together with the more moderate **Abbasi Madani**, registered the FIS as a political party in 1989. Belhadj personified the younger generation of the FIS, with a powerful appeal to the deprived and frustrated urban youth. A year later the party won a majority of votes in local elections. In 1991, however, the Algerian government proclaimed martial law and imprisoned Belhadj and Madani. In 1994 Belhadj was transferred to house arrest.

Ben Ali, Zine el-Abidine

President of Tunisia since 1987. Educated in France and the USA, he entered the army and became Minister of National Security (1984–86) and interior minister (1986–87). In October 1987 he became Prime Minister under the ageing Tunisian President **Habib Bourguiba**, whom he deposed in a bloodless coup in November 1987. Ben Ali was elected as President in 1989 and then re-elected in 1994 and again in October 1999.

Ben Bella, Ahmed

Born 1916, first President of Algeria from 1963 until 1965. Ben Bella served in the French army in the Second World War, thereafter becoming active in the Algerian struggle for **independence**. He was one of the nine members of the revolutionary committee that developed into the **Front de libération nationale (FLN—National Liberation Front)**. Ben Bella was imprisoned from 1956 until 1962, when the Evian Agreement was signed, and Algeria gained independence. He became President in 1962, but lost power to **Houari Boumedienne** in 1965, and was placed under house arrest until 1980.

Benin, Republic of

The Republic of Benin is bordered to the west by Nigeria, on the east by Togo and to the north by Burkina Faso and Niger. From a coastline of about 100 km on the Gulf of Guinea, it extends inland about 650 km to the Niger River. The coast is a straight sandbar, backed by lagoons. Rivers flow into these lagoons, and Lakes Ahémé and Nokoué are estuaries of large rivers whose exit to the sea is obstructed by the sandbar. North of Lake Nokoué the river Ouémé has a wide marshy delta. Benin's area is 112,622 sq km and its population about 6m. The administrative capital is Porto-Novo and the commercial capital Cotonou. The major ethnic groups in the country are: the **Fon** and **Adja**, which account for about 40% of the population, the **Yoruba** (12%), the Barba (9%) and the Betamarib (8%). The remainder of the population belong to some 40 other ethnic groups. The main languages are French (official), Fon, Yoruba and other ethnic languages. With regard to religion, those holding indigenous beliefs represent about 35% of the population, Christians another 35% and Muslims 30%.

Political profile

Benin is a **democracy**. The President, Head of State and head of the government is **Mathieu Kérékou**. The President is elected by popular vote for a five-year term of office. Kérékou, who has served continuously as President since 4 April 1996, was re-elected on 22 March 2001, having obtained 84.1% of the vote in the second ballot—contested by only one other candidate, Bruno Amoussou—of the presidential election; and, most recently, in 2003. The next presidential election is due to be held in March 2006. The President appoints the Council of Ministers. The legislature is the unicameral Assemblée nationale, comprising 83 seats to which deputies are returned by popular vote for a four-year term. Major political parties are **La Renaissance du Bénin (RB—Rebirth of Benin)**, the **Parti du renouveau démocratique (PRD—Parti of Democratic Renewal)**, the Parti social démocrate (PSD—Social Democrat Party), and the **Union pour le Bénin du futur (UBF—Union for Benin of the Future)**—a coalition of parties also known as the Presidential Movement).

History

Benin was the site of **Dahomey**, a prominent West African kingdom that rose in the 15th century. The territory became a French colony in 1872 and achieved **independence** on 1 August 1960, as the Republic of Benin. A succession of military regimes ended in 1972 with the rise to power of Maj. (later Brig.-Gen.) Mathieu Kérékou and the establishment of a government based on Marxist-Leninist principles. Following two attempted coups in 1988, popular discontent came to a culmination in 1989 in the form of prolonged strikes by teachers and civil servants, many of whom had not been paid since 1988. Kérékou allowed a sovereign national conference to be held, which drew up a new constitution and provided for multi-party elections, but he remained as President and head of the armed forces. The conference also designated Nicéphore Soglo, a former **World Bank** official, as Prime Minister, and an interim civilian government was appointed. This has been described as **sub-Saharan Africa**'s first 'civilian coup', whereby a single-party government, backed by the **military**, had been forced to cede power to a multi-party democracy. The conference also passed a resolution to change the country's name to the Republic of Benin, which took effect in 1991.

In March 1991 Kérékou was defeated in a presidential election by Soglo and he retired without any resistance. The avowed aim of the new (technocratic) government of President Soglo was to rebuild the economy, after years of misallocation of resources. On 1 April 1991 a freely elected multi-party Assemblée nationale was inaugurated, with 20 parties sharing 64 seats. Legislative elections contested by 30 parties in 1995 were generally calm and fair, although allegations of fraud led to polls being reheld in 13 constituencies. Soglo's supporters found themselves in a minority in the Assemblée nationale. In the first round of the presidential election held on 3 March 1996 Soglo obtained 34.9% of the votes and Kérékou 34.1%. In the second ballot that now became necessary as no candidate had obtained 51% of the vote in the first, Adrien Houngbedji—who had received 17% of the vote in the first ballot—announced his support for Kérékou. On 24 March the Constitutional Court proclaimed Kérékou the winner of the second ballot, with 54% of the vote to Soglo's 46%. There had been a turn-out of 86% in the first ballot and of 78% in the second. After a period of tension during which it was suggested that Soglo would not relinquish power, Kérékou was sworn in as President on 4 April. Houngbedji was rewarded for having supported Kérékou's candidacy with the post of Prime Minister. In May 1998, however, Houngbedji resigned, together with the other three ministers who were members of the PRD. The PRD had been the largest single party in the government coalition. Kérékou created a new government without PRD representation. Alliances within the Assemblée nationale remained fluid after Houngbedji's resignation. Following legislative elections held in 1990, the opposition held the majority of seats.

The presidential election that was held on 4 March 2001 was contested by 17 candidates, including Kérékou, Soglo and Houngbedji. More than 87% of those eligible to vote participated in the election—an exceptionally high number. Despite some administrative problems, such as the late arrival of voting cards, the national independent electoral commission reported that the voting process and counting of ballots had proceeded 'generally smoothly'. Kérékou and Soglo obtained, respectively, about 47% and some 29% of the votes. Houngbedji again finished in third place, having obtained 12% of the votes, while Bruno Amoussou, Minister of State in Kérékou's government, obtained 8%. As no candidate had received more than 50% of the votes, a second ballot should have been held between the two leading candidates. However, a second ballot was boycotted by Soglo, who claimed that irregularities had occurred during the first. Houngbedji also refused to participate in a second round of voting. The Constitutional Court confirmed the results of the first ballot, and in the second, held on 22 March, Kérékou received 84% of the votes and Amoussou 16%. Kérékou was duly inaugurated as President on 6 April. Throughout late 2001 and early 2002 he faced a series of nation-wide strikes, mainly by civil servants and employees in the health and **education** sectors, in support of pay claims and concerns about promotion criteria. Local elections were held on 15 December 2002. Partial results were declared on 7 January 2003, but run-offs were necessary in a number of areas. The ruling UBF party received 31.6% of the votes in total and thus returned most local councillors. Soglo became mayor of Cotonou. Legislative and presidential elections were next held on 30 March 2003. Kérékou was re-elected as President, but neither he nor Soglo will be able to contest the next presidential election in 2006 as the Constitution disqualifies candidates over the age of 70. Adrien Houngbedji is president of the Assemblée nationale.

International relations

Benin is a member of the **Economic Community of West African States (ECOWAS)** and of the **Union économique et monétaire ouest-africaine (UEMOA—West African Economic and Monetary Union)**, a regional organization based on membership of the West African **Franc Zone**. Both ECOWAS and UEMOA have free movement of people agreements. Benin is keen to achieve the full implementation of ECOWAS' free-trade zone and single passport, and has already dismantled some of its border posts with Nigeria. Benin provided troops to the ECOWAS Cease-Fire Monitoring Group that was dispatched to Guinea-Bissau in 1998, but these were withdrawn following the *coup d'état* there in 1999. Benin is involved in a dispute with Niger concerning some small islands in the Niger River. This dispute has been referred to the International Court of Justice for arbitration. In August 2003 Nigeria closed its borders with Benin for more than a week because of alleged criminal activity, including smuggling and human-trafficking. Benin, among others, complained that this contravened West Africa-wide agreements that guarantee the free movement of people and goods within the region.

Benin, economy

In 1999 Benin's gross domestic product (GDP) was US $2,200m., equivalent to $380 per head. GDP increased by 5% in 2001, in real terms. The rate of inflation was 9.8% in 1999. **Agriculture**, in particular the production of **cotton** and palm oil, is the mainstay of the economy, and the production of cement is an important industrial sector. Benin's major trading partners are Nigeria, France, the People's Republic of China and Brazil. The national currency is the franc de la **Communauté financière africaine (CFA)**—see the **Franc Zone**. In March 2005 the exchange rate was US $1 = 493.6500 francs CFA.

Benin, poor in natural resources, is traditionally a trading nation and its economy is heavily dependent on the success of, and on its trade with, its much larger neighbour, Nigeria. A large part of the economy is based on the re-export of goods to Nigeria. The agricultural sector in Benin contributes about one-third of GDP and employs an estimated 55% of the labour force. The main exports (in terms of value) are cotton, cottonseed and palm oil. Real GDP growth declined from 5.8% in 2000 to 5% in 2001, owing to lower-than-expected agricultural output. Benin is one of the first countries to have benefited from the framework of the **debt** initiative for **Heavily Indebted Poor Countries (HIPC)**. It will receive around $460m. in **debt relief**.

During the 1980s the economy went into serious decline as a result of unfavourable prices for its primary exports and the effects of the government's collectivization and nationalization measures. This was aggravated by devaluations of the Nigerian *naira*, which seriously damaged Benin's trade with Nigeria. This process was exacerbated by a decline in the Nigerian economy. The economy remains fragile and largely dependent on international aid, with inadequate agricultural diversification (cotton is the only major export crop, accounting for more than 80% of Benin's official exports and 40% of GDP), and a production base which is too narrow (cement is the only major industrial product).

The devaluation of the CFA franc in January 1994 came as a shock to most Beninois. Nicéphore Soglo, President since 1991, supported the devaluation (as an ex-**World Bank** official), and attempted to commend the move to his own people, holding public meetings with the trades unions and market traders. There was considerable social unrest and the government announced salary increases of 10% for all state employees. In July the Assemblée nationale approved increases in wages and student grants that exceeded those envisaged in the government's draft budget. Soglo announced that he would impose the budget by decree and was supported in this by the Constitutional Court. There were further tensions throughout the year between the executive and the legislature and in October 1995 it was rumoured that a coup would be attempted. Tensions increased in November when there was a rocket attack on a newly built conference centre where a major international conference was planned. In January 1996 Kérékou announced that he would contest the forthcoming presidential election and in March he was elected as President. A national economic conference was held in December 1996 with the aim of identifying and agreeing Benin's national economic objectives. The six-day meeting was attended by some 500 delegates from all economic sectors and by observers from the World Bank and the **International Monetary Fund (IMF)**. Addressing the conference, Kérékou expressed his belief that the further development of the private sector was essential to Benin's future economic prosperity and announced his commitment to eliminating **corruption** in all areas of public life.

In late 1997, the government was obliged to revise its budgetary provisions for 1998, after the Assemblée nationale rejected its proposals to end automatic promotions within the civil service. A series of general strikes, involving some 37,000 civil servants, caused considerable disruption and the crisis in the public sector deepened over the following year or so. In October 1999 an estimated 32,000 civil servants undertook a three-day strike over pay and promotion issues. In January 2000 Kérékou was obliged to impose the annual budget by decree, after the Assemblée nationale had rejected its provisions. At the same time, the armed forces demonstrated in Cotonou to complain about pay arrears. In June one of Benin's principal trade union federations, the Centrale syndicale autonome du Bénin, undertook a 48-hour strike in protest at the rapid rise in the cost of fuel. Popular discontent at price rises continued to escalate and an estimated 10,000 people attended a public demonstration in Cotonou in early July, organized by Benin's six trade union federations. Despite these difficulties, Kérékou was re-elected as President and formed a new government in May 2001. However, divisions between the executive and the legislature continued to disrupt economic policy-making. In late 2001 and early 2002 as many as 32,000 civil servants and workers, mainly in the public sector, went on strike over pay and promotion criteria. In February 2002, once again, the President was obliged to implement the state budget by decree following the failure of the Assemblée nationale to adopt the proposed draft. In early March the government reached agreement with six of the seven trade unions that had organized the strikes: wage arrears were to be paid and an increase in civil servants' salaries was to be granted while the issue of promotions was referred to the Assemblée nationale. President Kérékou has continued with his predecessor's pragmatic economic policies in close consultation with the World Bank and the IMF. There has been progress towards transparency and accountability in government, with the establishment of a Constitutional Court, empowered to try members of the government, including the President, and a public declaration of President Kérékou's assets. Twenty-eight of the country's 83 magistrates are at present in jail on corruption charges.

In November 2004 the World Bank approved a total of $125m. in guarantees for Benin, supporting the construction of a 678-km gas pipeline to transport **natural gas** from Nigeria to Benin, Ghana and Togo. The pipeline will improve the chronically poor **energy** situation in these countries. The gas is to be used initially for power generation, and later for other industrial and commercial purposes. The World Bank itself compares the situation with its approval of funds for the Chad–Cameroon **oil** pipeline, which had been the condition of several multinational companies for their participation in the project. The World Bank's contribution, which is only a small part of the total cost of the project—estimated at $600m.—opens the way for private investors to fund the project.

Benflis, Ali

Prime Minister of Algeria in 2000–03, until dismissed by President Benflika. Benflis opposed Benflika in the presidential election held in April 2004.

Berber(s)

Indigenous peoples of **North Africa** who were referred to by the Greeks as *barbaroi*, hence 'Berbers' (those who speak a language other than Greek). Used by all those who subsequently colonized North Africa, from the Romans to the French. In fact, the 'Berbers' speak a variety of dialects, and possibly languages, under the general rubric Tamazight. The Tuareg, who inhabit the central Sahara (southern Algeria, northern Mali and Niger), are also Berbers and speak Tamasheq. The Berbers today have a strong but controversial identity in Algeria, and, to a lesser extent, in Morocco, Libya, Tunisia and Mauritania. In 2003 around 300 schools in Morocco began to teach Tamazight. Education officials have stated that it will be available in all schools by 2008, a move that represents a victory for Berber rights activists. In Algeria, although Berber is widely recognized as a national language, Berber rights activists consider themselves discriminated against and have clashed with the police on several occasions in recent years.

Bérenger, Paul

Founder of the Mouvement Militant Mauricien (Mauritian Militant Movement) in Mauritius.

Berg Report

The **World Bank**'s response to the **Lagos Plan of Action** produced by the African governments. Elliott Berg was the chief author of the report, published in 1981 as *Accelerated Development in Sub-Saharan Africa*, which called for economic reform and structural adjustment in **sub-Saharan Africa** as a precondition for assistance. The report was an indication of polices to come, but was remarkably uncritical of previous policies adopted and purveyed by the World Bank. Samir Amin, a well-known Egyptian development economist, pointed out that 'more than half of the [US] $5 trillion in aid money spent in Africa between 1973 and 1980 came from the Bank. Most of the money went into 'green revolution' experiments, which failed miserably, while the small peasants were left to fend for themselves'. The Berg Report, however, blamed African governments and their polices—citing gross mismanagement, faulty exchange rate policies, excessive state intervention and, particularly, the protection of inefficient producers, the unnecessary subsidization of urban consumers, extraction of high rents from rural producers and general **corruption**. The central recommendation of the Berg Report was that the state should withdraw from intervention in African economies and liberate market forces by freeing foreign trade and exchanges from controls, which, it was anticipated, would reduce imports and increase exports so that the deficit on the foreign balance of payments could be cut and some of the outstanding debts repaid. Steps of this kind were to be made a precondition for structural adjustment loans and sectoral adjustment loans.

Berlin West Africa Conference

Organized by German Chancellor Otto von Bismarck in 1884–85, the Berlin West African Conference created a framework generally agreed by the major European powers for colonial expansion in order to avert any major conflict between them in a 'scramble for Africa'.

Bevin-Sforza Plan

After the Second World War the British and Italian governments devised a plan, named after their respective foreign ministers, whereby an independent Libyan state would come into being at the end of 10 years. In the mean time its existing three parts would fall under British or Italian tutelage: the Fezzan under Italian trusteeship, Tripolitania under the British for two years and Italian administration for eight, and Cyrenaica under British administration for the whole 10-year period. The political committee of the UN General Assembly accepted the plan but the

Assembly itself narrowly failed to endorse it. It was eventually agreed that Libya would become an independent tripartite constitutional monarchy under the emir of Cyrenaica, Said Mohammad Idris as-Sanussi, as King **Idris** of Libya.

Biafra

In May 1967 Lt-Col Odumegwu Ojukwu, who had been appointed military governor of the eastern region of Nigeria, concluded that, after the divisions that had emerged the previous year within the federation and particularly the massacres of **Ibos** in the east, the safety and long-term security of the Ibos could only be secured by the secession of the east from the rest of Nigeria. Dissuaded from taking this step at a conference held in January 1967 at Aburi, Ghana, Ojukwu nevertheless decided to proclaim the independent state of Biafra, and a **civil war** began that was to last three years.

Biafra War

The **civil war** between the forces of the secessionist Biafran state and the Nigerian army was a bitter one, in which historical and cultural divisions were emphasized and the entire structure of the Nigerian federation was called into question. Attempts at mediation by the **Organization of African Unity** in 1967 in Kinshasa, Democratic Republic of the Congo, in 1968 in Algiers, Algeria, and in 1969 in Addis Ababa, Ethiopia, all proved fruitless. The federal army, whose strength was expanded from 10,000 to more than 200,000, gradually prevailed, by sheer force of numbers and superior weaponry, despite tough Biafran resistance. While Britain and the USA supplied arms to the federal government, France assisted Biafra. Two of France's closest African associates, Côte d'Ivoire and Gabon, recognized the secessionist state, as did Zambia and Tanzania. By January 1970 Biafra was obliged to capitulate and, as such, ceased to exist. However, the northern Christian, **Yakubu Gowon**—who had taken over as army chief and Head of State when **Gen. Johnson Aguiyi-Aronsi**, his predecessor and an **Ibo**, was murdered when he suggested that a unitary constitution might be better for Nigeria than a federal one, leading some to infer a desire to see Nigeria united under Ibo dominance—proved statesmanlike, preaching, and practising, reconciliation. After the civil war, Nigeria was divided into 12 (later 19) states in order to reduce regional and national divisions.

Biko, Stephen Bantu

One of the founders of the Black Consciousness movement that developed rapidly in the 1970s across South Africa in the aftermath of the banning of the **African National Congress** and the **Pan-Africanist Congress**. It captured the black youth in particular and ignited the massive student uprisings that began in **Soweto** in June 1976 and destabilized the country for the next 10 months. Biko was described by Donald Woods as 'the most important political leader in the entire country and quite simply the greatest man I have ever had the privilege to know'. In August 1977 he was stopped at a roadblock near the Eastern Cape city of Grahamstown and detained for breaking a banning order which restricted him to his home district of King William's Town. News of his death in detention staggered the country and, despite an attempted cover-up, it soon became widely known that he had been severely ill-treated during September, while in detention, then sent to a prison hospital in Pretoria, where he died. The full story of the torture and brutality to which he had been subjected emerged later.

Bin Laden, Osama

Notorious international terrorist and Islamic extremist. Born in 1957 into great wealth as the son of a Yemeni-born owner of a leading Saudi construction company. In 1979 bin Laden left Saudi Arabia to support the Afghan *mujahidin* against the Soviet invasion of Afghanistan. The Afghan *jihad* was financially and militarily backed by the USA and supported by Saudi Arabia and Pakistan. While in Afghanistan bin Laden helped found the Afghan Service Bureau, which recruited and organized fighters from around the world and imported equipment to aid the Afghan resistance against the Soviet army. Many were from the Arab World and came to be known as the Afghan Arabs. After the Soviet withdrawal in 1989 the 'Arab Afghans' (bin Laden's faction) dispersed, some returning to their own countries, others continuing to fight as Islamists in ongoing struggles elsewhere (including Chechnya) while the 'base' of international *mujahidin* that he had established evolved into an international Islamist network, al-Qa'ida. Bin Laden returned to Saudi Arabia to work in the family construction business, but was expelled in 1991 because of his anti-government activities, which stemmed from his growing antagonism to the Saudi regime, which he regarded as corrupt and deviating from its strict Islamic foundations. He spent the next five years in Sudan until US pressure prompted the Sudanese government to expel him, whereupon bin Laden returned to Afghanistan to lead the operations of al-Qa'ida. Bin Laden's ideology is strongly anti-American, anti-Western, and also anti-Israeli. It has its foundations in Wahhabism and leads him (and many of his followers) to consider Saudi Arabia both as the fount of **Islam** and as a betrayer of Islam's fundamental principles and values. Some believe that al-Qa'ida is therefore a 'fundamentalist' Islamic movement, operating at a global level and seeking in some way to unite Islamic forces against 'the ungodly'. Bin Laden is alleged to have financed, inspired and even directly organized various terrorist attacks. According to the US government, he was, it seems, involved in at least five major attacks. First, the 1993 World Trade Center bombing. Second, the killing, in 1996, of 19 US soldiers in Saudi Arabia. Third, the bombing, in 1998, of US embassies in Kenya and Tanzania which killed more than 200 people. Fourth, the bomb attack, in October 2000, on the *USS Cole* in Yemen. Fifth, in September 2001, the multiple plane hijackings and co-ordinated attacks on the World Trade Center and the Pentagon. The World Trade

Center towers were destroyed, with a death toll of some 3,000 people. In response, the USA, with much international support, launched a war to remove the Taliban from power in Afghanistan. After the collapse of the Taliban regime, which had provided a safe haven as well as training and other facilities, bin Laden went into hiding. It is thought he may still be in Afghanistan.

Bioko

A small, mountainous, volcanic island in the Gulf of Guinea. Part of the archipelago that includes the other Equatorial Guinean island of **Pagalu**, and the islands of São Tomé and Príncipe, which together constitute the Democratic Republic of São Tomé and Príncipe.

Biya, Paul

Head of State in Cameroon since 1982. Born in 1933, Paul Biya was educated in Cameroon and France. Before becoming President himself, he spent his entire political career in the service of former President **Ahmadou Ahidjo**, becoming Prime Minister in 1975. As President, after Ahidjo's resignation in 1982, he set about replacing his predecessor's northern allies with southerners like himself. In 1983 he accused Ahidjo of organizing a coup against him, forcing the former President to flee Cameroon. He survived an attempted coup in 1984.

Black Economic Empowerment (BEE)

Black Economic Empowerment (BEE) is the main thrust of attempts by the government of South Africa to correct the imbalance in ownership of the economy and distribution of wealth inherited from the **apartheid** era. Its intention is to redress the exclusion of the majority of South Africans from the mainstream economy by supporting and favouring the economic empowerment of previously disadvantaged people in the private sector. In 2000 President **Mbeki** called on the black business community to devise a 'plan of action' to tackle the issue of empowerment. A Black Economic Empowerment Commission (BEEC), chaired by **Cyril Ramaphosa**, was formed and in 2001 presented a report to the government calling for targets such as 10% of retirement funds to be invested in BEE (prescribed assets); 25% of the JSE-listed companies to be black-owned within 10 years; at least 40% of non-executive and executive directors of JSE-listed companies to be black; 30% of state-owned enterprises due for restructuring to go to BEE firms. The report also called for an official definition of BEE to help companies meet their empowerment obligations and to clarify the business environment for investors. In March 2003, in response to the BEEC report, the government released a strategy document—*South Africa's Economic Transformation: A Strategy for Broad-Based Black Economic Empowerment*. The document provides a clear definition of BEE and guide-lines for businesses to follow. It included proposals for an Empowerment Act, which would confer powers on the Minister for Trade and Industry to establish a BEE Advisory Council. The Advisory Council will help sectors to formulate their own charters (a set of BEE objectives) where industry itself identifies the need for a Charter.

Boer(s)

The name given by the British in the 19th century to the South Africans of Dutch descent who trekked north-east out of the **Cape of Good Hope** to escape from the jurisdiction of the British and established farms in the **Orange Free State** and the Transvaal regions of South Africa. The Boers developed their own identity as **Afrikaners**, and came to regard themselves as Africans with rights to the land they had 'claimed', owned and farmed in the republics of the Orange Free State and the Transvaal. Towards the end of the 19th century they came into increasing conflict with the British, whose ambitions in **southern Africa** as a whole were considerable and who regarded South Africa as their rightful territory. Between 1899 and 1902 this conflict broke out into open warfare as the so-called **Boer War**.

Boer War

Britain's claims over much of the territory of **southern Africa** were challenged by the two **Afrikaner** republics of the **Orange Free State** and the Transvaal in what is now South Africa. The Afrikaners of the South African Republic under Paul Kruger were referred to by the British (and themselves) as the **Boers**—hence the Boer War. This was a bitter struggle, which lasted three years between 1899 and 1902. Britain overcame the two republics with great difficulty, and then left the Afrikaners, who formed the main element of the privileged white minority in the region, in control of a newly fashioned **Union of South Africa**, which was granted virtual **independence** in 1910.

Bokassa, Col Jean-Bédel

A military coup brought Jean-Bédel Bokassa to power in the Central African Republic, but he went on to declare himself Emperor and to head a regime that was characterized by great ostentation and cruelty. France, after having become embarrassingly closely associated with Bokassa's regime, assisted in its overthrow in 1979. In 1983 an attempt by Bokassa to return to power failed.

Bongo Ondimba, Omar (Albert-Bernard)

President of Gabon since 1967. Born in 1935, Bongo served in the French air force from 1958 until Gabon became independent. He returned to Gabon to join the foreign ministry, and after periods as chief of staff and defence minister under President Mba, he became Vice-President in 1966, succeeding Mba in the following year after his death. In 1968 Bongo declared Gabon a one-party state—a status that it retained until 1991—and in 1973 he converted to **Islam**, assuming the name of Omar el-Hadj. Bongo has been credited with encouraging foreign investment, but has also been accused of **corruption** and personal aggrandizement.

Borders

Most of the borders between today's states in Africa were the creation of the colonial period. Often these borders cut across pre-existing economic and social entities, creating new multinational and multiethnic states and dividing sections of many pre-existing economies and societies from each other. A prime example is that of the Horn of Africa, where the **Somalis** were divided at one time between three different European colonial powers—Britain, France and Italy—a division which had serious repercussions in the post-colonial period for the new Somalia (Somali Democratic Republic). The **Organization of African Unity**, established in 1963, broadly agreed that, in order to avoid controversy and conflict, the colonial boundaries should be accepted as the *de facto* boundaries of new African states and not challenged. Despite this, there have been border conflicts and disputes in many parts of Africa since that time, particularly in **North Africa**, the Sahel and the Horn of Africa.

Botha, P. W.

Former President of South Africa.

Botwsana, Republic of

The Republic of Botswana is a land-locked country situated in **southern Africa**. It shares **borders** with Namibia in the west and north, Zambia in the north, Zimbabwe in the north east and South Africa in the east and south. More than half of the country lies within the tropical zone north of the Tropic of Capricorn. The climate ranges from semi-arid through sub-tropical to temperate. The Kalahari Desert dominates southern and western Botswana; the climate of the extreme south west is near desert, while eastern Botswana enjoys temperate conditions with rainfall that is adequate to support arable farming. The Okavango Delta in northern Botswana is rich in animal and plant life and, together with Chobe, the Central Kalahari Game Reserve and the Tuli Block, is the focus of Botswana's growing tourist industry. The country is large, covering 581,730 sq km, but sparsely inhabited, with a population of 1.7m. (2001). The capital is Gaborone. Ba-Tswana account for 95% of the population, Kalanga, Basarwa and Kgalagadi for 4%, and whites 1%. The main languages are English and Se-Tswana. Most of the people of Botswana are Christians, although some hold indigenous beliefs.

Political profile

Botswana is a multi-party **democracy**. The Head of State and of the government is the President, who is elected by the National Assembly for a five-year term of office. At the most recent election, which took place on 30 October 2004, Festus Gonfebanye Mogae was returned to the presidency, having received 54.3% of the votes in the National Assembly. The President appoints the Vice-President, which office has been held since 13 July 1998 by Seretse Ian Khama. Should the President leave office between elections, the presidency is automatically assumed by the Vice-President. The legislature is bicameral, comprising a House of Chiefs and a National Assembly. The House of Chiefs is a largely advisory, 15-member body, comprising the chiefs of the eight principal tribes, four elected sub-chiefs and three other members who are selected by the aforementioned 12. The National Assembly contains 44 seats, to 40 of which deputies are directly elected by popular vote, while the remaining four are filled by appointees of the majority party. Deputies to the National Assembly serve a five-year term. Following the most recent elections to the National Assembly, held on 30 October 2004, seats were distributed as follows: **Botswana Democratic Party (BDP)**, 48; **Botswana National Front (BNF)**, 12; **Botswana Congress Party (BCP)**, 1.

History

Formerly the British protectorate of **Bechuanaland**, Botswana adopted its present name upon **independence** in 1966. In the period after independence Botswana pursued a policy of non-interference in the white minority governments that surrounded it, refusing, for instance, to harbour guerrilla operations against South Africa. It did, however, adopt an 'open-door' policy for political **refugees**, and prior to Zimbabwe's independence in 1980 Botswana became a refuge for guerrillas. In the years before a multiracial government was established in South Africa, Botswana was the target of South African reprisals. In 1974 Botswana was one of the original five front-line non-**apartheid** states whose alliance formed the core of what was to become the **Southern African Development Community (SADC)**. Since the end of apartheid in South Africa Botswana has enjoyed strong relations with all 14 members of SADC.

The first government of Botswana was formed by the BDP after multi-party elections in 1965. The BDP has been returned to power at each of the seven elections contested since independence. Sir Seretse Khama served as the first President of the Republic from 1966 until his death in 1980, when he was succeeded by Sir Ketumile Masire (co-founder of the BCP and former Vice-President). Masire relinquished power in 1998 and was succeeded by the current President, Festus Gonfebanye Mogae. The son of Sir Seretse Khama, Ian Khama, is the current Vice-President.

International relations

Botswana is a member of the SADC, which has its headquarters in Gaborone. Botswana Defence Force (BDF) troops formed part of the SADC Intervention Force that was deployed in Lesotho in September 1998 to restore law and order there after election results had triggered civil unrest. The BDF has also served with distinction in humanitarian and peace-keeping roles in Somalia and Mozambique. Botswana is also a member of the Southern African Customs Union (SACU, consisting of Botswana, South Africa, Namibia, Lesotho and Swaziland), which provides for tariff-free movement of most goods between its five members. Botswana also has separate trade agreements with Zimbabwe and Zambia.

In November 1998 an armed group of around 100 men crossed into Botswana following a failed secessionist attempt in the Caprivi region of north-east Namibia. Although the group fled after Namibian Defence Force units discovered their camp, more than 2,000 other secessionists crossed into Botswana shortly afterwards. The Botswana authorities, in consultation with the UN, granted most of them refugee status, although many have now returned to Namibia. There are several areas of the border between Botswana and Namibia's Caprivi Strip which are disputed. The most serious dispute was over Sedudu Island (called Kasikili by the Namibians). The case was referred to the International Court of Justice which, in 1999, ruled in Botswana's favour. Botswana began erecting a security fence along its north-eastern border with Zimbabwe in September 2003. This has been the result of pressure within the country to stem the flow of illegal immigrants crossing the border to flee the political and economic crisis in Zimbabwe.

Botswana, economy

In 2002 Botswana's gross domestic product (GDP) was US $5,700m., equivalent to $3,360 per head. GDP increased by 2.5% in 2001/02 and was forecast to increase by 5% in 2002/03. The rate of inflation was 8.1% in 2001, following the introduction of a value added tax, but was expected to fall in 2002. Important sectors of the economy are the mining of **diamonds**, **copper** and nickel, and beef production and tourism. Botswana's major trading partners are the **European Union**, Zimbabwe and fellow members of the **Southern African Customs Union**. In 2001/02 Botswana received £2m. in bilateral assistance. The national currency is the pula (100 thebe = 1 pula). In 2003 the exchange rate was US $1 = 4.9499 pula.

The economy of Botswana is essentially underpinned by the diamond industry, which still accounts for about one-third of the country's GDP and for approximately 50% of all foreign exchange earnings. Botswana is the largest producer (by value) of diamonds in the world. It is the development of the diamond industry and the sound management by the government of the revenues from the mining sector that have contributed to a post-**independence** era characterized by consistently high economic growth rates. Real GDP growth has averaged 7% over the past three decades, making Botswana one of the fastest-growing economies in the world, albeit starting from a low base. The government recognizes the need to shift the economy from its dependence on diamonds and is attempting to accelerate economic diversification. It is also actively pursuing foreign direct investment in services (particularly financial services) and manufacturing, as well as encouraging citizen-led private-sector development.

There has been little evidence of serious **corruption** in Botswana. The international corruption 'watchdog', Transparency International, has rated Botswana as the least corrupt country in Africa and ranks it as the 26th least corrupt country in the world. The government is determined to maintain its record. An independent body, the Directorate on Corruption and Economic Crime, that is directly answerable to the President, has been established to investigate any allegations of corruption, and a national chapter of Transparency International was launched in 2001 (President Mogae has for some time been a member of Transparency International's global board).

The government has managed to keep its recurrent expenditure within its revenue, allowing for investment in human and physical capital. The government's revenue from diamonds, as well as profits from the large foreign exchange reserves of the Bank of Botswana, have largely cushioned Botswana from the recessions that have buffeted most countries in the region. Through fiscal discipline and sound management, Botswana has transformed itself from one of the poorest countries in the world to a middle-income country with GDP per head of $3,360 in 2002.

Botswana Alliance Movement (BAM)

Political grouping in Botswana, founded in 1998 as an alliance of three opposition parties—the Independence Freedom Party, the United Action Party and the **Botswana People's Party (BPP)**—to contest the 1999 general election. The BPP withdrew from it in July 2000. The president of the alliance is Lepetu Setshwaelo and its chairman is Motsamai Mpho.

Botswana Congress Party (BCP)

Political party in Botswana, founded in 1998 following a split in the Botswana National Front. The BCP's president is Otlaadisa Koosaletse, its chairman Peba Sethantsho and its secretary-general Mokgweetsi Kgosipula.

Botswana Democratic Party (BDP)

Originally founded as the **Bechuanaland Democratic Party** in 1962 by Seretse Khama, former heir to the chieftainship of the Bamangwato, who had been forced to renounce his chieftainship in 1956 under pressure from the British, South African and Southern Rhodesian governments, after he married a white woman. Many white settlers supported the BDP in preference to the more radical **Bechuanaland People's Party (BPP)**. In **Bechuanaland**'s first direct legislative elections held under universal adult suffrage, in 1965, the BDP won 28 out of the 31 seats and Seretse Khama became Prime Minister. **Independence** followed in September 1966, when Bechuanaland became the Republic of Botswana, with Khama as

President. In the years following independence, the Bechuanaland Democratic Party, now renamed the BDP, was challenged by the BPP (particularly in urban areas) and by a new 'socialist' party, the **Botswana National Front (BNF)**. The BDP has, however, retained power over the last 40 years. In 1980, after Seretse Khama's death, the Vice-President, Dr (later Sir) Quett Ketumile Masire, a founder member of the BDP, succeeded to the presidency. His presidency was renewed in September 1984 when, in a general election to the National Assembly, the BDP again won a decisive victory. However, it lost control of most municipal councils in local elections held at the same time, with the notable exception of Selebi-Phikwe. Tension between the BDP and the BNF intensified in early 1987 and the BNF boycotted a national referendum on the electoral system. In October 1989 the BDP gained 65% of the votes and 31 out of 34 seats in the parliamentary elections. In the early 1990s the BDP split into two factions, largely due to the government's liberalization policies. In March 1992 Vice-President Peter Mmusi and Minister of Agriculture Daniel Kwelagobe resigned. Festus Mogae, the Minister of Finance and Development Planning, was appointed as Vice-President. In 1993 Masire was re-elected to the presidency and his new council of ministers included both Kwelagobe and Mogae. In November 1997 Masire announced that he would retire at the end of March 1998, and duly did so. Immediately on his retirement Mogae was inaugurated as President. The only new minister in his government was Lt-Gen. Ian Khama (son of the late Sir Seretse Khama), previously Commander of the Botswana Defence Force, who became Vice-President. Ponatshego Kedikilwe, who had been favoured for the position, was appointed as Minister of Finance and Development Planning instead. When Khama was elected to the National Assembly, Kedikilwe became Vice-President. In elections held in October 1999 the ruling BDP won all but seven of the 40 seats in the National Assembly and Mogae was elected as President. He also remains president of the BDP, while Ponatshego Kedikilwe is chairman and Daniel Kwelagobe is secretary-general.

Botswana Independence Party (BIP)

A splinter group from the first nationalist party in **Bechuanaland**, the **Bechuanaland People's Party**, founded in 1960.

Botswana Labour Party

Founded in 1989. The party's president is Lenyaletse Koma.

Botswana National Front (BNF)

Founded in 1966. The BNF's president is Otsweletse Moupo and its chairman Klaas Motshidisi.

Botswana People's Party (BPP)

Founded in 1960 as the **Bechuanaland People's Party**, the first nationalist party in **Bechuanaland**. It had close links with the **African National Congress** in South Africa. The BPP soon split in two, with one section becoming the **Botswana Independence Party** and the other the more important Botswana People's Party. Today the BPP's president is Motlatsi Molapisi, its chairman Joseph Mogotle and its secretary-general Kopano Chingapane.

Botswana Progressive Union

Political party in Botswana, founded in 1982. Its leader is G. Kaelo.

Botswana Workers' Front

Political party in Botswana, founded in 1993. Its leader is M. M. Akanyang.

Boudiaf, Mohammed

President of Algeria and head of the five-member High Council of State (HCS) from 1992 until 1994. One of the historical founders of the **Front de libération nationale (FLN—National Liberation Front)**, Boudiaf had quit politics in 1963, but was popular and charismatic. Intended as a figurehead, he became too active, assailing **corruption** within the government and bureaucracy, and was assassinated. He—and the HCS—was replaced by Gen. (retd) **Liamine Zéroual**, who was appointed as President in January 1994.

Ould Boulkheir, Messaoud

Mauritanian politician, leader of the Convention for Change.

Boumedienne, Houari

President of Algeria from June 1965 until December 1978. His original name was Muhammad Ibrahim Bukharruba. While studying in Cairo, Egypt, during the early 1950s he joined a group of expatriate Algerian nationalists that included **Ahmed Ben Bella**. Boumedienne secretly re-entered Algeria (1955) to join a group of guerrillas operating in the province of Oran. He was (1960–62) chief of staff of the exiled National Liberation Army in Tunisia and served as Algeria's Minister of Defence from the time of its **independence**. Boumedienne supported Ben Bella, and was his defence minister until 1965. However, after a series of disputes with Ben Bella, Boumedienne led a coup that overthrew his former ally's government. After the coup, Boumedienne assumed the posts of President, Prime Minister, and chairman of the revolutionary council until his death in December 1978.

Bourguiba, Habib

Former President of Tunisia. The son of a low-ranking government functionary in the Sahel (southern) town of Monastir, Bourguiba rose to become the charismatic leader of the nationalist Tunisian **Neo-Destour Party**, the founding father of modern Tunisia, Prime Minister and then President. He belonged to Tunisia's first nationalist party, the **Destour Party**, which was led by members of the traditional élites. Early on it became apparent to Bourguiba and his colleagues—who were mainly bright young men from the provinces who had received an education in Franco-Arab schools, especially at Saidik College, in Tunisia, and further **education** in France—that the nationalist movement needed to be broader-based than the Destour. They formed a new party, which included some members of the Destour and of the traditional urban élite but reached out to the mass of the Tunisan population, including those in the rural areas. He became Prime Minister of Tunisia in 1956 on **independence** and held this position until July 1957, when Tunisia formally became a republic. He then became President, holding office as Head of State for 30 years, from July 1957 until November 1987, when he was deposed after a bloodless coup. He was succeeded by **Zine el-Abidine Ben Ali**. He died on 6 April 2000 at the age of 96.

Bouteflika, Abdelaziz

President of Algeria from April 1999 after winning a heavily rigged presidential election from which six of the rival presidential candidates withdrew. Bouteflika had served as Algeria's foreign minister from 1963 until 1979 after being a charter member of the Oujda clan. Brought out of retirement to deal with the crisis, he attempted to reduce the level of the conflict within Algeria by offering an amnesty in June 1999 to the Islamist paramilitary opposition groups. Some of these groups took advantage of this to lay down their arms. Others, however, notably the **Groupe islamique armé (GIA—Armed Islamic Group)** and the **Groupe salafiste pour la prédication et le combat (GSPC—Salafist Group for Call and Combat)**, maintained the armed struggle against the state. Bouteflika was successful in the presidential elections held in April 2004, in which he won an overwhelming majority of the votes cast and significant political credibility as a consequence.

Boutros-Ghali, Boutros

Egyptian statesmen, born in 1922. Secretary-General of the UN in 1992–96. Educated in Cairo and Paris, France, he was professor of international relations at Cairo University in 1949–79, and was present at the negotiations that led to the Egypt-Israel Camp David Accords. He served as Egypt's delegate to the UN and held the posts of Minister of State for Foreign Affairs and Deputy Prime Minister for Foreign Affairs in the Egyptian government. Boutros-Ghali was the first African and Arab head of the UN. He sought to reorganize and streamline the UN secretariat, and to strengthen the UN's peace-keeping role. In 1996, after policy disagreements mainly with the USA, he was forced out of office. In 1997 he became secretary-general of La Francophonie, an organization of French-speaking nations.

Bozizé, Gen. François

President of Chad. Gen. François Bozizé took power in a coup in March 2003, while former leader Ange-Félix Patasse was out of the country. On taking power, Bozizé dissolved parliament and imposed a curfew. He promised to consult with the political opposition and to prepare for 'transparent elections' in 2004. Bozizé had been a presidential candidate in Chad's first democratic elections in 1993, but was defeated by Patasse. In 1983 Bozizé led an unsuccessful coup against military ruler André Kolingba. He was suspected of having been involved in another coup attempt, against President Patasse, in 2001, which was thwarted with the help of Libyan troops.

Brazzaville Group

The Brazzaville Group consisted of all of the former French colonies except Guinea, with the addition of Mauritania (whose claim to be independent and not a part of a 'greater' Morocco was accepted by the Group). It began as an *ad hoc* meeting in Abidjan, Côte d'Ivoire, in October 1960, at which the principal topic for discussion was Algeria. At Brazzaville, Republic of the Congo, in December, and at further meetings during 1961 at Dakar, Senegal, Yaoundé, Cameroon, and Antananarivo, Madagascar, it developed into a more permanent association, discussed ways of perpetuating the co-operation and common services which had existed in the colonial period, set up an organization for economic co-operation and considered joint institutions and defence arrangements. It was later joined by Libya, which had initially been part of the **Casablanca Group**.

Bread riots

Throughout the period from the mid-1970s to the mid-1990s, there was a virtual epidemic of popular protest and claims for social justice across Africa in response to economic reform policies that promoted '**structural adjustment**', effectively cut public expenditure, reduced subsidies and increased the price of basic goods. Widely referred to as 'bread riots', these waves of mass protest were an indication of growing opposition to the programmes of economic liberalization and structural adjustment which increased inequality and changed the relationship between the state and the ordinary mass of the people in terms of responsibility for basic welfare. Also termed 'food riots' and 'IMF riots' because of the perceived role of the **International Monetary Fund** (and the **World Bank**) in orchestrating and enforcing the 'austerity measures' that accompanied the reforms, this form of more-or-less spontaneous mass protest was increasingly replaced during the 1990s by more organized opposition, not only to the economic reform programmes but also to the regimes which continue to undertake the reforms. Political opposition, often encouraged by the conditions imposed by lending agencies on African governments, has increasingly demanded multi-party **democracy** and 'good governance'. Despite this general tendency towards the politicization of popular protest, 'spontaneous' protests have continued to occur in many countries in the region.

Brenthurst Group

A small forum of business leaders—including Harry Oppenheimer, patriarch of the founding dynasty of the **Anglo-American Corpn**—which met periodically in the 1990s with **Nelson Mandela** and other **African National Congress** leaders in Johannesburg to discuss economic issues and provide advice.

Bretton Woods Institutions

These are the two major international finance and lending agencies, the **International Monetary Fund** and the International Bank for Reconstruction and Development, better known as the **World Bank**, set up at Bretton Woods, USA, in 1944, initially to help provide the financial and economic basis for post-Second World War reconstruction and development, but increasingly to assist the newly independent countries of the developing world to implement policies to promote economic growth in an effective and efficient manner. Increasingly influential, particularly during the 1980s and 1990s, in providing a global framework and strategy, based on the rhetoric and principles of 'the free market' (i.e. economic liberalism) for the national economic development strategy of developing countries, the lending preconditions laid down have tended to lock developing countries into particular kinds of economic policies. During the 1990s a growing number of critics of the Bretton Woods institutions drew attention to their 'failures' (exemplified by continuing **poverty** and the growth of **debt**) and some even argued that 'Fifty Years is Enough'. The G7, at its meeting in Naples, Italy, in 1994 agreed to discuss reform at its next meeting, but it failed to do so. The increasing focus of the international development community, including the Bretton Woods institutions, through the last years of the 1990s and first few years of the 21st century on poverty alleviation and **debt relief**, was, however, in large part, a result of growing criticism and pressure from campaigning groups, including some international NGOs. The global framework for poverty reduction adopted in the early 2000s, however, still leaves the Bretton Woods institutions virtually unreformed and as influential as ever in determining the agenda for individual developing country governments, in Africa and elsewhere.

British Indian Ocean Territory (BIOT)

The British Indian Ocean Territory (BIOT) was formed in November 1965, through the amalgamation of the former Seychelles islands of Aldabra, Desroches and

Farquhar with the Chagos Archipelago, a group of islands 1,930 km north-east of Mauritius, and previously administered by the Governor of Mauritius. Aldabra, Desroches and Farquhar were ceded to Seychelles when that country achieved **independence** in June 1976. Since then BIOT has comprised only the Chagos Archipelago, including the coral atoll, Diego Garcia. BIOT was established to meet British and US military interests in the Indian Ocean. In May 2002 the British Overseas Territories Act reinstated the right to British citizenship of the people of the United Kingdom's Overseas Territories, including **Saint Helena** and dependencies. People who had been displaced from BIOT in 1969–73 were also to be allowed to apply for British citizenship.

Broederbond (Brotherhood)

A South African secret society of the **Afrikaner** right, which once evolved the **apartheid** ideology, controlled the South African Broadcasting Corporation and exerted a pervasive influence on the whole of Afrikanerdom. It is now a powerless forum for the exchange of ideas, the Afrikaner Bond.

'Buffalo Battalion'

A group of South African-trained mercenaries, believed to have participated in several regional conflicts in West Africa. Thought to have provided support to the **Frente Democrata Cristã (Christian Democrat Front)**, which took power in São Tomé and Príncipe in a bloodless coup in July 2003, while President **de Menezes** was in Nigeria. The coup was condemned by the international community, which demanded a return to civilian rule. Following successful mediation efforts, de Menezes returned to São Tomé in July 2003, accompanied by President **Olusegun Obasanjo** of Nigeria. Under an amnesty for the coup leaders, de Menezes was reinstated as President.

Buhari, Maj.-Gen. Muhammadu

Buhari became chief of the army and Head of State of Nigeria at the very end of 1983, replacing President Alhaji Shehu Shagiri through a military coup. The Buhari government was a comprehensive failure. It denounced **corruption** without reducing it; was brutally harsh on criminals without reducing crime; intensified economic austerity without any countervailing benefits; and forwent much needed aid from the **International Monetary Fund** by refusing to devalue the *naira*. It expelled large numbers of immigrants from neighbouring countries who had entered Nigeria in search of work and made little contribution to the **Economic Community of West African States**. It irritated its partners in the **Organization of Petroleum Exporting Countries** when it reduced the prices of Nigerian **oil** without warning. Within two years of seizing power Buhari had been evicted by one of the principal members of his ruling council, **Gen. Ibrahim Babangida**.

Burkina Faso

Burkina Faso is a land-locked country in West Africa, bordering Benin, Togo, Ghana, Côte d'Ivoire, Mali and Niger. The country can be divided into three parts: the Sudanian zone in the south, the wettest part; the Sudano-Sahelian zone in the centre, which covers 50% of the total area; and the Sahelian zone in the north, which is the drier part of the country. The total area is 274,190 sq km. In 2002 the population, in which more than 60 ethnic groups are represented, was 12.2m. The Mossi, based in central Burkina Faso and accounting for some 50% of the population, are the main group, while the Gurunsi, Senoufo, Lobi, **Mande** and **Fulani** are also significant. The official language is French. African languages of the Sudanic family are spoken by more than 90% of the population. Those professing indigenous/animist beliefs account for some 45% of the population, Muslims for about 30%and Christians (Roman Catholics) for about 14%. The capital is Ouagadougou.

Political profile

Burkina Faso is a constitutional republic. The Head of State is a directly elected President who formerly served a seven-year term—a constitutional amendment in 2000 reduced the term of the presidency to five years, with effect from 2005, and limited its incumbent to a single term. At the most recent presidential election, held on 15 November 1998, **Blaise Compaoré** was the successful candidate, receiving some 87.5% of the vote. The legislature is the 111-seat Assemblée nationale, to which deputies are returned by popular vote for a five-year term. Following the most recent legislative elections, held on 5 May 2002, the distribution of seats in the National Assembly was as follows: **Congrès pour la démocratie et le progrès (CDP—Congress for Democracy and Progress)**, 57; **Alliance pour la démocratie et la fédération-Rassemblement démocratique africain (ADF-RDA—Alliance for Democracy and Federation-Democratic African Rally)**, 17; **Parti pour la démocratie et le progrès-Parti socialiste (PDP-PS—Party for Democracy and Progress-Socialist Party)**, 10; **Coalition des forces démocratiques (CDF—Coalition of Democratic Forces)**, 5; **Parti africain de l'indépendance (PAI—African Independence Party)**, 5; others 17.

History

Formerly **Upper Volta**, the French colony gained **independence** in 1960. It has officially been known as Burkina Faso ('the land of the upright') since 1983. For a number of years political power alternated between civilian and military governments. The current President, Blaise Compaoré, came to power after a violent coup in 1987 in which his predecessor, **Thomas Sankara**, was killed. In June 1991 Compaoré dissolved his 'revolutionary' government and announced the formation of a transitional government leading to presidential and legislative elections. A constitution, endorsed by about one-half of the electorate in a national referendum, was enacted on 11 June 1991. A ban on political parties was lifted. However, Compaoré's refusal to comply with opposition demands for a National Conference led to riots and to a boycott by the opposition of presidential elections held in December 1991. Compaoré (as sole candidate) was elected—25% of the electorate participated in the poll—and was sworn in as President on 24 December 1991. The assassination of the leading opposition figure, Clément Ouédraogo, led to the postponement of legislative elections. When these were finally held in May 1992, Compaoré's party, the CDP, won a substantial majority. The CDP repeated this success in municipal elections in February 1995, and increased its majority in the May 1997 legislative elections. Compaoré was returned to power in a presidential election held in November 1998 in which 56% of the electorate participated. The government has had to contend with ongoing popular concern about human rights issues. These have included the circumstances surrounding Sankara's death; and the murder in December 1998 of an independent journalist, Norbert Zongo, who was investigating the business dealings of President Compaoré's younger brother (François) and, in particular, the torture and murder of his chauffeur, David Ouédraogo. The Zongo case, which has been the cause of a number of violent demonstrations, remains unresolved. The press in Burkina Faso operates freely. There is a vocal domestic human rights movement, and a national human rights commission was established in November 2001.

The government's commitment to promoting inclusive **democracy** has been questionable: in December 2000, for example, it issued a decree prohibiting all demonstrations of a non-religious nature. However, it has recently sought to increase dialogue with the opposition, and the legislative elections held in May 2002 represented a significant step forward. In a well-administered poll, which changed Burkina Faso's political landscape, the ruling CDP won 57 of the 111 seats in the Assemblée nationale (it had previously held 99), thus producing a viable opposition. Hermann Yaméogo's ADF-RDA won 17 seats, thus emerging as the leading opposition force.

Burkina Faso has been adversely affected by the crisis which erupted in neighbouring Côte d'Ivoire in September 2002. The governments of Côte d'Ivoire and Burkina Faso have reopened their common border, allowing crucial trade for landlocked Burkina Faso to continue, and this decision has been interpreted as a signal that Ivorians no longer consider Burkina Faso to support the rebels who oppose their President. The Council of Ministers announced the abolition of the upper parliamentary chamber, the Chambre des représentants, in January 2002. The Assemblée nationale subsequently approved constitutional amendments to that effect.

International relations

Compaoré's first official visit to France, which took place in June 1993, was widely interpreted as a recognition by the French authorities of his legitimacy following the installation of elected organs of state. Burkina Faso swiftly developed close relations with Jacques Chirac following his election to the French presidency in May 1995, and contacts have remained frequent. The 19th Franco-African summit took place in Ouagadougou in December 1996. Links with Libya have generally been strong under the Compaoré regime; Burkina Faso was, notably, a founder member of the Libyan-sponsored Community of Sahel-Saharan States and subsequently participated in a regional mediation effort, conceived by that organization, to resolve the political crisis in the Central African Republic (CAR). The Assemblée nationale authorized the contribution of a Burkinabè military contingent to the surveillance mission for the CAR in February 1997, and a Burkinabè force remained in the CAR as part of the UN peace-keeping force that succeeded the regional mission between April 1998 and February 2000.

Burkina Faso is a member of both the **Union économique et monétaire ouest-africaine (West African Economic and Monetary Union)** and of the **Economic Community of West African States (ECOWAS)**. It regularly hosts pan-African and international conferences. There have been concerns that Burkina Faso has played a destabilizing role in regional affairs; there is evidence, for example, that illegal exports of arms from Burkina Faso to Liberia occurred in 1999. President Compaoré has, in recent years, gained wide recognition for his efforts as a regional mediator and as a proponent of inter-African conflict-resolution initiatives. In the early 1990s, however, relations with some members of ECOWAS suffered a reversal, owing to the Compaoré government's support for **Charles Taylor**'s rebel National Patriotic Front of Liberia (NPFL) and Burkina Faso's refusal to participate in the military intervention by the ECOWAS cease-fire monitoring group **(ECOMOG)** in Liberia.

There has been tension between Côte d'Ivoire, which is home to a large West African immigrant community that includes as many as 2m. Burkinabès, and Burkina Faso. This worsened significantly in late 2002, following accusations by the Ivorians that Burkina Faso had provided support for the rebels who held the northern part of Côte d'Ivoire following a failed coup attempt in September. Significant numbers of Burkinabès returned from Côte d'Ivoire to Burkina Faso, or fled to other neighbouring countries as **refugees**. However, following progress in the Côte d'Ivoire peace process, Ivorian and Burkinabè ministers and officials began discussions in May/June 2003, with a view to restoring normal transport and trading links. Following the outbreak of unrest in Côte d'Ivoire in mid-September 2002, the Ivorian president **Laurent Gbagbo** alleged that an unnamed, neighbouring country (widely regarded as a reference to Burkina Faso) was implicated in a rebellion within Côte d'Ivoire. However, in late November, following an attack on the residence of the Burkinabè President in Abidjan, the Ivorian government expressed its regrets publicly for the attack. As a result of the upsurge in violence in Côte d'Ivoire, at least 350,000 Burkinabè citizens reportedly fled Côte d'Ivoire for Burkina Faso. Compaoré welcomed the peace agreement signed in France in January 2003, known as the Marcoussis Accords, which provided for a government of national reconciliation in Côte d'Ivoire, although at the end of the month the Burkinabè embassy in Abidjan was attacked and set on fire by opponents of the agreement. As greater stability appeared to return to Côte d'Ivoire later that year, the common border of the two countries, closed since the onset of the rebellion, was reopened in September. In

October the government of Côte d'Ivoire denied suggestions of Ivorian involvement in the alleged coup plot in Burkina Faso. Later in July, at a meeting in Abidjan, representatives of the two countries pledged to combat 'destabilizing acts' against their respective countries and agreed to increase co-operation in security and defence matters.

Burkina Faso, economy

In 2003 Burkina Faso's gross domestic product (GDP) per head, at US $220, was equivalent to $1,100 on a purchasing power parity basis. In 2002 economic growth of 4.5% was recorded. The rate of inflation was estimated at 3.9% in 2002. Important sectors of the economy are **agriculture**, in particular the **cotton** and livestock sectors. Mining for **gold** also makes a significant contribution to the economy. Burkina Faso's major trading partners are Côte d'Ivoire and France. The national currency is the franc de la **Communauté financière africaine (CFA**, see the **Franc Zone)**. In 2003 the exchange rate was US $1 = 581.20 francs CFA.

About 90% of the population are engaged in (mainly subsistence) agriculture, which is highly vulnerable to variations in rainfall. Industry remains dominated by unprofitable government-controlled corporations. Following the devaluation of the CFA franc in January 1994 the government updated its development programme in conjunction with international agencies, and exports and economic growth subsequently increased. Maintenance of macroeconomic progress depends on continued low inflation, reduction in the trade deficit and reforms designed to encourage private investment.

Despite achieving an average annual growth rate of 4.7% in 1996–2002, and a rate of 5.2 % in 2003, Burkina Faso's economic financial and social situation remains fragile largely as a result of three key factors. First, the country's heavy dependence on a limited number of export commodities (mainly cotton and cattle) and on external assistance. Second, the weakness of most social indicators including **education** and access to health services. And, third, high factor costs such as electricity, **water**, telephone and transportation which make doing business very expensive and reduce the competitiveness of Burkina Faso's goods internationally. More recently the land-locked economy has been adversely affected by the crisis in Côte d'Ivoire which has caused the closure of cross-border road and rail links needed for access to Côte d'Ivoire's ports. Levels of remittances from Burkina Faso's large community in Côte d'Ivoire have also fallen since the outbreak of the crisis.

In April 2002 Burkina Faso reached the completion point of the (Enhanced) **Heavily Indebted Poor Countries (HIPC) initiative**. The initiative makes available up to $100,000m. of **debt** 'forgiveness' to the world's poorest countries. However, Burkina Faso emerged with unsustainable debt and, as a result, the **World Bank** and the **International Monetary Fund (IMF)** agreed to grant the country exceptional **debt relief** ('topping up') to achieve debt sustainability and mitigate the adverse effects of external shock on the country's revenue. Since 1993 Burkina Faso has also satisfactorily implemented three IMF **Poverty Reduction and Growth Facility (PRGF)**-supported programmes. On 11 June 2003 the IMF granted the country a new three-year PRGF worth roughly $17m. The main aim of the programme over the medium term will be for Burkina Faso to implement appropriate macroeconomic policies and structural reform consistent with the Poverty Reduction Strategy Programme (PRSP) approved under the HIPC initiative. Paramount will be the effective privatization of loss-making public utilities (telecommunications, electricity and cotton parastatals), trade liberalization, economic diversification and good governance. The effective accomplishment of these objectives should help to attract much-needed foreign investment. Another key factor is Burkina Faso's need to address institutional and physical bottlenecks which currently prevent the effective absorption of resources freed through HIPC debt relief. The IMF's medium-term (2003–06) projection for average annual real GDP growth is 5.2%.

Burundi, Republic of

The Republic of Burundi is a land-locked country intersected by the three principal rivers of the Black, Red, and White Voltas. With an area of 27,834 sq km and a population that was estimated at 6,825,000 in mid-2003, Burundi is relatively densely populated. The capital is Bujumbura, whose population was estimated at 378,397 in mid-2003. Some 85% of the population are **Hutu** (Bantu), while a significant minority, of about 14%, belong to the **Tutsi** (Hamitic), and about 1% to the indigenous forest-dwelling **Twa** (Pygmy). Europeans (some 3,000) and Asians (about 2,000) are also present in small numbers. The main languages are Kirundi (official), French (official) and **Swahili** (along Lake **Tanganyika** and the Bujumbura area). Most (67%) of the population are Christians (Roman Catholics 62%, Protestants 5%), while there is also a significant minority (23%) that follow indigenous beliefs. About 10% are Muslims.

Political profile

The major political parties are the **Union pour le progrès national (UPRONA—Unity for National Progress)**, the **Front pour la démocratie au Burundi (FRODEBU—Front for Democracy in Burundi)**, the **Alliance burundaise-africaine pour le salut (ABASA—Burundi-African Alliance for Salvation)**, the **Rassemblement pour la démocratie et le développement économique et social (RADDES—Rally for Democracy and Economic and Social Development)**, the **Parti pour le redressement national (PARENA—Party for National Recovery)** and the **Parti pour la réconciliation du peuple (PRP—People's Reconciliation Party)**.

History

Burundi witnessed a slow downward spiral of violence after the murder of Prince Louis Rwagasore in 1961, immediately before **independence**. Rwagasore, as the leader of UPRONA, was the logical future Prime Minister. Despite a shared language, religion and culture, Burundians tended to be classified during the colonial period as either Hutu or Tutsi. The Tutsis were considered to have constituted a dominant group even before the colonial period. As a prominent member of the royal lineage, an anti- colonialist and a Tutsi married to a Hutu, Rwagasore embodied a trans-ethnic form of **nationalism**. UPRONA, furthermore, the clear majority party before independence, was constituted equally of Hutus and Tutsis. After Rwagasore's murder, however, Tutsi cadres immediately set about 'Tutsifying' the party and, thereafter, political parties became increasingly divided on ethnic lines and ethnicity (see **ethnic groups**) became the main determinant of political identity. During the next four decades political parties become increasingly organized on ethnic lines and extremist parties began to emerge amongst both Hutu and Tutsi groups. Hutu attempts to gain power met with devastating reprisals and massive numbers of deaths. The **genocide** of 1972, in which it is believed some 100,000–200,000 people, mainly Hutus, were killed, wiped out a whole generation of educated Hutus. For decades the violence in Burundi was not subject to international sanction or criticism and became increasingly entrenched. The main structures and institutions of society became largely controlled and dominated by the Tutsis and the army developed into a predominantly Tutsi force. Strong mechanisms of state control developed, the army and the security apparatus became largely unaccountable and maintained separate rights of intervention and control.

In 1987 Maj. Pierre Buyoya, a Tutsi, took control following a coup and initiated what was heralded as a five-year transition to **democracy**. This culminated in elections in June 1993, in which Buyoya was defeated by Melchoir Ndadaye, a Hutu. The main Hutu party, FRODEBU, took control of parliament in the first Hutu government in Burundi and introduced policies to promote Hutus. Elements of the Tutsi-dominated army attempted a coup in October 1993, assassinating President Ndayaye. The coup triggered massacres of more than 30,000 people, both Hutu and Tutsi. Under international pressure, a civilian government was reinstated under President Ntaryamira, a Hutu and a member of FRODEBU. In April 1994 Ntaryamira was killed when the aircraft in which he and President Habyarimana of neighbouring Rwanda were travelling was shot down near Kigali. In Rwanda the assassination of Habyarimana triggered a genocide perpetrated by Hutu extremists who killed as many as 1m. Tutsis and Hutu moderates. Burundi avoided renewed bloodshed, but inter-ethnic tensions increased. A new power-sharing government was formed in September 1994, led by Sylvestre Ntibantunganya. From early 1995 the mainly Hutu **Conseil national pour la défense de la démocratie (CNDD—National Council for the Defence of Democracy)**, led by Léonard Nyangoma, launched a guerrilla campaign against the army. The CNDD's armed wing, the Front pour la défense de la démocratie (Front for the Defence of Democracy), operated from refugee camps in what was then **Zaire** and (to a lesser extent) Tanzania. Other Hutu groups, especially the **Parti de libération du peuple hutu (PALIPEHUTU—Liberation Party of the Hutu People)**, were also active. The army and Tutsi youth gangs largely eliminated Hutus from Bujumbura in 1994–95. In July 1996 mounting insecurity culminated in a military coup that brought Buyoya back to power. Regional leaders reacted by imposing economic sanctions on Burundi. Buyoya tried to form an ethnically mixed government, suppressed the youth gangs and announced a three-year transition to civil rule. At the same time, regional leaders, led by former Tanzanian President **Julius Nyerere**, agreed at a summit meeting held on 31 July 1996 to impose sanctions on Burundi until it lifted the ban on political parties; restored parliament; and commenced negotiations with other parties to the conflict in Burundi. UN sanctions (imposed by UN Security Council Resolutions 918, 997 and 1011) imposed restrictions on the sale or supply of arms and related *matériel* to persons in states neighbouring Rwanda, including Burundi. As a result of the 1996–97 **civil war** in Zaire, Hutu rebels lost their sanctuary, tipping the balance of power in favour of the Burundi army. The rebels slowly recovered during 1997, but were subsequently weakened by splits within their ranks. Rebel activity remained strongest in the north west, around Bujumbura and in the far south.

The Arusha peace process, facilitated by the Nyerere Foundation, began in earnest in June 1998. Buyoya sought regional approval for his democratic reforms and the lifting of sanctions. Sanctions were finally suspended in January 1999 in recognition of progress made. **Nelson Mandela** took over as facilitator for the peace process in December 1999, following the death of Nyerere in October. His involvement injected a sense of urgency into the talks. On 28 August a peace agreement was signed in Arusha, Tanzania, by the government of Burundi and most of the rebel groups. On 23 July a regional summit convened in Arusha endorsed a proposal by Nelson Mandela that President Buyoya (a Tutsi) should lead a transitional government for the first 18 months of its three-year term. **Maj. Domitien Ndayizeye** (a Hutu) would be the Vice-President during this period and would then take over as President for the second 18-month period of transition. Both Buyoya and Ndayizeye signed an undertaking to abide by 11 conditions. These included reform of the armed forces; release of political prisoners on the advice of an international committee; protection of political leaders; and the inclusion of all signatory parties in the transitional government. A special protection unit composed of 701 troops from the South African Defence Forces was to be responsible for protecting political leaders and international personnel. The African Mission in Burundi took on this role. An additional undertaking was to work for equal representation of the Burundian communities in all public departments. The transitional government commenced its term on 1 November 2001.

Of the four rebel groups, three now signed a cease-fire with the government—the CNDD -Force pour la défense de la démocratie (CNDD-FDD, CNDD-Force for the Defence of Democracy, Jean Bosco Ndayikengurukiye faction) and PALIPEHUTU **-Forces nationales de libération** (PALIPEHUTU-**FNL—National Liberation Forces)**, led by Mugabarabona) in October and the largest rebel group, the CNDD-FDD (Nkurunziza faction), in December. Only the PALIPEHUTU-FNL (Rwasa faction) did not participate in the cease-fire. However, cease-fire violations still occurred on both sides between the CNDD-FDD (Nkurunziza) and the Burundian army. The December cease-fire agreement made provisions for a number of cease-fire verification and monitoring mechanisms. These included the Joint Cease-fire Commission and the multinational **African Union (AU)** peace-keeping force, the **African Mission in Burundi (AMIB)**. The AMIB was made up of South African, Mozambican and Ethiopian troops and had a total strength of around 3,000. The cease-fire between the Burundian armed forces and the CNDD-FDD envisaged by the agreement did not, however, enter into effect. Instead, fighting continued, particularly in areas where the CNDD-FDD intended to assemble its fighters. The CNDD-FDD sought to hold territory in these areas, and the armed forces fought to prevent this. With the need to deploy the AU force urgent, at a meeting in Addis Ababa, Ethiopia, on 12–13 January 2003, the governments of South Africa, Ethiopia and Mozambique agreed to contribute troops. Buyoya and Nkurunziza met in Pretoria, South Africa, on 27 January to discuss the implementation of the cease-fire agreement, and agreed that CNDD-FDD fighters should assemble in camps in Bubanza and Ruyigi provinces. This agreement immediately exacerbated the conflict in both provinces, however, as the CNDD-FDD intensified its efforts to capture territory, while the armed forces sought aggressively to retain it. Clashes were also reported in Gitega, Cibitoke, Kayanza, and Muramvya. Nkurunziza and Buyoya met once more in Pretoria on 21 February, but the discussions collapsed, with Nkurunziza accusing Buyoya of reneging on commitments made at their previous meeting. Regional Heads of State, Buyoya and the CNDD-FDD's secretary-general, Hussein Rajabu, met in Dar es Salaam, Tanzania, on 1 March. Both Buyoya and Rajabu reiterated their commitment to the cease-fire agreement, but the conflict between their forces continued unabated none the less.

In early March 2003 Buyoya tried to persuade the South African government that he should remain as Head of State until an effective cease-fire was in place, but the South African government disagreed, and so, on 28 March, Buyoya announced that he would transfer the presidency to Vice-President Ndayizeye of FRODEBU when his 18-month term expired at the end of April. President Buyoya stood down as agreed and the transfer of power for the second phase of transition took place peacefully on 1 May 2003. On 30 April Ndayizeye became President for a scheduled 18-month term, and Alfonse Kadege from the UPRONA (G10 Tutsi) party was nominated as Vice-President. Contingents of AMIB began to deploy in that month. (Meanwhile, in April, legislation was adopted that provided for the establishment of an international judicial commission of inquiry into war crimes committed since mid-1962.) Ndayizeye's first government, announced in early May, was little changed from Buyoya's, but included ministers representing Ndayikengurukiye's faction of the CNDD-FDD and Mugarabona's faction of the FNL. In May and June Ndayizeye travelled the region to introduce himself and his government's programme, visiting the Democratic Republic of the Congo, Tanzania, Uganda and Rwanda.

Civil conflict continued in parts of Burundi, however, with fierce clashes reported around Gitega and in border provinces. In early July hostilities escalated into a major offensive by FNL forces against Bujumbura, prompting the displacement of thousands of civilians. On 21 July 2003, at further peace discussions in Dar es Salaam, the government and Nkurinziza's faction of the CNDD-FDD reiterated their commitment to implementing the December 2002 cease-fire agreement, but failed to make any progress, and in late August further discussions between Ndayizeye and Nkurunziza on the outstanding issues, mediated by Zuma, again reached no firm conclusion. However, Zuma's persistence appeared finally to prove successful, when Ndayizeye and Nkurunziza signed a power-sharing agreement in Pretoria on 8 October. The CNDD-FDD agreed to abandon hostilities and order its combatants to assemble in cantonment camps, in return for substantial representation in the government and the armed forces, including four ministerial positions, the post of deputy speaker and one other executive position in the Assemblée nationale, representation of 15 parliamentary deputies, three of the country's 17 provincial governorships, and 40% of army command positions. Important decisions remaining unresolved in Pretoria included the proportion of the armed forces' membership to be allocated to the CNDD-FDD, the number of senatorships it would be awarded, and, crucially, the granting of immunity from prosecution to CNDD-FDD officials to allow them to take up the posts allocated to them in the agreement.

During its first few months of operation only South Africa supplied troops for AMIB, until the first Ethiopian contingent, numbering 226, was deployed in late September 2003, after funding pledges from the US government. The first 228-member AMIB contingent from Mozambique arrived in mid-October, following a guarantee of a grant of €25m from the **European Union**, and an assurance of further funds to support Mozambique's deployment. By October AMIB had reached its maximum authorized strength of 3,128 troops (of which South Africa contributed 1,629). In late October Ndayizeye and Nkurunziza returned to Pretoria, where the CNDD-FDD secured a government commitment to immunity of prosecution for its combatants, which was also extended to members of the armed forces. The immunity decision was denounced by Tutsi parties, and was also criticized by international human rights groups. Following resolution of the immunity issue, Nkurunziza's CNDD-FDD officially ended hostilities on 10 November, resulting in the cessation of fighting throughout most of the country, with the exception of Bujumubura rurale and Cibitoke provinces, where FNL forces remained active. On 16 November the peace agreement was formally signed at a summit meeting of regional Heads of State in Dar es Salaam, and on 23 November Ndayizeye announced the establishment of a new government of national unity, incorporating CNDD-FDD representatives. Nkurunziza was appointed to the newly created post of Minister of State for Good Governance and State Inspection, which was officially designated as the third most important position in the administration.

On 6 January 2004 Ndayizeye appointed a new 35-member military high command, comprising 21 members selected from the armed forces, and 14 from Nkurunziza's faction of the CNDD-FDD. Ndayizeye announced that the establishment of the high command was a prelude to the establishment of new, reconstituted armed forces, to be called the Forces de défense nationales (National Defence Forces). No representatives from either Ndayikengurukiye's faction of the CNDD-FDD, nor from Mugabarabona's minority FNL faction, were included in the high command, which, they alleged, violated the government's earlier agreements with them. Although the terms of the peace agreement required CNDD-FDD combatants to assemble in cantonment camps in preparation for disarmament, the faction began conducting joint operations with members of the armed forces against the FNL in Bujumbura rurale and Cibitoke, with heavy fighting ensuing. On 29 December 2003 FNL forces ambushed and killed the papal envoy in Burundi, Archbishop Michael Courtney, attracting widespread international condemnation. Clashes were also reported in Bururi province between supporters of Nkurunziza and those loyal to Léonard Nyangoma, the founder of the CNDD. Discussions between Ndayizeye and the FNL leadership that commenced in The Hague, Netherlands, in mid-January 2004 initially appeared positive, but in February ended with a unilateral suspension of dialogue by the FNL. During the following months continued heavy fighting between the FNL and CNDD-FDD, allied with members of the armed forces, caused the displacement of some 50,000 civilians. Ndayizeye convened a series of meetings with representatives of parties in the government during February and March in order to secure agreement on key unresolved issues, including the contents of a new draft constitution and electoral code. No agreement was reached, however, prompting Ndayizeye, who also cited concern at the ongoing civil war, to support a postponement in elections. In April Nkurunziza announced the suspension of the CNDD-FDD's participation in the transitional institutions, claiming that the government had failed to implement the November 2003 power-sharing accord. In May 2004 Ndayizeye announced a new draft electoral timetable, which scheduled the presidential poll for late 2005. This proposal was rejected by FRODEBU and the CNDD-FDD, which insisted instead on the original electoral timetable, but supported by predominantly Tutsi parties. After a meeting of political parties convened by Zuma in Pretoria failed to reach agreement on the issue, a summit meeting of regional Heads of State held in Dar es Salaam on 5–6 June 2004 ruled that elections must proceed according to the original schedule. Despite renewed contact between the FNL and Zuma just before the summit, the Heads of State condemned the militia for remaining outside of the peace process and imposed sanctions on its leadership, with further measures threatened. Six months after Zuma had made the initial request, on 21 May 2004 the UN Security Council approved the replacement of the AMIB with the UN Mission in Burundi (ONUB), which officially began to deploy on 1 June for a six-month period. Consequently, the UN, rather than South Africa, was henceforth to pay for the operation, which was to be expanded to include additional military personnel from a number of countries.

In July 2004 the international monitoring committee charged with overseeing the implementation of the power-sharing arrangements urged political parties to reach consensus in efforts to adopt a new constitution. A draft power-sharing accord, whereby the government and the Assemblée nationale would have 60% Hutu and

40% Tutsi composition, was reached in Pretoria later in that month, but was rejected by predominantly Tutsi parties. Also in July, the CNDD-FDD announced the resumption of its participation in the government of national unity. On 6 August the accord, which would allow elections to proceed on 31 October, was signed in Pretoria by 20 of the 30 delegations, with Tutsi parties, notably UPRONA, refusing to accept the proposed power-sharing arrangements. Despite continuing speculation that the elections would be postponed, a five-member independent electoral commission was established at the end of August. Elections were duly held and the CNDD-FDD was successful. After winning the parliamentary elections, the former main Hutu rebel group, the FDD, nominated its leader, Pierre Nkurunziza, to be the next President. By mid-2005 it appeared that Burundi was continuing its relatively peaceful transition from civil war to democracy.

Burundi, economy

In 2003 Burundi's gross domestic product (GDP) was estimated to have increased by 1.3% in real terms. The rate of inflation was estimated at 10.7% in 2003. **Coffee** and tea constitute Burundi's major exports. The United Kingdom, Switzerland, Germany and the USA are the most important destinations of Burundi's exports, while France, Zambia, Kenya and Tanzania are the major suppliers of the country's imports. The national currency is the Burundi franc (100 centimes = 1 Burundi franc). In March 2005 the exchange rate was US $1 = 1,113.5000 Burundi francs.

The mainstay of the Burundian economy is **agriculture**, which accounted for 46% of GDP in 1999. Agriculture supports more than 90% of the labour force, the majority of whom are subsistence farmers. Although Burundi is potentially self-sufficient in food production, over-population, soil erosion and **civil war** have all contributed to the contraction of the subsistence economy by 25% in recent years. As a result of the conflict, large numbers of internally displaced persons were unable to produce their own food and became largely dependent on international humanitarian assistance. In April 1997 UN officials reported that this large-scale movement, combined with the shortage of food aid, had resulted in widespread childhood malnutrition in the 'regroupment' camps. This, in turn, provoked more cross-border movement, as did the attacks against Burundian refugee camps in **Zaire** (now the Democratic Republic of the Congo—DRC) by Zairean rebels and Rwandan troops in October 1996. In April 1997 the neighbouring states partially ended the embargo to allow imports of food aid. Burundi's main cash crop is coffee, which in 1999 accounted for approximately 80% of export revenue. The ability to pay for imports therefore rests largely on the vagaries of the climate and the international coffee market. Coffee production is the largest state-owned enterprise. In recent years the government has tried to attract private investment to this sector, with some success. Efforts to privatize other publicly held enterprises have stalled, however. The country's other principal exports include tea and raw **cotton**. Little industry exists except the processing of agricultural exports. Although potential wealth in petroleum, nickel, **copper** and other natural resources is being explored, the poor security situation has in the past prevented meaningful investor interest. Some 40% of government expenditure was on the **military** during the 1990s. Industrial development is also hampered by Burundi's distance from the sea and high transport costs. Lake **Tanganyika** remains an important trading point. The trade embargo, although lifted in 1999, negatively affected trade and industry during the late 1990s. External **debt** was equivalent to 118% of GDP in 1998. There was little significant improvement in the economy, however, even after the suspension of sanctions in January 1999. Burundi ceased to service its international debt. It has accumulated arrears to bilateral creditors at an annual pace of about $10m. since 1995. In 2001 Burundi was one of the 34 sub-Saharan African countries designated by the UN as 'least developed countries'.

In the second half of 2001 a programme was initiated, and heavily monitored by the **International Monetary Fund (IMF)**, with the aim of stabilizing the macroeconomic situation, facilitating the mobilization of external assistance, and providing the basis for growth and **poverty** reduction. Little headway was made at first. Throughout 2002 the deterioration of the security situation resulted in new displacements of people fleeing violence, particularly in central and eastern provinces, and worsened the economic outlook for the country. It was clear that economic recovery was not likely without a durable peace. In fact, progress has been made in that regard during the last few years, and the outlook has now significantly improved. In mid-January 2004, at a conference organized by Belgium and the UNDP, donors pledged $1,032m. in assistance. This amount was supposed to finance budget and balance of payment support (about $440m.) in the following three years, assistance for displaced persons, returnees and **refugees**, and a demobilization and rehabilitation programme for the military ($500m.). The principal donor was the **European Union**, whose contribution totalled $279m., including a €172m.-package under the ninth European Development Fund aimed at financing rural development and agricultural projects, institutional support, good governance projects, and macroeconomic support. The other donors were the **World Bank** ($140m.), the USA ($135m.), the IMF ($93m.), the United Kingdom ($50m.), Germany ($46.2m.), Belgium ($46.2) and France ($25.5m.). These funds were supposed to contribute to covering the budget deficit for 2004.

In January 2004 the IMF extended a loan of $104m to Burundi within the framework of the **Poverty Reduction and Growth Facility**, which was intended to partially cover the estimated $200m. external financing deficit under the 2004 programme, and to help reschedule external debt arrears. The IMF considered that the staff-monitored programme, initiated in the second half of 2001, with the aim of stabilizing the macroeconomic situation, facilitating the mobilization of external assistance, and providing the basis for growth and poverty reduction, had generally made satisfactory progress in 2003, The IMF noted that Burundi's net international reserves were at comfortable levels, with the Burundi franc broadly stable in relation to major currencies. The external current-account deficit narrowed to

5.5% of GDP, compared with 6.5% in 2002. The IMF expressed the hope that implementation of the authorities' programme would provide conditions for a strong resumption of economic growth in 2004 and support the mobilization of additional foreign assistance. This was expected to enable Burundi to qualify for much-needed debt relief, under the enhanced **Heavily Indebted Poor Countries initiative**. On these assumptions, the IMF projected GDP growth of 5% and an inflation rate of 5.5%, reflecting lower food prices, and the continued implementation of a prudent monetary policy, for 2004. However, the IMF admitted that the short-term outlook remained uncertain, pending the expected return and relocation of nearly 1m. refugees and internally displaced persons. As Burundi continues its relatively peaceful transition from civil war to **democracy**, however, the longer-term outlook is promising.

Bushmen

European (English) term for the indigenous hunter/gatherer populations of **southern Africa**. Increasingly marginalized and reduced in numbers, over several centuries, as a result of intentional and unintentional pressures on their ecology, their way of life and culture, and their mode of subsistence, the peoples of the Kalahari and other dryland areas of South Africa, **South West Africa** and Botswana in particular, have become an increasing subject of concern on the part of various international human rights organizations and UN-sponsored agencies, which are increasingly working with these peoples to establish their rights with regard to their environment and sustainable development.

Busia, Dr Kofi A.

Veteran leader of the United Party—which maintained a consistent opposition to **Kwame Nkrumah** and his Convention People's Party while they were in power—and eventual Prime Minister of Ghana in 1969. By 1972, however, he had been defeated in part by the legacy of his predecessor and in part by his own liberal economic policy, which allowed an inflow of imported foreign goods that destroyed the balance of trade and crippled the balance of payments, and by a drastic currency devaluation that immediately doubled the foreign **debt**. Busia was ousted while in London, United Kingdom, and succeeded by an army committee that styled itself the National Redemption Council, under the chairmanship of **Col I. K. Acheampong**.

C

Cabral, Amílcar

Charismatic leader of the liberation struggle in Guinea-Bissau and Cape Verde in the 1960s and 1970s. In 1956 he founded the resistance movement—the Partido Africano da Independência do Guiné e Cabo Verde (PAIGC—African Party for the Independence of Guinea and Cape Verde) in Guinea Bissau and Cape Verde, and in 1963 launched an all-out **independence** struggle. He developed the Rádio Liberdade—Radio Liberation—which the PAIGC deployed to great effect. By 1972 the PAIGC was able to hold elections in 'liberated areas', and one year later announced the independence of Guinea-Bissau. In 1973, however, Cabral was murdered in Conakry.

Cabral, Luís

Former President of Guinea-Bissau, murdered in 1980.

Cameroon, Republic of

Cameroon lies in the Gulf of Guinea and borders Nigeria, Chad, the Central African Republic, the Republic of the Congo, Gabon and Equatorial Guinea. Geographically, the country comprises desert plains in the north, mountains in the central regions and tropical rainforest in the south and east. Its area is 475,000 sq km. In 2001 the population was estimated at 15.2m. The capital is Yaoundé, with a population of about 1m. Douala, with a population of about 1.5m., is Cameroon's largest city, and its main seaport and industrial and commercial centre. The population is divided into about 250 different ethnic groups. The languages of Cameroon are French (official), English (official), Fulfulde, Ewondo and various other African languages. About 50% of the population are Christians, some 20% Muslims and the remainder follow indigenous African religions.

Political profile

The Head of State is the President. At the most recent presidential election, in 1997, **Paul Biya** of the **Rassemblement démocratique du peuple camerounais (RDPC—Democratic Rally of the Cameroon People)** was re-elected, having received 92.57% of the votes. The next presidential election is scheduled to be held in 2009. The head of the government is the Prime Minister, who is appointed by the President. Ephraïm Inoni of the RDPC has been Prime Minister since 8 December 2004. The President appoints the Cabinet on the advice of the Prime Minister. The legislature is a unicameral Assemblée nationale of 180 seats, to which deputies are returned by direct popular vote for a five-year term of office. It is within the power of the President, to lengthen or curtail the term of the legislature. The Constitution calls for a second legislative chamber, the Sénat, but this has yet to be established. Major political parties, in addition to the RDPC, are the **Front démocratique et patriotique (FDP—Democratic Patriotic Front)**, the **Social Democratic Front (SDF)**, the **Union des populations camerounaises (UPC—Union of the Cameroon Peoples)**, the **Union nationale pour la démocratie et le progrès (UNDP—National Union for Democracy and Progress)**, and the **Union démocratique du Cameroun (CDU—Democratic Union of Cameroon)**.

History

The German protectorate of **Kamerun** was established in 1884. In 1916, during the First World War, the German administration was overthrown by French, British, and Belgian troops. In 1919, under League of Nations mandates, France was awarded administration of Eastern Cameroon, and Britain the Northern and Southern Cameroons, although both countries subsumed these regions into their neighbouring African colonies. These mandates were converted in 1946 into UN trusteeships, though still under British and French administration. The UN Charter promised self-determination for all inhabitants of trust territories and international and domestic pressure eventually led to a progression towards **independence**. Eastern Cameroon was granted self-government in 1958 with André-Marie Mbida as Prime Minister. He was soon succeeded by **Ahmadou Ahidjo**. Eastern Cameroon gained independence on 1 January 1960, and Ahidjo was elected as President. Following a UN-administered plebiscite, the Southern Cameroons joined the independent republic in a federal arrangement on 1 October 1961. The largely Muslim Northern Cameroons opted to join with Nigeria. Following federalization Ahidjo increasingly centralized political, economic and social institutions, outlawing all political parties but his own in 1966. From then until 1990, the Union nationale camerounaise—renamed the RDPC in 1986—represented the one-party state. With the greater electoral strength of the Francophone population, the federal republic became a United Republic after a referendum held in May 1972. The strong executive President, Assemblée nationale, and centralized system of administration has been a focus of resentment by many in the Anglophone minority ever since. The government sought to reduce the country's dependence upon France and adopted a non-aligned foreign policy. In June 1975 Paul Biya, formerly secretary-general in the President's office, was appointed as Prime Minister. President Ahidjo retired on the grounds of ill health and relinquished power to Biya in 1982. President Biya's position was confirmed by elections in January 1984. Tensions between Ahidjo and Biya had been increasing over the previous months, and in February 1984 Ahidjo was tried *in absentia* for alleged complicity in a 1983 coup attempt. There was a second coup attempt in April, this time by the élite republican guard. After intense fighting that caused many casualties, a military tribunal was established and 46 people were subsequently executed for their part in the failed coup. Although this coup attempt destabilized the regime, Cabinet reshuffles allowed Biya to retain control of the political situation.

In 1990, in response to growing civil unrest and political organization under the unofficial opposition SDF, Biya approved the legalization of a multi-party system. Legislative elections held in May 1992 were contested by 32 political parties. The first presidential elections to be held under a multi-party system, in October, were marked by controversy. President Biya was re-elected, defeating by a narrow margin the leading opposition candidate, **John Fru Ndi**, of the SDF. The elections were regarded as flawed by international observers. In legislative elections held in May 1997 the ruling RPDC won 109 of the 180 seats in the Assemblée nationale. There were claims of widespread fraud, results were referred to the Supreme Court and international election monitors were again critical of the polls. A report by a **Commonwealth** Observer Group made several recommendations, including that an independent electoral commission should be created. A National Elections Observatory was subsequently established in 2001, although it depended on the government for its mandate and funding.

The RDPC has thus been in power since independence. In 1990 the SDF was formed to press for multi-party **democracy**. Presidential elections were held in October 1997. They were boycotted by the three principal opposition candidates, however, who had had only 30 days to prepare for them, and who claimed, moreover, that the electoral system was seriously flawed and demanded an independent electoral commission. According to official figures, Biya received 92.57% of the votes in a poll in which 82% of the electorate participated. Most commentators considered the elections deeply flawed. The government subsequently entered into a dialogue with the opposition. Talks with the SDF stalled, although a UNDP member later joined the government. On 30 July 2002 legislative and local elections took place, in which the RDPC made significant gains. In the local elections the RDPC won control of 286 of the country's 337 councils—67 more than in 1996. The Supreme Court announced partial results of the legislative elections on Friday 19 July. The RDPC won 133 seats, the SDF 21, the CDU five, the UPC three, and the UNDP one. Following a Supreme Court decision, 17 seats were recontested on 15 September. Of these, the RDPC won 16 and the SDF one. The RDPC thus occupied149 seats in the Assemblée nationale, and the opposition 31. Opposition leaders complained of widespread irregularities, fraud and non-respect of the electoral law in the 2002 elections. Some called upon President Biya to cancel the result and threatened not to take up their seats in the legislature. The July elections had already been postponed from January 2002 to July, owing to concern that the newly established National Elections Observatory would not have had sufficient time or resources to prepare for them. Then, on 23 July, the day on which they were to be held, a presidential decree was issued, postponing them for a further week owing to a lack of preparation by the Ministry of the Interior. In many areas voting materials had not been distributed. Despite the presence of the National Elections Observatory, the conduct of July's elections has reinforced calls for the establishment of a fully independent body to supervise voting, as recommended by the Commonwealth Secretariat following the elections held in 1997.

The 2004 presidential election was won decisively by Paul Biya. However, Commonwealth election observers, who had been invited by the government to oversee the poll, concurred with the opposition, which had earlier claimed that government supporters had been provided with multiple voter cards and means of transport.

International relations

Nigeria and Cameroon are involved in a long-running dispute over their border, including the **oil**-rich **Bakassi Peninsula**. There were brief armed clashes in the 1990s. The Nigerian and Cameroonian foreign ministers met in Togo in February 1996 and declared in a statement that hostilities would cease. The case was referred to the International Court of Justice (ICJ), which ruled on the disputed territory on 10 October 2002. The ruling, largely in Cameroon's favour, was initially rejected by Nigeria. Through the mediation of the UN Secretary-General **Kofi Annan**, however, the ruling has been referred to a bilateral commission of the two countries. In August 2003 Nigeria and Cameroon adopted a framework agreement for the implementation of the ICJ's judgment, providing for the withdrawal of all military and administrative personnel from the Bakassi region. The bilateral commission requested that the international community support the cost of the exercise, which was estimated at some US $12m. In December 2003 the Nigerian government ceded control of 32 villages on its north-eastern border to Cameroon, but sovereignty over the disputed territory with petroleum resources remained under discussion. In January 2004 Presidents Biya and **Obasanjo**, meeting in Geneva, Switzerland, with UN mediation, agreed to exchange consular envoys, and to establish joint security patrols in the disputed region; the signing of a 'non-aggression' treaty was also envisaged.

Cameroon, economy

In 2001 Cameroon's gross domestic product (GDP) was estimated at US $8,600m., equivalent to $550 per head. The rate of inflation was 4.8% in 2002. Important sectors of the economy are **oil** production, forestry and the production of **cocoa**, **coffee**, **aluminium** and rubber. Cameroon's major trading partners are the France, Germany, Italy, Nigeria and Spain. Cameroon has qualified for the **Heavily Indebted Poor Countries (HIPC) initiative**, but has yet to reach completion point. The national currency is the franc de la **Communauté financière africaine (CFA)**. In 2004 the average exchange rate was US $1 = 528.29 francs CFA.

Cameroon experienced a boom in the first half of the 1980s, but the prices of oil, coffee, cocoa and **cotton** subsequently fell, leading to recession. In August 1997 the **International Monetary Fund (IMF)** agreed an Extended Structural Adjustment Facility for Cameroon, with tight controls owing to Cameroon's failure to meet the targets of previous agreements. The IMF commended Cameroon for its reform of macroeconomic policy under the **Poverty Reduction and Growth Facility (PRGF)** that ended in June 2000. However, it also stressed the need for further reforms, in particular to strengthen budgetary performance, improve transparency and speed up privatization in the agro-industrial sector. The IMF approved a new three-year PRGF at the end of 2000, following the government's adherence to the economic programme endorsed by the international financial institutions.

Macroeconomic performance has been satisfactory since 1996, with growth rates rising to almost 5% in 1996–2000. Encouraging progress has been made in macroeconomic stability, public finance, relations with external creditors, restructuring the banking system, privatization, economic liberalization, transportation and forestry. This 'first generation' of reforms has demonstrated the government's commitment to revamping the economy and to creating a more conducive basis for sustained growth. However, economic reform has so far brought few tangible benefits for the poor. **Poverty** reduction continues to be a daunting challenge: physical infrastructure is dilapidated and the public delivery of basic social services poor. On 10 October 2000 Cameroon became eligible for **debt** relief under the **HIPC** initiative. An IMF/**World Bank** mission visited Cameroon in late October 2001 to assess progress on poverty alleviation, and to discuss the adoption of the economic reform programme for a second year. Its assessment was positive and over the next two to three years Cameroon made significant progress, maintaining reasonable annual growth rates and low inflation. The 2004 IMF report confirmed there was still 'continued solid growth of Cameroon's economy amid low inflation'. The lack of control of government spending, however, was now 'putting at risk the macroeconomic stability that has been achieved in recent years'. The IMF felt that budget execution and the financial position of public enterprises had weakened, which had led to the accumulation of domestic arrears. In the discussion with the government, the IMF team stressed the importance of strengthening budgetary and financial management performance in the public sector in the immediate period ahead. Furthermore, the review suggested that progress in structural and financial sector reforms had been mixed during this period. Cameroonian authorities had pledged to reform and privatize public enterprises as part of the structural reform programme prescribed by the IMF. The government's proposed 2005 budget was regarded by the IMF team at the end of December 2004 as 'a first and important step to improve the use of public resources, foster economic activity, and increase the well-being of the population'.

While the IMF welcomed the proposed 2005 budget, it was strongly criticized by the opposition when presented in the Assemblée nationale. The budget included a surprising increase in taxation that was not paralleled by increased salaries.

According to the opposition, new taxes would not be necessary if **corruption** among government officials were eradicated.

Cameroon Anglophone Movement (CAM)

The Cameroon Anglophone Movement is a political movement that advocates a federal system of government for Cameroon and is particularly active in promoting the use of English in the country.

Compaoré, Blaise

President of Burkina Faso. Born in 1950 and trained as a soldier in Cameroon and Morocco, Blaise Compaoré served under **Thomas Sankara** as minister of state to the presidency, before deposing and executing him in 1987. He disarmed local militias and, despite his reputed left-wing leanings, embarked on a programme of privatization and austerity measures sponsored by the **International Monetary Fund**. After officially eschewing **socialism**, he was elected as President unopposed in 1991, and subsequently emphatically re-elected in 1998.

Cape Colony

Britain obtained the Cape Colony at the extreme south-western tip of the African continent by treaty at the end of the Napoleonic wars (1814) and soon found itself in conflict with both its white settlers of mainly Dutch origin (**Afrikaners** or **Boers**) and the many indigenous chiefdoms and kingdoms of the area.

Cape of Good Hope

The point of land furthest to the south west in South Africa. More generally, South Africa's most southwesterly region and province, of which Cape Town is the main city.

Cape Verde, Republic of

The Republic of Cape Verde consists of 10 main islands situated about 600 km off the coast of Senegal in West Africa. The climate is hot and dry and the islands suffer periodically from **drought**. The total land area is 4,033 sq km and at July 2001 the population was 405,163. The inhabitants are far outnumbered by the Cape Verde diaspora: at least 700,000 Cape Verdeans live outside of the country (in particular in the USA and Portugal). Their remittances provide an important source of revenue and investment for the islands. Almost all Cape Verdeans are of mixed African and Portuguese origin, in varying proportions. The languages of Cape Verde are Portuguese (the official language) and Crioulo, a local spoken language that mixes Portuguese and West African inputs. The majority of the population

(95%) are Roman Catholics, while the remaining 5% are either Protestants or else profess indigenous beliefs. The capital is Praia.

Political profile

The President, who is Head of State, is elected by popular vote for a five-year term of office. The current President, **Pedro de Verona Rodrigues Pires** of the **Partido Africano da Independência de Cabo Verde (PAICV—African Party for the Independence of Cape Verde)**, was returned to office in presidential elections held on 11 and 25 February 2001, having received 49.43% of the vote and thereby narrowly defeated **Carlos Veiga** of the **Movimento para a Democracia (MPD—Movement for Democracy)**, who obtained 49.42% of the vote. The next presidential is scheduled to be held in February 2006. The Prime Minister, who is head of the government, is nominated by the Assembléia Nacional and appointed by the President. José Maria Pereira Neves of the PAICV has been Prime Minister since 1 February 2001. The legislature is a unicameral Assembléia Nacional of 72 seats, to which deputies are returned by popular vote for a five-year term. Legislative elections were held most recently on 14 January 2001 and are next scheduled to be held in December 2005. In the elections held in January 2001 the vote was distributed as follows: PAICV, 47.3%; MPD, 39.8%; **Aliança Democrática para a Mudança (ADM—Democratic Alliance for Change)**, 6%; others 6.9%. The PAICV thus occupied 40 seats in the Assembléia Nacional, the MPD 30 and the ADM 2. Other major political parties are the **Partido da Convergência Democrática (PCD—Party of Democratic Convergence)**, the **Partido de Trabalho e Solidariedade (PTS—Party of Labour and Solidarity)** and the **União Caboverdiana Independente e Democrática—Partido Democrata Cristão (UCID—PDC, Independent Democratic Union of Cape Verde—Christian Democrat Party)**, all of which are part of the ADM coalition; and the **Partido da Renovação Democrática (PRD—Party of Democratic Renewal)**.

History

Cape Verde became independent from Portugal in 1975. Until 1981 the country was ruled by the Partido Africano da Independência do Guiné e Cabo Verde (PAIGC—African Party for the Independence of Guinea-Bissau and Cape Verde), a party that was united with that of the same name in Guinea-Bissau. Aristides Pereira, the secretary-general of the PAIGC, was the republic's first President. The governments of Cape Verde and Guinea-Bissau worked towards the eventual unification of the two countries. A coup in Guinea-Bissau, however, brought this association to an end, and in 1980 the Cape Verdean wing of the PAIGC became the PAICV. Pereira remained President until 1991, but Pedro de Verona Rodrigues Pires was appointed as Prime Minister, with effective control of the government. Until 1990 Cape Verde was ruled as a one-party state, but from the mid-1980s non-PAICV members began to take an increasingly prominent role in public and political life. In 1990 the PAICV began formally to consider a move towards multi-party politics and in April of that year a newly formed opposition group, the MPD demanded the immediate introduction of a multi-party system. In September Cape Verde officially became a multi-party state and the MPD held its first congress in November, at which Carlos Veiga was elected chairman and António Manuel Mascarenhas Gomes Monteiro, a former Supreme Court judge, was nominated as the party's candidate in the forthcoming presidential election. In legislative elections held in 1991 the MPD secured a clear victory, winning 56 out of 79 seats in the Assembléia Nacional, with the PAICV winning the remaining 23. Veiga was sworn in as Prime Minister of an interim government, pending the result of the presidential election—the first ever constitutional transfer of power to an opposition party in West Africa. Mascarenhas won a decisive majority against Pereira, receiving 74% of the votes cast. In the first multi-party local elections, held in December 1991, the MPD also achieved a decisive victory, winning control of 10 of the 14 local councils.

A new constitution, that of the Second Republic, was adopted in 1992. It reduced the power of the President and increased the role of the legislature. A new flag was adopted to indicate a clear break with the past. In December 1995 the MPD won a second emphatic victory in legislative elections. The incumbent President, Monteiro, supported by the MPD, was re-elected unopposed in February 1996. Over the next four years, however, divisions began to emerge within the MPD and in municipal elections held in February 2000 the MPD was defeated by the PAICV. The PAICV elected José Maria Pereira Neves as its president following the resignation of Pires, who announced his candidacy for the next presidential election. Veiga also resigned from his position as Premier in order to contest the presidential election and he was replaced as chairman of the MPD and as Prime Minister by António Gualberto do Rosário. In January 2001 legislative elections were held, and the PAICV was comfortably returned to power after10 years of opposition. The MPD now became the main opposition party. A new political force, the ADM, formed in October 2000 by the PCD, the PTS and the UCID, obtained two seats in the legislature in elections held in January 2001. Soon after the legislative elections Neves was appointed as Prime Minister. His new government stated that its priority would be the reduction of unemployment and the rehabilitation of public finances. Four candidates contested the first round of presidential elections held in February 2001. The favourites to win, the former Prime Ministers, Pedro Pires of the PAICV and Carlos Veiga of the MPD, emerged from the poll in first and second position. The second round of the election was characterized by a high turn-out and an extremely close result. Pires was declared the winner by a margin of only 17 votes by the National Electoral Commission. Veiga conceded defeat after the result had been upheld by the Supreme Court.

International relations

Owing to its history and geographic position, Cape Verde has little in common with its nearest neighbours in West Africa. Many Cape Verdeans retain closer links with the USA and Portugal. The bilateral relationship with Portugal remains by far Cape

Verde's most important. However, the country has been a member of the **Economic Community of West African States (ECOWAS)** since 1977. Cape Verde will have to make difficult decisions regarding its national currency, the escudo, as ECOWAS countries move towards a single currency. Cape Verde is also a member of the **Comunidade dos Países de Língua Portuguesa (CPLP—Community of Portuguese-speaking Countries)** and occupied the presidency of the organization in 1996–98. Cape Verde continues to try to develop its relations with other Lusophone African countries—an Angolan company has a stake in Cape Verde's state petroleum supplier. Cape Verde has also been a full member of Agence intergouvernementale de la francophonie since 1996.

Cape Verde, economy

In 2001 Cape Verde's gross domestic product (GDP) per head was estimated at US $1,500m. The rate of economic growth was estimated at 4.5% in 2004, and the rate of inflation at 3%. Important sectors of the economy are **agriculture**, in particular the production of bananas, maize, beans, sweet potatoes, sugar cane, **coffee** and groundnuts, and **fisheries**. Important industrial sectors are fuel, shoes, garments and hides. Services also make an important contribution to the economy. Cape Verde's major trading partners include France, Germany, Italy, Malaysia, Netherlands, Portugal, the United Kingdom and the USA. The national currency is the Cape Verde escudo. In March 2005 the exchange rate was US $1 = 82.2 Cape Verde escudos.

Cape Verde is poor in resources and experiences serious shortages of **water**, caused by cycles of long-term **drought**, and deficiencies in food production capacity (the country is a regular recipient of food aid). The agriculture and fishing sectors have great potential, but Cape Verde's economy is mainly service-oriented—tourism, commerce and public services account for some 70% of GDP. The tourism sector contributed approximately 8% of GDP in gross receipts in 2001, about twice as much as in 1999. The industry benefits from major investment by the government and from the remittances of expatriate Cape Verdeans. The country's economy has been generally well managed since **independence**. It has a low **debt** service ratio and an excellent repayment record. Cape Verde weathered a period of high macroeconomic uncertainty in the face of important fiscal deficits in the run-up to the 2000–01 legislative and presidential elections. An austerity programme was initiated. The economic growth rate fell from 8% in 2000 to 3% in 2001, but the fiscal turn-around limited the deficit to about 3% (including grants) in 2001, compared with 19% in 2000. The programme was backed by the country's first **Poverty Reduction and Growth Facility** in April 2002.

At the end of 2003 publicly held external debt was projected at $420m., and the government forecast that the economy would grow by more than 7% in 2004, with an inflation rate of only 0.1%. In the medium term economic growth was forecast at 6%–7% by the government, a calculation that was endorsed by a mission of the

International Monetary Fund (IMF) in 2004, and which contributed to the IMF's decision to remove Cape Verde from its list of 'least developed countries', due to its 'extraordinary development' in recent years. While Cape Verde's economic achievements have thus been recognized, potential receipts of foreign development aid have accordingly been reduced. Expenditure in the 2004 budget was focused on the social sectors, as well as on maintaining the fiscal balance. Total spending was projected to reach 32,000m. escudos (€360m.), with government revenue increasing by 4.5% in 2004. Total expenditure was capped at 32% of GDP, producing a financing gap of €26m. (US $32m.) for 2004. This was expected to be covered by external financing, and domestic borrowing was expected to remain low. Exports (including tourism receipts) remain limited, at about 27% of GDP, while imports represent about 60% of GDP.

Casablanca Group

In January 1961 a conference was held in Casablanca, Morocco, attended by the Heads of State of Egypt, Ghana, Guinea, Mali and Morocco (and Ceylon), and representatives of Libya and the provisional government of the Algerian Republic. Tunisia, Nigeria, Liberia and Togo declined an invitation to attend. An African Charter was adopted and it was decided to establish an African Military Command and an African Common Market. Mali had joined the Guinea-Ghana union in the previous year. Those participating came to be known as the Casablanca Group. They envisaged a broadly federal structure for a pan-African union. The group established permanent organs, including economic, cultural and political committees, a supreme command and a headquarters at Bamako, Mali. It opposed the **independence** of Mauritania (largely because of Moroccan interests in **Western Sahara**) and was initially pro-Lumumbist in the Congo. At its second conference, held in May in Cairo, Egypt, however, **Kwame Nkrumah** strongly opposed proposals to withdraw troops from the UN force and switch them to Gizenga, and persuaded his colleagues to adopt his view. Libya transferred soon afterwards to another association, known as the **Brazzaville Group**.

Casamance

Since 1982 an armed separatist movement in the Casamance region of southern Senegal, known as the Mouvement des forces démocratiques de la Casamance (MFDC), has been fighting ostensibly for **independence**. There have been numerous attempts at negotiated settlements since the early 1990s, but the MFDC is increasingly split into factions and most recent armed activity on the ground can be classified as banditry. The MFDC was supported clandestinely in the 1990s by the **military** in neighbouring Guinea-Bissau. This support ended in late 2000 with the death of Gen. Ansumane Mané in an aborted coup in Guinea-Bissau. Low-level violence continues. Most rebel activity is in the Bigniona region north of the Casamance River, although there are still pockets of rebels in the southern

Casamance. The political leadership of the MFDC does not appear to control all of the armed elements. The MFDC and the government have agreed to a new round of peace talks to be held in Guinea-Bissau, but these have yet to take place. In July 2004 the Assemblée nationale adopted legislation providing for an amnesty for all MFDC combatants. MFDC leaders none the less reiterated their demand for the withdrawal of government troops from Casamance.

Cell phones

The cell phone business is one of the most dynamic on the African continent and one of the most profitable. Even in some of the most politically unstable countries, the growth of cell phone use has been dramatic. In Somalia, for example, Mogadishu has the cheapest cell phone rates on the continent, largely because of the absence of government intervention in a country that has been without a central government for more than a decade.

CEN-SAD

Community of Saharan and Sahelian States.

Central African Federation

The Central African Federation came into being in August 1953, with Godfrey Huggins, former leader of the **United Party** in Southern **Rhodesia**, as federal Prime Minister and Roy Welensky of Northern Rhodesia as his deputy. The federal Constitution left the territorial constitutions untouched and also made it clear that the Federation could not hope for **independence** or dominion status until they were touched. The Federation lasted 10 years and its life was violent as well as short. In 1958 elections were held for the federal and Southern Rhodesian parliaments. In the former, Welensky, who had succeeded Huggins in 1956, achieved an overwhelming victory; in Southern Rhodesia, **Garfield Todd** was forced to resign, and was replaced by Sir Edgar Whitehead, although the Dominion Party (campaigning for independence by 1960) received more votes. The African population did not support the Federation and began to agitate against it from the outset. In 1957 George Nyandoro and Robert Chikerema re-animated the **African National Congress**, and in 1958 **Dr Hastings Banda** arrived to lead an anti-federation crusade. The main objective of this movement was secession followed by independence. In January 1959 there was a meeting between nationalist leaders (at which Banda was not present), which was afterwards represented as a murderous conspiracy. The governor of **Nyasaland** requested Rhodesian troops to help keep order and the government of Southern Rhodesia dispatched 3,000 troops and declared its own state of emergency. The governor of Nyasaland followed suit one week later. Between 2,000 and 3,000 Africans were rounded up throughout the Federation, the African National Congress parties in all three territories were dissolved and

Banda and his chief associates were among those jailed. The British colonial secretary, Alan Lennox-Boyd, stated that he had evidence of an impending massacre. A commission, under a High Court judge, appointed to investigate the affair found no evidence of any murder plot and specifically exonerated Banda. It also found that Nyasaland had temporarily become a police state in which it was unsafe to express approval of the policies of the Congress, to which the majority of Africans adhered. Shortly afterwards, the colonial office was placed in the more liberal hands of Ian Macleod, and the British Prime Minister, Harold Macmillan, began to recognize the need for change in Africa. In Northern Rhodesia a new constitution preceded elections in 1959, in which the United Federal Party (the new name for the local counterpart of the Huggins-Welensky party) was victorious. From 1960 there was a race between those forces that wished to extract independence for the federation out of the British government and those that wished to break up the federation and establish black rule in independent states. A commission of inquiry was sent out which, despite its focus on making the federation work, marked the turn of the tide in favour of break-up.

Central African Republic

The Central African Republic (CAR) is a large land-locked country. It is mainly savannah in the north and equatorial forest in the south. Chad borders the north of the country, Sudan lies to the east, the Democratic Republic of the Congo (DRC) and the Republic of the Congo (ROC) to the south, and Cameroon to the west. The main river, the Oubangui, forms part of the border with the DRC, and then flows south between the ROC and the DRC to the Congo Basin. The CAR is 622,984 sq km in area and its population was estimated at some 3.9m. in 2003. The capital is Bangui, whose population was estimated at 697,000 at mid-2003. The inhabitants belong to more than 80 different ethnic groups, of which the largest are the Baya (34%), the Banda (28%), the Sara (10%), the Mandja (9%), the Mboum (9%) and the M'baka (7%). French is the official language and the national language is Sangho. About one-half of the population are Christians—Protestants (25%) and Roman Catholics (25%)—with perhaps 15% Muslim and the largest group (35%) following indigenous beliefs.

Political profile

The Head of State is the President, who is elected by popular vote for a five-year term. The head of the government is the Prime Minister, who is appointed by the President. The legislature is a unicameral Assemblée nationale. Presidential and legislative elections were held most recently in March and May 2005. The major political parties are the Concertation des partis politiques d'opposition (CPPO—Dialogue of the Opposition Political Parties, an umbrella organization of 12 parties opposed to former President Patassé), the Coordination des patriotes centrafricains (CPC—Co-ordination of Central African Patriots), the **Mouvement**

pour la libération du peuple centrafricain (MLPC—Liberation Movement of the Central African People), the **Rassemblement démocratique centrafricain (RDC—Central African Democratic Rally)**, the **Mouvement pour la démocratie et le développement (MDD—Movement for Democracy and Development)**, the **Front patriotique pour le progrès (FPP—Patriotic Front for Progress)** and the **Parti social-démocrate (PSD—Social Democrat Party)**.

History

In 1885 the French, Germans, and Belgians began arriving in the area. The French consolidated their control in 1903 when they defeated the forces of the Sultan of Egypt and established a colonial administration. In 1910 the **Oubangui Chari** territory (largely present-day CAR) became one of the four territories of the federation of **Afrique équatoriale française (AEF—French Equatorial Africa)**, together with Chad, Congo (Brazzaville) and Gabon. The French presence centred on the extraction of raw materials, principally rubber, and trading companies were allowed to operate as *de facto* government authorities. Many were brutal in their treatment of local populations. The AEF fought for Charles de Gaulle's Free France during the Second World War, and in 1946 AEF inhabitants were granted citizenship of the French 'Union' encompassing all French colonies, and semi-autonomous local assemblies were created. Barthélemy Boganda, a Catholic priest, led the CAR assembly and, with the dissolution of the AEF in 1958, became head of government. Upon his death in 1959 his nephew, David Dacko, replaced him.

The CAR gained full **independence** from France in 1960, with Dacko as the country's first President. The French settler community and some local politicians favoured continuing attachment to the French Communauté. Dacko transformed the country into a one party state, with the **Mouvement de l'évolution sociale de l'Afrique noire (MESAN—Social Evolution Movement of Black Africa)** as the sole political party. Presidential elections were held in 1964 in which Dacko was the only candidate. With the country facing bankruptcy and a nation-wide strike pending, Dacko was ousted in 1966 in a swift and virtually bloodless coup led by **Col Jean-Bédel Bokassa**, the army chief of staff. Bokassa had virtually absolute power: he declared himself President for life in 1972, and in 1977 crowned himself Emperor of the Central African Empire.

Open opposition to his rule began in 1979 and several opposition groups were formed in exile, including the MLPC, led by Ange-Félix Patassé. In December 1979, following riots in Bangui and the murder of between 50–200 schoolchildren, Dacko deposed Bokassa in a coup supported by French troops dispatched from Gabon. He re-established the republic. President Dacko held elections in March 1981, which he won by a narrow margin. However, opposition pressure grew and he cancelled legislative elections due later in the year. He was unable to suppress subsequent outbreaks of violence and popular demonstrations by various opposition parties. Deprived of French support following a change of government in Paris, President Dacko resigned, relinquishing power to the army chief of staff,

Gen. André Kolingba. A coup attempt led by Patassé in March 1982 failed. He sought refuge in the French embassy and, at the insistence of the French, was guaranteed safe passage into exile in Togo. In 1986 Kolingba held a referendum that extended his mandate for a further six years and approved a draft constitution, which allowed for greater presidential powers. However, from late 1990 public unrest and disillusion with the regime increased, largely as a result of economic reforms and cutbacks. The government was plagued by sporadic strikes initiated by the trade union movement, into which opposition politicians now channelled their energies. Kolingba bowed to the demands of the opposition and international donor community to initiate a democratic transition. Multi-party presidential elections were held in October 1992. Kolingba received the least number of votes, but had the results annulled by the Supreme Court, with the support of other candidates, because of widespread irregularities. After several postponements, presidential elections were re-scheduled for October 1993. Ange-Félix Patassé defeated Dacko and Kolingba in the elections, thus ending 12 years of military rule.

Following a referendum in late 1994, Patassé introduced a new constitution and began work on decentralization. Despite this attempt at reform, in 1996 and 1997 there were three army mutinies against Patassé's government, provoked by salary arrears, labour unrest and ethnic tensions within the army. The French quelled the demonstrations and kept troops in the country to ensure stability. Regional leaders mediated between the mutineers and the government, leading to the signing of the so-called Bangui Accords by all parties in January 1997. Shortly after the declaration was signed, Michel Gbezera-Bria was appointed as Prime Minister and a new government was formed. In June 1997 there was fighting between the mutineers and the Inter-African peace-keeping force (MISAB). Mediators brokered another cease-fire and relative calm returned to Bangui. In April 1998 French forces based in the CAR withdrew and MISAB was replaced by MINURCA, a UN peace-keeping force of 1,350 troops. Legislative elections were held in November and December 1998. The presidential party, the MLPC, won 51 seats in the elections, the opposition alliance won 55, and three independent candidates were also elected. Before the opening of the Assemblée nationale the independents and one opposition member defected to the MLPC. The opposition reacted by routinely boycotting the Assemblée. This alarmed UN observers, who wished to see concrete progress on the implementation of the Bangui Accords through a functioning legislature. President Patassé was returned for a second term following elections held in September 1999, receiving slightly more than 50% of the votes in the first round of the polls. International observers considered the elections to have been broadly fair, and they were held with little disturbance. The political situation appeared to have stabilized and MINURCA withdrew from the CAR when its mandate finally expired on 15 February 2000. However, in late 2000 there was an increase in strikes in Bangui as civil servants protested at the non-payment of their salaries. A rally, organized by 15 opposition groups that accused Patassé of mismanagement and **corruption**, led to riots. In 2001 there were two further attempted coups: one in May by supporters of Kolingba, and one in November by followers of **Gen. François Bozizé**, former chief of defence staff. On both occasions Patassé's troops, with the help of Libyan and other forces, regained control of Bangui. A spate of revenge killings followed and many of Bangui's residents fled the city. Several thousand members of the Yakoma ethnic group fled the country to escape reprisals. After the attempted coup in May, Bozizé had been dismissed and a warrant issued for his arrest. Following his failed coup in November, he fled to Chad. Fighting again erupted in Bangui on 25 October 2002, between Bozizé's rebels and troops loyal to President Patassé. After several days of fighting, and with the intervention of the **Mouvement pour la libération du Congo (MLC—Movement for the Liberation of the Congo)** from the neighbouring DRC, the rebel forces were forced to retreat to the north of the country.

On 15 March 2003 forces loyal to Bozizé attacked Bangui and seized power. Patassé was out of the country at the time. He subsequently fled to Cameroon and later Togo. Upon taking power, Bozizé suspended the Constitution, dissolved the Assemblée nationale and established a transitional government. The 28-member transitional administration comprises representatives of civil society and all political parties. Its composition sends a signal of national unity and inclusion. It includes ministers from the CPPO, the CPC, the political arm of Bozizé's rebel force, the RDC of former President Kolingba, and the MLPC of Patassé. Gen. Bozizé is the self-appointed President and defence minister. The successful military coup followed at least two years of instability in the CAR. The international community condemned the military coup, but Bozizé has promised to hold elections within 18–30 months. He has also suggested that he will not stand for election himself. Bozizé has promised to establish a National Transitional Council to act as an advisory and transitional law-making organ, comprising representatives from politics, the unions, religion, commerce, the **military**, the judiciary and civil society. Former President Kolingba has been promised safe return from exile. Libyan and MLC troops have now left the CAR, although the peace-keeping force from the **Communauté économique et monétaire de l'Afrique centrale (CEMAC—Central African Economic and Monetary Community)** deployed to Bangui in December 2002 is still present, reinforced by Chadian forces. The current UN presence in Bangui (BONUCA) is a UN Peace-building Support Office under Gen. Lamine Cissé. It aims to support the government of the CAR in its efforts to: consolidate peace and the rule of law; strengthen democratic institutions; facilitate the mobilization of international political support and resources for national reconstruction and economic recovery; and follow up on security reforms.

International relations

The CAR is a member of CEMAC, together with Cameroon, Chad, Equatorial Guinea, Gabon and the ROC. The presence of large numbers of **refugees** in the Equateur Province of the DRC has caused tension in relations between the CAR and the DRC. Under Patassé, the CAR's relations with Chad were also tense, with each government accusing the other of supporting respective rebel movements, although this relationship has greatly improved under Bozizé, with Chadian troops protecting the new regime. Libya has been involved in the affairs of the CAR in the past—it provided troops in support of Patassé—but its forces have now been withdrawn. The CAR has traditionally had a close relationship with France, the former colonial power, with aid and trade complemented by the deployment of French peace-keeping troops following the coups in the 1990s.

Central African Republic, economy

In 2001 the Central African Republic's (CAR) gross domestic product (GDP) was US $1,100m., equivalent to $248.8 per head. The major sectors of the economy are **agriculture**, mining for **diamonds** and timber production. The CAR's principal trading partners are the Benelux countries, France, Cameroon, Spain and the People's Republic of China. The national currency is the franc de la **Communauté financière africaine (CFA**—see the **Franc Zone)**. In March 2005 the exchange rate was US $1 = 493.6500 francs CFA.

The CAR is one of the world's least developed countries and depends largely upon agriculture. The majority of the population is engaged in subsistence farming and the main crops are **cotton**, **coffee**, tobacco and food crops, such as bananas, cassava, maize, and yams. Economic development has been hampered by the country's land-locked location, poor transport system, a largely unskilled workforce and a legacy of misdirected economic policies. Subsistence agriculture and forestry account for almost 60% of export earnings. Timber and uncut diamonds are major sources of export revenue. The country is also rich in other natural resources, such as **gold**, and uranium, but these are largely unexploited, as are unconfirmed quantities of **oil** in the northern part of the country. Exports are largely reliant on the road route through Cameroon to the Gulf of Guinea, and the Oubangui River, both of which have often been affected by conflict in the country.

The CAR's economy has experienced severe difficulties in recent years because of fluctuations in the price of its raw material exports (notably cotton), poor economic policies and administration, increased indebtedness, and disruption caused by the repeated mutinies and coups from the 1990s. A number of strikes and non-payment of government salaries have further disrupted business activity and hindered domestic demand. Until confidence in the stability of the country increases, the situation will remain precarious. Arrears on **debt** service obligations continue to mount as government revenues fall short, control over budgetary expenditure remains weak and there have been delays in implementing structural reforms. The **World Bank** resumed its operations in the CAR in December 1999 with the approval of a fiscal consolidation credit and a development credit. However, in mid-August 2001 it suspended its disbursements for non-payment of amounts due. The **International Monetary Fund (IMF)** also suspended its **Poverty Reduction and Growth Facility (PRGF)** programme in the latter half of 2001 as a result of the coup. This combined with a deteriorating export sector to limit the CAR's ability to meet programme targets. In October 2001 the CAR embarked on a six-month (unfunded) Staff Monitored Programme (SMP). The CAR's difficulties in clearing arrears (mainly owed to the **African Development Bank**) delayed the presentation of the PRGF to the IMF Board until November 2002. This was again delayed following the coup that was attempted in October. The government hoped to qualify for **debt relief** by reaching enhanced **Heavily Indebted Poor Countries initiative** decision point in 2003, but this was reliant on first resuming a full PRGF. Without donor support and debt relief to clear external debt and civil service arrears the economic and political situation in the CAR will remain extremely fragile.

Ceuta

One of the two major ports (the other is **Melilla**) on the Moroccan Mediterranean coast still owned by Spain, with the special status of *praesidios* (garrisons). The Portuguese first occupied the town in 1415, but it was taken over by the Spanish in the 17th century and heavily fortified against attack from sea and from land. A peace treaty of 1860 with Morocco, after a war with Spain had led to Morocco's defeat, provided for the enlargement of the Ceuta (and Melilla) enclaves. Despite continuing demands by the Moroccan government since **independence** in 1956 for the return of these *praesidios*, both Ceuta and Melilla remain in Spanish hands.

CFA – *see* Communauté financière africaine

Chad, Republic of

The Republic of Chad is surrounded on three sides by mountain ranges. While there are fertile lowlands in the south, the country is arid in the centre and largely desert in the north. The population is concentrated in the south. Chad has borders with Libya, Niger, Cameroon, the Central African Republic (CAR) and Sudan. The total area is 1,284,000 sq km and the population was estimated to number only some 8.6m. in 2003. The capital is N'Djamena, whose population was estimated at about 793,000 in mid-2003. The population comprises around 200 ethnic groups, of which the Zaghawa are a major group in the north. The official languages are French and **Arabic**, but local languages are widely used (Sara in the south, Toubou in the north). Just over one-half of the population (55%) are Muslims, while the remainder are either Christians (35%) or else follow indigenous beliefs (15%).

Political profile

The Head of State is the President, who is elected by popular vote for a five-year term of office, renewable once. (If no candidate receives at least 50% of the vote in a presidential election, the two candidates receiving the most votes must contest a second ballot.) **Gen. Idriss Deby** has been President of Chad since 4 December 1990. He was most recently re-elected on 20 May 2001, when he received 63% of the votes in a presidential poll. The President appoints the Prime Minister, who is the head of the government, and, on the recommendation of the Prime Minister, the Council of Ministers. Pascal Yoadimnadji of the **Mouvement patriotique du salut (MPS—Patriotic Salvation Movement)** has been Prime Minister since 3 February 2005. The Constitution provides for a bicameral legislature, comprising a Sénat and an Assemblée nationale. However, the Sénat, of unspecified size, and whose members (one-third of whom are renewable every two years) are to serve a six-year term, has not yet been created. Deputies to the existing chamber, the 155-seat Assemblée nationale, are elected by popular vote for a five-year term. Following legislative elections held on 21 April 2002, the distribution of seats in the Assemblée nationale was: MPS, 110; **Rassemblement pour la démocratie et le progrès (RDP—Rally for Democracy and Progress)**, 12; **Fédération action pour la République (FAR—Action Federation for the Republic)**, 9; VIVA-Rassemblement national pour la démocratie et le progrès (VIVA-RNDP—National Rally for Democracy and Progress), 5; Union pour le renouveau et la démocratie (URD—Union for Renewal and Democracy), 5; Union nationale pour le développment et le renouveau (UNDR—National Union for Development and Renewal), 3; others, 11.

History

In 1959 the territory of the Federation of **Afrique équatoriale française (AEF—French Equatorial Africa)** was dissolved and Chad gained **independence** from France on 11 August 1960. **François Tombalbaye**, a southerner, became President. However, increasing centralization of power and southern-led government was widely resented. By the mid-1960s tax riots had broadened into a popular rebellion in the north and east which the army could not control. The **Front de libération nationale du Tchad (FROLINAT—National Liberation Front of Chad)** was formed in Sudan in 1966 and assumed leadership of the revolt. In 1968 French forces were sent to assist the government forces, and succeeded in pushing the rebel forces into isolated pockets. French intervention thus contained the rebellion, but did not defeat it. French troops left Chad in 1972. In 1975 Tombalbaye was killed by disaffected southern army officers in a coup led by **Gen. Félix Malloum**. In 1978 **Hissène Habré** was appointed Prime Minister, but divisions between him and Malloum soon emerged and fighting between their forces erupted in early 1979. Malloum fled the country, but fighting continued, with N'Djamena captured, recaptured and destroyed on several occasions by different factions. Central government broke down. In 1982 Habré captured N'Djamena and was inaugurated as President. Fighting continued, however. Rivalry and conflict within the government continued throughout the 1980s. In 1981 Libya entered the conflict in support of Habré's rival, Goukouni Oueddei, a northerner, and annexed the Aouzou Strip in northern Chad. In 1983 Libya supported a renewed offensive in northern and eastern Chad, provoking French intervention on behalf of President Habré. A cease-fire line was agreed on the 15th parallel prior to a withdrawal of all foreign forces in September 1984. In 1989 Idriss Deby, a northern Chadian and one of Habré's leading generals, defected and fled to Sudan, from where he launched a succession of attacks on Habré. In 1990, with Libyan assistance, Deby marched into N'Djamena under the banner of the MPS.

Multi-party politics were legalized in 1991, following Deby's coup in 1990, and Deby became President in February 1991. However, the country has remained divided on north/south, Muslim/Christian lines, with factions retaining arms obtained during the **civil war**. At the end of 1992, following both internal and external pressure, a National Conference was convened, attended by more than 1,000 people who were broadly representative of the whole country. A new constitution was adopted by referendum on 31 March 1996. Chad's first presidential elections since independence took place on 2 June 1996, and some 75% of the electorate was estimated to have participated in them. Deby received 43.8% of the votes and Gen. Kamougue (Malloum's chosen successor) 12.39%. Deby won the second round of voting to become Chad's first elected President. In December 1999 Nagoum Yamassoum became Prime Minister and the opposition UNDR acquired one ministerial portfolio in the government.

Since 1998 rebels belonging to the **Mouvement pour la démocratie et la justice au Tchad (MDJT—Movement for Democracy and Justice in Chad)**, led by Youssouf Togoimi, had skirmished with government and rebel troops in the Tibesti region, but little had been gained on either side. On 24 December 2001 the government and rebel forces concluded a peace agreement, brokered by Libyan leader **Col Muammar al-Qaddafi**, and signed a cease-fire agreement in early January 2002. The death of Togoimi in September 2002 cast doubt on the future of the peace process, but the level of the conflict has remained low. On the eastern border, a lesser-known rebel group, the Armée nationale de résistance (National Resistance Army) eventually signed a peace memorandum, in which rebels of the organization were granted a general amnesty prior to their reintegration into the civilian sector.

Chad is now a constitutional republic. Politics is dominated by a strong executive branch, led by President Deby. The President exercises considerable influence on the judiciary and the army, as well as on the Assemblée nationale through the MPS party structure. The most recently held presidential elections, which took place on 20 May 2001, were characterized by some observers as fair, although others noted irregularities, particularly in the distribution of voter registration cards. Some unrest followed the announcement of the results. Opposition leaders were arrested and released twice by the government. In legislative elections that took place on 21 April 2002 the presidential party and its allies won an overwhelming majority of 136 of 154 seats (in the previous legislative elections they had won 65 of 125 seats). The URD lost almost all of the seats it had held, and the FAR, having obtained 11 seats, became the main opposition party. The turn-out was 50% and the elections were reported to have been free on the day they were held. The **European Union**, however, considers that many irregularities occurred before they were held, in particular in respect of the updating of electoral lists. In June 2002 Haroun Kabadi was appointed as Prime Minister to head the new government.

International relations

Chad has recently been involved in border disputes with both Nigeria and the CAR. Chad has been accused of supporting Gen. **Bozizé**'s successful military coup of March 2003 in the CAR. Certainly the new government has achieved a remarkable *rapprochement* between the two countries. After the annexation of the Aouzou Strip by the Libyan-supported Goukouni, the International Court of Justice was requested to rule on its ownership. It ruled in Chad's favour in 1994. Chad was a founder member of the Community of Saharan and Sahelian States, established in 1997 by Libya to increase its influence in West Africa. Northern Chad, particularly the Tibesti and Faya-Largeau regions, were heavily mined during Chad's conflict with Libya in the 1970s and 1980s. The mines laid have not been cleared. Bilateral relations with Libya have gradually improved, and a border crossing and customs posts have been opened.

Chad, economy

In 2002 the gross domestic product (GDP) of Chad was estimated at US $1,600m., equivalent to $215 per head. In that year the rate of economic growth was estimated at 11.3%, and the rate of inflation at 6%. In 2001 the contribution of **agriculture** to GDP was estimated at 38%, that of industry at 13% and that of services at 49%. Chad's major industries are **oil**, **cotton**, meat and livestock. Chad's major trading partners are Portugal, Germany, Thailand, Costa Rica, South Africa, France and Nigeria. The national currency is the franc de la **Communauté financière africaine (CFA**—see the **Franc Zone)**. In March 2005 the exchange rate was US $1 = 493.6500 francs CFA.

Chad's economic development has been characterized by brief periods of growth interrupted by steep declines. The **World Bank** estimates that almost two-thirds of Chad's population live in extreme **poverty**. The country is largely dependent economically on continued development assistance from France. The tax collection structure is poor and public administration is weak. It is estimated that less than one-tenth of revenue actually reaches the treasury. In January 2000 the **International Monetary Fund** approved a three-year **Poverty Reduction and Growth Facility** for Chad, worth $49.9m. In order to complete this, the government of Chad will need to carry out privatization, judicial and fiscal reform and reform of such areas as health and **education**. Chad reached the **Heavily Indebted Poor Countries initiative** decision point in May 2001.

Cotton is currently the largest export, accounting for around 40% of total exports. However, the discovery of substantial oil reserves in the Doba basin has improved Chad's economic prospects. On 23 May 2000 the World Bank approved plans for a pipeline to transport this oil from Chad to the Cameroonian coast. The consortium involved in the project comprises Exxon (40%), Petronas (35%) and Chevron (25%). World Bank funds for the project were granted on condition that 40% of the revenue generated by it is put aside for future generations, with the remainder to be spent on improvements to the health and education sectors and the environment. This is one of the biggest projects in African history—World Bank and private-sector funding for it is estimated at more than $3,000m. The oilfields were expected to become operational in 2004. Doubts regarding the distribution of economic benefits within Chad were raised following the discovery in December 2000 that President Deby had used $4.8m. of World Bank funding to purchase arms.

Chadli, Benjedid

President of Algeria (1979–92). Benjedid Chadli was born in Sebaa, Algeria, in 1929. He joined the **Front de libération nationale (FLN—National Liberation Front)** shortly after the Algerian revolution began in 1954 and rose through the ranks of the guerrilla forces; by the early 1960s he was on the staff of Col (later President) **Houari Boumedienne**, and he played a decisive role in the latter's overthrow of President **Ahmed Ben Bella** in 1965. Subsequently serving in the Revolutionary Council and as acting Minister of Defence (1978), he was elected as President in February 1979 following the death of Boumedienne and re-elected in 1984 and 1988. When his democratization programme and the new multi-party system threatened to bring Islamic fundamentalists to power, he was forced to resign in January 1992 by a military-dominated junta, which took power as the High Council of State headed by **Mohammed Boudiaf** until January 1994.

Chagga

Major ethno-linguistic group in northern Tanzania. The Chagga are mainly agri-culturalists and **coffee** growers.

Chama Cha Mapinduzi (CCM—Revolutionary Party)

Signed a peace accord on 10 October 2001 with the Civic United Front in **Zanzibar**, Tanzania.

Chettiar, Angidi Varriah

Former President of Mauritius. Previously Vice-President, Chettiar assumed the presidency in February 2002, when **Cassam Uteem** resigned over controversial anti-terrorist legislation, only to resign himself within one month, relinquishing power to **Karl Offman**, who was elected as President in February 2002.

Chiluba, Frederick

Former President of Zambia. In November 2003 he pleaded 'not guilty' to 169 charges of theft of public funds, totalling US $30m.—equal to three days' income for every Zambian.

Chromium

Chromium is obtained from chromite. About 85% of total demand for chromite is from the metallurgical industry, 8% from the chemical industry and 7% from the refractory and foundry industries. World reserves of chromite are estimated at around 3,600m. metric tons. More than 80% of global reserves are in South Africa, with a further 4% in neighbouring Zimbabwe. South Africa produced almost 44% of estimated world chromite ore supplies in 2001 and is also the world's leading ferrochromium producer, accounting for about 43% of estimated world requirements. Zimbabwe currently accounts for about 5%. Other African producers include Madagascar and Sudan. Altogether, Africa accounts for just over one-half of total world output of chromium ore. In 1997 it was estimated that South Africa alone could account for 60% of world supplies by 2005. South Africa's ferrochromium sector has benefited from access to inexpensive electricity and relatively low labour costs. Over-supply in the early 1990s meant that export prices fell, but during the second half of the decade there was a significant recovery.

CHUMA (Islands' Fraternity and Unity Party)

A political party in the Union of the Comoros. Its leader is Assoumani Abdou.

Civil war

Civil war has been waged in a number of African countries in the last two decades. In Algeria, from 1992 onwards, the Islamist opposition, notably the **Front islamique du salut (FIS—Islamic Salvation Front)** was banned and went underground; several paramilitary groupings, including the **Groupe islamique armé (GIA—Armed Islamic Group)**, and the **Groupe salafiste pour la prédication et le combat (GSPC—Salafist Group for Call and Combat)** waged a bitter struggle over the next decade to overthrow the government and bring about an Islamic republic in Algeria. At the other end of the continent, the struggle against **apartheid** and the white-dominated regime in South Africa, which began in earnest in the 1960s and continued over the next two decades, spearheaded by the **African National Congress**, eventually—in 1994—achieved its objective of overthrowing the apartheid regime and bringing about a more democratic, non-racist political regime and society. In Burundi and, particularly, in Rwanda, a complex political emergency developed during the 1980s and 1990s, which increasingly took the form of inter-ethnic violence and conflict between **Hutus** and Tutsis, and led in the mid-1990s to **genocide** in which as many as 1m. people, mainly Tutsis, were massacred and many hundreds of thousands more were displaced. From the mid-1990s onwards the disintegrating central African state of **Zaire** was subject to growing conflict, which crystallized eventually as a major rebellion from the east which, in 1997, overthrew the regime of President **Mobutu** and installed **Laurent-Désiré Kabila** as President. The conflict continued, however, and during the latter part of the decade came to involve troops from several other African states, including Uganda, Rwanda, Angola and Zimbabwe, in a large-scale regional war, which only came to an end in the early 2000s, but left continued fighting in the Democratic Republic of the Congo (as it was now known), particularly in the east, until well into the mid-2000s. Many other African countries—including Sudan, Ethiopia, and Somalia in the north east, Uganda in **East Africa**, Mozambique, Zimbabwe and Angola in **southern Africa**, Sierra Leone, Liberia, Côte d'Ivoire and Equatorial Guinea in West Africa, and Mali, Niger and Chad in the Sahel—have also experienced civil war during the last two decades.

CLUB 2002

Political party in the Republic of the Congo, founded in 2002. Its president is William Nguesso.

Coalition des forces démocratiques (CFD—Coalition of Democratic Forces)

Political grouping in Burkina Faso, founded in 2002 as an alliance of six social democratic parties. Its leader is Ram Ouédrago. The CFD includes the Mouvement pour la tolérance et le progrès (Movement for Tolerance and Progress)/Moog Teeb Panpaasgo and Les verts du Burkina (Burkina Green Party).

Coalition for Unity and Democracy (CUD)

Recently formed opposition party in Ethiopia. The CUD offers a liberal alternative to the ruling Ethiopian People's Revolutionary Democratic Front.

Cobalt

Cobalt is usually mined as a by-product of another metal. In the case of African cobalt, this is principally **copper**, although it is also produced from nickel-copper-cobalt ores in Botswana and Zimbabwe and from platinum ores in South Africa. About 35% of all cobalt is used in metallic form as superalloys, hardfacing and stellite. Approximately 34% is applied to chemical uses in glass manufacture, paints and inks, rechargeable batteries and, increasingly, as catalysts in the processing of **oil** and petroleum feedstocks and synthetic materials. A further 10% is used in the manufacture of ceramics, 11% in magnetic alloys and 10% in the fabrication of hard metals. The USA is the world's major consumer of cobalt. The Democratic Republic of the Congo (DRC) possesses almost one-half of the world's identifiable cobalt reserves. These reserves also have the highest grade of the metal. Mining is conducted by a state monopoly, La Générale des Carrières et des Mines (GECAMINES). From 1990, however, the country's cobalt production was seriously disrupted by internal conflict and associated disintegration of the economy, and by theft, which in some years resulted in losses of 5%–25% of total output. Continuing political instability in the 1990s meant that output remained compromised. Despite this, in 2000 the DRC was the world's leading producer of cobalt, with output of some 7,000 metric tons, ahead of Zambia, its closest rival (4,600 tons). In 2001 both the DRC and Zambia produced around 7,000 tons. The privatization of Zambia Consolidated Copper Mines Ltd (ZCCM), one of the country's primary producers of cobalt, was completed in 2000. Together, Zambia and the DRC account for about 30% of world cobalt exports. The main African producers are the DRC, Zambia, Morocco, South Africa, Uganda, Botswana and Zimbabwe. Together they account for well over one-third of the world's total output. Morocco, the third largest African producer, has tended to export concentrates (about 1,305 tons in 2000) to the People's Republic of China, but an expansion in refining capacity may lead to a reduction of such exports in future as domestic production of refined cobalt increases. South African production totalled some 585 tons in 2000, with two mining companies producing cobalt as a by-product of platinum production. Botswana (with annual production of around 320–330 tons) exports mainly to Zimbabwe and to Norway for refining while Zimbabwe also produces its own cobalt (about 126 tons in 2000). Other African countries beginning to develop a production capacity include Tanzania, Côte d'Ivoire and Madagascar.

Cocoa

Cocoa first came to Europe from the New World in the 16th century and was introduced by the Spanish and Portuguese into Africa in the 19th century. It came first to the islands of **Fernando Póo** (now Bioko), São Tomé and Príncipe and Equatorial Guinea, and was established on the mainland by the end of the 19th century, first in Ghana and then in other countries. Cocoa is now widely grown in the tropics, mainly at altitudes less than 300 m above sea level. After tea and **coffee**, cocoa is the most important agricultural export commodity in world trade. Africa accounts for about two-thirds of all cocoa bean production. About 90% of all cocoa is used in chocolate-making. Cultivated cocoa trees may be divided into three groups. All West African cocoas belong to the Amazonian Forastero group, which now accounts for more than 80% of world output. It includes the Amelonado variety, suitable for chocolate-manufacturing, grown in Ghana, Côte d'Ivoire and Nigeria. Trinitario, which comprises about 15% of world output, is cultivated mainly in Central America and northern South America. Criollo cocoa is not widely grown and is used only for luxury confectionery. Processing capacity in West Africa was increased significantly in the 1960s after **independence** and processed products now account for a significant part of the value of cocoa exports from the region. The world's leading exporters of cocoa beans are Côte d'Ivoire, Ghana, Indonesia, Nigeria, Cameroon and Ecuador, with Côte d'Ivoire alone accounting for around 40% of total world output and 44% of world exports. Africa as a whole accounts for more than two-thirds of total world output and exports. World prices are highly sensitive to changes in supply and demand and the Cocoa Producers' Alliance was formed in 1962 with the aim of preventing excessive price fluctuations by regulating the supply of cocoa; but it was not until 1972 that the first International Cocoa Agreement (ICCA) was adopted by 52 countries, representing consumers as well as producers, although the USA, at that time the world's principal importer, did not participate. The International Cocoa Organization was established in the following year. The first ICCA lasted for three years, with a second ICCA operating during 1979–81, a third during 1981–87 and a fourth during 1987–90. Preliminary discussions on a fifth ICCA ended without agreement but eventually a fifth ICCA was agreed, and lasted from 1994 until 2001. A sixth was negotiated in 2001. Despite these agreements, cocoa prices have tended to be low in recent years, although there was an upward movement in 2001–02 as production was affected by a combination of poor weather and political unrest, particularly in Côte d'Ivoire.

Coffee

In 2004/05 African countries that were members of the International Coffee Organization accounted for some 14% of total coffee production world-wide. The principal African producing countries are Ethiopia, Uganda, Côte d'Ivoire, Cameroon, Kenya, Tanzania and the Democratic Republic of the Congo. Burundi and Uganda have traditionally relied heavily on coffee as a source of foreign exchange. As recently as 1997 coffee contributed 88% of Burundi's total revenue from foreign sales, although the proportion declined to only 50% in 2001. Coffee also makes a major contribution to Ethiopia's export revenues. Angola was formerly the world's leading exporter of robusta coffee, but output was severely disrupted by civil conflict in 1975–95. The rehabilitation of the sector, ongoing since the late 1990s, has proceeded slowly and is expected to span many years.

Collapsed states

While the governments of **failed states** maintain a degree of national legitimacy, while failing to exercise exclusive control over their **borders** and what happens within them, collapsed states have wholly disintegrated into warring factions, armies and components. A collapsed state retains little legitimacy—it lacks government and foreign policy; warlords and local fiefdoms with little claim to more general recognition at a national level struggle to increase their power and wealth. Collapsed states are easy prey to foreign intervention, whether economic, political or military. Somalia, Sierra Leone and the Democratic Republic of the Congo at various periods have had the appearance of collapsed states. In this region, the future of several other states remains unclear.

Colonialism

In broad terms, colonialism refers to the process and later the system whereby the major European powers intervened in, occupied, settled and defined as 'colonies' (or dependent territories of various kinds) most parts of what is now referred to as the developing world. For some, colonialism is a particular form of **imperialism**. In Africa, the process may be said to have started in the 16th century with Portuguese and Spanish settlements along the west coast, to have continued during the 17th and 18th centuries, with small predominantly coastal settlements (e.g. by the Dutch in the Cape). But the penetration and colonization of the African interior gathered pace only in the 19th century, starting with the French invasion (in 1830) of what came to be Algeria. Colonial intervention was patchy throughout the region, and affected different parts of the region differently at different times. The period from the late 19th century through the first half of the 20th century to the 1960s is the major period of colonialism in **sub-Saharan Africa**. A few territories gained a degree of independence in the aftermath of the First World War (e.g. Egypt), but it was not really until the late 1950s and the 1960s that political independence resulted from the rising tide of **nationalism** in the aftermath of the Second World War. Some territories were retained, for the most part ironically by the Portuguese and Spanish, until the 1970s, and the status of several territories remained unresolved into the 1980s and even beyond. A few territories (notably **Western Sahara**) have still to achieve final resolution of their political status. See also **Independence**.

Colon(s)

French (and Spanish) settlers or colonists, mainly in **North Africa** and particularly in Algeria. Former *colons*, who left Algeria to settle in France, usually in the southern provinces and particularly in the vicinity of or actually in Marseilles, are still referred to as *pieds noirs* and as *colons*.

Comissão de Libertação de São Tomé e Príncipe (CLSTP—Liberation Committee of São Tomé and Príncipe)

A nationalist group in São Tomé and Príncipe, formed in 1960, which eventually became the **Movimento de Libertação de São Tomé e Príncipe (Liberation Movement of São Tomé and Príncipe)** in 1972 under the leadership of **Dr Manuel Pinto da Costa**.

Comité politique d'action et de liaison (CPAL—Political Committee of Action and Liaison)

Political grouping in Chad, formed in December 1999, to co-ordinate the activities of the **Conseil démocratique révolutionnaire (CDR—Revolutionary Democratic Council)**, the Front national du Tchad renové (National Front for a New

Chad), the **Mouvement pour l'unité et la république (Movement for Unity and the Republic)** and the **Mouvement pour la démocratie et la justice au Tchad (Movement for Democracy and Justice in Chad)**, all political-military groups operating in Chad. The CPAL was led by Acheikh Ibn Oumar of the CDR.

Common Market for Eastern and Southern Africa (COMESA)

The treaty establishing COMESA was signed by member states of the Preferential Trade Area for Eastern and Southern Africa (PTA) in November 1993. COMESA formally succeeded the PTA in December 1994. It aims to promote regional economic and social development and its members comprise 20 African countries across north, east and southern Africa, namely: Angola, Burundi, Comoros, Djibouti, the Democratic Republic of the Congo, Egypt, Eritrea, Ethiopia, Kenya, Libya, Madagascar, Malawi, Mauritius, Rwanda, Seychelles, Sudan, Swaziland, Uganda, Zambia and Zimbabwe. The Authority, comprising the Heads of State of the member countries, is the supreme policy organ of COMESA and the Council of Ministers monitors COMESA activities, including supervision of the secretariat, recommends policy direction and development, and reports to the Authority. The inaugural session of the COMESA Court of Justice was held in March 2001. Its role is to settle disputes between member states and to adjudicate on matters concerning the interpretation of the COMESA treaty. The secretariat deals with trade, customs and monetary harmonization, investment promotion and private-sector development, infrastructure development, and information and networking. Since COMESA's establishment, there have been concerns on the part of member states, as well as of regional non-members, in particular South Africa, of potential conflict with the **Southern African Development Community (SADC)** and of a duplication of roles. Certainly the grouping is not one that makes a great deal of geographical or indeed economic and political sense. In 1997 Lesotho and Mozambique terminated their membership for that reason. Tanzania withdrew in September 2000, for the same reason. In 2003 Namibia withdrew from the organization, and in 2005 Libya was admitted as a full member. A joint COMESA/SADC co-ordinating force was established in 2001. In 2002 COMESA worked with other sub-regional organizations to finalize a common position on co-operation between African members of the **ACP** group of countries and the **European Union** under the **Cotonou Agreement** concluded in June 2000.

Commonwealth

The Commonwealth is a voluntary association of 54 independent states comprising more than one-quarter of the world's population. It is not a federation—there is no central government nor are there any rigid contractual obligations such as bind the members of the United Nations. The Commonwealth has no written Constitution but its members formally subscribe to the ideals of the Declaration of Commonwealth Principles approved by a meeting of heads of government in Singapore in

1971. It includes the United Kingdom and most of its former colonies and dependencies, Australia and New Zealand. All Commonwealth countries formally accept Queen Elizabeth II as the head of the Commonwealth. In 1985 there were 49 members of the Commonwealth (excluding Britain, Australia and New Zealand). At that time it was envisaged that in future Namibia and South Africa might join. Members of the Commonwealth in Africa today include: Ascension, Botswana, British Indian Ocean Territory, Cameroon, The Gambia, Kenya, Lesotho, Malawi, Mauritius, Mozambique, Namibia, Nigeria, Saint Helena, Seychelles, Sierra Leone, South Africa, Swaziland, Tanzania, Tristan da Cunha, Uganda, Zambia and Zimbabwe. Meetings of heads of government are private and informal and operate not by voting but by consensus. Meetings are normally held every two years in different capitals of the Commonwealth. Meetings at ministerial and official level are also held regularly. The Commonwealth Secretariat, established in 1965, operates as an international organization at the service of all Commonwealth countries. The Commonwealth has no specific aims, but proceeds by way of approving certain positions on international issues by way of Declarations, Accords and Statements expressing the agreed position of the Commonwealth member states. In 2000 the Secretariat adopted as its guiding mission 'working for all people of the Commonwealth as a force for democracy and good governance, as a platform for global consensus-building, and as a source of practical assistance for sustainable development'.

Commonwealth Fund for Technical Co-operation (CFTC)

The Commonweath Fund for Technical Co-operation (CFTC) provides experts, finances training and offers consultancy services in a variety of fields to member states. It is financed by voluntary subscriptions from all member governments. There were initially three technical assistance divisions: the general technical assistance division, the technical assistance group and the industrial development unit. In 1983 the human resource development group was formed to co-ordinate six existing **Commonwealth** programmes: the **education** programme, the fellowships and training programme, the management development programme, the medical programme, the **women** and development programme, and the Commonwealth youth programme. Other divisions of the secretariat are the science division, the economic affairs division, the export market development division and the food production and rural development division.

Commonwealth Heads of Government Meetings (CHOGMs)

Meetings of the heads of government of member states of the **Commonwealth** take place every two years. At these meetings the political leaders of the Commonwealth countries confer informally and take the decisions that are subsequently put into practice by the Commonwealth Secretariat. They may be held in any member country. The Commonwealth Secretariat in London, United Kingdom, prepares the

CHOGM agendas. The last of the old-style meetings—known as Imperial Conferences—took place in 1944, with Britain, Australia, Canada, New Zealand and South Africa participating. In 1949 a new formula was agreed to allow India to remain in the Commonwealth. In 1960 the issue of South Africa's continued membership, in the light of the persistence of the **apartheid** regime, was raised and in 1961, South Africa, which had just voted to become a republic, did not apply to remain in the Commonwealth and so left. In 1965 the meeting agreed to the establishment of a secretariat in London and was overshadowed by the issue of **Rhodesia**, which five months later (in November) made its **Unilateral Declaration of Independence**. Over the years, from the early 1970s onwards, the CHOGMs have produced a number of declarations, of which the first (The Declaration of Commonwealth Principles, Singapore 1971) set out some basic principles:

- We believe that international peace and order are essential to the security and prosperity of mankind
- We believe in the liberty of the individual
- We recognise racial prejudice as a dangerous sickness
- We oppose all forms of colonial domination and racial oppression
- We believe that the wide disparities in wealth now existing between different sections of mankind are too great to be tolerated
- We believe that international cooperation is essential.

Communauté économique de l'Afrique de l'ouest (CEAO—Economic Community of West Africa)

Formed in 1974 to replace the Union douanière et économique de l'Afrique de l'ouest (Customs Union of West Africa), the emphasis of this community is upon trade, although it also manages community development funds and initiates regional economic programmes. The main controlling bodies are the conference of Heads of State, the council of ministers, and the general secretariat. Its founder members were: Ivory Coast (now Côte d'Ivoire), Mali, Mauritania, Niger, Senegal and **Upper Volta** (now Burkina Faso).

Communauté économique des états de l'Afrique centrale (CEEAC—Economic Community of Central African States)

At a summit meeting in December 1981 leaders of the member states of the **Union douanière et économique de l'Afrique centrale (UDEAC—Customs Union of Central Africa)** agreed in principle to form an economic community of central African states, the CEEAC, to include UDEAC members and Burundi, Rwanda, São Tomé and Príncipe and **Zaire** (now the Democratic Republic of the Congo). CEEAC began operations in 1985. In June 1999 it was formally re-established as the **Communauté économique et monétaire de l'Afrique centrale (CEMAC—Economic and Monetary Community of Central Africa)**.

Communauté économique et monétaire de l'Afrique centrale (CEMAC—Economic and Monetary Community of Central Africa)

CEMAC was formally inaugurated in June 1999 as the successor to the **Union douanière et économique de l'Afrique centrale (UDEAC—Customs Union of Central Africa)**, which had been established in 1966. At a summit meeting in December 1981 UDEAC leaders agreed in principle to form an economic community of central African states—the **Communauté économique des états de l'Afrique centrale (CEEAC—Economic Community of Central African States)**, to include UDEAC members and Burundi, Rwanda, São Tomé and Príncipe and **Zaire** (now the Democratic Republic of the Congo). CEEAC began operations in 1985. CEMAC aims to promote the process of sub-regional economic integration within the framework of an economic and monetary union. CEMAC was also intended to comprise a parliament and sub-regional tribunal.

Communauté financière africaine

African Financial Community.

Comoros, Union of the

The Union of the Comoros (formerly the Federal Islamic Republic of the Comoros) is an archipelago in the Mozambique Channel, between the island of Madagascar and the east coast of the African mainland. The group comprises four main islands (Ngazidja, **Nzwani** and Mwali, formerly Grande-Comore, Anjouan and Mohéli respectively, and **Mayotte**. (The independent Comoran state claims the whole of the archipelago as its national territory. However, the island of Mayotte (Mahoré) is administered by France.) The area of the Comoros (the Union, excluding Mayotte) is 1,862 sq km and its population was estimated at 768,000 in mid-2003. The capital, which is situated on Ngazidja, is Moroni and the people are Comoran. Major languages are French, **Arabic** and Comoran. **Islam** is the main religion, and there is also a Christian (Roman Catholic) minority.

Political profile

The Head of State is the President, who is elected by popular vote for a five-year term. The current President, **Col Assoumani Azali**, was sworn in on 26 May 2002. (Azali initially assumed the presidency on 6 May 1999 following a bloodless coup. In January 2002 he relinquished office in order to contest a forthcoming presidential election that was held on 14 April. In the interim, Prime Minister Hamadi Madi 'Boléro' served as President.) In the second ballot of the presidential election held in April 2002 Col Azali was elected unopposed, his two qualifying opponents having withdrawn from the second round of voting. The next presidential election is scheduled to be held in 2007. Legislative power is vested in the Assemblée de l'Union, which is composed of 33 deputies, elected for a period of five years. Fifteen of the deputies are selected by the islands' local assemblies (five deputies per island) and 18 are directly elected by universal suffrage. At the most recent legislative elections, held in April 2004, a Coalition supporting the three regional Presidents won 11 of the 18 elective seats, the Convention pour le renouveau des Comores (Convention for the Renewal of the Comoros) 6 and **CHUMA (Islands' Fraternity and Unity Party)** 1. Other major political parties in the Comoros are the **Rassemblement national pour le développement (RND—National Rally for Development)**, the Front national pour la justice (FNJ—National Front for Justice), the **Forces pour l'action républicaine (FAR—Forces for Republican Action)** and the **Mouvement pour la démocratie et le progrès (MDP—Movement for Democracy and Progress)**.

History

The first European traders largely ignored the Comoros. France began formal colonization in 1843, when Mayotte was ceded as a protectorate. Grande-Comore, Anjouan and Mohéli followed in 1886. In 1912 all of the islands were declared a French colony, which was administered from Madagascar until 1947, when the Comoros became a separate territory. In 1961 the Comoros was granted a form of internal autonomy: a Chamber of Deputies was elected and a Comoran governing council assumed administrative tasks. However, a resident French commissioner retained considerable powers. On 15 June 1973 an agreement was signed in Paris, France, under which the Comoros would gain **independence** after five years, subject to popular approval in a referendum, which took place on 22 December 1974. The result was split: altogether there was a 96% vote in favour of independence, but in Mayotte there was a 64% vote against independence. Political tensions grew until, on 6 July 1975, the Comoros declared independence and Ahmed Abdallah Abderemane became the first President. France retained control of Mayotte but accepted the independence of the other islands.

Later in 1975 President Abdallah was deposed in a coup, to be replaced in 1976 by President Ali Soilih. After several coup attempts, he too was overthrown in 1978 by a group of French and Belgian mercenaries led by the notorious 'Colonel' Bob Denard. Abdallah, who had helped finance the coup, returned from exile in France and in 1978 was re-elected as President. He gradually became more authoritarian, relying on a system of patronage and the strength of the mercenary-trained and mercenary-led presidential guard. Denard became a key figure in the increasingly unpopular regime, and through him the Comoros became a conduit for the shipment of arms to Iran and to the Resistência Nacional Moçambicana rebel movement in Mozambique.

In 1989 President Abdallah secured a referendum victory allowing him to run for a third presidential term. France and South Africa reacted by calling for change and the replacement of the mercenaries. President Abdallah was killed in unclear circumstances during a meeting with Denard on 26 November 1989—Comoran and international opinion blamed Denard for his death. At the request of the interim

President, French warships arrived off shore. Denard later handed over control of the islands and returned to France (where, in May 1999, he was tried and acquitted of the late President Abdallah's assassination). Said Mohamed Djohar became President in 1990, defeating Mohamed Taki, the leader of the Union nationale pour la démocratie aux Comoros (UNDC—National Union for Democracy in the Comoros), in a second ballot. Later in that year the first multi-party Constitution came into force. Political tensions remained, however. Elections held in 1993 resulted in a clear majority for the newly formed pro-Djohar Rassemblement pour la démocratie et le renouveau (RDR—Rally for Democracy and Renewal), and the creation of a new opposition alliance, the **Forum pour le redressement national (FRN—Forum for National Recovery)**. In 1995 Denard returned to lead another coup, which was suppressed by French troops. Taki was victorious in the next presidential elections, held in March 1996, defeating Abbas Djoussouf of the FRN alliance. A new constitution was adopted in October 1996. In July 1997 a growing perception that Grande-Comore enjoyed an unfair share of government spending and donor aid led Anjouan to announcing its secession. An attempt to re-establish links with France, not least to gain financial support, was firmly rejected. President Taki died of a heart attack in November 1998. Tadjiddine Ben Said Massounde, Taki's first Prime Minister, reluctantly agreed to act as interim President pending elections to be held in 1999.

The **Organization of African Unity (OAU)** tried repeatedly to mediate between the three islands, sending military observers to maintain peace, and co-chairing an inter-island conference in Antananarivo, Madagascar, in April 1999. The conference was only partially successful: Grande-Comore and Mohéli signed an outline agreement, but the Anjouan delegation did not sign, and instead returned home to consult further. This sparked several days of violent protests in Grande-Comore, during which the 70,000-strong Anjouanese community was targeted and hundreds fled to Anjouan. On 30 April 1999 the army seized power in a bloodless coup. This was the 18th coup or attempted coup in Comoros since independence in 1975. Army chief of staff Col Assoumani Azali subsequently announced that he would head a transitional executive for one year until free elections were held. The OAU, **European Union (EU)**, UN and others repeatedly condemned the coup and called for the immediate restoration of the legitimate government. In August 2000 the military authorities and the secessionists negotiated an agreement aimed at settling the political and constitutional impasse, but the OAU did not accept the agreement. However, following further negotiations to find a solution acceptable within the terms of the Antananarivo Accord, agreement was reached on a way forward.

On 17 February 2001 the Fomboni Accord was signed by representatives of all three islands. The Accord called for the establishment of a committee of transition which would prepare a new constitution to be submitted to a referendum on the three islands. Each island would have its own President, constitution and legislative assembly. As well as island Presidents, the role of President of the Union would rotate between the three islands, with Grande-Comore providing the first such President. The draft Constitution was published in September 2001 and proposed a much greater degree of autonomy for each of the three islands of the Union (Grande-Comore, Anjouan and Mohéli). Some 77% of voters in the Comoros Islands endorsed the new Constitution in a referendum held on 23 December 2001, in which some 75% of the population participated. The next step was votes on each island to adopt its own constitution, which were held on 19 March 2002. The populations of Anjouan and Mohéli approved their respective constitutions, but on Grande-Comore the draft constitution was rejected (it was, however, approved in a vote that took place on 7 April). On 31 March presidential elections were held in Anjouan and Mohéli. Col Mohamed Bacar won the election in Anjouan outright. In Mohéli Mohamed Said Fazul was the successful candidate in a second ballot held for the presidency on 7 April. The election for the national President took place on 14 April, and Col Azali was elected unopposed, two of his three qualifying opponents having chosen to boycott the second ballot owing to allegations of irregularities.

On 19 May the voters of Grande-Comore elected Abdou Soule Elbak as the island's President.

Under the new constitutional arrangements, each island governor may appoint eight ministers to deal with local affairs, while the union authorities will control foreign affairs, finance, defence, justice and religious matters. However, there remain areas where the division of authority is unclear and this has led to political conflict.

International relations

The Comoros have never accepted the loss of Mayotte, and successive governments have lobbied for its return to Comoran control. However, the Mahorais (people of Mayotte) remain firmly against such a move. The islands' Islamic history means that links with the Gulf states (and Libya) remain strong. In an attempt to gain influence within the Islamic world, and increase donor aid, Taki increased the influence of **Islam** over the state, reintroducing the death penalty. However, the Comoros apply their own version of Islam, adapted to local traditions.

Comoros, economy

In 2002 the gross domestic product (GDP) of the Comoros was estimated at US $441m. In 2003 economic growth was estimated at 2.5%. The rate of inflation was estimated at 3.5% in 2001. The principal sectors of the economy are **agriculture**, **fisheries** and forestry. Major trading partners are France, the USA, Germany, Pakistan, South Africa and Kenya. The main exports are vanilla, cloves, ylang-ylang and perfume oil, and the principal imports are rice and petroleum products. The national currency is the Comoran franc. In 2004 the average exchange rate was US $1 = 396.214 Comoran francs.

The economy is underdeveloped and depends largely on remittances from the 70,000 Comorans (mainly from Grande-Comore) who reside in France, and on aid from France and from the **European Union**. Agriculture is the mainstay of the economy, in particular the production of vanilla and cloves (the main exports), ylang-ylang and copra. The sector generates about 40% of GDP and employs about 70% of the labour force. The economy has been adversely affected by sharp declines in world prices for these products. There is a small fishing industry, a minimal industrial base devoted mainly to processing vanilla, and a developing tourist industry. France is the Comoros' major trading partner, providing almost one-half of imports and receiving two-thirds of the islands' exports.

Sluggish economic growth, coupled with political uncertainties, has resulted in a decline in real per caput incomes during the past decade. Average real growth in GDP was only about 1% in 1995–2001. Revenue and expenditure movements have resulted in the halving of fiscal deficits (excluding grants) from 14% in 1996 to 7% in 2001; however, substantial financial needs exist because of the build-up of domestic and external arrears. Transfers from Comorans working abroad are helping to improve the current-account balance. The rate of inflation had declined to less than 5% by the end of 2000, but rose sharply in 2001, to 6.9%. Growth should be possible with greater political stability, improved economic management and strengthened fiscal discipline, and with private-sector involvement in efforts to bring about reform.

Comunidade dos Países de Língua Portuguesa (CPLP—Community of Portuguese-speaking Countries)

Association of former Portuguese territories and lusophone countries.

Conakat

A political party which operated in the latter years of the Belgian Congo, through which the Balunda aimed to exercise power in **Katanga** province, either within a federal state or independently. The party was led by **Moïse Tshombe**.

Confédération générale des entreprises marocaines (CGEM)

The Moroccan confederation of business leaders, representing industry, commerce and services. The official mouthpiece of 'business élites' in Morocco which has a close relationship with the state.

Confederation of South African Trades Unions (COSATU)

The post-**apartheid** confederation of South African trade unions. A powerful and increasingly dissident voice in contemporary South African politics, concerned with the continuing **poverty** and increased inequality in South Africa and the living and working conditions of the workers who form its constituency.

Conflict

Leaving aside the five North African states (Algeria, Egypt, Libya, Morocco and Tunisia), at the end of the 1990s one-fifth of all Africans lived in countries severely affected by wars, mainly civil wars. Most of those had occurred in or continued into the second half of the decade. There were major conflicts in the second half of the decade in Rwanda, the Democratic Republic of the Congo (DRC), Angola and Sudan. There were smaller but still significant conflicts in Madagascar, Burundi, Uganda, Somalia, the Central African Republic, Chad, Niger, Mali, Côte d'Ivoire, Liberia, Sierra Leone, Guinea, Guinea-Bissau and The Gambia. There were conflicts involving Eritrea and Ethiopia in the Horn of Africa, and between Morocco and the **Frente Popular para la Liberación de Saguia el-Hamra y Río de Oro (Frente POLISARIO—Popular Front for the Liberation of Saguia el-Hamra and Río de Oro)** in the **Western Sahara** in the **Maghreb**. Since the end of the 1990s the situation has improved somewhat. The conflicts in Sierra Leone and Angola have come to an end, as has the border conflict between Eritrea and Ethiopia. Liberia's ex-President, **Charles Taylor**, has been forced into exile; the rebels and the government in the DRC have signed a peace accord, as have the Sudan People's Liberation Army and the government of Sudan—although the prospects for peace in those two countries still appear distant.

Conflict resolution

Historically, it has been the UN and its 'peace-keeping' forces that have intervened to try to promote conflict resolution and to maintain or re-establish peace in post-conflict situations. That history was by no means always successful—indeed the earliest intervention, in the Congo in the 1960s, was remarkably inept and inadequate. In more recent years, US-led intervention under UN auspices has been a model that has also demonstrated severe weaknesses—as in the case of the US intervention in Somalia in the early 1990s. Increasingly, however, there have been efforts from inter-governmental organizations within the region, from the **Organization of African Unity (OAU)** and its successor the **African Union (AU)**, down to regional associations and institutions. The AU has proposed a 'rapid-reaction force', to stop wars while they can still be controlled. The plan is that by 2010 each of the five regions of Africa will have a brigade, under AU command, that will be ready to be deployed in areas of conflict at short notice. It is a brave attempt to tackle a real problem: peace-keepers dispatched by the UN Security Council do not generally arrive until three to six months after the event. However, the resources needed are more than appears to be available. The AU's annual allocation for the project is less than US $6m. Even assuming that the member states make their contributions on time, this is clearly inadequate. By way of comparison, the OAU spent $7.2m. to keep only 67 military observers in Burundi in 1993–96. The UN spends about $1,300m. annually on peace-keeping operations in Africa, with mixed results. However, with additional external funding and a core of trained troops based on existing strengths (Nigeria and South African forces), an African multinational force, capable of rapid and effective intervention, might emerge.

Congo (Democratic Republic of the Congo)

The Democratic Republic of the Congo (DRC, formerly **Zaire**) lies in Central Africa, bordered by the Republic of the Congo (ROC) to the north west, by the Central African Republic and Sudan to the north, by Uganda, Rwanda, Burundi and Tanzania to the east and by Zambia and Angola to the south. There is a short coastline at the outlet of the River Congo. The DRC is 2,344,885 sq km in area. At mid-2003 the population was estimated at 52,771,000. French is the official language. More than 400 Sudanese and Bantu dialects are spoken, Kiswahili, Kiluba, Kikongo and Lingala being the most widespread. An estimated 50% of the population are Roman Catholic, and there is a smaller Protestant community. Many inhabitants follow traditional (mostly animist) beliefs. The capital is Kinshasa, whose population was estimated at 5,276,958 in mid-2003.

Political profile

Following a comprehensive power-sharing agreement between the government and rebel factions, reached in December 2002, a new constitution was adopted on 4 April 2003, and **Maj.-Gen. Joseph Kabila** was inaugurated as President for a two-year transitional period on 7 April. A transitional government of national unity was installed in July. On 22 August a bicameral Parliament, comprising a 500-member lower chamber, the National Assembly, and a 120-member upper chamber, the Senate, was inaugurated. The National Assembly comprised a total of 94 members of the **Rassemblement congolais pour la démocratie**—Goma (RCD—Goma, Congolese Rally for Democracy—Goma), the **Mouvement pour la libération du Congo (MLC—Movement for the Liberation of the Congo)**, the former government, opposition political parties and civil society, while the RCD—Mouvement de libération (RCD—ML, RCD—Liberation Movement) was allocated 15 deputies, Mai-Mai militia 10, and the RCD—National (RCD—N, RCD—National) five. The Senate consisted of 22 representatives of the five main groups, four of the RCD—ML and Mai-Mai, and two of the RCD—N.

History

The DRC (first the Republic of the Congo and then Zaire) gained **independence** from Belgium in June 1960. Following a period of political instability—in which **Joseph Kasavubu** was the first President of the newly independent Congo, with **Patrice Lumumba** as Prime Minister, and then, after Lumumba's murder, **Moïse Tshombe** headed a move for mineral-rich **Katanga** to break away from the Congo, the UN intervened and a complex conflict developed which threatened to divide the country into a number of separate entities along largely regional lines—Col (subsequently Marshal) **Joseph-Désiré Mobutu**, the chief of the army, came to power in a military coup in 1965.

President Mobutu's regime was largely unchallenged throughout the 1970s and 1980s, although secessionist revolts took place in Katanga (Shaba) in 1977 and 1978. Mobutu, who bolstered his position by promoting members of his own tribe into positions of power and by dividing or co-opting opponents, presided over wide-scale **corruption** and built up a massive personal fortune. By the end of the 1980s President Mobutu was under increasing pressure to introduce **democracy**. The process of establishing a multi-party system was marked by divisions within the political class and army revolts (in 1991 and 1993). This was the period of the conflict within Rwanda. The European Community and member states imposed an arms embargo on the DRC (at that time Zaire) in 1993.

After the **genocide** in Rwanda in 1994, President Mobutu gave sanctuary and support to **Hutu** refugees and to members of the former Rwandan army. This exacerbated long-standing ethnic tensions with **Tutsi** inhabitants (**Banyamulenge**) in the east of the country. Elections were eventually scheduled for July 1995, but were postponed. In October 1996 the Banyamulenge, led by **Laurent-Désiré Kabila**, and other rebel groups formed the Alliance des forces démocratiques pour la libération du Congo-Zaïre (AFDL—Alliance of Democratic Forces for the Liberation of Congo-Zaire) and rose in revolt. The AFDL made dramatic gains against a demoralized Zairean army. They entered Kinshasa on 17 May. Kabila declared himself President and banned political parties. Mobutu fled to Morocco where he subsequently died.

Kabila's forces had worked closely with Rwanda and Uganda, but relations had deteriorated by mid-1998. In late July all foreign troops were ordered to leave the country within one week. Congolese rebels, supported by Rwanda and Uganda, seized major towns in the east in early August. Zimbabwe, Angola, Namibia and Chad intervened at President Kabila's request. In an attempt to normalize political relations on the domestic front, the ban on the formation of political associations was officially revoked in January 1999. Chad withdrew its forces in late May, but by this time rebel forces controlled large areas in the north and east and the war had become one of the largest regional conflicts ever. African leaders led efforts to find a negotiated settlement, with President **Chiluba** of Zambia chairing a series of summits under the auspices of the **Southern African Development Community (SADC)**. A cease-fire was part of the Lusaka Agreement that was signed in 1999. Until January 2001, however, there was little progress. On 16 January 2001 President Kabila was shot and killed by one of his bodyguards.

Maj.-Gen. Joseph Kabila, the son of Laurent-Désiré, was sworn in as the new President on 26 January 2001. He undertook to implement the Lusaka Agreement, open up internal politics, improve observance of human rights, and liberalize the economy. Joseph Kabila immediately presented a more measured and conciliatory approach both towards domestic politics and towards the wider conflict, making positive commitments to implement the Lusaka Agreement, setting out a framework for independently facilitated national dialogue and reconciliation. This intra-Congolese dialogue was intended to lay the foundations for free, democratic and transparent elections and the drawing up of a new constitution. In May remaining restrictions on the registration and operation of political parties were removed. Armed rebel movements remained active in the east of the country. The Heads of State of the DRC and Rwanda eventually signed a peace accord in South Africa. The Rwandan government pledged to withdraw all Rwandan forces from the DRC, while the Congolese authorities agreed to demobilize the Interahamwe militia in the DRC. In August the DRC reached an agreement with Uganda, in Angola, providing for the normalization of relations between the two countries and the full withdrawal of Ugandan troops from the DRC.

The UN had deployed a 90-strong military liaison mission in the DRC in September 1999. An expanded (5,537-strong) observer mission had been authorized in February 2000, but conditions in the DRC (lack of security, freedom of movement, co-operation by the parties) made deployment impossible. Following a review of the UN operation, a new plan to verify and monitor the disengagement of conventional forces under the Lusaka Agreement was authorized in February 2001. The UN Mission in the DRC (MONUC) comprised 550 military observers and up to 8,700 military personnel. The Security Council authorized the deployment of an Interim Emergency Multinational Force to Bunia on 30 May to stabilize the security situation there pending the deployment of UN forces later in the year. The Force was officially launched as an EU European Security and Defence Policy operation—known as **Operation Artemis**—on 12 June. France—the major contributor of forces—is Framework (lead) nation for the operation. On 30 July 2002 the Presidents of the DRC and Rwanda signed a peace agreement. The government of the DRC undertook to collaborate with MONUC in dismantling those forces, associated with the Rwandan genocide, which were operating in the DRC. In response, the Rwandan army made a full withdrawal from DRC territory in October 2002. The intra-Congolese dialogue seemed to have reached an impasse in early 2002, but active engagement by South Africa and the UN, supported by the international community, led in December to a deal signed in South Africa between the Kinshasa-based government, the main armed groups and members of the political opposition on the formation of a transitional national government. This was formally agreed by the parties on 2 April 2003 in Sun City, South Africa. In June French soldiers arrived in Bunia, spearheading a UN-mandated rapid-reaction force. President Kabila named a transitional government to lead the DRC until democratic elections were held in 2005. Leaders of the main former rebel groups were inaugurated as Vice-Presidents in July. A new National Assembly and Senate were inaugurated by President Kabila in August.

In March 2004, and again in June, attempted coups took place in Kinshasa. Both were quickly suppressed. According to the government, both coup attempts involved former presidential guards loyal to ex-President Mobutu. Reported serious fighting and human rights abuses in the east of the country, notably in Bukavu, in May and June, were attributed to supporters of Mobutu. In February 2005 nine Bangladeshi peace-keepers serving in the north east of the DRC were killed in what the UN described as 'the worst-ever attack against the UN's forces' in the country.

International relations

Relations with Uganda and Rwanda remain tense because of their involvement in the conflict in the DRC.

Democratic Republic of the Congo, economy

In 2003, according to estimates by the **World Bank**, the gross national income (GNI) of the Democratic Republic of the Congo (DRC), measured at average 2001–03 prices, was US $5,314m., equivalent to $100 per head (or $640 per head on an international purchasing-power parity basis). During 1990–2003, it was estimated, the population increased at an average annual rate of 2.7%, while gross domestic product (GDP) per head declined, in real terms, by an average of 6.6% per year. Overall GDP decreased, in real terms, at an average annual rate of 3.9% in 1990–2003; however, it increased by an estimated 5.0% in 2003. Annual inflation averaged 450.8% in 1993–2002. Consumer prices increased by 359.9% in 2001, by 31.5% in 2002, and by an estimated 12.8% in 2003. The DRC's major trading partners include Belgium, the USA, Finland, South Africa and Nigeria. The national currency is the Congolese franc. In 2003 the average exchange rate was US $1 = 405.34 Congolese francs.

The DRC has the third largest population, and the second largest land area in **sub-Saharan Africa**. It is rich in natural and human resources, including the second largest rainforest in the world, fertile soils, ample rainfall, and considerable and varied mineral resources. Historically, mining of **cobalt**, **diamonds**, **gold**, **copper** and other base metals, such as zinc, and petroleum extraction accounted for about 75% of total export revenue, and about 25% of the country's GDP. The country's formal economy has virtually collapsed in the last few decades largely due to political instability and internal conflict, but also to economic mismanagement. GDP per head in the 1980s was only one-third of that in 1962, and it declined even further in the 1990s. The already precarious economy was in a parlous state by mid-1998. Notwithstanding the central bank's tight monetary policy and the smooth introduction of the new Congolese franc in June, the authorities' fiscal plans were highly optimistic. Revenue shortfalls and increased spending on 'emergency security measures' were by mid-year already creating doubts about the sustainability of macroeconomic policies. The new Congolese franc depreciated by some 60% in the two months following its launch and has continued to depreciate since.

In January 2001 the new government announced a comprehensive change in economic policies. These policies include liberalizing the currency to end the parallel system of official and black market rates; lifting foreign exchange restrictions and ending the monopoly on diamond export sales. The government has also produced an Interim Economic Adjustment Programme backed by the World Bank and the **International Monetary Fund**. The stabilization measures launched by the government in May proved successful in breaking the spiral of hyperinflation and currency depreciation. Inflation declined from 630% in the second half of 2000 to 8.8% in the second half of 2001, and the exchange rate stabilized. The liberalization of prices resulted in increased availability of food products in major cities. Government revenues have increased and significant steps have been taken to centralize expenditure and improve budget execution. Partly because of the absence of substantial external financial assistance, however, the Congolese economy continued to decline and growth remained negative in 2001.

There were signs of recovery in the second half of 2001, however, and growth was expected to reach 2.5%–3% in 2002, and 6% in 2003. This growth could be fuelled in future by recovery in three sectors, where the DRC has important comparative advantages: mining, export **agriculture**, and forestry. However, ongoing conflict dramatically reduced government revenue, and increased external **debt**. Many foreign businesses curtailed formal operations owing to the ongoing conflict and because of increased government harassment and restrictions. However, the uncertain political situation, war, **corruption**, smuggling and a shortage of development capital have stifled the development of industry. The DRC is potentially one of the richest mining countries in Africa, with the copper-, cobalt- and diamond-mining industries having the potential to be the largest in Africa, while the gold-mining industry also has considerable potential.

Congo (Republic of the Congo)

The Republic of the Congo (ROC) is an equatorial country on the west coast of Africa. It has a coastline of about 170 km on the Atlantic Ocean, from which the country extends northward to Cameroon and the Central African Republic. The ROC is bordered by Gabon to the west and the Democratic Republic of the Congo (DRC, formerly **Zaire**) to the east, while in the south there is a short frontier with the Cabinda exclave of Angola. The ROC is 342,000 sq km in area. At mid-2003 the population was estimated at 3,724,000. The population comprises 15 main Bantu groups, the largest being the Bakongo, Vili, Bateke, M'Bochi, and Sangha. The official language is French; Kituba, Lingala and other African languages are also used. At least one-half of the population follow traditional animist beliefs and about 45% are Roman Catholics. There are small Protestant and Muslim communities. The capital is Brazzaville.

Political profile

Following the assumption of power by **Gen. Denis Sassou-Nguesso** on 15 October 1997, the 1992 Constitution was suspended. A Conseil national de transition was subsequently appointed, with 75 designated members, to act as an interim legislative body. A new constitution, which was approved by referendum on 20 January 2002, took effect following a presidential election in March–April and legislative elections in May–June. Under the terms of the 2002 Constitution, executive power is vested in a President, who is directly elected for a seven-year term, renewable only once. The President appoints a Council of Ministers. Legislative power is vested in a bicameral Parliament, comprising a 137-member Assemblée nationale, which is directly elected for a five-year term, and a 66-member Sénat, which is indirectly elected by local councils for a six-year term (with one-half of the membership renewable every three years).

In a presidential election held on 10 March 2002, Denis Sassou-Nguesso received 89.41% of the votes and was re-elected as President. Sassou-Nguesso had previously been inaugurated as President on 25 October 1997, having retaken by force the office that he had lost at the 1992 presidential election when he had sought a first presidential term under the 1992 Constitution. (Sassou-Nguesso had served two full and a partial third presidential terms under the Constitution in force prior to 1992.)

Following a general election held on 26 May and 23 June 2002, the distribution of seats in the Assemblée nationale was as follows: **Parti congolais du travail (PCT—Congolese Labour Party)** 53; **Forces démocratiques unies (FDU—United Democratic Forces**, an alliance of 29 parties) 30; **Union pour la démocratie et la République—Mwinda (UDR—Mwinda, Union for Democracy and the Republic—Mwinda)** 6; Union panafricaine pour la démocratie sociale (UPADS—Pan-African Union for Social Democracy) 4; Independents 19; Others 17; Vacant 8. (Figures include the results of voting in 12 constituences where the elections were rerun on 28–29 May 2002, owing to procedural irregularities on 26 May. Voting was postponed indefinitely in eight constituencies in the Pool region as a result of unrest.)

Following an election held on 11 July 2002, the distribution of seats in the Sénat was as follows: PCT 44; FDU 12; Parti pour la reconstruction du Congo (Party for the Reconstruction of the Congo) 1; Civil society organizations 2; Independent 1; Vacant 6. (Six seats remained vacant, as unrest had led to the postponement, in June 2002, of local elections in the Pool region.)

History

In 1910 the Republic of the Congo became the administrative centre of the federation of **Afrique équatoriale française (AEF—French Equatorial Africa)**. The federation comprised the ROC, Chad, Gabon and the Central African Republic. The AEF fought for Charles de Gaulle's Free France during the Second World War, and in 1946 all AEF citizens were granted French citizenship and allowed to establish local assemblies. The AEF was dissolved in 1958 and the ROC achieved full **independence** in August 1960 under President **Abbé Fulbert Youlou**. He resigned in 1963 and was replaced by Alphonse Massemba-Débat who created a one party state. Massemba-Débat formed the Mouvement national de la révolution (MNR—National Movement of the Revolution), a Marxist-Leninist group with an anti-Western foreign policy. In September 1968 he was overthrown in a military coup by Capt. Marien Ngoubai. The youth wing of the MNR took over the government, renaming itself the PCT. Ngoubai was assassinated in 1977. His successor, Col Jacques Joachim Yhombi-Opango, was swiftly replaced by Col (later Gen.) Denis Sassou-Nguesso in 1979.

The PTC, of which President Sassou-Nguesso was a member, was in power from 1969 until 1992, when it surrendered to opposition demands for change. A Sovereign National Conference was established to decide the shape of the country's political future and agree a timetable for elections. A new multi-party constitution was overwhelmingly endorsed in a referendum held in March. Pascal Lissouba, leader of the UPADs, was elected as President in August 1992, having received 61% of the votes. Bernard Kolélas, the leader of the **Mouvement congolais pour la démocratie et le développement intégral (MCDDI—Congolese Movement for Democracy and Integral Development)** received the second largest number of votes, while former President Sassou-Nguesso was eliminated in the first ballot and conceded defeat. Elections to the Assemblée nationale held in 1993 led to skirmishes between armed opposition supporters and the **military**. After a partial rerun under international supervision in October, the presidential group, comprising UPADS and its allies, won 67 seats compared to 58 for the opposition coalition, which included the PCT and the MCDDI. However, fighting broke out between the army and the opposition, whose leaders maintained dedicated militias. The 'Zulu' militia backed Lissouba, the 'Ninja' militia supported Kolélas, and the 'Cobras' supported Sassou-Nguesso. Hundreds were killed and the three militias remained in conflict until January 1995, when a new cross-party alliance under Yhombi-Opango assumed power. The militias signed a peace accord in December 1995, although the conditions were never met.

Six presidential candidates emerged to contest the presidential election held in 1997, including President Lissouba, Sassou-Nguesso and Kolélas. On 31 May 1997 they signed an agreement to conduct a peaceful campaign. On 2 June, however, fighting broke out between forces loyal to Lissouba and Sassou-Nguesso, after government troops surrounded Sassou-Nguesso's house and attempted to disarm his militia. Between June and October 1997, despite the efforts of the **African Union (AU)**, the UN and regional mediators, the country lapsed into **civil war**. Fighting was centred on Brazzaville, which was split into three zones occupied by the militias of the three leading candidates for the presidency. Some 5,000 foreign nationals were evacuated from Brazzaville by the French army. In all, 700,000 people fled Brazzaville, spreading throughout the country and to the DRC. In August President Lissouba appointed Kolélas as Prime Minister, leading to gains for the combined militias. However, in October Angolan troops entered Congo to support Sassou-Nguesso, altering the balance of power in his favour. He proclaimed himself President on 25 October. Lissouba and Kolélas fled the country. President Sassou-Nguesso formed a 'government of national unity' composed mainly of his supporters. The previous elected parliament was dissolved. Sassou-Nguesso then held a 10-day national forum of reconciliation at the end of which he appointed a 75-member transition parliament. He announced that legislative and presidential elections would be held at the end of a three-year flexible transition period. Uneasy calm was shattered in December 1998 when fighting and looting broke out in the Pool region of Brazzaville. Sassou-Nguesso claimed that it was an attempted coup by militias loyal to Lissouba and Kolélas, but there were widespread reports of looting and killing of civilians by government troops and armed militias. Hundreds of thousands of civilians were again displaced from Brazzaville. Peace agreements were signed in November and December 1999 by the government forces and all major rebel militias in the ROC. Lissouba and Kolélas have still not signed the agreements, however. In March 2001 the Conseil national de transition approved a draft constitution and the government drew up a timetable for a referendum on the proposed basic law and presidential, legislative and municipal elections, all of which took place in the first half of 2002. The new draft Constitution, providing for a presidency with executive powers and a seven-year mandate, was endorsed by referendum in January 2002. It also included provision for a bicameral legislature. In presidential elections held on 10 March 2002, Sassou-Nguesso was elected, having received 89% of the votes. Gen. Sassou-Nguesso now began a seven-year term, after achieving victory in a poll from which two of his main rivals—Lissouba and Kolélas—were excluded by a residency law, and a third contender (André Milongo) withdrew, alleging irregularities; and with a reformed constitution which tightened his hold on power. The first round of elections to the Assemblée nationale took place in May, but voting was postponed in the Pool region, owing to unrest. The second round took place in June. Local and municipal elections were also held in June, except in the Pool region, where unrest continued. Of the 137 seats, the PCT won 53, and a further 30 seats were won by candidates who were allied to it. Elections to the Sénat were held in July. In August a new Council of Ministers was formed, four days after the inauguration of Sassou-Nguesso as President.

Since 2002 the ROC has, generally, remained peaceful, although tensions remain in the Pool region. More than 630,000 of the 810,000 people displaced by the war have returned. In March 2003 the government signed agreements with 'Ninja' rebels, aimed at ending fighting in Pool region. 'Ninja' leader 'Pastor' Frédéric Ntoumi agreed to end hostilities and allow the return of the rule of law. Disarmament and reintegration of the rebel militias into the wider society has begun, but the process has proved slow and difficult. In April 2005, after an attack on a UN convoy, Ntoumi stated that he planned to disarm his forces, but would not surrender their weapons until he had reached a political agreement with the government. The political wing of the 'Ninja' militia hopes eventually to take part in elections, but the prospects for this remain poor. In effect, the civil war has abated and the level of violence is much reduced, following the peace agreement concluded between the government and the various rebel forces in 2003.

International relations

The ROC continues to be affected by the upheaval in the Great Lakes region. It is estimated that there are 117,000 **refugees** from the DRC in the Likouala region of the country. Humanitarian agencies have been able to help only 50,000 of these because fighting in the DRC's Equateur province interrupted navigation on the Oubangui and Congo Rivers. The difficulty of resolving these and other problems has been compounded by ongoing hostility between the ROC and the DRC, each accusing the other of supporting rebel militias. President Sassou-Nguesso has built alliances with fellow African leaders since he took power in October 1997. He has developed contacts with neighbouring countries and with Egypt, Morocco, Nigeria and South Africa. The ROC has very close relations with Angola, with which it signed a defence pact that ostensibly legitimized the presence of Angolan troops in the ROC until their withdrawal at the end of 2002.

The ROC has traditional ties with Gabon, the two countries having a number of ethnic groups in common. France is the ROC's main international partner. French companies retain significant investments in most sectors, and employ large numbers of expatriate personnel.

Republic of the Congo, economy

In 2003, according to estimates by the **World Bank**, the Congo's gross national income (GNI), measured at average 2001–03 prices, was US $2,643m., equivalent to $640 per head (and $710 on an international purchasing-power parity basis). During 1990–2003, it was estimated, the population increased at an average annual rate of 3.2%, while gross domestic product (GDP) per head declined, in real terms, by an average of 1.4% per year. Overall GDP increased, in real terms, at an average annual rate of 1.8% in 1990–2003; growth in 2003 was 1.0%. The annual rate of inflation averaged 0.4% in 1997–2003. Consumer prices increased by an average of 4.4% in 2002, but declined by an estimated 0.6% in 2003. Major sectors of the economy include petroleum, **natural gas**, phosphates and timber. The Congo's major trading partners are France, the USA, Belgium, the United Kingdom, Italy, Germany, Taiwan and the People's Republic of China. The national currency is the CFA franc (see the **Franc Zone**). In 2004 the average exchange rate was US $1 = 528.29 francs CFA.

The economy has suffered badly from continued disruption but is bolstered by large offshore **oil** reserves that have remained relatively unaffected by the **civil war**. Oil revenues make up more than one-half of the Congo's economy, with the sector dominated by the French company TotalFinaElf. **Agriculture** accounts for only 10%, which means that the country relies heavily on imports. Following the decline in petroleum prices in 1985, the system started to show signs of stress. The government maintained a large civil service through heavy borrowing, which has led to an unsustainable accumulation of **debt** (external public debt: $5,400m.). The country's extremely unfavourable economic situation was exacerbated by the five-month civil war in 1997 which claimed thousands of lives, severely damaged the city of Brazzaville, and caused 700,000 people to flee into the countryside or to neighbouring countries.

The government has agreed a Post-Conflict Assistance Programme with the World Bank, and the **International Monetary Fund (IMF)** approved a $14m. credit in November 2000 to aid post-conflict reconstruction. Under agreements with both the World Bank and the IMF, the government's main priorities are structural reform, the re-establishment of basic public services, and the promotion of post-conflict recovery through macroeconomic stabilization. Congo has arrears with most creditors, including the IMF and the World Bank.

Congo Free State

The name given in 1885 to the territory established and administered as a personal empire in the Congo Basin by King Léopold II of Belgium. Later taken over by the Belgian government and administered as the Belgian Congo.

Congrès pour la démocratie et le progrès (CDP—Congress for Democracy and Progress)

Major political party in Burkina Faso. Established in 1996 by the merger of the Organisation pour la démocratie populaire (Organization for Popular Democracy) and the Mouvement du travail (Labour Movement). Now the main political organization supporting President **Blaise Compaoré**. The CDP won almost one-half of the votes in the general election of May 2002 and occupied 57 legislative seats out of a total of 111. The CDP's president is Roch Marc Christian Kaboré.

Congrès national algérien (Algerian National Congress)

Algerian political grouping, established in 1999. Its leader is Abdelkader Belhaye.

Congrès national ittihadi (CNI—National Ittihadi Congress)

Moroccan political grouping, founded in 2001. The CNI's secretary-general is Abdelmajid Bouzoubaa.

Congrès pan-africain du Cameroun (CPC—Pan-African Congress of Cameroon)

Political party in Cameroon, established in 1991.

Congress of the People

A meeting convened in June 1955 by the **African National Congress (ANC)** in South Africa to formulate a vision of South Africa after **apartheid**. The ANC (which had not yet been banned) had formed an alliance with the **Indian National Congress**, the Coloured People's Congress, a white organization called the Congress of Democrats which contained many members of the Communist Party that had been outlawed five years before, and the trade union movement, then called the South African Congress of Trade Unions (SACTU). They all participated in the event. The ANC also invited the Liberal Party and the **United Party**, both predominantly white parties. They did not participate but the invitations were a significant indication of the ANC's commitment to the principles of multi-racialism. Three thousand delegates attended the meeting, held in what is now a part of **Soweto**. They drafted and adopted a **Freedom Charter**.

Conseil démocratique des partis politiques de l'opposition (CODEPO—Democratic Congress of the Political Parties of the Opposition)

Political grouping in the Central African Republic, comprising the Mouvement démocratique pour la renaissance et l'évolution de la République Centrafricaine (MDRERC—Democratic Movement for the Renaissance and Evolution of the Central African Republic) and the Parti républicain centrafricain (PRC—Central African Republican Party). COPEPO was established in 1995 and is led by Auguste Boukanga.

Conseil démocratique révolutionnaire (CDR—Revolutionary Democratic Council)

Political-military organization in Chad, led by Acheikh ibn Oumar.

Conseil de l'entente (Entente Council)

Founded in May 1959 as an economic and political association of four West African states—**Dahomey** (now Benin), Ivory Coast (now Côte d'Ivoire), Niger and **Upper Volta** (now Burkina Faso)—the Conseil was joined in 1966 by Togo. It aims to promote economic development in the region through its Mutual Aid and Loan Guarantee Fund. Its council consists of Heads of State and ministers according to the business to be conducted. The emphasis is in fact on economic affairs, although it began as a political as well as an economic association.

Conseil national pour la défense de la démocratie (CNDD—National Council for the Defence of Democracy)

Political party in Burundi, established in 1994. Predominantly **Hutu** membership.

Conté, Gen. Lansana

Elected President of Guinea since 1993. Conté seized power on the death of President **Ahmed Sekou Touré** in 1984, in a bloodless military coup, to become Head of State in Guinea. He suspended the Constitution, freed political prisoners and encouraged exiles to return, subsequently establishing an authoritarian regime. Born in the 1930s, after serving in the French army Conté returned to Guinea and became chief of staff in 1975. By 1992 he had organized a return to civilian rule, proceeding to win a presidential poll in 1993 and parliamentary elections in 1995. In 2001 he held a referendum which officially showed that voters supported the removal of a two-term limit that would have forced him to retire in 2003 and endorsed constitutional amendments that extended the presidential term to seven years. Critics describe the vote as a constitutional coup, which will ensure that he remains President for life. In June 2002 legislative elections took place and there was no obvious decline in the support he received indirectly through the polls. Abroad, Conté's government has enjoyed Western backing as a bulwark against instability in neighbouring Sierra Leone and Liberia.

Convenção Nacional Democrata de Angola (CNDA—National Democrat Convention of Angola)

Angolan political party, led by Paulino Pinto João.

Convention pour la démocratie et la fédération (CDF—Convention for Democracy and Federation)

Political party in Burkina Faso, established in 1998. The CDF is led by Amadou Diemdioda Dicko.

Convention pour la démocratie et le fédéralisme (CDF—Convention for Democracy and Federalism)

Political party in Chad, established in 2002. A socialist party that supports the establishment of a federal state. The CDF's leader is Ali Golhor.

Convention pour la démocratie et le salut (CODESA—Convention for Democracy and Salvation)

Political grouping in the Republic of the Congo. Established in 2002 as an alliance of opposition parties. CODESA's president is André Milongo.

Convention démocratique et sociale (CDS—Democratic and Social Convention)

Political party in Niger with 17 seats in the Assemblée nationale.

Convention libérale (CL—Liberal Convention)

Political party in Cameroon, established in 1991. The CL's leader is Pierre-Flambeau Ngayap.

Convention nationale (CN—National Convention)

Political party in the Central African Republic, established in 1991. The CN's leader is David Galiambo.

Convention nationale des démocrates progressistes (CNDP—National Convention of Progressive Democrats)

Political party in Burkina Faso, founded in 2000. The CNDP's leader is Alfred Kaboré.

Convention nationale démocratique et sociale (CNDS—National Democratic and Social Convention)

Political party in Chad, led by Adoum Daye Zere.

Convention nationale pour la République et la solidarité (CNRS—National Convention for the Republic and Solidarity)

Political party in the Republic of the Congo, established in 2001. The CNRS's leader is Martin Mber. Part of the **Convention pour la démocratie et le salut (Convention for Democracy and Salvation)**.

Convention pan-africaine sankariste (CPS—Pan-African Sankarist Convention)

Political grouping in Burkina Faso. Founded in 1999 by a merger of four parties. Expanded in 2000 to include two more. Promotes the policies of former President **Thomas Sankara**. The CPS's president is Nongma Ernest Ouédraogo.

Convention populaire de la résistance (CPR—Popular Resistance Convention)

Political-military group in Chad, led by Abdel-Aziz Abdallah Kodor.

Convergence nationale pour la paix et la réconciliation (CNPR—National Convergence for Peace and Reconciliation)

Political grouping in Burundi comprising the **Union pour le progrès national (Union for National Progress)**, a faction of the **Front pour la démocratie au**

Burundi (Front for Democracy in Burundi), and several **Tutsi** parties. Established in October 1999. The CNPR's president is Augustin Nzojibwami.

Convergência para la Democracia Social (CPDS—Convergence for Social Democracy)

Political party in Equatorial Guinea.

Coordination des mouvements armés et partis politiques de l'opposition (CMAP—Co-ordination of Armed Movements and Opposition Political Parties)

A political grouping of 13 politico-military organizations operating in Chad, established in December 1999. CMAP is led by Antoine Bangui of the Front extérieur pour la rénovation (FER—External Front for Renewal).

Copper

Copper is contained mainly in copper sulphide and copper oxide. These are mined both underground and by open-cast or surface mining. Copper is ductile, resists corrosion and is an excellent conductor of heat and electricity. Its industrial uses are mainly in the electrical industry (60% of copper is made into wire for use in power cables, telecommunications, domestic and industrial wring) and the building, engineering and chemical industries. Bronzes and brasses are typical copper alloys, used both for industrial and decorative purposes. There are, however, substitutes for copper is almost all of its industrial uses and in recent years, **aluminium** has presented a challenge in the electrical and transport industries. Reserves in Zambia and the Democratic Republic of the Congo (DRC) jointly account for about 11% of global reserves. Zambia, South Africa and the DRC are the three leading producers of copper ore, but Africa as a whole accounts for only a very small proportion of the world's copper output—about 492,000 metric tons in 2000 out of a total of 13.2m. tons. Copper production is the mainstay of the Zambian economy and copper sales historically accounted for about 85% of the country's export earnings. In the late 1990s, however, owing to the excess of supply over demand and low price of copper on the world market, the contribution declined substantially. In 1998 sales of copper accounted for about one-half of Zambia's export earnings. In general, there has been a trend towards increasing production and declining demand over the decades. In the early part of the present decade there was a significant copper surplus, affecting copper prices and the export earnings of copper producers.

Corruption

There has been much discussion of the nature of the post-colonial state in Africa and strong views have been expressed as to its legitimacy or lack of legitimacy. One of the key concerns often expressed has been that of the tendency of those in power to promote and take advantage of a personalization or privatization of public goods and resources. The extreme form of this has been referred to as kleptocracy—rule by thieves. A more general term widely used to refer to persistent and pervasive abuse of state power or bureaucratic position is corruption. In recent years, a number of organizations have assessed the extent to which corruption is thought to exist in a particular state. Transparency International is one of these. It produces an annual Corruption Perceptions Index, which reveals the perception of the level and extent of corruption existing across the world. The 2004 Index ranks 145 states, from 1 to 145, with the largest numbers being those perceived as most corrupt.

No African state appears in the 'best' 30 countries; 13 are ranked among the 'worst' 30 countries—the Republic of the Congo, Ethiopia, Sierra Leone, Zimbabwe, Niger, Sudan, Cameroon, Kenya, Angola, the Democratic Republic of the Congo, Côte d'Ivoire, Chad, and Nigeria, with Nigeria regarded as the 'worst of all' apart from Bangladesh and Haiti.

da Costa, Dr Manuel Pinto

Leader of the **Movimento de Libertação de São Tomé e Príncipe (MLSTP—Liberation Movement of São Tomé and Príncipe)**, a political party in São Tomé and Príncipe formed in 1972. First president of São Tomé and Príncipe after **independence**, from 1975 until 1991.

Côte d'Ivoire, Republic of

The Republic of Côte d'Ivoire (formerly Ivory Coast) lies on the west coast of Africa, between Ghana to the east and Liberia to the west, with Guinea, Mali and Burkina Faso to the north. The country is 322,462 sq km in area. At mid-2003 the population was estimated at 16,631,000. Some 60 ethnic groups make up the indigenous population. These include the **Akan** with its **Baoule** sub-group in the south, which is the largest single group. Others are the Sénoufou and the **Mande** (with the **Dioula** sub-group) in the north, and the Krou (with the Bété sub-group) in the west. The official language is French, and a large number of African languages are also spoken. At the time of the 1998 census it was estimated that some 34% of the population were Christians (mainly Roman Catholics), 27% Muslims, 15% followed traditional indigenous beliefs, and 3% practised other religions, while 21% had no religious affiliation. (However, it was thought that the proportion of Muslims was, in fact, significantly higher, as the majority of unregistered foreign workers in Côte d'Ivoire were believed to be Muslims.) The political and administrative capital is Yamoussoukro, although most government ministries and offices remain in the former capital, Abidjan, which is the major centre for economic activity. The population of Abidjan was estimated at 3,336,518 in mid-2003. At the 1998 census the population of Yamoussoukro was enumerated at 299,243.

Political profile

Under the terms of the Constitution of July 2000, executive power is vested in the President, as Head of State, who is appointed by direct universal suffrage for a term of five years, renewable only once. The President appoints a Prime Minister, and on the latter's recommendation, a Council of Ministers. Legislative power is held by the Assemblée nationale, which is elected for a term of five years.

In a presidential election held on 22 October 2000, **Laurent Gbagbo**, the candidate of the Front populaire ivoirien (FPI—Ivorian Popular Front), received 59.36% of the votes and was elected as President.

Following a general election held on 10 December 2000, the distribution of seats in the Assemblée nationale was as follows: FPI 96; Parti démocratique de la Côte d'Ivoire—Rassemblement démocratique africain (PDCI—RDA, Democratic Party of Côte d'Ivoire—African Democratic Rally) 94; Rassemblement des républicains (RDR—Republicans' Rally) 5; Parti ivoirien des travailleurs (PIT—Ivorian Workers' Party) 4; Union démocratique citoyenne (UDCY—Citizen Democratic Union) 1; Mouvement des forces d'avenir (MFA—Movement of the Forces of the Future) 1; Independents 22. (These figures include the results of voting in 26 constituencies where elections were postponed until 14 January 2001, owing to unrest. The RDR officially boycotted the elections and the seats assigned to it were won by a faction within the party that did not observe the boycott. Voting for two outstanding seats was postponed indefinitely.)

History

Côte d'Ivoire gained **independence** from France in 1960, with **Dr Félix Houphouët-Boigny** as President and chairman of the single ruling party, the PDCI. Houphouët-Boigny regarded himself as the father of the nation, and it was only in 1990 that a multi-party system was established. In the first contested presidential election, Houphouët-Boigny emphatically defeated Laurent Gbagbo of the FPI; another leading politician, Alassane Ouattara, was appointed as Prime Minister. Houphouët-Boigny died in December 1993, and was succeeded by the president of the Assemblée nationale, Henri Bédié, also of the PDCI. Ouattara subsequently resigned. In 1994 Bédié introduced a new electoral code, requiring presidential candidates to have two Ivorian parents and to have resided in the country for five years before the election. Both amendments were aimed at preventing Ouattara from contesting elections in 1995. Bédié and the PDCI, consequently, won an overwhelming victory in the elections. Subsequently, the government did little to deal with growing student and industrial unrest or with problems over pay and conditions in the **military**. Bédié encouraged the concept of 'Ivoirité'. Intended to emphasize cultural values, one of its effects was to increase ethnic divisions between the largely Muslim north and the more Christian south of the country. Further division stemmed from the fact that more than 25% of the population were nationals of other countries.

Bédié's popularity declined further in 1998 when he introduced constitutional amendments to lengthen the presidential term, raised the residence qualification for presidential candidates to 10 years, and failed to address widespread **corruption** and rising crime levels. Ouattara returned in August 1999 and obtained a nationality certificate. However, its cancellation in October led to unrest and the arrest of dozens of members of his party, the RDR. In December 1999 an army mutiny over pay and conditions turned into a coup led by former chief of staff, Gen. Robert Gueï. Bédié took refuge in the French embassy. Gueï promised a rapid return to **democracy**, and drafted a new constitution, again with stringent nationality conditions for presidential candidates. In a referendum, 86% of voters endorsed the Constitution. Gen. Gueï decided to contest the elections held in October 2000, from which both Ouattara and Bédié were excluded. When preliminary results indicated that Laurent Gbagbo was likely to win the presidency, Gueï suspended the electoral commission and declared himself the winner. Gbagbo's supporters staged mass demonstrations, supported by units of the army, and Gueï fled. Gbagbo was declared the winner by a reinstated electoral commission. He refused Ouattara's demand that he rerun the election, and several weeks of violence followed, largely between northerners and southerners. Legislative elections in December 2000 and municipal elections in March 2001 proceeded relatively smoothly, but strong support for the PCDI and the RDR (the latter participating in 2001 only) prompted President Gbagbo to organize a National Reconciliation Forum in October 2001. Gbagbo, Bédié, Ouattara and Gueï agreed a series of recommendations, including acceptance of the October 2000 election results. They met again in January 2002, when it became clear that Gueï had decided to support Ouattara's case for Ivorian nationality. Ouattara was again granted a certificate of nationality, but would still have been barred from contesting the presidency because of claims that he had held Burkinabé citizenship.

In September 2002 an attempted coup took place in Abidjan and in the north of the country. The uprising in Abidjan was quickly suppressed, although Gueï and the interior minister Boga Doudou were killed in the violence. In the north the rebels seized control of the major cities of Bouaké and Korhogo. They subsequently identified themselves as the Mouvement patriotique de la Côte d'Ivoire (MPCI—Patriotic Movement of Côte d'Ivoire) and included factions of the military; but they also drew wider support from those who opposed the existing political regime. The **Economic Community of West African states (ECOWAS)** responded swiftly, negotiating a cease-fire between the two sides on 17 October 2002. ECOWAS then chaired peace talks between government and rebels in the Togolese capital, Lomé. It was agreed to deploy a peace-monitoring force, to replace French troops, to whom the task of monitoring the cease-fire line had fallen. However, the situation became more complex following the emergence in November 2002 of two new rebel groups in the west, the Mouvement patriotique ivoirien du grand ouest (MPIGO—Ivorian Patriotic Movement of the Great West) and the Mouvement pour la justice et la paix (MJP—Movement for Peace and Justice). There was renewed fighting in the west, and also a number of cease-fire breaches in the north. France worked with ECOWAS to revitalize the peace process in January 2003, obtaining fresh commitments to the cease-fire from the government and the MPCI, and a truce between the government and the MPIGO/MJP. All Ivorian political parties and the three rebel groups attended discussions in January in Paris, France. They produced the Linas Marcoussis Agreement (LMA), which provided for a new government of national reconciliation and addressed the key issues underlying the crisis. President Gbagbo accepted this agreement at a summit in Paris in late January, which was attended by ECOWAS Heads of State and representatives of the wider international community.

Further talks, held in Accra, Ghana, in March 2003, resulted in an agreement over the allocation of ministerial portfolios in the new government, as well as in the establishment of a National Security Council to oversee defence/security issues and suggest consensus candidates for these two posts. By April, ministers from the Forces nouvelles (FN—New Forces) were willing to travel to Abidjan to take up their ministerial posts, and regular Cabinet meetings began. In May the new government presented its programme, closely based on the requirements of the LMA, to the Assemblée nationale. Following the declaration of a comprehensive cease-fire, the cease-fire line was successfully extended to the Liberian border in late May, and the situation in the west stabilized significantly. The Forces armées nationales de la Côte d'Ivoire (FANCI—National Armed Forces of Côte d'Ivoire) and the FN issued a joint declaration on 4 July declaring a permanent cessation of hostilities. The Assemblée nationale agreed an Amnesty Law on 6 August (this was not intended to provide amnesty for those who had committed serious human rights abuses or economic crimes). Despite considerable progress in the peace process, there remained significant challenges to overcome.

In January 2003 a peace treaty was signed in Lomé, Togo, by the leaders of the MPIGO and the MPJ, and the government. Although unrest continued, in late January unanimous agreement on a peace plan was reached by all parties involved in the negotiations. Under the negotiated settlement, Gbagbo was to remain as President until the expiry of his term of office in 2005, but would have to share power with a new Prime Minister. Rebel groups and opposition parties were to be integrated into the government. In February it was announced that Seydou Elimane Diarra was to serve as Prime Minister in the government of national reconciliation. However, the formation of a new government was delayed by the inability of all parties concerned to agree on acceptable candidates for the defence and security positions. In late April Félix Doh, the leader of the MPIGO, was captured and killed. In early May a cease-fire agreement was signed. In mid-June the national army and rebel forces agreed to the eventual confinement of troops, and despite occasional unrest and fighting, order was soon largely restored. In late June the UN Mission in Côte d'Ivoire (MINUCI—authorized by the UN Security Council in May) encouraged MPCI leaders to formally announce the end of the conflict. Legislation providing an amnesty for those involved in political unrest between 17 September 2000 and 19 September 2002 was enacted to encourage the re-establishment of the political process, although those involved in abuses of human rights or violations of international humanitarian law were to be excluded. The MPCI effectively absorbed the MPIGO and MJP, and announced that the organization was henceforth to be known as the FN.

In late August 2003 there were rumours of a plot to assassinate Gbagbo, and 30–50 people were arrested on suspicion of planning a *coup d'état*. Also in late August, two French solders were killed in clashes with rebels in central Côte d'Ivoire, becoming the first peace-keeping troops to lose their lives in the conflict; the FN subsequently apologized for the incident, and the alleged perpetrators of the killings were captured and brought before a military tribunal in early September. In that month the defence and security positions that had caused considerable disagreement were finally announced. While the appointments satisfied most, the FN and the RDR did not accept the nominations. On 22 September the FN suspended its participation in the government, accusing Gbagbo of delaying the process of reconciliation. The former rebels declared that they would not co-operate with the proposals for the disarmament and reintegration of former combatants. This led to sporadic fighting. French troops were forced on occasion to intervene. Ongoing diplomatic efforts, under the aegis of ECOWAS, to advance the peace process continued but had little success. The FN continued to demand greater security and increased devolution of powers from the President to the Prime Minister.

In early January 2004 French peace-keeping troops began to enter regions of northern Côte d'Ivoire, with the agreement of the FN, reportedly in order to assist in the provision of humanitarian aid, although tensions persisted, particularly in Korhogo. In late February the UN Security Council established the UN Operation in Côte d'Ivoire (UNOCI), with an authorized military strength of 6,240. The peace-keeping operation was to be deployed for an initial period of 12 months from 4 April. However, the process of national reconciliation now appeared to be stalling. At the end of February Guillaume Soro Kigbafori (of the political wing of the MPCI) announced that former rebel fighters would not disarm before the legislative and presidential elections scheduled for 2005. In early March, the PDCI—RDA announced that its ministers were to suspend their participation in the government, with immediate effect, in response to what it termed acts of humiliation and aggression against the party by supporters of Gbagbo. All parties represented in the government, with the exceptions of Gbagbo's FPI and the PIT, expressed support for the action of the PDCI—RDA. In late March, clashes occurred between members of the security forces and protesters following a demonstration in Abidjan, organized by seven of the 10 signatory parties of the LMA, known locally as the 'G7'. Following the outbreak of violence, the RDR, the FN and the MFA suspended their participation in the government and refused to negotiate with Gbagbo. The first contingent of UNOCI forces arrived in Côte d'Ivoire in early April.

In mid-April 2004 President Gbagbo acceded to the G7's principal demands in an attempt to restore some stability, agreeing to allow equal access to the state media to all political organizations, to respect the right to demonstrate and to ensure the security of the people. The peace process remained stalled, however, and in mid-May Gbagbo dismissed three opposition ministers from the government (including

Soro), replacing them with members of the FPI. Soro had previously urged FN ministers to return to Bouaké from Abidjan, after Gbagbo had threatened to suspend their salaries and restrict their freedom to travel in response to their boycott of government meetings. In early June the French embassy came under attack from the Coordination des jeunes patriotes (CJP—Co-ordination of Young Patriots) and other Gbagbo loyalists, who accused France of favouring the rebel movements. In late July 2004 all parties to the conflict attended a meeting of West African Heads of State in Accra, convened by the UN Secretary-General and the President of Ghana, at which they signed an agreement on means of implementing the LMA. The agreement, which was to be monitored by UNOCI, ECOWAS and the **African Union (AU)**, stated that disarmament of the rebels was to commence by 15 October. In mid-August, Gbagbo reinstated the three government ministers dismissed in May, and all ministers from opposition parties and rebel groups resumed participation in the government. Shortly afterwards, Gbagbo delegated some of his powers to the Prime Minister, pending elections in October 2005. However, the deadline for disarmament was not observed by the rebels, and in November the 18-month cease-fire was broken when the Ivorian Air Force launched bombing raids on Bouaké and targets in the north of the country.

In response to the breach of the cease-fire and the death of French troops from the peace-keeping contingent killed in the raids, French forces, acting on the direct orders of President Jacques Chirac, destroyed the Ivorian air force on the ground. This precipitated several days of violence, in Abidjan and elsewhere, against French and other foreign targets. French troops intervened to take control of Abidjan's airport and major thoroughfares and to protect French and other foreign nationals. On 15 November the UN Security Council voted in favour of imposing an arms embargo, drafted by France, on Côte d'Ivoire. In November and December 2004 the President of South Africa, **Thabo Mbeki**, designated as mediator by the AU, held talks with both the Ivorian government and the FN aimed at re-establishing the LMA as the basis for a resolution of the crisis. Political reforms and disarmament, both of which have failed to be fully implemented in the past, were again proposed. In June 2005 tensions escalated when 55 people were reportedly killed in the town of Duékoué, prompting fears that Côte d'Ivoire's fragile peace process was again under threat. However, in July residents of rebel-held northern Côte d'Ivoire voiced cautious optimism after government officials and rebel leaders signed an agreement setting out dates for fighters to disarm and prepare for elections in October.

International relations

Following the coup in 1999, most development assistance from the **European Union (EU)** was suspended while consultations took place between the EU and Côte d'Ivoire on returning the country to democracy. In 2001 the EU agreed to a partial resumption of development aid. Following a satisfactory review in May 2002 it was agreed to recommence European Development Funding assistance. However, since the current conflict began in September 2002 the implementation of EU assistance has been severely disrupted.

ECOWAS is also playing an active role in seeking to resolve the current crisis. Most of Côte d'Ivoire's immediate neighbours have been adversely affected by the crisis, having to cope with refugee flows, blockage of normal trade routes, and disruption of regional economic activity. The danger of the instability and ethnic tension in Côte d'Ivoire spreading to the wider region is also a significant issue.

Côte d'Ivoire has close ties with France, and France, too, is heavily involved in seeking a resolution to the current crisis.

Côte d'Ivoire, economy

In 2003, according to estimates by the **World Bank**, Côte d'Ivoire's gross national income (GNI), measured at average 2001–03 prices, was US $13,033m., equivalent to $660 per head (or $1,390 on an international purchasing-power parity basis). During 1990–2003, it was estimated, the population increased at an average annual rate of 2.8%, while gross domestic product (GDP) per head declined, in real terms, by an average of 1.3% per year. Overall GDP increased, in real terms, at an average annual rate of 1.4% in 1990–2003; however, real GDP declined by 1.6% in 2002 and by 3.8% in 2003. The annual rate of inflation averaged 2.7% in 1990–93. Consumer prices increased by an average of 26.1% in 1994 (following the devaluation of the currency at the beginning of the year); the inflation rate slowed to an annual average of 14.3% in 1995, and averaged 3.2% in 1996–2002. Consumer prices increased by 3.3% in 2003. Major sectors of industry include foodstuffs, beverages, wood products, **oil** refining, vehicle assembly, textiles, fertilizers and building materials. Côte d'Ivoire's major trading partners are France, the USA, the Netherlands, Germany and Italy. The national currency is the CFA franc (see the **Franc Zone**). In 2004 the average exchange rate was US $1 = 528.29 francs CFA.

According to World Bank estimates, **agriculture** accounts for just over 30% of Côte d'Ivoire's GDP. The country is the world's largest producer of **cocoa**, accounting for some 40% of global supplies, and the fifth largest producer of **coffee**. It is estimated that 650,000 farmers work solely on cocoa. In macroeconomic terms, cocoa crops represent 40% of GDP and 60% of export revenues. Heavy dependence on this sector has left the economy vulnerable to fluctuations in the prices of and revenues gained from these commodities. There has been more recently a concerted effort to move towards economic diversification, particularly in agro-industry, and petroleum products, **natural gas** and mineral reserves. The industrial sector accounted for 24.8% of GDP in 1999, while manufacturing activity has expanded rapidly, with Côte d'Ivoire producing a variety of goods for domestic and regional consumption. Services have also played a significant role in economic growth, with transport and trade accounting for approximately 44% of GDP. The economy's performance has been negatively affected by a downturn in international cocoa prices, and by the military overthrow of the Bédié government in December 1999, political instability in 2000–04 severely limiting new foreign investment. Real GDP continuously fell by an annual average of 2.1% in 2000–03. Fiscal and current-account deficits have become unmanageable.

Côte d'Ivoire is struggling to retain its position as a 'powerhouse' among francophone African countries, accounting for 40% of GDP produced by the **Union économique et monétaire ouest-africaine (UEMOA—Economic and Monetary Union of West Africa)**. It also plays a crucial role in the regional economy, primarily through remittances earned by immigrant workers from neighbouring countries such as Mali and Burkina Faso. This role as regional source of revenue is being severely undermined by the continuing political crisis. As a member of UEMOA, Côte d'Ivoire's exchange rate is fixed to the euro, with monetary policy controlled by the **Banque centrale des états de l'Afrique de l'ouest (BCEAO—Central Bank of West African States)**. Fiscal policy therefore remains the government's only instrument for realizing financial stability. However, Côte d'Ivoire's exporters benefited from the devaluation of the CFA franc in 1994.

In February 1998 a three-year Economic Structural Adjustment Facility (ESAF) was agreed with the **International Monetary Fund (IMF)**. In May international donors agreed to provide development assistance worth $4,100m. to support the economic reform programme. The discovery that **European Union (EU)** funds had been used fraudulently delayed further consideration of the second tranche of the ESAF. After the coup of December 1999 the economy declined. Two factors were responsible: political instability and a slump in world cocoa prices. At the beginning of 2001 a new factor arose, when donor communities, including the IMF and the EU, withheld payments and suspended financial aid. This was a result of the government's failure to pursue a policy of national reconciliation and to address the abuse of human rights by the security forces. However, in June the IMF implemented a six-month Staff-Monitored Programme (SMP) after two critical conditions for IMF re-engagement had been met, namely: the adoption of a prudent budget and successful EU-Côte d'Ivoire negotiations. Sound progress on the SMP, including the implementation of IMF conditions concerning domestic tax revenue, and domestic and external arrears, led to the resumption of IMF financial assistance in November, under a $366m **Poverty Reduction and Growth Facility (PRGF)**.

The priorities for Côte d'Ivoire under the PRGF will include clearing domestic and external payment arrears, liberalization of the oil sector, implementing an effective privatization programme, financial rehabilitation of the **water** utility and the restructuring of the state-owned postal savings system. Côte d'Ivoire was expected to receive significant **debt relief** by qualifying for enhanced **Heavily Indebted Poor Countries initiative** decision point at the end of 2002. However, the current political crisis has postponed the realization of this goal. Political uncertainty has jeopardized the economic prospects for 2005. Without a swift resolution, Côte d'Ivoire may soon face significant economic repercussions. More positively, international donors have offered $433m. of aid to fund reconstruction in the country over five years if a peace deal can be agreed and implemented.

Cotonou Agreement

Agreement signed in 2000 (with a term of 20 years), between the **European Union (EU)** and 78 **African, Caribbean and Pacific (ACP)** countries which were previously subject to the **Lomé Convention**. In 2004 the EU evaluated its budget support to 20 ACP countries in Africa, concluding that the experience of the new instrument for the allocation of development assistance funds had been generally positive. Conditions were attached in a reduced manner and a multi-stage process for further economic liberalization is being developed. This will involve the establishment of Economic Partnership Agreements (EPAs) as a means of breaking down the very large geographical area and three regions covered by the Agreement into sub-regions. In theory, what is proposed is: first, to create sub-regional groups of countries and promote their economic independence and competitiveness; second, to open these sub-regional markets carefully to the EU; and finally, to promote gradual, harmonious integration in the global economy as stipulated in the Maastricht Treaty. During this long phase of adjustment, the EU market will be open to ACP exports on a contractual basis. Those who support the approach argue that the EU is making a valuable contribution to sub-regional integration, but many are concerned that in practice these EPAs will cut across pre-existing regional and sub-regional associations and embryonic 'common markets' in the ACP region as a whole, thereby reducing the capacity of developing countries to build their own sub-regional markets. Thus, in Africa, the **Southern African Development Community (SADC)** would be divided, with different sub-sets of SADC countries having their own relationship with the EU, and South Africa having its own distinctive relationship with the EU. Already the **Arab Maghreb Union** has suffered from the way in which the **Euro-Mediterranean Partnership** has divided Algeria, Tunisia and Morocco (included) from Mauritania and Libya (excluded).

Cotton

Cotton is the world's leading textile fibre. But with the increased use of synthetics, its share in total world consumption of fibre declined from 48% in 1988 to 39% in 1998. About one-half of the cotton produced in the world is used for the manufacture of clothing, about one-third for household textiles and the remainder for numerous industrial products (tarpaulins, rubber reinforcement, abrasive backings, filters, high-quality papers). During the mid-1980s world cotton consumption failed to keep pace with the increase in output and the resultant surpluses led to a reduction in prices that had serious consequences for many African producers, which tend to rely heavily on cotton sales for a major portion of their foreign exchange. In the 1990s, prices improved as large areas of cotton production were turned over to food production and cotton sales declined. Towards the end of the decade and into the

2000s, prices once again fell, significantly. Although co-operation in cotton trading has a long history, there have been no international agreements governing the cotton trade. Proposals in recent years, to link producers and consumers in price stabilization arrangements, have been opposed by the USA (the world's largest cotton producer), by Japan and by the **European Union**. Cotton is the major commercial crop in Benin, Burkina Faso, the Central African Republic, Chad, Egypt, Mali, Mozambique and Togo. It is second in importance in Senegal and Sudan. Other countries where cotton is a major cash crop include Cameroon, Côte d'Ivoire, Nigeria, Tanzania and Zimbabwe. In 2001–02 exports from Mali, Burkina Faso and Benin alone accounted for almost 8% of total world exports. In all, African countries account for just under 10% of total world output, with Mali and Egypt the two largest producers.

Council of Arab Economic Unity (CAEU)

The Council of Arab Economic Unity (CAEU) held its first meeting in 1964. Thirteen Arab states, including Libya, Mauritania, Egypt and Sudan were members. Egypt's membership was suspended after 1978 when a peace agreement was concluded with Israel, but later was permitted to return. Under the aegis of the Council, an **Arab Common Market** was established in 1964, of which Mauritania, Libya and Egypt were members (with the same period of exclusion for Egypt). The objective was a full customs union.

D

Ould Daddah, Mokhtar

Born in the south east of Mauritania into a religious family. After a traditional Muslim and French primary education, Mokhtar moved to France, where he completed his secondary education, took a degree in law and met his future wife, whom he married in 1959. He returned to Mauritania, ran as a political candidate on a list of the Union progressiste mauritanienne (Progressive Mauritanian Union) and was elected territorial councillor of Adrar in March 1957. In May he was nominated as vice-president of the Council of the Government. In 1958 he campaigned for a 'yes' vote in the referendum held by French President Charles de Gaulle to keep the former French African colonies in the French-African Community. In 1961 he was elected as the first President of the independent Islamic Republic of Mauritania. He remained President of what was effectively a one-party state in Mauritania from 1961 until 1978 when he was overthrown in a military coup, after some years of economic crisis, exacerbated by **drought** and Mauritania's alliance with Morocco to take control of the former Spanish Sahara which led them to a costly war with the **Frente Popular para la Liberación de Saguia el-Hamra y Río de Oro (Frente POLISARIO—Popular Front for the Liberation of Saguia el-Hamra and Río de Oro)**, the political movement fighting for Sahrawi self-determination. In 1969 he secured the assistance of Algeria in the **Organization of African Unity** to secure recognition of Mauritania's sovereignty, which was previously disputed by Morocco, but from 1976 embroiled Mauritania in a war in the **Western Sahara** led by Morocco against the Frente POLISARIO. After his overthrow in 1978 he was detained for more than a year without trial in a remote fort by the leaders of the Military Committee for National Recovery (later the National Salvation Committee) who replaced him. However, he was allowed to travel to France for medical treatment after the intervention of French President Giscard d'Estaing, the Kings of Morocco, Saudi Arabia and Jordan, and some African leaders, and to remain there in exile. In his absence he was sentenced to hard labour for life, for treason, violation of the Constitution and undermining national economic interests. He spent 15 years in exile before the establishment of a multi-party regime encouraged him to consider returning to politics in Mauritania. However, although there was still support for him in the country and some opposition groups favoured his political return, ultimately he decided against it. Ould Daddah returned to Mauritania in July 2001, and died there in October 2003.

Dahomey – *see also* Benin

Formerly part of the colonial territory of **French West Africa**. The post-**independence** period (from 1960) was characterized by chronic political instability until Maj. (later Brig.-Gen.) **Mathieu Kérékou** took power in 1972 and established a more stable albeit highly centralized government. Under Kérékou, Dahomey was renamed Benin in 1975.

Dakar

Capital of Senegal. Major cultural and intellectual centre for much of West Africa.

Darfur

Region of western Sudan, historically the home of the Fur (hence Arabic *dar fur*). Darfur has come to international prominence in recent years owing to the bitter conflict there between (initially) rebels belonging to the Sudan Liberation Movement and pro-Sudanese government ethnic Arab militias—***Janjaweed***—which have allegedly conducted a campaign of **genocide** against black African sections of the region's population. In April 2005 the UN Security Council concurred in the recommendation of a UN-appointed commission, that the 'heinous crimes' committed in Darfur should be referred to the International Criminal Court (ICC). This was the first time that the Security Council has referred a case to the fledgling Court. The ICC's chief prosecutor was instructed to initiate an investigation into the two-year conflict, which has claimed an estimated 400,000 lives and driven an estimated 2m. people from their homes into other parts of Sudan, as internally displaced persons, and into neighbouring Chad and Uganda as **refugees**. A sealed list of 'prime suspects' has been compiled that reportedly includes the names of Sudanese officials, members of state-sponsored militias and Darfuri rebels. Sudan, meanwhile, has challenged the legality of the ICC's intervention. The ICC's statutes allow it to pursue cases only in countries that are unable or unwilling to do so themselves. The Sudanese government insists that it will try those who have committed crimes in Darfur. Attempts by the **African Union (AU)** to mediate between the government and the rebels had been unsuccessful as of mid-2005, but the AU had deployed 2,700 peace-keepers in Darfur and planned to deploy a further 5,000.

De Beers

One of Africa's most famous business corporations. A major diamond mining, trading and distribution group. Since 1998 its chairman has been **Nicky Oppenheimer**, whose grandfather, Sir Ernest Oppenheimer, bought into the De Beers group, originally founded in 1926 by **Cecil Rhodes**, and transformed it into a multinational business. The Oppenheimers also held a large stake in Anglo American and ran the two businesses together. In 2001 De Beers became a private company. As recently as the 1980s De Beers produced some 80% of the world's rough **diamonds** and distributed 65% of the total sold world-wide. Those respective shares have since fallen to about 40% and 50%, but the value of De Beers' sales in 2005 none the less totalled some US $5,700m. The smaller market share has taken off some of the regulatory pressure on De Beers that resulted from its dominant market position—until recently Oppenheimer could not visit the USA for fear of arrest under anti-trust laws. A De Beers subsidiary had been accused of conspiring with General Electric to fix prices in 1991 and 1992. De Beers pleaded guilty in order to ensure continued trading in the USA, even though the case against General Electric collapsed for lack of evidence.

Debt

Even in 1980 the total debt of African countries was equivalent to almost 30% of their combined gross national product (GNP) and 13% of their export earnings. At the end of the 1980s some 33 out of 52 African countries were heavily in debt. Twenty-six of them had debt service/export ratios above the average for their part of Africa and a further seven had outstanding debts in excess of their national income in the same period. Of the 33 heavily indebted countries, the vast majority been disrupted by civil unrest and internal conflict; but so too had eight of the countries with lighter debt burdens. Twelve countries where foreign debt was not overwhelming enjoyed relative peace. With regard to the difference between **North Africa** and Africa south of the Sahara, while the debt burden had been significantly greater in the former in 1980, it was generally less in 1988–91—equivalent to 66% of GNP compared with 88% previously. The most heavily indebted countries, whose debt was equivalent to more than their respective GNPs, were: Mozambique, Guinea-Bissau, São Tomé and Príncipe, Somalia, Mauritania, Republic of the Congo, Equatorial Guinea, Tanzania, Liberia, Côte d'Ivoire, Zambia, Madagascar, Ethiopia, The Gambia, **Zaire**, Egypt, Mali, Sudan. Those with low debts included: Benin, Botswana, Cape Verde, Central African Republic, Gabon, Libya, Mauritius, Namibia, Réunion, Seychelles, Swaziland and Tunisia. By the early 1990s, as a consequence of a decline in the terms of trade of Africa's products and growth in trade deficits and foreign debts, debt had come to exceed the combined gross domestic product of all of the African states, while debt-servicing consumed almost one-third of all export earnings. The situation continued, generally, to deteriorate throughout the 1990s, and, under increasing pressure from '**debt relief**' and 'debt forgiveness' campaigns across the developed (and developing) world, the international agencies began to consider seriously, for the first time, from the mid-1990s onwards a major debt relief initiative for Africa. Practical action, however, took longer to materialize, and it was not until the 21st century that the **World Bank** and the **International Monetary Fund**, together with many of the developed countries, began to put in place new frameworks and measures in pursuit of the **Millennium Development Goals** and the reduction of debt.

Debt relief

Debt relief and the doubling of aid to Africa were major items on the agenda of the meeting of the **G8** group of countries in Gleneagles, Scotland, in early July 2005. Since the campaign Jubilee 2000 was launched in 1998, there has been growing demand for some kind of debt relief. The decision to extend a conditional cancellation of some US $40,000m. of the debt of 18 poor countries, mainly located in sub-Saharan Africa, allowed G8 finance ministers to emphasize their global anti-**poverty** credentials. The decision means that those countries that reached the completion point of the **Highly Indebted Poor Countries (HIPC) initiative** and therefore already qualified for debt reduction will be forgiven all outstanding debts to the **World Bank**, the **International Monetary Fund (IMF)** and the **African Development Bank (ADB)**. However, the 'deal' will also require further measures of economic 'reform' by the 18 countries in question. That means deregulation, privatization and concessions to foreign traders and investors with the aim of 'opening' their economies. According to Christian Aid, however, 'two decades of [economic] liberalization have cost sub-Saharan Africa roughly what it has received in aid over the same period', and left the region in effect $272,000 worse off than it otherwise would have been. Furthermore, the debt cancellation applies only to loans from the World Bank, the IMF and the ADB, not to loans made by the World Bank's affiliates, the Inter-American Development Bank (IDB) or the Asian Development Bank, which hold much of the debt of countries participating in the HIPC initiative, which are the targeted recipients of the debt relief. Furthermore, aid from the IDB and the ADB, even to the favoured countries, will be reduced by the amounts forgiven. The G8 initiative may be regarded as either a welcome gesture or as a misleading one, but it will solve neither the issue of the debt nor the issue of poverty since it bears on only 2% of the external debt of developing countries. Several developing countries that will not benefit from these measures have expressed concerns. The Kenyan planning minister, Peter Anyang Nyongo, for example, claimed that countries that had always serviced their debts were being ignored while the unreliable debtors had been let off.

The debt relief to be extended would cost rich countries only about $1,500m. annually in compensation to the World Bank, IMF and ADB. Even if, as expected, the programme is expanded to cover a further nine countries and a total of $55,000m. of debt is cancelled, it is still a relatively small amount given the scale of the debt crisis.

Deby, Gen. Idriss

President of Chad since 1991. Born in 1952, Deby, a career army officer, helped **Hissène Habré** to overthrow Goukouni Oueddei in 1982. In 1989 he fled to Sudan after having been accused of plotting a coup. One year later his **Mouvement patriotique du salut (Patriotic Salvation Movement)** drove Habré into exile, and in 1991 Deby was proclaimed President. In 1996 he oversaw the inauguration of a multi-party constitution and later that year won the country's first presidential election. Deby was re-elected as President in 2001.

Declaration of Conakry

The Declaration of Conakry, in May 1959, established a union between Ghana and Guinea shortly after both had gained **independence**, in 1957 and 1958 respectively.

De Klerk, F. W.

Former President of South Africa—he succeeded **P. W. Botha**—and former leader of the **National Party (NP)**. He was largely responsible for negotiations with **Nelson Mandela** and the **African National Congress (ANC)** that initiated the process of political transformation in South Africa. De Klerk joined Mandela's government of national unity as Deputy President (together with **Thabo Mbeki**), but withdrew the NP prematurely after two years in June 1996 owing to the ANC's refusal to accept his notion of permanent 'power sharing'. Shortly afterwards he was replaced as leader of the NP by Marthinus van Schalkwyk.

Democracy

Most African states today would claim to be democratic and the majority are now characterized by multi-party political systems after a progressive change over the last decade or so. During the 1990s pressure, both internal and external, for greater and more effective representation of the interests of ordinary citizens and for 'good governance' combined to lead to the demise of many former one-party states and some of the more notorious authoritarian regimes, and their replacement by regimes which made at least some moves towards permitting a greater diversity of political views to be represented, usually by recognizing more than one political party. Military regimes, which from the 1960s until the 1980s were the norm across Africa, have generally been replaced by civilian regimes (although some remain), even if in some cases the previous military officer in command has re-defined himself as a civilian in order to assume the presidency or the position of Head of State. Some one-party regimes remain (e.g. Uganda) and in most African states party politics still tends to be dominated by a single party and many opposition parties operate under severe restrictions (as in Zimbabwe).

Democratic Alliance (DA)

In elections held in South Africa in 1999, the **Democratic Party (DP)** won 38 parliamentary seats, receiving more **Afrikaner** votes than the **New National Party (NNP)** and replacing it as the official opposition party. After the election the DP merged with the NNP to become a consolidated and overwhelmingly white opposition movement—the DA, with **Tony Leon** (the leader of the DP) as its leader and the NNP's Marthinus van Schalkwyk as deputy leader. After two years van Schalkwyk withdrew the NNP from the DA in favour of an informal relationship with the **African National Congress (ANC)**. The new ANC/NNP alliance subsequently gained control of the Western Cape provincial administration, which the DA had previously controlled, and of which van Schalkwyk eventually became Premier.

Democratic Party (DP)

An amalgamation of opposition groups from the **apartheid** era in South Africa, headed by the liberal **Progressive Party**, a predominantly white-supported party. Led by **Tony Leon**, it is still the residual home of white South African liberalism but has increasingly adopted a critical stance *vis-à-vis* the 'affirmative action' policy of the **African National Congress**.

Democratic Unionist Party (DUP)

Egyptian political party, founded in 1990. The DUP's president is Ibrahim Abd al-Moneim Turk.

The Dergue (Committee)

Ruling junta in Ethiopia from 1974 until 1991. It espoused a Marxist-Leninist political ideology and presided over a centralized one-party state.

Destour Party

The first party to challenge French colonial rule in Tunisia. The Destour was essentially a party of Tunisia's traditional leadership, based in the capital, Tunis: administrators, religious leaders, merchants, leaders of the most respected crafts and notables of the Ottoman beys. It was formed just after the end of the First World War. Active during the 1920s, it failed to mobilize popular support and was supplanted in the 1930s by the **Neo-Destour Party**, led largely by a new intelligentsia of modest social origins, with a significant power base in the provinces.

Development aid/assistance

Africa has always received a considerable proportion of global public development assistance. The largest recipient of aid in Africa (and seventh largest in the world) is Egypt, and Morocco and Tunisia both rank among the world's largest recipients of aid in overall value (in that order). According to one source, the West has spent US $450,000m. on aid to Africa over the past 40 years. By the mid-1980s Africa received 36% of all multilateral aid granted world-wide, although the combined population of the African countries was only 10% of the world total. On the other hand, over the past 15 years, the **G8** has increased aid to Africa by only $3 a head, while per caput incomes in G8 countries have risen by almost $6,000.

Devonshire Declaration

The Devonshire Declaration, in 1923, affirmed the primacy of African interests in Kenya. However, the settler community there assumed, and was allowed to continue to assume until the eve of **independence**, that its own powers and privileges were not threatened within the foreseeable future. Even in the 1950s both Africans and Europeans believed that a white government's commitment to the principles of self-determination and majority rule would stop short at placing a substantial white community under black rule.

Diamonds

Africa is the major producing region for natural diamonds. Botswana, where diamonds normally account for about 80% of export earnings, ranks as the world's largest producer in terms of value. Other major African producers are the Democratic Republic of the Congo (DRC), South Africa, Angola, Namibia, Central African Republic, Ghana, Sierra Leone and Guinea. In South Africa more than 90% of output derives from the operations of **De Beers** Consolidated Mines Ltd. De Beers, one of South Africa's most prominent business corporations, has traditionally been the principal conduit of African diamond sales, and, indeed, formerly enjoyed monopoly control of world diamond sales. That role has been evolving in recent years, however, in response, partly, to the entry into world markets of increasing quantities of diamonds mined in Australia, North America and Russia. In 2000 De Beers announced that it was to relinquish its monopoly on world diamond sales. Measures taken from the late 1990s to stem world trade in so-called 'conflict diamonds' (owing to their role, with particular reference to Angola, Sierra Leone and the DRC, in the financing of guerrilla insurgencies) culminated in 2000 in the initiation by southern African countries of the 'Kimberley Process', with the objective of ending their commercialization. As of August 2005 the Kimberley Process had 44 participants world-wide, including the member states of the **European Union**. Since 2003 the Kimberley Process Certification Scheme has imposed strict standards on all of its participants in respect of trade in rough diamonds.

Diouf, Abdou

Abdul Diouf succeeded **Léopold Sédar Senghor** as President of Senegal when Senghor retired in 1981. Diouf was confirmed in his position two years later by an overwhelming electoral victory, but was unsuccessful in dealing with Senegal's bitter sectarian rivalries and economic problems.

Diola

A major ethno-linguistic grouping in West Africa.

Dioula

The main vernacular spoken in the north of São Tomé and Príncipe. The **Mande**, together with the Dioula sub-group, constitute almost 30% of the total population of the country. Other ethno-linguistic groups are the **Baoule** in the south, the Krou in the west and the Senoufou, also in the north.

Direct Path (Assirat al-Moustaquim, *also known as* Righteous Path)

On 16 May 2003 13 suicide bombers killed themselves and 28 other people in a co-ordinated attack on five tourist and Jewish targets in Casablanca, Morocco. The worst carnage was in the Casa de España, a popular private club; other targets were the Israeli Alliance Club, a major business hotel, the Belgian consulate and a Jewish cemetery. A fourteenth suicide bomber, who fled from the attack on the hotel, identified eight colleagues, some of them Moroccans living abroad. Some indications suggest they were linked to a group calling itself Assirat al-Moustaquim (Direct Path). This group—several of whose members have recently been jailed—is believed to be a splinter group of another radical Islamist organization, **Salafist Jihad**. One of Salafist Jihad's main spiritual leaders, 28-year-old Ould Mohamed Abdelwahab Raqiqi, alias 'Abu Hafs', was jailed earlier in the year for inciting violence against Westerners.

Djibouti, Republic of

The Republic of Djibouti is in the Horn of Africa, at the southern entrance to the Red Sea. It is bounded on the north by Eritrea, on the north, west and south west by Ethiopia, and on the south east by Somalia. The area of the country is 23,200 sq km and the population was estimated at 703,000 at mid-2003. There are two main ethnic groups, the **Issa**, who are of Somali origin and comprise 50% of the population, and the Afar, who comprise 40% of the population and are of Ethiopian origin. Both groups are Muslims and they speak related Cushitic languages. The official languages are **Arabic** and French. The capital is Djibouti.

Political profile

The President of the Republic, who is Head of State and head of government, is directly elected, by universal adult suffrage, for a period of six years, renewable only once. The President nominates the Prime Minister and, following consultation with the latter, appoints the Council of Ministers. The legislature is the 65 member Assemblée nationale, which is elected, also by direct universal suffrage, for a period of five years.

Ismael Omar Gelleh of the Rassemblement populaire pour le progrès (RPP—Popular Rally for Progress) was first elected as President in April 1999. At the presidential election held on 8 April 2005 Gelleh secured 100% of the valid votes cast. Gelleh was the sole candidate at the election following the withdrawal, in March, from the contest of Mohamed Daoud Chehem of the Parti djiboutien pour la démocratie (PDD—Djibouti Democratic Party).

At the most recent general election to the Assemblée nationale, held on 10 January 2003, the Union pour la majorité présidentielle (UMP—Union for the Presidential Majority), a coalition comprising the Front pour la restauration de l'unité et de la démocratie (FRUD—Front for the Restoration of Unity and Democracy), the Parti national démocratique (PND—National Democratic Party) and the Parti populaire social-démocrate (PPSD—Popular Social Democrat Party) received 62.73% of the votes cast. In accordance with the electoral laws, as it had won the majority of the votes in each of the country's five constituences, the UMP secured all 65 seats in the Assemblée nationale. Despite receiving 37.3% of votes cast, the opposition coalition, the Union pour l'alternance démocratique (UAD—Union for Democratic Succession), comprising the Alliance républicaine pour la démocratie (ARD—Republican Alliance for Democracy), the Mouvement du renouveau démocratique (MRD—Democratic Renewal Movement) and the Union djiboutienne pour la démocratie et la justice (UDDJ—Djibouti Union for Democracy and Justice), failed to attain any legislative representation. The Council of Ministers was not altered following the election. Dileita Mohamed Dileita, who had first been appointed as Prime Minister in February 2001, remained as Prime Minister and continued to occupy that position in April 2005.

History

France secured a foothold in what is now Djibouti in the late1850s. In 1888 the territory became the colony of French **Somaliland**. In 1946 it became an overseas territory of France. Following agitation by Somali nationalists, a referendum held in 1967 reaffirmed the desire of most of the population to remain part of the French Community. In the same year the area was renamed as the French Territory of the Afars and Issas. **Independence** movements continued to agitate, however, and the territory eventually proceeded to independence as the Republic of Djibouti on 27 June 1977. **Hassan Gouled Aptidon** (an Issa) was chosen as the Republic's first President and was confirmed in office in presidential elections held in 1981. He was re-elected in 1987 and 1993. Ismael Omar Gelleh, the candidate of the ruling RPP, won the presidential election held on 9 April 1999 and thus succeeded his uncle, Aptidon, as Head of State. The RPP was declared the sole legal political party in 1981. (A new Constitution that was endorsed in a referendum in 1992 restored the multi-party political system.)

In November 1991 Afar rebels began assaults on government positions in the northern part of the country—the Afar areas. The rebel groups united as the FRUD, and gained control of two-thirds of Djibouti. (The FRUD did not, however, threaten the south, including the capital.) In 1993 government forces began a series of offensives against rebel-held areas and regained much of the territory that had previously been lost. The **civil war** was ended by the signature of peace and national reconciliation accords between the moderate elements of the FRUD and the government on 26 December 1996. On 12 May 2001 the Djiboutian Minister of the Interior signed a peace and reform agreement with Ahmed Dini, the leader of the (Afar) armed wing of the FRUD. Dini had led the Afar insurgency in northern Djibouti in 1991–94.

In December 2000 Gen. Yacin, chief of staff of the National Police Force, was removed from his post by presidential decree. In retaliation, Yacin and a faction of the police force surrounded the presidential palace and occupied Djibouti's telecommunications centre and television station. This revolt was quickly suppressed by the army, the gendarmerie and loyal factions of the police force. In September 2002 the limit on the number of political parties (previously fixed at four) was lifted. During the following months a number of political registered with the intention of participating in forthcoming legislative elections.

In July 2003 the government announced that owing to 'security and economic' reasons all illegal immigrants would be required to leave Djibouti by the end of August. The USA, which in August had warned of the possibility of terrorist attacks against Western targets in Djibouti, denied allegations that it had exerted pressure on the Djibouti government to expel the illegal immigrants.

Concerns over the freedom of the press escalated during 2004 following the imprisonment in April of Daher Ahmad Farah, the editor-in-chief of *Le Renouveau*. In June the authorities prevented the publication of the newspaper. The international organization Reporters sans frontiers denounced the government's actions as an attempt to silence the opposition press.

International relations

Djibouti provides most of Ethiopia's port needs, although relations between the two countries fluctuate—they have been strained by disputes over revised tariffs and Ethiopia's proposal to establish its own container port that would deny Djibouti a substantial amount of port work. There have been reciprocal visits by the leaders of Djibouti and Eritrea in an attempt to reconcile the differences that characterized relations between the two countries immediately before and during the war between Eritrea and Ethiopia. President Gelleh sponsored the peace and reconciliation conference—held under the auspices of the **Inter-Governmental Authority on Development (IGAD)**—which began on 2 May 2000 in Arta, Djibouti, which sought a solution to the civil conflict in Somalia. A Transitional National Assembly (for Somalia) convened for the first time in Djibouti in August 2000. The boycott by President Egal of 'Somaliland' (north-west Somalia) of the Arta conference effectively 'froze' relations between the two authorities. Relations have improved, however, since President Riyale succeeded President Egal in 2002.

Djibouti maintains close links with France, which provides significant amounts of aid and financial support. Some 2,700 French troops remain stationed in Djibouti under agreements signed at the time of independence. As part of the international 'war on terrorism', Djibouti also hosts 1,800 US troops and is the headquarters of a multinational Indian Ocean task force.

Djibouti, economy

In 2003, according to estimates by the **World Bank**, Djibouti's gross national income (GNI), measured at average 2001–03 prices, was US $641m., equivalent to $910 per head (or $2,200 on an international purchasing-power parity basis). During 1990–2003, it was estimated, the population increased at an average annual rate of 2.8% owing partly to an influx of **refugees** from neighbouring Ethiopia and Somalia, (although this figure was expected to decrease during 2004–05 due to mass expulsion of foreign migrants), while gross domestic product (GDP) per head decreased, in real terms, by an average of 2.9% per year. Overall GDP declined, in real terms, at an average annual rate of 0.2% during 1990–2003; however, growth of 3.5% was recorded in 2003. Consumer prices increased by an estimated 2% in 2003. Djibouti's major trading partners are Ethiopia, Somalia, Yemen, Saudi Arabia, France and Thailand. Djibouti has traditionally relied heavily on foreign assistance. The national currency is the Djibouti franc. The exchange rate has been fixed at US $1 = 177.721 Djibouti francs since February 1973.

Djibouti lacks any significant natural resources other than fishing grounds, geothermal potential and some mining activity. Due to soil infertility and poor rainfall, there is hardly any **agriculture**. **Fisheries** and **water** resources offer a promising but as yet unexploited potential owing to lack of domestic demand and non-competitive labour and pricing policies. Mining resources consist of a geothermal endowment and salt deposits that may have some potential for commercial exploitation. High unemployment, of 40%–50%, remains a major problem. Since **independence** the government has concentrated on developing Djibouti as a commercial and service centre, and the economy is now based on service activities connected with the country's strategic location and status as a free-trade zone in north-east Africa. Two-thirds of Djibouti's GDP in 1997 was derived from the servicing of the port and the railway to Ethiopia (more than 75% of the containers that arrive at the port are destined for Ethiopia) and the French garrison. The decision of France progressively to withdraw its military presence, and the accompanying decline in its financial assistance; the expansion of the port of Aden and other competing regional ports for trans-shipment; and the continued impact of the 1994 **civil war** gave rise to considerable macroeconomic instability.

Although Djibouti is severely handicapped both in terms of human capital and natural resources, it has many assets, such as its strategically-located port and relative stability in a region where armed conflict is frequent. Economic development on the basis of the resources noted above may be possible in the long term.

Economic restructuring, in collaboration with the **International Monetary Fundn (IMF)**, continues intermittently. In December 2004, however, the government characterized the economy and social situation as 'fragile', in spite of seven years of reform and anti-**poverty** efforts carried out under IMF-supported programmes.

Douala

The most populous city in Cameroon, with 810,000 inhabitants at the time of the 1987 census. The capital, **Yaoundé** had only 649,000 inhabitants at that time.

Drought

Africa has always suffered from drought. During the last 50 years, however, drought has apparently become more common and more severe. The first major drought faced by independent African countries was the great Sahelian drought of 1968–73. Another major drought, in 1983–85, also affected most of the Sahel, as well as Sudan, Ethiopia and other parts of the Horn of Africa. Subsequent droughts were experienced in southern Africa, across Zimbabwe and Mozambique in particular. In 2005, as a result of drought and crop losses to **locusts** in the previous year, an estimated 3m. people in Niger were in danger of starvation.

E

East Africa

Narrowly defined, East Africa usually comprises Uganda, Kenya and Tanzania (members of the erstwhile **East African Community**), but a broader definition would include Mozambique to the south and possibly the Horn of Africa—including Somalia, Ethiopia, Djibouti and Eritrea—to the north.

East African Community (EAC)

Immediately after **independence**, **Tanganyika**, Kenya and Uganda established a loose economic grouping, which included a common external tariff. Most of the foreign capital investment, however, flowed into Kenya, where British settlers continued to exercise a well-established pressure group in London. After proposals for federation collapsed, even the loose Community broke up in inter-state disputes that were aggravated by **Idi Amin**'s seizure of power in Uganda. More recently, attempts have been made to revive the EAC. In November 1991 the Presidents of Kenya, Uganda and Tanzania met in Nairobi, Kenya, and declared their commitment to developing mutual co-operation. In November 1994 the three leaders met at Arusha, Tanzania, and established a permanent tripartite commission for co-operation, with a view to reviving the defunct EAC. The EAC process was relaunched in 1997. A treaty for the re-establishment of the EAC (providing for the promotion of free trade among the member states, with the eventual introduction of a single currency; for the development of infrastructure, tourism and **agriculture** within the Community; and for the establishment of a regional legislative assembly and court) was signed on 30 November 1999 and ratified by the Heads of State of Kenya, Tanzania and Uganda in June 2000. The EAC was formally relaunched on 15 January 2001. Talks aimed at better integrating the economies of the EAC followed, and in June 2003 the three leaders met to discuss harmonizing tariffs and the creation of a customs union. The EAC has a secretariat, based in Arusha and staffed by officials from all the EAC countries, which has produced ambitious plans for further co-operation on development, including lowering customs tariffs and a single currency for the region. In March 2004 the three members of the EAC signed a protocol establishing the **East African Customs Union**.

East African Customs Union

In March 2004 the three members of the **East African Community (EAC)** signed a protocol establishing the East African Customs Union. In this, Kenya, Tanzania and Uganda committed themselves to reducing tariffs over the next five years, and were to apply a uniform tariff of 25% on imports of non-EAC finished goods, and of 10% on semi-processed imports. Although impediments to full implementation undoubtedly exist, there is the potential for creating a greater and more prosperous regional market for the three countries involved.

Economic Community of West African States (ECOWAS) Cease-fire Monitoring Group (ECOMOG): mission to Liberia, Guinea and Sierra Leone

In August 1999 a regional meeting was convened under the auspices of the **Economic Community of West African States (ECOWAS)** to attempt to defuse escalating tension between Liberia and Guinea following an incursion into northern Liberia by Guinean rebel forces. In September it was agreed to establish a monitoring body to supervise the situation in the border regions. Insecurity increased in 2000, particularly in southern Guinea, which was increasingly subjected to insurgencies by Sierra Leonean rebels belonging to the **Revolutionary United Front (RUF)** and clashes with Guinean troops, prompting large-scale displacement of local populations. Relations between the three countries deteriorated rapidly. In December the ECOWAS Authority approved the deployment of a 1,700-strong ECOWAS Cease-fire Monitoring Group (ECOMOG) force to act as a buffer in the Guinea-Liberia-Sierra Leone border region and to alleviate the growing humanitarian crisis there. In April 2001, in light of the fact that the Presidents of Guinea and Liberia had still not signed the Status of Force Agreement required to deploy the ECOMOG force, the ECOWAS Authority decided to postpone the deployment indefinitely. At the same time, an ECOWAS committee, comprising the Presidents of Mali, Nigeria and Togo, was established to mediate a resolution to the crisis.

Economic Community of West African States (ECOWAS) Cease-fire Monitoring Group (ECOMOG): first mission to Liberia

In August 1990 a Cease-fire Monitoring Group (ECOMOG) of the **Economic Community of West African States (ECOWAS)**—initially comprising about 4,000 troops from The Gambia, Ghana, Guinea, Nigeria and Sierra Leone—was dispatched to Liberia in an attempt to enforce a cease-fire between conflicting factions there, to restore public order and to establish an interim government, until elections could be held. In November a temporary cease-fire was agreed and an interim President was installed. A national conference, organized by ECOMOG in March 1991, established a temporary government pending elections that were to be held in early 1992. The elections were postponed, however, and even by September 1992 ECOMOG had failed to disarm two of the principal military factions, the National Patriotic Front of Liberia (NPFL) and the United Liberation Movement of Liberia for Democracy (ULIMO), and to establish effective control in substantial areas of the country. In October ECOMOG began offensive action against the NPLF. By April 1993 ULIMO had been disarmed, and in August an ECOMOG-brokered cease-fire was signed and began to take effect. ECOMOG was accused, however, of no longer being a neutral force and in September a UN mission (UNOMIL) was established to work alongside ECOMOG and to verify its impartiality. In September 1994 an agreement was signed that provided for a new, five-member Council of State, in the context of the cease-fire, to replace the expired interim executive authority, and established a timetable for democratic elections. In early 1995 peace talks collapsed, but under pressure from the international community the Liberian factions signed a new accord in August. This led to renewed efforts to strengthen ECOMOG and ensure its deployment throughout Liberia and along its borders. Clashes in the west of the country between ECOMOG troops and fighters of the dissident ULIMO-J faction disrupted the deployment of the multinational forces and the disarmament process. In April 1996, following a series of violations of the cease-fire, serious hostilities erupted in Monrovia, the Liberian capital, between government forces and dissident troops. Eventually, a further cease-fire agreement was concluded under the aegis of the US government, the UN and ECOWAS. At the end of May the country-wide deployment of ECOMOG was initiated, a new cease-fire was agreed and in November the disarmament process began. Elections were held in July, and in August, the new President, **Charles Taylor**, former leader of the NPFL, was inaugurated. It was agreed that ECOMOG would assist in the process of national post-conflict reconstruction and its mandate (officially due to expire in February 1998) would be extended. Increasing concerns on the part of the Taylor administration that ECOMOG was providing assistance to opposition groupings led to the movement of ECOMOG's headquarters from Monrovia to Freetown, Sierra Leone, towards the end of 1998. The ECOMOG mission to Liberia was effectively terminated in October 1999.

Economic Community of West African States (ECOWAS) Cease-fire Monitoring Group (ECOMOG): mission to Sierra Leone

In May 1997 the democratically elected President of Sierra Leone, **Alhaji Ahmed Tejan Kabbah**, was overthrown in a military coup mounted by officers of the national army and rebels belonging to the **Revolutionary United Front (RUF)**. Nigerian forces based in Sierra Leone as part of a bilateral defence pact attempted to restore order. At the end of June ministers of foreign affairs from the **Economic Community of West African States (ECOWAS)** agreed to try to restore a democratic government in Sierra Leone through dialogue and the imposition of economic sanctions. In July an ECOWAS committee together with representatives of the **Organization of African Unity (OAU)**, negotiated an agreement with the Armed Forces Revolutionary Council (AFRC) in Sierra Leone to establish an immediate cease-fire and to pursue efforts towards the restoration of constitutional order. In August ECOWAS condemned the removal of President Kabbah and officially endorsed a series of punitive measures against the AFRC. ECOMOG was mandated to maintain and monitor the cease-fire and to prevent all goods, except essential humanitarian supplies, from entering the country. In October the UN Security Council imposed an embargo on the sale, or supply, of arms to Sierra Leone and authorized ECOWAS to ensure the implementation of these measures. ECOMOG conducted a number of attacks against commercial and military targets and clashes occurred between ECOMOG troops and AFRC/RUF fighters. A peace agreement was, however, signed in Conakry, Guinea, at the end of October providing for an end to the fighting and the reinstatement of Kabbah's government by April 1998. In November 1997, however, the peace process was undermined by reports that ECOMOG forces had violated the cease-fire agreement and the response of the AFRC administration, which was to demand that ECOMOG withdraw from Sierra Leone. In mid-February 1998 ECOMOG forces assumed control of Freetown and arrested several members of the AFRC/RUF regime. A supervisory task force, which included the ECOMOG commander, was established to maintain order pending Kabbah's return from exile.

Economic Commission for Africa (ECA)

The UN Economic Commission for Africa (ECA) was founded in 1958 by a resolution of the UN Economic and Social Council. Its mandate is to initiate and take part in measures for facilitating the social and economic development of the African continent and its constituent states. Fifty-three African countries are members. The ECA has five sub-regional development centres, for Northern Africa, Eastern Africa, Western Africa, Central Africa and Southern Africa. The Commission has its headquarters in Addis Ababa, Ethiopia, but a sub-regional development centre for Northern Africa is based in Tangier, Morocco. The Commission has been guided by various regional strategies, including the Abuja Treaty establishing the African Economic Community, signed under the aegis of the **Organization of African Unity** in 1991, the UN System-wide Special Initiative on Africa, launched in 1996, and the UN New Agenda for the Development of Africa covering the period 1991–2000. The ECA was designated as the main body responsible for identifying and preparing programmes on economic and corporate governance under the **New Partnership for Africa's Development** launched in October 2001.

Economic Community of West African States (ECOWAS)

The Treaty of Lagos, establishing the Economic Community of West African States (ECOWAS), was signed in May 1975 by 15 African states with the objective of promoting trade, co-operation and self-reliance in West Africa. Outstanding protocols bringing certain key features of the Treaty into effect were ratified in November 1976. Cape Verde joined in 1977. A revised ECOWAS Treaty, designed to accelerate economic integration and to increase political co-operation, was drawn up in 1991–92 and signed in July 1993. As of mid-2005 the member states of ECOWAS were: Benin, Burkina Faso, Cape Verde, Côte d'Ivoire, The Gambia, Ghana, Guinea, Guinea-Bissau, Liberia, Mali, Niger, Nigeria, Senegal, Sierra Leone and Togo In December 1997 an extraordinary meeting of ECOWAS Heads of State and Government was convened to consider the future stability and security of the region. It was agreed that a permanent mechanism should be established for conflict prevention and the maintenance of peace. In March 1998 ministers of foreign affairs resolved that ECOMOG—an *ad hoc* cease-fire monitoring group established in August 1990—should become the region's permanent peace-keeping force, and in July 1998 a draft mechanism was agreed for conflict management, peace and security. A draft protocol was approved in December 1999 providing for both a Permanent Mechanism for the Prevention, Management and Settlement of Conflicts and the Maintenance of Peace in the Region, and for a Mediation and Security Council, to be supported by an advisory Council of Elders, comprising 32 eminent statesmen from the region. ECOMOG was to be transformed from an *ad hoc* cease-fire monitoring group into a permanent stand-by force available for immediate deployment to avert emerging conflicts in the region.

Economic growth in Africa

After two decades of disappointing economic growth and declining living standards across much of **sub-Saharan Africa**, the region has shown a stronger performance in recent years. Annual growth in the gross domestic product (GDP) of the region has averaged 3.8%, in real terms, during the first years of the new millennium, a substantial improvement compared to the rate of 3% that was achieved in the previous five years and significantly better than the rate of 1.8% recorded in 1980–95. In 2004 the *World Economic Outlook* produced by the **International Monetary Fund** estimated that economic growth in the countries of sub-Saharan Africa since 1986 had oscillated between 1.9%–3.5%. Growth in African GDP per caput is now running well ahead of rates of growth in the 1980s and early 1990s. A study by the merchant bank Goldman Sachs in mid-2005 suggested that the trend growth rate for the whole of sub-Saharan Africa was 5%. This is good but is below the 7% target set by African leaders for the next 15 years in order to achieve the **Millennium Development Goals**. If the higher rate is to be achieved, improvements in a number of areas, including investment and technical progress, will be required.

Education

Levels of education vary enormously by country across Africa. Gender differences in access to education are also particularly marked in Africa, with girls' enrolment at school generally significantly lower than that of boys. Africa is unlikely to achieve the **Millennium Development Goals** in respect to education or gender. Countries with the lowest spending on education include Egypt (2.3%). In **North Africa**, literacy rates are lowest in Mauritania (only an estimated 41.2% of the adult population in 2002), Morocco (an estimated 50.7% in 2002) and Egypt (an estimated 55.6% in 2002); countries with the highest primary school enrolment rates include Tunisia, Libya and Algeria.

Egypt, Arab Republic of

Located in north-east Africa, bordering the Mediterranean Sea, between Libya and the Gaza Strip. It borders Israel to the east, across the Sinai Peninsula, and Sudan to the south. Egypt controls the Sinai—the only land bridge between Africa and Asia—and the **Suez Canal**, which provides the shortest sea link between the Mediterranean and the Indian Ocean. It has an area of 1,001,450 sq km (of which 6,000 sq km is **water**). The capital is Cairo. For administrative purposes Egypt is divided into 26 governorates (*muhafazah*, plural *muhafazat*): ad-Daqahliyah, al-Bahr al-Ahmar, al-Buhayrah, al-Fayyum, al-Gharbiyah, al-Iskandariyah, al-Isma'iliyah, al-Jizah, al-Minufiyah, al-Minya, al-Qahirah, al-Qalyubiyah, al-Wadi al-Jadid, ash-Sharqiyah, as-Suways, Aswan, Asyut, Bani Suwayf, Bur Sa'id, Dumyat, Janub Sina', Kafr ash-Shaykh, Matruh, Qina, Shamal Sina' and Suhaj. In July 2002 the population was estimated at 70,712,345, of which Egyptians, **Bedouins** and **Berbers** constituted 90%, while Greeks, Nubians, Armenians and other Europeans (primarily Italian and French) accounted for 10%. The majority (94%) are Muslims (mostly **Sunnis**), with Coptic Christians and 'others' accounting for the remaining 6%. **Arabic** is the official language. English and French are widely understood by educated classes.

Political profile

Egypt is a republic. The Head of State is President **Hosni Muhammad Said Mubarak** (since 14 October 1981), the head of government is Prime Minister Dr Ahmad Mahmoud Muhammad Nazif (since 9 July 2004). The Prime Minister is appointed by the President, as is the Cabinet. Presidents are nominated by the People's Assembly for a six-year term. The nomination must then be validated by a national, popular referendum. A national referendum was last held on 26 September 1999 and the next was due to be held in September 2005. The legislative bicameral system consists of the People's Assembly or Majlis ash-Sha'b (454 seats; 444 elected by popular vote, 10 appointed by the President; members serve five-year terms) and the Advisory Council or Majlis ash-Shura—which functions only in a consultative role—(264 seats; 176 elected by popular vote, 88 appointed by the President). The People's Assembly is elected through a system of three-phase voting—elections were last held on 19 October, 29 October and 8 November 2000 (the next elections are scheduled to be held in November 2005). Elections to the Advisory Council were last held in May–June 2004. The legal system is based on English common law, Islamic Law and Napoleonic codes. Judicial review is by the Supreme Constitutional Court and the Council of State (which oversees the validity of administrative decisions). Egypt accepts compulsory International Court of Justice jurisdiction with reservations. The formation of political parties and NGOs must be approved by the government. There is a constitutional ban on religious-based parties, but the proscribed **Muslim Brotherhood** nevertheless constitutes the most significant political opposition to the government. Civil society groups are officially sanctioned, but constrained in practice; trade unions and professional associations are officially sanctioned.

Recognized political parties include:

- Nasserist Arab Democratic Party; Leader Dia' ad-din Dawud
- **National Democratic Party**; Leader Pres. Hosni Muhammad Said Mubarak; the governing party, formerly the Arab Socialist Union
- **National Progressive Unionist Group** (Tagammu); Leader Khalid Muhi ad-Din
- **New Wafd Party**; Leader No'man Goma; nationalist party
- **Socialist Liberal Party**

Religious parties and groups:

- Muslim Brotherhood
- Al-Jihad
- **Takfir wal-Hijra**

Egypt has numerous NGOs and informal groups. Some of the most vocal and prominent have been the informal Popular Committees supporting the Palestinian and Iraqi peoples and fighting against US aggression.

History

A unified kingdom first arose along the Nile in 3000–4000 BC and a series of dynasties ruled in Egypt for the next three millenniums. The last native dynasty fell to the Persians in 341 BC, who in turn were replaced, in succession, by the Greeks, Romans, and Byzantines. It was the Arabs who introduced **Islam** and the Arabic language in the 7th century and who ruled for the next six centuries. A local military caste, the Mamluks, took control in about 1250 and continued to govern after the conquest of Egypt by the Ottoman Turks in 1517. Following the completion of the Suez Canal in 1869, Egypt became an important world transportation hub, but also fell heavily into **debt**. Ostensibly to protect its investments, Britain seized control of Egypt's government in 1882, but nominal allegiance to the Ottoman Empire continued until 1914. Partially independent from the United Kingdom in 1922, Egypt acquired full sovereignty following the Second World War. In 1951 the Egyptian government abrogated the 1936 treaty with Britain and British troops occupied the Canal Zone. In 1952 Gen. **Muhammad Neguib** and Col **Gamal Abdel Nasser** seized power, ousting King **Farouk** in a military coup. In 1954

Nasser took full control. An Anglo-Egyptian agreement on the Canal Zone stipulated that the British base was to be evacuated within 20 months. In January 1956 Britain granted **independence** to Sudan in part as a move to pre-empt any union between Egypt and Sudan. The **World Bank**, the USA and Britain withdrew their offer of aid for the construction of the Aswan High Dam; instead the USSR offered to build it. The completion of the Aswan High Dam in 1971 and resultant Lake Nasser only increased the significance of the Nile in the **agriculture** and ecology of Egypt. A rapidly growing population, limited arable land, and dependence on the Nile all continue to create constraints and pressures. The government has struggled to prepare the economy for the new millennium through economic reform and massive investment in communications and physical infrastructure.

International relations
Egypt and Sudan each claim to administer triangular areas which extend north and south of the 1899 Treaty boundary along the 22nd parallel (in the north, the 'Hala'ib Triangle' is the largest, comprising 20,580 sq km); in 2001 the two states agreed to discuss an 'area of integration' and to withdraw military forces in the overlapping areas.

Egypt, economy

Egypt has the fifth largest economy in the Middle East (after Saudi Arabia, Turkey, Iran and Israel), with a gross national product of US $98,500m. Egypt improved its macroeconomic performance throughout most of the last decade by following the advice of the **International Monetary Fund** on fiscal, monetary and structural reform policies. As a result, it managed to bring inflation under control, reduce budget deficits and attract increased foreign investment. In the past three years, however, the pace of reform has slackened, and excessive spending on national infrastructure projects has widened budget deficits again. Lower foreign-exchange earnings since 1998 have resulted in pressure on the Egyptian pound and periodic dollar shortages. Islamist terrorist acts have had a negative impact on tourism. The country is dependent on imported technology. Monetary pressures have increased since 11 September 2001 because of declines in tourism, **Suez Canal** tolls, and exports, and Egypt has devalued the pound several times. The development of a **natural gas** export market is a major positive element of future prospects for growth. Other strengths include **oil** resources, a well-developed tourist industry, remittances from Egyptians working in the Gulf, Suez Canal tolls, **cotton**, light industry and manufacturing.

Egyptian Arab Socialist Party

Centrist party established by the **Sadat** regime in 1976, after a decision to 'open up' Egyptian politics. Its leader was Abu Wafa, who was related by marriage to Sadat. In 1978 it was renamed the **National Democratic Party**. **Hosni Muhammad Said**

Mubarak became its secretary-general, a post he retained on succeeding Sadat as President.

Egyptian Islamic Jihad

Egyptian Islamic extremist group active since the late 1970s. The original Jihad was responsible for the assassination in 1981 of Egyptian President **Anwar es-Sadat**. Led by **Ayman az-Zawahiri**, it sent fighters to Afghanistan and contributed significantly to the operations against Soviet troops and the Afghan army; it was part of the group that came to be known as the 'Arab Afghans'during the war in Afghanistan, and afterwards. In 1988, it linked up with al-Qa'ida and thereafter maintained links with that organization. It claimed responsibility for the attempted assassinations of interior minister Hassan al-Alfi in August 1993 and Prime Minister Atef Sidqi in November 1993. Historically Egyptian Islamic Jihad operated in the Cairo area, but most of its network is outside of Egypt, in Yemen, Afghanistan, Pakistan, Lebanon and the United Kingdom, among other places. It has not conducted an attack inside Egypt since 1993 and has never targeted foreign tourists there. It was responsible for the bombing of the Egyptian embassy in Islamabad, Pakistan, in 1995; and in 1998 an attempted attack against the US embassy in Albania by the organization was thwarted. It reportedly merged with al-Qa'ida in June 2001, but retained a capability to conduct independent operations. Egyptian Islamic Jihad's primary goals are to overthrow the Egyptian government and replace it with an Islamic state; and to attack US and Israeli interests in Egypt and abroad. Historically it has specialized in armed attacks against high-level Egyptian government personnel, including cabinet ministers; and car bombings against official US and Egyptian facilities. The Egyptian government claims that Iran supports the Jihad.

Egyptian-Israeli Peace Treaty

Treaty between Egypt and Israel, signed in March 1979, following the Camp David Agreements. The Treaty established a linkage between peace with Egypt and Palestinian autonomy. Though it was not fully implemented, the principle of recognition of the rights of Palestinians as well as that of the return of all territories implicit in the Treaty greatly influenced subsequent negotiations with the Palestinians and with Syria. On the other hand, Egypt was expelled from the **Arab League** and financial and economic assistance to Egypt from other Arab states was cancelled. Diplomatic relations were severed, with only Sudan, Somalia and Oman (all having a continuing dependence on Egypt) refusing to join in Egypt's effective exclusion. **Sadat**'s political and economic strategy, designed to bring Egypt more fully within the orbit of the USA and introduce economic reforms, also exposed him to opposition from within the country. It has been suggested that Sadat's assassination in 1981 was the most significant consequence of the Egyptian-Israeli Peace Treaty.

Energy

Algeria is the largest producer of energy in Africa, ranking 15th in the world, with output of 150m. metric tons of **oil** equivalent (higher than the United Arab Emirates, Iraq, Kuwait or Kazakhstan). Libya is the next largest, ranking 30th in the world, with output of 74m. tons of oil equivalent. Morocco is a high energy importer (and also the sixth most efficient user of energy in the world) and so too is South Africa. Among the least efficient African users of energy are Nigeria and Zambia (joint second least efficient, in world terms, after Uzbekistan). Algeria is one of the lowest energy importers in the world. The Democratic Republic of the Congo has tremendous potential as a producer of hydro-power, but little of this potential is currently being harnessed. Many African states (particularly the generally poor Sahelian states) have a high potential for solar power production, but, again, minimal existing capacity.

Equatorial Customs Union

Created in June 1959, but subsequently replaced by the **Union douanière et économique de l'Afrique centrale**.

Equatorial Guinea

The Republic of Equatorial Guinea consists of the islands of **Bioko** (formerly Fernando Póo and subsequently renamed Macías Nguema Biyogo under the regime of President Macías), Corisco, Great Elobey, Little Elobey and Annobón (previously known also as **Pagalu**), and the mainland region of **Río Muni** (previously known also as Mbini) on the west coast of Africa.

Cameroon lies to the north and Gabon to the east and south of Río Muni, while Bioko lies off shore from Cameroon and Nigeria. The small island of Annobón lies far to the south, beyond the islands of São Tomé and Príncipe. The area of the country, in total, is 28,051 sq km. At mid-2003 the population was estimated at 494,000. The official languages are Spanish and French. In Río Muni the Fang language is spoken, as well as those of coastal tribes such as the Combe, Balemke and Bujeba. Bubi is the indigenous language on Bioko, although Fang is also widely used, and Ibo is spoken by the resident Nigerian population. An estimated 90% of the population are adherents of the Roman Catholic Church, although traditional forms of worship are also followed. The capital is Malabo (formerly Santa Isabel).

Political profile

The Constitution that was approved by a national referendum on 16 November 1991 and amended in January 1995 provides for a plural political system and for a legislative House of Representatives (Cámara de Representantes del Pueblo). The term of the President is seven years, renewable on an indefinite number of occasions. The Cámara de Representantes serves for a term of five years. Both the President and the Cámara de Representantes are directly elected by universal adult suffrage. The President appoints a Council of Ministers, headed by a Prime Minister.

The President, Gen. (Teodoro) Obiang Nguema Mbasogo, first assumed office on 25 August 1979. He was elected as President on 25 June 1989, and re-elected on 25 February 1996; and, unopposed, on 15 December 2002, when he received 97.1% of votes cast following the withdrawal from the presidential contest of all other candidates.

As the result of a general election to the Cámara de Representantes del Pueblo held on 25 April 2004 the Partido Democrático de Guinea Ecuatorial (PDGE—Democratic Party of Equatorial Guinea) won 68 legislative seats, the Democratic opposition (a coalition of eight parties allied to President Obiang Nguema, including the Convención Socialdemocrática Popular (CSDP—Popular Social Democratic Convention), the Partido de la Convergencia Social Democráta (PCSD—Social Democrat Convergence Party) and the Unión Popular (UP—Popular Union)) 30 seats, and the Convergencia para la Democracia Social (CPDS—Convergence for Social Democracy) two seats. In June President Obiang Nguema appointed a new PDGE-dominated Council of Ministers, headed by Miguel Abia Biteo Boricó. In April 2005 Boricó remained Prime Minister of a Council of Ministers in which the PGCE, the Convención Liberal Democrática (CLD—Liberal Democrat Convention) and the Unión Democrática y Social de Guinea Ecuatorial (UDS—Democratic and Social Union of Equatorial Guinea) were represented.

History

In 1959 Spanish Guinea was awarded a status similar to that of the provinces of metropolitan Spain, including the right to return locally elected Equato-Guinean representatives to the Spanish parliament. Spanish Guinea achieved **independence** from Spain in March 1968 and became the Republic of Equatorial Guinea. Following multi-party elections, President Francisco Macías Nguema swiftly established absolute power. In 1970 he merged all political parties into the Partido Unico Nacional de los Trabajadores (PUNT—Sole National Workers' Party), and in 1972 assumed the title of President for Life. Up to one-third of the population fled the regime of Macías Nguema, including most of the skilled and trained workforce, and the economy collapsed. Relations with Spain deteriorated and Equatorial Guinea became dependent upon Eastern bloc countries for economic and military support. (Teodoro) Obiang Nguema Mbasogo, Francisco Nguema's nephew and commander of the National Guard, seized power in a coup in August 1979. Macías was arrested, tried and executed.

At first Obiang exercised power by means of the army. However, pressure from exiled political groups and an attempted coup in April 1981, combined with the country's need for foreign assistance, forced Obiang to grant some political concessions. A new constitution was approved by referendum in 1981. In legislative elections that were held in August 1983 voters were able to return representatives, from a total of 41 candidates, all nominated by the President, to a legislature that had no independent powers. In 1986, in response to a third attempted coup, President Obiang Nguema launched the PDGE, which was financed by obligatory levies on all wages and salaries. Legislative elections were held in July 1988 but were flawed. Another military coup was allegedly attempted in August. In June 1989 the first presidential election since 1968 was held, in which Obiang, the sole candidate, received 99.2% of the votes. In 1991, following international pressure and a referendum, President Obiang accepted the principle of multi-party **democracy**. A referendum held in November approved a new constitution that provided for a multi-party political system. This led to a transitional government in January 1992, but Obiang declared that legislative and presidential elections would be delayed until 1993 and 1996 respectively. In March 1993 the government and opposition concluded an agreement on the holding of elections, seeking funding from the international community. Potential donors responded with a five-point list of reforms that they required before the money would be forthcoming, including the redrawing of voter lists and the establishment of an electoral commission. Although the government failed to carry out these reforms, funding was eventually provided by France and legislative elections were held in November 1993. Amidst reports of violent clashes between the government's security forces and protesters, President Obiang declared a victory for the PDGE, which occupied 68 of the 80 legislative seats. Observers pronounced the elections flawed. In December President Obiang appointed a Council of Ministers that did not include any members of the opposition. The government also announced that any political gatherings would need official authorization. Local elections were scheduled for November 1994 but were postponed to allow for a population census, which was boycotted by opposition parties. The elections eventually took place in September 1995.

In April 1995 Severo Moto Nsa, the founding leader of one of the most influential exiled opposition parties, the Partido del Progreso de Guinea Ecuatorial (PPGE—Progress Party of Equatorial Guinea), and several other opposition politicians were found guilty of treason following an alleged coup plot. All of them were sentenced to long terms of imprisonment, but in August, after much international pressure, President Obiang announced that Moto would be released on humanitarian grounds, together with 11 other political prisoners. In June 1997 the PPGE was declared illegal by presidential decree. This occurred after another reported coup plot in which Moto was alleged to have been involved. Following his arrest and release, in September Moto took refuge in Spain, where he was granted political asylum. The PDGE continues to be dominated by the President and his family, who are members of the élite minority Fang tribe. There has been much speculation about President Obiang's health and who will eventually succeed him, leading to increased rivalry within both the government and the President's family network. However, the Constitution does not limit the number of presidential terms. During the approach to the presidential election held in December 2002, the government attempted to suppress political opposition. In June 144 people, including members of opposition parties, were arrested and tried in connection with an alleged coup attempt. It has been estimated that as many as one-third of Equato-Guineans may be living in exile abroad owing to political repression during the past 20 years.

International observers criticized the conduct of the presidential election held in December 2002, in which Gen. Obiang Nguema was re-elected unopposed following the withdrawal of all other candidates from the contest.

In mid-March 2004 the government announced that a group of 15 suspected mercenaries had been arrested on suspicion of planning a *coup d'état*, which President Obiang Nguema subsequently claimed had been funded by multinational companies and organized by Moto Nsa with the collusion of the Spanish government.

Following the death in custody of one of the accused, in November the remaining 14 defendants were found guilty of involvement in the coup attempt and received lengthy custodial sentences. Although Moto Nsa denied any involvement in the affair, he was sentenced *in absentia* by the court in Malabo to 63 years' imprisonment, while Nick du Toit, a former South African special forces officer who was alleged to have been the leader of the group in Equatorial Guinea, was sentenced to 34 years' imprisonment. Human rights groups condemned the trial for grave abuses of procedure. Meanwhile, in August 66 men, who had been detained by the Zimbabwean authorities at Harare airport in mid-March on suspicion of involvement in the coup attempt, were sentenced to terms of imprisonment ranging from 12 to 16 months for contravening immigration laws. They had been acquitted of any connection with those arrested in Equatorial Guinea in March for conspiring to overthrow the Equato-Guinean government, owing to a lack of evidence. However, Simon Mann, a South African-based British security consultant and the alleged leader of the coup plot, was convicted in September of attempting illegally to procure weapons and was sentenced to seven years' imprisonment (subsequently reduced to four). Also in August, Sir Mark Thatcher (a businessman and son of the former British Prime Minister Baroness Thatcher) was arrested in Cape Town, South Africa, on suspicion of having provided financial support for the alleged coup attempt. Thatcher initially denied any involvement in the affair, but in January 2005 he admitted contravening South African anti-mercenary legislation by agreeing to finance the use of a helicopter and was fined R3m. (more than US $500,000) and given a four-year suspended sentence.

Legislative and municipal elections were held concurrently on 25 April 2004. The PDGE won 68 of the 100 seats in an expanded Cámera de Representantes del Pueblo, while a coalition of eight parties allied to Obiang Nguema, styled the 'democratic opposition', secured a further 30 seats. International observers and the CPDS, which took the remaining two seats, denounced the results as fraudulent.

The PDGE and its allies also won 237 of the 244 council seats in the country's 30 municipalities. The rate of participation by eligible voters was estimated at 97%. In mid-June Prime Minister Rivas announced the resignation of his government and

Obiang Nguema subsequently appointed a new PDGE-dominated Council of Ministers, headed by Miguel Abia Biteo Boricó, hitherto Minister of State for Parliamentary Relations and Judicial Affairs.

Meanwhile, in May 2004 the authorities claimed to have averted another attempt to overthrow the government (this time originating in Gabon) and linked it to an opposition politician exiled in the USA since the 1970s. Five people were killed and five more captured by Equato-Guinean security forces following an attack on a military garrison on the island of Corisco. In response to this suspected coup attempt there followed several arrests in Bata and Libreville, Gabon, of persons linked to the PPGE.

In April 2005, the former opposition leader, Severo Moto, now in exile, was reported missing, prompting speculation that he had been murdered.

International relations

In September 2000 Equatorial Guinea and Nigeria achieved a resolution of a 10-year dispute between them over the demarcation of their maritime border in the **oil**-rich waters of the Gulf of Guinea. The agreement is likely to boost the exploitation of deep-water oil reserves located between Bioko Island and the Niger delta. Equatorial Guinea has also finalized negotiations with São Tomé and Príncipe over territorial waters.

Following a suspension in diplomatic relations between Spain and Equatorial Guinea during Macías's rule, Spain has revived its influence in the country. However, Equatorial Guinea has gradually shifted towards its Francophone neighbours within the **Communauté économique et monétaire de l'Afrique centrale (CEMAC—Economic and Monetary Community of Central Africa)**, and towards France itself. Owing to the volume of Equatorial Guinea's oil output, the USA has become the country's single largest foreign investor.

Equatorial Guinea, economy

In 2001, according to estimates by the **World Bank**, Equatorial Guinea's gross national income (GNI), measured at average 1999–2001 prices, was US $454m., equivalent to $930 per head. During 1990–2003, it was estimated, the population increased at an average annual rate of 2.6%, while gross domestic product (GDP) per head increased, in real terms, by an average of 17.7% per year. Overall GDP increased, in real terms, at an average annual rate of 20.7% in 1990–2003. Real GDP increased by 15.6% in 2003. The rate of inflation averaged 7.5% per year in 1990–98. The annual average rate of inflation was 7.5% in 2002 and an estimated 7.3% in 2003. Equatorial Guinea's major trading partners are the USA, Spain, France, Cameroon, the People's Republic of China, Japan and the United Kingdom. The national currency is the franc de la Coopération financière en Afrique centrale (CFA—see the **Franc Zone**). In 2004 the average exchange rate was US $1 = 528.285 francs CFA.

During the 1980s the economy of Equatorial Guinea was mainly agricultural. **Cocoa** and **coffee** were the main agricultural exports and the coffee sector remains a key sector. Timber was also an important source of foreign exchange in the 1980s. The decline in the terms of trade that occurred from the early 1990s, however, took their toll on the main exports. Today, none the less, Equatorial Guinea is one of the fastest growing economies in the world due to its recently discovered reserves of **oil** and **natural gas**. In 1984 the offshore Alba gas and condensate field was discovered by the Spanish company Repsol on behalf of Empresa Guineano-Española de Petróleos (Gepsa), a joint venture between the government and Repsol Production. The Equato-Guinean petroleum fields were also found to contain considerable reserves of natural gas. Initially, Equatorial Guinea was thought to have gas reserves of more than 110,000m. cu m. Its oil reserves have been estimated at 1,100m. barrels, and this figure is likely to rise further as a result of new discoveries. In February 1988 the US companies CMS Energy and Samedan Oil signed an agreement with the government to construct a petrochemical plant near Malabo, which has been forecast to generate as much as $300,000 per day in the coming years. The expansion of the petroleum sector gave rise to dramatic growth, of about 71.2%, in real terms, in GDP in 1997, of 22% in 1998 and of 15% in 1999. The contribution of the petroleum sector to total GDP was 17.9% in 1995, and rose to an estimated 61.8% in 1998. In 1996 67.7% of export earnings were derived from the petroleum sector, and the proportion rose to an estimated 90% in 2000. In 2001 the government instituted Guinea Ecuatorial de Petróleo (GEPetrol) in order to safeguard the country's interests in the sector. In 2002 oilfields were placed under state control. By 2002 petrochemicals had become the country's most valuable asset and Equatorial Guinea is forecast to become the third largest oil producer in **sub-Saharan Afric**a by about 2010, after Nigeria and Angola. It is thought that reserves are sufficient to last for another 10–20 years at current rates of production.

In theory, Equatorial Guinea should be one of the richest countries in sub-Saharan Africa, with a population of only 500,000 and oil revenues that totalled some $500m. in 2003. In reality, it ranks lowest in terms of the UN's human development indicators. Most of the revenue from the petroleum sector has apparently accrued to institutions under the control of the highest level of government and the impressive growth in GDP detailed above conceals stagnation in the rest of the economy and a wide **poverty** gap. Timber and **agriculture** are minor sources of exports. One of the biggest constraints on improved economic performance is the lack of educated or skilled personnel in all sectors of the economy that has resulted from many years of failure adequately to fund the **education** system. This is unlikely to improve without political reform and a shift in public spending towards social development. Despite the wealth created by oil, 65% of the population of Equatorial Guinea live in extreme poverty. An estimated 80% of national revenue is concentrated in the hands of the ruling oligarchy.

Eritrea

The State of Eritrea, which has a coastline on the Red Sea extending for almost 1,000 km, is bounded to the north west by Sudan, to the south and west by Ethiopia, and to the south east by Djibouti. Its territory includes the Dahlak islands, a low-lying coralline archipelago off shore from Massawa.

The total area of the country is 121,144 sq km. The population was estimated at 4,141,000 at mid-2003. The major language groups in Eritrea are Afar, Bilien, Hedareb, Kunama, Nara, Rashaida, Saho, Tigre and Tigrinya. English is rapidly becoming the language of business and is the medium of instruction at secondary schools and at university. **Arabic** is also widely spoken. The population is fairly evenly divided between Tigrinya-speaking Christians (mainly Orthodox), the traditional inhabitants of the highlands, and the Muslim communities of the western lowlands, northern highlands and east coast; there are also systems of traditional belief adhered to by a small number of the population.

Political profile

On 23 May 1997 the Constituent Assembly unanimously adopted the Eritrean Constitution. A presidential regime was instituted, with the President to be elected for a maximum of two five-year terms. The President, as Head of State, has extensive powers and appoints, with the approval of the National Assembly (the legislature), the ministers, the commissioners, the Auditor-General, the President of the central bank and the judges of the Supreme Court. The President's mandate can be revoked if two-thirds of the members of the National Assembly so demand. The current President, **Issaias Afewerki**, was elected to office by the National Assembly on 8 June 1993.

Under the Constitution, 'conditional' political pluralism is authorized. In May 1997, following the adoption of the Constitution, the Constituent Assembly empowered a Transitional National Assembly (comprising the 75 members of the People's Front for Democracy and Justice (PFDJ) Central Committee, 60 members of the former Constituent Assembly and 15 representatives of Eritreans residing abroad) to act as the legislature until elections were held for a new National Assembly. Pending the election of a new National Assembly, legislative power was to be held by a Transitional National Assembly. The Cabinet is headed by the President.

History

Eritrea did not exist as a distinct region until the Italians colonized it after their defeat by Ethiopia at the Battle of Adua in 1896. During the Second World War allied forces led by the British drove the Italian forces out of Ethiopia and Eritrea. Eritrea remained under British military administration until its post-war status could be settled. In 1947 a Four Power Commission (comprising the United Kingdom, the USA, the USSR and France) reported inconclusively on the wishes of the inhabitants. In 1950 a UN Commission was similarly divided between federation (with Ethiopia) and **independence**. The UN General Assembly voted on 2 December

1950 for Eritrea's federation with Ethiopia, granting in effect domestic autonomy to Eritrea. In 1958 the Eritrean Liberation Movement (ELM) was founded as an underground movement within Ethiopia. Towards the end of 1960 the Eritrean Liberation Front (ELF) was established in Cairo, Egypt, by the Eritrean community in exile there. For more than 30 years thereafter the ELM and the ELF fought each other as bitterly as they fought the Ethiopian regime from which they sought independence. In 1962, amid allegations of bribery, Eritrea's assembly voted to dissolve the federation and merge with Ethiopia, as its 14th province. This union was opposed by the Eritrean liberation movements.

In 1974 a mass uprising in Ethiopia led to the overthrow of the regime of **Haile Selassie** and the establishment of a 'revolutionary' military government, known as the '**Dergue**', with Haile Mariam Mengistu as Head of State. The new government was committed to the consolidation of the Ethiopian state and to the elimination of separatist movements. Fighting between the Ethiopian armed forces and the various (Eritrean, Tigrayan, Ogaden) separatist movements escalated greatly after 1974. The Eritrean liberation movement as a whole continued to struggle against the Ethiopian state with increasing success. By the end of 1977 all but five Eritrean towns were under the control of the 'liberation forces'. However, there was little progress in bringing together the ELF and the Eritrean People's Liberation Front (EPLF, which had been formed in 1970 as the Eritrean Popular Liberation Forces), each of which sought supremacy of the Eritrean liberation movement.

From 1981, when it virtually destroyed the ELF as a military force, the EPLF became, in effect, the principal liberation movement in Eritrea.

The war continued, with neither side achieving any decisive advantage until 1988, when the EPLF, having gained substantial ground, repulsed a major Ethiopian counter-offensive, inflicting devastating losses on the Ethiopian armed forces. Eventually, in mid-1991, the regime of Mengistu was overthrown by the Ethiopian Peoples' Revolutionary Democratic Front (EPRDF). At the same time as the EPRDF entered the Ethiopian capital, Addis Ababa, the EPLF entered Asmara, capital of Eritrea, and formed the provisional government of Eritrea.

Between May 1991 and the referendum that was held two years later, the EPLF consolidated its control by suppressing its actual and potential opponents. The referendum held in April 1993 which presented voters with a choice between continued association with Ethiopia or independence, was to decide the status of Eritrea. More than 90% of eligible voters participated in the referendum, 99.8% of them opting in favour of independence. On 27 April 1993 Issaias Afewerki, the head of the EPLF and secretary-general of the provisional government, declared Eritrea to be a sovereign and independent state. Ethiopia recognized Eritrea on 2 May 1993.

Following independence the Eritrean government declared a four-year transitional period, at the end of which democratic elections were to be held. During this transitional period, the People's Front for Democracy and Justice (PFDJ), which was formed from the EPLF, was to be responsible for running the country. A draft constitution was ratified by the National Assembly in 1997, but most of its provisions have yet to enacted. Elections were due to be held in 1997, but the government had made no progress in this respect by the time that conflict broke out with Ethiopia, over **borders**. Minor clashes during 1997 escalated into a more serious, if intermittent, military confrontation with Ethiopia that continued, despite attempts to achieve a peace agreement by the **Organization of African Unity (OAU)** and at the cost of many lives and the displacement of large numbers of civilians, until 2000, when a cease-fire agreement was concluded in Algeria. The agreement provided for a permanent cessation of all hostilities, the immediate return of all prisoners of war, the demarcation of the common border by an independent commission and the establishment of a Claims Commission to assess the issues of compensation and reparations. Furthermore, both countries pledged to co-operate with an independent investigation, which aimed to determine the origins of the conflict. From July a **United Nations Mission in Ethiopia and Eritrea (UNMEE)** had been deployed as a peace-keeping force inside a temporary security zone inside Eritrea, where it was to remain until the issue of the demarcation of the border had been settled. UNMEE's mandate was subsequently extended on numerous occasions up to April 2005, when the border remained intractably disputed.

Since the conclusion of the conflict with Ethiopia internal opposition to the Eritrean regime has been increasingly openly expressed, to which the government has responded by, among other things, the mass arrest of alleged dissidents and the closure of independent newspapers, prompting international criticism, notably by the **African Union**, whose Commission on Human and Peoples' Rights has declared the Eritrean government to be 'in violation' of four articles of the African Charter.

International relations

Djibouti suspended diplomatic relations with Eritrea in November 1998, following allegations by the Eritrean authorities that it was supporting Ethiopia in the Eritrea–Ethiopia border conflict detailed above. The two countries re-established diplomatic relations in March 2000, following Libyan mediation. The quality of Eritrea's relations with Sudan has fluctuated since the mid-1990s, but they have generally been characterized by mutual recriminations, in particular in respect of alleged support granted by both sides to opponents of their respective regimes. In December 2003 President **al-Bashir** of Sudan accused Eritrea of arming and training rebels in the **Darfur** region of Sudan and maintained that Eritrea was a destabilizing force in the region. Eritrea refuted the allegations. A dispute with Yemen concerning sovereignty over three Red Sea islands—Greater and Lesser Hanish and Zuquar—was resolved by an international tribunal in 1998.

Eritrea, economy

In 2003, according to estimates by the **World Bank**, Eritrea's gross national income (GNI), measured at average 2001–03 prices, was US $851m., equivalent to $190 per head (or $1,110 per head on an international purchasing-power parity basis). During 1990–2003, it was estimated, the population increased at an average annual rate of 2.6%, while gross domestic product (GDP) per head increased, in real terms, by an average of 2.4% per year during 1992–2003.

Overall GDP increased, in real terms, at an average annual rate of 5.1% in 1992–2003; growth in 2003 was 5.0%. The annual rate of inflation averaged 8.9% in 1996–2002. In 2001 Eritrea's principal trading partners (excluding suppliers of petroleum) were Italy, Saudi Arabia, the United Arab Emirates and Sudan. The national currency is the nakfa. At March 2005 the exchange rate was US $1 = 15 nakfa.

Since **independence** in 1993 Eritrea has faced the same economic problems that confront many other small, poor African countries. The economy is largely based on subsistence **agriculture**, in which 80% of the population is engaged. The damage that resulted from Ethiopia's offensive into northern Eritrea in May 2000 included the loss of livestock worth $225m., and also prevented the planting of crops in Eritrea's most productive region, causing food production to fall by 62%. Erratic rainfall and the delayed demobilization of agriculturalists from the armed forces has continued to impede cereal production and restrained growth in 2002–04. Even during the war, however, Eritrea was able to develop its transportation infrastructure. Since the war ended the government has taken firm control of the economy, expanding the use of the military and party-owned businesses to complete the country's development agenda.

The government has embarked on a demobilization and reintegration programme that aims to return soldiers to civilian life. Of the 1.1m. persons internally displaced by the recent war and affected by **drought**, about 48,000 remain in camps. A decade of progress has been reversed, and the economic and social damage caused by the conflict is significant.

Under a Recovery and Rehabilitation Programme initiated in 1993, emphasis was placed on improving agricultural productivity, promoting export-oriented industries, developing financial and tourism services, and restructuring the public administration. In November 1997 the government introduced the nakfa as the national currency in place of the Ethiopian birr. Trade with Ethiopia, which had previously provided markets for two-thirds of Eritrean exports, virtually ceased. Eritrea suffered severe drought and food shortages during 2003, with crop production at approximately one-quarter of its average level at mid-year. By early 2004 it was estimated that some 1.9m. Eritreans were in need of humanitarian assistance.

Eritrea is confronted by a severe shortage of foreign exchange shortage. Gross international reserves are insufficient to cover even one month's worth of imports. Food and other humanitarian assistance is needed in the near term because of the continued effects of the recent war and the most severe drought for more than a decade.

Ethiopia, Federal Democratic Republic of

The Federal Democratic Republic of Ethiopia is 1,133,380 km in area (twice the size of France) and has borders with Djibouti, Eritrea, Kenya, Somalia and Sudan. It is completely land-locked. For administrative purposes, the country is divided into nine regional states and two chartered cities—Addis Ababa, the capital, and Dire Dawa. At mid-2002 the population was estimated at 67,220,000; Ethiopia is thus one of the three most populous African countries (the other two are Nigeria and Egypt). The population is multi-ethnic; the major groups are the Oromo (40%), Amhara and Tigrean (32%), Sidamo (9%), Shankella (6%), Somali (6%), Afar (4%) and Gurage (2%). The official language is Amharic, but many other local languages, including Tigrinya, Oromigna, Guaragigna, Somali and **Arabic**, are also spoken. The Ethiopian Orthodox (Tewahido) Church, an ancient Christian sect, has a wide following in the north and on the southern plateau. In much of the south and east the inhabitants include Muslims and followers of animist beliefs.

Political profile

According to the Constitution adopted in 1994, the Head of State is the President, the candidate for which office is nominated by the House of People's Representatives. The nominee is deemed to have been elected if a joint session of the House of People's Representatives and the House of the Federation approves his candidacy by a two-thirds' majority vote. The term of the President is six years and no incumbent may serve more than two terms. The President fulfils mainly ceremonial functions, executive power being the preserve of the Prime Minister—who is elected by the House of People's Representatives—who appoints the Council of Ministers (subject to approval by the legislature). Lt Girma Wolde Giorgis was elected as President on 8 October 2001.

The legislature (Federal Parliamentary Assembly) comprises an upper house, the House of the Federation (Yefedereshn Mekir Bet), with 108 seats (members are selected by state assemblies and are drawn one each from 22 minority nationalities and one from each professional sector of the remaining nationalities, and serve for a period of five years), and a lower house of no more than 550 directly elected representatives, the House of People's Representatives (Yehizbtewekayoch Mekir Bet), who are also elected for a five-year term. Following the general election held on 15 May 2005, the distribution of seats in the House of People's Representatives was as follows: Ethiopian People's Revolutionary Democratic Front (EPRDF), 327; Coalition for Unity and Democracy (CUD), 109; United Ethiopian Democratic Forces (UEDF), 52; Oromo Federalist Democratic Movement (OFDM), 11; Somali People's Democratic Party (SPDP), 23; Benishangul Gumuz People's Democratic Unity Front (BGPDUF), 8; Afar National Democratic Party (ANDP), 8; Gambela People's Democratic Movement, (GPDM), 1; Sheko-Majenger People's Democratic Unity Organization (SMPDUO), 1; Harari National League (HNL), 1; Argoba National Democratic Organization (ANDO), 1; Independent, 1. The result in one constituency in Somali Regional State remained to be declared in August 2005. The EPRDF is an alliance of the Amhara National Democratic Movement (ANDM), the Oromo People's Democratic Organization (OPDO) and the Tigrai People's Liberation Front (TPLF). The chairman of the EPRDF, **Meles Zenawi**, was elected as Prime Minister in August 1995 and remained as Premier in April 2005.

History

Ethiopia is the oldest independent country in Africa. Even in the 19th century the ancient Ethiopian kingdom retained its **independence**, together with a certain immunity to the modernizing trends that accompanied **colonialism**. In 1935 Italy, dissatisfied with its part of **Somaliland**, exploited an incident at Wal Wal in the disputed Ogaden to conquer Ethiopia. Subjected for only five years in the 20th century (1936–41) to foreign (Italian) rule—when it became **Abyssinia**—Ethiopia resumed its independence, following the defeat of Italy in 1941, under Emperor **Haile Selassie**, who had first ascended the throne in 1930. In 1959 an international conference held in Oslo, Norway, attempted to resolve the issue of the Ethiopian-Somali frontier by producing a compromise that was agreeable to neither side. In 1960 Italian Somaliland, to which Italy had returned in 1950 to administer a 10-year trusteeship, became independent.

Haile Selassie remained in power in Ethiopia until 1974, when, having been pressed, and refused, to abdicate as Emperor, he was overthrown by a group of army officers. With the exception of the period of Italian rule in 1936–41, he had ruled Ethiopia since 1930. He was later to die in prison.

The mutiny was followed by the formation (in 1974) of the Provisional Military Administrative Council (PMAC)—a committee known as the '**Dergue**'—which now took power. The Dergue was supported by the USSR and Cuba and espoused a form of state **socialism**. The regime survived a series of conflicts with regional minority groups, including the **Somalis** and Eritreans, the Tigreans and the **Oromo**-speaking peoples of the south, all of whom were now struggling for self-determination and independence from Ethiopia. Col Mengistu Haile Mariam achieved ascendancy in the country in 1977. His authoritarian Marxist regime held power for almost 15 years before it was overthrown by the EPRDF in May 1991. Elections for a transitional government were held in June 1992.

Elections to a Constituent Assembly were conducted in Ethiopia in June 1994, in which the EPRDF won 484 of the 547 seats. The Constituent Assembly was inaugurated in October to debate a draft constitution, which it ratified in December. The new Constitution provided for the establishment of a federal government and the division of the country (renamed the Federal Democratic Republic of Ethiopia) into nine states and two chartered cities. It provided for regional autonomy, including the right of secession. A new legislature, the Federal Parliamentary Assembly, was to be established, comprising two chambers (see above).

The EPRDF and its allies won an overwhelming victory in elections to the House of People's Representatives and state assemblies in May 1995. Most opposition parties boycotted the polls. International observers accepted that the elections were conducted in a largely free and fair manner.

On 21 August 1995 legislative power was transferred from the transitional Council of Representatives to the Federal Parliamentary Assembly. On 22 August the transitional administration was terminated, and the country's new Constitution and designation as the Federal Democratic Republic of Ethiopia were formally instituted. Later that day Dr Negasso Gidada (formerly the Minister of Information), a member of the Oromo People's Democratic Organization (OPDO, which was in alliance with the EPRDF) and the nominee of the EPRDF, was elected President of the Federal Republic. A new Prime Minister, ex-President Meles Zenawi, was elected from among the members of the House of People's Representatives; Meles nominated a 17-member Council of Ministers, which was duly approved by the Federal Parliamentary Assembly.

Elections to the House of People's Representatives and the House of the Federation were held concurrently on 14 May 2000, except in the Somali regional state, where voting was postponed until 31 August, owing to severe **drought**. Voting was also repeated in several constituencies after accusations of irregularities were upheld by the National Electoral Board (NEB). According to results published by the NEB in September, the OPDO won the largest number of seats in the House of People's Representatives, taking 178 of the 546 available. The OPDO's major partners in the EPRDF coalition, the Amhara National Democratic Movement (as the EPDM had been renamed in 1994) and the TPLF, gained 134 and 38 seats, respectively, while a number of smaller groups in the EPRDF won a further 19 seats. The EPRDF thus comfortably retained its large majority in the lower chamber. In mid-October the new legislature was sworn in, and Meles was re-elected as Prime Minister.

On 8 October 2001 Lt Girma Wolde Giorgis, a former president of the parliament during Haile Selassie's reign and a member of the House of People's Representatives since 1995, was elected by the legislature to replace Gidada as President of Ethiopia.

During 2003 a number of new political parties and coalition organizations were formed with the intention of challenging the ruling EPRDF at the legislative elections scheduled for mid-2005. Meles also intended to reorganize the EPRDF, in order to transform it into a national, non-ethnic party, of which the TPLF, the ANDM and the OPDO would form regional branches. The most significant of the new groupings were the United Ethiopian Democratic Party, which was created by the merger of the Ethiopian Democratic Unity Party and the Ethiopian Democratic Party, and the United Ethiopian Democratic Forces (UEDF), under the leadership of Dr Beyene Petros.

In January 2004 Petros wrote to the Prime Minister requesting that he review and reform the electoral law and begin negotiations, with the aim of legalizing all opposition parties. In November the ruling EPRDF held its first ever meeting with opposition groups and announced its intention to review existing electoral legislation. However, despite unveiling a number of amendments to the electoral law in January 2005, which included granting opposition groups access to state-controlled media and the provision for opposition parties to call meetings and organize demonstrations, the government did not adhere to earlier pledges to alter the composition of the NEB.

International relations

Ethiopia's relations with Somalia have been problematic since the Ogaden War of 1977–78. In the 2000s they have generally been characterized by, on the hand, accusations by the Somali authorities that Ethiopia has lent support to their opponents; and, on the other, claims by Ethiopia that Somalia has harboured terrorist organizations. Relations with Sudan have generally improved since the mid-1980s, when full diplomatic ties were restored. In 2004 the two countries finalized (on paper) the demarcation of their common border. Relations with Kenya deteriorated during late 2000 and early 2001 after it was reported that some 50 Kenyans had been killed by Ethiopian militia forces. In January 2001 the two countries agreed to take steps to end disputes along their common border.

Ethiopia was at war with Eritrea from May 1998 until December 2000, when a cease-fire agreement was concluded. The agreement provided for a permanent cessation of all hostilities, the immediate return of all prisoners of war, the demarcation of the common border by an independent commission and the establishment of a Claims Commission to assess the issues of compensation and reparations. Furthermore, both countries pledged to co-operate with an independent investigation, which aimed to determine the origins of the conflict. From July a **United Nations Mission in Ethiopia and Eritrea (UNMEE)** had been deployed as a peace-keeping force inside a temporary security zone inside Eritrea, where it was to remain until the issue of the demarcation of the border had been settled. UNMEE's mandate was subsequently extended on numerous occasions up to April 2005, when the border remained intractably disputed.

Ethiopia, economy

In 2003, according to estimates by the **World Bank**, Ethiopia's gross national income (GNI), measured at average 2001–03 prices, was US $6,583m., equivalent to $90 per head (or $710 per head on an international purchasing-power parity basis): one of the lowest recorded levels of GNI per head for any country in the world. During 1990–2003, it was estimated, the population increased at an average annual rate of 2.3%, while gross domestic product (GDP) per head increased, in real terms, by an average of 0.6% per year. Overall GDP increased, in real terms, at an average annual rate of 2.8% during 1990–2003; it grew by 1.9% in 2002, but decreased by 3.9% in 2003. The annual rate of inflation averaged 2.2% in 1995–2003. Consumer prices increased by 1.5% in 2002, and by 17.8% in 2003. The **agriculture** and livestock sectors dominate the economy. In 2002 the principal source of imports was the People's Republic of China; other major suppliers were Italy, the USA, the United Arab Emirates, Japan, Saudi Arabia, Germany and India. The principal markets for exports in that year were Djibouti, Germany, Italy, Japan and Saudi Arabia. The national currency is the birr. At 29 October 2004 the exchange rate was US $1 = 8.647 birr.

With a population of around 70m., Ethiopia is by far the largest of the countries that rank among the final 10 in the UN Human Development Index. Ethiopia ranks 170th out of 177 countries in the Index, and is thus one of the poorest countries in the world. Real GDP per caput is among the lowest in the world, and only about one fifth of the sub-Saharan African average. In 1995 31.3% of the population lived on less than $1 per day, and as many as 76.4% on less than $2 per day. Rural Ethiopia is exceptionally poor and more than 85% of Ethiopians are subsistence farmers. Ethiopia has a mixed farming economy, raising both crops and animals. The major crops are grains, mainly teff, which is native to Ethiopia, wheat, barley, sorghum, millet and maize. **Coffee** accounts for a large share of merchandise exports. Manufacturing makes only a minor contribution to the Ethiopian economy. The country has one of the lowest rates of exports per caput in the world. The economy was especially badly affected by the collapse in the world price of coffee, traditionally Ethiopia's largest export. In addition to this vulnerability to fluctuations in the international price of coffee, millions of Ethiopians are also frequently affected by **drought**-induced **famine**.

In spite of the war with Eritrea, growth in GDP averaged 5.2% in 1993–2000. The proportion of the population living in absolute poverty has fallen slightly, from 45.5% in 1996 to 44.2% in 2000, according to the **International Monetary Fund**. In 2003, however, in addition to the low price of coffee, economic growth was also badly affected by a sharp fall in agricultural production that resulted from drought in 2002. An estimated 12.5m. people suffered food shortages. However, the economy has benefited from the combination of a commitment to sound macroeconomic policies, reduced military expenditure and **debt relief** under the **Highly Indebted Poor Countries initiative**, together with improved rains and a better harvest in 2003 and 2004. In 2003–05 rains have been good and the economy grew at a rate of more than 10% in 2004. None the less, the UN reported that 2.2m. Ethiopians would require emergency food assistance in 2005.

Ethnic group(s) and ethnicity

Many African states are characterized by societies of considerable ethnic diversity. That is to say that within the boundaries of the nation state and within the broader structure of 'national' identity, many people regard themselves as members of more specific groups—defined essentially by linguistic, cultural and/or tribal affiliations—which could be referred to as 'ethnic groups'. This form of affiliation is called 'ethnicity'. These groups are sometimes referred to as 'primordial groups' in the sense that loyalties to them often outweigh those to the nation state and its values and priorities. Examples in the region would include large groups (which some might say constitute 'peoples' or even 'nations'), such as the **Ibo**, the **Hausa** and the **Yoruba** (in Nigeria), and also groups which are to be found across several states, such as the **Berbers** of the **Maghreb** (found in Mauritania, Morocco, Algeria, Tunisia and Libya), the Tuareg of the Sahara (found in Libya, Algeria, Niger and Mali) and the **Fulani** of West Africa (Mali, Niger, Nigeria, Chad, Central African Republic and Senegal).

Euro-Mediterranean Economic Area (EMEA)

In June 1995, the European Council endorsed a programme to reform and strengthen the Mediterranean policy of the **European Union**. It envisaged the establishment of a Euro-Mediterranean Economic Area (EMEA) preceded by a gradual liberalization of trade within the region through bilateral and regional free-trade arrangements and through structural reforms in the countries of the Mediterranean involved. The Barcelona Declaration of 1995 set the objective of achieving a Euro-Mediterranean Free Trade Area by 2010.

Euro-Mediterranean Partnership (EMP)

The 15 foreign ministers of the **European Union (EU)** met with their Mediterranean counterparts—including those of Algeria, Egypt, Morocco and Tunisia—in Barcelona, Spain, in November 1995 to launch a Euro-Mediterranean Partnership (EMP) initiative, which called for the full liberalization of non-agricultural trade among the partner countries by 2010. Libya, until 1999 subject to UN sanctions for its alleged role in the **Lockerbie** bombing, was to have observer status in the EMP. The EU supported the Barcelona Declaration with a budgetary commitment over four years (1996–99) of ECU 4,799m. (US $5,000m.) in grants to finance projects preparing for free trade as well as for other social and developmental objectives. The actual allocation for the four-year period in question, however, was only ECU 3,800m. ($3,200m.)—a sum that is probably less than that remitted annually by migrant workers from the **Maghreb** countries—and states in the region are in effect surrendering their preferential access to European agricultural markets while progressively allowing the EU free access to their markets for industrial products. The partnership also cuts across pre-existing regional groupings forged within the Mediterranean area, such as the **Arab Maghreb Union**, which united the five countries of the Maghreb (Mauritania, Morocco, Algeria, Tunisia and Libya) in a programme for economic and social integration. From the perspective of the Mediterranean 'partners', the EMP appears somewhat unequal. Participation agreements have been signed and ratified with Tunisia and Morocco; negotiations with Egypt have been completed and some of the programmed bilateral funds have been disbursed to Algeria, without formal agreements. The primary financial instrument for the implementation of the EMP is the MEDA programme. Under MEDA II (a revised version of MEDA I), a long-term strategy for the period 2000–06 was drawn up.

European Union (EU)

Since its creation, the European Union (EU) has sought to establish a special relationship with a significant number of countries in the region, through a variety of mechanisms and institutional frameworks and agreements, including the **Euro-Mediterranean Partnership**. Individual partnership agreements signed with Tunisia and Morocco have been ratified; negotiations with Egypt have been completed and some of the programmed bilateral funds have been disbursed to Algeria without any formal agreement. 'Rapid reformers' are supposed to receive greater shares of the allocated funds than the more reluctant states. Funds are in any case limited and states in the region are surrendering their preferential access to European agricultural markets while progressively allowing the EU free access to their markets for industrial products. The EU has a special relationship with **African, Caribbean and Pacific countries**, through the successive **Lomé Conventions** and the more recent framework embodied in the **Cotonou Agreement**. The EU is still the major trading partner, for both imports and exports, with Africa as a whole, although efforts are being made by many African economies to diversify their trading partners.

European Union-Mauritania

Relations between the **European Union (EU)** and Mauritania fall outside the framework of the **Euro-Mediterranean Partnership**, even though Mauritania belongs to the **Arab Maghreb Union**, all other members of which, apart from Libya, are fully involved in its various arrangements. Mauritania belongs, for the EU, in the category of **African, Caribbean and Pacific countries**, with which successive treaties and agreements have been negotiated under the **Lomé Conventions**. It is the only Arab country within this grouping.

Ewe

Major ethnic or tribal grouping extending across the borders of Ghana and Togo.

Exports

The African continent as a whole plays a minor part in global trade. In 2000 **sub-Saharan Africa** accounted for only 2% of the total value of world trade, compared with about 5% in the 1980s. Nevertheless, for the past two decades the region has exported more goods than it has imported, achieving a balance-of-trade surplus. Africa depends heavily, however, on the export of primary products, particularly minerals, for its foreign exchange. **Oil** (from Egypt, Libya and Algeria in **North Africa**, and from several countries (notably Nigeria) in West Africa, is a major export. Metals are major exports from the Central African region, as are **diamonds**. **Gold** is exported, in particular by South Africa. Many countries are heavily dependent on a single export crop (**cotton**, **cocoa**, **coffee**, groundnuts, palm oil, tea, sugar and tobacco).

The export trade is strongly oriented outside the African continent, with the Western industrialized countries currently still providing the major markets for foreign sales and accounting also for as much as 80% of imports. Export trade between African states is limited, accounting for perhaps 5% of the total. Even the relatively well established **Southern African Development Community (SADC)** conducted only 4% of its total export trade among its 14 members in 2002.

F

Failed states

A term used to refer to states whose 'national' governments are no longer able to maintain exclusive control over their territory and population. Madeleine Albright, former US Secretary of State, defined them as 'countries with a weak or non-existent central authority'. Often, in a failed state, several competing authorities exercise varying degrees of power in different regions. It is generally argued that failed states arise from the political and economic disintegration of pre-existing states, under exceptional internal or external conditions. Arguably they may be the result of failed attempts to construct new regimes under inappropriate conditions. Loretta Napoleoni has used the term 'state-shells' to refer to emerging state-like forms within failed or disintegrating states which may develop their own economic and political and military regimes. Armed groups fill what is left of 'a mere geographical expression, a black hole into which a failed polity has landed'; they gain control of regions, create their own infrastructure, regulate markets and trade flows, and even attempt to establish foreign relations with neighbouring states. Failed states, however, retain some of the outward elements of sovereignty; even if they cannot retain control of their **borders**, or of all that occurs within them, they maintain the 'footprint' of territoriality. Failed states maintain diplomacy and a degree of legitimacy. Some would argue that this distinguishes them from **collapsed states**.

Famine

Sub-Saharan Africa is widely regarded as the region in the world where acute food shortages and famine are most likely to occur. **Drought** and famine across the Sahel and in Sudan and Ethiopia in the early 1970s and the early-to-mid-1980s have become part of the global folk-memory, and are still remembered in the regions affected as devastating. It is not only in the Sahel, however, that food shortages and famine develop. Across **southern Africa** also, where drought and floods have in recent years generated natural disasters, the capacity of governments and civil society to respond effectively with food distribution and adequate relief and recovery programmes has been shown to be limited. Famine is a consequence not only of natural disasters that affect food production and the local or regional availability of food supplies, but also of the failure of governments and non-government systems of food distribution, which result in large numbers of people—usually the poorer and socially disadvantaged sections of society (and children and older people)—experiencing acute food shortage, extreme malnutrition and death. Food shortages in Zimbabwe in 2004–05 were the result of a combination of poor weather conditions, interventions in the structure of landholdings and farming systems, and the inappropriate economic policies of the government of President **Mugabe**. In 2005 severe famine occurred in Niger owing to a combination of drought and **locusts**, and the incapacity of indigenous systems and lack of government resources to cope with the almost total loss of the harvest.

Fanti

Major ethnic group or people in Ghana.

Farouk

Born in 1920, died in 1965. King of Egypt in 1936–52. Son and successor of King **Fuad** I. After a short regency period he acceded to the throne in 1937. A constitutional monarch, Farouk was frequently at odds with the **Wafd Party**, the largest Egyptian party. Because of his pro-Axis sympathies during the Second World War, Britain imposed upon him a pro-British Premier in 1942. Egypt's defeat in the Arab–Israeli War (1948–49) and Farouk's own decadent lifestyle eventually led to the military coup of 1952, headed by Abdul al-Hakim and **Gamal Abdel Nasser**. Farouk was forced to abdicate; he fled the country and found refuge abroad.

Fédération action pour la République (FAR—Action Federation for the Republic)

Political party in Chad. Supports the establishment of a federal republic.

Fernando Póo

A Spanish-controlled island in the Bight of Biafra, renamed Macías Nguema Biyogo–together with **Río Muni**, an enclave in Gabon, became the independent state of Equatorial Guinea in 1968. Now known as **Bioko**.

Fighting Islamic Group (FIG—al-Jama'a al-Islamiyyah al-Muqatilah bi-Libya)

Emerged in 1995 among Libyans who had fought against Soviet forces in Afghanistan. Declared the government of Libyan leader **Muammar al-Qaddafi** unIslamic and pledged to overthrow it in order to establish an Islamic regime. Some members maintain a strictly anti-Qaddafi focus and organize against Libyan government interests, but others are aligned with **Osama bin Laden**'s al-Qa'ida organization or are active in the international *mujahidin* network. Claimed responsibility for a failed assassination attempt against Qaddafi in 1996 and engaged Libyan security forces in armed clashes during the mid-to-late 1990s. Continues to target Libyan interests and may engage in sporadic clashes with Libyan security forces. Probably maintains a clandestine presence in Libya, but since the late 1990s many members have fled to various Middle Eastern and European countries.

Fisheries

Most of the countries of the region that have significant coastlines are involved in fishing and many of these rely to an important degree on the fisheries sector for exports as well as for domestic consumption. In many countries in the region there is also fishing in inland lakes and in rivers, which provides for local subsistence and for local markets. The importance of fisheries for rural livelihoods and for urban consumers is generally underestimated. The major concerns facing the sector are increasing pollution and over-fishing. For countries for which fisheries constitute a major sector, particularly those with an Atlantic seaboard (Morocco, **Western Sahara** and Mauritania), over-fishing by foreign fleets is the main threat.

Fon

An ethnic and linguistic group in some West African countries. In Benin the Fon and **Adja** together constitute about 40% of the population.

Forces pour l'action républicaine (FAR—Forces for Republican Action)

Political party in the Union of the Comoros. Its leader is Col Abdourazak Abdulhamid.

Forces démocratiques unies (FDU—United Democratic Forces)

Grouping of 29 political parties (in 2002) in the Republic of the Congo, established in 1994. Formerly the Forces démocratiques et patriotiques (Democratic and Patriotic Forces). Supports the government of President **Sassou-Nguesso**.

Forces nationales de libération (FNL—National Liberation Forces)

Former armed wing of the **Parti de libération du peuple hutu (Freedom Party of the Hutu People)** in Burundi.

Forces pour le salut du Congo (FSC—Forces for the Salvation of Congo)

Established in June 2000 in the Democratic Republic of the Congo by former supporters of President **Mobutu**. The leader of the FSC is Jérôme Tshishimbi.

Forum civique (FC—Civic Forum)

Political party in the Central African Republic, led by Gen. Timothée Malendoma.

Forum démocratique (FODE—Democratic Forum)

Political party in Burundi, established in November 1999. The leader of the FODE is Deogratias Baburifato.

Forum démocratique pour la modernité (FODEM—Democratic Forum for Modernity)

Political party in the Central African Republic, established in 1998. Its president is Charles Massi.

Forum pour le redressement national (FRN—Forum for National Recovery)

Political grouping in the Union of the Comoros, formed in 1994. An alliance of 12 parties.

Franc Zone

The members of the Franc Zone are Benin, Burkina Faso, Cameroon, Central African Republic, Chad, Comoros, Republic of the Congo, Côte d'Ivoire, Equatorial Guinea, the French Overseas Territories, Gabon, Guinea-Bissau, Mali, Niger, Senegal and Togo. Prior to 1 January 2002, when the transition to a single European currency (euro) was finalized, the Franc Zone also included Metropolitan France, the French Overseas Departments (French Guiana, Guadeloupe, Martinique and Réunion), the French Overseas Collectivité Départementale (Mayotte) and the French Overseas Collectivité Territoriale (St Pierre and Miquelon). The French Overseas Territory (French Polynesia) and the French Overseas Countries (New Caledonia and the Wallis and Futuna Islands) have continued to use the franc CFP (franc des Comptoirs français du Pacifique, 'French Pacific franc').

Apart from Guinea and Mauritania, all of the countries that formerly comprised French West and Equatorial Africa are members of the Franc Zone. The former West and Equatorial African territories are still grouped within the two currency areas that existed before **independence**, each group having its own variant of the CFA franc, issued by a central bank: the franc de la **Communauté Financière d'Afrique** ('franc CFA de l'Ouest'), issued by the **Banque centrale des états de l'Afrique de l'ouest (BCEAO)**, and the franc Coopération financière en Afrique centrale ('franc CFA central'), issued by the **Banque des états de l'Afrique centrale (BEAC)**.

The following states withdrew from the Franc Zone during the period 1958–73: Guinea, Tunisia, Morocco, Algeria, Mauritania and Madagascar. Equatorial Guinea, formerly a Spanish territory, joined the Franc Zone in January 1985, and Guinea-Bissau, a former Portuguese territory, joined in May 1997.

The Comoros, formerly a French Overseas Territory, did not join the Franc Zone following its unilateral declaration of independence in 1975. However, the franc CFA was used as the currency of the new state and the Institut d'émission des Comores continued to function as a Franc Zone organization. In 1976 the Comoros formally assumed membership. In July 1981 the Banque centrale des Comores replaced the Institut d'émission des Comores, establishing its own currency, the Comoros franc.

The Franc Zone operates on the basis of agreements concluded between France and each group of member countries, and the Comoros. The currencies in the Franc Zone were formerly linked with the French franc at a fixed rate of exchange. However, following the introduction of the euro (European single currency) in January 1999, within the framework of European economic and monetary union, in which France was a participant, the Franc Zone currencies were effectively linked at fixed parity to the euro (i.e. parity was based on the fixed conversion rate for the French franc and the euro). From 1 January 2002, when European economic and monetary union was finalized and the French franc withdrawn from circulation, the franc CFA, Comoros franc and franc CFP became officially pegged to the euro, at a fixed rate of exchange. (In accordance with Protocol 13 on France, appended to the 1993 Maastricht Treaty on European Union, France was permitted to continue issuing currencies in its Overseas Territories—i.e. the franc CFP—following the completion of European economic and monetary union.) All the convertability arrangements previously concluded between France and the Franc Zone remained in force. Therefore Franc Zone currencies are freely convertible into euros, at the fixed exchange rate, guaranteed by the French Treasury. Each group of member countries, and the Comoros, has its own central issuing bank, with overdraft facilities provided by the French Treasury. (The issuing authority for the French Overseas Territories is the Institut d'émission d'outre-mer, based in Paris.) Monetary reserves are held mainly in the form of euros. The BCEAO and the BEAC are authorized to hold up to 35% of their foreign exchange holdings in currencies other than the euro. Franc Zone ministers of finance normally meet twice a year to review economic and monetary co-operation. The meeting is normally attended by the French Minister of Co-operation and Francophony.

Francophone Africa

Region or countries of Africa where French remains a major spoken and written language. It includes Benin, Burkina Faso, Cameroon, Chad, Central African Republic, Côte d'Ivoire, Gabon, Mali, Niger, the Republic of the Congo, Senegal and Togo. Former French colonies in **North Africa**, such as Morocco, Algeria and Tunisia, where French is also widely written and spoken, would not normally be referred to as Francophone, as **Arabic** is the major official language in those countries.

Free Officers' Movement

Following the 1948 Palestine war, the Free Officers' Movement was formed in 1949 from a revolutionary cell within the Egyptian army, composed of élite young officers hostile to and suspicious of the prevailing political order, which called for political reforms as well as deep-seated change in the structure of Egyptian society. **Gamal Abdel Nasser** became chairman of the organization in January 1950, and Gen. **Muhammad Neguib** was elected as president in December 1951. On 23 July 1952 the Movement, led by Nasser, seized power in a bloodless revolution. King **Farouk** was forced to abdicate in favour of his son and left the country for exile in Italy. The nine men who had constituted themselves as the committee of the Movement and led the 1952 revolution were Nasser, Maj. Abd al-Hakim Amir, Lt-Col **Anwar es-Sadat**, Maj. Salah Salim, Maj. Kamal ad-Din Husayn, Wing-Commander Gamal Salim, Squadron Leader Hasan Ibrahim, Maj. Khalid Muhi ad-Din and Wing-Commander Abd al-Latif al-Baghdadi. Maj. Husayn ash-Shafii and Lt-Col Zakariyya Muhi ad-Din also joined the committee later.

Freedom Charter

The Freedom Charter was drafted and adopted at a meeting—the **Congress of the People**—convened by the **African National Congress (ANC)** in June 1955 and held in what is now a part of **Soweto** in South Africa. Three thousand delegates participated. The Charter begins: 'We, the people of South Africa, declare for all our country and the world to know: that South Africa belongs to all who live in it, black and white, and that no government can justly claim authority unless it is based on the will of the people'. Then follows a manifesto of human rights and equality combined with a vision of radical political transformation, including the following critical passage: 'The national wealth of our country, the heritage of all South Africans, shall be restored to the people; the mineral wealth beneath the soil, the banks and monopoly industry shall be transferred to the ownership of the people as a whole; all other industries and trade shall be controlled to assist the well-being of all the people; all people shall have equal rights to trade where they choose, to manufacture and to enter all trades, crafts and professions'. There was also a passage which declared that the restriction on land ownership, which had been introduced with the Land Act in 1913, that prohibited blacks from owning land outside the tiny reserves which later formed the *bantustans* or so-called 'homelands', would be ended, and that 'all the land shall be re-divided amongst those who work it'. The Freedom Charter was adopted at a special congress of the ANC in the following year and became part of the formal policy of the organization.

Freedom Front

Afrikaner separatist party in South Africa, which won three seats in the National Assembly at the 1999 elections.

French Guinea

French Guinea was the second West African state to gain **independence** (after the **Gold Coast** became Ghana in 1957). It had been a part of the great colonial territory of **French West Africa** and, after the Second World War, one of the many Associated Territories of former West and Equatorial Africa. All of these had representatives in the French National Assembly and the Council of the Republic. In 1956 the French government under Guy Mollet introduced a *loi cadre* (framework law) which was intended to lead to a substantial degree of autonomy. This was elaborated by a series of decrees in 1957, which endowed the 12 West and Equatorial African territories with assemblies elected on a common roll and with councils of government elected by the assemblies. Some African leaders, including **Sekou Touré** of Guinea, suspected the *loi cadre* of being not a stage to sovereign independence but a device to postpone it indefinitely. When Charles de Gaulle returned to power in France in 1958 he presented the African territories with a choice: autonomy within a community in which France would retain control of the main economic levers, or independence—a polite term for expulsion from the **Franc Zone**. All but Guinea chose the first option. Guinea became an independent sovereign state in October 1958, discarded by its former French masters and forced to look towards the socialist bloc for assistance. It was not long, however, before many of the other French West African states began to press for more radical change.

French Protectorate of Morocco

Established in 1912, the French Protectorate in Morocco was the formal outcome of a gradual process of intervention and infiltration which had begun during the latter part of the 19th century. It involved most of Morocco, with the exception of the north, which came under Spanish rule (as 'the Spanish Protectorate). Use of the term 'protectorate' enabled France to maintain that its interest was essentially to 'protect' the Moroccan sultanate, although it became in effect a settler colonial state, with a substantial European (mainly French) expatriate community. The Protectorate came to an end in 1956 after many decades of growing pressure from the Moroccan nationalist movement.

French West Africa

The territories in West Africa acquired by France during the latter part of the 19th century were eventually brought together administratively as French West Africa in 1895 under a governor-general. The territory eventually comprised eight separate colonies and, after 1945, the two trust territories of Togo and Cameroon. Four equatorial (central African) territories were similarly federated as French Equatorial Africa **(Afrique équatoriale française)** in 1910. Further to the north, France established protectorates over Tunisia (1880) and Morocco (1912) to add to its existing colonial territory in **North Africa**, Algeria (annexed from 1830 onwards). In 1900 French advances from Morocco in the north, from Senegal in the west and from the Congo in the south, converged at Lake Chad. During the First World War France also acquired the island of Madagascar, most of the German territory of **Kamerun** (leaving a small region which passed to the British) and half of **Togoland**, which was also previously a German possession and was divided in 1919 between France and Britain as the powers in control of neighbouring **Dahomey** and the **Gold Coast** respectively.

After the fall of France in 1940 French West Africa opted for Vichy until the invasion of north-west Africa by the USA and Britain in 1942. An attempt by the Free French and British forces to seize **Dakar**, the capital of Senegal, in 1940, failed. At a conference in Brazzaville in 1944, African representatives were promised more participation in mixed Franco-African councils, more decentralization and a wider franchise. The first French Constitution of 1946 was rejected by the French people, and the second was less far-reaching. It created the French Union, comprising the French Republic, Associated States and Associated Territories (in addition to Overseas Departments and Overseas Territories which remained part of the French Republic). All of the West African territories became Associated Territories, with representatives in the French National Assembly and the Council of the Republic. In 1956, a *loi cadre* (framework law) was approved and in 1957 this was elaborated by a series of decrees giving the Territories assemblies elected on a common roll and councils of government elected by these assemblies. Every constituency in every Territory had a majority of black voters. The Rassemblement démocratique africain (Democratic African Rally), the principal nationalist party which operated throughout French West Africa, won the ensuing elections in Guinea, **Soudan**, **Ivory Coast** and **Upper Volta**. In 1958 de Gaulle offered the Territories a choice: autonomy within a French community, or **independence**. Only Guinea chose the latter alternative. Guinea became an independent state in 1958 but was excluded from the new community of autonomous West African republics. Soon, the other Territories began to press for independence. In 1959 Senegal, Soudan, Upper Volta and Dahomey decided to federate under the name of Mali and to request independence. Upper Volta and Dahomey changed their minds under French pressure and although Senegal and Soudan persisted, the resulting federation lasted only for about two months, after which Senegal withdrew, leaving Soudan with the new name of Mali.

Frente Democrata Cristã (FDC—Christian Democrat Front)

On 16 July 2003, while President **de Menezes** was in Nigeria, a small political party, the Frente Democrata Cristã (FDC), took power in São Tomé and Príncipe in a bloodless *coup d'état*. It was claimed that the FDC had connections with the former **'Buffalo Battalion'**, a group of South African-trained mercenaries who were believed to have participated in several regional conflicts. The FDC established a **'National Salvation Junta'**. The coup was condemned by the international community, which demanded a return to civilian rule. Following successful mediation efforts, de Menezes returned in July 2003 to São Tomé, accompanied by President **Olusegun Obasanjo** of Nigeria. Under an amnesty for the coup leaders de Menezes was reinstated as President.

Frente de Libertação do Enclave de Cabinda (FLEC—Cabinda Enclave Liberation Front)

A secessionist group that has been fighting for **independence** since the 1960s. Founded in 1963, it comprises several factions, claiming forces of some 5,000 guerrilla fighters. It seeks the secession of the Cabinda province of Angola. The FLEC's constituent groups include the Frente de Libertacão do Enclave de Cabinda-Forças Armadas Cabindesas and the Frente de Libertacão do Enclave de Cabinda—Renovada (FLEC—R), which merged under the above name in September 2004.

Frente de Libertação de Moçambique (Frelimo—Mozambique Liberation Front)

An alliance formed in 1962 by Eduardo Mondlane from the different groups that had started the struggle for liberation in Mozambique in the previous year. In 1964 Frelimo launched an armed struggle against the Portuguese in Mozambique. In 1969 Mondlane was assassinated, and power passed to a triumvirate: Uriah Simanga, Marcellino dos Santos and Samora Machel, the last of whom soon emerged as the effective new leader of Frelimo. Another six years of struggle ensued before an agreement—the **Lusaka Agreement**—was reached between Frelimo and the Portuguese government. Frelimo set June 1975 as the date for Mozambique's **independence**. The Europeans in Lourenço Marques (now Maputo) briefly seized power, but the revolt failed and Mozambique duly achieved its independence in June 1975.

Frente Nacional de Libertação de Angola (FNLA)

Angolan political party, established in 1962. The FNLA's president is Alvaro Holden Roberto.

Frente Popular para la Liberación de Saguia el-Hamra y Río de Oro (Frente POLISARIO—Popular Front for the Liberation of Saguia el-Hamra and Río de Oro)

The Frente POLISARIO was established to fight for the self-determination and **independence** of the Sahrawi people in 1973, at a time when the **Western Sahara** was under Spanish rule (Spanish Sahara). In 1975 the International Court of Justice ruled that the Sahrawis had a right to self-determination and that the Frente POLISARIO was their legitimate representative. Meanwhile, Spain had agreed a programme of withdrawal from the Spanish Sahara with Morocco and Mauritania (neighbours to the north and south respectively of the territory in question), which enabled them to intervene and take possession of the territory. As the Spanish left, Morocco and Mauritania began to take over. This take-over was resisted by the Frente POLISARIO, with support from Algeria. They declared a state of their own, the **Sahrawi Arab Democratic Republic (SADR)**. However, many Sahrawis were obliged to leave their homes and flee into south-western Algeria where they established refugee camps, with the help of the government of Algeria and the **UN High Commissioner for Refugees**. For 15 years the Frente POLISARIO fought a war of liberation, first against both Morocco and Mauritania and then, after 1978, when Mauritania agreed a cease-fire and subsequent peace with the Frente POLISARIO, with Morocco alone. The armed forces of the Frente POLISARIO were known as the Sahrawi People's Liberation Army (SPLA). In 1991 the UN produced a 'peace plan' and established a UN Mission (MINURSO) to oversee the 'peace process', which led first to a cease-fire between the warring parties and then to efforts to identify and register voters for a referendum on the future of the Western Sahara. Some 15 years later the status of the Western Sahara remained unresolved; voter identification and registration proved far harder to achieve than anticipated. The mandate of the MINURSO was continually extended but it failed to resolve the many difficulties generated by the conflicting interests and demands of the two main parties to the conflict, the Moroccan government and the Frente POLISARIO. POLISARIO remains, however, the sole representative of the Sahrawi people and continues to pursue self-determination and independence.

Front d'action pour le renouveau, la démocratie et le déevelop-pement-Alafia (FARD-Alafia—Action Front for Renewal, Democracy and Development-Alafia)

Political party in Benin, founded in 1994. Its secretary-general is Daniel Tawéma.

Front des alliés pour le changement (FAC—Allies' Front for Change)

Political grouping in Cameroon, founded in 1994. An alliance of 16 opposition movements. The FAC's leader is Samuel Eboua.

Front pour la démocratie au Burundi (FRODEBU—Front for Democracy in Burundi)

Political party in Burundi, founded in 1992. Split in June 1999. FRODEBU's membership is predominantly **Hutu**. FRODEBU's chairman is Jean Minani.

Front démocratique (FD—Democratic Front)

Algerian political party, established in 1999. The FD is led by Sid-Ahmed Ghozali.

Front démocratique (FD—Democratic Front)

Political party in the Union of the Comoros, established in 1982. The FD's chairman is Moustoifa Saïd Cheikh.

Front démocratique et patriotique (FDP—Democratic Patriotic Front)

Political grouping in Cameroon, established in 1994. The FDP comprises six opposition parties.

Front des forces démocratiques (FFD—Front of Democratic Forces)

Moroccan political grouping. Formed in 1997 after a split from the Parti du progrès **et** du socialisme. The FFD's secretary-general is Thami el-Khiari.

Front des forces sociales (FFS—Social Forces Front)

Political party in Burkina Faso, founded in 1996. A Sankarist party and member of the Groupe du 14 février (14 February Group) and opposition Collectif d'organisations démocratiques de masse et de partis politiques (Collective of Mass Organizations and Political Parties). The chairman of the FFS is Norbert Michel Tiendrébéogo.

Front des forces socialistes (FFS—Socialist Forces Front)

Algerian political party, established in 1963 and revived in 1989. The FFS is led by **Hocine Aït Ahmed**.

Front islamique du salut (FIS—Islamic Salvation Front)

An Algerian Islamist political party, founded in Algiers in 1989, after the riots of October 1988, and legalized in September 1989. The FIS quickly emerged as a force capable of mobilizing large numbers of supporters and sympathizers, possessing a nation-wide organization and appeal, extending its influence to other cities, such as

Oran, Mostagenem and Blida, over the period from 1989 until 1992. In June 1990 it took control of the popular assemblies in 32 out of Algeria's 48 provinces (*wilayat*) and in 853 out of the 1,539 communes, winning emphatic majorities in virtually all of the major cities in particular. It received at least 54% of the vote in an electoral turn-out of 65%; the support, therefore, of about one-third of the total electorate. It won nearly twice as many votes as the official **Front de libération nationale (FLN—National Liberation Front)**, which captured six provinces and 487 communes. Inspired by its success at the local electoral level, the FIS demanded that the general legislative elections be brought forward and that the electoral laws be amended. Taking to the streets, its slogans were often openly anti-democratic and the FIS was involved in clashes with the state security forces. While generally supporting the Algerian government's economic policy, the FIS—like **Hamas**, the **Mouvement de la renaissance islamique (MRI—Movement of the Islamic Renaissance)** and Rabita—has been primarily concerned with the reconstruction of the state on the basis of the **Shari'a** (Islamic Law) and with introducing the Islamic notion of *shura* in place of Western conceptions of pluralism and representative **democracy**. It differed from the other three movements in three main respects. It placed more emphasis on the capture of political power as the prerequisite for the reform of society on Islamic lines. It may be considered, therefore, to have been more 'revolutionary' than its main rivals, although it was prepared to operate within the framework of the 1989 Constitution, while reserving its right to state its principled objections to this Constitution as unIslamic. It was by far the most populist of the Islamist movements and parties in its political style and strategy. Its populism and its doctrinal eclecticism, while endowing it with a greater capacity than the other movements to gain and mobilize wide support, obliged it to accommodate a relatively high degree of social and political heterogeneity within its ranks. At the top of the FIS was a consultative council (*majlis ash-shura*) whose membership was highly guarded. It probably included Hachemi Sahnouni, an imam in Algiers, and Ben Azzouz Zebda, editor of the FIS newspaper *al-Munqidh* (*The Saviour*). More was known of the group's two main leaders, Professor **Madani Abbasi** and Sheikh **Ali Belhadj**. Madani Abbasi (as he was known) represented the 'old guard', while Sheikh Ali Belhadj, the imam of the al-Sunna mosque in the popular quarter of Bab el-Oued in Algiers, personified the younger generation of the FIS, with a powerful appeal to the deprived and frustrated urban youth.

The FIS had ties with Saudi Arabia and other Gulf regimes, and is known to have received substantial financial support from them. After Iraq's invasion of Kuwait, the FIS initially adopted a balanced, if not ambiguous, position, with Madani condemning the invasion early on, but also stating at a meeting on 17 August 1990 that there was no reason for frontiers to exist between Muslim countries, and Belhadj referring to Saddam Hussain in a derogatory fashion before denouncing the Kuwaiti regime for having amassed colossal fortunes 'against God's will'. He also suggested that the Holy Places belonged to all Muslims and that their management should be entrusted to the *ulema*—a not so veiled attack on the Saudi royal family.

The FIS maintained this attitude for several weeks. At a press conference in Algiers on 13 September 1990, Madani announced that the FIS was engaged in an effort at mediation and declared himself in favour of an Arab solution. He and Ali Belhadj travelled to the Gulf, visiting Jiddah three times and Baghdad twice in the hope of using the close link of the FIS with the Saudis to good effect. Their efforts were unsuccessful but the FIS persisted in its ambivalent posture, articulating the general view of its popular constituency without breaking the Saudi connection. As popular feelings moved towards support for Iraq, the FIS was also obliged to move steadily towards a pro-Iraqi position. It did this by making the Western military presence the major issue, stopping short of backing the Iraqi regime. Once the war started, however, the FIS emerged as the most vociferous and militant supporter of Iraq, notably at the huge demonstration held in Algiers on 18 January, which reportedly mobilized some 400,000 people and in which virtually all Algerian political parties took part. The FIS marched in this demonstration to slogans and under banners which were explicitly pro-Iraqi and which called on the government to set up training camps for volunteers wishing to go to Iraq to fight. It continued to show its strength, with another demonstration on 31 January, which mobilized some 60,000 supporters (some sources claim 100,000), with other parties staying away. In addition to calling for 'victory to **Islam** and the Muslims' in the war, the demonstrators also made clear the internal political issues at stake, by calling for a date to be fixed for the elections to the Assemblée populaire nationale. Despite the outcome of the war in Iraq, the FIS was able to maintain its political momentum within Algeria. The government decided that the elections to the Assemblée populaire nationale were to be held in two rounds, but measures were introduced which were designed to hamper, if not provoke, the FIS. Only the two parties winning the most votes in the first round would be allowed to contest the second in each constituency. This provision would have favoured the FLN across the country, and the FIS only where its support was safe from inroads from the other Islamist movements or the Mouvement pour la démocratie en Algérie (Movement for Democracy in Algeria). Moreover, in raising the number of constituencies from 295 to 542, the new law would have given much greater weight than before to the rural districts, where it was felt the FLN was relatively strong. Despite this, the FIS was able to maintain its high level of support, by prioritizing its popular base at home rather than its links with the Gulf states abroad. The FIS now made it very clear that, whatever the outcome of the war in Iraq, its objective was (as Madani declared) 'the building of an Islamic state in Algeria in 1991'. This may have cost it its formerly close links with Saudi Arabia in particular (although this is not certain), but it enabled it to mobilize considerable support in the first round of the elections. On 30 June 1991 Abbasi Madani and Ali Belhadj were both arrested and charged with conspiring to overthrow the government; they were subsequently released. Parliamentary elections, however, were to proceed in December 1991. The turn-out was low, but the success of the FIS was startling. It won 188 out of 231 seats, with 28 seats only left for a second round of voting that was to have been held on 1 January 1992. This did not take place. A military-backed 'palace coup' took place and the elections were stopped. A state of emergency was declared in February, and in March the FIS, together with other Islamist movements, was banned. Only the **MRI** and **Hamas** (since April 1997 the Mouvement de la société pour la paix—Movement of Society for Peace) remained able to operate legally. During the widespread unrest which followed, most of the leadership of the FIS—including Madani and Belhadj, were arrested. The FIS claimed that as many as 30,000 were arrested and detained, and that 150 people were killed. The government dissolved the 411 FIS-controlled local and regional authorities. Madani and Belhadj were arrested in June 1991, and in July 1992 were sentenced to 12-year terms of imprisonment. Abdelkader Hachani, in exile in Germany, directed the executive branch of the FIS. In February 1993 the state of emergency was renewed for an indefinite period. The FIS leadership was placed under house arrest in September 1994, but Belhadj was later returned to prison, where he remains. In the following years, the Islamist opposition in Algeria became fragmented and increasingly radicalized. Several groups emerged with more or less direct links with the FIS. To many Algerians, however, the FIS continued to be the dominant Islamist force within the country and these other groups were often regarded as no more than splinter groups of the FIS. The **Armée islamique du salut (AIS—Islamic Salvation Army)** was the armed wing of the banned FIS. Other paramilitary Islamist groups that emerged in the first few years included the **Groupe islamique armé (GIA—Armed Islamic Group)**, from which, later, in 1998, the **Groupe salafiste pour la prédication et le combat (GSPC—Salafist Group for Call and Combat)** was to split off. In 1996 Algeria introduced a new constitution which banned parties that defined themselves in exclusively religious or ethical terms. In 1997 the AIS took advantage of a government amnesty, accepted a cease-fire, and, in 1999, dissolved itself. At the end of January 1997 the executive branch of the FIS in exile condemned the wave of violent attacks perpetrated mainly by the GIA but also by some paramilitary sections of the FIS, and called for the formation of a national government. In mid-March 1997 the FIS excluded from membership some 40 of its leaders, who had refused 'to make peace at any price'. Its spokesman abroad, Abdelkrim Ould Adda, declared that the FIS did not seek a religious state or a theocracy in Algeria. However, according to a statement at the beginning of April 1997 by the same spokesman, the FIS would boycott the parliamentary elections. In November 1999, Abdelkader Hachani, who had returned from exile abroad, was killed in Algiers. The spokesperson for the FIS in exile became Annouar Haddam. FIS leader Madani remained under house arrest, allowed to receive visits but not to travel abroad, while Belhadj remained in prison. In 2000 the government refused to approve the new **Wafa wa al-Adl (Wafa)** party, on the grounds that it contained large numbers of FIS members. In August 2002 Rabeh Kabir, a former member of the FIS leadership, was ousted from party management at a Congress held in Belgium. At a further meeting in October, in Switzerland, Mourad Dhina was named as interim head of the party's executive.

Front de libération nationale (FLN—National Liberation Front)

Established in 1954, the Front de libération nationale (FLN—National Liberation Front) represented the unified nationalist movement until Algeria gained its **independence** in 1962 after many years of armed struggle and conflict. The FLN first came to power after the revolutionary movement with the same name led Algeria's war for independence against France. It was the only legal party in Algeria from in 1962–89, when a new constitution legalized other political parties. In elections held in 2002, FLN, led by Prime Minister **Ali Benflis**, more than tripled its number of seats in the 389-seat Assemblée populaire nationale, occupying a total of 199 compared with 64 previously. However, the boycott of the elections by key opposition parties, together with unrest among the country's sizeable **Berber** minority, seriously undermined **Abdelaziz Bouteflika**'s efforts to bring stability and more open politics to Algeria. The FLN's secretary-general is now Abdelaziz Belkhadem.

Front de libération nationale du Tchad-Conseil provisoire de la révolution (FROLINAT-CPR—National Liberation Front of Chad-Provisional Council of the Revolution)

Political-military group, based in Algeria but operating in Chad, and led by Goukouni Oueddai.

Front national pour la justice (FNJ—National Front for Justice)

Political party in the Union of the Comoros, of an Islamist orientation. Its leader is Ahmed Rachid.

Front national du Tchad renové (FNTR—National Front of Chad Renewed)

A political-military grouping in Chad, founded in 1996 in Sudan by former members of the Front national du Tchad, and led by Mahamat Moussa Abdelchafi. In June 2002 the FNTR announced that it was ending its armed struggle against the government of Chad.

Front patriotique pour le changement (FPC—Patriotic Front for Change)

Political grouping in Burkina Faso. Its president is Tahirou Ibrahim Zon.

Front patriotique pour le progrès (FPP—Patriotic Front for Progress)

Political party in the Central African Republic. Formed in 1972, it aims to promote political education and debate. The FPP's leader is Prof. Abel Goumba.

Fru Ndi, John

Chairman of the opposition **Social Democratic Front** in Cameroon. In presidential elections held in October 1992 Fru Ndi, the leading opposition candidate, was defeated by the incumbent President, **Paul Biya**, by a narrow margin. The elections were regarded as flawed by international observers.

Fuad, King

King of Egypt from 1917 until 1936.

Fuerza Democráta Republicana (FDR—Democratic Republican Force)

Clandestine political movement in Equatorial Guinea.

Fulani

Major ethno-linguistic group associated particularly with pastoralism and agro-pastoralism in West Africa. Found across southern Mauritania, Senegal, Burkina Faso, Mali, Niger and other adjacent countries. Also known as Peul or Peulh.

Fundamentalism

The *Concise Oxford Dictionary of Current English* defines *fundamentalism* as the 'strict maintenance of ancient or fundamental doctrines of any religion, especially Islam'. The term originated as a description of strict adherence to Christian doctrines based on a literal interpretation of the Bible. This usage derives from a late 19th and early 20th century trans-denominational Protestant movement that opposed the accommodation of Christian doctrine to modern scientific theory and philosophy. However, the term *fundamentalist* has been misused by the media to refer to terrorists who happen to be Muslim, or to anti-American Muslims. Fundamentalist Islam is simply the conservative wing of Islam, just as Fundamentalist Christianity is the conservative wing of Christianity.

G

G8

The group of the eight richest countries, which meets regularly to review 'world affairs' and particularly the state of the world economy and attempts to develop coherent strategies to deal with major global issues. The first meeting of the G6 (as it was then), at Rambouillet, France, in 1975 was organized by Valéry Giscard d'Estaing the French Prime Minister at a time when **oil** price increases and global recession were the major topics. In July 2005 the summit meeting of the G8 was hosted at Gleneagles, Scotland, by the British government and chaired by the Prime Minister, Tony Blair. Climate change and **debt relief** for Africa were among the main issues discussed. The meeting ended with an agreement to allocate US $50,000m. more to development assistance globally; $25,000m. was designated for African countries. Eighteen of the world's poorest countries (most of them in Africa) that have met debt relief criteria would be immediately eligible for 100% debt relief. Some progress was achieved on the issue of climate change, but no specific agreements. It was reported shortly after the G8 summit in 2005 that a group of small **European Union** member states (Belgium, Austria and Luxembourg) were arguing that the **International Monetary Fund** should exercise strict controls over the 18 eligible countries and the economic policies they proposed, thereby seeking to constrain eligibility.

G11

An alliance of 11 parties in the Central African Republic, established in 1997 to provide a coherent opposition to the **Mouvement pour la libération du people centrafricain (Liberation Movement of the Central African People)**, which supports exiled President Ange-Félix Patassé. Major parties that are members include the **Alliance pour la démocratie et le progrès (Alliance for Democracy and Progress)**, the **Front patriotique pour le progrès (FPP—Patriotic Front for Progress)**, the **Mouvement pour la démocratie et le développement (Movement for Democracy and Development)** and the **Rassemblement démocratique centrafricain (Central African Democratic Rally)**. G11 is led by Prof. Abel Goumba of the FPP.

G77

Group of 77, a group of countries in Africa, Asia and Latin America, established in the mid-1960s after the first UNCTAD meeting in 1964, to promote co-operation and collaboration between the developing countries and a degree of countervailing power in relations with the developed countries of the Organization of Economic Co-operation and Development and the **G8**. It now has far more than 77 members, but the name remains.

Gabon

The Gabonese Republic, or Gabon, sits on the Equator in western Africa and is bordered by Equatorial Guinea, Cameroon and the Republic of the Congo. About 85% of the country is covered with rainforest and the area is one of the most mineral-rich in Africa. With an area of 267,667 sq km and a population estimated at 1,329,000 in mid-2003, Gabon is a small country. The capital is Libreville, whose population was estimated at 611,033 in mid-2003. Ethnic groups include the Fang, Myene, Bapounou, Eschira, Bandjabi, and Bateke/Obamba. French is the official language, but Fang (in the north) and Bantu dialects (in the south) are also widely spoken. About 60% of the population are Christians, mainly Roman Catholics. Most of the remainder follow animist beliefs.

Political profile

The Constitution of March 1991 provides for a multi-party system, and vests executive power in the President, who is directly elected by universal suffrage for a period of seven years. The President appoints the Prime Minister, who is Head of Government and who (in consultation with the President) appoints the Council of Ministers. Legislative power is vested in the Assemblée nationale, comprising 120 members, who are elected by direct universal suffrage for a term of five years, and the 91-member Sénat, which is elected by members of municipal councils and departmental assemblies for a term of six years.

At the presidential election held on 6 December 1998 El Hadj **Omar (Albert-Bernard) Bongo Ondimba** was re-elected as President, having obtained 66.55% of the votes cast. President Bongo first took office as President in December 1967, was elected in February 1973, and re-elected in December 1979, November 1986 and December 1993.

Following legislative elections held on 9 and 23 December 2001 seats in the Assemblée nationale were distributed as follows: **Parti démocratique gabonais (PDG—Gabonese Democratic Party)** 86; independent candidates 12; Rassemblement pour le Gabon (RPG—Rally for Gabon) 8; **Parti gabonais du progrès (PGP—Gabonese Progress Party)** 3; Parti social-démocrate (PSD—Social Democrat Party) 2; Union du peuple gabonais (UPG—Union of the Gabonese People) 1; others 7. In by-elections held in June 2002 the PDG increased its representation to

88 seats. Elections to the Assemblée nationale are next scheduled to be held in December 2006.

In indirect elections to the 91-member Sénat held on 9 February 2003 the PDG won more than 60 seats, and the RPG secured eight seats.

History

In 1910 Gabon became one of the four territories of the federation of A **frique équatoriale française (AEF—French Equatorial Africa)**, together with Chad, Congo (Brazzaville) and the Central African Republic. The FEA fought for Charles de Gaulle's Free France during the Second World War, and in 1946 all FEA citizens were granted French citizenship and allowed to establish local assemblies. In 1958 Gabon voted to become an autonomous republic in the French communauté and in 1960 achieved **independence**. Léon M'Ba was elected as President in 1961. He was deposed in the only coup in Gabon's history in 1964, but was restored after French intervention. He ruled until his death in 1967, upon which Vice-President Albert-Bernard Bongo assumed the presidency, and in 1968, declared Gabon a one-party state, which it remained until 1991. President Bongo converted to **Islam** in 1973, taking the name Omar el-Hadj. Gabon enjoyed political stability throughout the 1970s, due largely to its rapid **oil**-driven economic growth. However, the social and political strains caused by such rapid growth and an ensuing economic decline became evident in the early 1980s. A moderate opposition group, the Mouvement de redressement national (MORENA—Movement for National Recovery), accused Bongo of **corruption** and formed a government-in-exile in Paris, France, nominating a candidate to stand against Bongo in the November 1986 presidential election. MORENA was unable to organize an electoral campaign, however, and Bongo was re-elected as President. In response to a number of strikes, the continued deterioration of the economy and MORENA's continued pressure for greater **democracy**, President Bongo convened a national conference to establish the principles for change.

In September 1990 multi-party elections to the Assemblée nationale were held for the first time in almost 30 years. The PDG, the party of the President, obtained an overall majority, although opposition parties were successful in Libreville and some provinces. In 1991 a new constitution was adopted that formalized the multi-party system. In the presidential election held in December 1993 President Bongo received 51% of votes cast in the first round of voting and was thus re-elected. International observers noted administrative flaws in the election, but no large-scale fraud. However, serious civil disturbances provoked the government and opposition elements to negotiate a political agreement and the Paris Accords were signed in November 1994. These provided for reform of the electoral code, the creation of an independent national electoral commission and the organization of free and fair elections. Recommended revisions of the Constitution were submitted to a referendum on 23 July 1995. In 1997 the Assemblée nationale approved the extension of the presidential term of office from five to seven years and created the position of

Vice-President, whose incumbent was to be appointed by the Head of State. Bongo named Divungui-Di-Ndinge Didjob as the first Vice-President. In the most recent presidential election, held in December 1998, Bongo received 66% of the votes cast in the first round of voting and was thus re-elected for a further 7-year term.

Following the most recent elections to the Assemblée nationale, held in December 2001, President Bongo offered four positions in the Council of Ministers appointed in January 2002 to opposition politicians, including Father Paul M'Ba Abessole, the founder of the **Rassemblement national des bûcherons (RNB—National Woodcutters' Rally)**, who had contested the presidential election in 1998.

Social tensions came to a culmination in June 2002 when protests at rising unemployment in Port Gentil escalated into riots. In July 2003 the Assemblée nationale voted to revoke the Constitution's limit on the number of terms for which the President is eligible to seek re-election. In September, in response to a series of strikes and protests, the government and representatives of labour groups signed a so-called 'social truce', which included commitments to lower the prices of essential items and to reduce the extent of political patronage over the following three years. However, renewed protests over reductions in state expenditure in early 2004 appeared to threaten the viability of the agreement.

International Relations

Gabon has traditionally maintained close relations with the Republic of the Congo (ROC). A number of **ethnic groups** are common to both countries. President Bongo has frequently mediated in regional disputes. He chaired the *ad hoc* committee of the **Organization of African Unity** that sought to resolve the border dispute between Chad and Libya, mediated in the ROC in 1999, and has supported peace-keepers of the **Communauté économique et monétaire de l'Afrique centrale (Economic and Monetary Community of Central Africa)** deployed in the Central African Republic. President Bongo has also played a leading role in the Arusha peace process in Burundi. Relations with the former colonial power, France, remain close although they have been strained by several financial corruption scandals that have been reported in the French media.

Gabon, economy

In 2003, according to estimates by the **World Bank**, Gabon's gross national income (GNI), measured at average 2001–03 prices, was US $5,205m., equivalent to $3,580 per head (or $5,700 per head on an international purchasing-power parity basis). During 1990–2003, it was estimated, the population increased at an average annual rate of 2.7%, while gross domestic product (GDP) per head declined, in real terms, by an average of 0.2% per year. Overall GDP increased, in real terms, at an average annual rate of 2.5% in 1990–2003; growth in 2003 was 3.4%. In 1996–2002 the average annual rate of inflation was 1.2%. Consumer prices increased by

0.5% in 2002. The most important sectors of the economy are **agriculture**, forestry and the **oil** industry. France, the USA and the Netherlands are major suppliers of imports to Gabon. The USA is the most important market for the country's exports. The national currency is the franc CFA, which is fixed to the euro (see the **Franc Zone**). In 2004 the average exchange rate was US $1 = 528.285 francs CFA.

Gabon is located in one of the most mineral-rich and fertile areas of Africa, but the country depends heavily upon the oil industry. In 1970–94 annual oil production increased from 5m. metric tons to 17.2m. tons, transforming Gabon into the richest country in **sub-Saharan Africa**, with GDP per head of $2,997. In 1999 GNP per caput was estimated at $3,300—well above the sub-Saharan African average. There are substantial reserves of manganese, uranium, and timber, and deposits of high-grade iron ore, **gold** and **diamonds**. Agricultural products include **cocoa**, **coffee**, rubber, sugar and pineapples. The development of agriculture and other sectors has until recently been largely neglected. However, efforts to reduce Gabon's dependence on oil have increased, in the form of greater investment in both mining and agriculture, and the creation, recently, of national parks to promote tourism. The economy still relies on oil, timber, manganese and other natural resources; accordingly it is highly susceptible to fluctuations in the price of commodities on world markets, and to external conditions in general. Gabon's economic growth was not sustained in the late 1990s, when the price of timber and of oil declined. The subsequent rise in oil prices eased the pressure only slightly. Gabon's oil output was in decline and substantial reserves had been sold forward at a loss; known oil reserves were diminishing and the prospects for new discoveries of oil were poor. Fluctuations in oil prices in the late 1990s, combined with the impact of a fall in East Asian demand for Gabon's timber and rubber and unfavourable exchange rate movements, led to a crisis in public finances that is hampering the government's ability to service its external **debt** promptly. Only two years ago the country faced a crisis as oil production was rapidly falling and government expenditure remained high. In October 2000 the **International Monetary Fund (IMF)** approved a $118m. 18-month stand-by arrangement. In a recent review of Gabon's economy, the IMF recommended the acceleration of the country's privatization programme, the encouragement of private-sector development, the enactment of anti-**corruption** legislation and the reform of the regulatory framework. Gabon has been criticized by the Paris Club and the IMF for its management of both its debt and its revenues. However, new discoveries of oil have since transformed Gabon's prospects.

The discovery by Royal Dutch/Shell and PanOcean of the Kouala oilfield close to Gabon's second largest port, Port Gentil, has added to the confidence and reliance on expanding oil resources from the new AWOKOU-1 well, in the Awoun Permit, and increased capacity discovered in the already established offshore Etame field. Gabon's proven oil reserves increased from 1,300m. barrels in 1996 to 2,500m. barrels in 2004. Gabon originally was to receive an IMF loan of $21m. at this stage, as part of an arrangement to support the country's economic reform programme. This, the Fund and Libreville authorities found, was no longer necessary. In a review of the Gabonese economy in March 2005 the IMF stated that the country no longer requires financial support from abroad. Higher prices for oil have consolidated the improvement in Gabon's economic prospects. Meanwhile, the potential of Gabonese agriculture and **fisheries** remains hugely under-developed. The country's annual fish catch, estimated at 40,000–50,000 tons, is insufficient to meet national demand and each year more than 7,000 tons of fish products have to be imported. The UN FAO launched a programme in March 2005 to boost the productivity of Gabon's fisheries in an attempt to increase food security.

Galaydh, Ali Khalif

Prime Minister of Somalia until October 2001, when a vote of 'no confidence' by the Somali Transitional National Assembly led to his dismissal.

Al-Gama'a al-Islamiyya (Islamic Group)

Egypt's largest militant group, active since the late 1970s; it appears to be loosely organized. It has an external wing with a world-wide presence. The group announced a cease-fire in March 1999, but its spiritual leader, Sheikh Omar Abdul ar-Rahman, incarcerated in the USA, withdrew his support for the cease-fire in June 2000. The Gama'a has not conducted an attack inside Egypt since August 1998. Rifa'i Taha Musa—a hardline former senior member of the group—signed **Osama bin Laden**'s *fatwa* in February 1998 that called for attacks against US civilians. The Gama'a has since publicly denied that it supports bin Laden and frequently differs with public statements made by Taha Musa. Taha Musa has sought to push the group towards a return to armed operations, but the Gama'a, which is still led by Mustafa Hamza, has yet to break the unilaterally declared cease-fire. In late 2000 Taha Musa appeared in an undated video with bin Laden and **Ayman az-Zawahiri**, threatening retaliation against the USA for Abdul Rahman's continued incarceration. The Gama'a's primary goal is to overthrow the Egyptian government and replace it with an Islamic state, but Taha Musa also may be interested in attacking US and Israeli interests. The Egyptian government believes that Iran, bin Laden and Afghan militant groups support the organization. It may also obtain some funding from various Islamic non-governmental organizations.

The Gambia, Republic of

The Republic of The Gambia is a narrow territory around the River Gambia on the west coast of Africa. Apart from a short coastline on the Atlantic Ocean, the country is a semi-enclave in Senegal. The area of the country is 11,295 sq km. At the census of 15 April 2003 the population numbered 1,364,507. English is the official language, while the principal vernacular languages are Mandinka, Fula and **Wolof**. About 85% of the inhabitants are Muslims; most of the remainder are Christians, and there are a small number of animists. The capital is Banjul.

Political profile

Under the terms of the Constitution of the Second Republic of The Gambia, which was approved in a national referendum on 8 August 1996, the Head of State is the President of the Republic, who is directly elected by universal adult suffrage. No restriction is placed on the number of times a President may seek re-election. Legislative authority is vested in the National Assembly, comprising 48 members elected by direct suffrage and five members nominated by the President of the Republic. The President appoints government members, who are responsible both to the Head of State and to the National Assembly.

In the presidential election held on 18 October 2001 **Col (retd) Alhaji Yahya A. J. J. Jammeh**, the candidate of the Alliance for Patriotic Reorientation and Construction (APRC), received 52.84% of the votes cast in the first round of voting and was accordingly re-elected as President. Jammeh was first proclaimed Head of State in July 1994, following a bloodless coup. He was first elected as President in September 1996.

Following a general election held on 17 January 2002, the distribution of seats in the National Assembly was as follows: APRC 45 (including 33 seats taken in constituencies where the party was unopposed); People's Democratic Organization for Independence and Socialism (PDOIS) 2; National Reconciliation Party (NRP) 1.

History

The Gambia became a British protectorate in 1894. It gained **independence** from Britain in 1965, with Dr (later Sir) **Dawda Kairaba Jawara** as Prime Minister. In 1970, following a referendum, The Gambia became a Republic, of which Jawara was elected as President. The Gambia was the smallest of the ex-British territories of West Africa, having originally been merely an enclave along the banks of the Gambia River inland from the sea. The economy was able to dispense with British aid after 1967, and relations with Senegal, which surrounds The Gambia, were good for some time. Indeed, in 1981 President Jawara was only saved from eviction by the intervention of Senegalese troops. However, confederation with Senegal, whereby The Gambia hoped to combine the benefits of association with a larger economy with those of independence, proved difficult. In particular, Senegal objected to Gambian smuggling. In July 1994 Lt (later Col) Yahya Jammeh overthrew Jawara in a bloodless coup. Jammeh's Armed Forces Provisional Ruling Council administered the country by decree and all political activity was banned. Under international pressure, presidential elections were held in 1996 and legislative elections in early 1997. A decree was passed that lifted the ban on political activity, although it excluded the three largest political parties. Four political parties were registered, including the APRC, of which Jammeh was and remains the leader. The leaders of the four registered parties contested the presidential election, in which Jammeh was the winning candidate, receiving 56% of the votes. The result was accepted by the international community, in spite of some alleged irregularities. In campaigning for the legislative elections held in January 1997 opposition parties complained of harassment, but the elections themselves proceeded peacefully. The APRC was the victorious party, winning 33 seats in the National Assembly, while the United Democratic Party (UDP) won seven and other opposition parties five.

The Gambia's political stability remained fragile after the elections, however. Few senior ministers retained their posts for long, rumours of coups regularly circulated and the independent media and opposition were regularly harassed for allegedly fomenting anti-government sentiment. In April 2000, during student demonstrations, the Gambian security services shot dead 16 people. A report by a commission of inquiry into the shootings did not lead to any action being taken against any of the individuals involved, among both the students and the security forces.

During the months that preceded the presidential election held in October 2001 there was a decline in the standard of governance. Concerns were raised over the suspension of the auditor-general, the dismissal of the chairman of the Independent Electoral Commission (IEC) and the removal of the deputy inspector-general of the police, all of whom had displayed reformist and independent tendencies. Harassment of the independent media by the security services continued. Amendments to the Constitution in May reduced the authority of the IEC and gave more power to the National Assembly (where the government held a majority).

In July 2001, after pressure from the international community Jammeh repealed Decree 89, which had banned members of the pre-coup government from holding public office. The repeal encouraged the two main opposition parties to form a coalition to contest the forthcoming presidential election. The alliance of the UDP and the People's Progressive Party (PPP) chose Ousanou Darboe as their candidate. The election, held in October, was contested by Jammeh, Darboe and three other candidates. Jammeh was the winning candidate, receiving 53% of votes cast in the first round of voting, while Darboe won 33%. Although the election was free and peaceful on the day it was held, the opposition candidates were handicapped by lack of access to the media and other resources. Opposition activists were also subject to intimidation. Furthermore, in the aftermath of Jammeh's victory, numerous abuses of human rights occurred, including the detention and torture of opposition activists and human rights campaigners and further harassment of the independent media. Civil servants who were regarded as sympathetic to the opposition were dismissed. The political situation subsequently stabilized, however. In December Jammeh made a reconciliatory and progressive inauguration speech, in which he offered an amnesty to former President Jawara to return to The Gambia. In elections to the National Assembly held in January 2002, the APRC won a huge majority—45 of the 48 elective seats—owing largely to their boycott by the UDP/PPP alliance. Only 15 seats were contested. The boycott, pursued because of unsubstantiated allegations of malpractice over the electoral register, was widely regarded as a misjudgement.

In May 2002 the National Assembly approved legislation that imposed stricter regulations over the print media, in accordance with which all journalists not working for the state-controlled media would be required to register with a National Media Commission. The law was condemned by the Gambia Press Union, which announced that it would not co-operate with the Commission. In early June Jawara returned to The Gambia from exile; at the end of the month he was officially received by Jammeh, and later tendered his resignation as leader of the PPP.

In October 2002 Lamine Wa Juwara, who had been expelled from the UDP, formed a new political party, the National Democratic Action Movement (NDAM). In November the opposition UDP-PPP-Gambian People's Party (GPP) coalition split, following the resignation of its chairman, Assan Musa Camara.

In June 2003 the National Media Commission was created, despite opposition from journalists, and was given far-reaching powers, including the authority to imprison journalists for terms of up to six months. Reports continued throughout 2003 and 2004 of journalists being arrested or subjected to harassment. In early December legislation providing for terms of imprisonment of up to three years for journalists found guilty of libel or sedition, and obliging members of the media to re-register with the state, was approved by the National Assembly. In January 2005 the National Alliance for Democracy and Development, a coalition of five opposition parties comprising the UDP, the National Reconciliation Party (NRP), NDAM, PDOIS and the PPP, was formed to participate in the presidential elections due to be held in late 2006.

International relations

After the 1994 coup The Gambia's traditional aid donors and trading partners suspended much co-operation. The Jammeh administration therefore sought new links. Diplomatic relations were restored with Libya in November, and numerous co-operation agreements ensued. The Republic of China (Taiwan) also became one of The Gambia's major sources of funding. The Gambia has offered to mediate in conflict between separatists in the southern Senegalese province of **Casamance** and the Senegalese government. Relations with Guinea-Bissau have improved since 2002, when that country's President accused Jammeh of involvement in a failed coup attempt in Guinea-Bissau and of supporting the Casamance rebels. In 2003 The Gambia contributed troops to the **Economic Community of West African States**' Mission in Liberia.

The Gambia, economy

In 2003, according to estimates by the **World Bank**, The Gambia's gross national income, measured at average 2001–03 prices, was US $411m., equivalent to $310 per head (or $1,820 on an international purchasing-power parity basis). During 1990–2003, it was estimated, the population increased at an average annual rate of 3.3%, while gross domestic product (GDP) per head increased by 0.2%. Overall GDP increased, in real terms, at an average annual rate of 3.5% in 1990–2003; GDP declined by 3.1% in 2002, but increased by 8.8% in 2003. The average annual rate of inflation was 4.6% in 1990–2002; consumer prices increased by an average of 17.0% in 2003. Services and **agriculture** were the most important sectors of the economy in 2003 in terms of their contribution to GDP. Agricultural exports include groundnuts and related products, fruit and vegetables. In 1999 the principal source of imports was Germany, while the two largest markets for exports were Belgium and the United Kingdom. The national currency is the dalasi. In 2002 the average exchange rate was US $1 = 19.918 dalasi.

The Gambia has no important mineral or other natural resources and has a limited agricultural base. About 75% of the population depend on crops and livestock for their livelihood. Small-scale manufacturing activity includes the processing of peanuts, fish, and hides. Re-export trade normally constituted a major segment of economic activity, but a pre-shipment inspection plan imposed by the government in 1999, the instability of the dalasi, and the stable political situation in Senegal have reduced these exchanges. In 1998 the government's seizure of the private peanut firm Alimenta eliminated the largest purchaser of Gambian groundnuts, and in the following two marketing seasons prices and sales were significantly lower. A decline in tourism in 1999–2000 also restrained growth, although there was a slight increase in tourist numbers in 2002. Unemployment and under-employment rates are extremely high. Short-term economic progress remains highly dependent on sustained bilateral and multilateral aid, on responsible government economic management, and on anticipated growth in the construction sector.

Since 1998, owing in part to favourable weather conditions and economic reforms, The Gambia has achieved consistent growth. Although the economy remains vulnerable to adverse external and domestic factors, it is beginning to diversify away from its traditional dependence on exports of groundnuts. With regard to fiscal matters, the 2001 elections led to an increase in government expenditure. As a result, and despite real GDP growth of 6% in 2001, there were significant budgetary slippages which continued in the first quarter of 2002. Expenditure was curbed in the second quarter of 2002. In order to address fiscal imbalances, the government has launched a comprehensive work programme to strengthen its capacity to execute and monitor the budget effectively. In 2002 the government presented a **Poverty Reduction Strategy Paper (PRSP)** to the **International Monetary Fund (IMF)** and the World Bank. The government is preparing a comprehensive technical assistance programme to support the PRSP. Also in 2002 the IMF approved a new three-year arrangement under the **Poverty Reduction and Growth Facility**. The budget for 2004 anticipated real GDP growth of 6%, partly because of a projected increase of 28% in domestic revenue. It was hoped that the establishment of a National Revenue Authority would improve the government's ability to collect taxes. The budget deficit was forecast to be equivalent to 11.6% of GDP. The Gambia Cotton Company was scheduled for privatization in 2004.

Garang, John

Long-time leader of the main southern rebel group in Sudan, the Sudan People's Liberation Movement (SPLM), who had been sworn in as the country's Vice-President only three weeks before he was killed in a helicopter crash in early August

2005. His death prompted fears that the peace agreement that had ended decades of civil conflict in Sudan might collapse. Garang was succeeded within the SPLM by his deputy, **Silva Kiir**. Garang had led the Sudan People's Liberation Army (SPLA) for 22 years and died just when a comprehensive peace agreement concluding the Sudanese civil conflict offered hope to southerners for an end to their repression and domination by the north. Provided the agreement does not collapse, the predominantly Christian and animist peoples of the south will be granted autonomy for a period of six years, at the end of which they will have the option to secede.

Gbagbo, Laurent

President of Côte d'Ivoire. A historian by profession, Laurent Gbagbo is a former trade union activist who, since the 1980s, has adopted a strongly nationalist position, espousing the concept of pure Ivorian parentage. He was imprisoned for two years in the early 1970s for 'subversive' teaching, and spent eight years in exile in France in the 1980s, returning to Côte d'Ivoire in 1988 to campaign for multi-party **democracy**. He proclaimed himself President in October 2000, following popular demonstrations in support of his candidacy in a recently held presidential election, and a declaration of support for him by the armed forces.

Gelleh, Ismael Omar

President of Djibouti. Ismael Omar Gelleh assumed the presidency following his victory in April 1999 in an election that his uncle, **Hassan Gouled Aptidon**, the incumbent (and first) President of Djibouti, had chosen not to contest. Gelleh favours the continuation of Djibouti's traditionally strong ties with France, and has played an important role in attempting to reconcile the conflicted factions in neighbouring Somalia.

General Agreement on Tariffs and Trade (GATT)

International framework and associated organization concerned with the regulation and liberalization of international trade; predecessor of the **World Trade Organization (WTO)**, which has effectively replaced it. The General Agreement on Tariffs and Trade (GATT) proceeded by a series of 'rounds' of discussion and debate that were designed to produce international agreement on specific trade issues, e.g. protectionism, tariffs and other barriers to 'free' trade. The final 'round' of talks was known as the **Uruguay Round**.

Genocide

A term used loosely to refer to the extinction or attempted extinction of a whole people; now subject to international definition by the United Nations. The history of European intervention in Africa was associated with large-scale violence in many of the territories 'discovered', settled and administered by the various European powers and in some cases significant sections of local societies and indigenous populations were subject to measures which led to very large numbers of deaths, either intentionally or unintentionally, through warfare, 'pacification' and disease. African indigenous society, particularly in West and parts of Central Africa, was characterized widely by **slavery** as an institution; and the involvement of Arabs in extensive slave trading across the Sahara from the Sahel to the **Maghreb**, from Sudan to Egypt and from the east coast of Africa across the Arabian peninsula developed from the Middle Ages onwards. However, it was not until growth in demand for labour in the New World and the associated Atlantic slave trade transformed indigenous slaving and slavery into a large-scale commercial enterprise, leading to a massive transfer of African populations out of Africa, that depopulation took place on a scale that might be classified as genocide. It was with direct European intervention and the beginning of the colonial period proper, characterized by European settlement and administration, that the extinction of whole peoples was initiated. Most vulnerable were the hunters and gatherers, whose way of life was most incompatible with that of the Europeans, and who in any case may already have been marginalized by the growth and expansion over many centuries of more 'developed' agricultural and agro-pastoral Bantu-speaking populations throughout much of the continent. In south and south-west Africa, where the so-called **'bushmen'** were hunted for sport at one time by Europeans and effectively reduced to small marginal populations, in **East Africa**, where they virtually disappeared, leaving only a few remnant populations in relatively isolated pockets, and in Central Africa, where the so-called **'pygmies'**, once widely spread throughout the extensive forest areas, were also pushed into the deep rainforest and reduced in numbers. Throughout Africa, indigenous populations of agriculturalists, agro-pastoralists and pastoralists were also subject to violence on a large scale during the colonial period, but arguably not to the point where the term genocide could be applied. It is not until the post-colonial period that Africa has experienced what has been identified as genocide. The most clear-cut case was in Rwanda in the early 1990s, when conflict and **civil war** between **Tutsis** and **Hutus** led to deaths on a massive scale and to the slaughter of millions of Tutsis, prompting the international community—which failed to intervene effectively to prevent it—to refer to this as a genocide. Similar conflicts in Burundi and in the Democratic Republic of the Congo (DRC) took place within the same broad time period (later in the DRC), in the case of Burundi also involving Tutsis and Hutus, and in the DRC involving a more complex mix of ethnic groups and tribes. In more recent years, the evolving conflict in the western part of Sudan in **Darfur**, where local 'African' populations (some organized in militias and constituting 'rebel' group, but most ordinary civilians) appear to have been systematically massacred by 'Arab' militias (known as ***janjaweed***). Once again, the international community has failed to intervene effectively, but has spent some time debating whether massacres on this scale could be termed genocide, or not.

German East Africa

Shortly after the **Berlin West Africa Conference** (1884–85), and the definition of **Togoland**, **Kamerun** and **South West Africa** as German colonial territories, Bismarck added German East Africa (including Ruanda-Urundi and the territory that was later **Tanganyika**, the mainland of modern Tanzania) to Germany's colonial possessions. After the First World War, the League of Nations awarded mandates over the colonial territories of the defeated Germany. Part of German East Africa went to Britain, and was renamed Tanganyika, while others went to Belgium and were renamed Rwanda and Burundi.

Al-Ghad

Al-Ghad ('Tomorrow') and its leader **Ayman Nour**, a 40-year old lawyer, are viewed, in the West in particular, as the new face of opposition in Egypt. In September 2005 Nour contested the first multi-candidate presidential election to be held in Egypt for more than 50 years.

Ghana, Republic of

The Republic of Ghana is situated on the southern West African coastline. It is bordered by Togo in the east, Burkina Faso in the north and Côte d'Ivoire in the west. A narrow grassy plain stretches inland from the coast, widening in the east. The south and west are covered by dense rainforest. To the north are forested hills, beyond which is dry savannah and open woodland. The Black and White Volta Rivers enter Ghana from Burkina Faso and lead to the largest man-made lake in the world, Lake Volta. The country has an area of 238,537 sq km. At mid-2003 the population was estimated at 20,922,000. The capital is Accra, whose population was estimated at 1,847,432 at mid-2003. English is the official language of Ghana, but there is a total of 75 spoken languages, each associated with a distinct ethnic group. The largest of these groups are the **Akan**, who account for approximately one-half of the population. Next in terms of size are the Mossi, the **Ewe** and the Ga-Adangme. Other significant groups and languages are Twi Fante, Ga and **Hausa**. Many of the inhabitants follow traditional beliefs and customs. Christians comprise an estimated 69% of the population.

Political profile

Under the terms of the Constitution, which was approved by national referendum in 1992, Ghana has a multi-party political system. Executive power is vested in the President, who is the Head of State and commander-in-chief of the armed forces. The President is elected by direct universal suffrage for a maximum of two four-year terms. Legislative power is vested in a 230-member unicameral Parliament, which is elected by direct universal suffrage for a four-year term. The President appoints a Vice-President, and nominates a Council of Ministers, subject to approval by the

Parliament. The Constitution also provides for a 25-member Council of State, principally comprising regional representatives and presidential nominees, and a 20-member National Security Council, chaired by the Vice-President, which act as advisory bodies to the President.

In a presidential election held on 7 December 2004 **John Agyekum Kufuor** received 52.45% of the votes cast in the first round of voting and was accordingly re-elected as President. He had first been elected as President in December 2000.

Following legislative elections held on 7 December 2004 the distribution of seats in the Parliament was as follows: New Patriotic Party (NPP) 128; National Democratic Congress (NDC) 94; People's National Convention (PNC) 4; Convention People's Party (CPP) 3; independents 1.

History

British colonial rule in the **Gold Coast** (as Ghana was then known) was established from 1874. It was extended under a League of Nations mandate to include part of the former German colony of **Togoland** in 1919. In 1957, following elections won by Dr **Kwame Nkrumah** and his party in the early 1950s, the Gold Coast became the independent state of Ghana—the first British dependency in **sub-Saharan Africa** to attain **independence** under majority rule. Ghana's first post-independence ruler, Kwame Nkrumah, was the pioneer of **'African socialism'** and advocated the application of European socialism, modified to take account of the circumstances of Africa. Nkrumah gradually developed close ties with the Soviet bloc. He was overthrown in a military coup in 1966. The new rulers' aim of rectifying Ghana's problems before returning it to civilian rule were undermined by deep-rooted political and economic malpractice. The pattern of fledgling civilian government aborted by military intervention continued to dog Ghana, culminating in a coup in 1979 led by **Flight-Lt Jerry Rawlings**. On that occasion Ghana was soon returned to civilian government. In 1981, however, Rawlings took power again in another coup that overthrew the civilian government of Dr Hilla Limann. He assumed chairmanship of the ruling Provisional National Defence Council (PNDC), abolished the Constitution, dissolved Parliament and proscribed opposition political parties. Significant abuses of human rights occurred under Rawlings's military regime of the 1980s. However, by the mid-1980s stability had returned to Ghana and its economy had started to recover. Following pressure for political reform, Rawlings lifted the ban on opposition parties. A new constitution was drawn up and approved in a referendum in April 1992.

In November 1992 the first presidential elections for 13 years were held. Rawlings, who contested them as the candidate of the NDC won with 58% of the vote. Although the elections were declared free and fair by international observers, opposition leaders were unhappy with their conduct and boycotted the parliamentary election held in December. Thus largely unopposed, the NDC won 189 of the 200 seats in the Parliament. In December 1996 Rawlings was re-elected for a second presidential term, with 57.5% of the vote. Parliamentary elections held at that time were contested by the opposition in the form of a Grand Alliance, comprising the NPP and the CPP, which won 65 seats—fewer than half of the number, 133, obtained by the ruling NDC.

In December 2000 President Rawlings relinquished office in accordance with the terms of the Constitution, which allows a maximum of two four-year presidential terms. In the subsequent presidential elections the NDC was represented by the Vice-President, Prof. John Atta Mills, and the opposition NPP by John Kufuor. Kufuor was the successful candidate, receiving 57% of the votes cast in the second round of voting.

International relations

Ghana's relations with Burkina Faso have generally improved since the mid-1980s. The two countries concluded co-operation agreements in 1998. Relations with Togo have stabilized since about the mid-1990s, full diplomatic links having been restored in 1994. In 2002 Ghana was the fifth largest contributor to UN peace-keeping missions world-wide. Ghana has played a prominent role in peace-keeping operations in Sierra Leone. The Kufuor administration has sought to increase Ghanaian involvement in conflict resolution within West and Central Africa, in particular in the Democratic Republic of the Congo and in Côte d'Ivoire.

Ghana, economy

In 2003, according to estimates by the **World Bank**, Ghana's gross national income (GNI), measured at average 2001–03 prices, was US $7,501m., equivalent to $320 per head (or $2,190 on an international purchasing-power parity basis). During 1990–2003, it was estimated, the population increased at an average annual rate of 2.3%, while gross domestic product (GDP) per head increased, in real terms, by an average of 2.1% per year. Overall GDP increased at an average annual rate of 4.4% in 1990–2003; growth in 2003 was 5.2%. In 1990–2002 the average annual rate of inflation was 25.3%. Consumer prices increased by 26.7% in 2003. **Agriculture**, in particular the production of **cocoa**, mining for **gold** and forestry are important sectors of the economy. Ghana's major trading partners include Nigeria, the United Kingdom, the USA, the Netherlands, Germany and Switzerland. The national currency is the cedi. In 2004 the average exchange rate was US $1 = 9,004.63 cedis.

Ghana's economy is mainly rural: cocoa, timber and pineapples are the main export crops. Exports of gold have become one of the country's principal sources of foreign exchange. The emerging industrial sector is based largely on products derived from cassava, fruits and cocoa. Ghana enjoyed the highest per caput income in the region at **independence**, but in the 1970s its economy declined. By the early 1980s income per head had fallen by one-third and the rate of inflation had risen above 100%. In 1983 the government launched a programme of stabilization and economic liberalization, seeking thereby to reduce budget deficits and create a market-friendly environment. In the decade that followed GDP growth averaged 5%, and physical and social infrastructure was largely rehabilitated.

However, from the second half of 1999 the terms of Ghana's trade began to suffer from declines in the price of its two principal exports, gold and cocoa, and from the rising price of imported petroleum. This, together with a delay in adjusting fiscal and monetary policy accordingly, led to a sharp deterioration in macroeconomic performance, including an accumulation of external arrears. In the latter part of 1999 the exchange rate depreciated rapidly and inflation increased significantly. These problems were compounded by delays in the adjustment of domestic petroleum prices and electricity rates, resulting in an accumulation of large bank debts owed by the state-owned monopoly importer, Tema Oil Refinery (TOR), that threatened the financial viability of the utilities. The exchange rate continued to depreciate and inflation to increase throughout 2000 as the terms of trade worsened. The authorities responded in early 2000 by tightening monetary policy, postponing public expenditures, and by raising the rate of value added tax. Fiscal and monetary discipline faltered once again, however, during the approach to elections in December.

The newly-elected government that took office in January 2001 inherited a difficult fiscal and social situation and an economy that was apparently in decline. Due to shortcomings in fiscal management and delays in the adjustment of public utility prices, the fiscal and quasi-fiscal deficit had reached an estimated 23% of GDP in 2000, while contingent fiscal liabilities were equivalent to 8% of GDP. These two factors created the prospect of a **debt** 'trap', with rising fiscal deficits being caused by domestic debt build-up and high real interest rates. The Kufuor administration has made tackling the economy a priority. Tough measures have been taken, including the raising of fuel duties by more than 90%. In 2001 Ghana applied to the **International Monetary Fund (IMF)** for heavily indebted poor country (HIPC) status in order to obtain **debt relief**. After much delay, the application was finally approved, and in February 2002 the IMF granted a disbursement of some $65m. to Ghana. This was followed by the approval of a three-year, $258m. arrangement under its **Poverty Reduction and Growth Facility** in May 2003. Political instability in Côte d'Ivoire from September 2002 coincided with a poor world-wide harvest to create a boom for Ghana's cocoa growers. The international price of cocoa briefly rose above $2,400 per metric ton in October 2002, and although it declined to $1,900 per ton in the following month this was still double the price in November 2001. By May 2003 the price had declined to $1,698 per ton, and the trend was moderately downward, the price falling to $1,552 per ton in May 2004. None the less, the rally in the price of cocoa provided a much-needed boost to confidence in Ghana's economic prospects. In 2003 significant new inward foreign investment and a successful cocoa harvest placed Ghana in a favourable economic position.

However, higher global petroleum prices, together with a removal of fuel subsidies in early 2003, increased inflation, which by January 2004 had risen to 22.4%. The 2004 budget set a target of reducing inflation to below 10% during the 2004/05 financial year and of stabilizing the cedi. In July 2004 the IMF, having completed a second review of economic performance under the PRGF arrangement, again commended the government's economic policy. The new government has achieved some major successes, but it has been assisted to a great extent by the recovery in the price of gold and fortuitously high cocoa prices. Generally prudent macroeconomic policies and substantial structural reforms have brought about steady economic growth and lower inflation. However, the economy remains reliant on cocoa and a few other primary products and has depended on bumper crops for economic growth, although some promising signs of diversification have emerged. Unemployment remains high and while **poverty** is declining, it is also deepening among more vulnerable groups, particularly food crop farmers. The outlook for 2005 and 2006 is for continued growth of about 6%, based on increased cocoa production and increased investment. In order to secure long-term growth, the Ghanaian government is seeking to increase the availability of credit and to reform the service sector and the **oil** industry.

Ghana-Guinea Union

Established in May 1959 by the Declaration of Conakry shortly after the two countries had become independent, the Ghana-Guinea Union proved to be of little practical consequence (either with or without Mali, which joined it in 1960), but it was an influential assertion of the political idea of transcending individual states to create larger associations, and informed the establishment of the **Casablanca Group** in 1961.

Gleneagles Agreement

The Gleneagles Agreement, made at the meeting of Commonwealth Heads of Government in London, United Kingdom, in 1977, at a time when the armed struggle in **Rhodesia** was reaching a climax, reaffirmed the total opposition of the **Commonwealth** as a whole to **apartheid**.

Globalization

A term increasingly used during the 1990s and early years of the 21st century to refer to the process of global economic (and social) integration as a consequence of international liberalization and domestic economic reforms and privatization.

Gold

Historically one of the main 'precious' minerals, linked to currencies the world over through the notion of a 'gold standard' and subsequently (after the abolition of the 'gold standard') a crucial element of the 'reserves' held by countries' national banks. The decision at the end of the 1990s by the central banks of many developed countries to sell off their gold reserves was a crucial development, particularly for the many gold-producing countries of Africa. For generations there had been a relationship between the number of bank notes a central bank issued and the amount of gold it held. But, increasingly, reserves could be held in other forms, that were as good as gold—such as US Treasury Bonds—and that would earn interest, which gold did not. Also, as interest rates globally have tended to decrease, so gold has lost its edge as a hedge against inflation. In addition to this, as more countries became gold producers, the supply increasingly outstripped demand, and the price fell. The price peaked in 1980 at above US $800 an ounce, and this sparked a rush of new exploration that caused gold production to grew by 8% annually over the next two decades. Output increased just as demand from central banks was declining. As prices fell, more and more mines across Africa became marginal, particularly where the costs of extraction were also rising. Among the new finds were a number of shallow and alluvial deposits, particularly in Australia and the USA. This new gold costs exactly half as much to mine as, for example, South African gold (see **Gold in South Africa**).

Gold in the Democratic Republic of the Congo

The lure of **gold** has fuelled atrocities in the north-east of the Democratic Republic of the Congo (DRC), with international companies and local warlords benefiting while local people suffer violence, torture and rape, according to a report—*The Curse of Gold*—produced by Human Rights Watch in June 2005. The organization reports that **AngloGold Ashanti**, part of the international mining conglomerate **Anglo-American**, developed links with the Front nationaliste et intégrationaliste (FNI—Nationalist and Integrationist Front) near the town of Mongbwalu in Ituri District and provided 'meaningful financial and logistic support' which led to substantial political benefits for the FNI, a group responsible for some of the worst atrocities. The company responded to the report by denying that it gave support to militia groups, but admitted that company employees had yielded to extortion by the FNI in an incident that would not recur. Anglo-Gold Ashanti drew a distinction between 'support' for a group like the FNI and 'some level of unavoidable contact', given the proximity of some of its mining operations to the local communities where the FNI was present. Human Rights Watch stated that fighting between armed groups for control of the gold-mining town of Mongbwalu had cost the lives of at least 2,000 civilians between June 2002 and September 2004. Gold from the DRC is being sent to Uganda, then shipped to global gold markets in Europe and elsewhere. The leading Swiss gold-refining company, Metalor Technologies, buys gold from Uganda.

Gold in South Africa

In South Africa, where the **gold** mined is usually some 3–4 km below ground, in narrow veins that average only 1 m in width, and in exceptionally hard rock, the costs of extraction have become increasingly prohibitive, as labour costs have increased. At the same time, profits have declined: whereas in 1980 1 kg of gold earned 120,000 rand (R) at a cost of R35,000 (giving a profit margin of R85,000), by 2000 it earned R60,000 at a cost of R55,000 (giving a profit margin of only R5,000). There was an increase in the price of gold (US $350 an ounce) in 2003, with the threat of war in Iraq, but this proved only temporary. In order to remain profitable, South African companies have restricted themselves to mining only the higher-grade veins, closing down shafts and even mines where that is not possible. Production has slumped, from 680 metric tons in 1980 to 428 tons in 2000. From contributing 50% of the value of all South Africa's exports in 1980, gold contributed a mere 15% by the early 2000s.

Gold Coast

Term used during the colonial period to refer to the coastal region of West Africa, including the territory now known as Ghana and formerly as the **Gold Coast Colony**. The name reflected the importance of **gold** mining and trans-Saharan trade in pre-colonial times from the region. Riots that broke out in Accra, the capital of the British Gold Coast Colony, in 1948 were started by ex-servicemen in protest at high prices. A commission of enquiry produced a radical report, which stated in effect that the colony's newly proposed constitution was out of date before even being introduced—to grant Africans a majority of seats in the legislative council was no longer enough. A new commission of Africans, with an African judge as chairman, was set up to devise a new constitution. At the same time, **Kwame Nkrumah** and other younger politicians were pressing for **independence** and self-government. As a result of these diverse forces, the Gold Coast became self-governing in 1955 and gained its independence in March 1957 as Ghana. In 1960 it became a republic.

Gold Coast Colony

Britain established the Gold Coast Colony in 1874, later conquering **Ashanti** and adding territory to the north as the 'scramble for Africa' continued; and sanctioned the advance of the Royal Niger Company into the heavily populated region that subsequently, as Nigeria, became Britain's most important West African colony.

Government, change of

The increasingly widespread use of elections to bring about changes of government in African states is relatively recent. In the period between 1960 and 2003, out of 195 changes of leadership in **sub-Saharan Africa**, 107 were by *coups d'état*, 19 involved retirement, 19 elections, 12 death from natural or accidental causes, five from assassination (not in connection with a coup) and 33 from 'other causes' (including the establishment of 'caretaker' or interim administrations). In the entire period from 1960 to 1989, 79 out of 118 changes of leadership were a result of coups and only one as of ouster by the electorate; nine were due to death by natural causes or accidents, three were due to assassinations and eight to retirement; eighteen occurred for other reasons. Between 1990 and 2003, 18 out of 77 changes of leadership occurred as a result of elections (although 28 were still due to coups), 15 of 'other causes', 11 of retirements, three of death from natural causes or by accident and only two took place as a result of assassinations. These statistics appear to suggest a gradual but significant shift from coups and assassinations to elections as the more usual mechanism for achieving a change of government.

Gowon, Col Yakubu

Col Gowon replaced **Gen. Johnson Aguiyi-Aronsi**, after his murder in mid-1966, as chief of the army and Head of State in Nigeria. He expressed his hopes for a rapid return to civilian rule and released a number of political prisoners. At a conference held in Lagos in September 1966, it was agreed that Nigeria should be organized as a loose, fourfold federal structure (north, east, west and mid-west), but this agreement coincided with a massacre of **Ibos** in the north and the flight of survivors to the eastern region. In May 1967 Lt-Col Odumegwu Ojukwu, who had been appointed military governor of the eastern region after the first coup of young Ibo officers in January 1966, took the eastern region out of the federation and declared the separate state of **Biafra**. There followed a bitter **civil war**, which eventually the superior forces of the federal army were able to win. In 1970 Biafra was forced to capitulate. Gowon proved a statesman in victory, preaching and practising reconciliation and reconstruction. The eastern region rejoined the federation and Nigeria embarked on a period of significant economic growth. With the growth of the economy came great wealth, for some, and increasing **corruption**. The army and the police force were particularly prone to corruption, but it was widespread in all sectors of the economy and society, private and public. Gowon's evident inability to manage Nigeria's growing complexity and problems led to his displacement in 1975 while out of the country. He was subsequently allowed, however, to leave the country safely, with his family and to settle in England. His successor, **Gen. Murtala Ramat Muhammed**, was assassinated shortly after.

Green Party

Egyptian political party, founded in 1990. Its chairman is Dr Abd al-Moneim el-Aasar.

Groupe islamique armé (GIA—Armed Islamic Group)

An Algerian Islamic extremist group, aiming at the overthrow of the secular regime in Algeria and its replacement with an Islamic state. The GIA began its violent activity in 1992–93 after the government had nullified the success of the **Front islamique du salut (FIS—Islamic Salvation Front)**, the largest Islamic opposition party, in the first round of legislative elections in December 1991. It claimed to be involved in a *jihad* or holy war. It was led initially by Abdelhak Layada. Many members of the banned FIS joined its ranks. Some of its members are thought to have been trained and to have fought in Afghanistan. It has also been suggested that some have had experience in Pakistan, Yemen, Syria, Sudan, Bosnia and Chechnya. The Algerian Islamist Khamareddine Kherbane, an Afghan veteran, was close both to the GIA and to the leadership of al-Qa'ida. At the outset the GIA focused its attention on the assassination of specific individual targets, particularly diplomats, clergy, industrialists, intellectuals, feminists, journalists, priests and foreigners. The intelligentsia, especially those thought to have been influenced by Western values (which often included **Berbers**), were branded 'false Muslims' or 'anti-Islamic civilians' and selectively targeted. After announcing a campaign of terror against foreigners living in Algeria in 1993, the GIA killed more than 100 expatriate men and women—mostly Europeans. It developed cells and networks among expatriate Algerians in Europe, mainly in France. In 1994 it hijacked an Air France flight to Algiers. In July 1995 one of its leaders, Zitouni, who had been in charge since October 1994, was assassinated. In 1996 there were splits within the GIA that led to a number of groups being formed. Antar Zouabri emerged as the leader of the main faction. From 1996 onwards the GIA campaign broadened in scale and scope. The group uses assassinations and bombings, including car bombs; many thousands of Algerian civilians have been killed, individually and in groups. There were massacres of whole communities. The level of violence associated with the GIA prompted four other North African Islamist groups—including the **Libyan Islamic Fighting Group** and Egyptian **Islamic Jihad**—to issue communiqués denouncing the cult of violence and by mid-1996 to withdraw their support from the GIA. On 8 September 1997 the GIA issued a declaration justifying the massacres, stating that the Algerian people were 'kaffirs [unbelievers], apostates and hypocrites' because they did not support the GIA against the government. It was claimed that all of its extreme actions were 'for the cause of Allah'. Al Qa'ida severed its links with the GIA leadership, denounced Antar Zouabri and encouraged Hassan Hattab, the head of the GIA's European network (who also disagreed with Muslims killing each other), to break away and join the **Groupe salafiste pour la prédication et le combat (GSPC—Salafist Group for Call and Combat)**, a group formed in May 1998 with several hundred former GIA members. Thereafter, al-Qa'ida support was concentrated on the GSPC, which it penetrated during the two years between 1998 and 2000. The GIA was led by nine 'emir' generals during its first eight years, all of whom were either killed or imprisoned. Antar Zouabri, the main 'emir' at the time, was killed together with two of his henchmen by security forces in February 2002 in his home town of Boufarik, near Algiers. According to unconfirmed reports, his successor, Rachid Abou Tourab, was killed by security forces in June 2002. The total number of GIA members is unknown. Estimates vary between 200 and several thousand. An estimated 1,000 GIA members surrendered to the Algerian authorities within the framework of the Law of Civil Harmony (Accord) in 1999–2000, but there remained an active hard core which continued to operate throughout the first half of the new decade. It is generally thought that the GIA recruits heavily from among the unemployed youth of the urban poor, but in fact relatively little is known in detail of its membership. Although in recent years, its activities have been reduced, there remain active cells in many parts of the country, including several of the larger towns, particularly Algiers—usually in the popular quarters (e.g. Bab el Oued, etc.).

Groupe islamique des combatants marocains (GICM—Islamic Group of Moroccan Combatants)

A Moroccan Islamist group believed to have been responsible for bomb attacks in Casablanca in May 2003, which killed 33 people and led to the deaths of 12 suicide bombers. The GICM is also thought to have been associated with bombings in Madrid, Spain, in March 2004. Some six Islamists suspected of carrying out the Madrid train bombings blew themselves up after being cornered by the police in a flat in the Madrid suburb of Leganes on 3 April. Shortly prior to that, explosives had been found on the Madrid–Seville high-speed railtrack.

Groupe salafiste pour la prédication et le combat (GSPC—Salafist Group for Call and Combat)

The GSPC was formerly a faction of the **Groupe islamique armé (GIA—Armed Islamic Group)**, from which it split in mid-1998. Its leader was Hassan Hattab. It has a fearsome reputation, but has pledged to avoid attacks on civilians as far as possible. It is linked to the radical wing of the **Front islamique du salut (FIS—Islamic Salvation Front)** and is thought to have links with al-Qa'ida. It responds to preaching by **Ali Belhadj**, one of the most prominent leaders of the banned FIS. It began operations in the region east of Algiers and Kabylia—in the region between Boumerdes province and Kabylia. Some of its 'emirs' are of **Berber** (Kabyle) origin. It is now reported to have groups in eastern Algeria, notably Jijel, Tizi Ouzou, Sétif and the area around Constantine. A GSPC group also operates in the Lakhdaria-Kadiria region, 70 km south of Algiers. The local 'emir' of this el-Farouk group is reportedly Ahmed Djebri. The GSPC operates in some cities, such as Boghni. Its numerical strength is unknown. Estimates range from several hundreds to several thousands inside Algeria. The GSPC has networks outside Algeria, notably in Europe. About 90 members reportedly surrendered under an amnesty in 1999–2000.

Growth, Employment and Redistribution (GEAR)

A document produced by a team of economists established by the South African Minister of Trade and Industry, Alec Erwin, in mid-1995 to rethink the **Reconstruction and Development Programme (RDP)** that had been adopted by the **African National Congress (ANC)** as an election manifesto and was the only major economic strategy document available to the new ANC government once it had decided to jettison that of the **Macroeconomic Research Group (MERG)**, *Making*

Democracy Work. The GEAR was an unashamedly liberal economic programme, well in line with the so-called '**Washington consensus**' and involving a combination of relaxed exchange rates, privatization, fiscal discipline and collaboration with the private sector to produce export-driven growth. GEAR marked the completion of a series of U-turns on the part of the ANC leadership with respect to economic strategy for development. It caused great acrimony within the alliance, with the **Confederation of South African Trade Union (COSATU)** and the South African Communist Party particularly feeling that their socialist concerns had been cast aside. What had added insult to injury was the fact that the GEAR had been presented by the ANC without even a debate in its National Executive Committee. Much criticized by those on the left, the GEAR became the framework for South Africa's economic development during the second half of the 1990s and into the new millennium. COSATU, which since 1991 had been developing its own policy documents, which informed the MERG discussions, felt that the abandonment of the MERG document, and the jettisoning of the RDP in favour of the neo-liberal GEAR, marked a shift to the right by the ruling ANC, and this has provided grounds for increasing tension between the two organizations and their respective leaderships. This was exacerbated by the GEAR's failure to achieve the five-year targets set for it in 1996. Rates of economic growth in the first two years of the new millennium were 3.4% and 2.2% respectively, rather than the anticipated 6%. There was a recovery in 2002 and the government was optimistic that 'the tide had turned' (as **Mbeki** put it in his State of the Nation speech in February 2003).

Guinea, Republic of

The Republic of Guinea is situated on the west coast of Africa and borders Guinea-Bissau, Senegal, Mali, Côte d'Ivoire, Liberia and Sierra Leone. The total area of the country is 245, 857 sq km. At mid-2003 the population was estimated at 8,480,000. The capital is Conakry, whose population was estimated at 1.4m. in mid-2003. There are four main ethnic groups in Guinea. The **Pulaar** or Fulani dominate the north west; the Malinke the eastern half of the country; and the Soussou the area around Conakry and along the coast. The southern forest region is inhabited by the Kissi, Loma and Kpelle peoples. The official language is French, but Soussou, Manika and six other national languages are widely spoken. Most of the inhabitants are Muslims, but some follow traditional animist beliefs. Around 2% are Roman Catholics.

Political profile

Under the terms of the Constitution promulgated on 23 December 1991, and amended in April 1992 and November 2001, the President of the Republic, who is Head of State, is elected for seven years by universal adult suffrage, in the context of a multi-party political system. The 114-member Assemblée nationale, which holds legislative power, is elected by universal suffrage for a five-year term. The

President of the Republic is also Head of Government, and in this capacity appoints the other members of the Council of Ministers.

At a presidential election held on 21 December 2003, **Gen. Lansana Conté** received 95.25% of votes cast in the first round of voting and was re-elected as President. Conté first came to power in Guinea in April 1984, following a bloodless coup. He was first elected as President in December 1993, and subsequently re-elected in December 1998.

Following a general election held on 30 June 2002, the distribution of seats in the Assemblée nationale was as follows: Parti de l'unité et du progrès (PUP—Party of Unity and Progress) 85; Union pour le progrès et le renouvean (UPR—Union for Progress and Renewal) 20; Union pour le progrès de la Guinée (UPG—Union for the Progress of Guinea) 3; Parti démocratique de Guinée—Rassemblement démocratique africain (PDG—RDA—Democratic Party of Guinea—Democratic African Rally) 3; Alliance nationale pour le progrès (ANP—National Alliance for Progress) 2; Union pour le progrès national—Parti pour l'unité et le développement (UPN—PUD—Union for National Progress—Party for Unity and Development) 1.

History

In September 1958, in a plebiscite, Guinea overwhelmingly rejected membership of the French **Franc Zone**. The French withdrew and on 21 October Guinea proclaimed itself a sovereign and independent republic with **Ahmed Sekou Touré**, leader of the PDG, as President. President Touré isolated himself from the international community, governed autocratically and repressed human rights and any opposition to his style of government. During his presidency more than 1m. Guineans fled the country. President Touré died in the USA in March 1984 and before his successor could be chosen the armed forces staged a bloodless coup. A Comité militaire de redressement national (CMRN—Military Committee for National Recovery) was set up, headed by Col (later Gen.) Lansana Conté. In 1990 a new constitution was introduced that provided for transition to a two-party democratic system over a period of up to five years. However, successive promised elections were postponed. A presidential election eventually took place in December 1993. Conté was the successful candidate, but his opponents complained that the ballot had been manipulated and results in opposition strongholds annulled. In December 1998 Conté won a second five-year mandate with a larger majority.

Alpha Condé was the leader of the opposition Rassemblement populaire guinéen (RPG) and contested the presidential election held in December 1998. His arrest two days after the election provoked international condemnation. Condé was subsequently charged with attempting to leave the country illegally in order to destabilize Guinea following his electoral defeat. In September 2000 he was convicted and sentenced to five years' imprisonment, together with seven of 47 co-accused Legislative elections that were scheduled to take place in November 2000 were posponed owing to widespread insecurity. In May 2001 President Conté unexpectedly freed Condé, although his civic and political rights were not restored and he subsequently left the country for exile in France. In November a referendum was held in which 96% of voters approved the amendment of the Constitution to allow the President to serve indefinitely and to lift the age restriction on the presidency. The referendum was widely criticized by independent Guinean newspapers and outside observers who regarded it as a set-back to Guinea's progress towards democratic change.

In legislative elections held on 30 June 2002 the PUP won 85 seats in the Assemblée nationale—a majority of about two-thirds. International observers declined to witness the poll as it was clear even before it was held that it could not be free and fair: among other things, the electoral commission was not independent of the government and voter lists had not been updated.

In early 2004 there was increasing speculation that the President's ill health would soon create a power vacuum. Conté was rarely seen in public, and during his reinstatement as President in January 2004, following a presidential election held in December 2003, his indisposition was evident. Two Prime Ministers resigned in rapid succession. The second of these, the former Minister of Foreign Affairs, François Louseny Fall, claimed that he had been obstructed in trying to carry out economic reforms. His resignation, in late April 2004, coincided with the arrest of former Prime Minister Sidya Touré and of a deputy army chief of staff, Col Mamadou Camara, who were charged with planning a *coup d'état*. In December 2004 Cellou Dalein Diallo was nominated as Prime Minister.

In January 2005 Antoine Gbokolo Soromou, leader of the opposition Alliance nationale pour le développement (who had been among those imprisoned with Alpha Condé between 1998 and 2001) was arrested, allegedly in connection with the forgery of national identity cards. He was released and placed under judicial control, but subsequently disappeared. Also in January it was announced that President Conté had survived an assassination attempt during an attack on his convoy in Conakry. There was speculation that Sierra Leonean and Ivorian elements had been involved in the incident, while opposition commentators denounced the attack as staged.

International relations

The **Mano River Union (MRU)** was formed in 1973 to establish a customs and economic union between Guinea, Liberia and Sierra Leone. Subsequently, members signed a mutual non-aggression pact and pledged to establish a permanent mechanism for conflict prevention. Despite this, relations between the three countries have not always been amicable and the MRU has failed to live up to its original ideals. There have been various initiatives aimed at restoring peace to the MRU, in particular the International Contact Group on Liberia. Guinea's relations with Liberia improved markedly from August 2003, when that country's President, **Charles Taylor**, was forced into exile and the incumbent government, rebel factions, political opposition and civil organizations in Liberia reached a peace agreement providing for the formation of a transitional power-sharing government and legislature. Relations between Guinea and Sierra Leone were complicated in the early 2000s by an ongoing dispute over ownership of the border town of Yenga, in a reportedly diamond-rich region of Sierra Leone, which Guinean troops had occupied in 1998. In a joint statement in September 2004, signed by President Conté and President Tabbah of Sierra Leone, it was announced that both countries recognised Yenga as belonging to Sierra Leone, on the basis of a border agreement of 1912 between the British and French colonial powers. However, it was reported in early 2005 that Guinean troops continued to occupy the area. Guinea has growing trade and tourism links on a bilateral basis with Mali and Guinea Bissau.

Relations with both the government of France and with private French interests strengthened considerably in the 1990s: official assistance from, and trade with, France is of great importance to the Guinean economy, as is French participation in the mining sector and in newly privatized organizations. However, in the early 2000s military assistance from France to Guinea was reduced and, to some extent, supplanted by support from other sources: Guinea signed a pact of military co-operation with Russia in 2001, and received military aid from the People's Republic of China in 2002, while in mid-2002 the US military participated in the training of Guinean troops.

Guinea, economy

In 2003, according to estimates by the **World Bank**, Guinea's gross national income (GNI), measured at average 2001–03 prices, was US $3,559m., equivalent to $430 per head (or $2,100 on an international purchasing-power parity basis). During 1990–2003, it was estimated, the population increased at an average annual rate of 2.5%, while gross domestic product (GDP) per head increased, in real terms, by an average of 1.3% per year. Overall GDP increased, in real terms, at an average annual rate of 3.8% in 1990–2003, with GDP growth of 2.1% recorded in 2003. Annual inflation averaged 5.2% in 1991–2003; consumer prices increased by an average of 12.9% in 2003. Mining, in particular of bauxite (see **aluminium and bauxite)**, but also of other minerals and of **gold**, is Guinea's main foreign-exchange earner—more than 80% of the country's exports derive from the mining sector. **Agriculture** and industry are also important to the economy. In 2004 the Republic of Korea, Russia, Spain, Ireland, the USA, Germany, France, Ukraine and Belgium were the main markets for Guinea's exports. France, the People's Republic of China, the Netherlands, Belgium, the USA, Italy, South Africa, Côte d'Ivoire and India were the principal suppliers of imports in that year. The national currency is the Guinean franc. In 2003 the average exchange rate was US $1 = 1,984.9 Guinean francs.

Guinea has abundant natural resources, including bauxite—25% of the world's known reserves—**diamonds**, gold and other metals. The country also has great potential for hydroelectric power. While bauxite and aluminium are currently the only major exports, the Guinean government plans to encourage the mining of other resources. Other industries include processing plants for beer, juices, soft drinks, and tobacco. Agriculture employs 80% of the country's labour force. The government encourages a free market economy and is determined to promote foreign investment. There is an ongoing privatization programme, in line with the government's **poverty**-focused model of development, which reserves a key role for the private sector.

Since 1984 a process of economic liberalization has been under way. Despite positive overall results in 1984–96 (including economic growth of 4% and single-digit inflation), performance was uneven, successes alternating with policy reversals, especially in 1995. Measures taken in the aftermath of the failed military coup in 1996, including a 50% pay increase for the **military**, had adverse fiscal consequences. Since July 1996, when a strong economic management team was put in place, remarkable progress has been made in the areas of macroeconomic management, fiscal discipline, budget elaboration and implementation, and addressing public-sector **corruption**. In 1997–98 real GDP grew at an average rate of about 4.7% and the rate of inflation averaged 3.5%. Performance in the fiscal sector was broadly satisfactory, and non-mining revenue rose from 7.3% of GDP to 7.9%. The primary balance averaged 2.7% of GDP in 1997–98, compared with 1.3% in 1996, and the external current account deficit was reduced from 7.6% of GDP at the end of 1996 to 6% in 1998. In 1999 declines in demand for and in the prices of bauxite and aluminium, together with the tenuous security situation in neighbouring countries, impeded Guinea's economic performance: growth in real GDP is estimated to have fallen to 3.7%.

In an attempt to remove domestic constraints on growth, the **Conté** regime introduced a series of policy reforms during the 1990s, in conjunction with the **International Monetary Fund** and the World Bank. These included the transfer of various state and para-statal enterprises to private interests, the liberalization of foreign trade and the abolition of price controls, together with monetary and banking reforms and a reduction in the number of civil-service personnel. These reforms appear to have had a significant effect, with real GDP growth in 1990–2002 averaging 3.9% per year. Real GDP continued to grow—by 4.2% in 2002 and by 3.0% in 2003. Continuing growth was attributed partially to these reforms, but principally to an expansion in mineral exports and some investment in infrastructure projects. Guinea's current growth levels, though encouraging, are still considered to be below potential, especially in view of the country's tremendous natural resource endowments. The national economy is still relatively undiversified, relying mostly on bauxite and mining revenue. There is also considerable room for improving revenue mobilization. Guinea's social indicators compare poorly with those of neighbouring countries in **sub-Saharan Africa**, although significant progress has recently been made in primary **education** and access to safe **water**.

Guinea-Bissau, Republic of

The Republic of Guinea-Bissau lies on the west coast of Africa, with Senegal to the north and Guinea to the east and south. The area of the country is 36,125 sq km. At mid-2003 the population was estimated at 1,493,000. The official language is Portuguese, of which the locally spoken form is Creole (Crioulo). There are 19 local languages, of which the most widely spoken are Balanta-Kentohe, **Pulaar** (Fula), Mandjak, Mandinka and Papel. The principal religious beliefs are animism and **Islam**. There is a small minority of Roman Catholics and other Christian groups. The capital is Bissau, whose population was estimated at 335,876 in mid-2003.

Political profile

Under the terms of the 1984 Constitution (revised in 1991, 1996 and 1999), Guinea-Bissau is a multi-party state, although the formation of parties on a tribal or geographical basis is prohibited. Legislative power is vested in the Assembléia Nacional Popular (ANP), which comprises 100 members, elected by universal adult suffrage for a term of four years. Executive power is vested in the President of the Republic, who is Head of State and who governs with the assistance of an appointed Council of Ministers, led by the Prime Minister. The President is elected by universal adult suffrage for a term of five years. However, on 14 September 2003 the elected President, **Kumba Yalá**, was deposed in a military coup led by the chief of staff of the armed forces, Gen. Veríssimo Correia Seabra. Yalá formally announced his resignation on 17 September. Transitional civilian institutions were inaugurated on 28 September, in accordance with an agreement signed by political organizations and the military authorities; **Henrique Pereira Rosa** became interim President. Elections to the ANP (which had been dissolved by Yalá in November 2002) took place on 28 and 30 March 2004. A presidential election was to be held 12 months later; however, in March 2005 it was announced that the election would not take place until July.

History

Portuguese Guinea (Guiné) was colonized by Portugal in the 15th century. Nationalist activism began to emerge in the 1950s. Armed insurgency commenced in the early 1960s, and by 1972 the **Partido Africano da Independência da Guiné e Cabo Verde (PAIGC—African Party for the Independence of Guinea and Cape Verde)** was in control of two-thirds of the country. The **independence** of the Republic of Guinea-Bissau was unilaterally proclaimed in September 1973, with **Luís Cabral** (the brother of the founder of the PAIGC, **Amílcar Cabral**) as President of the State Council. Hostilities ceased following the military coup in Portugal in April 1974, and on 10 September Portugal recognized the independence of Guinea-Bissau under the leadership of Luís Cabral. The PAIGC regime introduced measures to establish a single-party socialist state.

The PAIGC initially supervised both Cape Verde and Guinea-Bissau, the Constitutions of each remaining separate but with a view to eventual unification. These arrangements were terminated in November 1980, when President Cabral was deposed in a coup organized by João Vieira, the Chief State Commissioner, who was installed as Chairman of the Council of the Revolution. In March 1984 Vieira formally assumed the role of Head of Government. In May the ANP, which had been dissolved following the 1980 coup, was re-established, and the Council of the Revolution was replaced by a 15-member Council of State (Conselho de Estado), selected from among the members of the ANP. Vieira was subsequently elected as President of the Conselho de Estado and Head of State. The ANP immediately ratified the new Constitution, and formally abolished the position of Prime Minister.

In December 1990 the Central Committee of the PAIGC agreed to the adoption of a multi-party system, following a period of transition, and the holding of a presidential election in 1993. In May 1991 a series of constitutional amendments ending one-party rule were approved by the ANP, terminating the political monopoly of the PAIGC.

Legislation preparing for the transition to a multi-party democracy was approved by the ANP in February 1993, and in the following month a commission was appointed to supervise the forthcoming elections. In the elections, which were eventually held in July 1994, the PAIGC secured a clear majority in the ANP, while in the presidential election Vieira obtained 46.3% of the votes, and his nearest rival, Kumba Yalá of the Partido para a Renovação Social (PRS—Party for Social Renewal), secured 21.9% of the votes. As no candidate had obtained an absolute majority, the two leading candidates contested a second round of polling in August, in which Vieira was the victor. Vieira was duly inaugurated as President in September.

In June 1998 rebel troops, led by Brig. (later Gen.) Ansumane Mané, seized control of the Bra military barracks in the capital, as well as other strategic locations in the city. Mané subsequently formed a 'military junta for the consolidation of democracy, peace and justice' and demanded the resignation of Vieira and his administration. With the support of Senegalese and Guinean soldiers, troops loyal to the government attempted unsuccessfully to regain control of rebel-held areas of the city, and heavy fighting ensued. In November, under the aegis of the **Economic Community of West African States (ECOWAS)**, a peace agreement was concluded between the two sides, under the terms of which a previous cease-fire in August was reaffirmed, and it was resolved that the withdrawal of Senegalese and Guinean troops from Guinea-Bissau should be conducted simultaneously with the deployment of an **ECOWAS Cease-fire Monitoring Group (ECOMOG)** interposition force, which would guarantee security on the border with Senegal. It was also agreed that a government of national unity would be established, to include representatives of the rebel junta, and that presidential and legislative elections would be held no later than March 1999. (The elections did not take place as planned, however, owing to a further outbreak of conflict, followed by another cease-fire agreement.)

In May 1999 Vieira announced that the elections would take place on 28 December. However, on 7 May, to widespread condemnation by the international community, Vieira was overthrown by the rebel military junta. On 10 May Vieira signed an unconditional surrender. The President of the ANP was appointed acting

President of the Republic pending a presidential election, and the government of national unity (which had been announced in February) remained in office. At a meeting in late May of representatives of the government, the military junta and the political parties, agreement was reached that Vieira should stand trial for his involvement in arms-trafficking to the **Casamance** separatists (in Senegal) and for political and economic crimes relating to his terms in office. Vieira agreed to stand trial, but only after receiving medical treatment abroad, after which, he pledged, he would return to Guinea-Bissau. ECOMOG forces were withdrawn from the country in June. In that month Vieira went into exile in Portugal where he was offered political asylum.

Presidential and legislative elections took place in November 1999. Of the 102 seats in the enlarged legislature, the PRS secured 38, the Resistência da Guiné-Bissau—Movimento Bah-Fatah (RGB—MB, Guinea-Bissau Resistance—Bah-Fatah Movement) 28, the PAIGC 24, the Aliança Democrática (AD, Democratic Alliance—an alliance of the FD and the Partido da Convergência Democrática (PCD—Party of Democratic Convergence) four, the União par a Mudança (UM—Union for Change) three, the Partido Social Democrático (PSD—Social Democratic Party) three, and the Frente Democrática Social (FDS—Social Democratic Front) and the União Nacional para a Democracia e o Progresso (UNDP—National Union for Democracy and Progress) one each. As no candidate received the necessary 50% of the votes to win the presidential election outright, the leading candidates, Kumba Yalá of the PRS and Malam Bacai Sanhá of the PAIGC, contested a second round of voting on 16 January 2000, at which Yalá secured victory.

In September 2003 President Yalá was detained by the armed forces in a bloodless *coup d'état*, which was widely welcomed within Guinea-Bissau. The chief of staff of the armed forces, Gen. Veríssimo Correia Seabra, who led the coup, stated that the seizure of power had been a response to increasing unrest in the army and the worsening political and economic situation. Seabra proclaimed himself interim President of Guinea-Bissau, and President of a Comité Militar para a Recuperação da Ordem Constitucional e Democrática (Military Committee for the Restoration of Constitutional and Democratic Order). On 17 September Yalá officially resigned the presidency, and on 28 September Henrique Pereira Rosa and Artur Sanhá were sworn in as interim President and Prime Minister, respectively. On 2 October a transitional civilian government was appointed, in accordance with an agreement signed by political organizations and the military authorities. It was envisaged that elections to the ANP (which had been dissolved in November 2002) would be held within six months, and a presidential election within 18 months. A 56-member National Transition Council (NTC), composed of representatives of political and civil groups and the army, was to monitor government policy.

Elections to the ANP took place in March 2004, in which the PAIGC won 45 of the 100 seats, leaving it short of an absolute majority, while the PRS secured 35 and the Partido Unido Social Democrático (PUSD—United Social Democratic Party) 17.

International relations

In 1996 Guinea-Bissau was among the five lusophone countries in Africa which, together with Brazil and Portugal, officially established the **Comunidade dos Países de Língua Portuguesa**, a lusophone grouping for joint co-operation. Throughout the 1990s and subsequently Guinea-Bissau's relations with Senegal were marred by repeated Senegalese claims that the Guinea-Bissau government provided support to Casamance separatists, and by border issues. In 2001 the two countries issued a joint statement reaffirming their commitment to an agreement concluded in 2000 that provided for the establishment of a joint military force to patrol the border area. Relations between Guinea-Bissau and The Gambia were severely strained in June 2002, when President Yalá accused the government of The Gambia of harbouring and training Casamance rebels and former associates of Gen. Mané. Despite being generally welcomed in Guinea-Bissau, the coup of September 2003 was officially condemned by the international community, and sanctions imposed by the USA were not lifted until August 2004. However, President Rosa visited Portugal and a number of West African countries in late 2003 in an effort to gain support and financial aid for the transitional government, as well as the US headquarters of the UN, the **International Monetary Fund** and the **World Bank**.

Guinea-Bissau, economy

In 2003, according to estimates by the **World Bank**, Guinea-Bissau's gross national income (GNI), measured at average 2001–03 prices, was US $228.6m., equivalent to $140 per head (or $660 on an international purchasing-power parity basis). During 1990–2003, it was estimated, the population increased at an average annual rate of 3.0%, while gross domestic product (GDP) per head decreased, in real terms, by an average of 3.0% per year. Overall GDP decreased, in real terms, at an average annual rate of 0.5% in 1990–2003; real GDP declined by 7.2% in 2002 and by 1.2% in 2003. In 1990–2002 the average annual rate of inflation was 27.0%. Consumer prices decreased by 3.5% in 2003. **Agriculture** dominates the economy and industry typically involves the processing of agricultural products. In 2003 the principal source of imports was Portugal; other major suppliers were the People's Republic of China, Senegal, France and the Netherlands. In that year India was the principal market for exports. The national currency is the CFA franc (see the **Franc Zone**). In 2004 the average exchange rate was US $1 = 528.28 francs CFA.

One of the poorest countries in the world (ranking 205th out of 208 countries in terms of GNI per head, according to the **International Monetary Fund—IMF)**, Guinea-Bissau depends mainly on agriculture and fishing. Cashew growing has increased remarkably in recent years, and the country now ranks sixth in the world in cashew production. Guinea-Bissau exports fish and seafood along with small amounts of groundnuts, palm kernels and timber. Rice is the major crop and the staple food.

The conflict in 1998–99 destroyed much of the country's small industrial sector and some infrastructure. This left a substantial part of the economic infrastructure in ruins and resulted in a deepening of Guinea-Bissau's already widespread **poverty**. Following **Poverty Reduction and Growth Facility** and **Heavily Indebted Poor Countries initiative** decision point approval in December 2000, the country's macroeconomic performance has fallen short of expectations. In 2001 no economic growth was recorded, largely due to weak demand associated with a fall in the export price of cashew nuts and a sizeable loss of foreign assistance. In spite of some improvements in budget administration, the government was not able to bring the IMF Staff-Monitored Program back on track at the end of 2001. Following Yalá's dismissal and the transition to a new elected body, the World Bank and the IMF effectively halted negotiations on resuming assistance to Guinea-Bissau until after the legislative elections had taken place. The IMF has since expressed interest in starting a new programme to distribute and encourage further aid for post-conflict reconstruction. In December 2003 the UNDP established an Emergency Economic Management Fund to assist Guinea-Bissau through the period of transition. The Fund was to be managed jointly by the government, the IMF and the World Bank, UNDP and the **African Development Bank**. In January 2004 an 'emergency budget' for the year forecast expenditure totalling $108m., the bulk of which was for the payment of military and civil service salary arrears. However, not all pledges have so far been met and the government still faces significant budgetary shortfalls and continued strikes by unpaid workers. Indeed, the government's financial problems and its difficulties in paying civil servants' wages on time have generated an almost permanent state of labour unrest. Strikes continued in 2002–03—despite a decision, criticized by the IMF, to increase public-sector wages from September 2002—as by August 2003 many civil servants had not been paid for nine months. The interim administration has had some success in clearing the wage arrears that it inherited, and in early 2004 withdrew $2.5m. from the emergency budget to pay salaries for the period January–April 2004 for 11,000 civil servants.

Economic problems have also affected the banking system. Unpaid loans have placed the Banco Internacional da Guiné-Bissau on the brink of bankruptcy. Since its closure would be a severe blow to the fragile private sector, the central bank, the **Banque centrale des états de l'Afrique de l'ouest**, promised in late 2001 to grant it $9m. in order to offset $8m. of debts. However, this recapitalization was not forthcoming, obliging the government to announce the bank's closure in March 2002.

H

Habré, Hissène

A northerner who in 1979 overthrew President **Félix Malloum** of Chad, after having briefly formed an alliance with him against Habré's rival Goukouni Oueddai. Libya, Sudan and Niger engineered a superficial accord between Oueddai and Habré, but in 1980 Libya enabled Oueddai to put Habré to flight. In 1981 Chad and Libya announced their union and Libyan troops were withdrawn from the former. Habré was thus able to renew the conflict. Libya renewed its support for Oueddai, particularly from 1983, while Habré received support from **Zaire**, the People's Republic of China, the USA and France.

Ould Haidalla, Lt-Col Khouna

Head of State of Mauritania from January 1980 until December 1984, when he was overthrown by **Col Maaouiya Ould Sidi Ahmed Taya**.

Haile Selassie

Emperor, who, with the exception of five years of Italian rule in 1936–41, ruled Ethiopia in 1930–74. During this time he acquired an international reputation for longevity in politics (and in other respects), and as an African statesman. By 1973, however, Haile Selassie was being pressed to abdicate. He refused to do so, and in the following year a group of army officers mutinied. The mutiny led to a further revolt, and to the dethronement of the Emperor, who later died in prison.

Hamas (Algeria)

Al-Haraka li-Mujtama' Islami evolved from a previously non-political Islamic association, **al-Irshad wa'l Islah (Movement for Guidance and Reform)**, founded by Sheikh Mahfoud Nahnah. The new Hamas was established in December 1990, two months after a meeting (on 20 September) organized by Sheikh Nahnah, and attended, at his invitation, by more than 300 local Islamic associations and several minor parties which sought to unify the Islamist movement. Hamas was expected eventually to function like a political party. Its name was a direct allusion to the principal Islamist movement involved in the uprising (*intifada*) in the Occupied Territories of the West Bank and the Gaza Strip. In outlook Hamas could be situated in the tradition of the **Muslim Brotherhood** in the Middle East, but on the left wing of that tradition. It was anticipated that it would be likely to adhere to the evolutionary perspective of its predecessor, al-Irshad wa'l Islah, which tended to emphasize the need to reform society through Islamic missionary activity before it would be possible to reform the state in accordance with Islamic principles. This was in marked contrast to the 'revolutionary' perspective of the **Front islamique du salut (FIS—Islamic Salvation Front)**. Sheikh Nahnah expressed a more principled acceptance of the rules of the pluralist political process, in contrast to the purely tactical acceptance of it by the FIS. These differences, however, did not prevent Sheikh Nahnah from urging his followers to vote for Islamists in the June 1990 elections held in Algeria, and so, by implication, for the FIS, but they probably explain the decision to establish a distinct, rival party after the September 1990 meeting. The move was denounced as divisive by the FIS, which did not attend the meeting. Hamas had a strong following in Blida, a large town some 30 miles south of Algiers, where Sheikh Nahnah himself was based. It held well-attended meetings in southern Algeria and is reported to have expanded its membership throughout much of central Algeria. It was also reported in the early 2000s to have a nation-wide network of offices. Little information was available, however, concerning Hamas' leadership, other than that Sheikh Nahnah's deputy was Muhammad Bouslimani.

Hamrouche, Mouloud

Prime Minister of Algeria in 1989–91. Led a government committed to democratic political reforms and economic liberalization under the presidency of **Benjedid Chadli**.

Hassan II (Moulay Hassan Muhammadi ibn Yussuf)

Born in 1929, died in 1999. King of Morocco in 1961–99. Formerly crown prince until he succeeded his father as king. In 1960 Hassan was appointed as Minister of Defence and deputy Premier and successfully led the negotiations with France, Spain and the USA which ensured the withdrawal of foreign troops from Morocco. Coming to the throne in 1961, he was an authoritarian ruler, who made maximum use of his status as Commander of the Faithful as well as Head of State to ensure his religious and political dominance in Morocco. The main religious authorities (e.g. the *ulema*) and the political parties were orchestrated by him to establish what appeared to be a relatively open society but was in reality a highly controlled system of patronage and coercion. The survivor of three attempted assassinations, Hassan II was regarded with mixed feelings by his subjects. An effective secret police and heavy reaction to political opposition ensured political stability, or, rather, the absence of political activity and Hassan II was at times fiercely criticized by organizations in other countries for what were regarded as violations of human rights, political oppression and the cruel punishment of prisoners. However, he is also recognized as having been one of the more important participants in the peace process in the Middle East that was contemporaneous with more than 10 of the final years of his rule. Under Hassan II Morocco's relations with neighbouring countries (Algeria and Mauritania) were at times tense, and inside Morocco every effort was made to uphold the King's position and maintain the stability of the country. In 1962 he introduced a new constitution, which permitted a popularly elected legislature. In 1975 he initiated the Green March, whereby 350,000 civilians marched into the former Spanish colony, later named **Western Sahara**, claiming the territory as Moroccan and taking control over the northern two-thirds of it. By 1976 the part of Western Sahara occupied by Morocco in the preceding year had been officially annexed. The annexation is not recognized by any foreign state, however. In 1979, following the Mauritanian withdrawal from the southern part of Western Sahara, Morocco annexed the remainder of the territory, without taking control of the border town of La Gouera. The politics of Hassan II were among the most Western-friendly in **North Africa**, and in many cases Hassan played an important role in international affairs. In 1991 Morocco was the only **Maghreb** country to contribute troops to the UN actions against Iraq in Kuwait. Much of Hassan's domestic success, in particular his confrontation of Islamist elements, rested on his family's claim to be sharifs, descendants of the Prophet Muhammad, a claim that was widely accepted in Morocco as well as abroad. Moreover, Hassan took pains to preserve Moroccan heritage and religion. The world's highest mosque, completed in 1993, was built on his initiative and is named after him. Morocco, at the time of Hassan's death, suffered from high unemployment, an inappropriate educational system, an unresolved situation in Western Sahara and strong tensions within the population. On the other hand, Morocco had during the last decades of his rule developed an excellent infrastructure, and in some sectors, such as information technology and tourism, the Moroccan economy had achieved very positive growth.

Hausa

Major ethno-linguistic group in northern Nigeria.

Heavily Indebted Poor Countries (HIPC) initiative

The Heavily Indebted Poor Countries (HIPC) initiative was devised by the **G8** and other members of the Organisation for Economic Co-operation and Development to provide **debt relief** for the most heavily indebted poor countries, many of them in **sub-Saharan Africa**. Twelve African countries have reached the HIPC completion point: Benin, Burkina Faso, Ethiopia, Ghana, Madagascar, Mali, Mauritania, Mozambique, Niger, Senegal, Tanzania and Uganda. However, many of the countries that qualify for a cancellation of **debt** under the HIPC are in less desperate economic straits than some of those that do not. Kenya, for example, does not qualify for the HIPC initiative, but arguably has a greater need for inclusion at the present time than does Mozambique.

HIV/AIDS in Africa

Infection by the human immunodeficiency virus (HIV), the cause of acquired immunodeficiency syndrome (AID), is now widespread throughout most of Africa, particularly in the sub-continent south of the Sahara. Some 3.5m. people are newly infected each year and between 2–2.5m. die of AIDS in Africa each year. At the end of 2001 the number of adults and children living with HIV/AIDS in this region totalled 28.5m. Some 2.2m. Africans died of AIDS in 2001. The estimated number of children in the region who have been orphaned as a result of AIDS is 11m. It has been projected that in 2000–20, 55m. Africans will die earlier than they would have died in the absence of AIDS. (This projection is based on the assumption that prevention, treatment and care programmes will have a modest effect on the growth and impact of the epidemic in the next two decades.) The rate of transmission of the virus varies from population to population, depending on gender relations and sexual mores. Infection rates are lower in the Islamic north of the continent than in the more permissive southern and central regions. In Africa, unlike other regions of the world, more **women** than men have been infected, although rates equalize between the two sexes when they reach their mid-thirties as the women who became infected by the virus when young die and men become old and prosperous enough to begin to support younger mistresses. In much of eastern and **southern Africa** between one-fifth and one-third of adults are infected. In Botswana and Swaziland almost 40% are infected. Life expectancy is severely affected. In Zambia, a woman's life expectancy has been reduced to a little over 30 years, whereas it would have been closer to 55 years in the absence of AIDS; in Zimbabwe, female life expectancy has fallen to just over 30 years, whereas it would have been 70 had AIDS been absent. In other southern African countries (Botswana, Namibia and South Africa), the differences between actual life expectancy and what it might have been are probably similar. At least 10% of those aged 15–49 are infected in 12 African countries. Seven countries, all in southern Africa, now have prevalence rates higher than 20%: Botswana (38.8%), Lesotho (31%), Namibia (22.5%), South Africa (20.1%), Swaziland (33.4%), Zambia (21.5%) and Zimbabwe (33.7%).

In several of the worst-affected countries—including one of the earliest affected, Uganda—HIV prevalence appears to be levelling off. However, this reflects not so much a reduction in the rate of new infections as an increase in death rates. The human consequences of the HIV/AIDS epidemic in Africa are well documented; the economic impact is harder to predict. Some scientists believe for instance, that however grim at the household and local level, the epidemic will only reduce overall economic growth at the national level by a percentage point each year. As happened in Europe after the Black Death, labour may become scarcer and command higher returns; there may be more available agricultural land. But others are more concerned. HIV/AIDS strikes at adult earners and kills them slowly. Sick workers produce less and afflicted families are likely to spend more on medicines. Children, particularly daughters, will drop out of school to care for stricken parents. Those who have less **education** will be less able to contribute to the economy, except as labourers. Other diseases, such as **malaria** and tuberculosis, will increase in importance as those with depleted immune systems fail to ward them off and spread them more widely still. People will generally save less, work less, produce less and consume less. One recent study predicted that, unless the government moved quickly to tackle AIDS, South Africa's economy would collapse within four generations. There is evidence to suggest that HIV/AIDS spreads particularly rapidly in situations of war and conflict. Between 40%–60% of the soldiers who fought in the war in the Democratic Republic of the Congo (DRC) were HIV-positive. Five years of war, in which rape was frequently used as a weapon by Rwandan, Ugandan, Zimbabwean, Angolan and Congolese soldiers, has led to the infection of the population by a wide variety of HIV sub-types. HIV/AIDS may also itself contribute to political instability as those with little hope for the future turn to the immediate gratification of gaining spoils from criminal activity or military action.

So far, the countries that have managed to curb the epidemic have succeeded largely by persuading people to avoid risky sex. In Uganda, for example, after a campaign promoting abstinence, fidelity or the use of condoms, HIV prevalence has fallen to about 5%. In Senegal prompt government action to promote the use of condoms has helped keep HIV prevalence relatively low, at around 1%. It was estimated in June 2005 that roughly 4.7m. people in **sub-Saharan Africa** are in need of anti-retroviral (ARV) therapy, of which only about 11% are receiving it. The only region(s) with a lower rate is **North Africa** and the Middle East, where only 5% of a much smaller infected population are receiving ARV therapy. The price of the anti-retroviral medicines has fallen dramatically in recent years—from US $10,000 in 2000 to $150 in 2005, in many countries. More countries are making HIV/AIDS a national priority and are setting treatment targets and devising concrete plans to reach them. As treatment becomes available, more people are resorting to counselling and HIV-testing, which in turn helps prevention. There is also more money available and growing pressure for significant increases in development assistance, which are likely to be beneficial. In the future drugs will certainly play a greater role in treatment. As prices decline, drugs are being more widely used by African men and women. In 2002 only one HIV-positive African in 400 took anti-retrovirals; by 2005 it was hoped that some 3m. people would be taking these drugs, and many of these will be in Africa. However, the health programmes needed to deliver such levels of use will require greater commitment on the part of African governments and foreign development agencies to improving health delivery systems—and this means a substantial allocation of resources.

Houphouët-Boigny, Dr Félix

Born in 1905, Félix Houphouët-Boigny was a deputy in the French Assembly in 1946–48. As much at home in France as he was in Ivory Coast (now Côte d'Ivoire), he was one of the longest-lasting of the early African leaders. Conservative and pro-Western, he became President of Ivory Coast at **independence** in 1960, and remained in office nearly 30 years later, in 1988. He represented the evolutionary rather than the revolutionary wing of African **nationalism**, but his grip on the politics of Ivory Coast was never seriously threatened. In 1983, as a mark of respect, the government transferred the capital from Abdijan to Yamoussoukro, his birth-place. President and chairman of the single ruling party, the Parti démocratique de la Côte d'Ivoire (PDCI—Democratic Party of Côte d'Ivoire), Houphouët-Boigny regarded himself very much as the father of the nation, and he maintained a paternalistic system of personal rule through the PDCI until 1990, when a multi-party system was finally established. In the first contested presidential election, Houphouët-Boigny easily defeated his main opponent, **Laurent Gbagbo** of the Front populaire ivoirien (Ivorian Popular Front). Houphouët-Boigny died in December 1993, and was succeeded by the president of the Assemblée nationale, Henri Bédié, also of the PDCI.

Hutu(s)

Ill-defined majority group of the population of Burundi and Rwanda; also found in the Democratic Republic of the Congo. During the Belgian colonial administration of these three territories, the local population tended to be divided and classified into three main groups—the majority Hutu, the substantial minority **Tutsi** and the demographically (and economically and socially) marginal **Twa**. The last of these were also known as **pygmies** and were the original inhabitants, living as hunters and gatherers particularly in the forest regions. The Hutu tended to be agriculturalists and were regarded by the Belgians (and themselves) as the largest and most important social group. The minority Tutsis were historically pastoralists and agro-pastoralists and considered to be more recent immigrants than the Hutu. They also tended to dominate politically. Belgium systematized the previously relatively fluid distinctions between Tutsi and Hutu into a clear hierarchy (which some Belgian anthropologists likened to a 'feudal' system of estates), with the Tutsi as the dominant 'aristocracy' and the Hutu as the peasantry, and the Twa as the aborigines. In the period after **independence** these distinctions became the source of major social and political tension and eventually conflict, culminating in major civil wars in all three countries in which these 'ethnic' distinctions played a critical part in the **genocide** that took place.

I

Ibadism

Ibadism is a distinct sect of **Islam** that is neither **Sunni** nor **Shi‘a**. It exists mainly in Oman (where it is the majority religion), in Zanzibar, **East Africa**, and in the **Maghreb**—in the Nafus mountains of Libya, the island of Jerba in Tunisia and the Mzab valley of Algeria. The sect developed out of the 7th-century Islamic sect known as the Khawarij, and shares with that group the desire to found a righteous Muslim society and the belief that true Muslims are only to be found in their own sect. The Ibadis broke off early from the mainstream of Islam and are usually regarded as heretics.

Ibo(s)

Major ethnic or tribal grouping extending across the borders of Nigeria and Cameroon.

Idris I, Said Mohammad

Born in 1890, Said Mohammad Idris as-Sanussi was the first King of Libya, who reigned in 1951–69. A grandson of the founder of the Sanussi Muslim order, he became its leader in 1917. In 1920 he was acknowledged by Italy as Emir of Cyrenaica and, in 1921, after joining forces with the Tripolitanians, as Emir of Libya. He was forced to flee to Egypt in 1922 after quarrelling with the Italian Fascists. He was restored to power by Great Britain in 1943 and became Libya’s first king when **independence** was granted in 1951. He was deposed in September 1969 by the Libyan army under the leadership of **Col Muammar al-Qaddafi** in a bloodless coup. He went into exile in Egypt, where he remained until his death in 1983.

Imperialism

A term that is generally used to refer to a system of political and economic domination. Usually prefaced by reference to a particular dominant or imperialist state—e.g. US imperialism, British imperialism, Soviet imperialism. In the Marxist tradition the term is used more precisely to refer to ‘the highest stage of capitalism’ (following Lenin) and is usually associated with the period from 1870 until the First World War. In this context, **colonialism** refers to a particular form of imperialism associated with the annexation of territory, the creation of 'colonies' or 'colonial territories' and, in some cases, the establishment of settler colonial states.

Independence

During the final decades of the 19th century, there was a 'scramble' on the part of the European powers to gain control of territories in Africa and to establish various forms of colonial administration over these territories. The colonial period in Africa lasted in broad terms for around 80 years (from 1880 until 1960). In the aftermath of the Second World War the movements for independence and self-determination, that had arisen unevenly across the continent during the 1920s and 1930s, rapidly gained ground in many parts of Africa and independence was achieved in many colonial territories during the 1950s and 1960s. The first African states to be formally emancipated from colonial rule were Egypt, which gained nominal autonomy in 1922, but real independence only in 1952, and then, a few years later, Tunisia and Sudan, both of which became independent in 1955. They were soon followed, in 1956, by Morocco. The first state in Africa south of the Sahara to achieve independence was the **Gold Coast Colony**, which emerged as Ghana in March 1957. **French Guinea** became Guinea in October 1958. However, the *annus mirabilis* as far as political independence was concerned was 1960. In that year 17 African states emerged from French colonial rule (including Chad, Côte d'Ivoire—or Ivory Coast—Madagascar, Mali and Senegal), as did Nigeria, from British control, and what had been the Belgian Congo (which became the Republic of the Congo, then later **Zaire**, and then the Democratic Republic of the Congo). Several other new states appeared within a few years, including Algeria, Burundi, Rwanda and Uganda in 1962, Kenya in 1963 and Tanzania in 1964. The Portuguese colonies had in most cases to endure a prolonged and bitter struggle for independence, which was achieved only in the 1970s: Guinea-Bissau in 1974, Angola, Cape Verde, Mozambique and São Tomé and Príncipe in 1975. More prolonged still was the independence struggle in Southern Rhodesia, which did not gain independence, as Zimbabwe, until 1980, and that of **South West Africa**, which became Namibia only in March 1990. By the end of the millennium, however, the process of decolonization and achievement of political independence had been completed across virtually the entire continent, with the exception of **Western Sahara**, and a few smaller territories, owned by the British, French and Spanish.

Indian National Congress (INC)

Originally formed by Mohandas Gandhi in the early part of the 20th century in South Africa. For many years the Indian National Congress (INC) constituted the framework for the organization of the interests of 'Indians' or 'Asians' in South Africa. The INC joined with other organizations, representing different opposition 'racial' groups at the **Congress of the People**, convened by the **African National Congress (ANC)** in June 1955, which produced the **Freedom Charter** that was later adopted as ANC policy.

Informal economy

A term used to refer to the sector of the economy where government and other formal regulations and forms of protection are generally lacking; where registration of businesses, trade union organizations, health and safety measures, etc, are largely absent. In many African economies this is a substantial sector, comprising for the most part small and micro-enterprises employing very small numbers of workers or family members. It was estimated (in the **World Bank**'s annual *Doing Business* report) that in 2005 some 40% of the region's economy was informal—the highest proportion in the world.

Inkatha Freedom Party (IFP)

Political party in South Africa. Initially a **Zulu**-supported party, it has now gained somewhat wider support. After elections held in 1999 the Inkatha Freedom Party, led by Chief Buthelezi, held the third largest number of seats (33) in the National Assembly, while the **African National Congress** held 268 seats out of a total of 400 and the **Democratic Party** 39.

Intergovernmental Authority on Development (IGAD)

The Intergovernmental Authority on Development (IGAD) was established in 1996 to supersede the **Intergovernmental Authority on Drought and Development (IGADD)**, founded in 1986. It aims to co-ordinate the sustainable development of its member states, to respond to political and humanitarian issues, to combat the effects of **drought** and desertification and to promote regional food security. Located in Djibouti, IGAD's members are: Djibouti, Eritrea, Ethiopia, Kenya, Somalia, Sudan and Uganda. During the last decade IGAD has frequently been involved in efforts to mediate between conflicting parties within the region, for example in Sudan and Somalia, and in the border conflict between Eritrea and Ethiopia. In January 2002 IGAD agreed to establish a conflict early warning and response (CEWARN) mechanism, which held its inaugural meeting in June. In 2003–04 it was effective in bringing together the two main parties in the long-standing conflict in Sudan and achieving a peace agreement between them.

Intergovernmental Authority on Drought and Development (IGADD)

The Intergovernmental Authority on Drought and Development (IGADD) was established in 1986 by Djibouti, Ethiopia, Kenya, Somalia, Sudan and Uganda, in the aftermath of serious **drought** and **famine** in the region. Eritrea became a member in September 1993, following its **independence**. In April 1995 it was resolved to reorganize and expand the Authority, and in March 1996, the **Intergovernmental Authority on Development** was endorsed to supersede IGADD with an extended mandate to co-ordinate and harmonize policy in the areas of economic co-operation and political and humanitarian affairs, in addition to its existing responsibilities for food security and environmental protection.

International Bank for Reconstruction and Development – *see* World Bank

International Criminal Tribunal for Rwanda (ICTR)

In November 1994 the UN Security Council adopted Resolution 955, establishing an International Criminal Tribunal for Rwanda (ICTR) to prosecute persons accused of **genocide** and other serious violations of humanitarian law that had been committed in Rwanda and by Rwandans in neighbouring states. The ICTR comprises three three-member trial chambers and one appeals chamber with five additional judges. Its jurisdiction is limited in time to the period 1 January–31 December 1994. The first plenary session was held in The Hague, Netherlands, in June 1995; formal proceedings at its permanent headquarters in Arusha, Tanzania, were initiated in November. The first trial commenced in January 1997, and the ICTR imposed its first sentences in July. In September 1998 the former Rwandan Prime Minister, Jean Kambanda, and a former mayor of Taba, Jean-Paul Akayesu, both **Hutu** extremists, were found guilty of genocide and crimes against humanity. Kambanda subsequently became the first person ever to be sentenced (to life imprisonment) under the 1948 Convention on the Prevention and Punishment of the Crime of Genocide. In November 2000 the UN Security Council authorized the enlargement of the appeals chamber and the election of two further judges.

In March 2002 the ICTR established a commission to investigate allegations of mistreatment of witnesses from Rwanda. By July 59 people had been detained by the ICTR. Of the defendants in the nine completed cases at that time, one had been acquitted and six were already serving sentences in Mali. Prosecutions continue, although progress is slow. However, the ICTR only deals with the main perpetrators of the genocide. Around 120,000 detainees are in prisons in Rwanda. The Rwandan government will not countenance a mass amnesty for those suspected of involvement in the genocide, but the number of detainees is beyond its capability to deal with through the conventional judicial process.

International financial institutions

International lending agencies, such as the **International Monetary Fund** and the International Bank for Reconstruction and Development, better known as the

World Bank, established at Bretton Woods in 1944, and now lenders of last resort and major influences on macroeconomic policy throughout the developing world, including the Middle East. The term is sometimes also used with reference to UN institutions such as the International Fund for Agricultural Development. It is also used for regional banks such as the Asian Development Bank, the **African Development Bank** and European Development Bank.

International financing facility

The idea of an international financing facility for African countries, most recently espoused by British Chancellor of the Exchequer, Gordon Brown, has been under consideration since the 1950s. At the **G8** summit meeting held in Gleneagles, Scotland, in 2005, it was again discussed and a working group was established to study the possible parameters of such a facility. Meanwhile, steps towards the creation of such an institution have been taken by the private sector, in collaboration with the development agencies of some of the G8 countries, including the USA and the United Kingdom—see the **African Growth and Opportunity Act** and the **Investment Climate Facility for Africa**.

International Monetary Fund (IMF)

Established in July 1944 at the Bretton Woods Conference, the International Monetary Fund (IMF) is a multilateral institution based in Washington, DC, that lends money to governments to stabilize currencies and maintain order in international financial markets. For many decades, the Fund has imposed stringent loan conditions designed to improve financial stability and macroeconomic indicators. It has been criticized by its opponents for advocating measures that tend to lead to austerity, worsening income inequality and conditions for the majority of the population in the affected countries. Even more than its partner, the **World Bank**, the Fund is known for its rigid orthodoxy and often high-handed approach to indebted countries.

Investment Climate Facility for Africa (ICF)

Launched in July 2005, the Investment Climate Facility for Africa (ICF) aims to bring together the private sector and governments, in those 24 countries subjecting themselves to the scrutiny of their peers under the **New Partnership for Africa's Development (NEPAD)** initiative, 'to improve investment conditions in Sub-Saharan Africa'. Over its intended seven-year life period, the ICF hopes to double investment and raise the number of registered firms by 40%. As an independent trust, the ICF is relying on strong African private-sector representation on its board to find pragmatic solutions. The ICF will be financed by the United Kingdom's foreign-aid budget, the **World Bank** and the other **G8** countries, but 'driven and controlled by the private sector'. Backed by key African institutions, international agencies and large private-sector corporations, the ICF is currently attempting to raise US $550m. The fund will be launched by Niall Fitzgerald, now head of Reuters, but formerly chief executive of Unilever and before that Unilever's representative in **apartheid** South Africa. He wants the Facility to help create 'a healthy investment climate' that will offer Western companies 'attractive financial returns compared to competing destinations'. Anglo-American and Barclays have already volunteered to help.

Iran-Libya Sanctions Act (ILSA)

This US act was introduced to ban large scale investment in the two countries named, in view of their alleged support for **terrorism**. It has been recently renewed and tightened despite opposition from US oil companies, and efforts on various fronts by the regimes of both countries to show themselves not to be 'rogue states'. Pressure for a change in policy is likely to come from the Oasis consortium of US companies, which held major assets in Libya at the time sanctions were first imposed. These have been frozen by the Libyan government and held in trust despite repeated threats to re-allocate operating licences to other foreign oil companies. At present, firms such as ConocoPhillips and Marathon Oil have until 2005 to resume work or risk losing their assets. The promised pay-out to the **Lockerbie** victims could also soften the US administration's position on sanctions, at least as far as Libya is concerned.

Al-Irshad wa'l Islah (Movement for Guidance and Reform)

Algerian 'non political' Islamic movement, founded in 1974 by Mahfoud Nahnah. Regarded increasingly as a political movement by the Algerian authorities, especially during the 1990s, when it suppressed al Irshad wa'l Islah's activities and its adherents.

Islam

In **Arabic** means 'submission'. Major religion of the Middle East and **North Africa**. Established by the Prophet Muhammad (revered by Muslims as the Prophet of Allah). After his death in AD 632, his successors, the caliphs, spread Islam across the known world from North Africa to Spain, into eastern and central Europe, and eastwards to India and China. Islam is the fastest growing religion in the world. In the mid-1990s the annual growth of the Muslim population was 6.4%, compared with a growth rate of 1.46% for the Christian population.

Islamic banking

Usury or the taking of interest for loans is forbidden in **Islam**, so Islamic banking involves various different strategies to ensure viability and profitability.

Islamic banks have grown and become more significant in the years since the collapse of the Soviet Union and the demise of state **socialism** in eastern Europe. Unlike their Western counterparts, Islamic financial institutions were quick to come to the rescue of many former 'socialist' regimes which, deprived of support from Moscow, became highly dependent on Islamic finance; they have also become more involved in other regions where Western banks have been reluctant to invest—Africa, the Caucasus, parts of the Balkans and Central Asia, in particular. The fall of the Soviet system provided Islamic finance with its greatest opportunity for growth since its earlier revival in the mid-1970s. One of the most successful of the private Islamic banks, until its collapse, was the Bank of Credit and Commerce International. Inter-governmental banks also, such as the Islamic Development Bank, have proved very successful. The body that oversees modern Islamic finance is the **Shari'a** Supervisory Board of Islamic Banks and Institutions, better known as the Shari'a Committee. Today, Islamic banks operate all over the world, offering their services to the international Muslim community. More than 200 Islamic banks are active in the USA, and there are thousands in Europe, Africa, the Arab countries and Asia.

Islamic Development Bank (IDB)

The Islamic Development Bank (IDB) is an international financial institution, based in Saudi Arabia, established in pursuance of the Declaration of Intent issued by the Conference of Finance Ministers of the Organization of the Islamic Conference (OIC) held in Jiddah, Saudi Arabia, in December 1973. The Inaugural Meeting of the Board of Governors took place in July 1975 and the Bank was formally opened on 20 October 1975. Its aim is to encourage the economic development and social progress of member countries and of Muslim communities in non-member countries. The Bank formally opened in October 1975. The present membership of the Bank consists of 54 countries. Each member country is represented by a governor, usually the minister of finance and an alternate. The Board of Governors is the supreme authority of the Bank and meets annually. The Board of Executive Directors consists of 14 members, seven of whom are appointed by the seven largest subscribers to the capital stock of the Bank (Saudi Arabia, Kuwait, Libya, Iran, Egypt, Turkey and one other from Algeria, Indonesia and Pakistan); seven are elected by governors representing the other subscribers. The basic condition for membership is that the prospective member country should be a member of the OIC, pay its contribution to the capital of the Bank and be willing to accept such terms and conditions as may be decided upon by the Board of Governors. African members are: Algeria, Benin, Burkina Faso, Cameroon, Chad, Comoros, Djibouti, Egypt, Gabon, The Gambia, Guinea, Guinea-Bissau, Libya, Mali, Mauritania, Morocco, Mozambique, Niger, Senegal, Sierra Leone, Somalia, Sudan, Togo, Tunisia and Uganda. The purpose of the Bank is to foster the economic development and social progress of member countries and Muslim communities individually as well as jointly in accordance with the principles of **Shari'a**.

The Bank adheres to the principles of **Islamic banking** and provides interest-free loans (with a service fee)—mainly for infrastructural projects which are expected to have a marked impact on long term socio-economic development—technical assistance, equity participation in industrial or agricultural projects, leasing operations and instalment sale financing, and profit-sharing operations. The functions of the Bank are to participate in equity capital and grant loans for productive projects and enterprises besides providing financial assistance to member countries in other forms for economic and social development. The Bank is also required to establish and operate special funds for specific purposes including a fund for assistance to Muslim communities in non-member countries, in addition to setting up trust funds. It is also charged with the responsibility of assisting in the promotion of foreign trade, especially in capital goods, among member countries; providing technical assistance to member countries; and extending training facilities for personnel engaged in development activities in Muslim countries to conform to the Shari'a. It also funds a scholarship programme. Subsidiary organs include the Islamic Corporation for the Insurance of Investment and Export Credit (ICIEC) and the Islamic Research and Training Institute. The Islamic Development Bank has regional offices in Kazakhstan, Malaysia and Morocco.

In 1993, Saudi Arabia offered money to the Egyptian government of **Hosni Muhammad Said Mubarak** on the condition that it would encourage the Islamization of Egyptian society. Saudi Arabian **oil** revenues have poured into the IDB, which in turn has used its funds to promote the proliferation of Islamic investment houses and banks. Loans are conditional on strict adherence to Islamic laws and traditions. The Bank is used not only for strictly financial and banking purposes but also as a vehicle for the propagation of the Saudi fundamentalist interpretation of **Islam**, known as Wahhabism. It has wider political concerns as well, particularly where Islamic regimes are concerned. In 1998, several years after the closure of the Bank of Credit and Commerce International, it helped cover the economic penalties imposed on Pakistan for carrying out nuclear tests.

Islamic fundamentalism

A term widely used to refer to interpretations of **Islam** that urge a return to basic principles and, usually, to the more orthodox, conservative interpretations of the Koran and the Hadith. It differs, however, from Islamic traditionalism in that it attempts to confront the 'modern' world. Can refer to both **Sunni** or to **Shi'a** Islamic traditions.

Islamic government

Generally, government in accordance with principles derived from the Koran. While the governments of countries in **North Africa**, the Sahel and the Horn of Africa would claim to represent some form of Islamic government, the different Islamic and Islamist opposition movements in some of these countries would dispute such claims and emphasize the importance of their efforts (violent or peaceful) to establish 'true' Islamic government.

Islamic Group (al-Jama'a al-Islamiyya)

An Islamist political group in Morocco.

Islamic Jihad (al-Jihad al-Islami)

An Egyptian Islamist political grouping. Established following the imposition of a ban on the **Muslim Brotherhood**.

Islamic Martyrs Movement (IMM)

Libyan opposition movement. The IMM's spokesman is Abdallah Ahmad.

Issa(s)

Ethnic group in Djibouti.

Istiqlal

Original **independence** party established in Morocco in 1944 and led by Allal al-Fassi until his death in 1974. A split in 1959 led to the establishment of the Union des forces populaires, led by Mehdi Ben Barka. It remains a major political force. Istiqlal stresses Morocco's right to the **Western Sahara**. On the domestic front, it aims to raise living standards and to secure greater equality. Istiqlal's secretary-general is Abbas el-Fassi.

Ivory Coast – *see* Côte d'Ivoire

J

Al-Jabha al-Islamiyya li-Inqadh – *see* Front islamique du salut

Jamahiriya

In **Arabic** the term *jamahiriya* means 'a state of the masses', i.e. a republic. This is the type of government found in Libya. In theory *jamahiriya* is government by the people through local councils.

Jam'iyyat at-Takfir wa'l-Hijra (Society of Excommunication and Emigration)

Radical Moroccan Islamic group associated with a series of murders and preaching holy war. Some members of the group who have been arrested had spent time in **Osama bin Laden**'s training camps in Afghanistan and had fought with the Taliban.

Jammeh, Col (retd) Alhaji Yahya A. J. J.

Head of State of The Gambia since 1994. Born in 1965, Yahya Jammeh joined the army in 1984 upon leaving school. After serving with Gambian peace-keepers in Liberia, he returned to The Gambia and, together with a group of army veterans who had not been paid, overthrew the elected President, **Dawda Jawara**, who had led the country since **independence**. While he has established bodies to investigate **corruption** and recover misappropriated public funds, he has also been criticized for harassing opposition activists and journalists. Having first been elected as President in 1996, he was returned for a second five-year presidential term in 2001.

Janjaweed

A term applied to the so-called 'Arab' militias, which, with support from the government of Sudan, began terrorizing the so-called 'African' population of the western Sudan, in **Darfur**, in the early 2000s. The humanitarian crisis that developed as a result of the complex political emergency, of which the *janjaweed* militias were a part, was on a massive scale, affecting an estimated 1.5m. **refugees** and internally displaced persons. The failure of the international community to intervene in what the UN has considered to be, possibly, a **genocide** is almost as striking as the failure to intervene in Rwanda in the mid-1990s, when civil conflict on a vast scale led to what has been internationally recognized as a genocide (of the **Tutsi** population) and continued to affect East-Central Africa (including the Democratic Republic of the Congo) into the 21st century.

Jawara, Dawda Kairaba

Premier of The Gambia at **independence** in 1965, and thereafter Prime Minister until 1970, when, on The Gambia's decision to become a republic, he became President. In July 1994, exactly 100 years after The Gambia had become a British protectorate, Sir Dawda Kairaba Jawara's 30-year-long tenure of high political office was ended in a bloodless coup led by Lt **Yahya Jammeh**.

Jugnauth, Sir Anerood

President of Mauritius since October 2003. Formerly Prime Minister, Minister of Defence and Minister of the Interior. Born in 1930, Jugnauth studied law, worked as a lawyer and played an active role in **independence** negotiations in the 1960s. He served as Prime Minister in 1982–95. As leader of the Mouvement Socialiste Militant (Militant Socialist Movement), he became Prime Minister again after elections in September 2000.

K

Kabbah, Alhaji Ahmed Tejan

President of Sierra Leone since 1996. Born in 1932, Kabbah was educated in Sierra Leone and Britain. He began his career in public service in 1959, first as a district commissioner for the British colonial government and then, after **independence**, as a civil servant. After this he spent 21 years working for the UN Development Programme, based in New York, Lesotho and Tanzania. He returned to Sierra Leone in 1992 and was elected as President in March 1996, following war-time elections which brought a formal end to four years of military rule. Kabbah was overthrown by disaffected elements in the army in May 1997, but a West African intervention force, with British involvement, reinstated him within a year. Having gained considerable credit by bringing in an outside force to achieve control, Kabbah managed to agree a cease-fire in November 2000. This allowed the UN force to deploy throughout the country and to disarm combatants. In a presidential election held in May 2002 Kabbah was re-elected for a second five-year presidential term.

Kabila, Maj.-Gen. Joseph

President of the Democratic Republic of the Congo (DRC) since 2001. Joseph Kabila was a political novice when he became President in January 2001, following the assassination of his father, **Laurent-Désiré Kabila**, who had led a rebellion against President **Mobutu** in the 1990s and came to power, naming himself President of the DRC, in 1997. However, he had received military training in Rwanda and Uganda and had fought in his father's rebel army during the military campaign that brought him to power. Thereafter he served in the army as major-general and chief of staff, and headed the government forces in the fight against former rebel allies during the late 1990s. Within days of assuming power, Kabila expressed the wish that the **civil war** in the DRC would be concluded peacefully. This objective was not achieved for two more years, however, as fighting continued throughout much of the country, particularly in the eastern regions. In June 2003, following lengthy discussions, Kabila was able to name an interim government, which included portfolios for members of rebel groups and the political opposition. The main rebel leaders were sworn in as Vice-Presidents in the following month.

This interim government remained intact for two more years, until its term expired in June 2005, in spite of continued fighting in the east of the country.

Kabila, Laurent-Désiré

Laurent-Désiré Kabila was President of the Democratic Republic of the Congo (DRC) from May 1997, after he had overthrown President **Mobutu** Sese Seko, until his assassination in January 2001. He was succeeded by his son, **Joseph Kabila**. Born in November 1939, he was a member of the Ba-Luba tribe in Jadotville (formerly Likasi) in the **Katanga** province of the Belgian Congo. He studied political philosophy in France and attended the University of Dar es Salaam in Tanzania. When the Congo gained **independence** from Belgium in 1960, Kabila was a youth leader in a party allied to **Patrice Lumumba**. Lumumba became the first Prime Minister of the DRC, but was murdered in February 1961. Having fled, together with other supporters of Lumumba, into the jungle, in 1964 Kabila helped to organize a revolt in the Ruzizi region. The Cuban revolutionary Che Guevara assisted Kabila for a short time in 1965. The revolt was suppressed later that year.

In 1967 Kabila founded the Parti de la révolution populaire (PRP—People's Revolutionary Party). With the support of the People's Republic of China, the PRP created a secessionist Marxist state in South Kivu province, west of Lake **Tanganyika**. The PRP state came to an end in 1988. Kabila returned to the DRC in October 1996, leading ethnic **Tutsis** from South Kivu against **Hutu** forces, marking the beginning of the first Congo war. With support from Burundi, Uganda and the Rwandan minority Tutsi government, Kabila launched his forces in a full-scale rebellion against Mobutu as the Alliance des forces démocratiques pour la libération du Congo-Zaïre (AFDL—Alliance of Democratic Forces for the Liberation of Congo-Zaire). By mid-1997 the AFDL had made significant gains and, following the failure of peace talks in May, Mobutu fled the country. Kabila entered Kinshasa, the capital, in that month, proclaimed himself President, formed a transitional government and renamed the country—known as the Republic of Zaire since 1971—as the DRC. Kabila had been a committed Marxist, but the policies he pursued in power were a confusing mix of capitalism and collectivism, and he was soon ensnared by the seemingly inevitable idiosyncrasies and **corruption** that had likewise overwhelmed Mobutu. He was fatally injured in an assassination attempt by a member of his own staff in January 2001, dying in Zimbabwe, to where he had been flown for medical treatment.

Kagame, Maj.-Gen. Paul

President of Rwanda since 2000. Born in 1957, Paul Kagame, who is a **Tutsi**, grew up in Uganda, to where his parents had fled in order to escape **Hutu** violence. In Uganda he joined **Yoweri Museveni** in the fight to topple **Milton Obote**, rising to become Museveni's chief of intelligence. As President of Rwanda he has sought to avoid any ethnic agenda by presenting himself as a Rwandan and not a Tutsi.

Kamerun

A German protectorate was declared over Kamerun (later Cameroon) by Otto von Bismarck in 1884. After the First World War, the League of Nations divided mandates between the victors. **Togoland** and Kamerun were shared between France and Britain.

Kasavubu, Joseph

Aristocratic leader of Abako, a political party founded in the Belgian Congo in 1950 with predominantly Bakongo membership. It had the initial aim of restoring the old Kongo empire, but was converted to the idea of a Congo state, provided it remained a federal state. On **independence**, Kasavubu became the first President of the Democratic Republic of the Congo (Congo Kinshasa).

Katanga

Also known as Shaba. Wealthy mineral-producing region in the south east of the Democratic Republic of the Congo. After the Belgian Congo achieved **independence** in June 1960, strong efforts were made by **Moïse Tshombe** and his supporters to achieve independence for Katanga. Tshombe declared Katangan independence on 11 July 1960, but eventually, after considerable fighting and political negotiation, renounced it on 21 December 1961.

Katibat el-Ahoual

This Algerian group appears to have recently split from the **Groupe islamique armé (GIA—Armed Islamic Group)** and is reportedly one of the most active and dangerous armed groups in the centre-west of Algeria. Within this area it is said to operate mainly in El Ourenis in the east, Remka and Relizane in the west, and Chlef in the north.

Kaunda, Kenneth

Northern **Rhodesia**, which was henceforth known as Zambia, became an independent republic within the **Commonwealth** in October 1964, with Kenneth Kaunda, the leader of the United National Independence Party (UNIP), as its first President. In 1991, when multi-party politics were restored in Zambia (Kaunda had declared the country a one-party state in 1972), the UNIP was defeated in elections by the Movement for Multi-party Democracy (MMD), led by former trade union leader **Frederick Chiluba**, who was elected as President. UNIP became the main opposition party. Kaunda, who had retired, returned to active politics in 1994, and in the following year regained the leadership of the UNIP. Neither he nor the UNIP were able subsequently to regain political ascendancy in Zambia, however.

Keita, Modibo

Former Head of State of Mali, ousted in 1968 after having been in power since **independence** in 1960. Born in 1915, he dominated political life in Mali for 20 years both before and after independence. He applied Marxist principles to the problems of Mali and was frequently in conflict with the French authorities from the 1940s onwards. By 1956 he had become a deputy and vice-president of the French Assemblée nationale. In 1957 he became Secretary of State with responsibility for France's overseas territories. In 1959 Mali (then **Soudan**) and Senegal formed a union, but this collapsed two months after their joint independence in June 1960 owing to radical differences between Keita and **Léopold Sédar Senghor** of Senegal. Keita was replaced by a military junta in 1968.

Kenya, Republic of

The Republic of Kenya lies astride the equator on the east coast of Africa, with Somalia to the north-east, Ethiopia and Sudan to the north, Uganda to the west and Tanzania to the south. The area of the country is 580,367 sq km. At mid-2001 the population was estimated at 30,493,792. Kiswahili is the official language, while English is widely spoken and 22% and 13% of the population, respectively, speak **Kikuyu** and **Luo** as their mother tongue. Most of the country's inhabitants follow traditional beliefs. There is a sizeable Christian community, while Muslims form a smaller proportion of the population. The capital is Nairobi, whose population was estimated at 2,574,847 in mid-2003.

Political profile

Legislative power is vested in the unicameral National Assembly, with 224 members (210 elected by universal adult suffrage, the Attorney-General, the Speaker and 12 nominated members), who serve a term of five years, subject to dissolution. Executive power is held by the President, also directly elected for five years, who is assisted by an appointed Vice-President and Cabinet.

In a presidential election held on 27 December 2002, **Mwai Kibaki** received 62.3% of the votes cast in the first round of voting and was accordingly elected as President.

Following legislative elections held on 27 December 2002, the distribution of seats in the National Assembly was as follows: National Rainbow Coalition (NARC, an alliance comprising the Liberal Democratic Party—LDP, and the National Alliance Party of Kenya—NAPK) 125; **Kenya African National Union (KANU)** 64; Forum for the Restoration of Democracy for the People (FORD—People) 14; Forum for the Restoration of Democracy—Asili (FORD—Asili) 2; Safina ('Noah's Ark') 2; Sisi Kwa Sisi (SKS) 2; Shirikisho Party of Kenya (SPK) 1. The 12 nominated seats within the Assembly were distributed as follows: NARC 7; KANU 4; FORD—People 1.

History

Britain acquired Kenya in the late 19th century. The climate and terrain in certain parts of the country attracted settlers who soon came to have their own vested interests in the evolution of the territory. Unofficial members of the Kenyan legislative council began to be given ministerial appointments immediately after the end of the Second World War. They were, however, not black but white, representatives of the British settlers who had been coming to Kenya since the beginning of the century and had been acquiring and developing the excellent agricultural lands in what came to be called the White Highlands. In time this community came to dominate Kenyan politics. It hoped to rule Kenya either in lieu of the colonial authorities, or in a power-sharing arrangement in a multiracial state on a scale appropriate to its wealth and general superiority rather than to its numbers.

The first significant African nationalist organization was the **Kenya African Union (KAU)**. Founded in 1944, it drew support mainly from the Kikuyu, the largest ethnic group in Kenya. The Kikuyu were represented by **Jomo Kenyatta**, who had become president of the KAU in 1947. In 1952 the white settler community and the colonial authorities were faced with an outbreak of unrest among the Kikuyu, who had long resented the annexation of large areas of land by white settlers. In about 1948 the Kikuyu had formed a secret society, the **Mau Mau**, which rapidly developed into an organization that was hostile to continued white rule in Kenya. During 1952 the Mau Mau launched a campaign of terrorism that eventually prompted the government to declare an emergency, to seek reinforcements from neighbouring territories and from Britain, to arrest thousands of Kikuyu (including Kenyatta, who in 1954 was sentenced to seven years' imprisonment for his involvement with the Mau Mau) and to launch an all-out campaign of violence against the indigenous opposition.

On **independence** in 1963 Kenyatta became Head of State. On his death, in 1978, he was replaced by **Daniel arap Moi**, who ruled Kenya as a one-party state in 1978–92. The KAU was reorganized as the KANU, the sole legal party. In 1992 multi party **democracy** was restored, but the Kenyan political environment remained turbulent. In elections held in 1992 and 1997 KANU was able to defeat a divided opposition. President Daniel arap Moi, who was accused by many—with some justification—of maintaining an authoritarian personal regime, reshuffled the Cabinet in November 2001, including Uhuru Kenyatta, the son of the late President Jomo Kenyatta, among the new appointees. The National Development Party was dissolved in March 2002 and absorbed into the ruling KANU. In elections held in 2002 a united opposition won a convincing victory. Mwai Kibaki of the NARC was victorious in the presidential election, receiving more than 60% of the vote, while the NARC emerged as by far the largest party in the National Assembly. The elections were followed by a smooth transfer of power. Kibaki's election marked the first occasion since independence that Kenyans had elected a new Head of State. In September 2003 arap Moi announced his retirement from politics and relinquished the presidency of KANU. He was succeeded by Uhuru Kenyatta.

International relations

A treaty for the re-establishment of the **East African Community (EAC)**, which had been dissolved in 1977, providing for the promotion of free trade between the member states, the development of the regions' infrastructure and economy and the creation of a regional legislative assembly and court, was ratified by the Kenyan, Tanzanian and Ugandan Heads of State in 1999. The new EAC was officially inaugurated in 2001. Talks on integrating the economies of the three EAC members followed, and in March 2004 Kibaki, President **Yoweri Museveni** of Uganda and President Benjamin Mkapa of Tanzania signed a protocol on the creation of a customs union, which took effect from January 2005. During the late 1990s Kenya hosted a series of peace talks between the Sudanese government and opposition leaders, under the auspices of the **Intergovernmental Authority on Development (IGAD)**, in an attempt to resolve the conflict in southern Sudan. Further negotiations were held in Nairobi in September 2000 and June 2001, and in July 2002 the Sudanese government and the opposition Sudan People's Liberation Army (SPLA) signed an accord in Machakos, Kenya, which provided for the holding of a referendum on self-determination for southern Sudan after a transitional period of six years. In September 2003 Kenya and Sudan agreed to form a joint border committee. Talks aimed at achieving a final peace settlement between the Sudanese government and the SPLA continued in Kenya throughout 2003 and early 2004. Somalia has traditionally laid claim to part of north-eastern Kenya. The Kenyan government closed the two countries' common border in mid-1999, in response to rising insecurity in the area. The border was reopened in April 2000. In July 2001 Kenya again closed the border after numerous clashes, on the Somali side, were reported between forces of the interim Somali government and opposing rebel factions, which threatened to spill over into Kenya. agreed to reopen the border in November. An IGAD-sponsored Somali reconciliation opened in Kenya in 2002; the talks continued throughout 2003 and early 2004, when representatives from more than 20 factions in attendance reached agreement on the establishment of a new Somali parliament. In July 2003 President Kibaki appointed Kenya's first ambassador to Somalia for 13 years. Bilateral relations between Kenya and Ethiopia deteriorated in 2000 after it was reported that some 50 Kenyans had been killed, allegedly by Ethiopian militia forces, in cross-border clashes. In 2001 representatives from both countries met in Nairobi and agreed to initiate measures aimed at ending border disputes. In October 1995, despite strong condemnation from foreign governments, the Kenyan authorities refused to permit the international tribunal that was investigating war crimes committed in Rwanda during 1994 access to alleged Rwandan perpetrators of **genocide** who had fled to Kenya. In September 1996, however, the first arrest in Kenya was made of a Rwandan **Hutu** suspected of involvement in genocide. Relations between the Kenyan and Rwandan governments improved during 1997, when further Rwandan Hutus were arrested by the Kenyan security forces to stand trial on charges of genocide at the UN tribunal in Arusha, Tanzania. During a visit by President Moi to Rwanda in May 2000 the two countries agreed to reopen the Kenyan embassy in Kigali and to establish a joint commission for bilateral relations.

Kenya, economy

In 2003, according to estimates by the **World Bank**, Kenya's gross national income (GNI), measured at average 2001–03 prices, was US $13,663m., equivalent to $390 per head (or $1,020 per head on an international purchasing-power parity basis). During 1990–2003, it was estimated, the population increased at an average annual rate of 2.4%, while gross domestic product (GDP) per head declined, in real terms, by an average of 0.8% per year. Overall GDP increased, in real terms, at an average annual rate of 1.6% in 1990–2003. Real GDP increased by 1.3% in 2003. The annual rate of inflation averaged 12.8% in 1990–2003; consumer prices increased by an average of 10.8% in 2003. Industry generally involves the production, on a small scale, of consumer goods, the processing of agricultural products and tourism. In 2004 the principal suppliers of imports were the United Arab Emirates, Saudi Arabia, South Africa, the USA, the United Kingdom, the People's Republic of China, Japan and India. The main markets for Kenya's exports in that year were Uganda, the United Kingdom, the USA, the Netherlands, Pakistan, Egypt and Tanzania. The national currency is the Kenyan shilling (Ks.). In 2004 the average exchange rate was US $1 = Ks. 79.174.

Up to 80% of the population of Kenya work in **agriculture** and horticulture, producing crops such as tea (Kenya is one of the world's leading producers), **coffee**, and maize. Some 67% of Kenya is grassland, game parks and beach resorts and tourism is the country's second most important source of foreign exchange. The industrial sector currently contributes less than 20% of GDP, but is a growing source of exports to the East African region. Kenya has rich agricultural resources, a diverse private sector (including multinational investments) and a key regional position. Partial economic liberalization has brought benefits: a more open import/export regime, diversified financial services, deregulation, and steady progress on privatization. In addition to its position among the world's leading producers of tea and coffee, Kenya is also one of the largest producers of cut flowers (exports of which to the **European Union** were worth more than $100m. in 2000). However, the recurrent failure of rains and poor management of the **energy** sector have caused **drought** and power shortages.

Following the change of government in December 2002, relations with the international financial institutions improved considerably as the new administration began to demonstrate its credentials. The immediate policy priority was to press ahead with a comprehensive anti-**corruption** strategy. Legislation—including a bill to revive a strong Kenya Anti-Corruption Authority with both investigative and prosecution powers—was partially enacted. The passage of the legislation demonstrated the government's capacity to meet the conditions of the **International Monetary Fund (IMF)** for a resumption of international assistance. In January

2003 government representatives met with IMF to discuss the resumption of aid, suspended in the final years of Moi's regime for a variety of reasons, including corruption and mismanagement of the economy. In November the IMF approved a three year **Poverty Reduction and Growth Facility (PRGF)** for Kenya, and also approved a $252.2m. loan. This display of confidence and general approval of **Kibaki**'s government prompted other international agencies to pledge a total of $4,100m. to Kenya for 2004–06.

The full implications and effects of economic restructuring undertaken by the National Rainbow Coalition government are not yet apparent. The IMF awaits clear results from the anti-corruption strategy that is being pursued. Tax-relief incentives have been established to create a more enabling environment in which to do business in Kenya, and some tax changes aim to reduce the tax burden on the poorest citizens. The disadvantage of these tax cuts is that they erode the revenue base which is still recovering from mistakes made by the administration of **Daniel arap Moi**. In 2004 the greatest cause of concern was the continued high level of government domestic borrowing. Measures to strengthen the Kenya Revenue Authority were swiftly put into place in an attempt to combat these problems. In May 2004 the Central Bank of Kenya reported that total tax collection was 25.4% above target. Despite the dangers of a slim revenue base, the exchange rate remains stable, and inflation remains relatively low.

Kenya African Democratic Union (KADU)

Political party in Kenya, initially led by Ronald Ngala, which supported the idea of a federal constitution for Kenya to enable the smaller and weaker tribes to resist total domination by the **Kikuyu**. After a constitutional conference was held in London, United Kingdom, in 1960, Ngala, previously the leader of government business in the National Assembly, was made chief minister. However, elections held in May 1963 were won by **Jomo Kenyatta**'s Kikuyu-dominated **Kenya African National Union (KANU)**. After Kenya's **independence** in December 1963, its status was changed to that of a republic and the Constitution was rewritten to remove safeguards for minorities and regional rights. The absorption of the KADU into the KANU created a one-party state.

Kenya African National Union (KANU)

Originally formed to fight elections in May 1963, and based on the earlier **Kenya African Union**, the Kenya African National Union (KANU) formed a government at the end of 1963 when **independence** was achieved, together with a minority party, the **Kenya African Democratic Union (KADU)**, which represented minority ethnic groups, resented **Kikuyu** and **Luo** domination and hoped for the establishment of a federal state. The KANU eventually incorporated the KADU and excluded the breakaway radical **Kenya People's Union**, to become, in 1964, the only party in Kenya.

Kenya African Union (KAU)

Political grouping formed in 1944 by African intellectuals from several ethnic groups to press for political reform and to oppose the granting of self-government to the white settlers in Kenya. Largely ignored by the colonial administration, the Kenya African Union's (KAU) moderate political stance and demands were overtaken by the emergence of a guerrilla movement, known outside Kenya as the **Mau Mau**, which began an armed struggle to expel the white settlers and restore land appropriated by them, largely from **Kikuyu** farmers. In 1946 **Jomo Kenyatta** returned to Kenya from England and became president of the KAU. He was arrested and imprisoned. By 1952 local resistance had become a large-scale insurrection and the colonial administration adopted strong measures in order to crush the uprising. The Mau Mau revolt continued none the less in the 1950s. Meanwhile, the British government conceded African representation in the legislature and the **Kenya African National Union** won an overwhelming victory in the elections that it was formed to contest.

Kenya Commercial Bank (KCB)

A leading commercial banking group in **East Africa**, where it has the largest commercial network and includes the Kenya Commercial Bank (KCB) Tanzania among its subsidiaries. Renowned for its diversity and growth potential, the KCB maintains working arrangements with correspondent banks throughout the world.

Kenya People's Union (KPU)

Leftist political party, formed by Oginga Odinga, a prominent **Luo** politician in Kenya, in 1965 after he split from the **Kenya African National Union (KANU)**. After the assassination of his main rival, Tom Mboya, who had become the leading political figure in KANU after **Jomo Kenyatta**, the President, in July 1969, Odinga was sentenced to 15 months' imprisonment and the Kenya People's Union was banned.

Kenyatta, Jomo

Former President of Kenya. He studied in Kenya and in Britain, where he attended the London School of Economics, later publishing a book, *Facing Mount Kenya*, that was based on his thesis. He returned to Kenya in 1946 and became leader of the Kenyan liberation movement and president of the **Kenya African Union (KAU)**. Imprisoned for his alleged involvement in the **Mau Mau** uprising during the 1950s, he was nevertheless the key political figure with whom the British government and the colonial administration had to negotiate, although during this period two other political activists, Tom Mboya and Oginga Odinga, also came to prominence. Released from prison in August 1961, Kenyatta became the leader of the **Kenya African National Union (KANU)**, which won a conclusive victory in elections, held in May 1963, that it had been formed to contest. He became Prime Minister in June and **independence** followed in December 1963. Kenya was declared a republic, with Kenyatta as President, exactly one year later, in December 1964. By 1965 the KANU had divided into a radical wing, led by Odinga, and a conservative wing, led by Mboya. Odinga subsequently left the KANU to form the **Kenya People's Union (KPU)**. Following the assassination of Mboya in July 1969, Kenyatta banned the KPU and imprisoned Odinga for 15 months. Kenyatta remained as President in the 1970s: he was elected, unopposed, for a third five year term as President in September 1974. He died in August 1978 and was succeeded by **Daniel arap Moi**.

Kérékou, Mathieu

Former President of Benin. Kérékou was born in 1933 in the north of what was at that time **Dahomey**, and was educated in Senegal and Mali before joining the French army. He held senior posts in the Dahomean **military** before seizing power in October 1972, after repeated changes of government since **independence** in 1960. Maj. (later Brig.-Gen.) Kérékou proclaimed **Marxist-Leninism** as the official ideology of the new regime, earning for Dahomey the label 'Africa's Cuba'. In 1987 Kérékou left the army to become a civilian Head of State and made efforts to introduce a more representative administration. In 1989 Kérékou was re-elected for a further five-year presidential term, but his authority was subsequently undermined by persistent social and political difficulties. In February 1990 a national conference was convened, which decided on major changes to the political system—in effect a 'civilian coup'. The President of the Republic was henceforth to be elected by universal suffrage, with a five-year mandate, renewable only once. A draft Constitution was submitted to a referendum and approved. The registration of political parties began in 1990, and in February 1991 legislative elections were held place with 24 political parties participating. In March, in a presidential election, Kérékou was defeated by Nicéphore Soglo and subsequently withdrew from active politics. In January 1996, Kérékou announced his candidacy for a forthcoming presidential election, in which, in a second round of voting held in March, he was victorious. Kérékous was re-elected as President in 2001.

Khartoum Declaration

In 1988, 200 African delegates met in Khartoum, Sudan, under the auspices of the UN to study the papers of some 40 different experts on 'Human Dimensions of Africa's Economic Crisis' and agreed a vision of African renewal. They also spelled out certain concrete steps to be taken to begin to realize that vision. The Khartoum Declaration produced by the delegates to the conference identified five key areas:

1) structural adjustment programmes must be designed, implemented and monitored as part of the long-term framework of Africa's development;

2) the human dimension must be the fulcrum of the adjustment programmes;
3) the structural adjustment policies must incorporate the relevant adjustments of the social sector;
4) consideration must be given to the consequences of macro-policies on the poor and vulnerable, not only so as to design temporary and independent compensatory additional programmes, but to make the alleviation of absolute and relative poverty and the elimination of gender biases integral parts and factors of the adjustment programmes;
5) the entire process of monitoring the stabilization and structural adjustment programmes must incorporate the social aspects and criteria.

These general principles were expanded into detailed recommendations in the Declaration. They prompted the **World Bank** to design **PAMSCAD**—Programme of Actions to Mitigate the Social Costs of Adjustment—and to try it out first in Ghana.

Kibaki, Mwai

President of Kenya since December 2002, when he won an overwhelming victory in a presidential election. (The Constitution barred his predecessor, **Daniel arap Moi**, from seeking re-election.) Kibaki's National Rainbow Coalition (NARC) also won a parliamentary majority. President Kibaki declared that he would make the fight against **corruption** a priority during his presidency. He also promised to address Kenya's economic decline. Kibaki was born in 1931 and is a member of Kenya's largest tribe, the **Kikuyu**. He studied in Uganda and Britain before joining the **independence** movement in Kenya in the 1960s. He was elected as a deputy to the National Assembly in 1963. A respected economist, Kibaki served as finance minister and Vice-President in the 1970s and 1980s. He left the **Kenya African National Union (KANU)** in 1991 and founded the Democratic Party of Kenya. His electoral success in 2002 resulted to a large extent from his ability to create a 'rainbow alliance' in opposition to the ruling KANU party and the authoritarian regime of **Daniel arap Moi**. Kibaki has already made considerable progress in the fight against corruption and in restoring international confidence in the Kenyan government and its ability to manage the economy.

Kiir, Salva

Leader of the Sudan People's Liberation Army (SPLA), since the death, in August 2005, of **John Garang**, as whose deputy he formerly served. Like Garang, Salva Kiir is a member of the Dinka, one of the largest ethnic groups in southern Sudan, and is widely respected as a military commander. However, he was largely excluded from the final stages of peace negotiations with the government of Sudan and has little direct personal experience of the power-brokers in Khartoum.

Kikuyu

Major ethno-linguistic group in Kenya, where they constitute some 20% of the population. The Kikuyu were heavily involved in the **Mau Mau** uprising against British colonial rule in the early 1950s. Kikuyu leader **Jomo Kenyatta** was jailed during the Mau Mau rebellion, but was conditionally released in 1959 and allowed full freedom of movement in 1961. In 1963 his **Kenya African National Union (KANU)** party, which was overwhelmingly a Kikuyu party, won legislative elections and he became Prime Minister. In 1964 Kenya became a republic and one-party state, and the Constitution was rewritten to remove earlier safeguards for ethnic minorities and regional interests, thus ensuring Kikuyu political dominance in a centralized state.

Kufuor, John Agyekum

President of Ghana since 2001. Kufuor's victory in the presidential poll held in Ghana in December 2000 marked the first genuine transfer of power via the electoral system in Ghana. Born in 1938, he had previously served as deputy foreign minister; and as secretary for local government, in which role he initiated the policy that formed the basis of Ghana's present decentralized administration.

Kwa Zulu

The **Zulu** entity—both the **ethnic group** and the territory they inhabit.

L

Lagos Plan of Action

A programme for economic recovery and growth in Africa produced by African governments in the late 1970s, in response to a decade of decline in food production per head and general stagnation in average incomes. The **Berg Report** of 1981, *Accelerated Growth in Sub-Saharan Africa,* represented the **World Bank**'s response to the Lagos Plan of Action and called for **structural adjustment** and economic reform.

Lancaster House Agreement

The Lancaster House Agreement of December 1979 led, in 1980, to **independence** for what was previously Southern **Rhodesia**—following Ian Smith's illegal **Unilateral Declaration of Independence** in 1965—as Zimbabwe. The Agreement dealt with the Independence Constitution, pre-independence arrangements, and a cease-fire. The parties represented during the conference were the British government, the Zimbabwe-Rhodesia Administration and the Patriotic Front led by **Robert Mugabe** and **Joshua Nkomo**.

Leon, Anthony (Tony)

Leader of the **Democratic Party (DP)** in South Africa. A charismatic and energetic critic of the **African National Congress (ANC)**, whose party gained only seven legislative seats in the first democratic election in South Africa, but which managed to galvanize public opinion through a campaign aimed blatantly at winning the white vote by criticizing the ANC's affirmative action policy as potentially racist. In legislative elections held in 1998 the DP won 38 seats, receiving more **Afrikaner** votes than the **New National Party (NNP)** and ousting it as the official opposition. After the 1998 elections the DP merged with the NNP to become the **Democratic Alliance (DA)**, a consolidated and overwhelmingly white opposition movement, led by Leon, with Marthinus van Schalkwyk of the NNP as deputy leader. After two years, however, van Schalkwyk withdrew the NNP from the alliance in favour of an informal relationship with the ANC.

Lesotho, Kingdom of

The Kingdom of Lesotho is a land-locked country, entirely surrounded by South Africa. The area of the country is 30,355 sq km. At May 2002 the population was estimated at 2,200,000. More than 99% of the population belong to the Basotho ethnic group. The official languages are English and Sesotho. About 90% of the population are Christians. The largest denominations are the Roman Catholic, Lesotho Evangelical and Anglican Churches. The capital is Maseru, whose population was estimated at 169,554 in mid-2003.

Lesotho is an hereditary monarchy. Under the terms of the Constitution, which came into effect following the March 1993 election, the King, who is Head of State, has no executive or legislative powers. The College of Chiefs is theoretically empowered, under traditional law, to elect and depose the King by a majority vote. Executive power is vested in the Cabinet, which is headed by the Prime Minister. Legislative power is exercised by the National Assembly, which is elected, at intervals of no more than five years, by universal adult suffrage in the context of a multi-party political system. A system of mixed member proportional representation was introduced at the general election of May 2002, when the National Assembly was expanded to 120 members (80 elected by simple majority in single-member constituencies and 40 selected from party lists). The upper house, the Senate, comprises traditional chiefs and 11 nominated members.

The reigning monarch is HM King Letsie III, who acceded to the throne on 7 February 1996.

Following legislative elections held on 25 May 2002, the distribution of seats in the National Assembly was as follows: Lesotho Congress for Democracy (LCD) 77; Basotho National Party (BNP) 21; Lesotho People's Congress (LPC) 5; National Independent Party (NIP) 5; Basotho Congress Party (BCP) 3; Basutoland African Congress (BAC) 3; Lesotho Workers' Party (LWP) 1; Marematlou Freedom Party (MFP) 1; National Progressive Party (NPP) 1; Popular Front for Democracy (PFD) 1. (Voting in two constituencies was postponed, owing to the death of candidates.)

History

Lesotho, formerly **Basutoland**, a British protectorate from 1868, became independent on 4 October 1966. The Constitution provided for a monarch (King Moshoeshoe II), with limited powers, and an elected National Assembly based on universal suffrage. The Prime Minister at **independence** was Chief Leabua Jonathan of the BNP. In 1970 Chief Jonathan, anticipating defeat by the BCP, a pan-Africanist group led by Dr Ntsu Mokhehle, in the country's first post-independence elections, declared a state of emergency and suspended the Constitution. King Moshoeshoe was placed under house arrest and subsequently exiled, although he returned in December after accepting a government order banning him from participating in politics. The country was thus effectively under the Prime Minister's personal control.

In January 1986 Chief Jonathan's government was overthrown in a coup led by Maj.-Gen. Justin Lekhanya, the head of the armed forces. A Military Council, chaired by Lekhanya, was established. The 1983 Parliament Act (which had repealed the emergency order of 1970 that had suspended the Constitution) was revoked, and it was announced that executive and legislative powers were to be vested in King Moshoeshoe, assisted by the Military Council and a (mainly civilian) Council of Ministers.

In February 1990 Lekhanya dismissed three members of the Military Council and one member of the Council of Ministers. When Moshoeshoe refused to approve new appointments to the Military Council, Lekhanya suspended the monarch's executive and legislative powers, which were assumed by the Military Council in March. Moshoeshoe (who remained Head of State) was exiled in the United Kingdom. Lekhanya announced that a general election would take place during 1992; however, party political activity remained outlawed. In June 1990 a National Constituent Assembly (including Lekhanya, members of the Council of Ministers, representatives of banned political parties, traditional chiefs and business leaders) was inaugurated to draft a new constitution. In October Lekhanya invited the King to return from exile. Moshoeshoe responded that his return would be conditional upon the ending of military rule and the establishment of an interim government, pending the readoption of the 1966 Constitution. On 6 November 1990 Lekhanya promulgated an order dethroning the King with immediate effect. Lesotho's 22 principal chiefs elected Moshoeshoe's elder son, Prince David Mohato Bereng Seeiso, as the new King; on 12 November he acceded to the throne, as King Letsie III, having undertaken to remain detached from politics.

On 30 April 1991 Lekhanya was deposed in a coup organized by disaffected army officers. Col (later Maj.-Gen.) Elias Phitsoane Ramaema succeeded Lekhanya as Chairman of the Military Council. Ramaema repealed the ban on party political activity, and by July the National Constituent Assembly had completed the draft Constitution.

In the general election that was held on 27 March 1993 the BCP secured all 65 seats in the new National Assembly, winning 54% of the votes cast. The BNP—which received 16% of the votes—rejected the result, alleging that there had been widespread irregularities, and later declined the new administration's offer of two seats in the restored Senate. On 2 April Dr Ntsu Mokhehle was inaugurated as Prime Minister, and King Letsie swore allegiance to the new Constitution, under the terms of which he remained Head of State with no executive or legislative powers; executive authority was vested in the Cabinet.

In August 1994 King Letsie announced that he had dissolved the National Assembly, dismissed the government and suspended sections of the Constitution, citing 'popular dissatisfaction'. Hae Phoofolo, was appointed chairman of a transitional Council of Ministers, and the secretary-general of the BNP, Evaristus Retselisitsoe Sekhonyana, was appointed Minister of Foreign Affairs. Phoofolo identified as a priority for his administration the amendment of the Constitution to facilitate the restoration of Moshoeshoe; in the mean time, King Letsie was to act as executive and legislative Head of State. In September King Letsie and Mokhehle signed an agreement that provided for the restoration of Moshoeshoe II as reigning monarch and for the restitution of the elected organs of government. Moshoeshoe was restored to the throne on 25 January 1995, undertaking not to interfere in politics. Letsie took the title of Crown Prince.

King Moshoeshoe was killed in a motor accident on 15 January 1996. The College of Chiefs subsequently elected Crown Prince David to succeed his father, and the prince was restored to the throne, resuming the title King Letsie III, on 7 February. Like his father in January 1995, King Letsie undertook not to involve the monarchy in any aspect of political life.

In elections to an expanded National Assembly held on 23 May 1998 the LCD secured an overwhelming victory, winning 78 of the Assembly's 80 seats; the BNP was the only other party to win representation. The opposition protested that the outcome of the poll reflected fraud on the part of the LCD, and in August, following mass demonstrations, the establishment of an independent commission to investigate the conduct and results of the May election was announced. In September the commission declared itself 'unable to state that the invalidity of the elections had been conclusively established', precipitating widespread unrest and, in response, the intervention of a peace-keeping force of the **Southern African Development Community**. An Interim Political Authority was subsequently installed, pending new elections to the National Assembly.

In January 2002 amendments to electoral legislation were approved that provided for the expansion of the National Assembly to 120 members, with 80 to be elected on a constituency basis and 40 selected by proportional representation. The LCD won a resounding victory at the general election, which took place on 25 May, retaining 77 of 78 contested constituency seats. The BNP became the second largest legislative party, securing 21 of the 40 seats allocated by proportional representation (known as compensatory seats); the LPC won one constituency seat and four compensatory seats. Of the remaining 15 compensatory seats, the National Independent Party secured five, the BAC and the BCP both won three, while four smaller parties each took one seat.

International relations

Lesotho's internal affairs are strongly influenced by South Africa. Long-standing problems of border security and, in particular, the issue of disputed land in South Africa's Free State (formerly **Orange Free State**) have periodically caused friction between the two countries. During a visit to Lesotho by President **Thabo Mbeki** of South Africa in April 2001, it was agreed to replace an intergovernmental liaison committee that had been established following SADC intervention in 1998 with a joint binational commission at ministerial level, with the aim of enhancing bilateral relations. Relations between Lesotho and South Africa were further enhanced in May 2002, when their ministers of foreign affairs signed the Joint Bilateral

Commission of Co-operation programme, which aimed to raise Lesotho from its current status as a 'least developed country' by 2007.

Lesotho, economy

In 2003, according to estimates by the **World Bank**, Lesotho's gross national income (GNI), measured at average 2001–03 prices, was US $1,337m., equivalent to $590 per head (or $3,120 per head on an international purchasing-power parity basis). During 1990–2003, it was estimated, the population increased at an average annual rate of 1.0%, while gross domestic product (GDP) per head increased, in real terms, by an average of 3.0% per year. Overall GDP increased, in real terms, at an average annual rate of 3.5% in 1990–2003; growth in 2003 was 3.9%. The annual rate of inflation averaged 10.4% in 1990–2002; consumer prices increased by 8.1% in 2003. Manufacturing, in particular of clothing, footwear and road vehicles, food and livestock and tourism are important sectors of the economy. Lesotho's major trading partners are the members of the Southern Africa Customs Union (SACU—South Africa, Namibia, Botswana and Swaziland); Hong Kong, the Republic of China and Germany, as suppliers of imports; and the USA, Canada and the Benelux countries, as markets for exports. The national currency is the loti (plural: maloti). In 2004 the average exchange rate was US $1 = 6.4597 maloti.

Lesotho is a low-income country, whose economy is inseparably linked to that of South Africa. The main natural resource is **water**, which Lesotho sells to South Africa. Other advantages include self-sufficiency in power and potential for the development of tourism in the highlands. More than 85% of the population is engaged mainly in **agriculture** and informal activities. Agriculture contributes only about 14% of GDP, but has remained a crucial supplementary source of income since about one-half of rural household income is remitted by family members working in mining and other sectors in South Africa. Although declining, these migrant earnings still constitute about 30% of Lesotho's gross national product (GNP). Income from the sale of water and workers' remittances are complemented by SACU receipts. However, the latter may decline in future owing to changes to SACU's rules and to the liberalization of trade between **southern Africa** and Europe.

In recent years the large-scale retrenchment of Basotho miners from the South African **gold**-mining sector have had a negative effect on the economy. The rate of unemployment is estimated at about 45%. However, jobs have been created in the expanding garment-manufacturing industry, which has benefited from greater trade with the USA as a consequence of that country's **African Growth and Opportunity Act**. Lesotho is the second largest exporter in **sub-Saharan Africa** of garments to the USA.

Despite uncertainties and rapid changes in economic affairs, Lesotho achieved average real growth in GDP of about 10% in 1995–97. Growth subsequently slowed, however, following the political crisis of 1998, but was boosted by the construction of the Lesotho Highlands Water Project, which supplies water to South Africa, and by the rapid expansion of the manufacturing sector in the late 1990s.

Since then **drought** has caused agricultural output to fall. In April 2002, for example, the government declared a state of **famine** in response to adverse weather conditions. In February 2004 Lesotho was again confronted by famine as a result of sustained drought. It was estimated that some 57,000 metric tons of food aid would be required to feed 600,000–700,000 people in 2004. Lesotho was, none the less, able to raise its international credit ratings and improve job-creation. Export revenues have risen mainly owing to the contribution of the textiles sector. There is concern, however, that the expiry of the Multi-Fibre Agreement of the **World Trade Organization** in January 2005 may make Lesotho's textiles far less competitive than those of, for example, the People's Republic of China, India and Bangladesh. Much depends on Lesotho's ability to raise standards and productivity.

Government efforts to improve educational standards are hampered by the high incidence of **HIV/AIDS** among the country's teachers. Indeed, in all sectors of the economy Lesotho's work-force is, like those of its neighbours, seriously affected by the HIV/AIDS pandemic. The rate of infection with HIV/AIDS among people aged 15–49 stood at 28.9% at the end of 2003, one of the highest in the world. Anti-retroviral drugs have been made available to pregnant women infected with HIV in order to reduce mother-to-child transmission. It was estimated by the **International Monetary Fund** that expenditure on treatment of HIV/AIDS would amount to 3% of Lesotho's GDP by 2010.

Liberia, Republic of

The Republic of Liberia lies on the west coast of Africa, with Sierra Leone and Guinea to the north and Côte d'Ivoire to the east. The area of the country is 97,754 sq km. At mid-2003 the population was estimated at 3,367,000. English is the official language but the 16 major **ethnic groups** (including Kpelle, Bassa, Gio and Kru peoples) speak their own languages and dialects. Liberia is officially a Christian state, although some Liberians hold traditional beliefs. There are about 670,000 Muslims. The capital is Monrovia, whose population was estimated at 550,200 in 2003.

Political profile

Under the Constitution of January 1986, legislative power is vested in the bicameral National Assembly, comprising the 26-member Senate and the 64-member House of Representatives. Executive power is vested in the President, who holds office for a six-year term (renewable only once). The President, who appoints the Cabinet (subject to the approval of the Senate), is directly elected by universal adult suffrage, as are members of the Assembly. Members of the House of Representatives are elected for a term of six years, and senators for a term of nine years. Following a peace agreement in August 2003, a power-sharing National Transitional Government and a 76-member unicameral legislature, the National Transitional Legislative Assembly (NTLA), replaced the previous organs of government on 14 October for a two-year period, after which a democratically elected administration was to be established. (The National Transitional Government was officially inaugurated on 23 March 2004.)

On 11 August 2003 President **Charles Taylor** relinquished office before leaving Liberia for exile in Nigeria. Representatives of the incumbent government, rebel factions, political opposition and civil organizations reached a comprehensive peace agreement on 18 August, providing for the establishment of a transitional power-sharing government and legislature. On 21 August Gyude Bryant was elected as chairman of a National Transitional Government, defeating Ellen Johnson-Sirleaf and Rudolph Sherman.

History

Founded by liberated black slaves from the southern USA, Liberia became an independent republic in 1847. In 1980, following a military coup, Master Sgt (later Commander-in-Chief) Samuel Doe assumed power as chairman of the newly established People's Redemption Council, suspending the Constitution and proscribing all political parties. In 1985 Doe was elected as President. From 1989, when an armed insurrection was launched by rebel forces belonging to the National Patriotic Front of Liberia (NPFL), led by a former government official, Charles Taylor, until 2003 Liberia was destabilized by a civil conflict in which, at various times, many different factions and groups participated. Charles Taylor was elected as President of Liberia in July 1997.

On 18 August 2003, Taylor having relinquished power before leaving Liberia for exile in Nigeria, delegates of the incumbent government, rebel factions, political opposition and civil organizations, under the aegis of the UN, reached a comprehensive peace agreement, which provided for the establishment of a transitional power-sharing government and legislature, to comprise representatives of the participating groupings. Under the accord, Moses Zeh Blah (formerly the Vice-President, to whom Taylor had relinquished power) was to transfer power to the new administration on 14 October, all armed militia were to be disbanded, and democratic elections were to be conducted by October 2005. On 21 August 2003 the delegations elected Gyude Bryant, the leader of the Liberian Action Party (LAP), as chairman of the transitional administration. By the end of August a UN Joint Monitoring Committee had been dispatched to Monrovia, and ECOWAS Mission in Liberia (ECOMIL) troops were slowly taking control of rebel-held territory.

In September 2003 the UN Security Council formally established the UN Mission in Liberia (UNMIL), which was mandated to support the transitional authorities and the implementation of the August peace agreement. On 14 October, under the terms of the peace agreement, Bryant was officially inaugurated as chairman of the two-year power-sharing administration, the National Transitional Government, while the leader of the United People's Party, Wesley Johnson, became vice-chairman. At the same time a 76-member unicameral legislature, the NTLA, comprising representatives of the groupings signatory to the August agreement and 15 deputies nominated by the counties, was installed. A prominent member of Liberians United for Reconciliation and Democracy (LURD), George Dweh, was subsequently elected speaker of the new Assembly. Later in October the former administration, LURD and the Movement for Democracy in Liberia (MODEL) (which were each allocated five ministries in the National Transitional Government) submitted ministerial nominees for approval by the legislature. Of the former Taylor loyalists, Daniel Chea retained the post of Minister of Defence, while LURD representatives were awarded the portfolios of justice and finance, and the leader of MODEL, Thomas Nimely Yaya, became Minister of Foreign Affairs. (However, the political opposition and civil society groups failed to agree on how representatives for the remaining six portfolios divided between them would operate effectively.) In early December the International Criminal Police Organization issued an arrest notice against Taylor (who remained in Nigeria) for suspected war crimes. In December, in accordance with the peace agreement, UNMIL began a programme of disarmament and demobilization. The disarmament process, under which a total of some 96,000 former combatants had relinquished armaments, ended on 2 November 2004, with a ceremony at which the former armed factions were also officially dissolved involving an estimated 40,000 former combatants.

In February 2005 the National Elections Commission announced that the presidential and legislative elections would be conducted on 11 October. A total of 18 political parties had already registered to contest the elections, while the approval of a further 18 was expected. Some 40 prospective presidential candidates had also emerged, notably including George Weah, a Liberian national who had gained international renown as a footballer, and in November 2004 had returned to the country and announced his intention to contest the elections. In April 2005 Sekou Conneh of the LURD also announced his intention to contest the forthcoming presidential election as the candidate of his new political grouping, the Progressive Democratic Party.

International relations

The **Mano River Union (MRU)** was formed in 1973 to establish a customs and economic union between Guinea, Liberia and Sierra Leone. Subsequently, members signed a mutual non-aggression pact and pledged to establish a permanent mechanism for conflict prevention. Despite this, relations between the three countries have not always been amicable and the MRU has failed to live up to its original ideals. There have been various initiatives aimed at restoring peace to the MRU, in particular the International Contact Group on Liberia. Liberia's relations with Guinea improved markedly from August 2003, after President Charles Taylor was forced into exile and the incumbent government, rebel factions, political opposition and civil organizations in Liberia reached a peace agreement. The protracted **civil war** resulted in the presence of large numbers of Liberian **refugees** in Côte d'Ivoire in the 1990s.

The possible infiltration of refugee groups by Liberian fighters, together with sporadic incursions into eastern Côte d'Ivoire by Liberian armed factions, proved a significant security concern of the Ivorian authorities in the mid-1990s. Liberian troops, militia groups and mercenaries were involved in fighting in the west of Côte d'Ivoire during the civil conflict that erupted in that country in the late 1990s.

Liberia, economy

In 2003, according to the **World Bank**, Liberia's gross domestic product (GDP) was US $378m., equivalent to $130 per head. During 1990–2003, it was estimated, the population increased at an average annual rate of 2.5%, while GDP per head declined by 0.2%. Overall GDP increased, in real terms, at an average annual rate of 2.3% in 1990–2003; there was no discernible increase in GDP in 2003. Consumer prices increased by 12.1% in 2001, by an estimated 14.2% in 2002 and by an estimated 15.0% in 2003. In 2003 the principal suppliers of imports to Liberia were Japan, Singapore and Germany. The most important markets for Liberia's exports in that year were Germany, Poland, Greece and the USA. The national currency is the Liberian dollar (L $). In 2003 the average exchange rate was US $1 = L $59.3788. **Agriculture** accounted for about 40% of Liberia's GDP before the outbreak of **civil war**. The rubber industry generated more than US $100m. in export earnings annually. The discovery of significant iron ore deposits attracted substantial foreign investment in the 1960s and 1970s. The export-oriented concession sector formerly generated about one-third of government revenue. By 1996 real GDP had fallen to as low as 10% of its pre-war level. Most foreign business left the country during the civil war. Depletion of iron ore deposits, damage to mines and the impact of the war on rubber production caused the value of recorded exports to fall from $440m. in 1988 to $25m. in 1997. However, real GDP doubled in 1997 and increased further, by an average rate of 25%–30% in 1998–2000, reflecting a post-war surge in output of rice, timber and rubber.

Nevertheless, real income per head remains at about one-third of its pre-war level. According to a UN survey conducted in 2002, 76% of the population subsisted in **poverty** on incomes of less than $1 per day; of these, about two-thirds had daily incomes of less than $0.50. Liberia's GDP per head, estimated at $900 in 2005, has become one of the lowest in the world.

Intense fighting in the capital in June–August 2003 resulted in a humanitarian crisis and the disruption of most commercial activity. In 2004 agriculture continued to provide a subsistence living for the majority of the population, although many of the approximately 300,000 Liberian **refugees** and a further 260,000 internally displaced persons were reliant on international humanitarian aid. The transitional government has so far focused its efforts on producing a political climate in which UN sanctions applied to Liberia's timber and **diamonds**, on which the country's export trade is based, can be lifted. The UN Security Council renewed an embargo on the export of diamonds from Liberia in May 2002. Liberia's economic prospects depend on progress being made towards peace, on radical changes in governance, on the removal of UN sanctions and on the delivery of substantial foreign aid.

Libya (Great Socialist People's Libyan Arab Jamahiriya)

Libya is located in **North Africa**, bordering the Mediterranean Sea, between Egypt and Algeria. It borders Tunisia to the east, Niger and Chad to the south and Sudan to the south west. More than 90% of the country is desert or semi-desert. Its total area is 1,759,540 sq km. The capital is Tripoli. At mid-2002 the population was estimated at 5,445,000, of which **Berbers** and Arabs constitute more than 95%. Most of the population are **Sunni** Muslims. The official language is **Arabic**. Italian and English are widely understood in the major cities.

Political profile

The form of government in Libya is that of a ***jamahiriya***, in Arabic a 'state of the masses' or republic. The country is thus governed, in theory, by the people through local councils. In practice, ultimate control rests with **Col Muammar al-Qaddafi** and his close associates. *De facto* Head of State since 1 September 1969, Revolutionary Leader Col al-Qaddafi in fact holds no official title. The head of government is the Secretary of the General People's Committee (Premier), Shukri Muhammad Ghanem (since 14 June 2003).

The General People's Committee is established by the General People's Congress. National elections are held indirectly, through a hierarchy of about 2000 people's committees; the head of government is elected by the General People's Congress—the most recent election was held on 2 March 2000. The legislature is the unicameral General People's Congress whose members are elected indirectly through a hierarchy of people's committees.

The legal system is based on the Italian civil law system and the **Shar'ia**, or Islamic law. There is no constitutional provision for judicial review of legislative acts. There is a Supreme Court and separate religious courts. Libya has not accepted compulsory International Court of Justice jurisdiction. Political parties were banned in 1971. Various opposition groups with almost negligible memberships function clandestinely, or from exile in Egypt and Sudan. Political dissidents, including Islamist militants, have been heavily suppressed. Some Libyan dissidents abroad have also been murdered.

History

Since he took power in 1969 in a military coup, Col Qaddafi has imposed his own political system—a combination of **socialism** and **Islam**—which he calls the Third International Theory. Regarding himself as a revolutionary leader, in the 1970s and 1980s he used **oil** funds to promote his ideology outside of Libya, even supporting subversives and terrorists abroad to hasten the end of **Marxism** and capitalism. Libyan military adventures failed: the prolonged foray of Libyan troops into the Aozou Strip in northern Chad, for example, was finally repulsed in 1987. Libyan support for **terrorism** decreased after UN sanctions were imposed in 1992. Those sanctions were suspended in April 1999. Since then Libya has been drawn gradually back into diplomatic and economic relations with the international community.

International relations

Chadian rebels from the Aozou region reside in Libya. Libya claims about 19,400 sq km of territory in Niger as well as part of south-eastern Algeria in currently dormant disputes.

Libya, economy

Libya's command-economy depends primarily upon revenues from the **oil** sector, which contributes practically all export earnings and about one-quarter of the country's gross domestic product (GDP). These oil revenues and a small population give Libya one of the highest levels of GDP per head in Africa, but little of this income flows down to the general population. Import restrictions and inefficient resource allocations have led to periodic shortages of basic goods and foodstuffs. The non-oil manufacturing and construction sectors, which account for about 20% of GDP, have expanded from processing mostly agricultural products to include the production of petrochemicals, iron, steel and **aluminium**. Climatic conditions and poor soils severely limit agricultural output, and Libya imports about 75% of its food. Higher oil prices in 1999 and 2000 led to an increase in export revenues, which improved macroeconomic balances and helped to stimulate the economy. The suspension of UN sanctions in 1999 also boosted growth. In January 2002 a 51% devaluation of the official exchange rate of the dinar was a positive fiscal move, although it will lead to higher inflation.

Libyan Change and Reform Movement

Libyan opposition party. Breakaway group from the **National Front for the Salvation of Libya**.

Libyan Conservatives' Party

Libyan opposition party, founded in 1996.

Libyan Constitutional Grouping

Libyan opposition group.

Libyan Democratic Authority

Libyan opposition party, founded in 1993.

Libyan Democratic Conference

Libyan opposition party, founded in 1992.

Libyan Democratic Movement

Libyan opposition party, founded in 1977. An external group.

Libyan Islamic Fighting Group (Al-Jama'a al-Islamiyyah al-Muqatilah bi-Libya)

The Libyan Islamic Fighting Group emerged in 1995 among Libyans who had fought against Soviet forces in Afghanistan. It declared the government of Libyan leader **Col al-Qaddafi** to be unIslamic and pledged to overthrow it. Some members maintain a strictly anti-Qaddafi focus and organize against Libyan government interests, but others are aligned with **Osama bin Laden**'s al-Qa'ida organization or are active in the international *mujahidin* network. The group claimed responsibility for an unsuccessful attempt to assassinate Qaddafi in 1996 and engaged Libyan security forces in armed clashes in the mid- and late 1990s. It continues to target Libyan interests and may engage in sporadic clashes with Libyan security forces. It probably maintains a clandestine presence in Libya, but since the late 1990s many of its members have fled to various Middle Eastern and European countries.

Ligue islamique de la daawa et le djihad (LIDD—Islamic League of Call and Jihad)

Algerian Islamist opposition group, led by Sheikh Ali Benhadjar. Part of the LIDD joined the cease-fire announced by the **Armée islamique du salut (AIS—Islamic Salvation Army)** in October 1997 and dissolved itself after the 1999 amnesty in January 2000. A dissident splinter group of the LIDD continued fighting in eastern Algeria.

Locusts

Locusts are a major scourge of the Saharan and, particularly, the Sahelian regions of Africa, although they also affect **southern Africa**. Breeding usually in remote areas, their swarms periodically sweep across vast areas, destroying pastures and standing crops. Early warning systems exist to give notice of emerging swarms and their probable direction, but these are not always effective and governments and other agencies are in any case frequently unable to respond swiftly enough or on a sufficient scale to deal with them effectively. Spraying (particularly aerial spraying) is generally effective, but costly, and logistically difficult; locals generally depend on beating, but this has little effect on large swarms. Together with **drought,** locusts are a major contributory factor in the creation of preconditions for **famine** in Africa.

Lockerbie

On 21 December 1988 Pan-Am Flight 103 to New York exploded in mid-air over Lockerbie, a small town in Scotland. All 259 people on board died in the crash. Libya was accused of involvement and, after numerous delays, eventually, in 1999, surrendered two suspects for trial. In 2001 a Scottish court convicted one of the Libyan accused and sentenced him to life imprisonment. The evidence and the responsibility for the crash remain disputed. There is some evidence to suggest that the Palestinian group, the Popular Front for the Liberation of Palestine—General Command, might have been involved. Libya, however, agreed in August 2003 to pay US $4m. to the families of each of those killed. The UN Security Council immediately commenced the removal of the sanctions that had been applied against Libya. However, the families of the victims were not able to receive the full amount of compensation from Libya until the USA lifted its unilateral sanctions, which it was still not prepared to do. The USA did not block the Security Council vote, but retained its own sanctions because of Libya's alleged human rights violations, role in perpetuating regional conflicts and pursuit of weapons of mass destruction. US sanctions have been applied since 1986, when the USA, under President Reagan, bombed Tripoli in retaliation against alleged Libyan **terrorism**. More sanctions were imposed in 1996 when the D'Amato Act targeted Libya and Iran for their alleged support of terrorism and efforts to acquire weapons of mass destruction. In 2001 the Act was renewed until 2006. If the USA were to lift sanctions on Libya, the Lockerbie relatives would receive a further $4m. If Libya is removed from the US Department of State's list of sponsors of terrorism, they would receive an additional $2m. and compensation would thus total $10m. in all. If the USA does not lift sanctions before May 2004, the families will receive only $1m. more—$5m. in total. Although the government of Libya formally accepted responsibility for the Lockerbie explosion in return for being allowed to rejoin the international community after a decade of isolation, there are some (including Libya's Prime Minister, Shukri Ghanem) who have indicated that Libya was not actually responsible.

Lomé Convention(s)

The First Lomé Convention (Lomé I) that came into force in April 1976 replaced the **Yaoundé Convention** and the Arusha Agreement, and was designed to provide a new framework of co-operation between the European Community (now the **European Union (EU)**) and the **African, Caribbean and Pacific (ACP) countries**, taking into account the varying needs of developing countries. Lomé II was concluded at Lomé, Togo, in October 1979, and came into force in January 1981. Lomé III was signed in December 1984 and came into force in March (trade provisions) and May (aid) 1985. The Fourth Lomé Convention, which had a 10-year commitment period, was signed in December 1989; its trade provisions entered into force in March 1990, and the remaining provisions in November 1991. In February 2000 negotiations on a successor arrangement to the Lomé Convention were concluded. The new partnership accord was signed by ACP and EU heads of state or government in Cotonou, Benin, in June 2000, and was to enter into force following ratification by the European Parliament and ACP national legislatures. Pending the entry into force of the **Cotonou Agreement** and the conclusion of new economic and trade arrangements, existing EU-ACP preferential trade agreements remained in effect.

Lord's Resistance Army (LRA)

The Lord's Resistance Army (LRA), operating in the north west of Uganda, is a rebel group led by Joseph Kony, who considers himself to be semi-divine. For 18 years it has waged a brutal campaign against the local population, notably the northern Acholi, and government forces deployed to suppress its rebellion. The aims of the movement are by no means clear. Kony, who was raised as a Roman Catholic, claims to have been sent by God to save his people from evil, including Ugandan President **Yoweri Museveni**, and all forms of witchcraft. He has stated that he wishes to rule Uganda in accordance with the Ten Commandments, but has more prosaic demands for **education** for all, an independent judiciary and policies to encourage foreign investment. Almost 2m. people, representing 90% of the population of the three main Acholi provinces of Gulu, Kitgum and Pader, are thought to have fled the LRA and now live in refugee camps. Pressure on the LRA has increased since the government of Sudan agreed in 2002 to cease supporting it. It has allowed Ugandan government forces to attack LRA bases in the southern Sudan and in March 2005 the two countries collaborated in a joint military operation against the LRA.

Ould Louly, Lt-Col Mohammed Mahmoud

Head of State of Mauritania from June 1979 until January 1980, when he was overthrown by **Lt-Col Khouna Ould Haidalla**.

Lumumba, Patrice

One of the founder members of the Mouvement national congolais (MNC—National Congolese Movement) in 1958. Lumumba was a popular political figure in the years before the Belgian Congo became independent. Although imprisoned by the Belgian authorities in 1959, he retained his good standing with the Belgians until the eve of **independence**. He was eventually installed as Prime Minister of a broad coalition government in the newly independent Republic of the Congo (ROC), of which **Joseph Kasavubu** was President. Shortly after independence was declared (on 30 June 1960), the armed foreces mutinied, sparking a series of conflicts and confrontations. **Moïse Tshombe** declared the independence of **Katanga**, the wealthy mineral-producing region of the south east, on 11 July, prompting Belgium to immediately renounce its recently signed treaty of friendship with the Congo and to transfer support (and armed forces) to Tshombe. On 14 July the UN dispatched troops to the region to maintain order and displace the Belgians, but it was unclear whether they were also to subject Katanga to the authority of the central government. During this difficult initial period relations between Kasavubu and Lumumba were co-operative. In September, however, Kasavubu dismissed Lumumba and appointed a new government. The Assemblée nationale supported Lumumba, maintaining that his dismissal had been illegal. However, the UN intervention, as a result of which all airports were closed and telecommunications severed, effectively gave the advantage to Kusavubu by preventing Lumumba from stating his case either over the air or by travelling the country. He was forced to remain in Léopoldville in his official residence, while Col Joseph-Désiré **Mobutu**, the army chief of staff, seized power. Mobutu declared his support for Kasavubu. From virtual house arrest, Lumumba fled Léopoldville by car at the end of November, hoping to reach Stanleyville, where he had strong support. He was overtaken with the help of aircraft and imprisoned in Thysville, from where he escaped to the Katangan capital of Elisabethville on 17 January, only to be captured again, and murdered. Lumumba's supporters, led by Antoine Gizenga in Stanleyville, broke away from the centre. At one point it seemed that the USSR would recognize the Stanleyville party as the government of the Congo and supply it with arms. However, Gizenga did not formally declare the secession of Stanleyville and when new governments were appointed, first in February 1961 under Ileo and then, in August, under Adoula, Gizenga accepted a post as Deputy Prime Minister on the understanding that force would be used if necessary to end the Katanga secession. As well as in Stanleyville, support for Lumumba remained strong in the eastern region (Orientale province); indeed, generally, as far as could be ascertained, he remained the most popular of leaders. The murder and the charisma of Patrice Lumumba, and a sense of 'what might have been', haunted Congolese politics for many decades after his murder.

Luo

The Luo are an important ethno-linguistic grouping in Kenya, where they constitute some 13% of the population.

Lusaka Agreement

An agreement concluded between Portugal and the **Frente de Libertação de Moçambique (Frelimo—Mozambique Liberation Front)** in 1974, after more than a decade of war in Mozambique, that set June 1975 as the date for Mozambique's **independence**.

Lusaka Protocol

Agreement for a process (the Lusaka Process) to bring about (under UN auspices) a cease-fire and eventual peace accord in the Angolan **civil war**. The acceptance by the **União Nacional para a Independência Total de Angola (UNITA—National Union for the Total Independence of Angola)** of the results of elections held in 1992 led to renewed talks between the government and UNITA in Lusaka in October 1993. This resulted in the signature of a second peace agreement, known as the Lusaka Protocol, on 20 November 1994. A formal cease-fire took effect two days later.

M

Macroeconomic Research Group (MERG)

Group charged with the responsibility of developing a coherent macroeconomic policy for the new South Africa, chaired by Vella Pillay, a long-time economic adviser to the **African National Congress (ANC)** and consultant to the Bank of China. Set up in mid-1992 shortly after the ANC's *Ready to Govern* document was adopted, MERG drew on the experience of 100 economists, most of them foreign academics, and included leading figures from the ANC, the **Confederation of South African Trade Unions (COSATU)** and the South African Communist Party. In November 1993, six months before the ANC came to power as the leading partner in a government of national unity, MERG presented a 300 page document entitled *Making Democracy Work*. The report, however, which broadly set out a programme involving substantial state intervention and a heavily-managed capitalist development strategy of the kind popular on the left in European academic circles during the 1980s, and practised by a number of developing countries, including the emerging Asia Tigers, was shelved by the ANC when it came to power and moved more towards the liberal economic policies encouraged by the **International Monetary Fund (IMF)** and the **World Bank** in the 1980s and 1990s. Already, and even as Pillay presented his report in November, the ANC's two leading economists, Trevor Manuel and Alec Ewin, were drafting a secret letter of intent to the IMF seeking a loan of US $850m. loan and accepting the kind of conditions that would have been anathema to the majority of MERG members. Having discarded the MERG document, the new ANC government had to rely on a document called the **Reconstruction and Development Programme**, which had been hastily crafted in preparation for the election campaign. In mid-1995, however, a new team was set up to develop a more coherent macroeconomic framework. This team produced a policy document called **Growth, Employment and Redistribution**, which Manuel presented to government in June 1996.

Madagascar, Republic of

The Republic of Madagascar comprises the island of Madagascar, the fourth largest in the world, and several much smaller offshore islands, in the western Indian

Ocean, about 500 km east of Mozambique, in southern Africa. The area of the country is 587,041 sq km. At mid-2004 the population was estimated at 16,908,000. The official language is Malagasy, and government acts are published in both Malagasy and French. Hova and other dialects are also widely spoken. More than 50% of the population follow animist beliefs, while about 41% are Christians and the remainder are Muslims. The capital is Antananarivo (formerly Tananarive), whose population was estimated at 1,111,392 in 2001.

Political profile

The Constitution of Madagascar provides for a bicameral legislature, comprising a Senate (established in March 2001) and a National Assembly. Two-thirds of the members of the Senate are elected by the autonomous provinces, and the remaining one-third of the members are appointed by the President, while the National Assembly is elected by universal suffrage for a five-year term of office. The constitutional Head of State is the President, who is elected for a term of five years, and can be re-elected for two further terms. The President appoints the Prime Minister and, on the latter's recommendation, the other members of the Council of Ministers. **Marc Ravalomanana** was inaugurated as President in May 2002, following a disputed election in December 2001 (see below).

Following a senatorial election held on 18 March 2001, the distribution of seats in the Senate was as follows: Association pour la renaissance de Madagascar (AREMA—Association for the Renaissance of Madagascar) 49; LEADER/Fanilo (Torch) 5; Independents 3; Ny asa vita no ifampitsara (AVI—People are judged by the work they do) 2; Asa, Fampandrasoana, Arinda (AFFA) 1. Appointments to an additional 30 seats were made by the President.

Following a legislative election held on 15 December 2002, the distribution of seats in the National Assembly was as follows: Tiako i Madagasikara (TIM—I Love Madagascar) 104; Front Patriotique (PF—Patriotic Front) 22 (of which the constituent AVI held 20 and the Rassemblement pour le socialisme et la démocratie—RPSD, Rally for Socialism and Democracy—2); RPSD nouveau (New RPSD) 5; AREMA 3; LEADER/Fanilo 1; Independents 23.

History

A French possession since 1896, Madagascar became an autonomous state within the French Community in October 1958, as the Malagasy Republic. In May 1959 Philibert Tsiranana, leader of the Parti social démocrate (PSD—Social Democrat Party), was elected President. The country achieved full **independence** on 26 June 1960. In May 1972, following civil unrest, President Tsiranana transferred full powers to the Army Chief of Staff, Gen. Gabriel Ramanantsoa. In February 1973 all political parties were suspended.

Since the mid-1970s political affairs in Madagascar have been characterized to a large extent by constitutional issues. In a referendum in December 1975 more than 94% of voters approved a new Constitution, which provided for radical administrative and agrarian reforms, and the appointment of Lt-Commdr (later Adm.) Didier Ratsiraka as President of the Republic for a term of seven years. The country's name was changed to the Democratic Republic of Madagascar, and a 'Second Republic' was proclaimed. In January 1976 the civilian element in the government was increased, and in March the Avant-garde de la révolution malgache (AREMA—Antoky Ny Revolosiona Malagasy) was founded as the nucleus of the Front national pour la défense de la révolution socialiste malgache (FNDR), the only political organization permitted by the Constitution. In March 1990 the government formally permitted the resumption of multi-party politics.

A draft Constitution of the Third Republic, as submitted to the government in April 1992, envisaged a unitary state and provided for a bicameral legislature, comprising a Senate and a National Assembly. Two-thirds of the members of the Senate were to be selected by an electoral college, with the remaining one-third to be appointed by the President, while the 184-member National Assembly was to be elected by universal suffrage, under a system of proportional representation, for a four-year term. The authority of the President was reduced, and executive power was vested in the Prime Minister, who was to be appointed by the National Assembly. (A stipulation in the draft Constitution that the President be restricted to two terms of office had, however, been withdrawn.) Ratsiraka demanded that a draft providing for a federal system of government also be submitted to a forthcoming referendum, as an alternative to these proposals. The new Constitution was approved by 72.2% of votes cast in a national referendum on 19 August.

In January 1998 Ratsiraka (who had been elected as President in 1996) invited political leaders to attend discussions on constitutional reform, although Hery Miara-dia, an opposition grouping led by former President Albert Zafy, and members of the Panorama Group, a more moderate alliance led by Francisqe Ravony and Norbert Ratsirahonana, refused to participate. None the less, Ratsiraka subsequently announced that a constitutional referendum would take place in March 1998, to be followed by legislative elections. The draft amendments to the Constitution envisaged a 'federal-style' state, composed of six autonomous provinces, and also provided for increased presidential powers. The referendum proceeded on 15 March 1998, when the extensive revisions proposed were narrowly endorsed by 50.96% of votes cast.

A presidential election took place on 16 December 2001, contested by six candidates, including Ratsiraka, Zafy, Herizo Razafimahaleo and Marc Ravalomanana. According to the official results, Ravalomanana, whose candidacy was supported by a number of opposition parties, most notably the AVI, the RPSD and the Mouvement pour le pouvoir prolétarien (Mpitolona ho aminny Fonjakanny Madinika—MFM, Movement for Proletarian Power), secured 46.21% of the votes cast and Didier Ratsiraka 40.89%, thereby necessitating a second round of voting. However, Ravalomanana's own electoral observers disputed this result, claiming that he had won an outright victory, with 52.15% of the votes, and demanded a public comparison of voting records. The opposition was supported in these demands by international electoral observers. A re-count was subsequently conducted, and on 25 January 2002 the Constitutional High Court endorsed the official results and ruled that a second round of voting should take place within 30 days. Ravalomanana rejected this verdict and called for a national strike in protest. Some 500,000 people responded by gathering in Antananarivo. A political crisis ensued.

Following the completion of a further re-count, in late April 2002, the Constitutional High Court ruled that Ravalomanana had secured the presidency, with 51.46% of the votes cast, while Ratsiraka had won 35.90%. Ratsiraka refused to accept the Court's decision, but Ravalomanana was none the less inaugurated as President on 6 May, largely without international recognition, and appointed a new Council of Ministers later that month. Four of the country's six provincial governors, who were loyal to Ratsiraka, subsequently threatened to secede. In June heavy fighting occurred as troops loyal to Ravalomanana conducted a military offensive against areas controlled by Ratsiraka, securing two provincial capitals, Mahajanga and Toliary, in mid-June. At the end of June the USA recognized Ravalomanana as the legitimate leader of Madagascar; endorsement soon followed from France and, in contravention of the policy of the **Organization of African Unity (OAU)**, Senegal. Meanwhile, the OAU suspended Madagascar from its meetings, pending the staging of free and fair elections leading to the establishment of a legitimate government; this decision was upheld by the **African Union (AU)**, which replaced the OAU in July. Madagascar's suspension from meetings of the AU—hitherto the only remaining significant authority not to have recognized the new government—was formally revoked in July 2003; the legitimacy of the Ravalomanana administration was thus considered finally to have been established.

International relations

Madagascar's foreign policy is officially non-aligned: while it formerly maintained close links with communist countries, the Zafy government established relations with Israel, South Africa and the Republic of Korea. Relations with France have been affected by disputes over compensation for nationalized French assets and over the continuing French claim to the Iles Glorieuses, north of Madagascar, and three other islets in the Mozambique Channel. In February 2000 it was agreed that the Iles Glorieuses would be co-administered by France, Madagascar and Mauritius, without prejudice to the question of sovereignty. Relations with the People's Republic of China were strengthened in January 1999, when agreements were signed on the expansion of bilateral economic relations and China's provision of preferential loans to Madagascar. In September 2000 the representative office for Taiwan in Madagascar was closed down, following an official visit by the Malagasy Minister of Foreign Affairs to China.

Madagascar, economy

In 2003, according to estimates by the **World Bank**, Madagascar's gross national income (GNI), measured at average 2001–03 prices, was US $5,378m., equivalent to about $290 per head (or $800 per head on an international purchasing-power parity basis). During 1990–2003, it was estimated, the population increased at an average annual rate of 2.9%, while gross domestic product (GDP) per head decreased, in real terms, by an average of 1.4% per year. Overall GDP increased, in real terms, at an average annual rate of 1.4% in 1990–2003; GDP decreased by 12.7% in 2002, but increased by 9.6% in 2003. The annual rate of inflation averaged 15.7% in 1990–2001; consumer prices increased by 16.5% in 2002 but decreased by 1.7% in 2004. Mining, fishing, tourism, the production of paper, food and tobacco, chemicals, and cement, and the refining of petroleum and metalwork are all important sectors of the economy. Madagascar's principal exports are **coffee**, shellfish, vanilla and (as re-exports from the free-trade zone) cloves, pepper, **cotton**, **chromium**, graphite and sapphires. France, the USA, Germany, the United Kingdom and Mauritius are Madagascar's principal trading partners. A new national currency, the ariary, was introduced in July 2003. In 2004 the average exchange rate was US $1 = 1,868.9 ariary. **Agriculture** (including livestock production and forestry) dominates the Malagasy economy, accounting for about one-third of GDP and employing some 86% of the workforce. Although traditional crops of **coffee**, vanilla, cloves and pepper continue to make up a large part of agricultural exports, the contribution of fish, in particular prawns, has also increased. The industrial sector, which contributes only about 13% of GDP, is focused on **energy**, textiles, wood, cement, paper, beverages and soap products, and the processing of agricultural produce. Madagascar is rich in mineral resources, including sapphires, emeralds and ilmenite, and may have reserves of **oil** and **natural gas**. However, virtually all mining activity is in the private sector and the general population derives little benefit from it. Services account for about 55% of GDP. Over the last three decades, the annual rate of economic growth has averaged only about 0.6%. As the population has increased by about 3% annually during the same period, income per head has declined sharply. After Ratsiraka took power in 1975, the Malagasy economy, which had been on a similar level to those of Thailand or Botswana, steadily declined. Over the last three decades, according to the World Bank, Madagascar has recorded the fifth lowest rate of GDP growth in the world—0.5% per annum—and that without involvement in any war, at home or abroad. In recent years, however, the economy has improved, thanks to a programme combining resumed donor **structural adjustment** support, debt rescheduling, liberalization, privatization and the establishment of the zone franche, concentrating mainly on garment manufacture. In the period 1999–2001, despite widespread **corruption**, the annual rate of GDP growth rose from 4% to almost 6%. The rate of inflation was being steadily reduced, and in 2001 fell to around 7%. However, the political crisis of 2002, when many companies ceased their activities and the majority of the 160,000 zone franche employees lost their jobs, reversed previous gains. At about 12% of GDP, fiscal revenue is low. This constraint on public finances makes the government budget dependent on donor flows. In turn, the **International Monetary Fund** seeks a greater effort to combat fraud.

While new export industries have been developed, some traditional agricultural exports have been affected by low world prices (coffee) or ageing plantations. Imports have also risen as a result of liberalization, putting pressure on the balance of payments: foreign exchange has been liberalized, import licences have been removed and some state monopolies ended. Future prospects depend heavily on restoring domestic and foreign private-sector confidence: this had been improving before the recent crisis, although inadequate transparency and lack of application of the law remained persistent problems. The new government has pledged to address these issues. It is also committed to reducing **poverty** and fighting corruption, as well as to the principles embodied in the **New Partnership for Africa's Development (NEPAD)**. The greater role envisaged for tourism may be impeded by generally weak infrastructure, in particular for transport, a lack of transparency in the legal system, and ambivalence over land tenure for foreigners. The depreciation of the national currency in 2004, combined with severe cyclone damage and the high international price of petroleum, had an inflationary effect on the economy, leading to national discontent and international concern. The response by the international community has been positive: the UN's World Food Programme quickly provided support in the aftermath of the cyclone, while the European Commission approved grants totalling some €165m. to aid development in 2005–11. In mid-2004, France announced that it would forgive the remaining public **debt** owed to it by Madagascar, while the USA announced that Madagascar had been selected to receive supplementary aid from the **Millennium Challenge Account**, which would increase the level of bilateral aid from that country by 50% over three years.

Madani, Abbasi

Referred to widely in the foreign language press as Madani, as though this were his surname, in fact Madani is his given name and Abbasi his family name. Madani was a founder member of the **Front de libération nationale (FLN—National Liberation Front)** in 1954 and spent most of the Algerian war of **independence** in prison. He became a university teacher after independence and subsequently obtained a doctorate from the Institute of Education at the University of London in the mid-1970s. Married to an Englishwoman, he personifies the middle-class, middle-aged and pragmatic element within the **Front islamique du salut (FIS—Islamic Salvation Front)**. In the late 1970s he helped found Islamic welfare organizations in the slums to meet the growing needs of the impoverished. He became politically active and organized protests against the Algerian government for which he was jailed for two years in 1982. In 1989 he assumed the leadership of the FIS, an umbrella group of some six organizations seeking Islamic social, political and economic reform. The FIS achieved victories in local elections and was on the verge of winning national legislative elections in 1992 when the **military** took power and aborted the electoral process. The FIS was banned and Madani was arrested together with other Islamic leaders. The Algerian **civil war** erupted as a result with radicalized Islamic groups, especially the **Groupe islamique armé (GIA—Armed Islamic Group)**, resorting to violence. Madani was released in 1997 and is now under house arrest.

Maghreb

Term used to refer to the countries of North West Africa—usually Mauritania, Morocco, Algeria, Tunisia and Libya (see also **Arab Maghreb Union).** Literally means the land of the setting sun, hence 'the west'. Term used in the Arab World to refer to its western part (i.e. **North Africa**). In Algeria the term is used to refer to Morocco.

Al-Mahdi, Sadiq

Major political opponent of President **Gaafar Muhammad Nimeri** in Sudan during the 1970s, who represented an Islamic tradition as opposed to the authoritarian populism of Nimeri. A reconciliation, marked by al-Mahdi's election to a vice-presidency of the Sudanese Socialist Union, was ruptured in 1979. Al-Mahdi was jailed by Nimeri from September 1983 until December 1984. His release came as Nimeri himself was beginning to move towards the introduction of Islamic law throughout Sudan and had begun to refer to himself as Imam. In April 1984, after **bread riots** and social unrest had developed into a movement of political opposition, Nimeri was overthrown by the army (although he was visiting the USA at the time) in a pre-emptive coup to forestall more radical action. The succeeding military government held power only temporarily while traditional political parties negotiated the formation of a civilian coalition with al-Mahdi as Prime Minister. Al-Mahdi, too, was only Head of State for a relatively short period before he was replaced by **Lt-Gen. Omar Hassan Ahmad al-Bashir** following a military coup.

Malaria

A major scourge of the African sub-continent. Of the estimated 1.2m. deaths caused by malaria annually world-wide, 85% occur in Africa. In the past the spraying of DDT and other insecticides contributed to a significant decline in numbers of the malaria-carrying mosquito, but the emergence of resistant strains of mosquito and failure to maintain levels of insecticide spraying have resulted in its resurgence and a higher incidence of malaria. The provision on a large scale of mosquito nets impregnated with insecticide would provide a major boost to the campaign to control the disease. The cost is relatively low—US $4 per net—and the estimated reduction in risk of mortality for infants high—14%–63%. However, mosquito nets cost more to distribute than they do to produce and adequate mechanisms for their effective distribution and use have yet to be developed.

Malawi, Republic of

The Republic of Malawi is a land-locked country in southern central Africa, with Zambia to the west, Mozambique to the south and east, and Tanzania to the north. Lake Malawi forms most of the eastern boundary. The area of the country is 118,484 sq km. At mid-2003 the population was estimated at 12,105,000. Among the many different ethnic and tribal groups the Chewa preponderate. The official language is English, although Chichewa is being promoted as the basis for a 'Malawi Language'. More than 70% of the population profess Christianity, while a further 20%, largely Asians, are Muslims. Most of the remaining Malawians follow traditional beliefs, although there is also a Hindu minority. The capital is Lilongwe, whose population was 440,471 at the census of September 1998.

Political profile

The Head of State is the President, who is elected by universal adult suffrage, in the context of a multi-party political system, for a term of five years. Executive power is vested in the President, and legislative power in the National Assembly, which has 193 elective seats. Members of the Assembly are elected for five years, by universal adult suffrage, in the context of a multi-party system. Cabinet ministers are appointed by the President.

In a presidential election held on 20 May 2004 Bingu wa Mutharika, the candidate of the United Democratic Front (UDF), received the largest share of the total votes cast (35.89%) and was accordingly elected as President.

Following legislative elections held on 20 May 2004, the distribution of seats in the National Assembly was as follows: Malawi Congress Party (MCP) 56; UDF 49; Republican Party (RP) 15; National Democratic Alliance (NDA) 8; Alliance for Democracy (AFORD) 6; People's Progressive Movement (PPM) 6; Movement for Genuine Democratic Change (MGODE) 3; Congress for National Unity (CONU) 1; People's Transformation Party (PETRA) 1; Independents 39. The RP, the PPM, the MGODE and PETRA all contested the election as part of the Mgwirizano Coalition, which also comprised the Malawi Democratic Party (MDP), the Malawi Forum for Unity and Development (MAFUNDE) and the National Unity Party (NUP). In June 2004 the MGODE and the RP signed a memorandum of understanding on co-operation with the UDF. As of June 2004 disputed results in three constituencies remained under investigation, while voting in a further six constituencies was not conducted owing to irregularities.

History

Malawi was formerly the British protectorate of **Nyasaland**. In 1953 it was linked with two other British dependencies, Northern and Southern **Rhodesia** (now Zambia and Zimbabwe), to form the Federation of Rhodesia and Nyasaland. Elections in August 1961 gave the Malawi Congress Party (MCP), led by **Dr Hastings Kamuzu Banda**, a majority of seats in the Legislative Council. Dr Banda became Prime Minister in February 1963, and the Federation was dissolved in December. Nyasaland gained **independence**, as Malawi, on 6 July 1964. The country became a republic and a one-party state, with Banda as its first President, on 6 July 1966. In 1971 Banda was named Life President. Until 1993 all Malawian citizens were obliged to be members of the MCP; no political opposition was tolerated, and only candidates who had been approved by Banda were allowed to contest elections to the National Assembly.

In June 1993 a referendum on the introduction of a multi-party system took place. Despite evidence of MCP attempts to disrupt the opposition's activities prior to the poll, 63.2% of those who participated (some 63.5% of the electorate) voted for an end to single-party rule. Banda rejected opposition demands for the immediate installation of an interim government of national unity. He agreed, however, to the establishment of a National Executive Council to oversee the transition to a multi-party system and the holding of free elections, and of a National Consultative Council to implement the necessary amendments to the Constitution. Both councils were to include members of the Government and the opposition. Banda announced an amnesty for thousands of political exiles, and stated that a general election would be held, on a multi-party basis, within a year. In late June the Constitution was amended to allow the registration of political parties other than the MCP. In November the National Assembly approved a Constitutional Amendment Bill, which, *inter alia*, abolished the institution of life presidency and ended the requirement that election candidates be members of the MCP. Malawi's first multi-party parliamentary and presidential elections took place on 17 May 1994. In the presidential election the secretary-general of the UDF, **(Elson) Bakili Muluzi** (a former government minister and MCP secretary-general), received 47.3% of the votes cast, defeating Banda (who won 33.6% of the votes). Eight parties contested the legislative elections: of these, the UDF won 84 seats in the National Assembly, the MCP 55 and AFORD 36. (Voting was repeated in two constituencies where irregularities had been found, as a result of which the UDF and MCP each won a further seat.)

Presidential and legislative elections were held on 15 June 1999. Muluzi was re-elected to the presidency, securing 51.37% of the votes cast. In elections to the expanded National Assembly the ruling UDF won 93 seats, while the MCP secured 66 seats, AFORD 29 and independent candidates four. (Owing to the death of a candidate, voting in the remaining constituency was postponed until October, when the seat was won by the UDF.) Although the opposition disputed the results, Muluzi was inaugurated later in June.

At the presidential election held on 20 May 2004 Bingu wa Mutharika, representing the ruling UDF, was the successful candidate. At concurrent elections to the National Assembly, however, the MCP emerged as the largest party, winning 56 of the 193 seats in the legislature, while the UDF gained 49 seats and the Mgwirizano Coalition 25. International observers criticized the conduct of the polls and opposition parties disputed the results. Mutharika was sworn in as President on 24 May amid rioting by opposition supporters. The new President subsequently pledged to take measures to combat **corruption**, and to introduce economic reforms.

International relations

Despite being the only African country to have maintained full diplomatic relations with South Africa during the **apartheid** era, Malawi joined the Southern African Development Co-ordination Conference (subsequently the **Southern African Development Community**), which originally aimed to reduce the dependence of southern African countries on South Africa.

Malawi, economy

In 2003, according to estimates by the **World Bank**, Malawi's gross national income (GNI), measured at average 2001–03 prices, was US $1,687m., equivalent to $170 per head (or $600 per head on an international purchasing-power parity basis). During 1990–2003, it was estimated, the population increased at an average annual rate of 2.0%, while gross domestic product (GDP) per head increased, in real terms, by an average of 0.9% per year. Overall GDP increased, in real terms, at an average annual rate of 2.9% in 1990–2003; real GDP increased by 5.9% in 2003. The annual rate of inflation averaged 28.8% in 1990–2002; consumer prices increased by an average of 9.6% in 2003. In 2004 the main destinations of Malawi's exports were South Africa, the USA, Germany, Egypt and the United Kingdom. The principal suppliers of imports in that year were South Africa, India and Tanzania. The national currency is the Malawi kwacha. In 2003 the average exchange rate was US $1 = 97.4325 kwacha.

Malawi's economy is based largely on **agriculture**, from which the country derives more than 90% of its export earnings, and which contributed 38.1% of GDP in 2003. Malawi has some of the most fertile land in the region. Almost 70% of total agricultural production is by small-holder farmers. Land distribution is unequal: more than 40% of small-holders cultivate less than 0.5 ha. The country's export trade is dominated by tobacco, tea, **cotton**, **coffee** and sugar. Agricultural GDP increased at an average annual rate of 5.4% in 1990–2002. An estimated 82% of the working population were engaged in agriculture in mid-2003.

The UN Human Development Index ranks Malawi 159th out of 174 countries, and as the sixth poorest country in the world, with income per head of $600. Its few exploitable resources, apart from land, are at serious risk of degradation as a result of population pressure and poor farming methods. About 90% of the agricultural labour force are engaged in subsistence farming. In February 2002, after adverse weather conditions had reduced the maize harvest, President **Muluzi** declared a state of **famine** in Malawi.

Tobacco contributes some 60% of export earnings, with sugar, tea and coffee each contributing, approximately, a further 5%. The tobacco auctions have repeatedly been closed during the selling season as Malawian growers protest against low prices offered by global buyers. Two such closures occurred in 2002, and the 2003 season was halted in May.

Malawi undertook significant commercial borrowing in the mid-1970s in order to finance development programmes. International organizations (e.g. the **African Development Bank**, the **International Monetary Fund (IMF)**, and the World Bank) have become the main source of foreign funding, but the United Kingdom and South Africa have remained significant donors of aid. Other major donors are the **European Union** (currently the main donor overall), France, Canada, the USA, Germany, Denmark and Japan. As a proportion of outstanding **debt**, commercial borrowing increased from less than 2% in 1976 to more than 24% in 1980. World Bank figures for 1994 indicated that the Muluzi government inherited a total external debt equivalent to 163.2% of Malawi's GNI in that year. By 2001/02 debt-servicing was the largest single expenditure, absorbing 25% of total revenue—more than was spent on **education** or health. This remained the case even under the **Heavily Indebted Poor Countries initiative**, reaching $2,860m. by 2004.

The privatization of major banks in late 2001 was encouraged by the IMF as part of a continued attempt to reform the banking sector. In order to qualify for further IMF loans, Malawi's economic planners were required to reduce monetary growth, achieve a balanced fiscal position, deepen structural reform, strengthen governance and prioritize expenditure to benefit the poor. Specifically, the IMF insisted that intervention in maize marketing and the subsidization of petroleum should not be resumed. In June 2004 the Fund noted that growth was not sufficient to meet the development goals that had been espoused, that **poverty** in Malawi was 'widespread', and criticized the government. IMF spending was suspended in mid-2004 pending further discussions: the priority of the Mutharika government is to improve relations with donors and creditors and alleviate fears that the budget for 2005–06, which is pegged at 113,000m. kwacha (761m. euros), will cause inflation to rise further, raising commodity prices to unaffordable levels.

Mali, Republic of

The Republic of Mali is a land-locked country in West Africa, with Algeria to the north, Mauritania and Senegal to the west, Guinea and Côte d'Ivoire to the south, and Burkina Faso and Niger to the east. The area of the country is 1,240,192 sq km. At mid-2003 the population was estimated at 13,007,000. The principal ethnic groups are **Mande (Bambara**, Malinke, **Soninke**), **Peul**, Voltaic, Songhaï, Tuareg and Moor. The official language is French but a number of other languages, including Bambara, Fulfulde, Sonrai, Tamashek, Soninke and Dogon, are widely spoken. It is estimated that about 80% of the population are Muslims and 18% follow traditional animist beliefs; under 2% are Christians. The capital is Bamako, whose (*de jure*) population at the census of 1998 was estimated at 1,016,167.

Political profile

Executive power is vested in the President of the Republic, who is elected for five years by universal suffrage. The President appoints a Prime Minister, who, in turn, appoints a Council of Ministers. Legislative power is vested in the 147-seat unicameral Assemblée nationale, elected for five years by universal suffrage. Elections take place in the context of a multi-party political system.

In the second ballot of the most recent presidential election, held on 12 May 2002, **Gen. (retd) Amadou Toumani Touré**, an independent candidate, received 65.01% of the votes cast, defeating Soumaïla Cissé, a candidate of the Alliance pour la démocratie au Mali—Parti pan-africain pour la liberté, la solidarité et la justice (ADEMA, Alliance for Democracy in Mali—Pan-african Party for Liberty, Solidarity and Justice), who received 34.99% of the votes.

Following a general election held on 14 and 28 July 2002, the distribution of seats in the Assemblée nationale was as follows: ADEMA 53; Rassemblement pour le Mali (RPM—Rally for Mali) 46 (including 20 seats won in coalitions with other parties); Congrès national d'initiative démocratique—Faso Yiriwa Ton (CNID—Faso Yiriwa Ton, National Congress of Democratic Initiative—Faso Yiriwa Ton) 13; Rassemblement pour la démocratie et le travail (RDT—Rally for Democracy and Labour) 7; Parti de la solidarité africaine pour la démocratie et l'indépendance (SADI—Party of African Solidarity for Democracy and Independence) 6; Convention démocratique et sociale (CDS—Democratic and Social Convention) 4; Bloc pour la démocratie et l'intégration africaine—Faso Jigi (BDIA—Faso Jigi, Bloc for Democracy and African Integration—Faso Jigi) 3; Union soudanaise—Rassemblement démocratique africain (US—RDA, Sudanese Union—Democratic African Rally)/Rassemblement national pour la démocratie (RND—National Rally for Democracy) 3; Mouvement patriotique pour le renouveau (MPR—Patriotic Movement for Renewal) 2; Rassemblement malien pour le travail (RAMAT—Mali Rally for Labour) 2; Parti pour la démocratie et le renouveau—Dounkafa Ton (PDR—Dounkafa Ton, Party for Democracy and Renewal—Dounkafa Ton) 1; Parti pour la renaissance nationale (PARENA—Party for National Rebirth) 1; Independents 6. (The figures above include the results of voting in eight constituencies where were the elections were rerun on 20 October 2002.)

History

Mali, as the former French West African colony of **Soudan**, merged in April 1959 with Senegal to form the Federation of Mali, which became independent on 20 June 1960. Senegal seceded two months later, and the remnant of the Federation was proclaimed the Republic of Mali on 22 September 1960. Its first President was **Modibo Keita**, the leader of the US—RDA), who pursued authoritarian socialist policies. Mali withdrew from the **Franc Zone** in 1962, and developed close relations with the communist bloc. Economic difficulties caused Mali to return to the Franc Zone in 1968, although the country was not fully reintegrated into the Zone's monetary union until 1984.

Keita was overthrown in November 1968 by a group of junior army officers, who assumed power as the Comité militaire pour la libération nationale (CMLN). Lt (later Gen.) Moussa Traoré became Head of State and President of the CMLN. Thereafter, Mali remained under a single party military dictatorship until 1991, when, in March, it was announced that Traoré had been arrested. A military Conseil national de réconciliation (CNR), led by Lt-Col Amadou Toumani Touré, assumed power. In legislative and presidential elections held in 1992, ADEMA emerged as the largest party in the Assemblée nationale, and Alpha Oumar Konaré, ADEMA's leader, was elected as President. Konaré was re-elected to the presidency in 1997. The final results of legislative elections held in 1997 allocated 130 of the 147 seats to ADEMA, eight to PARENA, four to the CDS, three to the Union pour la démocratie et le développement (UDD—Union for Democracy and Development) and two to the Parti pour la démocratie et le progrès (PDP—Party for Democracy and Progress). Gen. Amadou Toumani Touré was elected as President in April 2002. In legislative elections held in 2002 ADEMA emerged, ultimately, as the largest single party in the Assemblée nationale.

International relations
The presence of large numbers of **refugees** from a conflict in northern Mali (which began in 1990 as large numbers of Tuareg nomads, who had migrated to Algeria and Libya at times of **drought**, began to return to West Africa) dominated Mali's relations with its neighbours during the 1990s. Bilateral relations between Mali and Mauritania were strengthened by a military co-operation agreement regarding border security signed in January 2005. France remains an important trading partner and the principal donor of bilateral aid to Mali. President Konaré regarded the development of a wider international role for Mali as a priority in foreign policy, and Mali has contributed actively to UN peace-keeping forces. Konaré has also sought to emphasize the role of Mali in the **Economic Community of West African States**. Mali has in recent years forged closer relations with Libya, and was a founder member of the Community of Sahel-Saharan States established in 1997.

Mali, economy

In 2003, according to estimates by the **World Bank**, Mali's gross national income (GNI), measured at average 2001–03 prices, was US $4,156m., equivalent to $290 per head (or $960 on an international purchasing-power parity basis). During 1990–2003, it was estimated, the population increased at an average annual rate of 2.5%, while gross domestic product (GDP) per head increased, in real terms, by an average of 2.3% per year. Overall GDP increased, in real terms, at an average annual rate of 4.8% in 1990–2003. According to the World Bank, real GDP increased by 6.0% in 2003. The annual rate of inflation averaged 3.6% in 1990–2003. Consumer prices increased by 5.0% in 2002, but declined by 1.4% in 2003. Industrial activity includes food processing, construction and mining for phosphates and **gold**. In

2004 the major markets for Mali's exports were the People's Republic of China, India, Italy, Bangladesh, Thailand, Germany and Taiwan. France, Senegal, Côte d'Ivoire and Germany were the main supplier of imports in that year. The national currency is the CFA franc (see the **Franc Zone**). In 2004 the average exchange rate was US $1 = 528.29 francs CFA.

Mali has limited natural resources, high vulnerability to external shocks, and acute social needs. The 50% devaluation of the CFA franc in January 1994 brought some positive results to the rural population of Mali, including increased regional sales of beef and cereals. The gold-mining sector is flourishing, but the economy generally remains fragile. Difficulties arose in 2000 owing to a crisis in the **cotton** sector, combined with poor rains and an increase in **oil** prices, and worsened in 2001, when GDP increased by only 1.5% and the rate of inflation rose to 5.2% (reflecting an increase in cereal prices caused by the reduced output and a rise in the cost of electricity). Mali's economy relies primarily on subsistence farming and animal husbandry, with cotton the major source of foreign exchange earnings, making it highly dependent on adequate rainfall. Rainfall was poor in 2002 and the effects of conflict in Côte d'Ivoire led to an increase in the price of several basic consumer goods.

Mali remains heavily dependent on aid. Net aid, of which France is the main donor, constitutes 20% of gross national product. In recent years Mali's particular vulnerability has been recognized by international agencies. In 2002 France announced the cancellation of 38% of **debt** owed it by Mali. Mali is also eligible for **debt relief** under the **Heavily Indebted Poor Countries initiative**. In 2004 the **International Monetary Fund (IMF)** approved a three-year programme for Mali under the **Poverty Reduction and Growth Facility**.

In a review of Mali's economic performance completed in 2005, the IMF noted that while the authorities had adhered to reform agreements made with the Fund, 'economic performance has been adversely affected by the economy's vulnerability to exogenous shocks'. Low world market prices for cotton and the price of imported oil had severely damaged Mali's terms of trade. Agricultural output suffered in 2004 from the infestation of the Sahel by the desert **locust**. Conflict in neighbouring Côte d'Ivoire hindered access to Abidjan, Mali's nearest port, sustaining the cost of transport and imports. Slower economic growth necessitated corrective fiscal measures by the Malian authorities in 2005, in order to meet budgetary targets. These measures included a reduction in non-**poverty**-focused spending and the absorption of the higher world price of oil into domestic prices. Growth improved in 2005, and the government has forecast strong growth in 2006 and 2007.

Malloum, Gen. Félix

President of Chad in 1975–79. Malloum, who succeeded **François Tombalbaye** after his assassination, inherited a war with the northern **Front de libération nationale du Tchad (FROLINAT—National Liberation Front of Chad)**, which was supported by, and had its headquarters in, Libya. When the leaders of the various FROLINAT factions quarrelled, France withdrew its support from the government of Chad. **Col al-Qaddafi** of Libya now backed Goukouni Oueddei, who promised to cede the Aozou Strip and its uranium deposits to Libya. Oueddei's rival **Hissène Habré** formed a brief alliance with President Malloum before seizing power in 1979.

Mande

Ethno-linguistic group, which, together with the **Dioula** sub-group, constitutes about 30% of the population of São Tomé and Príncipe.

Mandela, Nelson

Nelson Mandela's lifelong commitment to the fight against racial oppression in South Africa has won him international recognition, a Nobel Peace Prize and the position of Head of State of South Africa. As president of the **African National Congress (ANC)** and head of South Africa's anti-**apartheid** movement, he was instrumental in moving the nation toward multiracial government and majority rule. He relinquished office as President in June 1999, but has remained active as an international statesman, in Africa and globally, intervening in support of human rights and racial equality on numerous occasions.

Born in Tembu, a small village in the Transkei region of South Africa, on 18 July 1918, and named Rolihlahla Mandela, his father, Henry Mgadla Mandela, was chief councillor to Thembuland's acting paramount chief David Dalindyebo. When his father died, Mandela (aged 10) became the chief's ward and was groomed for the chieftainship. He matriculated at Healdtown Methodist Boarding School and began studying for a BA degree at Fort Hare. As a member of the Student Representative Council, he participated in a student strike and was expelled, along with **Oliver Tambo** who he met while at Fort Hare, in 1940. He completed his degree by correspondence from Johannesburg, trained as an articled clerk and enrolled for an LLB at the University of Witwatersrand. In 1944 he helped found the radical ANC Youth League—an offshoot of the ANC, which Mandela had joined in 1942. The Youth League's Programme of Action was adopted by the ANC in 1949. Following the electoral victory, in 1948, of the **Afrikaner**-dominated National Party, with its apartheid policy of racial segregation, Mandela was prominent in the ANC's Defiance Campaign of 1952. He became the ANC's national volunteer-in-chief, in which capacity he travelled the country organizing resistance to discriminatory legislation. Following his involvement in the Defiance Campaign, Mandela was tried and received a suspended sentence. Shortly afterwards, a banning order confined him to Johannesburg for six months. During this period, he was also instrumental in formulating the 'M Plan', which broke ANC branches into underground cells in anticipation of the outlawing of the organization. He took the attorney's admission examination and was admitted to the legal profession.

Together with Oliver Tambo, he opened the first black legal firm in the country, representing those who had been ejected from their land and who would otherwise have had no legal representation. Repeated attempts were made to constrain the legal challenges posed by Mandela and Tembo. However, a petition by the Transvaal Law Society to strike Mandela off the roll of attorneys was refused by the Supreme Court, which found that Mandela 'had been moved by a desire to serve his black fellow citizens and nothing he had done showed him to be unworthy to remain in the ranks of an honourable profession'.

During the early 1950s Mandela played an important role in leading the resistance to the Western Areas removals and to the introduction of Bantu Education. He also played a significant role in popularizing the **Freedom Charter** adopted by the **Congress of the People** in 1955. In the late 1950s Mandela's attention turned to the struggles that were then beginning against the exploitation of labour, the pass laws, the nascent Bantustan policy, and the segregation of the open universities. Mandela arrived at the conclusion very early on that the Bantustan policy was a political swindle and an economic absurdity. He predicted, with dismal prescience, that ahead there loomed a grim programme of mass evictions, political persecutions, and police terror. On the segregation of the universities, Mandela observed that the friendship and inter-racial harmony that is forged at mixed universities constituted a direct threat to the policy of apartheid and *baasskap*, and that it was to remove that threat that the open universities were being closed to black students. Throughout the 1950s Mandela was the victim of various forms of repression. He was banned, arrested and imprisoned. For much of the latter half of the decade, he was one of the accused in the protracted Treason Trial, at great cost to his legal practice and his political work. When the ANC was banned, after the **Sharpeville** massacre in 1960, Mandela was detained until 1961 when he went underground to lead a campaign for a new national convention.

In June 1961 the ANC executive considered Mandela's proposal on the use of violent tactics and agreed that those members who wished to involve themselves in Mandela's campaign would not be prevented from doing so by the ANC. The **Umkhonto we Sizwe**—the military wing of the ANC—was established in the same year. Under Mandela's leadership it launched a campaign of sabotage against government and economic installations. In 1962 Mandela left the country to arrange military training for MK members. On his return, on 5 August 1962, he was arrested for having left the country illegally and for incitement to strike. There was speculation that the US Central Intelligence Agency might have played a role in informing the police of his whereabouts. He conducted his own defence in court, applying for the recusal of the magistrate on the grounds that, in such a prosecution, a judiciary controlled entirely by whites was an interested party and therefore could not be impartial. He was convicted and jailed in the Johannesburg Fort in November 1962. He began his jail sentence in Robben Island Prison, a maximum security prison on a small island 7 km off the coast near Cape Town.

Some 20 years later, in April 1984, he was transferred to Pollsmoor Prison in Cape Town and in December 1988 was again moved to the Victor Verster Prison near Paarl, from where he was eventually released. While serving his sentence, he was charged, in the Rivonia trial, with sabotage and sentenced to life imprisonment. Over the course of the 26 years that he served in prison, Mandela was able to release statements to the ANC calling for the party to unite in the battle against apartheid. He became increasingly associated with opposition to apartheid, to the point where the slogan 'Free Mandela' became the rallying cry for all anti-apartheid campaigners around the world. While in prison, Mandela flatly rejected offers made by his jailers of a remission of his sentence in exchange for his accepting the Bantustan policy by recognizing the independence of the Transkei and agreeing to settle there. Again, in the 1980s, Mandela rejected an offer of release on condition that he renounced violence. 'Prisoners cannot enter into contracts. Only free men can negotiate', he stated.

After more than two decades in prison, Mandela decided on a new approach. After painstaking preliminaries, and in great secrecy, negotiations began with the ruling white South African government on both his own release and also on the nation's transition from apartheid to **democracy**. On 2 February 1990 President **F. W. de Klerk** lifted the ban on the ANC and announced Mandela's imminent release, which took place on 18 February 1990. Mandela immediately returned to politics and to the struggle against apartheid, of which he had become the leading figurehead. In 1991, at the first national conference of the ANC held inside South Africa since its banning in 1960, Mandela was elected as president of the ANC, while his lifelong friend and colleague, Oliver Tambo, became the organisation's national chairperson. Mandela was inaugurated as the first fully democratically elected State President of South Africa on 10 May 1994—a post he held until June 1999.

Mandela presided over the transition from minority rule and apartheid, winning international respect for his advocacy of national and international reconciliation. While some radicals were disappointed with the social achievements of his five-year term of office, he was broadly applauded by the international and national community. After his retirement, Mandela admitted that he may have failed his country by not paying more attention to the **HIV/AIDS** epidemic. Mandela was also criticized for his close friendship with such leaders as Fidel Castro of Cuba and Col Muammar al-Qaddafi of Libya, whom he called his 'comrades in arms'. After his retirement as President in 1999, Mandela went on to become an advocate for a variety of social and human rights organizations. He received many foreign honours, including the Order of St. John from Britain's Queen Elizabeth II, the Presidential Medal of Freedom from President George W. Bush of the USA and the Bharat Ratna, India's highest civilian award.

In 2003, in a number of speeches, Mandela attacked the foreign policy of the US administration of George W. Bush, in particular its failure to comply with the UN and its African secretary-general, **Kofi Annan**, on the issue of the war in Iraq: 'Is it because the secretary-general of the United Nations is now a black man? They never did that when secretary-generals were white,' was one of the most controversial statements in respect of the war. In June 2004, aged 85, Mandela announced that he would be retiring from public life. He has overlooked this decision, however, for the fight against AIDS, of which his eldest son, Makgatho Mandela, died in 2005. In July 2004 he travelled to Bangkok, Thailand, to speak at the XV International AIDS Conference, and he has taken many opportunities since then to highlight the tragedy of AIDS in South Africa and Africa more generally. He has also lent his influential support to the Make Poverty History Campaign, announcing that, although officially retired, 'as long as poverty, injustice and gross inequality persist in our world, none of us can truly rest'.

Mandinke

Major ethno-linguistic grouping in West Africa.

Mano River Union (MRU)

The Mano River Declaration was signed in 1973 to establish a customs and economic union between Liberia and Sierra Leone. A common external tariff was agreed in 1977. Guinea joined the Union in 1980. Members of the Mano River Union are also members of the **Economic Community of West African States**.

Margai, Sir Albert

Sir Albert Margai succeeded his brother, **Sir Milton Margai**, on his death in 1964 as Prime Minister of Sierra Leone. His plans for constitutional change, however, were rejected by the electorate in 1966. The army intervened briefly, chiefly in order to keep **Siaka Stevens** from power, but in 1968 Stevens became Prime Minister and, in 1971, President of the newly proclaimed republic of Sierra Leone.

Margai, Sir Milton

Sir Milton Margai was the first Prime Minister of Sierra Leone. He was succeeded on his death in 1964 by his more radical brother, **Sir Albert Margai**.

Mars 23 (23 March)

Moroccan left-wing political group. Established in 1970 following a split in the **Union nationale des forces populaires (UNFP—National Union of Popular Forces)**, Mars 23 was led by Mohamed Ben Said. In 1978 and 1979 it split over attitudes towards the **Union socialiste des forces populaires (USFP—Socialist Union of Popular Forces)** and the **Western Sahara** issue. One faction joined the USFP; other factions remained outlawed, and some of their members were jailed for their beliefs.

Marxism

A political ideology and approach to the analysis of social change, which has proved attractive to a significant minority of African intellectuals over the years. More widely and strongly espoused in the late colonial period and early days of political **independence** than in recent years (particularly after the collapse of the state socialist regimes of Eastern Europe and the disintegration of the USSR). The influence of Marxism in the region has been significant largely in the ideological and political formation of smaller left-wing groups and movements. The establishment of Communist Party branches took place in most of the colonial territories from the 1920s onwards, but in most cases they remained very much minority parties. **Nationalism** remained a dominant ideological and political force throughout the period from the 1920s to the 1960s and most regimes or dominant parties adopted versions of Arab or African nationalism, which tended to espouse an authoritarian populism or 'national socialism', rather than the classic Marxist-Leninist '**socialism**' as a transitional phase in a process of transformation leading to communism. Communist parties were often marginalized by such dominant movements and proscribed or banned when they came to power. Many more, however, pursued the idea of a distinctively **African socialism**, which denied the applicability of classical Marxist-Leninist theory to African economies and societies. Relatively few states have adopted classical Marxist-Leninist ideology and principles, although distinctive African versions could be identified at specific periods in specific African states (e.g. Benin and Mozambique). Military governments, like the various civilian populist 'African or Arab socialist' governments, have also tended to emphasize national unity and to identify class-based politics as 'divisive'. During the 1970s and 1980s, the rise of political **Islam** and Islamism sometimes generated efforts to reconcile Marxism and Islam—interesting examples of such efforts are to be seen in the writings of several Egyptian intellectuals, such as Adel Hussein and, more practically, in the political ideology of many Muslim African states (e.g. Sudan, Libya, Mauritania).

Marxist-Leninism

A political theory and practice derived from the work and political practice of Karl Marx and Vladimir Ilyich Lenin. Popular among left-wing intellectuals in Africa during the late colonial and early post-colonial period, and adopted by a number of regimes and governments in Africa during the 1960s and 1970s.

Masai

Major ethno-linguistic group in Tanzania and Kenya. The Masai are mainly agro-pastoralists.

Mashreq

The eastern region of the Arab world. Includes Egypt, Jordan, Palestine, Lebanon, Syria and Iraq.

Mau Mau

Secret society formed by the **Kikuyu** of Kenya in about 1948. Its activities were a militant expression of a deep-seated nationalist movement among a people concerned about land expropriation and colonization by Europeans. It developed a distinctive campaign of violence and guerrilla warfare during the 1950s, binding its members to loyalty by oaths and rituals. Most of its victims were, in fact, other Kikuyu, regarded as collaborators with the white settler regime. The African victims of Mau Mau totalled some 8,000; the number of Europeans killed was 68. In response to the unrest, the government declared an emergency, called for military reinforcements from neighbouring territories and from Britain, arrested thousands of Kikuyu, including **Jomo Kenyatta** (who was sentenced in 1954 to seven years' imprisonment for organizing Mau Mau activities), and adopted its own brutal programme of repression and violence. The state of emergency was ended in 1956. Gross human rights violations and murders were perpetrated by the forces deployed by the colonial administration.

Mauritanian African Liberation Forces (MALF)

Organized in 1983 to oppose what were perceived as repressive policies towards blacks, the Mauritanian African Liberation Forces (MALF) were believed to have been responsible for an 'Oppressed Black' manifesto which was widely distributed in Mauritania and at the non-aligned summit in Zimbabwe in 1986. Based partly in Dakar, Senegal, the group also condemned reprisals against blacks by the **Ould Taya** regime following an alleged coup attempt in 1987. Many MALF supporters were reported to be among those who fled or were expelled to Senegal in 1989. Subsequently engaged in guerrilla activity, MALF leaders announced in July 1991 that they were suspending 'armed struggle' in response to the government's general amnesty and promulgation of a new Mauritanian constitution. MALF endorsed Ahmed Ould Daddah in the January 1992 presidential election, after which it renewed its anti-governmental military campaign near the Senegalese borders. Leaders of the group stated in early 1995 that they were neither secessionists nor terrorists, reiterating their support for the establishment of a federal system that would ensure an appropriate level of black representation in government while protecting the rights of blacks throughout Mauritanian society.

Mauritania, Islamic Republic of

Mauritania is bordered to the north by the **Western Sahara** and Algeria, to the east and south-east by Mali, to the south by Senegal, and to the west by 754 km of

Atlantic coastline, stretching from the Senegal River to the peninsula of Nouadhibou and Guera. The northern three-quarters of this vast country (with an area of 1,030,000 sq km) consists largely of the Sahara (desert) while the southern quarter is essentially Sahelian (semi-desert). Most of the population is concentrated in the cities of Nouakchott (the capital) and Nouadhibou, and along the Senegal River in the southern part of the country. In mid-2002 the population was estimated at 2,807,000. With regard to religion, the entire population is **Sunni** Muslim. The official languages are **Arabic** and **Wolof**. Pulaar, Soninke and French are also spoken. **Col Maaouiya Ould Sidi Ahmed Taya**, who first came to power in December 1984 through a *coup d'état*, but was elected as President in the first multi-party elections, held in January 1992. The President is elected by popular vote for a six-year term of office. Presidential elections were held in December 1997 and December 2003, and Ould Taya was re-elected on both occasions. Ould Taya was deposed in a military coup in August 2005 by Col Ely Ould Mohamed Vall. The Prime Minister is appointed by the President. The current Prime Minister (since 8 August 2005) is Sidi Mohamed Ould Boubakar. There is a Council of Ministers. The legislature consists of the Assembly of Sheikhs (Majlis ash-Shuyukh) comprising 56 seats, to some of which elections are held every two years; members are elected by municipal leaders to serve six-year terms) and the National Assembly (Majlis al-Watani), comprising 81 seats, whose members are elected by popular vote to serve five-year terms. Elections for the Assembly of Sheikhs were last held in April 2004 (the next are scheduled to be held in April 2006), and those for the National Assembly were last held in October 2001 (the next being scheduled for 2006). The judiciary consists of the Supreme Court and Courts of Appeal. The legal system is a combination of **Shari'a** or Islamic law and French civil law. Political parties were legalized by the Constitution that was ratified in July 1991, although politics remains strongly tribally-based. Political organizations include the Convention for Change, the Alliance for Youth and Democracy, the Democratic and Social Republican Party (DSRP, the ruling party), the Mauritanian Party for Renewal and Construction, the National Union for Democracy and Development, the Rally for Democracy and Unity and the Union of Progressive Forces.

History

In 1891 France and Spain agreed a boundary between their respective possessions in north-west Africa and in 1898 two major Moorish groups accepted French arbitration in a local '**civil war**', increasing French influence north of the Senegal River and paving the way for French penetration between 1902 and 1904 of the Trarza and the Brakna regions, in the south west of what is now Mauritania. It was not until 1934, however, that the entire territory was pacified. During the colonial period, St Louis on the Senegal River was the capital for the French administration of Mauritania, which constituted an 'economic appendix' to Senegal. For much of the colonial period, Mauritania remained a transition zone between the two major regions of French **colonialism** in north-west Africa: the **Maghreb** (Morocco,

Algeria and Tunisia) and French West Africa (Senegal and other territories). The first political reform of French colonial policy in Mauritania began after the Second World War, when the territory was allowed to elect a representative to the French National Assembly. The second political reform was the election of territorial assemblies in the French West African colonial territories. One of those elected in March 1957 was **Mokhtar Ould Daddah**, one of Mauritania's first university graduates, who was nominated as Vice-President of the first Council of the Government in May 1957.

By the late 1950s the black ethnic minorities had grown from virtually nothing to constitute some 20% of the total population, and already ethnic divisions were beginning to affect Mauritanian politics. In 1958 the Association of Mauritanian Youth (Rabitat ash-Shabab al-Muritany), which had been established in 1955, founded the Mauritanian National Renaissance Party (Hizb an-Nahda al-Wataniya al- Muritaniya), inspired by Arab nationalism. The party opposed integration within **French West Africa** and many of its members sought a federation with Morocco, claiming that Mauritania was a part of 'Greater Morocco'. Ould Daddah, then Prime Minister, declared in 1958 that if there were to be a choice between a federation with the Maghreb or a federation with French West Africa, the Maghreb would be preferred. On the other hand, the Union of Natives of the South (Union des originaires du sud), created in Dakar, Senegal, and the Democratic Bloc of Gorgol (Bloc démocratique du Gorgol), founded in 1957, sought a federation within the framework of French West Africa.

There was to be no federation, either way, until 30 years later (and the establishment of the **Arab Maghreb Union—AMU**), although Mauritania was declared an Islamic republic on **independence**, which was achieved from France on 28 November 1960. Ould Daddah, whose Mauritanian Assembly Party (MAP) had won all the seats in the previous year's general election, became Head of State. All parties subsequently merged with the MAP to form the Mauritanian People's Party(MPP), and Mauritania was declared a one-party state in 1964. Mauritania was a founder member of the **Organization of African Unity** when it was established in 1963, and only joined the **Arab League** a decade later, in 1973. Gradually, as a result of efforts to break free from the neocolonial ties that had been maintained with France (and French capital in the mining sector) after independence, there emerged a compromise between a genuine Mauritanian **nationalism** and a form of authoritarian populism, comparable in many ways to regimes that had emerged elsewhere in Africa and the Middle East. The regime adopted an increasingly radical position on international issues, supporting African national liberation movements and developing closer relations with the People's Republic of China. It left the West African Monetary Union and French army personnel were withdrawn.

At home, the regime remained strongly opposed to the growth of political opposition movements (notably the clandestine Democratic Movement, which began as a leftist student movement but grew to become a significant political force) and to trade unions. In September 1970 it was announced that 'no trade union or group of any kind in Mauritania has the right to express political ideas which contradict those of the party'. The Mauritanian Workers' Union was brought under the control of the MPP and the government in 1973, and in 1975 the MPP adopted a 'party charter' and declared that the political system was to be 'Islamic, national, centrist, and socialist'.

Towards the end of 1975 the Mauritanian government signed a tripartite agreement with Morocco and Spain that ended Spanish occupation of the Western Sahara (then the Spanish Sahara) and transferred the territory to Morocco and Mauritania. This was opposed by the **Frente Popular para la Liberación de Saguia el-Hamra y Río de Oro (Frente POLISARIO—Popular Front for the Liberation of Saguia el-Hamra and Río de Oro)**, the main vehicle of the Sahrawi nationalist movement, established in 1973, which sought self-determination and independence for the Western Sahara. The case was referred to the World Court at The Hague, Netherlands, which ruled in favour of Sahrawi self-determination. Morocco launched a blitzkrieg against the POLISARIO forces, and Mauritania became involved in the war that followed. Participation in the conflict cost Mauritania dearly; its adverse effect on the economy was made worse by **drought**. Opposition to Mauritania's involvement in the war and dissatisfaction with government policy and the Ould Daddah regime more generally led to the overthrow of the President (and the banning of the MPP) in July 1978 by a group of army officers, who established a Military Committee for National Salvation (CMSN). The 10 July Movement—a faction within the CMSN, which took its name from the date of the coup—had three declared aims: withdrawal from the war and neutrality with regard to the conflict, economic recovery and the restoration of **democracy**.

Between 1978 and 1980 there were three different military Heads of State and frequent changes of personnel within the CMSN. Lt-Col Ould Haidalla took over as Head of State in January 1980, having negotiated an effective cease-fire with the Frente POLISARIO, and in December a civilian Prime Minister was appointed to head a transitional government and a constitution was drafted, which provided for a multi-party state with a presidential system of government. Ould Haidalla's position was not, however, unchallenged. The main opposition came from the Alliance for a Democratic Mauritania (AMD), established by the supporters of Ould Daddah and members of the banned MPP and based in Paris, France, but also receiving support from Senegal and Morocco. The AMD sponsored a failed coup attempt against Ould Haidalla in March 1981. The move towards political liberalization was halted: the Constitution was suspended, army officers returned to key government posts as members of the CMSN, and known members of the AMD within Mauritania were arrested and either jailed or executed. Angered by the support given by Morocco to the attempted coup, Ould Haidalla signed a peace agreement with the Frente POLISARIO and a friendship treaty with Algeria, POLISARIO's main backer. However, Ould Haidalla faced continuing opposition at home, with one former military Head of State and a former Prime Minister involved in plots to remove him from power. In 1982 the Democratic Movement called for the formation of a united national front with the participation of all political groupings. This appeal was rejected by the CMSN, which supported the development of the official mass movements established in 1978 (and maintained as the basis for 'mass mobilization' by Ould Haidalla in 1980), known as the Structures for the Education of the Masses.

Successive droughts marked the early 1980s and the economic crisis deepened; in 1983, the government declared the whole country a disaster area and requested aid from the international community. In December 1984 Ould Haidalla was replaced as chairman of the CMSN and Head of State, following a coup led by Col Maaouiya Ould Sid'Ahmed Taya. Ould Taya stated that his government would respect human rights, free political prisoners and 'end the use of cruel, inhuman and degrading punishment'; he did not, however, announce any plan for the restoration of the Constitution or for a return to civilian government. Administrative decentralization was initiated and elections were held for mayors in the capital, Nouakchott, and the 12 regional capitals in 1986, but political parties remained proscribed and strict rules on forms of association were maintained. Ould Taya's government recognized the **Sahrawi Arab Democratic Republic** and brought the war with the Frente POLISARIO officially to an end. It also embarked on a programme for economic and financial adjustment for the period 1985–88, which coincided with a period of economic recovery and growth.

Opposition parties were legalized and a new constitution was approved in 1991. Two multi-party presidential elections held subsequently, in which Ould Taya was elected, were widely regarded as flawed, but legislative and municipal elections held in October 2001 were generally free and open. Mauritania remains, in reality, a one-party state. The country continues to experience ethnic tensions between its black minority population and the dominant Maur (Arab-**Berber**) populace.

International relations

The establishment of full diplomatic relations between Mauritania and Israel in 1999 precipitated intense diplomatic activity in the Middle East. Mauritania recalled its ambassador to Iraq after the Iraqi government criticized the upgrading of relations as harmful to the interests of the Arab nation. There has also been criticism from opposition figures in Mauritania itself, as well as from the Iranian government. Libya has had talks on the decision—which it described as a dangerous violation—with the other three members of the AMU, as well as with Egypt and Sudan. Previously, Egypt and Jordan were the only Arab states to have full diplomatic relations with Israel.

Since September 2001 the government has on several occasions reiterated its determination to combat international terrorism. In June 2003 an attempted coup against the government of Maaouiya Ould Taya by elements of the army was effectively suppressed within days. In the month prior to the attempted coup 36 alleged Islamic militants had been arraigned for allegedly having plotted against the constitutional order, and nine politicians from the Ba'ath movement had been sentenced to terms of imprisonment (suspended) of three months for the creation of an unauthorized association and the reorganization of a dissolved political party. The state remains wary of all opposition movements considered to be a threat to the regime and is clearly intent on maintaining tight control on domestic politics while adopting a pragmatic strategy in foreign relations.

Mauritania, economy

One-half of Mauritania's population still depends on **agriculture** and livestock for a livelihood, even though most of the nomads and many subsistence farmers were forced into the cities by recurrent **drought** in the 1970s and 1980s. Mauritania has extensive deposits of iron ore, which account for 50% of total exports. The decline in world demand for this ore, however, has led to cutbacks in production. Mauritania's coastal waters are among the richest fishing areas in the world, but over-exploitation by foreign fleets threatens this key source of revenue. The country's first deep-water port opened near Nouakchott in 1986. In the past drought and economic mismanagement resulted in an accumulation of foreign **debt**. In February 2000 Mauritania qualified for **debt relief** under the **Heavily Indebted Poor Countries initiative** and in December 2001 received strong support from donor and lending countries at a triennial Consultative Group review. Mauritania withdrew from the **Economic Community of West African States** in 2000 and subsequently increased commercial ties with **Arab Maghreb Union** members Morocco and Tunisia, most notably in telecommunications. In 2001 exploratory **oil** wells sunk 80 km off shore indicated potential viable extraction at the then prevailing international price of oil. However, the refinery in Nouadhibou historically has not exceeded 20% of its distillation capacity and handled no crude at all in 2000. A new Investment Code approved in December 2001 improved the opportunities for direct foreign investment.

Mauritius, Republic of

The Republic of Mauritius lies in the Indian Ocean. The principal island, from which the country takes its name, lies about 800 km east of Madagascar. The other main islands are Rodrigues, the Agalega Islands and the Cargados Carajos Shoals (St Brandon Islands). The area of Mauritius is 2,040 sq km. At 31 December 2004 the population, who are mainly of Indian descent, was estimated at 1,238,043. The most widely spoken languages in 2000 were Creole (38.6%) and Bhojpuri (30.6%). English is the country's official language, and Creole (derived from French) the lingua franca. The principal religious group are Hindus, who comprise more than 50% of the population. About 30% are Christians and 17% are Muslims.

Political profile

The constitutional Head of State is the President of the Republic, who is elected by a simple majority of the National Assembly for a five-year term of office. Legislative power is vested in the unicameral National Assembly, which comprises the Speaker, 62 members elected by universal adult suffrage for a term of five years, up to eight 'additional' members (unsuccessful candidates who receive the largest number of votes at a legislative election, to whom seats are allocated by the Electoral Supervisory Commission to ensure a balance in representation of the different ethnic groups), and the Attorney-General (if not an elected member). Executive power is vested in the Prime Minister, who is appointed by the President and is the member of the National Assembly best able to command a majority in the Assembly. The President appoints other ministers, on the recommendation of the Prime Minister. **Sir Anerood Jugnauth** has been President of Mauritius since 7 October 2003.

Following a general election held on 3 July 2005, the distribution of seats in the National Assembly was as follows: Social Alliance 38; Mouvement Socialiste Militant (MSM—Militant Socialist Movement)/Mouvement Militant Mauricien (MMM—Mauritian Militant Movement) 22; Organisation du Peuple Rodriguais (OPR—Organization of the People of Rodrigues) 2.

History

The islands of Mauritius and Rodrigues, formerly French possessions, passed into British control in 1810. The first elections under universal adult suffrage, held in 1959, were won by the Mauritius Labour Party (MLP), led by Dr (later Sir) Seewoosagur Ramgoolam. Mauritius became independent, within the Commonwealth, on 12 March 1968, with Ramgoolam as Prime Minister.

During the 1970s political opposition to successive coalition governments formed by Ramgoolam was led by a radical left-wing group, the MMM, founded by **Paul Bérenger**. At a general election in June 1982 the MMM, in alliance with the Parti Socialiste Mauricien (PSM—Mauritian Socialist Party), won all 60 contested seats on the main island. Anerood (later Sir Anerood) Jugnauth, the leader of the MMM, became Prime Minister, and Bérenger Minister of Finance. In 1983 Jugnauth formed a new party, the MSM, which subsequently merged with the PSM. From 1984 the MSM participated in all governing coalitions until 1995, when an alliance of the MMM and the MLP achieved a decisive electoral victory. In December 1991 the Legislative Assembly approved the constitutional framework for the country's transition to a republic within the **Commonwealth**. The Republic of Mauritius was proclaimed on 12 March 1992.

In August 2000 an alliance between the MSM and the MMM was officially declared, in advance of an imminent general election, on the basis that Jugnauth would lead as Prime Minister for three years in the event of victory, before assuming the more honorary role of President, thus allowing Bérenger (the leader of the MMM) to become Prime Minister for the remaining two years. This arrangement took effect after the MSM/MMM alliance achieved a significant electoral victory in September.

Following the general election held in July 2005 the Social Alliance, a grouping of various parties led by the MLP, occupied the largest number of seats in the

National Assembly. Dr Navinchandra Ramgoolam, the leader of the MLP, was Prime Minister of the new government formed following the 2005 election.

Mauritius, economy

In 2003, according to estimates by the **World Bank**, Mauritius' gross national income (GNI), measured at average 2000–03 prices, was US $5,224m., equivalent to $4,090 per head (or $11,260 per head on an international purchasing-power parity basis). During 1990–2003, it was estimated, the population increased at an average annual rate of 1.1%, while gross domestic product (GDP) per head increased, in real terms, by an average of 3.9% per year. Overall GDP increased, in real terms, at an average annual rate of 5.1% in 1990–2003; growth in 2003 was 3.2%. The annual rate of inflation averaged 7.2% in 1990–2004. Consumer prices increased by an average of 3.9% in 2003 and 4.7% in 2004. Industrial activity mainly involves textiles and the processing of sugar. Tourism is also important. In 2004 the main destinations of Mauritius' exports were the United Kingdom, France, the USA and Madagascar. The main suppliers of imports in that year were France, South Africa, India, the People's Republic of China, Germany and Singapore. The national currency is the Mauritian rupee. In 2004 the average exchange rate was US $1 = 29.498 rupees.

The economy of Mauritius is stable and relatively sound. Singapore is the model for Mauritius' free port, the expansion of offshore banking, manufacturing base and modernization of traditional industries. Aware that the traditional industries of textiles and sugar will not be sufficient to ensure future wealth and job creation, the government is giving high priority to the development of the IT sector with the aim of transforming Mauritius into a 'cyber island'. Tourism continues to flourish and to attract new investment. Mauritius' economic performance remains good by international standards, although growth has slowed somewhat and unemployment is rising. Mauritius' competitiveness is also jeopardized by the emergence of new, low-cost rivals, the expiry of preferential trade agreements, and the saturation of tourism space. The country's challenges are to improve the economic growth rate through higher productivity; to develop human capital through educational reforms to raise skill levels; to invest in a second generation of industries that corresponds better to Mauritius' evolving comparative advantage; to reform the welfare state to focus on the neediest; and to reduce the size and increase the productivity of the civil service in order to meet the needs of an expanding population with the highest life expectancy in the region. In response to these challenges, the government has embarked on an ambitious economic programme, the Economic Agenda for the New Millennium (NEA). The NEA is expected to advance Mauritius to the next phase of development. Its three key objectives are to: (i) increase Mauritius' competitiveness; (ii) to bring about deeper social development and social cohesion; and (iii) to preserve and protect Mauritius' fragile environment. The NEA is expected to further diversify the Mauritian economy into a high-skill services sector endowed with an efficient public sector that delivers quality services, and that is based on a modern infrastructure. The NEA is also expected to provide more opportunities for those who have not fully benefited from the country's past economic performance, as well as those selected groups who may be negatively affected by the transformation of the economy. The NEA provides mechanisms for ensuring that growth remains sustainable and does not negatively affect Mauritius' natural environment.

The abolition of the global quota system for textile production in January 2005 will have serious consequences for economies based heavily on textile production, such as that of Mauritius, where some 75,000 out of a working population of about 549,000 are employed in the clothing sector.

Mayotte

Mayotte forms part of the Comoros archipelago, which lies between the island of Madagascar and the east coast of the African mainland. The territory comprises a main island, Mayotte (Mahoré), and a number of smaller islands. The area of Mayotte is 374 sq km. At the census of 30 July 2002 the population was enumerated at 60,265. The official language is French but Shimaore (Maorese) and Shibushi are also spoken. Islam is the main religion. The capital is Dzaoudzi, whose population at the 2002 census was enumerated at 12,308.

Political profile

Mayotte is the sole French overseas Collectivité départementale. It is an integral part of the French Republic and is administered by a Prefect, who is appointed by the French government. Under the terms of its status, which was approved by the French parliament in July 2001, executive power was transferred from the Prefect to the President of the locally elected General Council (Conseil général) in April 2004, and the position of Prefect was to be dissolved by 2007. Mayotte elects one deputy to French Assemblée nationale and one representative to the Sénat in Paris. The Collectivité départementale is also represented in the European Parliament.

The Conseil général comprises 19 members who are elected by universal suffrage. At elections held on 21 and 28 March 2004, the Union pour un Mouvement Populaire (UMP—Union for a Popular Movement) won eight seats in alliance with the Mouvement Populaire Mahorais (MPM—Popular Movement of Mayotte), which secured one seat, while the Mouvement Départementaliste Mahorais (MDM—Departmentalist Movement of Mayotte) and the Mouvement des Citoyens (MDC—Citizens' Movement), also in alliance, obtained five and two seats, respectively; independent candidates were elected to the remaining three seats.

History

Since the Comoros unilaterally declared **independence** in July 1975, Mayotte has been administered separately by France. The independent Comoran state claims sovereignty of Mayotte, and officially represents it in international organizations, including the UN. In December 1976 France introduced the special status of Collectivité territoriale for the island. Following a coup in the Comoros in May 1978, Mayotte rejected the new government's proposal that it should rejoin the other islands under a federal system, and reaffirmed its intention of remaining linked to France. In December 1979 the Assemblée nationale approved legislation that extended Mayotte's special status for another five years, during which the islanders were to be consulted. In October 1984, however, the Assemblée nationale further prolonged Mayotte's status, and the referendum on the island's future was postponed indefinitely. The UN General Assembly has adopted a number of resolutions in support of the sovereignty of the Comoros over the island. Until 1999 the main political party on Mayotte, the Mouvement Populaire Mahorais (MPM), demanded full departmental status for the island, but France was reluctant to grant this in view of Mayotte's lack of development.

At the general election to the Assemblée nationale in March 1986, Henry Jean-Baptiste, a member of the Centre des Démocrates Sociaux (CDS—Centre of the Social Democrats), which was affiliated to the Union pour la Démocratie Française (UDF—Union for French Democracy), was elected as deputy for Mayotte. (Jean-Baptiste was re-elected in 1988, 1993 and 1997.) In the second round of the French presidential election, which took place in May 1988, François Mitterrand, the incumbent President and the candidate of the Parti Socialiste (PS—Socialist Party), received 50.3% of the votes cast on Mayotte, defeating Jacques Chirac, the candidate of the Rassemblement pour la République (RPR—Rally for the Republic). In the first round of the French presidential election in April 1995, Edouard Balladur received the highest number of votes on Mayotte (although Jacques Chirac subsequently won the election). In the first round of the French presidential election, which was held on 21 April 2002, Chirac received the highest number of votes on Mayotte, winning 43.0% of the valid votes cast; the second round, held on 5 May, was also won resoundingly by Chirac, who secured 88.3% of votes cast on the island, defeating the candidate of the extreme right-wing Front National, Jean-Marie Le Pen. At elections to the Assemblée nationale, held in June, Jean-Baptiste did not stand. Mansour Kamardine, representing the Union pour la Majorité Présidentielle (UMP, which incorporated the RPR, the Démocratie Libérale (Liberal Democracy) and significant elements of the UDF), defeated the MDM-UDF candidate.

In July 2000, in a referendum, the population of Mayotte voted overwhelmingly in favour of granting Mayotte the status of Collectivité départementale for a period of 10 years. The French parliament approved Mayotte's status as a Collectivité départementale in July 2001.

Mayotte, economy

Mayotte's gross domestic product (GDP) per head in 1991 was estimated at 4,050 French francs. Between the censuses of 1991 and 2002 the population of Mayotte increased at an average annual rate of 10.1%.

The economy is based mainly on **agriculture**, in which almost 20% of the population are engaged. Rice, cassava and maize are cultivated for domestic consumption, and vanilla, ylang-ylang, **coffee** and copra are the main exports. Industry, which is dominated by the construction sector, engaged 21.5% of the employed population in 1997. Most (almost 60%) of the population, however, are engaged in services, notably those associated with tourism. Mayotte has a substantial trade deficit and in the late 1990s some 40% of the population, a large proportion of them under 25 years of age, were unemployed. Substantial aid from France, deployed mainly in the transport infrastructure to facilitate tourism as a major industry, is intended to promote the island's development, and in September 2000 an economic and social development agreement involving substantial amounts of financial and technical assistance was signed for the period 2000–04. Mayotte's geographical remoteness, however, limits the prospects for future economic development.

M'Ba, Léon

President of Gabon from 1960 until 1967, when he was succeeded, on his death, by **Albert-Bernard Bongo**.

Mbeki, Thabo

President of South Africa since 1999. Mbeki assumed the presidency when **Nelson Mandela** relinquished office in mid-1999, but he is considered to have to have effectively ruled the country almost since the **African National Congress (ANC)** formed South Africa's first democratically elected government in April 1994. Born on 18 June 1942 in the Transkei region of South Africa, both of Thabo Mvuyelwa Mbeki's parents were teachers and activists. His father, Govan Mbeki, was a leading figure in the ANC in the Eastern Cape and a member of the South African Communist Party. Mbeki joined the ANC Youth League at the age of 14 and quickly became active in student politics. After his **education** was interrupted by a strike in 1959, he completed his studies at home. While studying for his British A-levels, he was elected as secretary of the African Students' Association (ASA). He went on to study economics as a correspondence student at London University. The ASA collapsed following the arrest of many of its members, at a time when political movements were increasingly being attacked by the state. Mbeki left South Africa in 1962 under orders from the ANC. He moved to Britain where he completed a master's degree in economics at Sussex University in 1966. Remaining active in student politics, he played a prominent role in building the youth and student sections of the ANC while in exile. Following his studies, he worked at the London office of the ANC with **Oliver Tambo** and Yusuf Dadoo before being sent to the USSR in 1970 for military training. Later that year he arrived in Lusaka, Zambia, where he was soon appointed assistant secretary of the Revolutionary Council. In 1973–74 he was involved in discussions with the government of Botswana about the opening of an ANC office in Botswana. In 1975 he was acting ANC representative in

Swaziland. Appointed to the National Executive Committee of the ANC in 1975, he served as ANC representative to Nigeria until 1978.

On his return to Lusaka Mbeki became political secretary in the office of Oliver Tambo, and then director of information. From this position he played an important role in turning the international media against **apartheid**. His other role in the 1970s was in building the ANC in Swaziland and developing underground structures inside South Africa. During the 1980s Mbeki rose to head the department of information and publicity that co-ordinated diplomatic campaigns to involve more white South Africans in anti-apartheid activities. From 1989 Mbeki headed the ANC's Department of International Affairs, and was a key figure in the ANC's negotiations with the former government. Following the general election held in 1994 Mbeki was chosen by Nelson Mandela to be the first Deputy President of the new government of national unity. After the National Party withdrew from the government of national unity in June 1996, Thabo Mbeki became the sole Deputy President. At the ANC's 50th national conference in Mafeking in December 1997, Thabo Mbeki became the president of the ANC. In June 1999 he was inaugurated as President of South Africa.

Mbeki has been pivotal in the formation of the New Partnership for Africa's Development and in the development of the role played by the African Union in brokering peace agreements in Rwanda, Burundi and the Democratic Republic of the Congo. Mbeki has attempted to restore dialogue between Zimbabwe's President Robert Mugabe and the opposition Movement for Democratic Change, headed by Morgan Tsvangirai. His policy of 'quiet diplomacy' and tacit support for Mugabe within the international community has attracted much criticism. In 2004 Archbishop Desmond Tutu publicly criticized President Mbeki for surrounding himself with 'yes-men' and for not doing enough to improve the position of the poor. Mbeki's views on the causes and treatment of HIV/AIDS have also been criticized, notably his defence of a small group of scientists who have claimed that HIV infection is not the cause of AIDS. Though applauded by AIDS activists for its successful legal challenge to action brought by multinational pharmaceutical companies seeking to prevent the local manufacture of cheaper, 'generic' anti-AIDS drugs, Mbeki's government has been accused of failing to respond adequately to HIV/AIDS in South Africa, which is now believed to affect more than 21% of the country's adult population.

Mediterranean Free Trade Area

The long-term objective of the **EU-Mediterranean Partnership** established in the mid-1990s and involving the **European Union** with a number of Mediterranean countries, initially Tunisia and Morocco.

Melilla

One of two ancient ports on the Mediterranean coast of Morocco seized by the Spanish and still held by them under the special status of garrisons (praesidios) – the other is **Ceuta.** Melilla was taken by the Spanish in 1497. After 1499, there were those in Spain who urged the permanent occupation of the **Maghreb** and foundation there of a Spanish empire, but the strategy adopted instead was to establish garrisons along the Mediterranean coast of **North Africa**, as far east as present day Tunisia. Despite demands by Morocco, since **independence**, that the two remaining Spanish *praesidios* be returned, Spain continues to hold them. Melilla is today a major centre of smuggling (including human 'trafficking') between Morocco and Spain. A ferry runs between Melilla and Malaga.

Mende

Major ethno-linguistic grouping in West Africa, particularly in Sierra Leone.

De Menezes, Fradique

President of São Tomé and Príncipe since 2001. De Menezes is a wealthy **cocoa** exporter who relinquished his Portuguese citizenship (he was a national of both Portugal and São Tomé and Príncipe by birth) in order to be able to contest the presidential election in 2001. He studied in Portugal and Belgium and held several political and diplomatic posts, including foreign minister and ambassador in Europe. De Menezes has stated that **agriculture** must remain the basis of São Tomé and Príncipe's development, and his wish to dynamize the country, combat excessive bureaucracy and improve public-sector management. He also wishes revenues that are expected to be generated from new offshore oilfields to be used to improve public services. He is also keen to reduce São Tomé and Príncipe's isolation and favours stronger ties with West Africa. In July 2003 de Menezes was overthrown in a military coup while he was visiting Nigeria. He returned to São Tomé and Príncipe after an agreement to restore democratic rule was made with the coup's leaders.

Middle Congo

Now the Republic of the Congo. Formerly part of the colonial territory of **French Equatorial Africa** that was established in 1910.

Migration

The movement of people and populations is a common feature of African economy and society. In the dry areas of the continent, particularly in the Saharan and Sahelian regions but also in the Horn of Africa, **East Africa** and parts of **southern Africa**, livestock production takes the form of pastoralism, in which herders move with their animals, often over long distances, in search of **water** and grazing land; more common is seasonal movement of people and animals over shorter distances associated with agro-pastoralism. Rural-urban migration has given rise to a substantial growth in the proportion of the population living in urban areas in recent decades as men (and to a lesser extent **women**) search for economic opportunities in the rapidly expanding **informal economy** in the towns, and thereby contribute to it. In some regions long-distance labour migration has a long history—in southern Africa, for example, the mines of South Africa have attracted labour from surrounding territories and countries for more than a century, while long-distance migration was also commonplace in West Africa. Today, international migration has become increasingly common, as economic growth and employment opportunities in some African countries attract labour from countries where opportunities are fewer and less attractive. Migration out of the continent has been a feature of the North African economies for many years, certainly since the post-war period, when many migrant workers from the **Maghreb** travelled north into Europe seeking employment and then settled to create the North African immigrant communities found in France and elsewhere today. In addition to what is termed 'economic migration' there is involuntary or forced migration, in which people are forced to move because of **drought**, **famine** or conflict. Large-scale forced migration is also a characteristic of Africa today. Periodic drought and famine has, over the last three to four decades (particularly in the early 1970s and mid 1980s), affected large numbers of people in the Sahel, Sudan, Ethiopia and the Horn of Africa, resulting in substantial movement of population away from the areas affected, either to other parts of the same country (internal displacement) or across national boundaries into other countries as **refugees**.

Military

Historically, the military have played a major role in African politics. Often in newly independent states, the armed forces have represented a distinctive organized and effective force, with educated officers and technical capacities beyond those of the ordinary civilian, and have intervened to provide effective leadership when they considered that the civilian rulers and leaders had failed to do so. In some cases the armed forces of the newly independent state were a reincarnation of the guerrilla forces involved in the liberation struggle which eventually took power and transformed themselves into the military; in other cases, they were professionals who took power to replace what they considered ineffective or (often) corrupt governments. Usually they have ruled 'in the name of the people', presenting themselves as a radical and modernizing force, but in some cases they too have represented more selfish vested interests and have proved as corrupt and often more repressive than the governments they replaced. Increasingly, in Africa today, those governments which rule as or through the military are becoming less common, as the process of democratization progresses. Even so, there are still many Heads of State who come from a military or guerrilla/rebel background (e.g. **Col al-Qaddafi** in Libya, **Col Jammeh** in Gambia, **Gen. Museveni** in Uganda, **Maj.-Gen. Kabila** in the Democratic Republic of the Congo, **Robert Mugabe** in Zimbabwe). As recently as August 2005 a military coup took place in Mauritania, in which the civilian

President (who had himself previously been a colonel in the army) was replaced by a Military Council for Justice and Democracy.

Military expenditure

Many African states devote a considerable share of their state budget and public expenditure to the military, ostensibly for 'defence' but often, in fact, as part of the government's efforts to retain power.

Millennium Challenge Account (MCA)

A fund, established by US President George W. Bush, held by the **Millennium Challenge Corporation** to enable it to allocate money to honest governments pursuing sound economic policies. Countries eligible for allocations of funds were identified relatively quickly, but approval of their projects has been slow. The first grant, of US $110m., was made in April 2005, to Madagascar. The criteria for allocation of funds are based on 16 different indicators of a country's honesty and soundness, including its credit rating, level of inflation, level of **corruption**, treatment of civil liberties, spending on health and **education**, how long it takes to start a business, etc. A country cannot qualify for assistance from the Millennium Challenge Account (MCA) unless it ranks in the upper half of a corruption index. The indicator for corruption is based on figures compiled by Daniel Kaufmann and Aart Kraay of the **World Bank**. Many of the standards are relative and countries are in fact in competition between themselves. Kaufmann and Kraay are themselves concerned that their corruption index is imprecise—while they could be 90% certain that Sudan and Burundi were correctly classified in the lower half of the table they compiled in 2000–01, ranking 61 countries in total, they could not be so sure of the other 28 countries that fall into the lower half.

Millennium Challenge Corporation

An institution established by US President George W. Bush in 2002 to provide funds (from the **Millennium Challenge Account)** to honest governments pursuing sound economic policies. Its first grant, of US $110m., was made in April 2005, to Madagascar. A number of other African countries are eligible for grants, including: Benin, Cape Verde, Ghana, Lesotho, Madagascar, Mali, Mozambique, and Senegal. Others are on the 'threshold': Burkina Faso, Kenya, Malawi, São Tomé and Príncipe, Tanzania, Uganda and Zambia.

Millennium Development Goals (MDGs)

The Millennium Development Goals (MDGs) are targets adopted at a UN summit in 2000 in a number of areas—economic and social—which the international community has committed itself to help the governments of developing countries to achieve within a defined period of time (usually by 2010 or 2015). The goals include halving **poverty** and hunger, arresting disease and environmental degradation, helping newborn babies survive infancy and providing better access to **education** for both girls and boys. At the present rate of progress, Africa south of the Sahara will meet none of the goals. For six out of the eight major goals, there has been little improvement and some deterioration; only in primary education and gender equality has some progress been made. In January 2005 it was noted that sub-Saharan Africa has met or is on track to meet not a single MDG. Even where it is making some progress, the change is too slow to bring the MDG within reach. Several analysts have suggested that major **debt relief** and **development assistance** for Africa is required if real progress is to be made. *The Economist* estimated in July 2005 that if the MDGs were to be fulfilled for Ghana, Tanzania and Uganda, it would require the equivalent of an additional US $49, $60 and $47 per person per year in the three countries respectively, with the largest amounts allocated to health and education.

Mineral production

The African sub-continent is a major producer and exporter of minerals. The major minerals produced are: **aluminium and bauxite**, **chromium**, **cobalt**, coltan, **copper**, **diamonds**, **gold**, iron ore, manganese, petroleum, phosphates, platinum and uranium.

MINURSO

The United Nations Mission for the Referendum in **Western Sahara** was established in April 1991 to verify a cease-fire in the disputed territory of Western Sahara, which came into effect in September 1991, to implement a settlement plan, involving the repatriation of Sahrawi **refugees**, the release of all political prisoners on both sides of the conflict (with Morocco) and to organize a referendum on the future of the territory. Originally scheduled for January 1992, the referendum has been continually deferred and has not yet taken place. There were serious disagreements between the **Frente Popular para la Liberación de Saguia el-Hamra y Río de Oro (Frente POLISARIO—Popular Front for the Liberation of Saguia el-Hamra and Río de Oro)**, representing the Sahrawi people, and the Moroccan government with regard to who was eligible to vote in a referendum and this—together with other difficulties—has resulted in a stalemate, in which little progress towards the referendum has been made in a decade. The identification and registration process was eventually formally started in August 1994, but in December 1995 the UN Secretary-General reported that the identification of voters had stalled, owing to persistent obstructions on both sides. In early 1997 the new UN Secretary-General, **Kofi Annan**, attempted to revive the possibility of an imminent resolution of the dispute amidst increasing concerns that the cease-fire would collapse and be followed by a resumption of hostilities. In October 1997 the mission was strengthened, to enable it to supervise nine voter identification centres.

By early September 1998 the initial identification process had been completed, with a total of 147,350 voters identified. Debates continued, however, regarding three particular tribal groups. A new timetable envisaged the referendum being held in July 2000. In December 1999 the UN Security Council acknowledged that persisting disagreements obstructing the implementation of the settlement plan precluded any possibility of conducting the planned referendum before 2002. In June 2001 the personal envoy of the UN Secretary-General elaborated a new draft Framework Agreement which envisaged the disputed area remaining part of Morocco but with substantial devolution of authority. Any referendum would be postponed. The Security Council agreed to extend MINURSO's mandate until November 2001 and then again until February 2002. In January the new special representative visited the region and the mandate of MINURSO has been extended several times.

Mlambo-Ngcuka, Phumzile

President **Thabo Mbeki** of South Africa appointed Phumzile Mlambo-Ngcuka, Minister of Minerals and Energy, to replace **Jacob Zuma** as Vice-President, in late June 2005. He hailed her appointment as 'an opportunity to further strengthen the participation of women in the executive'. Mlambo-Ngcuka already sits on the National Executive Committee of the **African National Congress (ANC)**. As Minister of Minerals and Energy she has been instrumental in devising the first charter for 'black economic empowerment', South Africa's version of affirmative action. Mlambo-Ngcuka is a strong supporter of the broadly liberal economic policy adopted by the President and it is thought that she may be a future presidential candidate.

Mobutu, Joseph-Désiré (Mobutu Sese Seko)

Overthrew President **Joseph Kasavubu** in 1965 to seize power in the Democratic Republic of the Congo (DRC). Col (and, subsequently, Marshal) Mobutu had earlier played a leading role in the military coup through which Kasavubu had achieved power. Under Mobutu, who was elected (unopposed) as President in 1979, the DRC was renamed the Republic of **Zaire** and Mobutu renamed himself Mobutu Sese Seko as part of a national policy of 'authenticity' that sought to discard European influences. Mobutu's regime was characterized by, on the one hand, disastrous economic mismanagement, of which the efforts of the President and his associates to enrich themselves were a salient feature, and the suppression of all political opposition on the other. Efforts, pursued from the 1990s, to introduce political reform were unsuccessful in restoring the economy and from 1996 domestic opposition was reinforced by **Tutsis** whom Mobutu had sought to expel from Zaire. In 1997 Mobutu was overthrown by the Alliance des forces démocratiques pour la libération du Congo-Zaïre and replaced by **Laurent-Désiré Kabila**. He died in exile in Morocco later in the same year.

Modise, Joe

Former head of **Umkhonto we Sizwe** ('Spear of the Nation'), the military wing of the **African National Congress (ANC)**. Modise was appointed as Minister of Defence in the ANC government of South Africa that took office in 1994.

Mohammed VI, King

Grandson of Mohammed V and son of **Hassan II**, kings of Morocco, Mohammed VI succeeded his father as King of Morocco and Head of State in July 1999. The king in Morocco is also a religious leader, known to his people as Commander of the Faithful (Emir al-Mouminin). Expected to make some significant political and social changes, Mohammed VI has proved extremely cautious, but has made efforts to introduce social reforms, particularly with regard to **women**'s rights in Morocco. He initially made gestures which led some to believe that he would initiate changes affecting human rights (a subject of criticism by international human rights agencies during his father's reign), but has remained obdurate on the issue of the **Western Sahara**.

Moi, Daniel arap

Daniel arap Moi succeeded **Jomo Kenyatta** as President of Kenya on Kenyatta's death in 1978. He was first elected (unopposed) as President of Kenya in 1979 and remained in office until 2002, when he did not contest the presidential election in which **Mwai Kibaki** was the winning candidate. Moi maintained a one-party state and comparative stability, surviving an attempted coup in 1982 and a semi-covert challenge from Charles Njonjo, one of Kenyatta's colleagues, in spite of an economic slump and continuing tribal tensions. His period of government was characterized, however, by considerable repression and **corruption**. Britain, which provided substantial technical and financial assistance to Kenya, was particularly concerned and on several occasions reduced and threatened to sever aid in response to Moi's policies.

Momoh, Maj.-Gen. Joseph

President of Sierra Leone in 1985–92. Momoh succeeded **Siaka Stevens** as President, and promised to end the **corruption** that had characterized the outgoing regime, of which he himself had been a member for more than a decade He was overthrown in a military coup in 1992 and fled Sierra Leone for Guinea.

Monrovia Group

Between October 1960 and March 1961, three conferences were held by French-speaking African countries, at Abidjan (Côte d'Ivoire), Brazzaville (Republic of the Congo) and Yaoundé (Cameroon). None of the 12 countries that attended these meetings had been represented at the Casablanca Conference of January 1961, which had given rise to what came to be called the **Casablanca Group**. In September these states signed a charter establishing the Union africaine et malgache, later the **Organisation commune africaine et mauricienne (OCAM)**. The Monrovia Group was a grouping of African states which came together following a conference held in Monrovia, Liberia, in May 1961, attended by the Heads of State or representatives of 19 countries—Cameroon, Central African Republic, Chad, the Republic of the Congo, Côte d'Ivoire, **Dahomey**, Ethiopia, Gabon, Liberia, Madagascar, Mauritania, Niger, Nigeria, Senegal, Sierra Leone, Somalia, Togo, Tunisia and Upper Volta. It thus included the whole of the **Brazzaville Group**, and, in addition, Libya and a majority of former British territories. The Monrovia Group met again (with the exception of Tunisia and with the addition of the ex-Belgian Congo) in January 1962 in Lagos, Nigeria, to establish a permanent secretariat and a standing committee of finance ministers, and to accept a draft charter for an Organization of Inter-African and Malagasy States. Owing largely to the prominence of Nigeria, it acquired an anti-Ghanaian and anti-**Nkrumah** orientation. The group envisaged a loose association of African states, in contrast with the Casablanca Group, which preferred a closer federal arrangement and had, at the Casablnce Conference in 1961, agreed an African Charter and proposed the establishment of an African Military Command and an African Common Market.

Mont Fleur scenarios

In 1992, at the Mont Fleur conference centre in South Africa's Western Cape, a group of economists, political, trade union and civil organization leaders met to develop a series of scenarios for the post-**apartheid** economy of South Africa. Initially, 32 scenarios were presented, but the number was eventually reduced to four. These were: the Ostrich Act, in which the old regime refused to settle in the face of the liberation movement demands that it regarded as too radical, and decided to use its military/security strength to retain power for at least another decade; the Lame Duck, in which a constitutional settlement was reached which tried to allay white fears by ensuring a long transition of five–eight years, with many 'sunset' clauses giving the old regime a right to veto economic policies; Icarus, in which the new government embarked on a policy of macroeconomic populism, trying to pump-prime the demand side of the economy with large wage increases and government spending; and the Flight of the Flamingos, in which the parties negotiated a political system with a high degree of legitimacy and the new regime made considerable social investment within a framework of fiscal discipline and adopted balanced economic policies aimed at creating conditions to attract fixed investments and a reorientation of the industrial sector towards the export of manufactured goods. The Flight of the Flamingos attracted most support and two months later the **African National Congress** held a major policy conference and drafted a comprehensive set of policy guide-lines called Ready to Govern. The section on the economy was a watershed, downplaying the role of the state in the economy (primarily to oversee, and to provide infrastructure and welfare payments) and envisaging a dynamic private sector.

Morocco, Kingdom of

The Kingdom of Morocco is situated in **North Africa**, bordering the North Atlantic Ocean and the Mediterranean Sea, between Algeria to the east and **Western Sahara** to the south. Morocco is in a strategic location opposite Spain and the Straits of Gibraltar. The country's total area is 446,550 sq km (of which 250 sq km is **water**). The capital is Rabat. In July 2002 the population was estimated at 31,167,783, comprising Arabs (70%), **Berbers** (29%), 'others' 0.8% and Jews (0.2%). The religious composition of the country is: Muslims (mostly **Sunni**) 98.7%, Christians 1.1%, Jews 0.2%. **Arabic** is the official language. Berber dialects are also spoken and French is often used in business, government and diplomacy.

Political profile

Morocco is a constitutional monarchy. The Head of State is King **Mohammed VI** (since 23 July 1999). The head of government is Prime Minister Driss Jettou (since 9 October 2002). A Council of Ministers is appointed by the monarch. The monarchy is hereditary and the Prime Minister is appointed by the monarch following legislative elections. Gradual political reforms in the 1990s resulted in the establishment of a bicameral legislature in 1997.

Legislative elections held in 1997 resulted in a tripartite division of the parliament. The eventual formation of a socialist-led government was regarded as a clear expression of the increasing role of the party system. The bicameral parliament consists of a Chamber of Counsellors (upper house) and a Chamber of Representatives (lower house). The Chamber of Counsellors has 270 seats. Members of the Chamber are elected indirectly by local councils, professional organizations and labour syndicates for nine-year terms. One-third of the members are renewed every three years. The Chamber of Representatives has 325 seats and members are elected by popular vote for five-year terms. The most recent elections to the Chamber of Counsellors were held on 15 September 2000. The most recent elections to the Chamber of Representatives were held on 27 September 2002. The next elections to the Chamber of Representatives will be held in 2007.

There is a Supreme Court, to which judges are appointed on the recommendation of the Supreme Council of the Judiciary, which is presided by the monarch. The legal system is based on **Islamic Law** and on the French and Spanish systems of civil law. Judicial review of legislative acts takes place in the Constitutional Chamber of the Supreme Court.

Political Parties and groups

With Mohammed VI's succession to the throne the Islamists have been tolerated. In 2000 the leader of the banned Islamic movement 'Justice and Good Deeds' was released after 10 years' imprisonment without trial.

- Action Party; Leader Muhammad El Idrissi
- Alliance of Liberties; Leader Ali Beljaj
- Annahj Addimocrati; Leader Abdellah El Harif
- Avant Garde Social Democratic Party; Leader Ahmed Benjelloun
- Citizen Forces; Leader Abderrahman Lahjouji
- Citizens' Initiatives for Development; Leader Mohamed Benjamou
- Constitutional Union; Leader Mohamed Abied
- Democratic and Independence Party; Leader Abdelwahed Maach
- Democratic and Social Movement; Leader Mahmoud Archane
- Democratic Socialist Party; Leader Aissa Ouardighi
- Democratic Union; Leader Bouazza Ikken
- Environment and Development Party; Leader Ahmed El Alami
- Front of Democratic Forces; Leader Thami El Khyari
- **Istiqlal** Party (Independence Party); Leader Abbas el-Fassi
- Justice and Development Party (formerly the Party of Justice and Development); Leader Abdelkrim El Khatib
- Moroccan Liberal Party; Leader Mohamed Ziane
- National Democratic Party; Leader Abdallah Kadiri
- National Ittihadi Congress Party; Leader Abdelmajid Bouzoubaa
- National Popular Movement; Leader Mahjoubi Aherdane
- National Rally of Independents; Leader Ahmed Osman
- National Union of Popular Forces; Leader Abdellah Ibrahim
- Parti Al Ahd (Al Ahd); Chair. Najib El Ouazzani
- Party of Progress and Socialism; Leader Ismail Alaoui
- Party of Renewment and Equity; Leader Chakir Achabar
- Party of the Unified Socialist Left; Leader Mohamed Ben Said Ait Idder
- Popular Movement; Leader Mohamed Laenser
- Reform and Development Party; Leader Abderrahmane El Kouhen
- Social Centre Party; Leader Lahcen Madih
- Socialist Union of Popular Forces; Leader Abderrahman El-Youssoufi

History

As an **Alawite**, the King of Morocco, Mohammed VI, claims descent from the Prophet Muhammad through the 17th-century Sultan Moulay Ismail and the Filali dynasty. Morocco was never incorporated into the Ottoman Empire and, although divided in the time of the colonial protectorate regime into a French zone (the majority of the country) and a Spanish zone (in the north and to the south), it maintained its monarchy throughout the colonial period.

The nationalist movement, established during the early 1930s, maintained good relations with the palace. In 1936–37 efforts were made to extend the nationalist movement from a small nucleus into a mass movement. Riots that broke out in Meknes in 1937 increased French repression of the movement and for the next decade all nationalist activity had to be undertaken semi-clandestinely. Allal al-Fassi was in exile from 1937 until 1945. Pressure for **independence** from France increased, however, during the Second World War, and US President Roosevelt, meeting privately with the Sultan in January 1943 in Casablanca (at the time of his meeting there with Winston Churchill and Charles de Gaulle) led him to believe that he would promote Moroccan independence after the war. In January 1944 the National Party announced the establishment of a new party, the Istiqlal (Independence) Party. Over the next five years the Sultan identified himself ever more closely with the ambitions for independence expressed by the Istiqlal. In August 1953, as a result of his uncompromising position, the Sultan was exiled to Madagascar. However, after the end of the Second World War, Allal al-Fassi returned to Morocco, the nationalist leadership regrouped and the membership of the Istiqlal grew from 10,000 in 1947 to around 100,000 by 1951.

For many years, during the 1930s and 1940s, and even the 1950s, the nationalists were dominated by an urban élite, which allied itself with and gave unconditional support to the Sultan. Allal al-Fassi epitomized this conservative bourgeois nationalist leadership, which combined a sense of **nationalism** with a full sense of Morocco's religious and political history as a sultanate. Referred to as Sheikh Allal (an honorific title suggesting a religious status), Allal al-Fassi was increasingly associated, as the Istiqlal party began to split between the conservatives and the radicals, with 'the old turbans' as the former were known (the latter became known as 'the young Turks' and included the leftist ideologue, **Mehdi Ben Barka**).

Morocco's long struggle for independence from France ended in 1956. The internationalized city of Tangier was transferred to the new country in the same year. Morocco virtually annexed **Western Sahara** during the late 1970s, but no final resolution has been achieved with regard to the status of the territory.

Morocco claims and administers the Western Sahara, but sovereignty remains unresolved. Off the coast of Morocco Spain controls the islands of Penon de Alhucemas, Penon de Velez de la Gomera, the Islas Chafarinas and two autonomous communities on the coast of Morocco—Ceuta and Melilla. Morocco rejected Spain's unilateral designation of a median line from the Canary Islands in 2002 to explore undersea resources and to interdict illegal **refugees** from Africa.

Morocco, economy

Morocco faces the problems typical of developing countries—restraining government spending, reducing constraints on private activity and foreign trade, and achieving sustainable economic growth. Following **structural adjustment** programmes supported by the **International Monetary Fund**, the **World Bank**, and the Paris Club, the dirham is now fully convertible for current account transactions, and reforms of the financial sector have been implemented. Droughts depressed activity in the key agricultural sector and contributed to the stagnation of the economy in 1999 and 2000. Favourable rainfall in 2001 led to economic growth of 5%. Formidable long-term challenges include: servicing the external **debt**; preparing the economy for freer trade with the **European Union**; and improving **education** and attracting foreign investment to boost living standards and job prospects for the country's youth.

Mosisili, Bethuel Pakalitha

Prime Minister of Lesotho. Bethuel Mosisili came to power in May 1998 after his party, the Lesotho Congress for Democracy (LCD), won an emphatic electoral victory. Protests by the opposition Basutho Congress Party (BCP) and Basotho National Party (BNP) against the results subsequently escalated into unrest, which was suppressed by an intervention force from neighbouring countries. A new electoral system was subsequently devised to make the legislature more representative.

Moto, Severo

Exiled opposition leader of Equatorial Guinea, whom British-led mercenaries sought to install in power in an abortive coup in 2005, with the alleged involvement of Mark Thatcher, son of the former British Prime Minister, Margaret Thatcher.

Mouvement africain pour la démocratie et le progrès (MADEP—African Movement for Democracy and Progress)

Political party in Benin, founded in 1997. Supports President **Mathieu Kérékou**. The party is led by El Hadj Séfou L. Fagbohoun.

Mouvement africain pour la nouvelle indépendance et la démocratie (MANIDEM—African Movement for New Independence and Democracy)

Political movement in Cameroon. Formerly a faction of the **Union des populations camerounaises (UPC—Union of Cameroon Peoples)**. MANIDEM's leader is Anicet Ekane.

Mouvement algérien pour la justice et le développement (MAJD)

Algerian political group established in 1990. A leftist reformist party supporting the policies of former President **Boumedienne**. The MAJD is led by Moulay Habib.

Mouvement des citoyens pour la République (MCR—Citizens' Movement for the Republic)

Political organization in the Union of the Comoros, established in 1998. The MCR's leader is Mahamoud Mradabi.

Mouvement congolais pour la démocratie et le développement intégral (MCDDI—Congolese Movement for Democracy and Integral Development)

Political party in the Republic of the Congo, established in 1990. The MCDDI's leader (in exile) is Bernard Kolelas, its president Michel Mampouya.

Mouvement pour la défense de la République (MDR—Movement for the Defence of the Republic)

Political party in Cameroon, established in 1991. Its leader is Dakole Daissala.

Mouvement des democrates socialistes (MDS—Movement of Socialist Democrats)

Tunisian political party; favours a pluralist political system; participated in the 1981 election and was officially recognized in November 1983. The secretary-general of the MDS is Ismail Boulahya.

Mouvement pour la démocratie et la citoyenneté (MDC—Movement for Democracy and Citizenship)

Algerian political grouping, established in 1997 by dissident members of the **Front des forces socialistes (FFS)**. Based in Tizi Ouzou and led by Said Khelil.

Mouvement pour la démocratie et le développement (MDD—Movement for Democracy and Development)

Political party in the Central African Republic, established in 1993. Its aims are safeguarding national unity and the equitable distribution of national wealth.

Mouvement pour la démocratie et le développement (MDD—Movement for Democracy and Development)

Political-military group in Chad consisting of two factions, led, respectively, by Issa Faki Mahamat and Brahim Mallah.

Mouvement pour la démocratie, l'indépendance et le progrès social (MDI-PS—Movement for Democracy, Independence and Social Progress)

Political party in the Central African Republic. The secretary-general of the MDI-PS is Daniel Nditifei Boysembe.

Mouvement pour la démocratie et la justice au Tchad (MDJT—Movement for Democracy and Justice in Chad)

Political-military group in Chad. In January 2002 the government of Chad signed a peace agreement with the deputy leader of the MDJT, Adoum Togoi, although this was later rejected by elements close to former leader, Youssouf Togoimi (who died in September 2002). A number of former MDJT rebels subsequently joined the government forces.

Mouvement pour la démocratie et le progrès (MDP—Movement for Democracy and Progress)

Political party in Cameroon, established in 1992. The MDP's leader is Samuel Eboua.

Mouvement pour la démocratie et le progrès (MDP—Movement for Democracy and Progress)

Political party in the Union of the Comoros. A founder member of the **Forum pour le redressement national (FRN—Forum for National Recovery)**, from which it withdrew in May 1999. The leader of the MDP-NGDC is Abbas Djoussouf.

Mouvement démocratique et social (MDS—Democratic and Social Movement)

Algerian political party, formed in 1998 by former members of Ettahadi. A left-wing party with about 4,000 members. The secretary-general of the MDS is Hachemi Cherif.

Mouvement démocratique et social (Democratic and Social Movement)

Moroccan political party, founded in 1996 as the Mouvement national démocratique et social (National Democratic and Social Movement) after splitting from the Mouvement national populaire (National Popular Movement). Adopted its current name in November 1996. Its leader is Mahmoud Archane.

Mouvement de l'évolution sociale de l'Afrique noire (MESAN—Social Evolution Movement of Black Africa)

A political party established in 1949 in the Central African Republic. It comprises two factions, led, respectively, by Fidèle Ogbami and Joseph Ngbangadibo.

Mouvement pour la jeunesse du Cameroun (MLJC—Movement for the Youth of Cameroon)

Political movement in Cameroon, led by Dieudonné Tina.

Mouvement pour la libération et le développement du Cameroun (MLDC—Movement for the Liberation and Development of Cameroon)

Political party in Cameroon, formed by a breakaway faction of the **Mouvement pour la jeunesse du Cameroun (MLJC—Movement for the Youth of Cameroon)**. The MLDC's leader is Marcel Yondo.

Mouvement pour la libération du Congo (MLC—Movement for the Liberation of the Congo)

Political party in the Democratic Republic of the Congo, established in 1998. A Ugandan-supported rebel movement, whose strength is estimated at more than 30,000. The MLC is led by Jean-Paul Bemba.

Mouvement pour la libération du peuple centrafricain (MLPC—Liberation Movement of the Central African People)

Political party in the Central African Republic, established in 1979. Leading party in government since October 1993. The president of the MLPC is Ange-Félix Patassé, who was elected as the President of the Central African Republic in September 1999.

Mouvement pour la liberté

Algerian political party, established in 1999 in opposition to President **Bouteflika**. It is led by **Mouloud Hamrouche**.

Mouvement national populaire (MNP—National Popular Movement)

Moroccan political party of the centre, founded in 1991. Its leader is Mahjoub Aherdane.

Mouvement national pour une société de développement-Nassara (MNSD-Nassara—National Movement for a Development Society-Nassara)

Leading political party in Niger, with 47 seats in the national assembly.

Mouvement patriotique du salut (MPS—Patriotic Salvation Movement)

Political grouping in Chad. Established in 1990 as an association of several opposition movements. Other opposition groups joined during the November 1990 offensive against the regime of **Hissène Habré**, and following the movement's accession to power in December 1990.

Mouvement populaire (MP—Popular Movement)

Moroccan political party, formally established in February 1959. Initiated by Mahjoub Aherdane, then governor of Rabat province, at a press conference in November 1957, the new party had no finances, no programme and was not even legal. It was more than one year before it was formally recognized. A Provisional Committee of Direction was established to draw up a programme and secure financial support. It held its constituent Congress in November 1959. The party drew on rural support, particularly in areas where the Liberation Army had been active, such as the Rif, and proposed to challenge the dominance of the **Istiqlal**. In some ways it presented itself as a rural/**Berber** party as opposed to the urban/Arab Istiqlal, although the distinction was rarely explicit. It gave loyal support to the King, and joined the Front pour la défense des institutions constitutionnelles (Front for the Defence of Constitutional Institutions) in the 1960s. It was allocated four ministerial posts after the 1977 elections. In elections held in 1984 it obtained 47 seats in the Chamber of Representatives, helping relegate the Istiqlal party into fourth place. Today it is a less powerful force than in the past. Its secretary-general is Mohand Laenser.

Mouvement populaire anjouanais (MPA—Popular Movement of Anjouan)

Political party in the Union of the Comoros and principal separatist movement on **Nzwani** (Anjouan). Established in 1997 by the merger of the Organisation pour l'indépendence d'Anjouan (Organization for the Independence of Anjouan) and the Mouvement separatiste anjouanais (Separatist Movement of Anjouan).

Mouvement populaire pour la démocratie (MPD—Popular Movement for Democracy)

Moroccan political party, led by M. el-Khatib.

Mouvement populaire de la révolution (MPR—Popular Movement of the Revolution)

Political party in the Democratic Republic of the Congo. Established in 1966 by President **Mobutu**. Sole legal political party in **Zaire** until November 1990. Advocates national unity and opposes tribalism. The MPR's secretary-general is Kithima bin Ramazani.

Mouvement de la réforme nationale (MRN—Movement of National Reform)

Algerian political group, formed in 1998 but based on the earlier **Mouvement de la renaissance islamique**. Its leader is Sheikh Abdullah Djaballah.

Mouvement de la renaissance islamique/Harakat an-Nahda al-Islamiyya (MRI—Movement of the Islamic Renaissance)

Algerian Islamist political grouping. The MRI received official legal approval in December 1990, although its leader, Sheikh Abdullah Djaballah, claimed that it had existed clandestinely since 1974. Like **Hamas**, the MRI was close in spirit and outlook to the **Muslim Brotherhood**, although not organizationally linked to it (any more than Hamas in Algeria appeared to be). Unlike the **Front Islamique du Salut (FIS—Islamic Salvation Front)** and Hamas, the MRI opposed the Algerian government's economic reform measures, defending the public sector against further privatization. It has therefore appeared to be trying to establish a distinctive position for itself on the left wing of the Islamist movement. In the early 1990s it was argued that the MRI did not appear to have much of a popular constituency, but it was reported to have a substantial following among intellectuals, particularly in Constantine, the cultural capital of eastern Algeria, where Sheikh Djaballah was based, and to be more coherent intellectually than the FIS. Sheikh Djaballah called for people to vote for the FIS in June 1990, but the MRI was expected to contest elections to the National People's Assembly in 1991. The MRI was banned in 1992.

Mouvement de la résistance pour la réhabilitation du citoyen (MRC-Rurenzangemero—Resistance Movement for the Rehabilitation of the Citizen)

Political party in Burundi, established in June 2001. The MRC's leader is Col Epitace Bayaganakandi.

Mouvement social pour la nouvelle démocratie (MSND—Social Movement for New Democracy)

Political party in Cameroon, led by Yondo Black.

Mouvement pour le socialisme et la démocratie (MSD—Movement for Socialism and Democracy)

Political party in the Union of the Comoros, founded in 2000 by a splinter group of the **Front démocratique (FD—Democratic Front)**. The MSD is led by Abdou Soefou.

Mouvement de la tendance islamique (MTI—Islamic Tendency Movement)

Under the leadership of **Habib Bourguiba**, who held power in 1956–87, and backed by Western governments, Tunisia's post-**independence** government pursued an aggressive programme of secularization and modernization. The government abolished the **Shari'a** courts, closed the Zaytouna (a renowned centre of Muslim learning), banned the headscarf for women, and debilitated the *ulema*. These events led to the formation in 1979 of the MTI, led by Rashid Ghannoushi. Though initially apolitical, it sought a humanitarian restructuring of society and the economy based on Islamic principles, together with participation in the democratic political process, rejecting violence as a means of change. The group's status changed in January 1978 when Bourguiba used the **military** to suppress protesters associated with the group. This event, in combination with the success of the Islamic Revolution in Iran, convinced Ghannoushi and the movement of the need to move beyond broad ideological statements and to relate **Islam** directly and specifically to the real, everyday political, economic, and social problems of the people. Ghannoushi was arrested in 1981, and sentenced to 11 years' imprisonment, but was released in 1984. Rearrested in 1987, he was released following **Ben Ali**'s ouster of Bourguiba. When Ben Ali replaced Bourguiba, the former also refused to allow the MTI to participate in public life. Instead, he voiced a 'firm belief in the need not to mix religion and politics, as experience has shown that anarchy emerges and the rule of law and institutions is undermined when such a mixing takes place'. Yet, the MTI's actual agenda did not represent an attempt to establish a militant Islamic state. Instead, it included a reassertion of Tunisia's Islamic-Arabic way of life and values, the restriction of Tunisia's Westernized (Francophile) profile, and the promotion of **democracy**, political pluralism, and economic and social justice. Due to its Islamist affiliations, however, secular leaders automatically classified the party with pro-Iranian groups such as **Islamic Jihad** and Hezbollah. As a result, MTI was banned from formal political participation despite its widespread legitimacy among the Tunisian people and its relatively progressive nationalist agenda.

In 1988 Ghannouchi restyled the organization as the **an-Nahda (Renaissance Party)**.

Mouvement pour l'unité et la République (MUR—Movement for Unity and the Republic)

Political-military group in Chad, founded in 2000 by a faction of the **Mouvement pour la démocratie et le développement (MDD—Movement for Democracy and Development)**. The MUR is led by Gaileth Gatoul Bourkoumandah.

Movement for Democratic Change (MDC)

In 1999 in Zimbabwe **Morgan Tsvangirai** helped to create the Movement for Democratic Change (MDC) out of the radical trade union organization with which he was involved. Within months, the new party had defeated the government over its referendum on constitutional reform, which included clauses allowing the seizure of white-owned farms without compensation. It was the most dramatic political set-back for President **Mugabe** since **independence**, but even this was eclipsed by the MDC's subsequent electoral performance. In the general election held in June 2000 the MDC—despite harassment by ZANU—PF supporters—won 57 of the constituency-based legislative seats, while Mugabe's ruling **Zimbabwe African National Union—Patriotic Front (ZANU—PF)** won 62—a result without precedent in Zimbabwe, where opposition parties had never held more than a handful of seats. Tsvangirai himself was not elected. Turning down the opportunity of a seat in one of the cities, where the MDC's support is strongest, the MDC's leader chose instead to stand in his home district, which, like most rural constituencies, was won by ZANU—PF. In elections held in March 2005 elections ZANU—PF regained overall control, although the MDC won some seats and, supported by the United Kingdom and the USA, claimed that widespread electoral fraud had occurred. In spite of continued repression, the MDC still represents the only coherent opposition to Mugabe's increasingly dictatorial regime.

Movement of Patriotic Libyans

Libyan opposition movement, founded in 1997.

Movimento para a Democracia (MPD—Movement for Democracy)

Governing party in Cape Verde since January 1991. Advocates administrative decentralization. The MPD's chairman is Agostinho Lopes.

Movimento Democrático Força da Mudança-Partido Liberal (MDFM-PL—Force for Change Democratic Movement-Liberal Party)

Political party in São Tomé and Príncipe, founded in 2001. The MDFM-PL gained nearly 40% of the vote in the legislative election held in 2002 and constitutes the main coalition partner in a government of national unity with the **Movimento de Libertação de São Tomé e Príncipe-Partido Social Democrata (Liberation Movement of São Tomé and Príncipe-Social Democrat Party)**.

Movimento de Libertação de São Tomé e Príncipe—Partido Social Democrata (MLSTP—PSD, Liberation Movement of São Tomé and Príncipe-Social Democrat Party)

Political Party in São Tomé and Príncipe. Following legislative elections held in 2002 the MLSTP-PSD formed a government of national unity with the **Movimento Democrático Força da Mudança-Partido Liberal (Force for Change Democratic Movement-Liberal Party)**.

Movimento Popular de Libertação de Angola (MPLA—Popular Liberation Movement of Angola)

The Movimento Popular de Libertação de Angola (MPLA), a successor to the oldest Angolan anti-colonial movement, the Partido da Luta Unida dos Africanos de Angola (Party of the United Struggle of the Africans of Angola), was considered to be dominated by the Mbundu people, who inhabit the area around the capital, Luanda, and by the views of urban intellectuals, mostly *assimilados* (Europeanized Africans granted Portuguese citizenship) and *mesticos* (people of mixed European and African descent), as personified by its first leader, **Mário de Andrade**. From its inception in 1956, the MPLA displayed a strong leftist orientation and had strong links with the Portuguese Communist Party. This enabled it to attract substantial support from the countries of the Soviet bloc. During 1961–74 the MPLA conducted guerrilla operations against Portuguese colonial rule in Angola. The MPLA was significantly bolstered in 1974 by the appointment as president of the movement of **Dr Agostinho Neto**, a Mbundu *assimilado* and former political prisoner. In 1975 Angola achieved **independence** and the MPLA became the governing party. Known as the MPLA-Partido de Trabalho (MPLA-PT—MPLA-Workers' Party) between 1977 and 1992, in December 1990 it formally replaced its Marxist-Leninist ideology with a commitment to 'democratic socialism'. The chairman of the MPLA is **José Eduardo dos Santos**, who was elected President of Angola in September 1992, and the party's secretary-general is João Manuel Gonçalves Lourenço.

Mozambique, Republic of

The Republic of Mozambique lies on the east coast of Africa, bordered to the north by Tanzania, to the west by Malawi, Zambia and Zimbabwe, and to the south by South Africa and Swaziland. The country has a coastline of about 2,470 km on the shores of the Indian Ocean, and is separated from Madagascar, to the east, by the Mozambique Channel. The area of the country is 799,380 sq km. At mid-2004 the population was estimated at 18,972,396. Portuguese is the official language, while there are 39 indigenous languages, the most widely spoken being Makhuwa, Tsonga, Sema and Lomwe. Many of the inhabitants follow traditional beliefs. There are about 5m. Christians, the majority of whom are Roman Catholics, and 4m. Muslims. The capital is Maputo (formerly Lourenço Marques), whose population was estimated at 1,220,632 at mid-2003.

Political profile

The Constitution of 30 November 1990 (amended in 1996 and 2004) provides for a multi-party political system. Legislative power is vested in the Assembléia da República, with 250 members, who are elected for a five-year term. Members are elected by universal, direct adult suffrage in a secret ballot, according to a system of proportional representation. The President of the Republic, who is Head of State, is directly elected for a five-year term; the President holds executive power and governs with the assistance of an appointed Council of Ministers. A Council of State advises the President, who, however, has no obligation to follow its advice. Provincial governors, appointed by the President, have overall responsibility for the functions of government within each of the 11 provinces.

In a presidential election held on 1–2 December 2004 Armando Guebuza, the candidate of the **Frente de Libertação de Moçambique (Frelimo—Mozambique Liberation Front)**, received 63.74% of the votes, thus defeating all of the four other candidates who contested the poll.

Following a general election held on 1–2 December 2004, the distribution of seats in the Assembléia da República was as follows: Frelimo 160; Resistência Nacional Moçambicana—União Eleitoral (Renamo—UE, National Mozambican Resistance—Electoral Union) 90. The election was also contested by the Partido para a Paz, Democracia e Desenvolvimento (PPDD—Party for Peace, Democracy and Development), the Partido para a Liberdade e Solidariedade (PAZS—Party for Freedom and Solidarity), the Partido de Reconciliação Nacional (PARENA—Party of National Reconciliation), the Partido Independente de Moçambique (PIMO—Independent Party of Mozambique) and the Partido Social de Moçambique (PASOMO—Social Party of Mozambique), among others, none of which received the minimum 5% of the vote required in order to secure representation in the Assembléia.

History

Mozambique became a Portuguese colony in the 19th century and an overseas province in 1951. Nationalist groups began to form in the 1960s. Frelimo was formed in 1962 and launched a military campaign for **independence** in 1964. After a military coup in Portugal in April 1974, negotiations between Frelimo and the new Portuguese government resulted in a period of rule in Mozambique by a transitional government, followed by full independence on 25 June 1975. The leader of Frelimo, Samora Machel, became the first President of Mozambique. In February 1977 Frelimo was reconstituted as the Frelimo Party, a 'Marxist-Leninist vanguard party', with restricted membership.

After Zimbabwean independence in April 1980, South Africa adopted **Rhodesia**'s former role as supporter of the Mozambican opposition guerrilla group, Renamo. From the early 1980s the Mozambique government and Renamo fought a **civil war** that was not concluded until 1992.

Presidential and legislative elections were held on 27–29 October 1994. In the presidential election Joaquim Alberto Chissano, the candidate of Frelimo, secured an outright majority (53.3%) of the votes. His closest rival was Afonso Macacho Marceta Dhlakama, the leader of Renamo, who received 33.7% of the votes. In the legislative elections Frelimo also secured an overall majority, winning 129 of the 250 seats in the Assembléia da República; Renamo obtained 112 seats, and the União Democrática (UD—Democratic Union) the remaining nine.

Presidential and legislative elections took place on 3–5 December 1999. In the presidential contest, Chissano defeated Dhlakama (his sole challenger), taking 52.3% of the valid votes cast. Frelimo secured an outright majority in the legislative elections, winning 133 of the 250 seats in the Assembléia da República; Renamo—UE obtained the remaining seats.

President Chissano announced in May 2001 that he would not stand for re-election on the expiry of his term in 2004. Presidential and legislative elections took place on 1–2 December 2004. In the presidential election Armando Guebuza, the secretary-general of Frelimo, won 63.7% of the votes cast, while Dhlakama received 31.7%. In the legislative elections, Frelimo won 62.0% of the votes, securing 160 of the available 250 seats, while Renamo took 29.7% and 90 seats (a significant decline compared with the 117 seats it had won in the 1999 elections).

International relations

After independence, Mozambique developed strong international links with the USSR and other countries of the communist bloc, and with neighbouring African states: it is a member of the **Southern African Development Community**. In 1993 full diplomatic relations were established with South Africa. In 1995 Mozambique was admitted, by special dispensation, as a full member of the Commonwealth. In early 2005 more than 200 Mozambican troops were participating in the United Nations Operation in Burundi.

Mozambique, economy

In 2003, according to estimates by the **World Bank**, Mozambique's gross national income (GNI), measured at average 2001–03 prices, was US $4,097m., equivalent to $210 per head (or $1,070 per head on an international purchasing-power parity basis). During 1990–2003, it was estimated, the population increased at an average annual rate of 2.2%, while gross domestic product (GDP) per head increased, in real terms, by an average of 4.1% per year. Overall GDP increased, in real terms, at an average annual rate of 6.4% in 1990–2003; growth in 2003 was 7.0%. According to the **International Monetary Fund (IMF)**, the average annual rate of inflation was 11.9% in 1998–2002; consumer prices in Maputo increased by an average of 13.3% in 2003, and by 9.1% in 2004. **Agriculture** and **fisheries** are important sectors of the economy. Industrial activities include the production of **aluminium**, **natural gas** and hydro-power. Services and tourism are also being developed. In 2004 the main markets for Mozambique's exports were Belgium, Italy, Spain, Germany and Zimbabwe. South Africa, Australia and the USA were the main suppliers of imports in 2004. The national currency is the metical (plural: meticais). In 2004 the average exchange rate was US $1 = 22,581.3 meticais.

Mozambique is one of the world's poorest countries, ranking 168th among the 174 countries included in the UN's Human Development Index. GDP per head was $193 in 2001, well below the average for **sub-Saharan Africa** ($480), and about 70% of Mozambicans live in absolute **poverty**. The fight against poverty is the government's top priority. In 1999 the government published an Action Plan for the Reduction of Absolute Poverty (PARPA) that aims to extend the benefits of economic growth to the general population. Key donors have increasingly been delivering development flows through support to the budget, attempting to improve coherence and strengthen government ownership and capacity to deliver its own programmes to combat poverty. Key areas on which the new Guebuza government has pledged to concentrate are **education**, health, infrastructure and agriculture, but it has also placed emphasis on public-sector reform, good governance and the private sector.

Agriculture accounts for 26% of GDP, employs 83% of the labour force and, before the Mozal state-of-the-art aluminium smelter near Maputo began operations, accounted for 80% of exports. The sector is heavily dependent on adequate rainfall. Mozambique's main agricultural exports are prawns, cotton, cashew nuts, sugar and coconuts. The country also has considerable resources of **oil**, natural gas, minerals and hydro-electricity. The industrial base, severely weakened by war, poor management and the loss of skills when the Portuguese left in 1975, is now expanding again, although in 2000 and 2001 temporary set-backs occurred owing to floods. Mozamibique is also slightly affected by the current regional **drought**. The three main ports, at Maputo, Beira and Nacala have rail/road links to neighbouring countries. Some ports and transport links are being rehabilitated.

Although it started from a relatively low base, Mozambique's recent economic performance has, in general, been good. Combating the effect of floods in 2000, in which 10% of cultivatable land was destroyed, has obstructed economic growth. The government has concentrated on tackling **corruption**, crime and issues of governance. The 2004 budget focused on establishing transparency in government expenditure and accountability in order to encourage donations, aid and investment. Direct budget support of $157.7m. was projected for 2004, a 33% increase on 2002.

The currency is stable at present and inflation has been brought under control. Macroeconomic policy is prudent. Problems in the banking sector are being addressed, although they continue to need close attention. The government is making efforts to improve its revenue base by fiscal, public financial management, customs and income tax reforms. Other critical reforms—particularly in the public sector—have been launched. Defence and security expenditure has been cut sharply, allowing higher social spending. Customs revenue collection has increased by 125% since 1997. Clearance times for cargo have been reduced from weeks to days.

In recent years many state enterprises have been privatized, including the largest commercial bank and a number of sizeable manufacturing firms. Other privatizations are pending in the areas of transportation, **energy** and telecommunications. The $1,300m. Mozal aluminium plant opened in 2000 and second-phase expansion, costing a further $900,000, is well under way. Maputo port is being concessioned. In parallel with the concessioning of the railway that runs from the port to South Africa, this is expected to catalyze considerably larger volumes of cross-border trade with South Africa and other interior neighbours in coming years.

One major focus of current investment is the Maputo Development Corridor, the transport axis between Gauteng—the industrial heart of South Africa—and Maputo. The respective governments are working together to attract investment to the corridor as part of a wider development programme. The Mozambican and Malawian governments are also keen to promote the Nacala Development Corridor, aimed at attracting investment, and hence economic growth, to the areas near the railway line which links the two countries, including the relatively poor and isolated northern Mozambique. The Beira Development Corridor, linking central Mozambique and Zimbabwe, is less buoyant, but there are prospects for concessioning the Sena railway line and exploiting the Moatize coal reserves as part of Mozambique's plans to revitalize the Zambezi valley area. Other large projects are for mining of heavy sands in two areas of the country, and the $1,800m. Mpanda Ncua hydropower project downstream from Cahora Bassa.

Mozambique continues to be supported by substantial foreign development assistance and **debt relief**. In November 2001 the Paris Club group of major bilateral (government) creditors agreed to suspend all of Mozambique's **debt** payments following completion of the **Heavily Indebted Poor Countries (HIPC) initiative**. The debt remaining after this relief was about one-quarter of the US$2,700m. that would have been owed without HIPC assistance. The main challenges facing the Mozambican economy relate to achieving more equitable distribution of wealth. Growth has depended quite heavily on large, capital-intensive private-sector investments, whose impact on poverty reduction has been difficult to evaluate. Also, there are perceptions that the centre and north of the country, further away from the South African economy, have been excluded from the economic benefits of peace. Continued efforts are needed to improve the policy environment for the private sector, to promote SMEs, and to catalyse agricultural production and value added projects.

Mubarak, Hosni Muhammad Said

President of Egypt since the assassination of **Anwar es-Sadat** in 1981. Born in Lower Egypt in 1928, Hosni Mubarak has a military background. Appointed chief-of-staff of the air force in 1969 and commander-in-chief in 1972, he was promoted to the rank of general after the Arab-Israeli War of 1973. In April 1975 he was appointed Vice-President by Sadat. He was confirmed as President of Egypt in a referendum held shortly after Sadat's assassination. Re-elected in 1987, 1993 and 1999, Mubarak has broadly maintained the continuity of Egyptian policy at home and abroad, attempting to modify it without every really breaking with Sadat's legacy. Under Mubarak Egypt has restored its relationship with the other Arab states after being temporarily marginalized (following the Camp David accords and the peace treaty with Israel) and continued to support the position of the Arab states as a whole and the leadership of the Palestine Liberation Organization with respect to the Palestinian issue. It has remained a close ally of the USA, benefiting from this relationship considerably in terms of economic aid and political support. President Mubarak was the first Arab leader to be contacted by President George W. Bush following Iraq's invasion of Kuwait and was a key ally in the US-led coalitions against Iraq in 1990–91 and in 2003. Good relations (both diplomatic and commercial) have also been re-established with Russia.

At home, Mubarak has presided over a slow and uneven process of economic restructuring and has managed, by and large, to contain the militant Islamist groups. Major social and economic inequalities continue to exist, however, and **poverty** and social welfare remain to be effectively tackled. Mubarak's regime maintains strict control over political expression. Some commentators have referred to Egypt under Mubarak as a 'stalled state'. In 2005 a small political opening was achieved when it was agreed that, for the first time, there would be more than one candidate in the forthcoming presidential election, following a proposal by the government that was endorsed by a referendum. In the election, held in September, Mubarak was re-elected for a further term of office.

Mugabe, Robert Gabriel

One of Africa's most controversial leaders, Robert Mugabe became the head of government in Zimbabwe (formerly **Rhodesia**) on its **independence** in 1980, first becoming Prime Minister and later President. A former Marxist and guerrilla leader, involved for several years in the armed struggle against white minority rule, Mugabe has recently become notorious outside the country for his sweeping land reforms and other policies that have contributed to Zimbabwe's economic decline and current crisis. His repression of opposition to the ruling **Zimbabwe African National Union-Patriotic Front (ZANU-PF)** party has led to international concern.

Born in Zvimba District, north-west of what is now Harare in what was Southern Rhodesia, Mugabe was raised as a Roman Catholic and was educated in Jesuit schools. After qualifying as a teacher, he left to study at Fort Hare University in South Africa, where he met **Joshua Nkomo**, his future collaborator, whom he would defeat to become the first black Zimbabwean President. In 1960, after further studies abroad, Mugabe returned to Rhodesia, where, together with Nkomo, he established the National Democratic Party (NDP), which was later to become the Zimbabwe African Peoples Union (ZAPU), banned by Ian Smith's government. Mugabe later left ZAPU in 1963 to establish the ZANU, together with Rev. Ndabaningi Sithole and Herbert Chitepo. Sithole, ZANU's initial leader, nominated Mugabe as secretary-general of the party. ZANU was influenced by the **Pan-Africanist Congress** in South Africa, and also by Maoism—an association with the People's Republic of China was to remain a feature of Mugabe's international relations—while ZAPU was an ally of the **African National Congress** and supported a more orthodox pro-Soviet line on national liberation.

With other nationalist leaders, Mugabe was detained by the Rhodesian government in 1964 and remained in prison for 10 years. In 1974, on his release, he left Rhodesia for Mozambique and led the Chinese-financed military wing of ZANU, the Zimbabwe African National Liberation Army (ZANLA), in the war against Ian Smith's government. After Chitepo's death in a bomb attack in 1975, Mugabe unilaterally assumed control of ZANU from Mozambique. Later in 1975, after quarrelling with Sithole, Mugabe formed a militant ZANU faction, leaving Sithole to lead the moderate ZANU (Ndonga). Under increasing pressure from the international community, white minority rule could not continue indefinitely. In 1978 a process was agreed upon that would lead to an interim government, under Lord Soames, a British governor, in preparation for democratic elections. Elections to a new House of National Assembly were held in 1979, from which the United African National Council, which enjoyed British support, emerged as the majority party. Following elections held in 1980 Mugabe became Prime Minister of the first government of Zimbabwe.

Mugabe sought to incorporate the ZAPU into the ZANU-led government and ZAPU's military wing into the army. ZAPU's leader, Nkomo, was appointed to Mugabe's government, but was dismissed in 1983, prompting fighting between ZAPU supporters in the Ndebele-speaking region of the country and the ruling ZANU. Between 1982 and 1985 the **military** suppressed armed resistance in Ndebeleland and Mugabe's rule was secured. A peace accord negotiated in 1987 resulted in the merger in 1988 of ZAPU with the ZANU-PF. Mugabe brought Nkomo into the government once again, as Vice-President. In 1987 the position of Prime Minister was abolished, and Mugabe assumed the new office of executive President of Zimbabwe, gaining additional powers. He was re-elected in 1990, 1996 and, controversially, in 2002. In the presidential election held in March 2002 Mugabe was challenged by **Morgan Tsvangirai**, the leader of the **Movement for Democratic Change (MDC)**. Mugabe emerged as the winning candidate, receiving 56% of the vote, compared with 42% obtained by Tsvangirai.

In 2004 the African Union criticized the repressive nature of the Zimbabwean government. In legislative elections held in 2005 the ZANU-PF increased its majority. While South African observers characterized the result as reflecting 'the free will of the people of Zimbabwe', the MDC alleged that there had been widespread fraud.

When Mugabe became Prime Minister 70% of Zimbabwe's arable land was owned by approximately 4,000 descendants of white settlers. However, he reassured white landowners that they had nothing to fear from black majority rule. Mugabe initially favoured a 'willing buyer, willing seller' as a basis for the gradual redistribution of land. However, in 1999 and 2000 Mugabe used force to transfer land ownership from whites to blacks, and encouraged the forcible and often brutal expulsion of white settlers. This policy has attracted international condemnation. The land reform programme has led to a drastic decline in agricultural productivity: in a country that was formerly a net exporter of food some 5m. people now rely on food aid.

The USA has applied sanctions against Mugabe and other leading politicians in Zimbabwe, 'freezing' their assets and barring US citizens from engaging in any transactions or dealings with them. In December 2003, in protest against Zimbabwe's continued suspension from the Commonwealth, Mugabe withdrew the country from that organization. Increasingly excluded from many sections of the international community, Zimbabwe has renewed it ties with the People's Republic of China, which has been willing to exchange aid and loans for minerals concessions.

Muhammed, Gen. Murtala Ramat

Brig. (later Gen.) Murtala Ramat Muhammed replaced **Col Yakubu Gowon** as Head of State in Nigeria in 1975, following a coup. He was vigorous in his attempts to eradicate **corruption**, but was assassinated after only a few months in office.

Muluzi, (Elson) Bakili

President of Malawi in 1994–2004. Muluzi succeeded **Dr Hastings Banda**, in whose Cabinet he had formerly served. Initially welcomed with great enthusiasm, after the dictatorship of Banda, he freed political prisoners and allowed greater freedom of expression. Muluzi initiated the introduction of multi-party politics. However, he was obliged to reshuffle his Cabinet at the end of 2000 after donor countries and agencies, opposition parties, religious leaders and civil rights groups had criticized his inaction *vis-à-vis* reports of fraud and **corruption** in his government. In July 2002 the National Assembly rejected a proposed constitutional amendment that would have allowed Muluzi to seek a third five-year presidential term. In January 2003 popular protests led to the abandonment of a further attempt by Muluzi to extend his tenure of office.

Museveni, Gen. Yoweri Kaguta

President of Uganda since 1986. Born in 1944, Museveni attended university in Tanzania, where he became involved with the **Frente de Libertação de Moçambique (Frelimo—Mozambique Liberation Front)**, from which he learnt the techniques of guerrilla warfare. After briefly serving in the Ugandan government, Museveni fled to Tanzania in 1971 when **Idi Amin** overthrew **Milton Obote**, returning in 1980. In 1986 Museveni overthrew the regime of Lt-Gen. Basilio Okello following a military campaign waged by the National Resistance Army, the military wing of the National Resistance Movement, which was led by Museveni. In 1996 Museveni was elected as President for the first time. In a presidential election held in 2001 he was re-elected. In June 2005 the Ugandan Parliament approved a constitutional amendment to allow Museveni to seek a third presidential term of office in 2006.

Muslim Brotherhood

Islamic organization established by Hassan al-Banna, which has branches virtually throughout the Middle East and **North Africa**. Now an effective and recognized political organization in Egyptian politics after many years of being harassed and marginalized by successive regimes. Considered 'moderate' in comparison with many of the more extremist Islamist groups.

Mwanawasa, Levy Patrick

President of Zambia since 2002, following his victory in a presidential election, held in December 2001, which the incumbent President, **Frederick Chiluba**, had chosen not to contest. Since his election Mwanawasa removed aides of the former President from the government and embarked on a programme of economic reform and privatization. He has also initiated the investigation of **corruption** alleged to have occurred under Chiluba, and has pressed for Chiluba's immunity from prosecution to be lifted.

N

An-Nahda (Renaissance Movement)

Algerian Islamist political grouping, led by Lahbib Adami. Suppressed after the declaration of a state of emergency in March 1992.

An-Nahda (Renaissance Party)

Outlawed Tunisian Islamic fundamentalist party. Its membership are, for the most part, in jail, in hiding or in exile. Led by Rachid Ghannouchi, the an-Nahda party was originally established in the 1960s as the **Mouvement de la tendance islamique (MTI—Islamic Tendency Movement)**, a peaceful Islamic movement dedicated to creating an Islamic society in Tunisia. It has been illegal ever since, despite widespread support in the country, and has regularly been brutally suppressed.

Namibia, Republic of

The Republic of Namibia (formerly known as **South West Africa**) lies in south-western Africa, with South Africa to the south and south-east, Botswana to the east and Angola to the north. The country has a long coastline on the Atlantic Ocean. The narrow Caprivi Strip, between Angola and Botswana in the north-east, extends Namibia to the Zambezi river, giving it a border with Zambia. The arid Namib Desert stretches along the west coast, while the easternmost area is part of the Kalahari Desert. Namibia is 824,292 sq km in area. At mid-2003 the population was estimated at 1,987,000. The official language is English; however, most of the African ethnic groups have their own languages. At the 1991 census the most widely-spoken languages were Ovambo (used by 50.6% of the population), Nama (12.5%) and Kavango (9.7%). In addition, **Afrikaans** and German are widely used. About 90% of the population are Christians. The capital is Windhoek, whose population was estimated at 236,517 at mid-2003.

Political profile

Executive authority is held by the President, who is the Head of State. According to the Constitution, the President shall be directly elected by universal adult suffrage for a term of five years, and permitted to hold office for a maximum of two terms. (In late 1998 legislation was approved whereby the Constitution was to be exceptionally amended to allow the incumbent President to seek a third term of office.) Legislative power is vested in the National Assembly, comprising 72 members directly elected by universal adult suffrage and as many as six non-voting members nominated by the President. The National Assembly has a maximum term of five years. An advisory National Council, comprising two representatives from each of the country's 13 regional councils, elected for a six-year period, operates as the second chamber of parliament.

In a presidential election held on 15–16 November 2004 Hifikepunye Pohamba, the candidate of the SWAPO Party of Namibia (SWAPO), was the successful candidate, receiving 76.44% of the votes.

Following a general election held on 15–16 November 2004, the distribution of seats in the National Assembly was as follows: SWAPO 55; Congress of Democrats (CoD) 5; Democratic Turnhalle Alliance of Namibia (DTA) 4; National Unity Democratic Organisation (NUDO) 3; United Democratic Front (UDF) 3; Republican Party 1; Monitor Action Group (MAG) 1. The Namibia Movement for Democratic Change (NMDC) and the South West African National Union (SWANU) both contested the election but failed to win any seats in the National Assembly.

History

South West Africa became a German possession in 1884. During the First World War South African forces occupied South West Africa in 1914, and in 1915 Germany surrendered the territory. In 1920 the League of Nations entrusted South Africa with a mandate to administer South West Africa. No trusteeship agreement was concluded with the UN after the Second World War, and in 1946 the UN refused South Africa's request for permission to annex South West Africa. In 1950 the International Court of Justice issued a ruling that the area should remain under international mandate and that South Africa should submit it to UN control. South Africa refused to comply with this judgment. Namibia did not finally achieve **independence** until 21 March 1990.

Namibia's first post-independence presidential and legislative elections in December 1994 resulted in overwhelming victories for **Samuel Nujoma**, the leader of the external wing of the South West Africa People's Organization (SWAPO) who had been elected as Namibia's first President by a Constituent Assembly in 1990, and SWAPO. Nujoma was elected for a second term as President, receiving 76.3% of the votes cast; his only challenger was the President of the DTA, Mishake Muyongo. SWAPO secured 53 of the elective seats in the National Assembly, while the DTA won 15 seats and the UDF two. The remaining two seats were won by the Democratic Coalition of Namibia and the MAG. In October 1997 an exceptional constitutional amendment, that would allow Nujoma to seek re-election for a third term as President, was approved by the National Assembly.

In 1999 Nujoma declared a state of emergency in the Caprivi region following an armed attack by members of an organization styling itself the Caprivi Liberation Army (CLA) on targets in the regional capital, Katima Mulilo.

Presidential and legislative elections held on 30 November and 1 December 1999 resulted in an overwhelming victory for Nujoma and SWAPO, while the CoD apparently won support at the expense of the DTA. In the presidential election Nujoma was returned for a third (and final) term of office with 76.8% of the votes. SWAPO won 55 of the elective seats in the National Assembly, while the CoD and the DTA each won seven seats.

In elections held on 15–16 November 2004 Hifikepunye Pohamba, the candidate of SWAPO, was elected, receiving 76.4% of the votes cast, while his nearest rival, Ben Ulenga (the founder of the CoD), secured 7.3%. SWAPO also achieved a decisive victory in the elections to the National Assembly, retaining 55 of the 72 seats with 76.1% of the national vote. The CoD increased its share of the vote but won only five seats, compared with seven in the 1999 elections. The DTA took four seats, the UDF three and the MAG one seat, while two newly reactivated parties, the NUDO and the Republican Party, won three seats and one seat, respectively. (Following claims of electoral irregularities by members of the opposition a recount was held in March 2005: with the exception of the CoD all parties received a smaller number of votes, however, the overall allocation of seats remained the same.)

International relations

Following the attack on Katima Mulilo by Caprivi separatists in August 1999, the Namibian government alleged that the **União Nacional para a Independência Total de Angola (UNITA)** was lending military and logistical support to the CLA. There was considerable speculation that not only was Caprivi an important supply route for UNITA, but also that the Angolan rebel movement was attempting to divert resources of the Namibian armed forces away from the conflict in the Democratic Republic of the Congo (DRC). Tensions in the region of the Namibia–Angola border escalated from late 1999, after the two countries began joint patrols targeting UNITA, and the Namibian government authorized the Angolan armed forces to launch attacks against UNITA from Namibian territory. In 2002 the Namibian government welcomed the signing of a formal cease-fire agreement by the Angolan government and UNITA. Following independence, Namibia became a member of the UN, the **Commonwealth**, the **Organization of African Unity** and the Southern African Development Co-ordination Conference—now the **Southern African Development Community (SADC)**. Namibia has forged close links with post-**apartheid** South Africa. From August 1998 Namibia, which was participating in regional efforts to resolve the conflict in the DRC, supported a Zimbabwean-led initiative by members of SADC (notably excluding South Africa) for military intervention in support of the regime of President **Laurent-Désiré Kabila**; as many as 2,000 Namibian troops were subsequently dispatched to the DRC. All Namibian troops had been withdrawn by the end of 2002. Germany has been a major aid donor to Namibia since independence, and relations are generally close, although members of Namibia's Herero ethnic group have sought compensation from Germany for suffering inflicted on the Herero under German rule.

Namibia, economy

In 2003, according to estimates by the **World Bank**, Namibia's gross national income (GNI), measured at average 2001–03 prices, was US $4,839m., equivalent to US $1,870 per head (or $6,620 per head on an international purchasing-power parity basis). During 1990–2003, it was estimated, the population increased at an average annual ratc of 2.8% per year, while gross domestic product (GDP) per head increased, in real terms, by an average of 0.7% per year. Overall GDP increased, in real terms, at an average annual rate of 3.9% in 1990–2003. Real GDP increased by 3.7% in 2003. The annual rate of inflation averaged 8.6% in 1992–2003 and was 7.3% in 2003; consumer prices increased by 7.2% in 2003. Mineral production, cattle ranching, fishing, tourism are important sectors of Namibia's economy. In 2001 the major markets for Namibia's exports were the members states of the **European Union (EU)** and the USA. The EU and the USA were also the principal suppliers of imports in that year. The national currency is the Namibian dollar (N $). In 2004 the average exchange rate was US $1 = N $6.4597.

Namibia's economy relies heavily on the extraction and processing of minerals, on the processing of fish and on other manufactures for export. Namibia is the world's fifth largest producer of uranium and a primary source of gem-quality **diamonds**. Concerns about the depletion of its diamond reserves were assuaged in 2005 by the discovery of new productive sources, especially around the Marshall Fork deposit off Lüderitz. Minerals provide 54% of Namibia's exports, of which diamonds account for 34% and uranium 10%. Cattle and sheep grazing dominate **agriculture**, and the country has one of the richest potential **fisheries** in the world. The main economic challenges facing the government in the short term are to reduce the public-sector budget deficit, reform the civil service, create new jobs by attracting inward investment, improve efficiency and sustainability of social sector spending and use resources more efficiently. In the medium and longer term, Namibia has a narrow economic base, which makes it vulnerable to external influences. Namibia's economy is still dominated by South Africa, with the Namibian dollar pegged to the South African rand. More than 80% of its trade is with, or via, South Africa.

A major challenge is to develop new sources of growth by diversifying away from primary products. An example of such diversification is tourism. The government has a strategy of promoting low-volume, high quality tourism that will have a limited impact on the environment. The depreciation of the South African rand and events elsewhere in the world have the potential to increase tourism in Namibia and the region as a whole.

The government is also seeking to encourage foreign investment. It has created an export processing zone (EPZ) around the deep-water port of Walvis Bay. The development of transport links, in particular the trans-Kalahari and trans-Caprivi highways connecting the South African province of Gauteng and the Zambian and Katangan copperbelts with Walvis Bay, would provide a potentially significant boost to the economy. Manufacturing capacity remains limited, however, and provides little employment. One promising new development is the Ramatex garment plant (a Malaysian investment) outside Windhoek. Growth of 5.7% in the manufacturing sector in 2004 was an encouraging sign that the hitherto narrow base of the Namibian economy was beginning to expand. The central bank forecast that real GDP would increase by 3.8% in 2004–05, owing to increased output by the diamond sector, strong growth in manufacturing and improved yields from agriculture and fishing. Serious challenges for the government include the economic development of the impoverished northern region of the country and tackling **HIV/AIDS**. The indirect costs of HIV/AIDS, added to the direct costs of medical care, have been predicted to produce losses to the Namibian economy equivalent to some 20% of GDP over 2005. Combating this impact and seeking a solution will remain crucial to Namibia's continued prosperity.

Nasser, Gamal Abdel

Egyptian Prime Minister in 1954–56 and President in 1956–70. A pragmatic populist regarded as the pioneer of **Arab socialism** and the leader of the Arabs in one of the most critical periods in their history, Nasser was born on 15 January 1918 in the poor Alexandrian suburb of Bacos to southern Egyptian parents. Nasser was able to attend the Royal Military Academy in Cairo after the signature of the 1936 pact which, for the first time, allowed the lower class youth to join it. He graduated in July 1938 and joined the Egyptian army. He fought in the first Arab–Israeli War in 1948, which increased his awareness of the Palestinian problem and of the contemporary Arabic case. Dissatisfied with the continuing British occupation and the **corruption** of the regime of King **Farouk**, he formed a semi-underground organization, the **Free Officers** (el-Dhobatt el-Ahrar), which ousted Farouk in 1952, forcing him to leave Egypt. The son of King Farouk, Ahmad **Fuad**, was declared king, although only a child. In 1953 the Free Officers deposed Fuad and declared Egypt a republic, with **Muhammad Neguib** as its first President. The remaining British troops were requested to evacuate the country and, by 1954, had done so. Neguib was himself deposed in 1954 by Nasser, who became Prime Minister. In 1956 he announced the nationalization of the **Suez Canal**—a move that was followed by the Suez Crisis and military intervention by Israel, Britain and France in a short-lived attempt to reverse the move. US pressure ended the efforts of the former colonial powers to intervene directly. Nasser was elected President for a six-year term. He was re-elected twice and remained President until his death in 1970. In the Middle East Nasser was highly praised for his nationalization of the Suez Canal, his subsequent agrarian reforms and his radical populism, and he achieved unprecedented popularity throughout the Arab World. He was admired for his support of Arab nationalism, and his domestic economic and social reforms that sought to modernize Egypt in the name of the Egyptian masses. He became recognized as a major international power-broker in the politics of the developing world. He was a founding leader of the **Non-aligned Movement**, together with India's Nehru and Indonesia's Sukarno. The defeat of the Arab armies in the Arab–Israeli War (1967) virtually destroyed Nasser and he resigned, retracting his resignation after demonstrations of popular support. In November 1967 he accepted **UN Security Council Resolution 242**, which called for the peaceful coexistence of Israel and Arab states in return for Israel's evacuation of the occupied Arab territories. Nasser remained a figure of major importance in Arab politics, acting as the elder statesman of the progressive Arab World, mediating between the Palestine Liberation Organization (PLO) and Lebanon to achieve the Cairo Agreement of 1969, and again between the PLO and the Jordanian army in 1970. He died of a heart attack in 1970.

Nasserism

An ideology or socio-political doctrine based on the thoughts and actions of **Gamal Abdel Nasser**. It emerged as a series of practical responses to the problems—domestic and foreign—that were encountered by Egypt following the **Free Officers**' coup. A form of populist authoritarianism, it emphasizes the role of the one-party state in economic and social progress at home and a radical anti-imperialist, **Third World** nationalist stance in foreign affairs. It remains an important current in the political life in Egypt.

Nasserist Party

Egyptian political party, founded 1991. Its chairman is Diaa ed-Din Daoud.

National Congress

Political grouping in Sudan, created in early 1999 by President **al-Bashir**. The National Congress is believed to be a proxy for the **National Islamic Front (NIF)**.

National Congress for Popular Forces

Egyptian political coalition.

National Democratic Party (NDP—Hizb al-Dimuqratti al-Wattaniyya)

Originally the Egyptian Arab Socialist Party, the Party was renamed in August 1978. Thereafter President **Sadat** himself took a considerable interest in the NDP, which was closely identified with the regime. With the resignation of Prime Minister Salem in 1978 from the Misr Party, more than 250 members of the

People's Assembly joined the NDP and after 1979 it became the dominant political party in Egypt, winning sweeping majorities in elections that year, and consequently achieving an overwhelming majority in the People's Assembly. Following the assassination of Sadat in 1981, **Hosni Mubarak** took over as President of the Republic and became chairman of the NDP as well as the Party's general secretary. For 20 years it dominated Egyptian politics, making Egypt in effect a one-party state. In parliamentary elections held in 2000, however, the NDP won only 388 of the 442 seats in the People's Assembly (compared with 410 in the previous election), which was considered a relatively poor performance. Following these elections, the NDP initiated an internal reform process in order to develop both its structures and principles.

National Entente Movement (MEN)

Algerian political grouping, led by Ali Boukhazna.

National Front for the Salvation of Libya (NFSL)

Libyan opposition group, founded in 1981 in Khartoum, Sudan. It aims to replace the existing regime in Libya by a democratically elected government. The Front's leader is Muhammad Megarief. In May 1984 Libyan intelligence uncovered a plot by the NFSL to assassinate Col **Qaddafi**. The plotters' hideout was attacked and a fierce gun battle ensued. 'Abu Nidal' was visiting Libya at the time and was staying in a nearby villa, waiting to leave for the airport.

National Islamic Front (NIF)

Sudanese political grouping. Founded by **Muslim Brotherhood** leaders (particularly Hassan at-Turabi, who, as attorney general under President **Nimeri**'s, played a key role in introducing Islamic law in Sudan), the NIF is widely regarded as the main political force behind the 1989 military coup. The **National Congress**, created in early 1999 by President **al-Bashir**, is believed to be a proxy for the National Islamic Front, which continues to dominate the Sudanese government.

National Pact (Tunisia)

On 7 November 1988 President **Ben Ali** invited Tunisia's seven political parties to join with representatives of the business community, the trade unions, the human rights community, the farmers' association, national **women**'s organizations and the lawyers' guild in co-writing the National Pact, a major consensus-based document establishing the rules of political engagement in a republican **democracy**, as well as the basic economic and foreign policy orientations of the country.

National Party (NP)

Political party supported overwhelmingly by **Afrikaners** in South Africa. The National Party (NP) came to power in 1948 committed to implementing a system of 'separate development' called **apartheid**, and to the entrenchment of Afrikaner-dominated white rule. This became the overwhelming 'national' objective, with increasing suppression of alternative views and political tendencies. The predominantly English **United Party** was initially regarded as the enemy in this 'nationalist' vision, as was the English-language press. It was not until the late 1950s and early 1960s, with the growth of black resistance at home, followed by a wave of African **independence** across the continent, that the possibility of a black African opposition even became conceivable. Even then, the major ostensible focus was on the danger of 'communism' as the universal threat—hence the introduction of the Suppression of Communism Act, later subsumed into a general law called the Internal Security Act. Even as late as 1982 an opinion survey showed that 80% of South African whites believed the government line that communism, not black discontent, was the greatest threat to South Africa's future. As the black African resistance movement took shape, however, the NP government banned the **African National Congress** and the **Pan-Africanist Congress** (in 1960), bringing them under the 'security' law as well. In 1977 19 Black Consciousness organizations were banned; in 1987, a decade later, 17 other black political organisations. National security became an excuse for a range of legislation that effectively restricted or repressed freedom of speech, and for the construction of an ever more elaborate system of apartheid. National identity increasingly became that of the **Afrikaner** nation, embattled in its laager (defensive circle) against all opposition from within, and, as world opinion moved increasingly towards hostility and sanctions, outside as well. After the resignation of **F. W. de Klerk** as leader (succeeded by Marthinus van Schalwyk) in 1996, the NP was renamed the **New National Party**.

National Progressive Unionist Group or National Union Progressive Party (Egypt—Hizb at-Tagamaa al-Watani at-Taqaddam al-Wahdawi)

The Egyptian Tagammu party was founded in 1976 as a party of the left in the tradition of the Arab Socialist Union. It was originally known as the National Progressive Unionist Organization and was led by Khalid Mohi ad-Din (Muhiyyidin), one of the few **Free Officers** from July 1952 still prominent in politics, and a Marxist. The party regards itself as a coalition of leftist forces and has historically included Nasserists, Marxists and Arab nationalists. It was critical of the 1978 Camp David Accords and Egypt's March 1979 peace treaty with Israel. It supports a more radical foreign policy and opposes the **National Democratic Party**'s privatization agenda, favouring instead a return to a national command economy. It made some attempts to break away from its élitist core and reach out to the grassroots, but it lacks a strong popular base, partly because government controls on labour organization and unions restrict its ability to mobilize its natural constituency among the Egyptian working class. It was only able to gain about 4% of the vote in the 1984 elections. The party has moved noticeably to the centre in recent years, dropping the word 'socialist' from its title in 1995 and voting to abstain from rather than to oppose **Mubarak**'s re-election referendum in 1999. Khalid Mohi ad-Din remains its leader, while Tagammu's secretary is Dr Rifa'at es-Said. It has a membership of about 160,000.

National Reform Movement (MRN)

Algerian political grouping, led by Abdellah Djaballah.

National Renewal Party (PRA)

Algerian political grouping.

National Salvation Junta

On 16 July 2003, while President **de Menezes** was in Nigeria, a small political party, the Frente Democrata Cristã (FDC), took power in a bloodless *coup d'état* in São Tomé and Príncipe. It was claimed that the FDC had connections with the former **'Buffalo Battalion'**, a group of South African-trained mercenaries who were believed to have participated in several regional conflicts. The FDC established a 'National Salvation Junta'. The coup was condemned by the international community, which demanded a return to civilian rule. Later in July, following successful mediation efforts, de Menezes returned to São Tomé, accompanied by President **Olusegun Obasanjo** of Nigeria. Under an amnesty for the coup leaders, de Menezes was reinstated as President.

National Union Movement

The official party of the Egyptian and Syrian regions of the **United Arab Republic** (UAR), from 1958 until 1961, when it was replaced by the Arab Socialist Union (ASU).

Nationalism

A political ideology claiming the existence of a 'nation' or people with a legitimate right to self-determination and political **independence**. Thus, Sahrawi nationalism identifies 'the Sahrawi people' as a nation with rights of self-determination and political autonomy. In most cases within the region, nationalism emerged as a political-ideological response to colonial occupation and the creation of a distinctive colonial society of Europeans and indigenous peoples and led to the development of 'nationalist' movements and nationalist struggles for liberation. Nationalism may also apply, however, to wider groups who identify themselves as a people—as in the case of 'African nationalism', in which 'the Africans' are identified as a people struggling for independence and autonomy against first European and subsequently 'Western' economic, social, cultural and political domination. In the contemporary situation, where the majority of nationalist movements have achieved the goal of formal political independence, but various forms of '**neo-colonialism'** or 'Western imperialism' are widely felt to prevail, new forms of 'nationalism' have emerged, crossing state boundaries and forging new alliances and networks. 'Islamism' (what many refer to as **Islamic fundamentalism**) as a political force may be seen as a form of cultural/religious nationalism, uniting people defined as a 'community' of Muslims against a common threat.

Nationalist Party

Egyptian political party.

Natural gas

Many of the major **oil**-producing countries are also producers and exporters of natural gas. Algeria ranks as the largest producer of natural gas in Africa, and as the fifth largest producer in the world.

Ndayizeye, Maj. Domitien

President of Burundi. Domitien Ndayizeye, a **Hutu**, succeeded Maj. Pierre Buyoya, a **Tutsi**, as head of Burundi's three-year transitional government on 30 April 2003. The government was established in November 2001 as part of efforts to end eight years of **civil war**. It provided for power to be shared between the Tutsi minority, which has traditionally ruled the country, and the Hutu majority. Ndayizeye served as Vice-President during Buyoya's 18-month term of office. Ndayizeye, a senior figure in the largest Hutu party, the **Front pour la démocratie au Burundi (FRODEBU—Front for Democracy in Burundi)**, faced the formidable challenge of maintaining good relations with Burundi's Tutsi-led government army while persuading Hutu rebels to stop fighting. Burundi's three previous Hutu presidents had been overthrown by the **military**. A transitional Constitution (which was drafted in accordance with a peace accord signed in August 2000) came into effect at the end of October 2001 and on 1 November a new government was installed. A new transitional legislature was inaugurated in the first week of January 2002. On 28 March 2003 Buyoya announced that he would transfer the presidency to Vice-President Ndayizeye when his 18-month term expired at the end of April. He stood down as agreed and power was transferred peacefully. At the same time as Ndayizeye became President, Alfonse Kadege of the **Union pour le progrès national (UPRONA—Union for National Progress)** was nominated as Vice-President.

Ndebele

Major ethnic or tribal grouping in Zimbabwe.

Neguib, Muhammad

Muhammad Neguib was born in Khartoum, Sudan, in 1901. He was educated at the Cairo Military Academy and during the Second World War he joined the **Free Officers' Movement**. The failed 1948 Palestine campaign reinforced Neguib's view that the Government of Farouk I was inefficient and corrupt. In July 1952 Gen. Neguib, Col **Gamal Abdel Nasser**, Abdul al-Hakim and the Free Officers forced Farouk to abdicate through a *putsch*. After the Egyptian Revolution Neguib became commander-in-chief, Prime Minister and President of the republic while Nasser held the post of Minister of the Interior. The young officers considered Neguib to be too moderate and in November 1954 he resigned as President and retired from public life, to be replaced by Nasser.

Neo-colonialism

A term used to refer to the system of economic, political and cultural links, which continue to tie a formally independent state to a former colonial power, thereby reducing its real autonomy and **independence**.

Neo-Destour Party

Established in the 1930s by **Habib Bourguiba** and his colleagues (including Mahmoud Materi, Taher Safer and Bahri Guiga) to replace the **Destour Party**—which had been the first political organization to challenge French colonial rule in Tunisia—as the vehicle for the nationalist movement in Tunisia. The Neo-Destour leadership had little in common with the traditional élites that dominated the Destour Party. They were, for the most part, members of a new intelligentsia of modest social origins with their roots in the provinces, educated in Franco-Arab schools, especially Sadiki College, in Tunisia and at university in France. The group who founded the Neo-Destour originally participated in the Destour, but decided early on that an effective nationalist movement would require a larger popular base. The new party included some members of the traditional élite, but reached beyond the privileged minority to involve ordinary urban and rural Tunisians. The Neo-Destour regarded itself as leading a mass nationalist movement whose objective, after **independence**, was modernization under the tutelage of intellectuals. It stressed the unified, corporate nature of Tunisian society and the ability of the party to represent the interests of this society as a whole. In fact, however, despite this strong political ideology, the Neo-Destour relied heavily on funding from the large rural landowners and merchants, and on the mobilization of the rural masses, for its success in displacing the Destour as the main vehicle for the nationalist movement.

Neto, Dr Agostinho

Early president of the **Movimento Popular de Libertação de Angola (MPLA—Popular Liberation Movement of Angola)**, Dr Agostinho Neto was a Mbundu *assimilado* and former political prisoner. In 1975 Angola achieved **independence** and the MPLA became the ruling party. Neto became the country's first President. He was succeeded on his death in 1979 by **José Eduardo dos Santos**.

New African Initiative – *see* New Partnership for Africa's Development (NEPAD)

New National Party (NNP)

South African right-wing, conservative political party, formerly the **National Party**. The New National Party (NNP) was led from 1996 by Marthinus van Schalkwyk from 1996 after the resignation as party leader of **F. W. de Klerk**, former President of South Africa.

New Partnership for Africa's Development (NEPAD)

In July 2001 the **Organization of African Unity (OAU)** adopted a New African Initiative, which was subsequently renamed the New Partnership for Africa's Development (NEPAD). NEPAD was launched in October at an inaugural meeting held in Abuja, Nigeria. NEPAD's founding documents were jointly formulated by the Heads of State of Egypt, Algeria, Nigeria, Senegal and South Africa. Its aim was to develop a 'holistic, comprehensive integrated, strategic framework for the socio-economic development of Africa. The priorities included: i) creating peace, security and stability; ii) investing in people; iii) promoting industrialization; iv) increasing information and communications technology; and v) developing basic infrastructure. Following discussions on NEPAD at a summit meeting of the **G8** group of industrialized nations in Canada in June 2002, an Africa Action Plan was announced. However, the Plan's provisions were widely criticized as inadequate by aid agencies and the international media. The extent to which the provisions will be implemented has also been called into question, given the difficulties experienced over the decades with attempts by the various African states to act co-operatively, collectively and effectively. The OAU was replaced in 2001–02 by the **African Union (AU)**, which has assumed responsibility for the NEPAD. NEPAD is ultimately answerable to the AU Assembly.

New Wafd Party (Hizb al-Wafd al-Jadid)

The Egyptian New Wafd Party, founded in February 1978, disbanded in June 1978 and reformed in 1983, gains some strength from its association with the old **Wafd Party**, which was founded in 1919 and enjoyed great popularity for its strenuous resistance to British interference in Egyptian affairs, but was banned in 1952. On the other hand, the party has not been helped by the fact that its leader, Fuad Seraq ad-Din, was associated with the party's prior history of **corruption**. The New Wafd has tried to place itself at the ideological 'centre' between the main historic traditions in Egypt of **Arab socialism** and private capitalism. It has been critical of the government's encouragement of foreign private investment and advocated a more balanced approach to the relationship between private and public sectors. It is led now by Nu'man Jum'ah, with Ibrahim Farag as secretary-general.

Nguema Mbasogo, Gen. (Teodoro) Obiang

President of Equatorial Guinea since 1979. An ethnic Fang, Obiang Nguema was born in 1942 in mainland Equatorial Guinea. He received his military training in Spain and, after **independence**, served under his uncle, President Francisco Macías Nguema, first as military governor of **Bioko** and then as presidential aide-de-camp. In 1979 he overthrew his uncle, who was subsequently executed. Although Obiang Nguema proclaimed an amnesty for **refugees** and released some 5,000 political prisoners, he retained the absolute control he had inherited. In the most recent presidential election in Equatorial Guinea, held in December 2002, President Obiang Nguema reportedly received almost 100% of the votes cast, opposition candidates having withdrawn owing to alleged electoral fraud and irregularity.

Niger, Republic of

The Republic of Niger is a land-locked country in western Africa, with Algeria and Libya to the north, Nigeria and Benin to the south, Mali and Burkina Faso to the west, and Chad to the east. Niger is 1,267,000 sq km in area. At mid-2003 the population was estimated at 11,972,000. The official language is French, but numerous indigenous languages, including **Hausa** (spoken by about one-half of the population), Tuareg, Djerma and **Fulani**, are also used (10 national languages were identified in 1991). Some 95% of the population are Muslims, the most influential Islamic groups being the Tijaniyya, the Senoussi and the Hamallists. Most of the remainder of the population follow traditional beliefs, and there is a small Christian minority. The capital is Niamey, whose population was estimated at 889,977 at mid-2003.

Political profile

The Constitution of the Fifth Republic, promulgated on 9 August 1999, envisages a balance of powers between the President, government and legislative Assemblée nationale. The President, who is elected by universal adult suffrage, is Head of State, and is accorded 'broad ordinary and arbitral powers'. The government, under a Prime Minister appointed by the President, is responsible to the Assemblée nationale, which is competent to remove the Prime Minister by vote of censure. The Assemblée nationale is similarly elected by direct adult suffrage.

In the second round of a presidential election held on 4 December 2004 **Col (retd) Mamadou Tandja**, the candidate of the Mouvement pour une société de développement—Nassara (MNSD—Nassara, Movement for a Development Society—Nassara) received 65.53% of the votes, thus defeating Mahamadou Issoufou, the candidate of the Parti nigérien pour la démocratie et le socialisme—Tarayya (PNDS—Tarayya, Niger Party of Democracy and Socialism), who received 34.47% of the votes.

Following a general election held on 4 December 2004, the distribution of seats in the Assemblée nationale was as follows: MNSD 47; PNDS 25 (including eight seats won by parties in coalition with the PNDS, namely the Parti nigérien pour l'autogestion (PNA—Niger Self-management Party), the Parti progressiste nigérien pour le rassemblement démocratique africain (PPN-RDA—Niger Progressive Party for the Democratic African Rally), the Union pour la démocratie et la République (UDR—Union for Democracy and the Republic) and Union nigérienne des indépendants (UNI—Niger Union of Independents)); Convention démocratique et sociale—Rahama (CDS—Rahama, Democratic and Social Convention—Rahama) 22; Rassemblement social-démocratique—Gaskiya (RSD—Gaskiya, Social Democratic Rally—Gaskiya) 7; Rassemblement pour la démocratie et le progrès—Jama'a (RDP—Jama'a, Rally for Democracy and Progress—Jama'a) 6; Alliance nigérienne pour la démocratie et le progrès—Zaman Lahiya (ANDP—Zaman Lahiya, Niger Alliance for Democracy and Progress—Zaman Lahiya) 5; Parti social-démocrate nigérien—Alheri (PSDN—Alheri, Niger Social Democrat Party—Alheri) 1.

History

Formerly a part of **French West Africa**, Niger became a self-governing member of the French Community in December 1958 and was granted **independence** on 3 August 1960. Hamani Diori, leader of the Parti progressiste nigérien (the local section of the Ivorian-dominated Rassemblement démocratique africain) and Prime Minister since December 1958, became Head of State. Diori was elected President in November 1960, and re-elected in 1965 and 1970.

In a military coup in April 1974 Diori was arrested, and Lt-Col (later Maj.-Gen.) Seyni Kountché, the armed forces Chief of Staff, became President. The new administration, headed by a Conseil militaire suprême (CMS), suspended the Constitution; the legislature was replaced by a consultative Conseil national de développement (CND), and political activity was banned. A draft 'national charter' was approved by a reported 99.6% of voters in a referendum in June 1987. In November Kountché died and Col (later Brig.) Ali Saïbou, the army Chief of Staff, was inaugurated as Chairman of the CMS and Head of State. In August 1988 Brig. Saïbou formed a new ruling party, the MNSD. In May 1989 an MNSD congress elected a Conseil supérieur d'orientation nationale (CSON) to succeed the CMS. A draft Constitution was endorsed by a reported 99.3% of voters in a referendum in September. At elections in December Saïbou (as President of the CSON, the sole candidate) was confirmed as President of the Republic for a seven-year term, while 99.5% of voters endorsed a single list of CSON-approved deputies to a new, 93-member Assemblée nationale.

A process of transition to civilian rule initiated in 1991 culminated, in 1993, in elections to the 83-member Assemblée nationale in which the MNSD won the greatest number of seats (29), but was prevented from resuming power by the rapid formation, following the elections, of the Alliance des forces de changement (AFC—Alliance of the Forces of Change), which included six parties with a total of 50 seats in the legislature; and in a presidential election, in the second round of which Mahamane Ousmane, the leader of the CDS, was the winning candidate. At legislative elections held in 1995 the MNSD won 29 seats and subsequently formed a 43-strong majority group with its allies in the Assemblée nationale. In January 1996 the elected organs of state were overthrown by the military. The coup leaders, who formed a Conseil de salut national (CSN), chaired by Col (later Brig.-Gen.) Ibrahim Baré Maïnassara. The CSN suspended the Constitution and dissolved the Assemblée nationale and suspended political parties. A revised Constitution was approved by some 92.3% of the votes cast at a referendum in May and the ban on political activity was lifted shortly afterwards. In a presidential election held in July Maïnassara was the successful candidate. In legislative elections held in November the pro-Maïnassara Union nationale des indépendants pour le renouveau démocratique (UNIRD—National Union of Independents for Democratic Renewal) won 52 of the Assemblée nationale's 83 seats. The CSN was formally dissolved in December.

In April 1999 it was announced that Maïnassara had been killed in an accident, although it was generally perceived that he had been assassinated in a *coup d'état*. A military Conseil de réconciliation nationale (CRN), under the chairmanship of Maj. Daouda Mallam Wanké, was to exercise executive and legislative authority during a transitional period, prior to the restoration of elected civilian institutions. A new constitution was approved by referendum in July. In the second round of voting in a presidential election held in October, Mamadou Tandja, of the MNSD, was the successful candidate. The MNSD was similarly successful in concurrent elections to the Assemblée nationale, winning 38 of the 83 seats.

In the second round of a presidential election held in December 2004 Tandja was re-elected to office. At elections to the newly enlarged 113-seat Assemblée nationale, held concurrently with the second round of voting in the presidential election, the MNSD won the largest number of seats, obtaining 47, while allied pro-presidential parties secured a further 41 seats.

Northern Niger was destabilized from the late 1980s by a rebellion by Tuareg nomads, avowedly in pursuit of a federal system of governance. A peace agreement concluded between the government and rebel organizations in 1995 was subsequently undermined when Tuareg groups made common cause with groups of former Chadian **refugees** settled in the north east who sought greater autonomy. Neither insurgency had been brought to a definitive conclusion by early 2005.

International relations
The assumption of power by the CRN in April 1999 was condemned by the USA, France and Niger's other Western creditors. In 2000, however, the USA announced an end to sanctions imposed after Maïnassara's death. French co-operation was also resumed from 2000. Niger has forged closed relations with Libya, although that country, too, denounced the military take-over in 1999. Niger and Benin presented their final submissions concerning the disputed ownership of a number of small islands along their common border to the International Court of Justice for arbitration in early 2005. In June 2001 Niger and Nigeria announced that joint border patrols of their common frontier would be instigated, in order to combat increasing cross-border crime and smuggling in the region. In March 2004 it was reported that the governments of Algeria, Chad, Mali and Niger were to reinforce security co-operation in the regions of their common borders.

Niger, economy

In 2003, according to estimates by the **World Bank**, Niger's gross national income (GNI), measured at average 2001–03 prices, was US $2,718m., equivalent to $200 per head (or $820 on an international purchasing-power parity basis). During 1990–2003, it was estimated, the population increased at an average annual rate of 3.4%, while gross domestic product (GDP) per head declined, in real terms, by an average of 0.9% per year. Overall GDP increased, in real terms, at an average annual rate of 2.4% in 1990–2003; growth was 4.0% in 2003. Consumer prices increased by an annual average of 5.7% during 1990–2002, although in 1994, following a 50% devaluation of the CFA franc, the rate of inflation averaged 36.1%. Consumer prices increased by 2.7% in 2002, but decreased by 1.6% in 2003. The mining of uranium and the raising of livestock are important sector of the economy. In 2004 the major markets for Niger's exports were France, Nigeria, Japan and the USA. Niger's principal suppliers of imports in that year were France, Côte d'Ivoire, Italy, Nigeria, Germany, the USA and the People's Republic of China. The national currency is the CFA franc (see the **Franc Zone**). In 2004 the average exchange rate was US $1 = 528.29 francs CFA.

Niger is one of the poorest countries in the world, with extremely poor social indicators and a land-locked, undiversified economy that is heavily dependent on a narrow export base (uranium, livestock). Moreover, Nigeriens are much poorer today than they were 30 years ago: GDP growth has been highly volatile and very low on average, while the population has more than doubled. An extremely poor natural resource base and low levels of human capital investment hamper Niger's growth prospects. The primary sector (which contributed about 41% of GDP in 2003) is dominated by rain-fed **agriculture**, while livestock production accounts for about one-third of the value added in the sector. Of the national population actively employed, 84% of men and 97% of women are involved in growing crops or raising livestock. Agro-pastoral GDP grew at an average annual rate of only 0.6% in real terms in 1969–2000, mainly as a result of an increase in the area cultivated. This has translated into an annual decline in agricultural GDP per head of more than 2%, and in an increase in the number of households lacking food security. Unlike most other Sahelian countries, which have experienced productivity gains in cereals, yields of Nigerien staples (millet, sorghum) are low and declining. Although economic performance improved in 2001–03, owing to a series of successful harvests, the effect of **drought** and **locust** infestation on the agricultural sector had a negative impact on growth in 2004 and created the preconditions for serious food shortages in 2005. Despite warnings by many agencies on the ground and requests for special assistance, the response of the international community was slow, and by mid-2005 a severe **famine** had developed in which more than 3m. people (including 1m. children) were at serious risk.

Economic growth is to a large extent determined by factors such as climatic conditions, and is heavily reliant on external assistance. Niger achieved sustained growth for a short period in the late 1970s, when activity was stimulated by high prices for uranium. In 1983–93, however, real GDP growth averaged -0.6%, owing to declining demand for uranium, two severe droughts, the real overvaluation of the currency and other market distortions, as well as poor management of public finances. This prolonged downturn, coupled with persistently high population growth, has been a main cause of the country's increasing **poverty** over the last two decades. The devaluation of the CFA franc in January 1994 restored some competitiveness to the economy, helping to invigorate growth, which reached an annual average of 4.3% after the change in parity. After increasing dramatically during the uranium boom, the share of the secondary sector in total production has stagnated around the current level of 18% over the past 10 years. Long-term growth in the tertiary sector (which provides about 41% of GDP) has been stagnant, although there has been a moderate improvement since 1995. The state's share in the formal economy remains important, but has been reduced in recent years.

Niger reached the enhanced **Heavily Indebted Poor Countries (HIPC)** initiative decision point in December 2000, a factor that should have resulted in more than $500m.-worth of **debt relief** by the time Niger reaches completion point of the initiative. Niger has recently reached the final phase of a three-year **Poverty Reduction and Growth Facility** programme worth approximately $42m. The aims of the programme remain consistent with Niger's **Poverty Reduction Strategy Paper**, agreed as part of the HIPC initiative. The objectives include the implementation of prudent macroeconomic policies, aimed at containing inflation and raising growth levels to 4%; and structural reforms, particularly in the area of public finance, and the privatization of key utilities. So far Niger has shown commitment to implement the programme of the **International Monetary Fund (IMF)**, and with improved weather conditions and the restoration of stability in Côte d'Ivoire, growth rose to 4% in 2003–04. The divestiture of the state petroleum company and restructuring of the state electricity company led the IMF to forecast growth of

4.2% in GDP in 2005. Further IMF loans of $12.4m. were promised to aid the continued improvement of economic performance.

Nigeria, Federal Republic of

The Federal Republic of Nigeria is a West African coastal state on the shores of the Gulf of Guinea, with Benin to the west, Niger to the north, Chad to the north-east, and Cameroon to the east and south-east. Nigeria is 923,768 sq km in area. The population was estimated at 124,009,000 at mid-2003. In 1963 the most widely spoken languages were **Hausa** (20.9%), **Yoruba** (20.3%), **Ibo** (16.6%) and **Fulani** (8.6%). English is the country's official language. In 1963 the principal religious groups were Muslims (47.2%) and Christians (34.5%), while 18% of the total population followed animist beliefs. The capital is Abuja, to which the Federal Government was formally transferred in December 1991; however, many non-government institutions remained in the former capital, Lagos. The population of Abuja was enumerated at 107,069 in the census of 1991. At mid-2003 the population of Lagos was estimated at 10,103,459.

Political profile

Under the terms of the Constitution of the Federal Republic of Nigeria, which entered into effect on 31 May 1999, executive power is vested in the President, who is the Head of State. The President, who is elected for a term of four years, nominates a Vice-President and a Cabinet, subject to confirmation by the Senate. Legislative power is vested in the bicameral National Assembly, comprising a 360-member House of Representatives and a 109-member Senate, which is elected by universal suffrage for a four-year term. Nigeria is a federation of 36 states, comprising 774 local government areas. The executive power of a state is vested in the Governor of that state, who is elected for a four-year term, and the legislative power in the House of Assembly of that state.

In a presidential election held on 19 April 2003, the incumbent (since 1999) President, **Gen. (retd) Olusegun Obasanjo**, the candidate of the People's Democratic Party (PDP), received 61.94% of the votes and was duly re-elected.

Following an election held on 12 April 2003, the distribution of seats in the House of Representatives was as follows: PDP 213; All Nigeria People's Party (ANPP) 95; Alliance for Democracy (AD) 31; United Nigeria People's Party (UNPP) 2; All Progressive Grand Alliance (AGPA) 2; National Democratic Party (NDP) 1; People's Redemption Party (PRP) 1; People's Salvation Party (PSP) 1. (The distribution of seats is based on votes cast in 346 of the 360 constituencies of the House of Representatives, received on 2 May 2003.)

Following an election held on 12 April 2003, the distribution of seats in the Senate was as follows: PDP 73; ANPP 29; AD 6. (The distribution of seats is based on votes cast in 107 of the 109 districts of the Senate, received on 2 May 2003.)

History

The territory of present-day Nigeria, except for the section of former German-controlled Cameroon, was conquered by the United Kingdom, in several stages, during the second half of the 19th century and the first decade of the 20th century. In 1947 the United Kingdom introduced a new Nigerian Constitution, establishing a federal system of government, based on three regions: Northern, Western and Eastern. On 1 October 1960 the Federation of Nigeria achieved **independence**, initially as a constitutional monarchy. In 1961 a revised Constitution was adopted, and the country was renamed the Federal Republic of Nigeria, although it remained a member of the **Commonwealth**.

In 1964, in the first national election after independence, to the federal House of Representatives, the Nigerian National Alliance, which was dominated by the Northern People's Congress (NPC), achieved a large majority. In 1966, following two coups, the **military** assumed power. Following a further, bloodless coup in 1975, power was eventually transferred to newly elected civilian authorities in 1979 and a new constitution came into effect. In 1983, however, the civilian government was again deposed in a military coup. Following a further military coup in 1985, led by **Maj.-Gen. (later Gen.) Ibrahim Babangida**, a new military administration, the Armed Forces Ruling Council (AFRC), was established, with Babangida as President. Programmes of transition, pursued under the regime of Babangida and that of his successor (from 1992), Gen. **Sani Abacha**, with the aim of returning Nigeria to civilian rule were thereafter repeatedly delayed, postponed or otherwise impeded.

In 1986 Nigeria's acceptance as a full member of the Organization of the Islamic Conference prompted concern in the non-Muslim sector of the population at increasing 'Islamization' in Nigeria. In 1990 the Movement for the Survival of the Ogoni People (MOSAP) was formed to co-ordinate opposition to the exploitation of petroleum reserves in territory of the Ogoni ethnic group (Ogoniland), the south-central Rivers State, by the Shell Petroleum Development Company of Nigeria. In November 1995 the execution of nine Ogoni MOSOP activists, who had been convicted of involvement in the murder, in 1994, of four Ogoni leaders, prompted Nigeria's suspension from the Commonwealth. In 1998, following Abacha's death, Maj.-Gen. Abdulsalami Abubakar, was inaugurated as Head of State. Civilian rule was restored in 1999, when, in elections held in January to a newly constituted bicameral legislature, the PDP secured 215 seats in the 360-member House of Representatives and 66 seats in the 109-member Senate; and, in February, Olusegun Obasanjo was elected as President. Following Obasanjo's inauguration as President, Nigeria was readmitted as a full member of the Commonwealth.

From late 1999 there was increased religious and ethnic unrest in northern and central Nigeria, owing to the introduction in some northern, preponderantly Muslim States, of Islamic, or Shari*'a*, law. This unrest intensified in mid-2001, when some 1,000 people were killed in fighting between Christians and Muslims in Bauchi (which had become the 10th northern state to adopt Islamic law). In federal legislative elections held in April 2003, the PDP emerged with an overwhelming majority in both legislative chambers (213 seats in the House of Representatives and 73 in the Senate), while the ANPP was the only other party to secure significant representation (95 seats in the House of Representatives and 28 in the Senate). At the presidential election held on 19 April (the first to be organized by civilian authorities for 19 years), Obasanjo was elected for a second term by 61.9% of the valid votes cast.

International relations
Nigeria has taken a leading role in African affairs and is a prominent member of the **Economic Community of West African States (ECOWAS)** and other regional organizations. Nigerian forces were prominent in peace-keeping and monitoring operations undertaken under the auspices of ECOWAS and of the UN in Liberia and Sierra Leone from the early 1990s. In 2002 the International Court of Justice ruled that the Bakassi peninsula, in the Gulf of Guinea, whose ownership was disputed by Nigeria and Cameroon, belonged to Cameroon. A commission, comprising Nigerian, Cameroonian and UN officials, was subsequently established to undertake the redemarcation of boundaries between Nigeria and Cameroon.

Nigeria, economy

In 2003, according to estimates by the **World Bank**, Nigeria's gross national income (GNI), measured at average 2001–03 prices, was US $44,172m., equivalent to $320 per head (or $900 per head on an international purchasing-power parity basis). During 1990–2003, it was estimated, the population increased, in real terms, at an average annual rate of 2.7%, while gross domestic product (GDP) per head rose by 0.5%. Overall GDP increased, in real terms, at an average annual rate of 3.2% in 1990–2003; growth was 10.6% in 2003. The annual rate of inflation averaged 24.8% in 1990–2003; consumer prices increased by 14.0% in 2003. The petroleum sector dominates the economy, and agricultural is also important. In 2004 the most important markets for Nigeria's exports were the USA, India, Spain, Brazil and Japan. The main suppliers of Nigeria's imports in 2004 were the USA, the People's Republic of China, the United Kingdom, Netherlands, France, Germany and Italy. The national currency is the naira. In 2004 the average exchange rate was US $1 = 132.888 naira.

As the most populous African nation and the leading sub-Saharan **oil** producer, Nigeria has vast but largely unfulfilled economic potential. Its generally poor macroeconomic performance in recent years reflects fundamental structural problems, notably poor infrastructure, especially in the power sector, and the independence of state governments, which has made implementation of national economic policy difficult. Most significantly, perhaps, economic development has been hindered by institutionalized and pervasive **corruption**. All of this has prevented diversification from the hydrocarbons sector, which contributes almost all revenue from merchandise exports. Strikingly, in 2002 some 66% of all Nigerians were living below the national **poverty** level, compared with 43% in 1985.

Nigeria and the **International Monetary Fund (IMF)** approved a one-year Standby Arrangement on 4 August 2000. However, this lapsed by mutual consent in October 2001 owing to inadequate performance in some of the major areas of economic reform. One area of relative success in structural reform has been a privatization programme. However, the timetable for this suffered a significant set-back through the collapse, in early 2002, of the sale of the national telecommunications carrier, NITEL. In March 2002 Nigeria and the IMF agreed that they would not pursue a further formal programme until after the next presidential election. Nigeria cannot apply to the Paris Club of official creditors for a programme of **debt** rescheduling or relief until an IMF programme is in place and a satisfactory track record of reform has been established. Growth in real GDP, which was only 3.83% in 2000, increased to 6.2% in 2004, largely as a result of higher oil prices and high levels of government spending. Poor budgetary controls and inadequate monetary management, however, contributed to high inflation, which, in turn, led to an unsustainable disparity between the official and parallel exchange rate for the naira.

Nigeria is a heavily indebted country, owing approximately $28,000m. to external creditors. The overwhelming majority of this debt ($22,000m.) is owed to official bilateral creditors (governments), which are members of the Paris Club. The remainder is owed in roughly equal amounts to private creditors and multilateral institutions (the World Bank and the **African Development Bank**). Despite these long-term concerns, however, recent statistics indicate healthy economic growth. In 2005, for the first time in decades, non-oil sectors were growing faster than the oil sector. Successful and credible economic reforms in 2004 have re-established confidence in Nigeria as a foreign investment location. Some $2,000m. in new foreign direct investment has reportedly been committed.

Nimeri, Gaafar Muhammad

President of Sudan in 1969–85. Towards the end of his presidency Nimeri aggravated tensions between the 'Arab' north of the country and the 'African' south by imposing Islamic law. This, together with popular discontent at the economic mismanagement of Nimeri's regime, was among the factors that prompted the bloodless military coup in which he was overthrown in 1985.

Nkomo, Joshua

Born to missionary parents in Matabeleland (now part of Zimbabwe) in 1918, Nkomo was educated in South Africa, where he came into contact with **Nelson Mandela** and other regional nationalist leaders. He returned in 1948 to Bulowayo where he became active as a trade unionist. In 1962 he founded the Zimbabwe African People's Union (ZAPU), which was almost immediately banned by the white Rhodesian government. Nkomo served prison sentences for his activism in 1964–74. His support was among the **Ndebele** people and this ethnic support base led him increasingly into conflict with **Robert Mugabe**, whose main support came from the majority **Shona** people. As tensions within **Rhodesia** increased, Nkomo left for Zambia, from where ZAPU and its military wing, the Zimbabwe People's Revolutionary Army, waged a guerrilla campaign against the white regime in Rhodesia. Nkomo was backed by the USSR, while Mugabe received support from the People's Republic of China. An alliance— the Patriotic Front—between ZAPU and Mugabe's **Zimbabwe African National Union (ZANU)**, co-ordinated the armed struggle. Zimbabwe eventually achieved **independence** in 1980.

Nkomo remained for several years a major political figure in independent Zimbabwe, but both he and his ZAPU followers were increasingly marginalized as Mugabe increased his influence in national politics, becoming President and effectively controlling the government and military. In 1982 Nkomo was accused of planning a coup against Mugabe, was dismissed from government, deprived of his passport and confined to Bulowayo. In the early 1980s conflict between the two main factions of the former nationalist movement deepened and Zimbabwe sank into a virtual **civil war**. Thousands of civilians were killed in Matebeleland. In 1987 Nkomo was appointed as one of Zimbabwe's two Vice-Presidents, but the position was little more than a sinecure. Mugabe moved Zimbabwe towards a one-party state and ZAPU effectively disintegrated. Without a power base or organized support, Nkomo was effectively neutralized and withdrew from politics. He died at the age of 82 in 1999.

Nkrumah, Kwame

Nkrumah, the driving political figure behind the **Gold Coast**'s campaign for **independence** from British colonial rule, became the first Prime Minister of Ghana in 1957, when independence was achieved. Nkrumah, a leading proponent of Pan-Africanism, was born in Nkroful, Gold Coast, and educated at a Roman Catholic seminary in Amisano. In 1935 he travelled to the USA to study and became active within the African Students' Organization of America and Canada, of which he was elected president. Subsequently, in the United Kingdom, he began campaigning in earnest for the independence of the Gold Coast.

Nkrumah returned to the Gold Coast in 1947 and joined to join the United Gold Coast Convention (UGCC). In the same year, however, he left the UGCC to form the Convention People's Party (CPP), whose aim was immediate independence. In 1949 he encouraged opposition to British rule through boycotts, strikes, and civil disobedience, for which he was arrested in 1950. Active internal resistance was orchestrated to a large extent by Nkrumah and this increased the international pressure which precipitated Britain's withdrawal from the Gold Coast. In 1951 Nkrumah's CPP won 34 out of 38 seats in the legislative assembly. He was released from prison in February of that year and agreed to a request that he should lead the new government, in co-operation with the British, towards independence.

On 6 March 1957 Ghana was declared fully independent and Nkrumah became Prime Minister. He was, accordingly, Head of State of one of the first countries in sub-Saharan Africa to gain independence. He envisaged for the future not only a strong, centralized and prosperous Ghana, but also a united Africa, in which independent states co-operated closely for the good of all. However, Nkrumah's style of leadership confrontational, as well as collaborative, and alienated many. The CPP, whose main strength was in the coastal areas, was opposed by local chiefs, and by the United Party, led by **Kofi A Busia** and J. E. Appiah. Nkrumah's increasingly dictatorial and suspicious manner alienated opinion at home and abroad. In 1964 he declared himself President for Life and banned all political opposition. In an attempt to retain power, human rights were disregarded as many potential opponents were arrested.

In February 1966, while Nkrumah was visiting Viet Nam, the Ghanaian army effected a *coup d'état*. It is widely believed that the coup was orchestrated with the aid of the US Central Intelligence Agency, which at this period was actively seeking to overthrow radical regimes world-wide. The CPP was banned and Nkrumah was dismissed as President. He died in 1972 in Romania.

Non-aligned Movement (NAM)

The NAM is an international organization of states which consider themselves not formally aligned with or against any major power bloc. It was formed in 1961 on the initiative of Josip Broz Tito, then President of Yugoslavia. The first conference of non-aligned heads of state, at which 25 countries were represented, was convened at Belgrade in September 1961, largely through the initiative of Tito, who had expressed concern that an accelerating arms race might result in war between the Soviet Union and the USA. Subsequent conferences involved ever-increasing participation by developing countries. The 1964 conference in Cairo, at which 47 countries were represented, featured widespread condemnation of Western colonialism and the retention of foreign military installations. Thereafter, the focus shifted away from essentially political issues to the advocacy of solutions to global economic and other problems.

North Africa

The region of the African continent north of the Sahara. It is usually defined as including Morocco, Algeria, Tunisia, Libya and Egypt, and may also include Western Sahara (the disputed territory between Morocco and Mauritania, whose right to self-determination was recognized as long ago as 1976 by the International Court of Justice, but which is claimed by Morocco) and Mauritania.

Nour, Ayman

Leader of the **al-Ghad** ('Tomorrow') political party in Egypt. A 40-year old lawyer, he and his party are viewed, particularly in the West, as the new face of political opposition in Egypt. In 2005 Nour contested the presidential election in Egypt—the first multi-candidate presidential election for more than 50 years—but was defeated by incumbent President **Mubarak**.

Nouvelle convention (NC)

Political party in Cameroon.

Nujoma, Dr Samuel Daniel

President of Namibia in 1994–2004. Leader of the South West Africa People's Organszation (SWAPO) which fought for liberation and self-determination in the 1970s and 1980s, and achieved **independence** for Namibia in 1990. Born in 1929, Nujoma assumed the leadership of SWAPO in 1962 and launched an armed struggle against South African rule, maintaining that struggle for almost 30 years. Nujoma was elected by a Constituent Assembly as the first President of the newly independent Namibia.

Nyasaland

Previous name for Malawi, after Lake Nyasa which borders the country.

Nyerere, Julius

President of Tanzania in 1965–85. Born in 1922, Nyerere's father was a local chief. In 1954, after studying abroad, Nyerere entered politics when he helped to establish the Tanganyika African National Union (TANU). TANU subsequently merged with the Afro-Shirazi Party of Zanzibar to form the People's Revolutionary Movement (PRM), which then became the main vehicle of the struggle for **independence**. As president of TANU and leader of the PRM, Nyerere campaigned throughout the country for independence from colonial rule, speaking on behalf of TANU to the United Nations in 1954. He served as Chief Minister of Tanganyika before it gained independence in 1961.

In 1964, Tanganyika and Zanzibar merged to form the United Republic of Tanzania, of which Nyerere was elected the first President in 1965. For the next two decades, as Head of State of Tanzania, Nyerere played a key role not only at home but also in regional politics. Within Tanzania he espoused a distinctive form of 'African socialism', maintaining Tanzania as a one-party state with a unified and coherent policy of 'self-reliance' for development. Nyerere's TANU government introduced a policy of forced collectivization, under the rubric of *ujamaa* or 'familyhood', which was resisted by the peasantry and failed to boost agricultural output. By 1976, at the end of the collectivization programme, Tanzania had been transformed from the largest exporter to the largest importer of agricultural products in Africa. Nyerere admitted his failure before relinquishing power in 1985.

Nzwani

Nzwani, formerly Anjouan, is one of the four main islands that constitute the Union of the Comoros. In 1997 the merger of two separatist movements, the Organisation pour l'indépendence d'Anjouan (Organization for the Independence of Anjouan) and the Mouvement séparatiste anjouanais (Separatist Movement of Anjouan), led to the establishment of the **Mouvement populaire anjouanais (MPA—Popular Movement of Anjouan)**, now the principal separatist movement on the island. In 2001 two attempted military coups on the island were suppressed. In that year some 76% of the electorate in the Comoros voted in favour of a new constitution, which provided for a greater devolution of power to the separate islands and renamed the Federal Islamic Republic of the Comoros as the Union of the Comoros.

O

Obasanjo, Gen. (retd) Olusegun

Born in 1937, Olesugun Obasanjo is an ethnic **Yoruba** and a Christian from the south west of Nigeria. He joined the army in 1958 and came to prominence in 1970 as the officer who accepted the surrender of Biafran forces in the 1967–70 **civil war**. Gen. Olseugun Obasanjo succeeded **Gen. Murtala Muhammed** as army chief and Head of State of Nigeria in 1975, after Muhammed's assassination—shortly after he had himself replaced **Col Yakubu Gowon**. Obasanjo made **corruption** and Nigeria's political difficulties his priorities. In 1979 he became the first modern African military leader to hand over power to civilian rule. Obasanjo returned to power as President of Nigeria in 1999. He was elected as civilian Head of State in 1999. Obasanjo was re-elected to the presidency in 2003, winning more than 60% of the votes in Nigeria's first civilian-administered presidential poll for 20 years. He has presided over the longest period of civilian rule in Nigeria since **independence**.

Internationally, Obasanjo helped to devise a common plan for Africa's economic recovery—the **New Partnership for Africa's Development (NEPAD)**. Within the **Commonwealth**, Obasanjo reluctantly supported Zimbabwe's suspension over political violence in March 2002. Obasanjo has been praised for improving Nigeria's poor infrastructure, but his management of the economy generally has been criticized.

Obote, Milton

Leader of the Uganda People's Congress, which in 1961 entered into an alliance with the Bugandan home rule party, Kabaka Yekka, to win a parliamentary majority. Obote replaced Benedikto Kiwanuka as Prime Minister. **Independence** followed in October 1962, and in the following year Uganda became a republic in the British **Commonwealth** and the Kabaka of Buganda became President. The alliance did not last. Early in 1966 Obote assumed emergency powers, dismissed and arrested a number of his ministers and dismissed the President. Two months later he introduced a new constitution, which precipitated a fresh clash between himself and the *lukiko* (the Bugandan assembly), and appointed himself President. Obote survived an assassination attempt in 1969, but was overthrown in a military coup in January

1971 while he was in Singapore attending a Commonwealth conference. He was replaced by **Idi Amin**. In September 1972, after having first gone to Sudan and then been forced to leave when **President Nimeri** pacified the south, Obote led an unsuccessful attempt to invade Uganda from Tanzania with a force of about 1,000. Seven years later, after Amin had been overthrown, Obote was able to return to Uganda. The provisional government installed by Tanzanian forces (whiched had helped overthrow Amin), under Dr Yusufu Lule, was dissolved by the National Consultative Council and Lule was deposed. He was replaced by Godfrey Binaisa, a lawyer who had previously held ministerial office under Obote. Binaisa was then himself deposed by the army and placed in detention while a pro-Obote Council took over the government of the country. At the end of 1980 Obote succeeded, by a small (and disputed) margin, in being elected as President again. He remained in power until 1985, when he was overthrown in a coup led by Brig. Basilio Okello.

Odinga, Oginga

Left-wing Kenyan politician. Vice-President and main rival to President **Jomo Kenyatta**, who had him removed from the vice-presidency and placed in detention.

Offman, Karl

President of Mauritius in February 2002–October 2003. Offman was elected as President by an extraordinary session of the National Assembly after the two previous incumbents—**Cassam Uteem** and Angidi Varriah Chettiar—had resigned, in rapid succession, over controversial anti-terrorist legislation.

Ogoni

Indigenous group in the Delta region of Nigeria. Known internationally for the Ogoni rights movement led by **Ken Saro-Wiwa** in opposition to the regime of **Gen. Sani Abacha**; and for the execution of Saro-Wiwa and other activists by that regime in 1995.

Oil

Oil is important to the gross domestic product and gross national product of many African countries. Nigeria is the largest oil-producing country in Africa, but Angola, Gabon, Equatorial Guinea, Egypt, Libya and Algeria, Sudan and the Republic of the Congo (ROC) have all also benefited from the exploitation and sale of oil. In many of these countries, however, oil has fuelled private accumulation, through **corruption** and kleptocracy on the part of the élites, rather than economic growth and improved living standards for the poor. Often, links between the national élites and the major oil corporations have been in part responsible. In the ROC, for example, the government is involved in increasingly tortuous deals with the oil industry in order to avoid financial scrutiny from the **World Bank** and the **International**

Monetary Fund (IMF), and its own citizens. In Angola, where about one-quarter of the country's oil revenues are unaccounted for each year, the state oil company, Sonagol, continues to receive secret signature bonuses from Western oil companies, which are concealed in offshore bank accounts.

Oil prices have tended to rise in recent years, particularly after the US-led intervention in Iraq and in the light of political uncertainties in the Middle East (particularly as regards Iran's nuclear policy), and in June 2005 broke through the $60 per barrel marker for the first time. The implications of high oil prices for non-producing African countries are likely to be quite severe, and it is not at all clear that oil-producers will benefit in any simple fashion, although there are already signs of growing interest on the part of the big oil-importing countries in developing closer links with governments in the African oil-producing countries and in various forms of collaboration to ensure access to new oil discoveries.

Olympio, Sylvanus

Head of State of Togo from 1961 until his assassination in 1963. He was succeeded by Nicholas Grunitzky, who was himself ousted a few years later by Etienne Eyadama.

Operation Artemis

The UN Security Council authorized the deployment of an Interim Emergency Multinational Force to Bunia, in the east of the Democratic Republic of the Congo, on 30 May 2001 in order to stabilize the security situation there, pending the deployment of UN forces later in the year. The Force was officially launched as a European Security and Defence Policy (ESDP) operation of the **European Union**—known as Operation Artemis—on 12 June. France, the main contributor of forces to Operation Artemis, was 'Framework (lead) Nation' for the operation.

Operation Licorne

French peace-keeping operation in Côte d'Ivoire from 2003 onwards.

Operation Murabambatsvina

Operation Murabambatsvina, or 'Operation Clear out the Trash/Rubbish' was initiated by the government of Zimbabwe in June 2005 in order to remove settlements that had grown up on the outskirts of major towns across the country in previous years. The programme was launched in the wake of a fiercely contested election, in which President **Robert Mugabe** had been unsuccessfully challenged by the **Movement for Democratic Change (MDC)**. The bulk of the clearances were in the capital, Harare, but they took place across the entire country. There are no reliable figures as to how many lost their homes as a result of this programme of 'slum clearance': the government figure is 120,000, while opposition groups have claimed as many as one million. Aid agencies suggest the total is about 300,000. The government's justification for this large-scale destruction (of what, in many cases, were quite substantial houses and not merely cardboard or corrugated iron shacks) and creation of homelessness on a mass scale was threefold: that the settlements consisted of illegal structures which constituted a health hazard and damaged Harare's fragile infrastructure; that they bred crime; and that the 'parallel market' of unauthorized businesses that flourished in these settlements, dealing in currency, goods and fuel, constituted a serious threat to the country's economy. Mugabe's opponents, however, regard it is a punishment of those from the settlements who voted so heavily against him in the recent elections and for the MDC, and a measure to disperse and disarm those who might foment an uprising against his regime.

Operation Palliser

British peace-keeping operation in Sierra Leone, from 2000 onwards.

Orange Free State

Afrikaner republic established in the 19th century, together with the Transvaal. The Orange Free State's refusal to accept Britain's plans for a Union of South Africa prompted the British government to embark on the **'Boer War'**.

Organisation commune Africaine et mauricienne (OCAM— Common African and Mauritian Organization)

In early 1961 a group of 12 French-speaking countries (which had met three times between October 1960 and March 1961) signed a charter establishing a Union Africaine et Malgache, later to be the Organisation commune Africaine et mauricienne (OCAM). In May 1961 a larger group of 19 met at Monrovia, Liberia (and thus came to be known as the **Monrovia Group**), and in 1962 accepted a draft charter for an Organization of Inter-African and Malagasy States. OCAM created a number of useful agencies, which were sometimes more effective than those of the **Organization of African Unity**, but politically its members were often divided. In the 1960s it was regarded as a weapon for **Félix Houphouët-Boigny** of Côte d'Ivoire against **Kwame Nkrumah** and in support of **Moïse Tshombe** in the Congo. In the Nigerian **civil war**, in which it tried in vain to mediate, Côte d'Ivoire and Gabon recognized **Biafra**, while the remainder were strongly anti-separatist. Some members had relations with the People's Republic of China, some with Taiwan. As the colonial period receded, the common French colonial heritage became a weaker link. There were a number of absentees at the 8th Congress, held at Lomé, Togo, in 1972 and **Zaire**, under Mobutu, withdrew from OCAM.

Organisation pour la mise en valeur du fleuve Sénégal (Organization for the Exploitation of the Senegal River)

Para-statal organization, established with Mauritanian and Senegalese government involvement, to develop the irrigation potential on either bank of the Senegal River. Has achieved some success, but much less than initially anticipated.

Organization of African Unity (OAU)

At the Conference of Addis Ababa (Ethiopia), convened in 1963, which brought together the foreign ministers of 32 African states in a preparatory meeting and then the Heads of State in the Heads of State Conference, the creation of an Organization of African States was discussed and a Charter of the Organization of African Unity (OAU) was drawn up, and signed by 30 Heads of State on 25 May 1963. The Charter was essentially functional and reflected a compromise between the concept of a loose association of states favoured by the **Monrovia Group** and the stronger federal idea supported by the **Casablanca Group**, and in particular by Ghana. In July 2001 the OAU adopted a **New African Initiative**, which was subsequently renamed the **New Partnership for Africa's Development (NEPAD**) and launched in October 2001. The OAU was replaced by the **African Union** in 2001–02.

Organization of Arab Petroleum Exporting Countries (OAPEC)

Established 9 January 1968. Its aim is to promote co-operation in the petroleum industry. Its member states are Algeria, Bahrain, Egypt, Iraq, Kuwait, Libya, Qatar, Saudi Arabia, Syria and the United Arab Emirates.

Organization of Petroleum Exporting Countries (OPEC)

OPEC was established in 1961 but began to exert its strength first in 1969, when Libya was able to challenge the smaller foreign **oil** companies and effectively nationalise its oil industry, under the new 'revolutionary' regime of **Muammar Qaddafi**. In 1974, OPEC restricted output and the price of oil rose sharply on world markets. Another price increase took place in 1979. These had a significant effect, exacerbating divisions between oil producing and oil importing countries in Africa, with the majority in the second category. The foreign **debt** incurred at this time was to have a nefarious impact on growth in many African economies during the 1980s and lead to the growing debt crisis of the 1990s. OPEC was willing and able to provide financial assistance to some African countries, but most of its aid went as 'fraternal solidarity' to other Muslim countries (e.g. Sudan).

Oromia

Largest region of Ethiopia, inhabited by the **Oromo**-speaking minority, where secessionist movements still exist and which has suffered from considerable repression by the Ethiopian regime.

Oromo

Major ethno-linguistic group that inhabits **Oromia**, in Ethiopia.

Oubangui Chari

Formerly part of the colonial territory of **Afrique équatoriale française (French Equatorial Africa)**. Now the Central African Republic.

Ould Daddah, Mokhtar – *see* Daddah

Ould Taya – *see* Taya

P

Pagalu

A small, mountainous, volcanic island in the Gulf of Guinea, which, together with **Bioko**, forms part of Equatorial Guinea and is part of the archipelago that includes the islands of São Tomé and Príncipe, which together constitute the Democratic Republic of São Tomé and Príncipe.

PAMSCAD

Programme of Actions to Mitigate the Social Costs of Adjustment. One of the early programmes introduced by the **World Bank** to mitigate the social costs of structural adjustment, unveiled for Ghana at a meeting in Geneva, Switzerland, in 1988. PAMSCAD was introduced largely in response to the criticisms contained in the **Khartoum Declaration** earlier in 1988.

Pan-African Conference

The first Pan-African Conference was held in 1900, followed by a second in Paris, France, during the peace conference of 1915. These first meetings were dominated by West Indian blacks, but the sixth, held in Manchester, United Kingdom, at the end of the Second World War, was attended by the principal African leaders—**Kenyatta**, **Nkrumah**, **Akintola**, **Nyerere** and **Banda**. It voiced demands for **independence** that would have seemed fanciful five years earlier.

Pan-African Parliament

Launched in 2004 by the **African Union (AU)**, the Pan-African Parliament (PAP) was the concrete expression of African leaders' determination to improve governance and alleviate **poverty** in Africa. It has had more than one year to set up its structures, nominate office bearers and organize itself, but its performance has been mixed so far. While parliamentarians agreed to send peace missions to Côte d'Ivoire and the Democratic Republic of the Congo, and made recommendations on the **Darfur** conflict, they missed opportunities to exercise a crucial function of parliaments, that of oversight. Among the key issues on the agenda of the March 2005 session was the **African Peer Review Mechanism (APRM)**, a voluntary appraisal of national governments' economic and political performance by fellow Africans. The assembly did pass a resolution, calling on national parliaments to urge their governments to accede to the APRM as a demonstration of their commitment to **democracy** and good governance. The parliamentarians did not go as far as they could have done, however. The APRM requires that each country's review report and recommended plan of action be publicly tabled in parliament. At every successive sitting, the assembly should compel members from APRM countries to report on their government's progress in implementing the national action plan in the five-year period between the reviews. This process has not yet been implemented. However, it could have a powerful impact on governance and economic policies in Africa, if the members take their role seriously. The assembly passed resolutions commending the AU's prevention of an unconstitutional take-over of power in Togo, but was conspicuously silent on widely reported abuses of election guide-lines in Zimbabwe's March election, failing to challenge transgressions that are tacitly backed by many African governments. Although the fledgling parliament has no legislative power in its early years, it can debate issues of continental importance and make its views felt through recommendations to the African Union Commission and the Heads of State. The Pan-African Parliament will be as powerful as the members of the Pan-African Parliament (MPAPs) enable it to be. If parliamentarians are supposed to represent their country's citizens rather than their government's, then MPAPs from countries such as Uganda, in effect a one-party state, lack a certain credibility, while Libyan MPAPs are even less representative, as Libya has no national assembly. Even South Africa has been criticized for failing to include a member of the official opposition in its delegation. MPAPs are not directly elected to the Pan-African Parliament, but it is of vital importance that they represent and are seen to represent the interests of all their national 'constituencies' and apply appropriate pressures and scrutiny both to their own governments and to the structures and apparatus of the AU Commission, and the Peace and Security Council. Only if the elected representatives of states with better records of democracy dare to raise the level of the debate and scrutiny will the PAP become more than a 'talking shop'.

Pan-Africanist Congress of Azania (PAC)

A black militant party in South Africa, which won three seats in the National Assembly in elections held in 1999.

Parti africain de développement (PAD—African Development Party)

Political party in the Central African Republic.

Parti africain de l'indépendance (PAI—African Independence Party)

Political party in Burkina Faso, founded in 1999. The PAI's secretary-general is Soumane Touré.

Parti comorien pour la démocratie et le progrès (PCDP—Comoros Party for Democracy and Progress)

Political party in the Union of the Comoros.

Parti congolais du travail (PCT—Congolese Labour Party)

Political party in the Republic of the Congo (ROC), formed in 1969. The PCT was the sole legal political party in the ROC in 1969–90. Formerly a member of the **Forces démocratiques unies (FDU—United Democratic Forces)**. The president of the PCT is Gen. Denis Sassou-Nguesso.

Parti démocrate et social chrétien (PDSC—Christian Social Democrat Party)

Political party in the Democratic Republic of the Congo, established in 1990. The president of the PDSC is André Bo-Boliko.

Parti des démocrates camerounais (PDC—Party of Cameroon Democrats)

Political party in Cameroon, established in 1991. The PDC's leader is Louis-Tobie Mbida.

Parti pour la démocratie et le progrès-Parti socialiste (PDP-PS—Party for Democracy and Progress-Socialist Party)

Political party in Burkina Faso, founded in 2001 by the merger of the PDP and the Parti socialiste burkinabè (Socialist Party of Burkina Faso). Third largest party in the Assemblée nationale after winning 7% of the votes and 10 seats in the general election of May 2002. The national president of the PDP-PS is Joseph Ki-Zerbo.

Parti pour la démocratie et la réconciliation (Party for Democracy and Reconciliation)

Political party in Burundi, established in May 2002 and led by Augustin Nzojlbwami.

Parti pour la démocratie et le socialisme (PDS—Party for Democracy and Socialism)

Political party in Burkina Faso, led by Félix Soubéiga.

Parti démocratique gabonais (PDG—Gabonese Democratic Party)

Political party in Gabon, founded in 1969. The PDG was the sole legal party in 1968–90. The PDG is led by **Omar Bongo**.

Parti gabonais du progrès (PGP—Gabonese Progress Party)

Political party in Gabon, founded in 1990. The PGP is led by Pierre-Louis Agondjo-Okawé.

Parti indépendant des travailleurs (PIT—Independent Workers' Party)

Political party in Burundi, founded in 1993. The membersship of the PIT is predominantly Tutsi.

Parti libéral (PL—Liberal Party)

Political party in Burundi, established in 1992. The membership of the PL is predominantly **Hutu**. The leader of the PL is Joseph Ntidendereza.

Parti libéral-démocrate (PLD—Liberal Democrat Party)

Political party in Cameroon, founded in 1991. The PLD is led by Njoh Litumbe.

Parti libéral-démocrate (PLD—Liberal Democrat Party)

Political party in the Central African Republic, led by Nestor Kombo-Naguemon.

Parti de libération du peuple Hutu (PALIPEHUTU—Liberation Party of the Hutu People)

Political party in Burundi. Originally formed in Tanzania in 1980 with the objective of advancing the interests of the Hutu people.

Parti pour la liberté et le développement (PLD—Party for Freedom and Development)

Political party in Chad, established in 1993. Boycotted the legislative elections in 2002. The PLD's secretary-general is Ibn Oumar Mahamat Saleh.

Parti nigérien pour la démocratie et le socialisme (PNDS—Niger Party for Democracy and Socialism)

Political party in Niger, founded in 1990. The leader of the PNDS is Mahamadou Issoufou.

Parti du peuple (PP—People's Party)

Political party in Burundi, established in 1992. Mainly **Hutu** membership. The leader of the PP is Shadraik Niyonkuru.

Parti populaire pour la réconstruction et le développement (PPRD—Popular Party for Reconstruction and Development)

Political party in the Democratic Republic of the Congo, established by **Joseph Kabila** during the Sun City negotiations in 2003. It comprises some 250 founding members, the majority of whom are former members of **Laurent-Désiré Kabila**'s government and members of Joseph Kabila's transition government.

Parti populaire pour le développement (PPD—Popular Party for Development)

Political party in Cameroon, established in 1997.

Parti pour la réconciliation du peuple (PRP—People's Reconciliation Party)

Political party in Burundi, established in 1992. The PRP's membership is predominantly Tutsi. The party is led by Mathias Hitimana.

Parti pour le redressement national (PARENA—Party for National Recovery)

Political party in Burundi, established in 1994. PARENA is led by Jean-Baptiste Bagaza.

Parti de la renaissance nationale (PAREN—Party of National Rebirth)

Political party in Burkina Faso, founded in 2000. PAREN's president is Kilachia Laurent Bado.

Parti du renouveau démocratique (PRD—Party of Democratic Renewal)

Political party in Benin, founded in 1990. The PRD is led by Adrien Houngbédji.

Parti républicain des Comores (PRC—Republican Party of the Comoros)

Political party in the Union of the Comoros, established in 1998. The leader of the PRC is Mohamed Saïd Abdallah M'Changama.

Parti républicain et démocratique social (PRDS—Republican and Social Democratic Party)

The ruling party in Mauritania, led by former **President Ma'aouya Ould Sid Ahmed Taya**.

Parti républicain du peuple camerounais (PRPC—Republican Party of the Cameroon People)

Political party in Cameroon, founded in 1991. The PRPC is led by Ateba Ngoua.

Parti du salut (PS—Salvation Party)

Political party in Benin, founded in 1994. The PS is led by Damien Modéran Zinsou Alahassa.

Parti social démocrate (PSD—Social Democrat Party)

Political party in Burundi, founded in 1993. Predominantly Tutsi membership. The PSD is led by Godefroid Hakizimana.

Parti social-démocrate (PSD—Social Democrat Party)

Political party in the Central African Republic. The PSD is led by Enoch Derant Lakoué.

Parti socialiste camerounais (PSC—Cameroon Socialist Party)

Political party in Cameroon. The PSC is led by Jean-Pierre Dembele.

Parti socialiste démocratique (PSD—Democratic Socialist Party)

Political party in Cameroon, established in 1991. The PSD is led by Nsame Mbongo Joseph.

Parti socialiste démocratique du Cameroun (PSDC—Democratic Socialist Party of Cameroon)

Political party in Cameroon. The PSCD is led by Jean-Michel Tekam.

Parti socialiste unifié (Unified Socialist Party)

Political party in Burkina Faso, founded in 2001 by members of the former Parti socialiste burkinabè (Socialist Party of Burkina Faso). The party's leader is Benoït Lompo.

Parti des travailleurs (PT—Workers Party)

Algerian political grouping, led by Louisa Hanoun, who contested the Presidential election held in April 2004.

Parti de l'unité nationale (PUN—Party of National Unity)

Political party in the Central African Republic. The PUN is led by Jean-Paul Ngoupandé.

Partido Africano da Independência de Cabo Verde (PAICV—African Independence Party of Cape Verde)

Major political party in Cape Verde. Established in 1956 as the Partido Africano da Independência da Guiné e Cabo Verde (PAIGC—African Party of Independence of Guinea and Cape Verde). Changed its name in 1981, following the 1980 coup in Guinea-Bissau. Sole authorized party in Cape Verde in 1975–90. After 1991 the PAICV became the major opposition party, until gaining 40 seats in the national assembly at the legislative elections of January 2001, when it won nearly half of the votes. The PAICV's president is José Maria Neves.

Partido de Aliança de Juventude, Operários e Camponêses de Angola (PAJOCA—Angolan Youth, Workers' and Peasants' Alliance Party)

Political organization in Angola.

Partido Angolano Independente (PAI—Angolan Independent Party)

Political party in Angola, led by Adriano Parreira.

Partido da Convergência Democrática (PCD—Party of Democratic Convergence)

Political party in Cape Verde. Established in 1994 by former members of the **Movimento para a Democracia (MPD—Movement for Democracy)**. The PCD is a member of the **Aliança Democrática para a Mudança (ADM—Democratic Alliance for Change)** formed in October 2000 by the PCD, the **Partido de Trabalho e Solidariedade (PTS—Party of Labour and Solidarity)** and the **União Caboverdiana Independente e Democrática (Independent Democratic Union of Cape Verde)**.

Partido Democrático Angolano (PDA—Angolan Democratic Party)

Political party in Angola, led by António Alberto Neto.

Partido Democrático Liberal de Angola (Liberal Democratic Party of Angola)

Political party in Angola, led by Honorato Lando.

Partido Democrático para o Progresso—Aliança Nacional de Angola (PDP—ANA, Democratic Party for Progress—National Alliance of Angola)

Political alliance in Angola, led by Mfufumpinga Nlandu Victor.

Partido Liberal Democrático (PLD—Liberal Democratic Party)

Political party in Angola, led by Anália de Victória Pereira.

Partido Nacional Democrata de Angola (PNDA—National Democrat Party of Angola)

Political party in Angola. The PNDA's secretary-general is Pedro João António.

Partido Reformador de Angola (PRA—Reform Party of Angola)

Political party in Angola, led by Rui de Victória Pereira.

Partido da Renovação Democrática (PRD—Party of Democratic Renewal)

Political party in Cape Verde. Established in 2000 by former members of the **Movimento para a Democracia (MPD—Movement for Democracy)**.

Partido Renovador Democrático (PRD—Democratic Renewal Party)

Political party in Angola, led by Luís dos Passos.

Partido Renovador Social (PRS—Social Renewal Party)

Political party in Angola. The president of the PRS is Eduardo Kwangana.

Partido Social Democrata (PSD—Social Democrat Party)

Political paty in Angola, led by Bengui Pedro João.

Partido Social Democrata de Angola (PSDA—Social Democrat Party of Angola)

Political party in Angola, led by André Milton Kilandonoco.

Partido Socialista Democrático (PSD—Democratic Socialist Party)

Political party in Cape Verde, established in 1992. The PSD's secretary-general is João Além.

Partido de Trabalho e Solidariedade (PTS—Party of Labour and Solidarity)

Political party in Cape Verde, established in 1998. Member of the **Aliança para a Mudança Democrática (ADM—Alliance for Democratic Change)**, a coalition formed in October 2000 by the **Partido da Convergência Democrática (PCD—Party of Democratic Convergence)**, the PTS and the **União Caboverdiana Independente e Democrática (Independent Democratic Union of Cape Verde)**.

Peasants' and Workers' Defence Committees

Political organizations established by **Jerry Rawlings** in Ghana to support his coup in December 1981. The response to their formation was reported to have been 'slow, suspicious and cynical'—see also **Workers' and Soldiers' Defence Committees**.

Pemba

One of the islands that forming **Zanzibar**, now a part of Tanzania.

Peul – *see* Fulani

Pires, Pedro de Verona Rodrigues

President of Cape Verde since 2001. A veteran left-wing politician, Pedro Pires was elected to the presidency by a margin of only 17 votes more than his nearest rival, **Carlos Veiga**. He succeeded António Mascarenhas Monteiro. Pires and Veiga have been Cape Verde's dominant political personalities since **independence** in 1975. Both men are former Prime Ministers of Cape Verde.

POLISARIO Front – *see* Frente Popular para la Liberación de Saguia el-Hamra y Río de Oro

Popular Unity Party (PUP—Parti de l'unité populaire)

Tunisian political party.

Population growth

Half of the population of sub-Saharan Africa is under 16 and more than 70% were born after **independence**. Regional population growth rates are highest in Somalia (4.17%), Liberia (4.05%), Sierra Leone (3.80%), Eritrea (3.65%), Niger (3.62%) and Uganda (3.24%).

Portuguese Guinea – *see* Guinea-Bissau

Poverty

Sub-Saharan Africa is the poorest region in the world by most criteria. In terms of gross domestic product (GDP) per head (in terms of purchasing power parity), Africa achieves about US $1,500, compared with $2,400 for South Asia and around $4,000 for East Asia and the Pacific. It is the only region that has experienced an overall decline (from about $1,800 in 1975) in this measure over the last decade. While the percentage of the population living on less than $2 a day is only 23.8 in South Africa, in Kenya it is 58.6, in Tanzania 59.7, in Malawi 76.7, in Ghana 78.5, in Zambia 87.4, and in Uganda 96.4.

Poverty Reduction and Growth Facility (PRGF)

A facility provided by the **International Monetary Fund (IMF)** under specific conditions to poor developing countries. Linked increasingly with the obligation to produce a **Poverty Reduction Strategy Paper** and to adhere to specific guide-lines produced by the IMF and the **World Bank**.

Poverty Reduction Strategy Paper (PRSP)

From the turn of the millennium the **World Bank** and the **International Monetary Fund (IMF)** began to develop a new framework for **poverty** reduction, with the idea that developing countries should sign up to a defined programme of public expenditure as part of a national poverty reduction strategy and should produce a policy paper (or PRSP) to clarify the main elements of this strategy, in collaboration with a wide range of national stakeholders, including groups and organizations drawn from civil society. These PRSPs, as they are known, now provide a framework widely accepted by the bilateral and multilateral lending agencies and donors, for the allocation of development assistance. Many countries in sub-Saharan Africa now have produced a PRSP, including: Benin, Burkina Faso, Cameroon, Chad, Djibouti, Ethiopia, Gambia, Ghana, Guinea, Madagascar, Malawi, Mali, Mauritania, Mozambique, Niger, Rwanda, Senegal, Tanzania, Uganda and Zambia. For some, this framework provides a new and more effective way of promoting poverty reduction and the 'ownership' of national strategies. Others, however, are critical of what remains a predominantly external and more or less standardized policy framework determining the preconditions for development assistance—often with very little real difference from the broadly neo-liberal measures recommended over the last 25 or so years by the IMF and the World Bank—despite its emphasis on national 'ownership' and widespread involvement by many domestic stakeholders in shaping the strategy to be adopted.

Private Military Companies (PMCs)

The growth of the involvement of private military companies (PMCs) in conflicts in Africa has been a significant phenomenon over the last two decades. Since the South African-based PMC Executive Outcomes (EO) first emerged publicly in late 1992, international attention has been increasingly focused on the role and influence of these private companies in securing and stabilizing—or destabilizing—national and regional security. Many PMCs are organized along corporate lines (including boards of directors, share holdings, and corporate structures), their work has a clear contractual aim and obligation to their clients, and they engage in activities involving arms and other military-type equipment across the spectrum, from small-scale security, intelligence-gathering, training and advisory services to more extensive combat operations. Among the better known examples are EO (South Africa), Sandline International (United Kingdom), DSL (UK) and MPRI (USA). Others include Keenie Meenie Services (KMS) and its subsidiary Saladin Security, The Corps of Commissionaires, BDM International/Vinnell Corporation, and Air-Scan—all based in the USA—Secrets and Service and Security (both French), Levdan and Silver Shadow (both Israeli), Omega Support Ltd., Panasee, Bridge Resources, Corporate Trading International, Grey Security and Strategic Concepts Pty Ltd (all based in South Africa) and Gurkha Security Guards Ltd (United Kingdom).

Generally involving former special forces personnel from the US, UK, Israeli, South African, Southern Rhodesian (and, after 1989, Eastern European or former Soviet) official armed services, they increasingly possess capabilities which many African state services do not. While most often involved in the training and retraining, and reequipping, of national armed services, they have also participated in combat operations to secure and stabilize strategic mineral- or petroleum-producing regions from rebel movements, to support government forces against rebels, or to assist rebel movements in overthrowing national governments.

Often perceived to be operating outside the laws of warfare and strictly for pay—as mercenaries have done for centuries—the actual *modus operandi* of these private companies providing professional fighters has been one of the grounds for concern. Another has been the social and political affiliations that some of them are known to have. The involvement of non-governmental organizations in African conflicts is not new, but whereas the activities of NGOs involved in relief, humanitarian or development work are rarely criticized or subject to intensive scrutiny, those of the organizations actively engaging in the conflict, on one side or the other, or in the role of intermediary 'peace-keepers', are more contentious. The emergence of PMCs has been a concern for governments and for the international community of states, less as regards the effectiveness of their security operations than as regards their regulation. Under the existing international system, in theory at least, national military forces are controlled through the civilian political leaders in their respective countries who in turn regulate and control the activities of these forces in order to ensure that their use falls within national or international legal statutes and controls. At a regional and global level, regional associations and the United Nations provide a framework within which the deployment of military forces for security purposes can be regulated and controlled. The privatization of these activities introduces a new dimension. On the other hand, they play a role which it seems the governmental and inter-governmental structures and forces are often unable to fulfil, in helping to resolve political and military crises and conflicts.

Privatization

Since the 1980s part of the advice given to African governments regarding economic reform and economic restructuring has been the need to embark on a serious programme of privatization of state enterprises. This advice remains highly controversial and in many African countries extremely unpopular, particularly when it involves the privatization of public utilities, such as power, **energy** and **water**. Governments have sometimes embraced privatization enthusiastically, sometimes reluctantly and sometimes have prevaricated or refused. In May 2005 the government of Tanzania withdrew from a deal that had been arranged with the British company Biwater to privatise water supplies in Dar es Salaam.

Progressive Democratic Party

Tunisian political party.

Progressive Party

Former political party, and part, together with the conservative **United Party**, of the parliamentary opposition in the 'old' South Africa. Led by **Frederik van Zyl Slabbert** and including long-standing politician and critic of the **apartheid** regime, the party's only parliamentary representative, Helen Suzman.

Protectionism

Under the new regime of global liberalization espoused and supported by the **World Trade Organization (WTO)**, most African economies have significantly reduced the levels of effective protection by reducing trade tariffs and other barriers. The informal barriers that continue to exist still remain a sufficient disincentive, however, to international investment, particularly within the African continent. A number of African countries have established export-processing zones, offering special tax concessions and trade facilities to foreign companies. Relatively few of these have proved very effective in attracting foreign direct investment, apart from Mauritius—which had specific advantages, including a Chinese émigré colony with links with large Hong Kong textile companies interested in bypassing the quota limits on imports into northern markets from Hong Kong. On the other hand, African exporting economies face considerable continuing protectionism in North American, European and Japanese markets, despite the rhetoric of global liberalization strongly advocated by these developed economies and by international financial institutions.

Pulaar (Pular, Peuhl, Fulani)

Major ethno-linguistic grouping found in several West African countries, including Senegal, Burkina Faso and the Central African Republic.

Puntland

The Puntland State of Somalia. Puntland is the self-administered north-eastern territory of Somalia. During the late 1990s Puntland, like **Somaliland**, enjoyed relative peace and stability. The Puntland Regional Government was established in July 1998 with a 69 member parliament. However, in July 2001 a political crisis developed when the tenure of President Col Abdullahi Yusuf expired. The President refused to stand down as required under the Constitution. Puntland's clan elders appointed Yusuf Haji Nur as interim President until elections could be arranged. In August 2001 there were several clashes (particularly in the port of Bosasso) between militias loyal, respectively, to Yusuf and Nur. A conference of traditional leaders took place in late 2001 to elect a new President. In November Jama Ali Jama chosen as President. However, clashes between militias loyal to Col Yusuf and Jama Ali Jama continued. In early May 2002 Col Yusuf's forces drove Jama Ali Jama and his supporters out of Bosasso, effectively ending Yusuf's control of the whole of Puntland.

Pygmies

A term used by Europeans (English) to refer to the indigenous hunter/gatherer peoples of central Africa, whose way of life has been increasingly circumscribed over the last few centuries by the expansion of agriculture and agro-pastoralism and of those peoples who have adopted and developed these farming systems and effectively destroyed the habitat within which the hunters and gatherers previously existed. European settlement and the demands of the colonial administration with respect to the resources of the colonial economy provided an added and more recent driving force, marginalizing the hunter/gatherer communities even further and forcing them out of many of the territories they previously occupied. Generally relatively small in stature, these groups include the **Twa** of Burundi, Rwanda and the Democratic Republic of the Congo (DRC), especially in the Ituri forest region in the north east of the DRC.

Q

al-Qaddafi, Col Muammar Abu Minyar (1942–)

President and Head of State of Libya. He was born in Sirte in 1942. He came to power in 1969 as a member of a military coup by young officers, directed against **King Idris I** and launched a cultural revolution to remove traces of imported ideology. He has supported a broad range of militant groups including the Irish Republican Army and the Palestine Liberation Organization. Alleged Libyan involvement in attacks in Europe in 1986 led to US military strikes against Tripoli. For several decades Qaddafi tried to portray himself as a regional leader in both the Arab World and Africa. His attempts to create alliances, and his interventions, particularly in **North Africa** and the Sahel, earned him limited credit and a reputation for adventurism. His support for various militant groups, in the Arab World and beyond, also attracted hostility from the West. However, in 1999, following the surrender of the suspects in the **Lockerbie** bombing, Qaddafi sought improved relations with western European nations and issued a denunciation of **terrorism**. In 2004 Qaddafi's willingness to accept UN inspection of his nuclear weapons facilities and a visit by UK Prime Minister Tony Blair marked another step towards Libya's international rehabilitation.

R

Ramaphosa, Cyril

Former trade union leader who became the chief constitutional negotiator and secretary-general of the **African National Congress**. It was Ramaphosa who first promoted the idea of 'empowerment charters'. He left politics after losing to **Thabo Mbeki** in the contest to become **Nelson Mandela**'s successor. Later became a business tycoon and is now considered to be one of the richest men in South Africa.

Rassemblement congolais pour la démocratie (RCD—Congolese Rally for Democracy)

Political party in the Democratic Republic of the Congo, established in 1998. Advocates the introduction of a democratic political system. Split into two factions in 1999, of which the Ilunga faction (Goma) is supported by Rwanda.

Rassemblement congolais pour la démocratie—Mouvement de libération (RCD—ML, Congolese Rally for Democracy—Liberation Movement)

Political party in the Democratic Republic of the Congo, established in 1999 when it broke away from the main RCD. The RCD—ML is supported by Uganda.

Rassemblement congolais pour la démocratie—National (RCD—N, Congolese Rally for Democracy—National)

Political party in the Democratic Republic of the Congo. Broke away from the **Rassemblement congolais pour la libération—Mouvement de libération (RCD—Liberation Movement)** in October 2000. The leader of the RCD—N is Roger Lumbala.

Rassemblement constitutionnel démocratique (RCD—Constitutional Democratic Rally)

Tunisian political grouping.

Rassemblement pour la démocratie et le développement (RDD—Rally for Democracy and Development)

Political party in the Republic of the Congo, established in 1990. Advocates a mixed economy and forms part of the **Convention pour la démocratie et le salut (CODESA—Convention for Democracy and Salvation)**.

Rassemblement pour la démocratie et le développement économique et social (RADDES—Rally for Democracy and Economic and Social Development)

Political party in Burundi, established in 1992. Predominantly Tutsi membership. RADDES's chairman is Joseph Nzeyzimana.

Rassemblement pour la démocratie et la République (RDR—Rally for Democracy and the Republic)

Political party in the Republic of the Congo. Member of the **Forces démocratiques unies (FDU—United Democratic Forces)**. The RDR is led by Gen. (retd) Raymond Damase Ngollo.

Rassemblement pour la démocratie et le panafricanisme (RDP—Rally for Democracy and Pan-Africanism)

Political party in Benin, founded in 1995. The RDP is led by Dominique O. Houngninou and Gilles Auguste Minontin.

Rassemblement pour la démocratie et le progrès (RDP—Rally for Democracy and Progress)

Pro-government political party in Chad. Established in 1992, the RDP seeks to create a secure political environment by the establishment of a reformed national army. The RDP is led by Lol Mahamat Choua.

Rassemblement démocratique centrafricain (RDC—Central African Democratic Rally)

Political party in the Central African Republic. Established in 1987 and sole legal political party from then until 1991. Largest opposition party in the Assemblée nationale following the general elections of November–December 1998. The RDC is led by Gen. André Kolingba, who the presidential election held in 1999.

Rassemblement démocratique du peuple camerounais (RDPC—Democratic Rally of the Cameroon People)

Political movement in Cameroon. Founded in 1966 as the Union nationale camerounaise (National Cameroon Union), by the merger of the Union camerounaise (Cameroon Union), the Kamerun National Democratic Party and four opposition parties. It adopted its present name in 1985. The RDPC was the sole legal party in 1972–90. The movement's president is **Paul Biya**.

Rassemblement démocratique du people sans frontières (RDPF—Democratic Rally of the People without Frontiers)

Political movement in Cameroon, founded in 1997.

Rassemblement national des bûcherons (RNB—National Woodcutters' Rally)

Political party in Gabon.

Rassemblement national démocratique (RND—Democratic National Rally)

Algerian centrist political party, established in 1997. Ahmed Ouyahia is secretary-general of the RND.

Rassemblement national pour le développement (RND—National Rally for Development)

Political party in the Union of the Comoros, founded in 1996. The RND's chairman is Omar Tamou.

Rassemblement pour une nouvelle société (RNS—Rally for a New Society)

Political party in the Democratic Republic of the Congo.

Rassemblement pour le peuple du Burundi (RPB—Rally for the People of Burundi)

Political party in Burundi, established in 1992. Predominantly Hutu membership. The RPB is led by Balthazar Bigirimana.

Rassemblement du peuple togolais (RPT—Rally of the Togolese People)

A political party in Togo, founded in 1969. Sole legal party in 1969–91.

Rassemblement populaire pour la reconstruction de la Centrafrique (RPRC—Popular Rally for the Reconstruction of Central Africa)

Political party in the Central African Republic. The RPRC is led by Gen. François Bozizé.

Rawlings, Flight-Lt Jerry

In 1979 Flight-Lt Jerry Rawlings carried out a coup against the regime of **Gen. F. W. K. Akuffo** in Ghana, promising to end **corruption**, reverse economic decline and restore civilian rule. In his three months in power, he succeeded only in the last of these objectives, completing an electoral process that had already been set in motion and which installed Dr Hilla Liman as President of a country with a collapsing economy and aggravated social tensions. At the end of 1981 Liman was ousted and Rawlings returned to combat economic decline once again, as well as sporadic plots and riots.

Ravalomanana, Marc

President of Madagascar since May 2002. Marc Ravalomanana was born in the village of Imerikasina, not far from Antananarivo. A successful businessman, he entered politics in 1999 and created a large base of support in Antananarivo. Ravalomanana claimed outright victory in presidential elections held in December 2001 and a bitter six-month struggle for power with veteran leader Didier Ratsiraka ensued. Shortly after the USA and France had recognized Ravalomanana as the legitimate President of Madagascar, Ratsiraka flew to France and his forces on the island transferred their allegiance to Ravalomanana. Ravalomanana promised to use his entrepreneurial flair to fight **poverty** and unemployment.

Reconstruction and Development Programme (RDP)

Having jettisoned the **Macroeconomic Research Group (MERG)** policy document in 1993, the new **African National Congress (ANC)** government in South Africa had to rely on the Reconstruction and Development Programme (RDP), which had been hastily crafted in preparation for the election campaign. Jay Naidoo, general secretary of the **Confederation of South African Trade Union (COSATU)**, prepared the first draft of the RDP. In all it went through six drafts and emerged as a compromise document, strong on rhetoric but weak on how to deliver its promises. It set ambitious targets, for land distribution, **water** and sanitation, housing, electrification and access to **education**, health and telecommunications. The economic section, however, was riddled with ambiguities. As Minister without Portfolio, Naidoo was in charge of the RDP, but he had no department or ministry of his own and no clear line of authority within the administration. Various problems of co-ordination arose. In mid-1995 a new team was set up by Alec Erwin in the Ministry of Trade and Industry, to develop a more coherent macroeconomic framework. This team produced a policy document called **Growth, Employment and Redistribution (GEAR)**, which Manuel presented to government in June 1996. It was accepted, and the government has insisted ever since that GEAR did not replace the RDP, but was simply a strategy to fund the RDP. However, GEAR was based on an openly free-market programme, more directly in line with 'the Washington consensus' than with any 'Asian tiger' strategy. Naidoo's job disappeared and he became Minister of Posts, Telegraphs and Broadcasting. The RDP office was closed and the programme's goals were assigned to the various government departments.

Refugees

Refugees are defined by the international agencies as involuntary migrants or displaced persons finding refuge outside their own country. Large scale involuntary or forced migration has increased in recent decades as local conflict and major **civil wars** have affected numerous countries throughout Africa. The number of involuntary migrants, internally displaced persons (IDPs) and refugees across national frontiers has grown to an alarming extent in recent years. Many take refuge in neighbouring countries, themselves unable to provide adequate conditions for settlement or resettlement; a smaller but still substantial number try to find opportunities even further afield, sometimes crossing many national borders to reach a place of refuge. The **UNHCR** struggles for lack of funds and logistical support to respond adequately to this growing problem; local governments are often also unable to provide the necessary assistance and support, and the international relief and humanitarian aid agencies are often unable to respond sufficiently quickly or on a sufficient scale to provide effective relief and rehabilitation. (See also **Migration**.)

La renaissance du Bénin (RB—Rebirth of Benin)

Political party in Benin, founded in 1992. The honorary resident of the RB is Nicéphore Soglo, former President of Benin. In elections to the Assemblée nationale in 2003 the RB won15 of the 83 seats, the second highest number occupied by any single party.

René, France Albert

In 1977 in the Seychelles, only one year after **independence**, Albert René staged a bloodless coup against the country's first President, **James Mancham**, and was declared President, retaining that office until 2004, when he relinquished power to Vice-President James Michel. Throughout the many years of René's one-party socialist dictatorship, Michel had held key positions in the ruling Seychelles People's Progressive Front and ministerial portfolios. The country moved gradually towards greater political openness and multi-party elections were eventually held in 1993. Michel served as Vice-President from 1996 onwards. René was re-elected as President of Seychelles in the last presidential election, held in September 2001, before he relinquished power.

Réunion

French Overseas Possession. Elections to the French Assemblée nationale took place in **Mayotte** and Réunion in mid-June 2002.

Revolutionary United Front (RUF) – *see* Sierra Leone, Republic of, *History*

Rhodes, Cecil

British explorer, traveller and entrepreneur who, in the late 19th century, gained control of a huge territory in southern Africa on behalf of the British government. In 1889 he and his company, the British South Africa Company, were asked to administer the protectorate of **Bechuanaland**, a huge, largely desert region to the north of the **Cape Colony**. He accepted and subsequently advanced northwards to conquer the Matabele and Mashona and establish what was later referred to as Southern Rhodesia. From there he continued across the Zambezi and won concessions from the sovereign (or *litunga*) of Barotseland and other local chiefs, who were probably unaware of precisely what they were conceding. The territory under his control—now Northern and Southern Rhodesia—was supplemented by **Nyasaland**. The administrative rights over these territories were eventually taken back and Nyasaland became a British protectorate in 1907 and Southern Rhodesia, which had become an area of white settlement, became a self-governing colony in 1923. Northern **Rhodesia**, eventually, became a British protectorate in 1924. The British South Africa Company was, however, allowed mineral rights, which ultimately proved to be highly lucrative, particularly after the opening of Northern Rhodesia's **copper** mines. Rhodes' Company sold the mineral rights he had acquired in Southern Rhodesia in 1933 to the government of Southern Rhodesia. The legitimacy of the land rights he had 'acquired'—which he claimed gave him possession of the whole land area of Southern Rhodesia—proved more controversial. In 1914 some 8.5m. ha had been 'reserved' for the native population, but in 1923 at the time of self-government, Rhodes' Company, which had previously resold about 12.5m. ha, transferred a balance of some 18.2m. ha to the new government.

Rhodesia

Former name of present-day Zimbabwe (previously Southern Rhodesia) and Zambia (previously Northern Rhodesia). Named after **Cecil Rhodes**, the British explorer, traveller and entrepreneur whose British South Africa Company was chartered by the British government at the end of the 19th century to explore and annex territories in southern Africa for Britain. In 1896–97 he fought and conquered the Matabele and Mashona and became ruler of what was later to be called Southern Rhodesia. He then continued across the Zambezi and won concessions from various local rulers to take possession of vast tracts of land in what would later be called Northern Rhodesia and **Nyasaland**. In 1914 some 8.5m. ha in Southern Rhodesia were 'reserved' for the native population, but in 1923 Southern Rhodesia, which had become an area of white settlement, became a self-governing colony. The British government transferred control of the colony's internal affairs to the white community and, subject only to certain safeguards and reservations, withdrew from direct participation. The possibility of uniting Southern Rhodesia with South Africa was raised but rejected by white Rhodesians. In 1930 the whole country was divided by the land Apportionment Act into European areas, Native purchase areas, Unoccupied areas and Forests. Despite numerous discussions throughout the 1940s and 1950s on the possibility of some sort of federation between Southern Rhodesia, Northern Rhodesia and Nyasaland, this failed to materialize until 1953, when Godfrey Huggins of Southern Rhodesia became federal Prime Minister of a new Central African federation, with Roy Welensky of Northern Rhodesia as his deputy and a six-member Cabinet. In Southern Rhodesia Huggins was succeeded by **Garfield Todd** as Prime Minister and leader of the United Party.

Río Muni

Fernando Póo, a Spanish-controlled island in the Bight of Biafra, renamed Macías Nguema Biyogo, together with Río Muni, an enclave in Gabon, became the independent state of Equatorial Guinea in 1968.

Río de Oro

Former Spanish territory in **Western Sahara**.

Rosa, Henrique Pereira

Interim President of Guinea-Bissau in 2003–05. Appointed by Gen. Veríssimo Correia Seabra, who had overthrown the regime of President **Kumba Yalá** in September 2003. Rosa was succeeded by João Bernardo Vieira, who was elected as President of Guinea-Bissau in July 2005.

Rwanda (Rwandan Republic)

The Rwandan Republic is a land-locked country in eastern central Africa, just south of the Equator, bounded by the Democratic Republic of the Congo (DRC) to the west, by Uganda to the north, by Tanzania to the east and by Burundi to the south. Rwanda is 26,338 sq km in area. At mid-2003 the population was estimated at 8,387,000. There are three ethnic groups: **Hutu** (85%), Tutsi (14%) and **Twa** (1%). French, English and Kinyarwanda, the native language, are all in official use, and Kiswahili is widely spoken. About one-half of the population adhere to animist beliefs. Most of the remainder are Christians, mainly Roman Catholics. There are Protestant and Muslim minorities. The capital is Kigali, whose population was estimated at 656,153 at mid-2003.

Political profile

Under the terms of the Constitution, which entered into force on 4 June 2003, legislative power is vested in a bicameral Parliament, comprising a Chamber of Deputies and a Senate. The Chamber of Deputies has 80 deputies, who are elected for a five-year term. In addition to 53 directly elected deputies, 27 seats are allocated, respectively, to two youth representatives, one disabilities representative, and 24 female representatives, who are indirectly elected. The Senate comprises 26 members, of whom 12 are elected by local government councils in the 12 provinces, and two by academic institutions, while the remaining 12 are nominated (eight by the President and four by a regulatory body, the Parties' Forum). Members of the Senate serve for eight years. Executive power is exercised by the President (Head of State), assisted by an appointed Council of Ministers. The President is elected by universal suffrage for a seven-year term, and is restricted to two mandates.

In a presidential election held on 25 August 2003, **Maj.-Gen. Paul Kagame** was re-elected for a second term. Kagame was first elected as President (by members of the Transitional National Assembly and the government) in April 2000, becoming the first Tutsi Head of State of Rwanda since 1959.

Following legislative elections held on 29 September–3 October 2003, the distribution of seats in the Chamber of Deputies was as follows: Front patriotique rwandais (FPR, Patriotic Front of Rwanda, which contested the elections with the Parti démocratique centriste (PDC—Centre Democratic Party), the Parti démocratique idéal (PDI—Ideal Democratic Party), the Union démocratique du peuple rwandais (UDPR—Democratic Union of the Rwandan People) and the Parti socialiste rwandais (PSR—Rwandan Socialiste Party)) 40; Parti social-démocrate (PSD—Social Democrat Party) 7; Parti libéral (PL—Liberal Party) 6.

History

Rwanda, with the neighbouring state of Burundi, became part of German East Africa in 1899. In 1916, during the First World War, it was occupied by Belgian forces from the Congo. From 1920 Rwanda was part of Ruanda-Urundi, administered by Belgium under a League of Nations mandate and later as a UN Trust

Territory. Long-standing dissension between the majority Hutu tribe and their former overlords, the Tutsi, caused a rebellion and the proclamation of a state of emergency in 1959. In September 1961 it was decided by referendum to abolish the monarchy and to establish a republic. Full **independence** followed on 1 July 1962. Serious tribal conflict erupted in December 1963, and massacres (of an estimated 20,000) were perpetrated by the Hutu against the Tutsi. During 1964–65 large numbers of displaced Rwandans were resettled in neighbouring countries. In 1969 Grégoire Kayibanda, the new Republic's first President, was re-elected, and all 47 seats in the legislature were retained by the governing party, the Mouvement démocratique républicain (MDR), also known as the Parti de l'émancipation du peuple Hutu (Parmehutu).

A legacy of the outbreaks of persecution by the Hutu regime in 1959 and 1963 (and again in 1973) was the presence in Uganda of some 250,000 Rwandan **refugees** in Uganda (mainly members of the Tutsi minority), who had fled their homeland. In October 1990 rebel forces, based in Uganda, invaded northern Rwanda, occupying several towns. The 4,000-strong rebel army, known as the FPR, which mainly comprised Rwandan Tutsi refugees, aimed to overthrow the regime of President Juvénal Habyarimana and secure the repatriation of all Rwandan refugees. The invasion marked the beginning of a **civil war** that caused severe political and economic disruption as the 1990s progressed. A further consequence of the war was the aggravation of tribal polarization, which culminated, in 1994, in the massacre of hundreds of thousands of Tutsi and moderate Hutu Rwandans and the displacement of many hundreds of thousands of more, both Tutsi and Hutu. In particular, there was an intensification of the inter-ethnic violence and killings immediately after the death, in April 1994 of President Habyarimana, who was killed when the presidential aircraft, returning to Rwanda from Tanzania, was fired on, above Kigali airport, and exploded.

The FPR, which by the time of Habyarimana's death was in control of most of Rwanda, rejected the legitimacy of the interim government that succeeded his regime, and in July 1994 announced the composition of a new government of national unity, with the leader of a moderate faction of the MDR, Faustin Twagiramungu, as Prime Minister. The majority of cabinet posts were assigned to FPR members (including the FPR military chief, Maj.-Gen. Paul Kagame, who became Minister of Defence and also assumed the newly created post of Vice-President. In September the **European Union** recognized the government of national unity. A National Transitional Assembly was formally inaugurated in December. In May 1995 this legislature adopted a new constitution, which was based on selected articles of the 1991 Constitution, the terms of the Arusha peace accord of 1993, the FPR's victory declaration of July 1994 and a multi-party protocol of understanding concluded in November of that year.

In February 1995 the UN Security Council adopted Resolution 977, whereby Arusha, in Tanzania, was designated the seat for an International Criminal Tribunal for Rwanda (ICTR). The Tribunal was inaugurated in June. It was reported that the

ICTR intended to investigate allegations made against some 400 individuals of direct involvement in the planning and execution of crimes against humanity perpetrated in Rwanda during 1994. The ICTR reached its first verdict in September 1998. By early 2004 the ICTR had convicted 18 and acquitted three defendants.

Following the 1994 **genocide**, some 2m. Rwandan Hutus fled to **Zaire** (now the Democratic Republic of the Congo—DRC), Tanzania and Burundi. The international community provided relief to refugees in camps established in the border areas. These became havens for former members of Hutu-dominated Forces armées rwandaises (FAR—Rwandan Armed Forces) and the extremist Hutu Interahamwe militia, which carried out guerrilla raids over the border with the objective of destabilizing the FPR government and killing survivors of the genocide. In October 1996 the Armée patriotique rwandaise (ARP—Patriotic Rwandan Army) broke up many of the refugee camps in eastern Zaire (DRC), facilitating the return of some 700,000 Rwandan refugees to Rwanda. Around 370,000 were thought to have remained in DRC, including elements of ex-FAR/Interahamwe. Further large-scale returns of refugees occurred from 1997.

Political reforms undertaken by the FPR regime culminated, in 2003, in the adoption by the Transitional National Assembly, of a new constitution. At a national referendum, which took place on 26 May, the draft Constitution was endorsed by 93.4% of the electorate. The first presidential election to take place in Rwanda since the single candidate poll of 1988 (when Habyarimana had been re-elected) was conducted on 25 August 2003 (thereby marking the end of the nine-year transitional period). Maj.-Gen. Paul Kagame was returned to power, having received about 95.1% of votes cast. In elections to the Chamber of Deputies in September, an FPR-led coalition secured 40 seats, while the PSD won seven seats and the PL six.

International relations

Rwanda's involvement in the conflict in the DRC damaged its relations with those countries that supported President **Kabila**—Zimbabwe, Angola and Namibia. However, on 30 July 2002 the Presidents of the DRC and Rwanda signed a peace agreement in an attempt to finally end the war. The government of the DRC undertook to collaborate with the UN Mission in the DRC (MONUC) in dismantling the forces responsible for the Rwandan genocide still operating in the DRC. The government of Rwanda withdrew its forces from the DRC in October. In 2004 the international community and the UN voiced concerns over threats by the Rwandan authorities to launch a military intervention in the DRC. The UN's concern was that Rwandan military action on Congolese territory 'would disrupt the vital transitional process in the DRC, and the UN demanded that any Rwandan troops be withdrawn from the DRC.

Rwanda, economy

In 2003, according to estimates by the **World Bank**, Rwanda's gross national income (GNI), measured at average 2001–03 prices, was US $1,662m., equivalent to $220 per head (or $1,290 per head on an international purchasing-power parity basis). During 1990–2003, it was estimated, the population increased at an average annual rate of 1.3%, while gross domestic product (GDP) per head rose, in real terms, by an average of 0.2% per year. Overall GDP increased, in real terms, at an average annual rate of 1.6% in 1990–2003; growth in 2003 was 3.2%. In 1992–2003 the average annual rate of inflation was 11.4%. Consumer prices increased by 6.9% in 2003. In 2004 the main destinations of Rwanda's exports were Indonesia, the People's Republic of China and Germany. The main suppliers of imports to Rwanda in that year were Kenya, Germany, Belgium, Uganda and France. The national currency is the Rwanda franc. In 2004 the average exchange rate was US $1 = 574.622 Rwanda francs.

Rwanda is a poor rural country where about 90% of the population are engaged in (predominantly subsistence) **agriculture**. The 1994 **genocide** wrecked Rwanda's fragile economic base, severely impoverished the population and eroded the country's ability to attract private investment. However, Rwanda has made substantial progress in stabilizing and rehabilitating its economy to pre-1994 levels, although **poverty** levels are higher now. GDP has rebounded, having increased by 70% in 1994–97. In subsequent years growth remained relatively high (6%–9%), but it took until 2000 for GDP to return to its 1990 level.

In the aftermath of the genocide growth was led by manufacturing, commerce, and services—spurred by the presence of a large number of international NGOs and relief agencies. Since 1998 agriculture and construction have been the main sources of growth. In parallel, inflation was rapidly brought under control after 1994 and has remained low. Rwanda reached its **Heavily Indebted Poor Countries** initiative decision point in December 2000, which helped alleviate the burden of a substantial external **debt** ($1,200m., or 63% of GDP). Revenue performance has been disappointing, with revenues equivalent to only 9.9% of GDP in 1999 and 2000. The introduction of VAT in January 2001 contributed to the achievement of the revenue target of 11.4% of GDP in 2001. Rwanda began to reform its economy in 1995. The reforms have focused on the exchange and trade regime, the privatization of state enterprises, the reform of public administration, the budget and financial management, and private-sector development. Following successful compliance with conditions imposed by the **International Monetary Fund** since 1994, Rwanda's major creditor countries agreed to cancel 100% of the country's remaining debt to them in 2005. This currently amounts to more than US $90m., according to the Paris Club.

Rwanda completed its **Poverty Reduction Strategy Paper (PRSP)** in June 2002. This helped to focus public interventions on poverty reduction, with rural development and agricultural transformation the main priorities. Other priorities for public actions included governance, human development, economic infrastructure, private-sector development and institutional capacity-building. The PRSP aims at an annual real GDP growth rate of 6%–7%, which will help Rwanda to reduce the level of poverty from 60% of households in 2001 to 30% in 2015, and to meet the other **Millennium Development Goals**.

Rwandan genocide

It took **Hutu** death squads only three months from early April 1994 to murder an estimated 800,000 Tutsis and moderate Hutus. The international community and the UN failed to respond adequately in time, although most governments and international agencies were well aware of what was happening. The US administration under President Bill Clinton was certainly aware of the killings; senior officials privately used the word genocide two to three weeks after the start of the slaughter, but chose not to do so publicly because the President had already decided not to intervene. Intelligence reports obtained using the freedom of Information Act showed 10 years later (in 2004) that the administration and almost certainly the President had been told of a planned 'final solution to eliminate all Tutsis' before the killing reached its peak. However, the USA was still recovering from the impact of its disastrous intervention in Somalia and Rwanda was considered a small Central African country with no minerals or strategic value. Other Western governments also had sufficient information to suggest an enormous human catastrophe, but chose not to provide more support for the token force of UN peace-keepers, which was overwhelmed by the scale and rapidity of events. On a visit to the Rwandan capital, Kigali, in 1998, Clinton did apologize for not having acted quickly enough and not openly calling the crimes 'genocide'. In November 1994 the UN Security Council adopted Resolution 955, that established an **International Criminal Tribunal for Rwanda (ICTR)** to prosecute those persons responsible for the genocide and other serious human rights violations committed in Rwanda and by Rwandans in neighbouring states. In September 1998 the former Rwandan Prime Minister, Jean Kambanda, and a former mayor of Taba, Jean-Paul Akayesu, both Hutu extremists, were found guilty of genocide and crimes against humanity. Kambanda subsequently became the first person ever to be sentenced under the 1948 Convention on the Prevention and Punishment of the Crime of Genocide.

S

Es-Sadat, Anwar

President of Egypt in 1970–81. Born in 1918, Sadat entered the Abbasia Military Academy in 1936, where he became friendly with **Gamal Abdel Nasser** and other fellow cadets committed to Egyptian **nationalism**. A German agent during the Second World War, he was imprisoned by the British authorities in 1942, but escaped after two years in jail. He was jailed again in 1946–49 for his involvement in terrorist acts against pro-British Egyptian officials. Sadat took part in the *coup d'état* by the **Free Officers** in 1952 that deposed King **Farouk**. Between 1952 and 1968 he held a variety of government positions, including director of army public relations; secretary-general of the **National Union Movement**, Egypt's only political party; and president of the National Assembly. In 1969 he was appointed as Vice-President by Nasser, on whose death in 1970 he succeeded to the presidency. Less charismatic than his predecessor, Sadat was nevertheless able to establish himself as Egypt's 'strongman' and a leader of the Arab World. He assumed the premiership in 1973 and in October of that same year led Egypt into war with Israel. He became an Arab hero when Egyptian troops recaptured a small part of the Sinai Peninsula, taken by Israel in 1967. A pragmatist, Sadat indicated his willingness to consider a negotiated settlement with Israel and shared the 1978 Nobel Peace Prize with Menachem Begin as a result of the Camp David Accords. Together with the launching of the *infitah* laws, he transferred Egypt's allegiance from the USSR to the West during the Cold War. He was assassinated by Muslim extremists during a military parade in 1981.

Saharan Republic

In the 1970s Libyan leader **Col al-Qaddafi** planned to establish a Saharan Republic which would have included Libya, Tunisia, Algeria, the **Western Sahara**, Mauritania, Niger and Chad, under Libyan leadership. In 1973 he took advantage of the **civil war** in Chad to further his expansionist designs. Offering its support to military leader Goukouni Oueddai against **Hissène Habré**, Libya occupied the Aozou Strip in the north of Chad, a region rich in manganese and uranium. There was an immediate reaction from France, which dispatched 3,500 troops to support Habré, who succeeded in defeating Oueddai. The war continued for many years and cost Libya dearly. Libya eventually withdrew from Aozou and the idea of a Saharan Republic was abandoned.

Sahrawi Arab Democratic Republic (SADR)

Declared by the **Frente Popular para la Liberación de Saguia el-Hamra y Río de Oro (Frente POLISARIO—Popular Front for the Liberation of Saguia el-Hamra and Río de Oro)** in 1976, the SADR is recognized by 76 states. It fought for effective **independence** from 1976 onwards against Morocco and Mauritania, and then, from 1979 onwards, after signing a peace treaty with Mauritania, against Morocco alone. The SADR was admitted, despite strong Moroccan opposition, as the 51st member of the **Organization of African Unity** in February 1982. It agreed a cease-fire in 1991, after UN intervention to initiate a 'peace process'. The SADR has consistently tried to move towards the referendum planned by the UN and MINURSO, but this has been stalled by Moroccan objections and filibustering. The SADR is a state in exile, with much of its territory under Moroccan occupation since 1976. Its main organs are a 33-member National Secretariat, a 101-member Sahrawi National Assembly and a 13-member government. The Head of State and President of the SADR is Muhammad Abdel Aziz.

Sahrawis

The people of the **Western Sahara** (former Spanish Sahara). A significant majority of the population has been living in refugee camps in south-west Algeria, near Tindouf, since the Moroccan invasion of the former Spanish Sahara in late 1975; a smaller number have been living under Moroccan occupation in the western coastal regions of the territory. Sahrawi opposition to Spanish colonial rule led to the establishment in 1973 of the **Frente Popular para la Liberación de Saguia el-Hamra y Río de Oro (Frente POLISARIO—Popular Front for the Liberation of Saguia el-Hamra and Río de Oro)** and, in 1976, to the declaration of an independent state—the **Sahrawi Arab Democratic Republic**.

Saint Helena

Saint Helena lies in the South Atlantic Ocean about 1,930 km from the south-west coast of Africa and some 2,000 km from Cape Town. **Ascension Island** and the group of islands of **Tristan da Cunha**, also in the South Atlantic, are dependencies of Saint Helena. The British East India Company first established a settlement there in 1659. The island was captured and briefly held by the Dutch in 1673. In the same year King Charles II confirmed the status of the island as a British outpost and it was occupied and settled by the British East India Company. During 1815–21 the British government assumed temporary direct control of the island, owing to the exile there of Napoléon Bonaparte and in 1834, the British Foreign and Colonial office formally took over the administration of the island as a colony. Its importance as a port of call on the trade route to India declined after the opening of the **Suez Canal** in 1869. Temporary revivals during the **Zulu** and Anglo–Boer Wars and during the First and Second World Wars were followed by periods of economic depression. At a general election held in 1976, all but one of the 12 members returned to the Legislative Council supported a policy of maintaining close economic links with the United Kingdom; this position has been adopted by subsequent Legislative Councils up to the present time. Owing to the limited range of economic activity on the island, Saint Helena is dependent on development and budgetary assistance from the United Kingdom. From 1981, and the adoption of the British Nationality Act, which effectively removed the islanders' traditional right of residence in Britain, opportunities for overseas employment were limited to contract work, principally in Ascension and the Falkland Islands. In July 1997 private legislation was introduced in the British Parliament to extend full British nationality to islanders, and in March 1999 the British government published draft legislation proposing that full British nationality was to be restored to the population of Saint Helena and its dependencies under the reorganization of the British Dependent Territories as the United Kingdom Overseas Territories. In May 2002 the inhabitants of Saint Helena celebrated both the 500th anniversary of the island's discovery and the restoration of British citizenship to the inhabitants of Saint Helena and its dependencies, under the British Overseas Territories Act.

Salafist Jihad

In May 2003, suicide bombers killed themselves and 28 other people in a co-ordinated attack on five tourist and Jewish targets in Casablanca, Morocco. Those involved appear to have been linked to a group called Assirat al-Moustaquim (The Righteous Path). This group, several of whose members have been jailed previously, is believed to be a splinter group of the Salafist Jihad, one of whose leaders, Ould Mohamed Abdelwahab Raqiqi, alias 'Abu Hafs', was jailed earlier in 2003 for inciting violence against Westerners.

Ould Mohammed Salek, Lt-Col Mustapha

Head of State of Mauritania from July 1978, after the coup which overthrew **Mokhtar Ould Daddah**. Forced to resign in June 1979, he was succeeded by Lt-Col **Mohammed Mahmoud Ould Louly**.

Sama, Koffi

Appointed as Prime Minister of Togo in 2002. In July Sama announced the formation of a new government.

Sanniquellie Declaration

On 19 July 1959, at the village of Saniquellie in Liberia, President **Tubman** of Liberia, President **Touré** of Guinea and President **Nkrumah** of Ghana formulated the principles for achieving a Community of Independent African States. Liberia was to part ways with Ghana and Guinea shortly afterwards, when in January 1961 the **Casablanca Group** (of which Ghana and Guinea were members) and in May 1961 the **Monrovia Group** (of which Liberia was a member, President Tubman having called the meeting in Monrovia) established themselves to advocate and promote somewhat different visions of a union of African states. But these meetings and debates eventually led to the creation of the **Organization of African Unity** in May 1963, now the **African Union**.

Sankara, Thomas

In 1983 a civilian government in **Upper Volta** was replaced in a military coup by Capt. Thomas Sankara, who changed the country's name to Burkina Faso. Sankara developed close relations with Benin, where President **Mathieu Kérékou** had a somewhat similar background and orientation. A union with Ghana was planned, but did not materialize.

dos Santos, Fernando da Piedade Dias

Fernando dos Santos was appointed as Prime Minister of Angola on 6 December 2002, but this is not a position of real power, as the Head of State and head of government remains **José Eduardo dos Santos**, the President.

dos Santos, José Eduardo

President of Angola since 1979 and president of the **Movimento Popular de Libertação de Angola (MPLA—Popular Liberation Movement of Angola)**. Born in 1942, dos Santos enlisted in the MPLA's guerrilla army at the age of 19. He gained qualifications in petroleum engineering and radar telecommunications in the former USSR, and held ministerial posts before (at the age of 37) succeeding Angola's first President, **Dr Agostinho Neto**, when he died in 1979. In the 1992 presidential elections he won a narrow victory over the leader of the **União Nacional para a Independência Total de Angola (UNITA—National Union for the Total Independence of Angola)**, **Dr Jonas Savimbi**, who rejected the result and resumed guerrilla war. In August 2001 President dos Santos had announced that he would not contest the next presidential election. However, he was elected as president of the MPLA at its Fifth Congress in December 2003 and subsequently selected as the party's presidential candidate.

São Tomé and Príncipe, Democratic Republic of

The Democratic Republic of São Tomé and Príncipe lies in the Gulf of Guinea, off the west coast of Africa. There are two main islands, São Tomé and Príncipe, and the country also includes the rocky islets of Caroço, Pedras and Tinhosas, off Príncipe, and Rôlas, off São Tomé. The area of the country is 1,001 sq km. At mid-2003 the population was estimated at 161,000. Portuguese is the official language, and native dialects are widely spoken. Almost all of the inhabitants profess Christianity, and the overwhelming majority (some 83%) are adherents of the Roman Catholic Church. The capital is the town of São Tomé (on São Tomé island), whose population was estimated at 53,570 at mid-2003.

Political profile

Under the 2003 Constitution, legislative power is vested in the Assembléia Nacional, which comprises 55 members, elected by universal adult suffrage, for a term of four years. No limit is placed on the number of political parties permitted to operate. Executive power is vested in the President of the Republic, who is Head of State, and who governs with the assistance of an appointed Council of Ministers, led by the Prime Minister. The Council of State acts as an advisory body to the President, who is elected by universal suffrage for a term of five years. The President's tenure of office is limited to two successive terms. The Prime Minister, who is appointed by the President, is, in theory, nominated by the deputies of the Assembléia Nacional.

In 1994 the Assembléia Nacional granted political and administrative autonomy to the island of Príncipe. Legislation was adopted establishing a seven-member regional assembly and a five-member regional government; both are accountable to the government of São Tomé and Príncipe.

In an election held on 29 July 2001 **Fradique de Menezes** received 56.31% of the votes and was duly elected to the presidency.

Following a general election held on 3 March 2002, the distribution of seats in the Assembléia Nacional was as follows: **Movimento de Libertação de São Tomé e Príncipe—Partido Social Democrata (MLSTP—PSD, Liberation Movement of São Tomé and Príncipe—Social Democrat Party)** 24; **Movimento Democrático Força da Mudança-Partido da Convergência Democrática (MDFM-PCD—Force for Change Democratic Movement-Party of Democratic Convergence)** 23; **Uê Kédadji** (a coalition of the **Acção Democrática Independente (ADI—Independent Democratic Action)**, the Partido de Coligação Democrática (CÓDÓ—Party of Democratic Coalition), the Partido Popular do Progresso (PPP—Popular Progress Party), the **Partido de Renovação Democrática (PRD—Party of Democratic Renewal)** and the União Nacional para Democracia e Progresso (UNDP—National Union for Democracy and Progress) 8.

History

The two main islands of São Tomé and Príncipe were uninhabited until the Portuguese arrived in 1493. The islands became an overseas province of Portugal in 1951. A nationalist group, the **Comissão de Libertação de São Tomé e Príncipe (CLSTP—Liberation Committee of São Tomé and Príncipe)** was formed in 1960 and became the **Movimento de Libertação de São Tomé e Príncipe (MLSTP—Liberation Movement of São Tomé and Príncipe)** in 1972 under the leadership of **Dr Manuel Pinto da Costa.** Following the military coup in Portugal in 1974, the Portuguese government recognized the right of the islands to **independence**. Portugal appointed a transitional government that included members of the MLSTP, which was recognized as the sole legitimate representative of the people.

At elections for a constituent assembly held in July 1975, the MLSTP won all 16 seats. Independence as the Democratic Republic of São Tomé and Príncipe took effect on 12 July, with Pinto da Costa as President and **Miguel Trovoada** as Prime Minister. The Constitution promulgated in November 1975 effectively vested absolute authority in the hands of the President and the Central Committee of the MLSTP, leaving Trovoada and the Cabinet with few real powers. Radical socialist policies were introduced and any activity deemed contrary to MLSTP directives was defined as treason. In 1976–82 serious ideological as well as personal divisions arose within the MLSTP and a number of prominent members who favoured a more moderate approach to social, economic and agrarian reforms were forced into exile. In March 1978 Angolan soldiers were brought to the islands to provide protection for the President and his associates following an alleged coup attempt. In April 1979 Trovoada was dismissed as Prime Minister. In September he was arrested, charged with complicity in the 1978 coup attempt and detained until 1981 when he was permitted to leave the islands. Another alleged coup attempt was forestalled in November 1980. In December 1981 rioting broke out on Príncipe, where food shortages had led to agitation for the island's autonomy. During 1982 Leonel Mário d'Alva, a former Prime Minister and Minister of Foreign Affairs, fled to exile in Cape Verde and Daniel Daio, the Minister of Defence and National Security, was dismissed, but remained in the country. In 1989 the MLSTP (now known as the MLSTP—PSD), after a strenuous debate in an extraordinary meeting of the MLSTP Central Committee, embarked on a transition to full multi-party **democracy**. In August 1990, in a national referendum, 72% of the electorate voted in favour of introducing the Constitution proposed by the Central Committee.

The new Constitution was adopted on 10 September 1990. It defined São Tomé and Príncipe as a sovereign, unitary and democratic state, and provided for a multi-party political system, the abolition of the death penalty, guarantees on human rights and a maximum of two five-year terms of office for the President. Legislative power is vested in the Assembléia Nacional, which has 55 members and holds two sessions a year. There are six district assemblies on São Tomé. The island of Príncipe has had a seven-member Regional Assembly since being granted political and administrative autonomy in 1994. The first multi-party elections to the Assembléia Nacional took place in January 1991. The newly formed opposition PCD-Grupo de Reflexão (PCD-GR—PCD-Reflection Group), led by Daniel Lima dos Santos Daio, won the election with 54% of the vote. In the presidential election held in March 1991 Miguel Trovoada, returning from exile to stand as an independent but with the support of the PCD-GR, was elected unopposed. Since 1991 there have been seven governments and political life has been dominated by power struggles between the President and government, party infighting, widespread **corruption** and administrative paralysis. There was one coup attempt in 1995. There has also been unrest in the army since then, owing to reductions in numbers, poor and late pay and poor conditions.

Fradique de Menezes, a businessman, won the presidential elections held in July 2001 in the first round, receiving 56% of the votes. His closest rival, former President Manuel Pinto da Costa, received 38%, and the other three candidates received no more than 5% among them. In March 2002 elections were held to the Assembléia Nacional. No party won a clear majority, so the government was formed by the MLSTP-PSD (24 seats) and the coalition group known as MDFM-PCD (23 seats). The remaining eight seats are held by Uê-Kédadji. In April a government of national unity was formed, led by the newly appointed Prime Minister, Gabriel Arcanjo Ferreira da Costa. Analysts feared instability, as it was considered likely that the two major parties would disagree on the most basic political decisions. There was also alleged tension because President Fradique de Menezes was closely linked with the MDFM-PCD coalition. On 16 July 2003, while President de Menezes was in Nigeria, a small political party, the **Frente Democrata Cristã (FDC—Christian Democrat Front)**, took power in a bloodless *coup d'état*. It was claimed that the FDC had connections with the former **'Buffalo Battalion'**, a group of South African-trained mercenaries who were believed to have participated in several regional conflicts. The FDC established a '**National Salvation Junta**'. The coup was condemned by the international community, which demanded a return to civilian rule. Later in July, following successful mediation efforts, de Menezes returned to São Tomé, accompanied by President **Olusegun Obasanjo** of Nigeria. Under an amnesty for the coup leaders de Menezes was reinstated as President.

International relations

Throughout the 1970s and 1980s São Tomé and Príncipe maintained close economic ties with the People's Republic of China (PRC) and the German Democratic Republic. Cuba and the USSR provided the regime with military advisers. Neighbouring Gabon viewed these developments with disquiet and relations between the two countries deteriorated. São Tomé and Príncipe extended its range of its international contacts by joining the **International Monetary Fund** in 1977, by acceding to the **Lomé Convention** in 1978 and by participating in the foundation of the **Communauté économique des états de l'Afrique centrale (CEEAC)** in 1983. The bulk of the country's trade continued to be transacted with Western Europe and relations with Portugal remained generally cordial. In 1985, confronted with the threat of the complete collapse of the economy, Pinto da Costa began to abandon economic ties with the Eastern bloc in favour of the West. Trade agreements with

Eastern bloc countries were allowed to lapse on expiry. Pinto da Costa and his ministers made extensive visits to Western Europe and North America to solicit support for economic liberalization initiatives. The two main European nations seeking to exert influence were Portugal and France: however, trade with Portugal was much more substantial than trade with France and negotiations concerning São Tomé and Príncipe's admission to the **Franc Zone** were ultimately inconclusive. The USA accredited its first ambassador to São Tomé and Príncipe in 1985 and provided the country with a limited amount of military aid. Relations with the PRC deteriorated when President Trovoada established diplomatic relations with Taiwan on 6 May 1997. This step was taken despite opposition from the government and parliament.

São Tomé and Príncipe has maintained trade links with nearby Gabon, Cameroon and Equatorial Guinea. In November 1999 the country was a founder of the seven-member Gulf of Guinea Commission, whose objective was to resolve inter-state conflict and act as a mediator between the nations. In 2000 São Tomé and Príncipe began talks to establish a joint development zone (JDZ) for the exploitation of petroleum and mineral resources with Nigeria. In January 2002 the Presidents of both countries inaugurated a development authority to oversee the affairs of the JDZ.

São Tomé and Príncipe, economy

In 2003, according to estimates by the **World Bank**, São Tomé and Príncipe's gross national income (GNI), measured at average 2001–03 prices, was US $50m., equivalent to $320 per head. During 1990–2003, it was estimated, the population increased at an average annual rate of 2.4%, while gross domestic product (GDP) per head, in real terms, remained constant. Overall GDP increased, in real terms, at an average annual rate of 2.4% in 1990–2003; growth was 4.5% in 2003. Annual inflation averaged 23.5% in 1996–2003. Consumer prices increased by an average of 10.0% in 2003. In 2004 the main markets for São Tomé and Príncipe's exports were the Netherlands, the People's Republic of China, Germany, Belgium, the Philippines and France. São Tomé and Príncipe's principal suppliers of imports in that year were Portugal, Germany, the USA, the Netherlands and South Africa. The national currency is the dobra (Db). In 2003 the average exchange rate was US $1 = Db 9,347.6.

The economy of São Tomé and Príncipe is based almost exclusively on **cocoa** production, which accounts for more than 94% of total exports (**coffee** and cocoa were brought to the islands in the 19th century). Other export crops include palm kernels and coffee. **Agriculture** accounted for 16% of GDP in 2004 and employed 37% of the country's workforce. Land reform has broken up the great plantation estates and given most families sufficient land for subsistence and production of export crops. Other than agriculture, the main economic activities are fishing and a small industrial sector producing a few basic consumer goods. The government is keen to promote tourism.

São Tomé and Príncipe is poor and burdened by a high ratio of **debt** per head. In view of the fragility of the undiversified economy and the uncertain prospects for cocoa, the country requested help with an adjustment programme (still ongoing) from the **Bretton Woods institutions** in 2000 in order to stabilize the macroeconomic situation, introduce structural reforms, and benefit from the **Heavily Indebted Poor Countries (HIPC) initiative**. The **International Monetary Fund (IMF)** considered that the government was making satisfactory progress in 2003 towards fulfilling the conditions specified for the reinstatement of a **Poverty Reduction and Growth Facility** arrangement, under the HIPC programme. São Tomé and Príncipe remains a major recipient of external aid. In August 2004 the World Bank granted a total of $6m. and commenced negotiations with a view to cancelling the country's external debt. In December the central bank reported that the rate of economic growth in 2004 had been below 4%, while the rate of inflation was 15%. The 2005 budget provided for a 25% increase in public-sector salaries and forecast a reduction in the rate of inflation to about 10%, while GDP growth of 5% was forecast. The discovery of petroleum in Santomean waters is an encouraging development for the economy and should help the country meet its targets for increased GDP. In February 2005 ChevronTexaco made the first of payments that were to total $49m. for exploration rights to bloc one of the oilfields shared with Nigeria.

Savimbi, Dr Jonas

Long-time leader of the rebel **União Nacional para a Independência Total de Angola (UNITA—National Union for the Total Independence of Angola)**. Prior to the formation in April 1993 of a government of national unity and reconciliation in Angola, Jonas Savimbi was the principal rival to President **José Eduardo dos Santos** in the presidential elections of September 1992. Savimbi received only 40% of the votes, however, while dos Santos polled 50%. Savimbi was killed in February 2002 by government forces. Savimbi's successor, António Dembo, died shortly after him.

Saro-Wiwa, Ken

Leader of the **Ogoni** rights movement in the early 1990s in Nigeria. Saro-Wiwa became internationally known after he and eight colleagues were arrested on fabricated charges and executed by the regime of **Gen. Sani Abacha** in 1995.

Sassou-Nguesso, Gen. Denis

President of the Republic of the Congo since October 1997, when he retook by force the office that he had lost at the 1992 presidential election. (Sassou-Nguesso had served two full and a partial third terms under the Constitution in force prior to the 1992 election.) Born in 1943, Denis Sassou-Nguesso first seized power in a coup in

1979. Sassou-Nguesso's seizure of power in 1997 was backed by Angolan forces. A French-trained soldier, Sassou-Nguesso is viewed as a pragmatist. During his first presidential term in 1979–92 he loosened the country's links with the Soviet bloc and allowed French, US and other Western **oil** companies to play a major role in oil exploration and production. He abandoned the one-party system in 1992, forcing the **Parti congolais du travail (PCT—Congolese Labour Party)** to contest with other parties for political power after more than 20 years as the sole party. A new Constitution was approved by referendum in January 2002. In March Gen. Sassou-Nguesso began a new seven-year presidential term, after winning elections from which two of his main rivals—former President Pascal Lissouba and former Prime Minister Bernard Kolélas—were excluded by a residency law, and a third contender, André Milongo, withdrew, alleging irregularities. Reform of the Constitution has enabled Gen. Sassou-Nguesso to consolidate his position in power.

Senegal, Republic of

The Republic of Senegal lies on the west coast of Africa, bordered to the north by Mauritania, to the east by Mali, and to the south by Guinea and Guinea-Bissau. In the southern part of the country The Gambia forms a narrow enclave extending some 320 km inland. Senegal is 196,722 sq km in area. At mid-2003 the population was estimated at 10,095,000. Ethnic groups include the **Wolof** (43.3%), the **Pulaar** (Pular, Peulh or Fulani—23.8%), the **Serer** (14.7%), the **Diola** (3.7%), the Mandinka (3%) and the **Soninke**. French is the official language; the most widely spoken national languages at the time of the 1988 census were Wolof (spoken by 49.2% of the population), Peul (22.2%), Serer (12.8%) and Diola (5.1%). At the 1988 census almost 94% of the population were Muslims, and some 4% Christians, mostly Roman Catholics; a small number followed traditional beliefs. The capital is Dakar, whose population was estimated at 2,166,861 in mid-2003. In December 2002 the government announced that a new administrative capital, Mékhé-Pékesse was to be developed east of Dakar.

Political profile

Under the terms of the Constitution, approved by popular referendum in January 2001, executive power is held by the President, who is directly elected for a mandate of five years, which is renewable only once. (President **Wade** will, however, complete the seven-year mandate to which he was elected in March 2000 by the terms of the former Constitution.) Legislative power rests with the Assemblée nationale, with 120 members elected for five years by universal adult suffrage. There is no restriction on the number of political parties, although the formation of parties on an ethnic, religious or geographical basis is prohibited. The President appoints the Prime Minister, who, in consultation with the President, appoints the Council of Ministers.

In the second ballot of a presidential election held on 19 March 2000, Abdoulaye Wade, the candidate of the Parti démocratique sénégalais (PDS—Senegalese

Democratic Party), received 58.49% of the votes, while his second-round opponent, **Abdou Diouf**, the candidate of the Parti socialiste du Sénégal (PS—Socialist Party of Senegal), received 41.51%. Wade was accordingly elected to the presidency.

Following a general election held on 29 April 2001, the distribution of seats in the Assemblée nationale was as follows: Sopi Coalition (a coalition of some 40 parties and movement, led by the PDS) 89 (including 62 seats won by majority voting within departments); Alliance des forces de progrès (AFP—Alliance of the Forces of Progress) 11 (including two seats won by majority voting within departments); PS 10; Union pour le renouveau démocratique (URD—Union for Democratic Renewal) 3 (including one seat won by majority voting within departments); And Jëf—Parti africain pour la démocratie et le socialisme (AJ—PADS, And Jëf—African Party for Democracy and Socialism) 2; Parti libéral sénégalais (PLS—Senegalese Liberal Party) 1; Parti pour le progrès le la citoyenneté (PPC—Party for Progress and Citizenship) 1; Alliance pour le progrès et la justice—Jëf-Jël (APJ—JJ, Alliance for Progress and Justice—Jëf-Jël) 1; Rassemblement national démocratique (RND—National Democratic Rally) 1; Parti de l'indépendance et du travail (PIT—Party of Independence and Labour) 1.

History

Senegal was a French colony until **independence** in 1960. Dakar was the administrative capital of **French West Africa**. President **Léopold Sédar Senghor** (a Christian) was Senegal's first President and presided over a moderate, partly-democratic system (Senegal was a one-party state in 1966–75). Senghor nominated Abdou Diouf as his successor in 1980. The PS dominated Senegalese political life until 2000, winning elections that were mostly fairly conducted in the 1980s and 1990s. President Diouf and the PS won elections held in 1983 and 1988 with large, although diminishing, majorities. The election results of 1988 prompted serious rioting in Dakar, amid allegations of electoral malpractice. In the 1990s Diouf introduced multi-party government by inviting members of the opposition to join the government on two occasions. When not in the government, Abdoulaye Wade of the PDS remained the main opposition figure. In 1997 the former interior minister, Djibo Ka, began a campaign to modernize the PS and formed the URD, which won seats in the 1998 election. In 1999 former foreign minister Moustapha Niasse formed the AFP. These splits in the PS marked the end of its electoral invincibility.

Eight candidates contested the presidential election held in 2000. Abdou Diouf received 40% of the votes in the first ballot and was opposed by Abdoulaye Wade in a second. Wade rallied almost all of the other candidates and won comfortably in the second round. Diouf conceded defeat rapidly and there was a peaceful transition to the country's first ever non-PS government. Moustapha Niasse, the leader of the AFP, was appointed as Prime Minister in Wade's government—a coalition comprising seven political parties. The PS continued to dominate the Assemblée nationale. In a referendum held on 7 January 2001 minor amendments to the

Constitution were approved by more than 90% of voters. After a long period of conflict prior to the legislative elections, Wade appointed Mame Madior Boye as Prime Minister in place of Niasse in March 2001. After strong campaigning by Wade, the PDS won a landslide victory in the April elections, occupying 80 of the 120 seats in the Assemblée nationale. The PS lost much of its support and the AFP made few gains. On 4 November 2002, in a Cabinet reshuffle, Wade appointed Idrissa Seck (of the PDS) as Prime Minister in place of Boye. In a continued attempt to persuade opposition groups to participate in a new government, and despite their continued refusal, for the most part, to do so, Wade dismissed Seck's government in April 2004, appointing Macky Sall, hitherto Minister of the Interior, as the new Prime Minister.

Since 1982 an armed separatist movement in the **Casamance** region of southern Senegal, known as the Mouvement des forces démocratiques de Casamance (MFDC—Movement of the Democratic Forces of the Casamance) has been fighting ostensibly for independence. There have been numerous attempts to negotiate a settlement since the early 1990s, but the MFDC is increasingly split into factions and most recent armed activity on the ground can be classified as banditry. The MFDC was supported clandestinely in the 1990s by the **military** in neighbouring Guinea-Bissau. This support ended in late 2000 after the death of Gen. Ansumane Mané. Low-level violence continues, however. Most rebel activity is in the Bigniona region, north of the Casamance River, although there are still pockets of rebellion in the southern Casamance. The MFDC and the government have agreed to renew negotiations for peace in Guinea-Bissau, but these have yet to take place. The Casamance is the richest agricultural area in Senegal, but, owing to the rebellion, is underdeveloped and lacks basic infrastructure and good links to the rest of Senegal. A ferry, which used to link the Casamance with Dakar, Le Joola, sank in September 2002 with the loss of more than 1,800 lives. Demining operations, which had commenced in July 2003, continued into 2004. In July 2004 the Assemblée nationale adopted legislation providing for an amnesty for all MFDC combatants. In response, MFDC leaders reiterated their demand for the withdrawal of government forces from Casamance.

International relations

Relations with The Gambia in recent years have been difficult owing to trade and transport issues. The Gambia's intentions *vis-à-vis* the Casamance conflict are also viewed with suspicion in Senegal. The Presidents of Senegal and The Gambia exchanged state visits in early 2002, but a major transport dispute negated any improvement in relations. Senegal's relations with Guinea-Bissau have improved since the end of **civil war** and democratic elections in that country in 1999, and especially since the death of ex-junta leader Ansumane Mané. The two countries' armed forces have a good working relationship, which has resulted in a decline in rebel activity in the border area. Relations with neighbouring Mauritania have been difficult since a serious border dispute in 1989, which led to expulsions of each other's citizens and many deaths. There was a further deterioration in relations in 2000 over the Senegal River border.

Senegal pursues the main agendas of its active and moderate regional foreign policy via the **Economic Community of West African States (ECOWAS)** and the **Union économique et monétaire ouest-africaine (UEMOA)**. Senegal occupied the presidency of both organizations in 2002. President Wade sometimes pursues an independent policy within the African international community (e.g. towards Madagascar, when Senegal disregarded the consensus of opinion within the **African Union** to recognize the government of **Marc Ravalomanana** there). President Wade and President **Obasanjo** of Nigeria are, respectively, vice-chairman and chairman of the Implementation Committee of the **New Partnership for African Development (NEPAD)**. NEPAD is an African-led initiative directed to the achievement of sustainable development in Africa. It was endorsed by the whole of Africa at the Lusaka summit meeting of the **Organization of African Unity** in July 2001. More detailed programme proposals for implementation are under development. NEPAD represents a new-found political will on the part of African leaders to assume responsibility for addressing the continent's challenges, including dealing with conflict.

Senegal has good relations with Western countries, especially France, which provides the largest contribution of external aid. However, under President Abdoulaye Wade, Senegal has made a major alliance shift from France towards the USA. Senegal is the latest focus point of the US Department of Defence in Africa. The USA has obtained a wide range of concessions at a Dakar airfield, which has already been used as a landing point for several military operations in West Africa. Senegal also maintains good relations with the **European Union** and many European countries, and with Taiwan. Some Middle Eastern states also provide substantial aid. A number of Senegalese hold high positions in international organizations.

Senegal, economy

In 2003, according to estimates by the **World Bank**, Senegal's gross national income (GNI), measured at average 2001–03 prices, was US $6,404m., equivalent to $550 per head (or $1,660 on an international purchasing-power parity basis). During 1990–2003, it was estimated, the population increased at an average annual rate of 2.5%, while gross domestic product (GDP) per head increased by an average of 1.1% per year. Overall GDP increased, in real terms, at an average annual rate of 3.6% per year in 1990–2003; growth in 2003 was 6.5%. In 1990–93 consumer prices declined by an annual average of 0.8%. However, following the 50% devaluation of the CFA franc, inflation averaged 32.3% in 1994; inflation subsequently slowed to an annual average of 1.8% in 1995–2002. Consumer prices increased by an average of 2.3% in 2002. Senegal's industries include the processing of agricultural products and fish, phosphate mining, production of fertilizers, petroleum refining and production of construction materials. Output by the agricultural sector includes groundnuts, millet, maize, sorghum, rice, **cotton**, tomatoes, and green vegetables. Cattle, poultry and pigs are also raised. The national currency is the CFA franc (see the **Franc Zone**). In 2004 the average exchange rate was US $1 = 528.29 francs CFA.

Senegal has few natural resources. The agricultural base of the economy has been eroded by periodic **drought** and gradual desertification. The agricultural sector's contribution to GDP declined from around 24% in 1970 to 16.3% in 2002. The main agricultural crop is groundnuts, but the sector is in long-term decline. Other sources of foreign exchange are **fisheries**, tourism and phosphates. Senegal is a member of thc Franc Zone of French West African countries, whose common currency is linked to the euro. Economic growth has been generally good since the mid-1990s, but the economy has many structural problems and poor social indicators—high unemployment, high illiteracy rates and some poor health statistics, especially in rural areas. Senegal is a major recipient of foreign development aid. Apart from the World Bank and the **International Monetary Fund (IMF)**, France, the **European Union**, Germany, the USA, Japan, Taiwan and some Middle Eastern countries are major donors. French companies and the local Lebanese community are the main domestic investors. In recent years Senegal has made successful attempts to reduce its **debt** burden; in June 2000, it became eligible to receive support under the **Heavily Indebted Poor Countries (HIPC) initiative**. In 2001 Senegal was reclassified as a Least Developed Country by the UN and ranked 154th (out of 173) in the UNDP's Human Development Index. The HIPC completion point is contingent on macroeconomic performance and on progress in the health and **education** sectors.

Economic growth was slow in 2002, after a poorly organized groundnut collection in the spring and weak rains in the summer. Implementation of sectoral and structural reforms has been uneven, with significant progress in the trade sector, but with unfinished privatization agendas in the power and groundnut sectors. However, there was strong growth in real GDP in 2003, and inflation has fallen markedly. GDP growth of 6.1% has been forecast for 2005. Senegal has, on the whole, pursued policies that are approved by the IMF/World Bank, including privatization. Despite problems, the efforts of the Wade government were commended by the IMF in 2005 for having made 'significant progress'.

Senghor, Léopold Sédar

Former President of Senegal. Senghor retired in 1981 and was peacefully succeeded by **Abdou Diouf**, who was confirmed in his position by an overwhelming electoral success two years later, but failed to provide the necessary initiative to stem fierce sectarian rivalries and to retrieve an economy that was over-dependent on unwanted groundnuts and afflicted by **drought**.

Serer

A major ethno-linguistic grouping in West Africa.

Seychelles, Republic of

The Republic of Seychelles comprises about 115 islands, widely scattered over the western Indian Ocean. Apart from the Seychelles archipelago, the country includes several other island groups, the southernmost being about 210 km north of Madagascar. The total area is 455.3 sq km. At mid-2004 the population was officially estimated at 82,474. In 1981 Seselwa, a creole spoken by virtually all Seychellois, replaced English and French as the official language. Almost all of the inhabitants are Christians, of whom more than 90% belong to the Roman Catholic Church. The capital is Victoria (on the island of Mahé), whose population was estimated at 20,050 in mid-2003.

Political profile

Under the 1993 Constitution, executive power is vested in the President, who is Head of State and Commander-in-Chief of the Armed Forces. The President, who is elected by direct popular vote, appoints and leads the Council of Ministers, which acts in an advisory capacity to him. The President also appoints the holders of certain public offices and the judiciary. The President may hold office for a maximum period of three five-year terms. The legislature is the unicameral National Assembly, presently comprising 34 members, of whom 25 are directly elected for five years and nine allocated on a proportional basis. Constitutional changes, introduced in July 1996, provide for an enlargement to 35 members: 25 directly elected and a maximum of 10 allocated on a proportional basis.

In a presidential election held on 31 August–2 September 2001 **France Albert René**, the candidate of the Seychelles People's Progressive Front (SPPF), received 54.19% of the votes and was thus re-elected. René had first been declared President in 1977, after an armed coup, and remained in office until 14 April 2004, when he resigned and was succeeded by James Mancham, hitherto Vice-President.

Following an election held on 4–6 December 2002, the distribution of seats in the National Assembly was as follows: SPPF 23; **Seychelles National Party (SNP)** 11.

History

Seychelles was proclaimed a French colony in 1756 but the first French settlers did not arrive until 1770. France ruled the islands with delegated powers from Mauritius. Both Britain and France were keenly interested in the strategic value of the islands and during the late 1790s and early 1800s Seychelles changed hands several times. Following the Napoleonic wars, Seychelles was ceded to the United Kingdom in 1814 and was administered from Mauritius until 1888, when an administrator was appointed to govern from Victoria. Seychelles became a separate Crown Colony in 1903.

The campaign for **independence** began in 1964 and culminated in Seychelles becoming a republic within the **Commonwealth** in June 1976. Initially a coalition government headed by President James Mancham ruled the country. However, he was overthrown in a coup on 5 June 1977 and was replaced by France Albert René, the former Prime Minister. President René administered the country as a one-party state for 14 years, surviving three unsuccessful coups, plotted by exiled opponents and involving foreign mercenaries—in April 1978, November 1979 and November 1981—and a suppressed mutiny (in August 1982). In December 1991 President René announced an unexpected transition to multi-party **democracy**. This followed pressure for change from foreign governments and exiles overseas. Presidential and parliamentary elections were held in July 1993, and were described by Commonwealth observers as free and fair. The SPPF (the party of the President) won the legislative elections convincingly, receiving 57% of the total votes, while Mancham's Democratic Party (DP) received 33% and the United Opposition (UO) 10%. In the presidential election René received 59% of the votes, Mancham 37% and Rev. Wavel Ramkalawan (of the DP) 4%. In June 1996 the Constitution was amended to create the post of Vice-President, to which the finance minister James Michel was appointed.

The SPPF won another large majority in the National Assembly in elections held on 20–22 March 1998. Rev. Ramkalawan replaced James Mancham as leader of the opposition and became the only directly elected member of the National Assembly who was not a member of the ruling party. Ramkalawan's party, the SNP (formerly the UO), secured an extra two seats through proportional allocation, but was ranged against a government holding 30 seats in the Assembly. The DP was allocated one seat. In the presidential election René received 67% of the votes, Ramkalawan 19%, and Mancham 14%.

A President is currently allowed to serve a maximum of three terms, each of five years. In May 2000, however, the National Assembly amended the Constitution to allow the President to seek a new mandate before the end of his term (provided he has held office for one year and is not in his third term). Following months of speculation, on 12 July 2001 President René announced an early presidential election. This was originally scheduled for 10–12 August, but after opposition parties complained that this did not allow them sufficient time to organize their campaigns, the elections were rescheduled and held on 31 August–2 September. President René was re-elected, but with a significantly reduced majority. The main opposition candidate, Rev. Ramkalawan, received 45% of the votes, compared with 54% for René. An independent candidate, Philippe Boulle, received only 481 votes. The DP did not contest the election. The balance in the National Assembly remains unchanged. National Assembly elections were held on 4–6 December 2002. In a turn-out of 85%, the SPPF won 54% of the votes and therefore retained control of the National Assembly, while the SNP received 42% of the votes. In early 2003 President René officially acknowledged Vice-President Michel as his successor, and relinquished power on 14 April 2004 after 27 years as President, although he retained his position as president of the SPPF. James Michel was inaugurated as President on the same day and Joseph Belmont was appointed as Vice-President.

International relations
Seychelles follows a non-aligned foreign policy. It has often sided with the more radical members and causes of the **Non-aligned Movement**, but has not allowed this to interfere with essentially pragmatic decisions directly affecting Seychellois interests. It has enjoyed close relations with France and Britain, as well as with the USSR/Russia, the People's Republic of China, India and Cuba. It has sought to promote economic relations particularly with countries from which it might receive loan assistance. Seychelles is a member of the Indian Ocean Commission—a group promoting economic and trade co-operation between the islands of the Indian Ocean; and of the Indian Ocean Rim-Association for Regional Co-operation. Seychelles has been particularly active in promoting the Indian Ocean as a peace zone. It is an active member of the **African Union**. It also participates in meetings of the **Common Market for Eastern and Southern Africa**. The Seychelles chose to withdraw from the **Southern African Development Community (SADC)** in favour of stronger regional co-operation in the Indian Ocean region. This shift in foreign policy away from southern Africa was completed in January 2004 when effective disassociation from SADC was completed. Seychelles has sought to strengthen ties with Mauritius and other Indian Ocean island nations.

Seychelles, economy

In 2003, according to estimates by the **World Bank**, Seychelles' gross national income (GNI), measured at average 2001–03 prices, was US $678m., equivalent to $7,480 per head (or $15,960 per head on an international purchasing-power parity basis). During 1990–2003, it was estimated, the population increased at an average annual rate of 1.4%, while gross domestic product (GDP) per head increased, in real terms, by an average of 1.5% per year. Overall GDP increased, in real terms, at an average annual rate of 2.9% in 1990–2003. Real GDP increased by 0.3% in 2002, but declined by 5.1% in 2003. The annual rate of inflation averaged 3.0% in 1995–2003; consumer prices increased by an average of 3.3% in 2003. Tourism and tuna fishing/canning are important sectors of the economy. Fish (canned tuna and prawns), together with re-exports of petroleum, constitute Seychelles' principal exports. In 2004 the main destinations of Seychelles' exports were the United Kingdom, France, Spain, Japan, Italy, Germany and the Netherlands. The principal suppliers of imports in that year were Saudi Arabia, Spain, France, Singapore, Italy, South Africa and the United Kingdom. The national currency is the Seychelles rupee. In 2004 the average exchange rate was US $1 = 5.5000 rupees.

Seychelles is now classed as an upper middle-income country. GDP increased by 1.4% in 2000 and by 1.0% in both 2001 and 2002. GDP per head is higher than anywhere on the African continent. Growth slowed in 1998–2002, and fell in 2003 owing to the sluggish performance of both the tourist and tuna sectors, but resumed in 2004, erasing a persistent budget deficit. The tourist sector employs about 30% of the workforce. In 2000 tourist numbers rose by 7% over 1999 and tourist revenues increased by 9%. However, Seychelles has felt the impact of the global downturn in this area that followed the events on 11 September 2001 in the USA. The government continues to encourage foreign investment in order to upgrade hotels and other services, in the face of stiff regional competition (especially from Mauritius and the Maldives). In response to strong regional competition in and the volatility of the tourist sector, the government has attempted to reduce Seychelles' reliance on the sector by promoting the development of farming, fishing, and small-scale manufacturing. Tuna fishing/canning accounted for 78% of GDP from exports in 2002, generating $154m. The government entered into negotiations for new and preferential fishing agreements with the **European Union** in 2004 and hopes to expand revenues by selling fishing rights and increase catches through joint ventures.

For some years the main feature of the economy has been a chronic shortage of foreign exchange. The simple foreign exchange pipeline system, introduced in 1994, was ineffective and businesses that relied on imported goods had to wait for as long as six months for foreign exchange. A more complex version involving prioritized allocations was subsequently introduced but again proved ineffective. The pipeline has now been notionally abandoned in favour of the allocation by commercial banks of permitted retentions of hard currency, backed up by new sanctions on the black market. However, it can still take many months for invoices to be paid and the price of the rupee on the black market is half the official exchange rate. In 1995, in order to attract foreign investment and ease the foreign exchange problems, President René introduced the Economic Development Act (EDA), which allowed sweeping immunities from prosecution and sequestration of assets to anyone investing $10m with the government. (The Economic Citizenship Programme was also introduced in 1996, selling Seychelles passports for $25,000 or more, but was later officially abandoned.) The EDA caused great concern to other governments owing to its implications for money-laundering and funds accruing from drugs-trafficking. In 1996, as a result of these concerns, President René announced that the EDA would never be used, although it was not repealed until August 2000.

In November 2000 the **International Monetary Fund (IMF)** expressed concern that economic conditions in Seychelles had steadily deteriorated since July 1998. Of greatest concern were the wide fiscal and balance of payments deficits that were being financed, in part, by accumulating large external **debt** arrears. The IMF noted that growth in capital spending, as a percentage of GDP, far exceeded that of countries of similar size and wealth. However, the government has largely ignored the IMF's remedial advice (including that on currency devaluation), instead pursuing major infrastructural projects, such as the ambitious East Coast Land Reclamation Project. New foreign currency regulations introduced on 1 June 2001 oblige visitors to pay for hotel rooms and services, car hire, guided tours and other recreational activities in hard currency. In July 2003 the government announced major economic reforms, encompassing taxation, welfare, the privatization of government properties, incentives to productive sectors and a review of the public service. Following Michel's assumption of the presidency a new economic policy was promised in 2005.

Seychelles National Party (SNP)

Formerly the United Opposition party in Seychelles, led by Rev. Wavel Ramkalawan.

Shagari, Alhaji Shehu

In 1979 Alhaji Shehu Shagari became President of a new Nigerian federation comprising 19 states, with a total population of well over 80m. The Shagari regime proved ineffective at dealing with Nigeria's mounting problems: blatant **corruption**, an economy no longer buoyed up by **oil** (the price of which had fallen by 10%, while, partly as a result of mismanagement, output had declined by almost 25%), interminable disputes over the Constitution and religious disorder in the north. At the end of 1983 the army returned to power and **Maj.-Gen. Muhammadu Buhari** replaced President Shagari as Head of State.

Shari'a

Islamic Law. Literally means the 'way' or the 'road'. Based on divine revelation in the form of the Koran and prophetic practice, Sunna (as recorded in the Hadith), the Shari'a governs the individual and the social life of the believer. The Shari'a is the only valid basis for judging acts as good or evil, lawful or unlawful. As the Koran and the Hadith do not cover all eventualities, Islamic jurists later included *ijma* (consensus) and *ijtihad* (reasoning) as integral to the interpretation of the Shari'a.

Sharpeville

Remembered in South Africa as the location of a massacre of unarmed African protesters in the 1960s.

Shi'a or Shi'ite Muslims

The minority strand of Islamic thought and belief, with relatively few adherents in Africa. The largest Shi'a sect is that of the Ithna'ashriya (Twelvers), who acknowledge a succession of 12 imams. Another group is that known as the Seveners, or Ismailis, who believe that the last imam on earth was Ismail. The Seveners are divided into several sub-groups, on the basis of their beliefs regarding the succession from Ismail onwards.

Shona

Major ethnic or tribal grouping in Zimbabwe.

Sierra Leone, Republic of

The Republic of Sierra Leone lies on the west coast of Africa, with Guinea to the north and east, and Liberia to the south. Sierra Leone is 71,740 sq km in area. At mid-2003 the population was estimated at 4,971,000. Eighteen identified groups make up the indigenous population; the **Temne** in the north (30%) and the **Mende** (29%) in the south are the largest groups. English is the official language, while Krio (Creole), Mende, Limba and Temne are also widely spoken. The majority of the population follow animist beliefs, but there are significant numbers of Islamic and Christian adherents. The capital is Freetown, whose population was estimated at 920,717 in mid-2003.

Political profile

Under the terms of the Constitution of 1991, executive power is vested in the President, who is directly elected by universal adult suffrage. The President appoints the Cabinet (subject to approval by the legislature). The maximum duration of the President's tenure of office is limited to two five-year terms. Legislative power is vested in a unicameral Parliament, which is elected for a four-year term and comprises 112 members elected by a system of proportional representation, in 14 constituencies, and 12 Paramount Chiefs, who represent the provincial districts.

In a presidential election held on 14 May 2002 **Alhaji Ahmed Tejan Kabbah**, the candidate of the Sierra Leone People's Party (SLPP), received 70.06% of the votes and was duly re-elected. (Kabbah was first elected as President in 1996, but was deposed in a coup in 1997. He was reinstated in 1998.)

Following a general election held on 14 May 2002, the distribution of seats in the Parliament was as follows: SLPP 83; All-People's Congress (APC) 27; People's Liberation Party (PLP) 2.

History

Sierra Leone gained **independence** from Britain in 1961. It became a republic in 1971 under President **Siaka Stevens** of the APC. In the post-independence period there has rarely been stability in Sierra Leone as economic mismanagement and **corruption** has marginalized the majority of Sierra Leoneans who live in the provinces in favour of a Freetown élite. Stevens imposed his authority on the country in 1978 by outlawing multi-party politics. He remained President until 1985, when he transferred power to **Brig.-Gen. Joseph Momoh**. Momoh failed to reverse the economic decline. A brutal internal conflict began in April 1991 when the Revolutionary United Front (RUF), led by an obscure former army corporal, Foday Sankoh, supported by President **Charles Taylor** of Liberia, invaded Sierra

Leone from Liberia, ostensibly to oust the corrupt APC. Momoh was powerless to deal with the insurgents, and was overthrown in a military coup in 1992 that installed Capt. Valentine Strasser as head of a National Provincial Ruling Council (NPRC). Strasser promised to rid the country of corruption and defeat the RUF, but failed. He was in turn overthrown by Capt. Julius Maada Bio in early 1996. Under pressure from civil society, Bio organized multi-party elections in February 1996. Ahmed Tejan Kabbah of the SLPP won the presidency, defeating Dr John Karefa Smart in a second ballot. In the mean time, rebel activities prevented the government from exercising its authority in more than half of the country.

In 1997 disaffected soldiers of the Sierra Leone Army (SLA) staged a coup and requested Maj. Johnny Paul Koroma, at the time imprisoned on treason charges, to be their leader. Koroma assumed power and formed the Armed Forces Revolutionary Council (AFRC). In an effort to halt further challenges, Koroma invited the RUF to ally itself with his administration. Koroma's military junta failed to attract international support and was shunned by the people of Sierra Leone. The Nigerian-led **Economic Community of West African States (ECOWAS) Monitoring Group (ECOMOG)**, aided by the Sierra Leone Civil Defence Force (CDF) led by Sam Hinga Norman, removed the military junta from Freetown in February 1998, and President Kabbah, whose government had sought refuge in neighbouring Guinea, returned to Freetown on 10 March in that year. Rebel groups—mainly AFRC and ex-SLA members—attacked again, occupying most of Freetown in January 1999, but ECOMOG forces eventually expelled them. During the rebel action more than 5,000 people were killed and most of the eastern suburbs of Freetown were destroyed. Abuses of human rights by both the rebels and by ECOMOG forces were reportedly widespread. A cease-fire was agreed in May 1999.

The cease-fire led to the Lomé Peace Agreement, signed in Togo on 7 July 1999, between the government and the RUF. The agreement was widely criticized because it offered amnesties for crimes committed prior to its signature. It also provided for cease-fire monitoring; transformation of the RUF into a political party; security guarantees; disarmament, demobilization and reintegration (DDR) of former combatants; restructuring of the armed forces; withdrawal of mercenaries; release of prisoners of war; delivery of humanitarian assistance; dealing with human rights violations; a Truth and Reconciliation Commission; and four (out of 18) Cabinet positions as well as four Deputy Minister positions for the rebels.

In May 2000, after 10 months of relative stability, RUF rebels attacked UN peace-keeping personnel and destroyed DDR camps. A number of UN peace-keepers and journalists were killed and more than 500 others detained. British forces were deployed to Freetown to evacuate UK citizens and secure the airport to allow the arrival of UN reinforcements. Foday Sankoh, the leader of the RUF, and more than 100 RUF personnel, including all RUF government ministers, were arrested by the government under emergency powers. In November the government and the RUF signed the Abuja Agreement, a cease-fire agreement brokered by ECOWAS in Nigeria. The agreement included: disarmament; the return of weapons seized from the **United Nations Observer Mission in Sierra Leone (UNOMSIL)**; freedom of movement throughout Sierra Leone (including the areas where **diamonds** were mined) for UNOMSIL; and a commitment to return to the peace process. In early 2001 more than 50% of the country was under the control of the RUF rebels. A UN peace-keeping force, the **United Nations Assistance Mission in Sierra Leone (UNAMSIL)** was deployed throughout the country. The government restored its authority throughout the country and gradually extended basic services into areas that had not been under government control for almost 10 years.

In January 2001 President Kabbah declared that disarmament was complete and the war over. By March the state of emergency had been lifted. Work began on several fronts to consolidate the fragile peace. In peaceful and credible elections, held in May 2002, Kabbah was re-elected as President. In parliamentary elections the SLPP achieved an emphatic victory.

International relations

In 1973 the **Mano River Union (MRU)** established a customs and economic union between Guinea, Liberia and Sierra Leone. Subsequently, members signed a mutual non-aggression pact and pledged to establish a permanent mechanism for conflict prevention. Despite this, relations between the three countries have not always been amicable. There is an unresolved dispute between Sierra Leone and Guinea over the demarcation of the border around Yenga.

In 2000 the UN deployed a peace-keeping force (UNAMSIL) in Sierra Leone to oversee the implementation of the 1999 Lomé Agreement. UNAMSIL began a gradual withdrawal from Sierra Leone in late 2002, but it is anticipated that there will be a UN presence in the country for some time to come. There are currently about 13,000 UNAMSIL personnel in Sierra Leone.

Sierra Leone, economy

In 2003, according to the **World Bank**, Sierra Leone's gross national income (GNI), measured at average 2001–03 prices, was US $764m., equivalent to $150 per head (or $530 per head on an international purchasing-power parity basis). During 1990–2003, it was estimated, the population increased at an average annual rate of 2.2%, while gross domestic product (GDP) per head declined, in real terms, by an average of 4.4% per year. Overall GDP declined, in real terms, at an average annual rate of 2.2% in 1990–2003; however, growth was 6.3% in 2002 and 6.5% in 2003. The annual rate of inflation averaged 16.1% in 1992–2003. Consumer prices declined by 3.3% in 2002, but increased by 7.6% in 2003 and by an estimated 12.0% in 2004. Mining, principally of **diamonds** and rutile, but also of **gold** and other minerals, is the country's main source of income. **Agriculture** and forestry are also important sectors, and tourism has the potential to become one. In 2004 the main destinations for Sierra Leone's exports were Belgium, Germany and the USA. The principal suppliers of imports in that year were Germany, the United Kingdom, Côte d'Ivoire, the USA, Ukraine, the Netherlands, the People's Republic of China and Denmark.

The national currency is the leone. In 2004 the average exchange rate was US $1 = 2,701.30 leones.

Sierra Leone has substantial mineral, agricultural and fishery resources. Agriculture employs about two-thirds of the working population, with subsistence agriculture dominating the sector. The mining of diamonds, bauxite and rutile provides the major source of hard currency. Manufacturing consists mainly of the processing of raw materials and of light manufacturing for the domestic market. In 1991–99 serious efforts were made to stabilize the economy and lay the foundation for sustainable economic growth. These efforts were interrupted, however, by recurrent violence and political instability.

In the three years to March 1994 Sierra Leone successfully implemented an adjustment programme supported by the **International monetary Fund (IMF)** under the Rights Approach. In 1992 the International Development Association supported the government's efforts through the Reconstruction Import Credit aimed at improving fiscal management. Economic performance improved significantly. The rate of inflation declined from more than 100% to 20%, and real GDP growth recovered gradually, rising to a positive rate in 1994, after several years of economic decline. In 1995 all programmes encountered serious difficulties, however, following the escalation of rebel activity, which spread to the mining areas. After rebel activity was brought under control at the end of 1995, in 1996 the democratically elected government adopted a new economic recovery programme that was supported by the IMF with a second annual arrangement under the Enhanced Structural Adjustment Facility (ESAF). Despite the fragile security situation, the 1996 programme was implemented in a satisfactory manner and remained on schedule. Economic performance improved markedly, with real GDP growth rising to 5% in 1996 and inflation declining to about 6%.

Economic activity began to recover in 2000—real GDP increased by 3.8%, following a cumulative decline of 25% in 1997–99. Moreover, the price level, which rose by 80% in 1998–99, fell by 3% in 2000—owing mainly to the expansion of external assistance that financed a twofold recovery in imports and an appreciation of 27% in the leone. The recovery accelerated in 2001, when GDP rose by 5.4%. Consumer and investor confidence increased with a much greater freedom of movement of people and goods; resettlement and rehabilitation activities; greater agricultural output; and a 74% increase in power supply. Power supply is to be further improved through the 50-MW Bumbura hydroelectric power station, which is scheduled to commence operations in 2006. Fiscal and monetary policies contained inflation to 3.4% in 2001, despite the large, healthy realignment of domestic relative prices—the leone depreciated by 30% in 2001, reversing its sustained appreciation during 2000. However, economic growth remains dependent on sustained peace. For this reason the United Nations Assistance Mission in Sierra Leone will remain in Sierra Leone until at least December 2005.

The Revolutionary United Front's control of Sierra Leone's major diamond fields provided the means to fuel the conflict and sustain the rebels during the war. An embargo prohibiting the direct or indirect import of any rough diamonds not covered by a specially devised Government Certificate of Origin Scheme was allowed to expire in June 2003. The Certification Scheme was the precursor to the Kimberley Process, to which Sierra Leone is now a signatory. Lasting stability in Sierra Leone will depend partly on managing the diamond fields that accounted for 91.3% of total export earnings in 2003. Reconstruction and regaining investor confidence has been slow. Sierra Leone remains heavily dependent on external financial aid, and on assistance in maintaining peace. However, diamonds are contributing to the recovery of the economy as a result of the Kimberly certification process and of increased output. Revenues from diamond exports have risen by 60% since 2003 as the government has regained control over the industry. Another positive development has been the reopening of rutile mines in 2005. Before 1995 Sierra Leone provided 25% of the world's production of rutile and it is estimated that rutile deposits will be worth more than $3,000m. once they have been fully exploited.

Sisulu, Walter

Elder statesman of the **African National Congress** in South Africa, who, like **Nelson Mandela**, was imprisoned for 25 years by the **apartheid** regime.

Slabbert, Frederik van Zyl

Former leader of the **Progressive Party** of South Africa and leader of the opposition in the South African parliament before 1994.

Slavery

Since before the arrival of the Europeans in Africa, slavery had been practised by local African peoples, particularly in West Africa. Arab traders on the East African coast also became involved in the slave trade from the Middle Ages onwards. With the Europeans, however, came a new drive to enslave people as labour to produce commodities for sale. The Atlantic slave trade grew from small beginnings into a massive, forced transmigration of African populations during the 18th and 19th centuries and transformed many African communities as a consequence. It is hard to determine the scale of this transformation, or the demographic consequences, both for those societies actively involved in slaving and those communities that provided the human raw material. Undoubtedly, much of West and Central African society was significantly affected. Abolitionism came to have an effect eventually and the slave trade declined during the latter part of the 19th century, but slavery as an African institution, transformed through the previous centuries, remained relatively widespread. In many of the territories in which the Europeans intervened more directly, converting them into protectorates and colonies, institutionalized forced labour—whether organized by private enterprise or by the colonial state itself—tended to replace local slavery across many parts of West and Central Africa.

Slavery itself as an institution lasted in some places throughout the colonial period and even after **independence**. The colonial authorities were often loath to intervene in 'local' matters, especially where it might antagonize the local rulers and chiefs through whom the colonial administration worked and on whom it usually depended, and slavery was one of those 'local' matters. Slavery continued in Africa in many places into the 1970s. In the Portuguese colonies of São Tomé and Angola, contract workers on sugar and **cocoa** plantations and on **cotton** plantations were treated as virtual slaves as late as the 1970s. In Mauritania and parts of Mali and Niger, the institution of slavery continued even later, and in Mauritania and parts of Sudan (and possibly to a limited extent elsewhere in the remoter desert areas of the Sahel and Sahara) continues today.

Slovo, Joe

Leader of the South African Communist Party and Chief of Staff of the guerrilla army of the **African National Congress (Umkhonto we Sizwe—Spear of the Nation)**.

Smuts, Jan

Prime Minister of South Africa during the Second World War.

Social Democratic Front (SDF)

Political party in Cameroon, established in 1990. The SDF's chairman is **John Fru Ndi**.

Social Democratic Movement (SDM)

Political party in Cameroon. Established in 1995, following a break with the **Social Democratic Front**. The SDM's leader is Siga Asanga.

Social Democratic Party (SDP)

Political party in Botswana, founded in 1994. The SDP's leader is O. Marumo.

Social Justice Party

An Egyptian political party, founded in 1993. Its chairman is Muhammad Abd al-Aal.

Social Liberal Party

Algerian political grouping, led by Ahmed Khelil.

Socialism

Many political movements and parties, particularly during the three decades after the Second World War, and many governments, particularly during the 1960s and 1970s, in Africa have claimed to be 'socialist', to be following a path towards socialism through a process of 'socialist construction'. Many, however, were reluctant to adopt the Marxist-Leninist understanding of socialism, in which class struggle played a central role in the revolutionary transformation of economy and society, and preferred instead to speak of a distinctively '**African socialism**', in which radical economic and social reform was initiated in the name of the mass of the people, often by a ruling élite who considered themselves the main force for radical change, and often through authoritarian and centralized regimes and one-party states. The ideologies and political practices of 'African socialism' were often more reminiscent of national socialism' in Europe and of 'authoritarian populism' in Latin America and the Middle East, than of socialism in Europe.

Socialist Labour Party (Hizb al-Amal al-Ishtiraki)

The Socialist Labour Party of Egypt, like the **New Wafd Party**, has pre-1952 origins. It has historical links with a proto-fascist movement, the Green Shirts or Egyptian Youth (Misr al-Fatat). Under the leadership of Ibrahim Shukri, it generally supported the liberalization policies of President **Sadat**, but criticized the peace treaty with Israel. Until the 1984 presidential elections, it was designated the official opposition party by the regime. It has links with the higher echelons of the labour movement, but little to do with the rank and file. It is less of a socialist party in the European sense than a party of national **socialism** in the corporatist or fascist tradition.

Socialist Liberal Party (Hizb al-Ahrar al-Ishtiraki)

The Egyptian Socialist Liberal Party, which represents the interests of liberal capitalism, is led by Hilmi Murad. The party was mildly critical of Egypt's peace treaty with Israel, but broadly supportive of the economic policies of Presidents **Sadat** and **Mubarak**. It is very much a party that emerged as a result of reforms made in the mid- and late 1970s. It has limited political support, and received only 7% of the vote in elections held in 1984.

Société internationale financière pour les investissements et le développement en Afrique (SIFIDA)

Established in 1970 by 120 financial institutions, including the **African Development Bank**. Following a restructuring in 1996, the main shareholders are now the Banque Nationale de Paris (BNP)/Paribas Group and its six banking affiliates in West and Central Africa. SIFIDA is active in the fields of project and trade finance in Africa and also provides financial advisory services, notably in the context of privatization and **debt** conversion.

Solidarité pour la défense des minorités (SOJEDEM—Solidarity for the Defence of Minorities)

Political association in Burundi.

Somalia (Somali Democratic Republic)

The Somali Democratic Republic is situated in **East Africa**, with a coastline that borders the Gulf of Aden and the Indian Ocean and faces the Arabian Peninsula across the sea. It shares land borders with Djibouti, Ethiopia and Kenya. Somalia has a land area of 637,657 sq km in area. At mid-2003 the population was estimated at 9,890,000. The people are mainly Somali (85%), the remainder comprising Bantu and Arabs. The national language is Somali, but **Arabic** is also in official use. English and Italian are widely spoken. The state religion is **Islam**, and the majority of **Somalis** are Sunni Muslims. There is a small Christian community, mostly Roman Catholics. The capital is Mogadishu, whose population was estimated at 1,174,881 in mid-2003.

Political profile

In July 2000 a Somali national reconciliation conference approved a national Charter, which envisaged the Somali Republic adopting a federal system of government, comprising 18 regional administrations, after a three-year interim period. The Charter provided for the creation of a Transitional National Assembly (TNA), which was to exercise legislative power in Somalia during the interim period. The 245-member TNA, comprising members of the four major clans and of an alliance of smaller clans, as well as 20 influential Somalis, was inaugurated in August and elected a President of Somalia. In October the President nominated a Prime Minister, who formed a Cabinet. Despite the expiry of its mandate in August 2003, the TNA remained in place, pending the election of a new legislative body. In late January 2004, following protracted negotiations in Kenya, an agreement was signed that provided for the establishment of a new 275-member national parliament, to comprise 61 representatives from each of the four major clans and 31 from an alliance of smaller clans. Members were sworn in to the Transitional Parliament in late August. Once established, the parliament elected a national President, who, in turn, nominated a Prime Minister to form a government.

Col Abdullahi Yussuf Ahmed was elected as President of Somalia by the Transitional Parliament in October 2004.

History

The region was divided in the latter part of the 19th century into a British protectorate in the north and an Italian colony in the south. In 1935 Italy, which was dissatisfied with the barrenness of its part of 'Somaliland' or Somalia, exploited an incident at Wal Wal in the disputed Ogaden to conquer Ethiopia, which it held in 1936–41. Italy was suspected of wishing to establish a 'Greater Somalia', which would annex British Somaliland, but its defeat in 1941 revived the independent Ethiopian empire and left the **Somalis** still subject and divided. Discussions on the Ethiopian-Somali frontier proceeded slowly until 1950, when a compromise was agreed in Oslo, Norway, that satisfied no one, and Italian Somaliland became the UN Trust Territory of Somalia, placed under Italian administration for a 10-year period prior to **independence**.

The Trust Territory's first general election was held in March 1959, in which the Somali Youth League (SYL) won 83 out of 90 seats in the Legislative Assembly. Britain accelerated the independence of British Somaliland, so that it could be joined with the ex-Italian colony to form an independent state. A movement in French Somaliland in favour of accession to Somalia had been circumvented two years earlier when that territory's assembly voted in favour of remaining a French Overseas Territory. French Somaliland was eventually to become Djibouti. In June 1960 the independent Somali Republic was declared, the president of the southern Legislative Assembly was proclaimed Head of State and the two legislatures merged to form a single National Assembly. A coalition government was formed by the SYL.

Immediately after attaining independence in July 1960, the former British Somaliland Protectorate and the Italian-administered UN Trust Territory of Somalia merged to form the Somali Republic. Despite an initial period of political stability, inter-clan tensions threatened the coalition government. At the Lancaster House conference on Kenya in 1962, a request by the Somalis for a plebiscite in the Northern Frontier District of Kenya and its union with Somalia was denied. Later that year there was discussion of an East African federation, which would embrace not only Somalia and the British East African territories, but also Ethiopia. Kenya was adamant, however, that it would retain the Northern Frontier District. In 1963 hostilities erupted between Somalia and Ethiopia—the Somalis did not accept the 1897 treaty by which Britain had ceded part of British Somaliland to Ethiopia, and the border between Italian Somaliland and Ethiopia was not established. Fighting continued until 1967 when a new Somali government asked President **Kaunda** of Kenya to mediate. Diplomatic relations were restored in 1968.

Following the unsuccessful war with Ethiopia, and a presidential assassination, the army, under Gen. Mohamed Siad Barre, seized power in October 1969. During the 1970s Barre established a regime based on 'scientific **socialism**' that became increasingly militaristic and dictatorial. In 1977 Barre embarked on a disastrous war with Ethiopia to liberate the Ogaden from Ethiopia, which led to a Somali defeat in 1978. By the early 1980s opposition groups had begun to form in the north west and in north-eastern regions. One such group in north-west Somalia (formerly British Somaliland), the Somali National Movement (SNM), launched an unsuccessful offensive in 1988 against the forces of Siad Barre based in the north-west. Barre's forces countered with great violence, resulting in thousands of civilian deaths and the almost total destruction of Hargeisa (the region's capital).

By October 1990 other rebel groups were in active opposition to the Barre regime, including the **United Somali Congress (USC)**, whose military wing was led by **Gen. Aideed**. In January 1991 the USC gained control of Mogadishu. Barre fled to his south-western homeland (and in 1992 took refuge in Nigeria). The ensuing power vacuum triggered an intense struggle between the self-appointed interim President, Ali Mahdi, and Gen. Aideed. This later escalated into full-blown **civil war** over Mogadishu.

UN involvement in Somali began in January 1992 with a small Cease-fire Observer Force and was subsequently developed into a peace-keeping operation, the **United Nations Operation in Somalia (UNOSOM)**. In September 1992 'Somaliland' stated its categorical opposition to the deployment of UN troops within its borders. The impetus was humanitarian with the primary aim of ensuring the safety of relief operations to help the **famine**-stricken population in the south of the country. However, factional opposition to UNOSOM I led to the adoption of UN Security Council Resolution 794, which provided for the use of all necessary measures to establish a secure environment for relief operations. A US-led coalition force **(UNITAF)** began operations in December 1992. The main relief centres in the starvation area were secured by January 1993. Following the success of this exercise, UN Security Council Resolution 814 was adopted, which provided for the deployment of 28,000 UN troops and 2,800 civilians, to take over from UNITAF for six months from 1 May 1993. This operation was called UNOSOM II. In June 1993 UN forces were attacked by militia belonging to the USC/SNA, led by Gen. Aideed. Subsequently UN Security Council Resolution 837 was adopted, which authorized all necessary measures against those responsible, including their arrest and detention for trial. The UN Secretary-General's Special Representative, Adm. Howe, ordered the arrest of Gen. Aideed.

In September 1993 UN Security Council Resolution 865 was adopted, which supported UNOSOM's efforts but called for greater emphasis on the political front. Meanwhile, hundreds of Somalis were killed as UN troops searched unsuccessfully for Aideed in Mogadishu. Following the deaths of 12 US troops in early October, US President Clinton announced that all US armed forces would be withdrawn by March 1994. Subsequently, UN Security Council Resolution 885 was adopted, which suspended the arrest actions against Gen. Aideed. UN Security Council Resolution 886 extended UNOSOM's mandate until 31 May 1994, but made it clear that it was the prime responsibility of the Somalis themselves to find a solution to the crisis. UN Security Council Resolution 897 called for a reduced force of up to 22,000 troops, mainly to protect airports and ports, keep open supply routes for humanitarian aid and assist with the repatriation of **refugees**. Resolution 897 also made clear that the Somalis would bear the ultimate responsibility for setting up viable national political institutions and for reconstructing their country.

In view of the very limited progress achieved in political reconciliation, the UN had to consider whether it was necessary to prepare options for UNOSOM's mandate and future operations. The Security Council therefore dispatched a mission to Somalia to explain that the future of UNOSOM was in doubt. The UN Secretary-General subsequently issued a report recommending the withdrawal of UNOSOM forces. The last troops left Mogadishu on 3 March 1995. Since the withdrawal of UNOSOM, the UN has maintained a political office in Nairobi, Kenya, from where it monitors internal political developments.

For the next five years the political situation in Somalia remained extremely unclear, and external commentators increasingly referred to Somalia as a **failed state**. After the UN withdrawal, the **Inter-governmental Authority on Development (IGAD)** made efforts to find a solution to the Somali crisis. In 2000 IGAD focused on developing greater participation by Somali civil society, rather than the 'warlords', in the peace process. President **Gelleh** of Djibouti sponsored an IGAD peace and reconciliation conference that began on 2 May 2000 in Arta, Djibouti. The conference was attended by more than 2,000 Somalis, either as delegates or observers. Seats for a Transitional National Assembly (TNA) were allocated on the basis of the clan structure of Somali society: 44 to each of the four main clans, 24 to an alliance of smaller clans, 25 for **women** and a further 20 appointed by President Gelleh. The self-administered areas of Somalia—Somaliland in the north west and **Puntland** in the north east —and some prominent warlords in the Mogadishu area did not participate in the Djibouti conference and were not represented in the TNA. The TNA convened for the first time in Djibouti on 13 August, and on 25 August Abdiqassim Salad Hassan, former Deputy Prime Minister and interior minister in Siad Barre's government, was elected as President. In October the interim President formed a Transitional National Government (TNG), which transferred from Arta to Mogadishu.

A declaration by the **European Union (EU)** of 8 September 2000 stated that the EU was, *inter alia*, willing to support the new Somali authorities' efforts to rebuild the country once it had established its authority. The EU also urged the new authorities to establish a constructive dialogue with the authorities in Somaliland and Puntland. In late 2001, as the TNG struggled to provide peace and stability and as regional states became increasingly dissatisfied with Somalia's continued instability, President **Moi** of Kenya convened two Somali reconciliation conferences in Nairobi between the TNG President (Abdiqassim) and factions opposed to the TNG. The meetings achieved little, however. At an IGAD summit held in Khartoum, Sudan, in January 2002, regional leaders agreed to hold a large Peace and Reconciliation Conference within two months in Nairobi. Kenya, Ethiopia and Djibouti as the three 'front-line states' were tasked with organizing it.

Since its creation, the TNG has tried, with only limited success, to establish its authority on the ground. Significant militia forces opposed its formation, and 2001 there were major clashes between warlords and TNG militia in Mogadishu, Baidoa and Kismayo. On 22 March 2001 Somali faction leaders opposing the TNG met in Awash, Ethiopia, to establish the Somali Reconciliation and Restoration Council (SRRC). The SRRC aims to bring about an all-inclusive reconciliation conference and transitional representative government. The SRRC established its provisional headquarters in Baidoa—the stronghold of the Rahanweyn Resistance Army (RRA), which had taken tentative steps to establish a regional administration as early as 1999. On 1 April 2002 the SRRC announced the formation of the South-west Regional Government, with its capital in Baidoa and with the RRA Chairman, Col Hassan Mohamed Nur Shatigudud, as its first President. Two Vice-Presidents, 19 ministers, 19 assistant ministers and 145 members of a parliament were to be elected. The new state claimed to incorporate six regions: Bay, Bakool, Gedo, Lower Shebelle, Middle Juba and Lower Juba. However, only the administrations of Bay and Bakool recognized the new government.

A new transitional federal government, consisting of a 275-member parliament, was established in October 2004 but remains located in Nairobi, and has not established effective governance inside Somalia. The 'Head of State' of this administration is Abdullahi Yusuf Ahmed, leader of the Puntland region of Somalia, who was elected as President in October, and the 'head of government' is Ali Muhammad Ghedi, who was nominated in December. A Cabinet was appointed by the Prime Minister and approved by the Transitional Parliament.

International relations

Relations with Arab and Gulf states are historically good. Relations with Ethiopia are more fragile, however, owing to Somalia's occupation of the Ogaden in 1977/78. Ethiopia is also concerned by the activities of armed opposition groups operating inside its territory, supplied through lawless southern Somalia. Kenya also has an interest in the restoration of stability to Somalia, not least to prevent an increase in Somali refugees and the flow of illegal arms.

Somalia, economy

In 1990, according to estimates by the **World Bank**, Somalia's gross national income (GNI), measured at average 1988–90 prices, was US $946m., equivalent to $150 per head. According to UN figures, in 2001 gross domestic product (GDP) was $1,000m., equivalent to $110 per head. During 1990–2003, it was estimated, the population increased at an average annual rate of 2.3%. GDP declined, in real terms, at an average annual rate of 3.3% in 1990–99; however, growth of 2.1% was recorded in 1999. In 1990–2001 the average annual rate of inflation was 20.6%. Consumer prices increased by 11.5% in 2001. Somalia's economy is based on **agriculture**, in particular the production of bananas, and livestock-rearing. In 2004 the main markets for Somalia's exports were Thailand, the United Arab Emirates (UAE), Yemen, India, Oman and the People's Republic of China. The principal suppliers of imports in 2004 were Djibouti, Kenya, India, Brazil, Oman and the

UAE. The national currency is the Somali shilling. At 30 November 2004 the exchange rate was US $1 = 13,475 Somali shillings.

Somalia is one of the world's poorest and least developed countries. Civil unrest has been the primary obstacle to economic policy-making and development. Economic management is also hampered by the country's reliance on mainly dryland farming and pastoralism, which are vulnerable to climatic conditions. Agriculture is the most important sector, with livestock accounting for about 40% of GDP and about 65% of export earnings.

Foreign exchange earnings from exports of livestock and livestock products are supplemented by a regular and large-scale influx of remittances (estimated at about $400m. annually) from the diaspora. A reduction in remittances caused by the closure of **al-Barakaat**, formerly Somalia's largest remittance company, and branches of other remittance companies, in addition to a ban on livestock exports, have worsened the economic situation. Public-sector management is poor and there is an almost complete lack of economic and monetary policies and regulation. This lack of effective management, combined with the lack of institutional support, continues to have a paralysing effect on the economy and its few unguarded natural resources. Furthermore, with the breakdown of the public health system, falling numbers of health personnel, and the collapse of **water** and sanitation systems, Somalia's poor national health status has continued to decline steadily over the past decade. The contribution of continuous conflict has also been significant. The average Somali lifespan declined from 48 years in 1990 to 44.6 years for men and 47.8 years for women in 1997. Somalia now has the worst health indicators in Africa.

Somaliland

Generally, the territory inhabited by **Somalis**. More specifically the 'Republic of Somaliland'. In May 1991 the north-west region of Somalia declared its **independence** as the 'Republic of Somaliland'. It claims the borders of the former British Protectorate of Somaliland, but it has remained unrecognized as a sovereign state by the international community. A government was elected for an initial two-year period at a conference in Boroma in May 1993. Here an agreement was reached on the formation of a new, inter-clan government of Somaliland. Clan representatives elected former Somali Prime Minister Mohamed Ibrahim Egal as President. He was re-elected for a five-year term by the National Communities Conference in Hargeisa in February 1997. Following parliamentary elections (for which members were nominated by the clans participating in the Congress), a new government was formed and a constitution approved. A referendum on the Constitution (which reasserts Somaliland's claim for independence) took place on 31 May 2001. Ninety-seven per cent of voters reportedly supported a new constitution confirming the region's unilateral secession from the rest of Somalia.

Somali National Alliance (SNA)

A US-led coalition force (**UNITAF**) began humanitarian relief operations in Somalia in December 1992. The main relief centres in the starvation area had been secured by January 1993. Following the success of this exercise, UN Security Council Resolution 814 was adopted, providing for the deployment of 28,000 UN troops and 2,800 civilians, to take over from UNITAF for six months from 1 May. This operation was called **UNOSOM** II. In June 1993 UN forces were attacked by militia belonging to the **United Somali Congress**/Somali National Alliance (USC/SNA), led by **Gen. Aideed**. Subsequently UN Security Council Resolution 837 was adopted, authorizing all necessary measures against those responsible for the attack, including their arrest and detention for trial. The UN Secretary-General's Special Representative, Adm. Howe, ordered the arrest of Gen. Aideed. Between June and October 1993, a total of 70 UN troops were killed. UN Security Council Resolution 865 (passed on 22 September) supported UNOSOM's efforts, but called for greater emphasis on the political front. However, Somali deaths totalled several hundreds in clashes, as UN troops hunted unsuccessfully for Aideed in Mogadishu. Following the deaths of 12 US troops in early October, US President Clinton announced that all US forces would be withdrawn by March 1994. Subsequently, UN Security Council Resolution 885 was adopted, suspending the arrest actions against Gen. Aideed.

Somalis

The Somalis are a Cushitic and **Arabic**-speaking Muslim population in the Horn of Africa. The population is mainly divided into a number of major clans—including the Digil and Rahanwin, who speak a distinctive dialect and are predominantly agro-pastoralists, and the Dir, Isaaq, Hawiye and Darod, who are primarily pastoralists, apart from the Hawiye along the Shebelle Valley who are more involved in cultivation. The territory between the Shebelle and Juba rivers is the richest part of the country in agricultural terms and it is here that the remnants of Bantu groups, partly of ex-slave origin, are to be found. Today the Somalis extend across the borders of Ethiopia, Somalia and Kenya. They were subjected in the latter part of the 19th century, first by France and then by Britain and Italy. Britain declared a protectorate over northern Somalia in 1886 and Italy established a colony in the south at about the same time. The British colony of Kenya extended northwards over territory that was predominantly that of the Somalis, and Ethiopia appropriated it into its Ogaden province territory to which the Somalis laid claim.

Soninke

A major ethno-linguistic group in West Africa. Found in Mauritania and Senegal.

Soudan

Part of colonial **Afrique occidentale française (French West Africa)**. Now Mali.

South Africa, Republic of

The Republic of South Africa occupies the southern extremity of the African mainland. It is bordered by Namibia to the north west, by Botswana and Zimbabwe to the north, by Mozambique to the north east, and by Swaziland to the east. Lesotho is completely surrounded by South African territory. South Africa is 1,219,090 sq km in area. At mid-2004 the population was estimated at 46,586,607. The official languages are Sepedi, Sesotho, Setswana, siSwati, Tshivenda, Xitsonga, Afrikaans, English, isiNdebele, isiXhosa and isiZulu. About 77.8% of the population are black, 10.2% are white, 8.7% are Coloured (of mixed race), and 2.5% are Asian (mainly of Indian origin). Most of the inhabitants profess Christianity, although traditional African religions are still adhered to. There are also small minorities of Hindus (nearly all Asians) and Muslims (mainly Coloureds and Asians). The administrative capital is Pretoria, the legislative capital is Cape Town, and the judicial capital is Bloemfontein, whose populations at the 2001 census were enumerated at, respectively, 1,985,983, 2,893,247 and 111,698.

Political profile

Under the terms of the Constitution, which was adopted on 8 May 1996 and entered into force on 4 February 1997, legislative power is vested in a bicameral Parliament, comprising a National Assembly and a National Council of Provinces (formerly the Senate). The National Assembly is elected by universal adult suffrage under a system of proportional representation and has between 350 and 400 members. The 90-member National Council of Provinces comprises six permanent delegates and four special delegates from each of the provincial legislatures (see below). The President, who is elected by the National Assembly from among its members for a five-year term, exercises executive power in consultation with the other members of the Cabinet. Any party that holds a minimum of 80 seats in the National Assembly (equivalent to 20% of the national vote) is entitled to nominate an Executive Deputy President. A Constitutional Court ensures that the executive, legislative and judicial organs of government adhere to the provisions of the interim Constitution.

Each of the nine provinces has a legislature, which is elected under a system of proportional representation. Each legislature is entitled to draft a constitution for the province, subject to the principles governing the national Constitution, and to elect a Premier, who heads an Executive Council. Parties that hold a minimum of 10% of seats in the provincial legislature are entitled to a proportional number of portfolios in the Executive Council.

The current Head of State, **Thabo Mbeki**, was inaugurated as President in June 1999, on the retirement of **Nelson Mandela**. He was re-elected by vote of the National Assembly in April 2004.

Following a general election held on 14 April 2004, the distribution of seats in the National Assembly was as follows: **African National Congress (ANC)** 279; **Democratic Alliance (DA)** 50; **Inkatha Freedom Party (IFP)** 28; United Democratic Movement (UDM) 9; Independent Democrats (ID) 7; **New National**

Party (NNP) 7; **African Christian Democratic Party (ACDP)** 6; Freedom Front Plus (FFP) 4; United Christian Democratic Party (UCDP) 3; **Pan-Africanist Congress of Azania (PAC)** 3; Minority Front 2; **Azanian People's Organization (AZAPO)** 2.

Summary of Recent History, 1989–2001
1989: **F. W. de Klerk** replaces **P. W. Botha** as President, meets Nelson Mandela. Public facilities desegregated. Many ANC activists freed. 1990: Ban on the ANC rescinded. Mandela released after 27 years in prison. 1991: Start of multi-party talks. Remaining **apartheid** laws repealed and international sanctions lifted. Armed conflict between the ANC and the Zulu Inkatha movement. 1993: Agreement reached on interim constitution. 1994 (April): ANC wins first non-racial elections. Mandela becomes President. Government of national unity formed. **Commonwealth** membership restored. Remaining sanctions lifted. South Africa takes seat in UN General Assembly after 20-year absence. 1996: **Truth and Reconciliation Commission** chaired by Archbishop Desmond Tutu begins hearings on human rights crimes committed by former government and liberation movements during apartheid era. Parliament adopts new constitution. National Party withdraws from government. 1998: Truth and Reconciliation Commission releases its report, branding apartheid a crime against humanity and finding the ANC accountable for human rights abuses. 1999: ANC wins general election. Thabo Mbeki replaces Mandela as President. 2000: In local elections the ANC wins control of most of the 237 local councils (59%), but the DA—created five months earlier by a merger of the **Democratic Party**, the **New National Party (NNP)** and the Federal Alliance—receives almost one-quarter of the votes. The IFP wins 9%. 2001: The NNP splits from the DA and announces an alliance with the ruling ANC.

South Africa is now politically dominated by its black majority (about 78% of the population), which is represented by the ANC. The vote for the ANC has increased over three general elections (held in 1994, 1999 and 2004) from 62% to 67% and subsequently to almost 70%. After the 1999 election, the ANC held 268 of the 400 seats in the National Assembly, the DP 39, the IFP 33 and the NNP 28 seats (compared with 82 after the election in 1994). The black militant PAC and the **Afrikaner** separatist **Freedom Front** won three seats each, while AZAPO and the ACDP each won one.

After the 2004 election the ANC held 285 seats in the National Assembly, while the main opposition grouping, the DA, held only 50. The DA is supported by some three-quarters of South Africa's white population and by perhaps half of the coloured (mixed-race) population. White support for the ANC is perhaps as low as 2%. Many have been alienated by the ANC's—and President Thabo Mbeki's—intolerance of criticism and opposition. At the same time, it is clear that while **poverty** rates among whites and Indians remain below 5% and 10% respectively, they are higher among coloureds (20%) and blacks, more than 55% of whom were 'in poverty'—defined as less than 678 rand, or US $90, in 2003.

Unemployment rates also continue to be strikingly unequal across the different racial groups—8% for whites, but 20% and 30%, respectively, for Indians and coloureds, and around 50% for blacks (in 2003). As long as this structural inequality remains, there will be a tendency for politics to fracture along racial lines. While the DA argues that emphasis should be placed on economic growth, **education**, deregulation and a freer market, the ANC maintains its rhetoric and policy of black empowerment and its drive towards 'representivity'. It also points to the composition of the government—six of the 28 strong Cabinet are non-black (including three whites), together with 10 of the 21 deputy-ministers (of whom six are white). Mbeki seems to be particularly keen to reach out and embrace Afrikaners, once the blacks' chief oppressors, regarding them as 'genuinely African people'.

The political structure and administration of South Africa has been transformed over the last decade. A country that consisted previously of four provinces and 10 nominally autonomous 'homelands', or Bantustans, four of them independent, has been reorganized into one of nine completely new provinces with their own premiers, executives and legislatures, and with the so-called homelands eliminated as separate entities and subsumed into the provinces. At the city, town and country level, a mixture of local institutions (rooted in the complex apartheid system, under which the races were segregated physically and politically) has been restructured into a compact system of six metro- or mega-cities, 47 district councils and 231 local councils. In December 2000 30,477 candidates from 79 political parties and 690 independents contested local government elections to fill these new local governing bodies.

Big businesses, such as Anglo-American, the mining and manufacturing conglomerate, appear to have made their peace with the ANC—out of fear, it has been suggested. But many businesspeople regard the empowerment charters, which propose incremental increases in the proportion of blacks in management and in the amount of black-held equity, as a price to pay if the private sector is to be permitted to operate reasonably freely and business to flourish. There is no doubt that a relatively prosperous black middle class is beginning to emerge, although progress towards the economic and social development for the mass of blacks promised in the early days after the ending of apartheid remains painfully slow. South Africa remains divided, in part by race but most significantly by class, into a world of relative comfort and plenty and a world of poverty and disease.

Many whites fear that politics will become more racially divided. It is likely that more than 250,000 have left South Africa since 1994, and an increasing number have become uneasy regarding the country's long-term future. There is also more widespread concern that the ANC is not truly committed to a pluralistic, liberal **democracy**, although the party has not attempted to tamper with the highly liberal post-apartheid Constitution. Some—particularly the liberals—feel that the ANC covets the one-party state and strong controls over all aspects of economic, social and political life; others—on the left—that it is not moving fast enough to deal with the real basic needs of the mass of the people and is too easily prepared to work with private capital at home and abroad and compromise its radical and transformative heritage as a powerful social and political movement.

One issue that concerns many is the reluctance of the President to face the reality of the **HIV/AIDS** epidemic, which has already killed some 1.5m. South Africans. With some 5m. infected with the HIV virus, South Africa has one of the highest prevalence rates in the world. More South Africans now die each month from AIDS than were killed during the two decades of political violence before liberation. The government is belatedly implementing a plan to distribute anti-retroviral drugs, but lacks a real sense of urgency, partly as a result of worries that the issue was open to racist interpretations of transmission rates and rates of infection. The fear of violent crime also blights many South Africans' lives, particularly in the urban areas. The murder rate is lower than a decade ago, largely because political killings have stopped, but South Africans are still five times more likely to be murdered than are US citizens.

The ANC government has established Africa's largest welfare state, through the provision of old age pensions. But this was done while maintaining fiscal discipline. The budget deficit has been reduced from 9.1% of gross domestic product in 1993 to an estimated 2.4% in 2003. Economic growth, which averaged only 0.6% annually in 1981–93, rose to 2.8% annually in 1994–2002, easily outstripping the annual rate of population growth—1.8%. The more dynamic and open economy has, however, not benefited the less prosperous as much as it has the better off. The richest 25% of the black population, whose incomes rose by 40% in 1974–94 as the worst restrictions of apartheid were relaxed, have experienced a further 30% rise since 1994. Poor blacks have not experienced such an improvement; indeed, the income of the bottom 45% of the black population, which halved in 1974–94, has contracted by another 10% since then. The main reason is that unskilled South Africans are finding it harder to find work: unemployment among blacks increased from 24% in 1970 to 40% in 1994 and has now reached more than 50%.

International relations

South Africa was rapidly reintegrated into the international community after the isolation of the apartheid years. It was readmitted to the Commonwealth in 1994 and hosted the annual Commonwealth Heads of Government Meeting (CHOGM) in 1999. South Africa assumed the chairmanship of the **Non-aligned Movement** in August 1998. It played a prominent role in the **Organization of African Unity (OAU)** and hosted the inaugural meeting of the **African Union**, which succeeded it. South Africa is also a key member of the **Southern African Development Community**. South Africa has recently hosted two UN conferences: the World Conference Against Racism, held in Durban in August 2001; and the World Summit for Sustainable Development, held in Johannesburg in August 2002.

Traditionally, South African foreign policy has had two foci: the West, and the immediate region. President Mbeki's primary focus is Africa. This has manifested itself in a more active diplomatic role for South Africa in the region, notably in Zimbabwe, the Democratic Republic of the Congo (DRC), Burundi and Angola.

President Mbeki personally intervened in the Inter-Congolese Dialogue held in Sun City, and was instrumental in resolving differences, which led to the Pretoria Accord. South Africa has also demonstrated its willingness to play an active role in peace support operations. It has committed more than 700 troops to Burundi, and planned to support peace operations in the DRC following the Pretoria Accord.

President Mbeki has also attempted to raise international awareness of issues of importance to Africa, such as **debt**. He and Presidents **Obasanjo** of Nigeria and **Bouteflika** of Algeria were instrumental in securing undertakings from the **G8** Summit in Kyushu-Okinawa (July 2000) to engage the international community further on issues such as debt, poverty reduction and market access. President Mbeki's speech to the World Economic Forum in January 2001 referred to a Millennium Action Plan (MAP), a pan-African process focusing on these sorts of issues and aiming to address the challenges of globalization. The MAP, now known as the **New Partnership for Africa's Development (NEPAD)**, was launched by Mbeki at the G8 summit in Genoa, Italy, in June 2001 and endorsed by the OAU summit in July 2001. The G8 meeting in Kananaskis, Canada, in June 2002 focused on development and Africa. The UN Secretary-General and four African leaders (including President Mbeki) attended. It was agreed to provide an additional US $1,000m. for **Heavily Indebted Poor Countries** and for an Africa Action Plan.

NEPAD is a continental strategy directed to the achievement of sustainable development in Africa. It gives firmer expression to the idea of African renaissance, first proposed by Mbeki in 1998. Its leadership recognizes their responsibility to end conflict, to improve economic and political governance and to develop regional integration. They seek the support of the international community to achieve this. In the context of tackling poverty, they also seek help in ending Africa's acute economic marginalization, with measures including increased resource flow, improved trade access, **debt relief**, support for infrastructure, agricultural diversification and human development (health and education).

South Africa's relations with Zimbabwe are characterized by extensive trade and investment, mutual dependency in **energy**, a shared history of opposition to white minority rule and common social problems, such as HIV/AIDS. The issue of land reform also has a strong resonance in both countries. For these reasons, South Africa has chosen to engage President **Mugabe** throughout Zimbabwe's current crisis. South Africa has spoken out during particular incidents of violence in Zimbabwe and shares many of the concerns of the international community. On 19 March 2002 a Commonwealth Troika (Presidents Mbeki of South Africa and Obasanjo of Nigeria and Prime Minister Howard of Australia) agreed to suspend Zimbabwe from the Councils of the Commonwealth.

South Africa, economy

In 2003, according to estimates by the **World Bank**, South Africa's gross national income (GNI), measured at average 2001–03 prices, was US $156,511m., equivalent to $2,780 per head (or $10,270 per head on an international purchasing-power parity basis). During 1990–2003, it was estimated, the population increased at an average annual rate of 2.0%, while gross domestic product (GDP) per head, in real terms, remained constant. Overall GDP increased, in real terms, at an average annual rate of 2.0% in 1990–2003, according to the World Bank; growth was 1.9% in 2003. The annual rate of inflation averaged 8.7% in 1990–2002; consumer prices increased by 5.8% in 2003 and by 4.3% in 2004. South Africa's major industries include mining (the country is one of the world's largest producer of platinum, **gold** and **chromium**), automobile assembly, machinery, textiles, iron and steel, chemicals, fertilizers and foodstuffs. Major trading partners in 2001 were the United Kingdom, the USA, Japan and Germany. The national currency is the rand. In 2004 the average exchange rate was US $1 = 6.4597 rand.

South Africa's abundant mineral and **energy** resources form the core of the country's economic activity. Much of manufacturing is based on mining, and exports are led by gold and **diamonds**. In part, South Africa has a sophisticated economy based on manufacturing, mining and financial services—in which macroeconomic indicators such as interest rates and the strength of the rand are critical. However, it also has an economy consisting of the very poor who eke out a living through near-subsistence **agriculture** or the informal sector, to whom economic statistics are meaningless. Relatively small improvements in living standards, including government-funded improvements in utilities, can make a huge difference to their lives. Economic growth remains slow—around 2.5% in 2003 rising to above 3% in 2004. Growth is badly needed to solve the problems of **poverty** and deprivation. High unemployment levels, ranging from the official figure of 26% to broad measures of 36% (including the **informal economy**), remain a serious problem. Labour experts argue that growth of at least 4% is required to stimulate employment. A thorough reorganization of the **education** system is also needed to provide the human capacity development necessary to promote growth and employment.

The structure of the economy is changing. The agricultural subsidies provided for predominantly white, predominantly **Afrikaner** farmers under the **apartheid** regime—which, at their peak in 1970, consumed the largest proportion of the national budget—have been drastically reduced, with dramatic effects. Between 1980 and 2000 the number of farmers declined from 70,000 to 50,000, the number of farm workers from more than 1.2m. to 914,000, and agriculture's contribution to GDP shrank from 6% to 3.4%. In 1980 gold sales accounted for 15% of South Africa's GDP; in 2000 they accounted for less than 3%. Manufactured exports increased, from about 7% of GDP in 1990 to almost 40% in 2000. Industrial output grew by 7.1% in the year to April 2005. Even so, the trade balance declined by 2.1% over the same period and the current account by 7%.

In the post-apartheid era the government has focused on controlling the deficit while at the same time striving to increase spending on social programmes to combat inequality. Since 1994 the government and the central bank have used tight macroeconomic policies to control inflation. Public spending is well under control.

The government views the restructuring of the economy through privatization as fundamental for growth and employment generation in the long term, despite short-term transitional costs. The privatization process so far has been disappointing. Political difficulties in implementing privatization have been reflected mainly through the left-leaning and union elements within the ANC government, which are strongly opposed to the transfer of state assets to what is still a white dominated business sector, despite the relatively rapid emergence of a black middle class. The ANC's alliance partner, the **Confederation of South African Trade Unions**, has pledged to resist any move on restructuring that the government may make.

Southern Africa

The region consisting of South Africa, Swaziland, Lesotho, Botswana, Namibia, Angola, Mozambique, Zimbabwe and Zambia.

Southern African Development Community (SADC)

The first Southern African Development Co-ordination Conference (SADCC) was held at Arusha, Tanzania, in July 1979, to harmonize development plans and to reduce the region's economic dependence on South Africa. In August 1992 the 10 member countries of the SADCC signed a treaty establishing the Southern African Development Community (SADC), to replace the SADCC, now that South Africa appeared to be moving beyond the **apartheid** state. The treaty states that the objective of the organization is to promote economic integration towards a fully developed common market. A tribunal was to be established to arbitrate in case of disputes between the member states. By September 1993 all of the member states had ratified the treaty, which came into effect in October. A protocol on the long envisaged tribunal was adopted in 2000. The Protocol on Politics, Defence and Security Co-operation, established in June 1996, was adopted and opened for signature in August 2001. A troika system, comprising the current, incoming and outgoing SADC chairmanship operates at the level of the Summit, Council of Ministers and Standing Committee of Officials. Other member states may be co-opted into the troika as required. A system of SADC national committees, comprising representatives of government, civil society and the private sector, oversees the implementation of regional programmes at the country level and helps formulate new regional strategies. The SADC institutions underwent a major reorganization in 2002.

Southern Cameroons National Council (SCNC)

Political movement in Cameroon, founded in 1995. It supports the establishment of an independent republic in anglophone Cameroon. The SCNC is led by Martin Luma.

South West Africa

South West Africa became a German possession in 1884. After the defeat of Germany in the First World War, the League of Nations passed the administration of its colonial territories to the victors as mandates. South Africa obtained South West Africa and administered it until, finally, the territory achieved **independence** in 1990 as Namibia, after a long struggle by the **South West Africa People's Organisation**.

South West Africa People's Organisation (SWAPO)

The struggle for the liberation of South West Africa and self-determination of its people was waged by the South West Africa People's Organisation (SWAPO), with some assistance from Angolan-based Cuban troops and elements of the Angolan army. As the struggle intensified during the 1980s, the South African regime, increasingly concerned about the growth of the black opposition within South Africa itself, began to contemplate the possibility of **independence** for South West Africa.

Soweto

South African township outside Johannesburg. Centre of a bloody uprising in 1976, triggered by black students protesting against compulsory instruction in **Afrikaans**.

Spanish Morocco

Also known as the Spanish Protectorate of Morocco, which lasted from 1912 until 1956. Located along the Mediterranean coastline in the north of the country, it included the Rif mountains and the two Spanish presidiums, Ceuta and Melilla. Formally reunited with the main part of Morocco, which had been under the **French Protectorate of Morocco** since 1912, at **independence** in 1956, it was effectively reunited with the rest of Morocco after 1958.

Spanish Sahara

Large desert territory to the south of Morocco, occupied by Spain until 1975/76, when it withdrew, leaving Morocco and Mauritania to invade and occupy most of the territory, against the declared wish of the local inhabitants, the **Sahrawis**, for self-determination and independence. Former name of **Western Sahara**.

Stevens, Siaka

Siaka Stevens became Prime Minister of Sierra Leone in 1968. In 1971 he succeeded **Sir Albert Margai** as President of the country. The one-party state that Stevens established was characterized by economic decline and **corruption**. Stevens resigned in 1985 and was succeeded as President by **Maj.-Gen. Joseph Momoh**.

Structural Adjustment

A term widely used in the 1980s, when the two **Bretton Woods institutions**, the **World Bank** and the **International Monetary Fund**, made economic reforms and structural adjustment—involving essentially a reduction in state intervention in the economy, cuts in public expenditure, privatization and the promotion of market forces—a precondition for further loans and 'assistance'. Strongly encouraged as a recipe for recovery and growth after the difficult decade of the 1970s in the so-called **Berg Report** (named after the chief author, Elliott Berg), *Accelerated Development in Sub-Saharan Africa* published by the World Bank in 1981, structural adjustment was widely adopted as a key concept in economic reform programmes across Africa during the first half of the 1980s in particular. The World Bank's review of the experience—*Africa's Adjustment and Growth in the 1980s*—purported to show that countries that had adopted structural adjustment policies had performed better than those which had not. However, this assessment was contradicted by the findings of the **Economic Commission for Africa**, published in the same year (1989).

Sub-Saharan Africa

A term used to distinguish the majority of African countries from those of **North Africa**. Often the basis for statistical data relating to 'Africa' as a whole; also widely used to refer to 'Africa', particularly by commentators outside the region. A misnomer, because many of the states included in this 'entity' have substantial areas of Sahara desert within their boundaries—these are the countries of the African Sahel (Senegal, Burkina Faso, Mali, Niger, Chad and, sometimes, Sudan).

Sudan, Republic of

The Republic of Sudan lies in north-eastern Africa. The largest country in Africa, Sudan is bordered by Egypt to the north, by the Red Sea, Eritrea and Ethiopia to the east, by the Central African Republic, Chad and Libya to the west, and by Kenya, Uganda and the Democratic Republic of the Congo (DRC, formerly **Zaire**) to the south. Sudan is 2,505,813 sq km in area. At mid-2003 the population was estimated at 33,610,000. The people are mainly black African, belonging to various ethnic and linguistic groups, but a significant minority, constituting some 39% of the total, are Arabs, and a small minority Beja. **Arabic** is the official language, although other languages are spoken and English is widely understood. Most northern Sudanese are Muslims, while in the south most of the inhabitants are animists or Christians. The capital is Khartoum, whose population was estimated at 4,285,542 in mid-2003.

Political profile

In October 1993 the Revolutionary Command Council for National Salvation (RCC), which had assumed power after the military coup of 30 June 1989, was dissolved after appointing **Lt-Gen. Omar Hassan Ahmad al-Bashir** as President and head of a new civilian government. In April 1998 a new Constitution was endorsed by the National Assembly, and was presented to President al-Bashir. The document was endorsed by 96.7% of voters in a national referendum held in May. Under its terms, executive power is vested in the Council of Ministers, which is appointed by the President, but is responsible to the National Assembly. Legislative power is vested in the National Assembly. The 360-member National Assembly serves a term of four years. Of its 360 members, 270 are directly elected in single-seat constituencies, 35 members represent **women**, 26 represent university graduates and 29 represent trade unions.

In early July 2005 the National Assembly approved an interim Constitution as part of the Comprehensive Peace Agreement signed in January between the Sudanese government and the Sudan People's Liberation Army (SPLA). The interim Constitution provided for the establishment of a government of national unity, representation in which was to be divided between northerners and southerners, with the former holding 70% of the posts and the latter 30%. The interim Constitution also stipulated that, pending legislative elections, which were to be held no later than the end of the fourth year of the interim period, the National Assembly shall be composed of 450 members who shall be appointed by the President of the Republic in consultation with the First Vice-President, according to the 70%/30% north and south ratio.

Provision was also made in the interim Constitution for the election of the President of the government of Southern Sudan and the establishment of a transitional Southern Sudan Assembly. The President of the government of Southern Sudan shall be elected directly by the people of Southern Sudan for a five-year mandate, renewable only once. The transitional Southern Sudan Assembly shall be an inclusive, constituent legislature composed of 170 appointed members with 70% representing the SPLA; 15% representing the National Congress; and 15% representing the other Southern Sudanese political forces.

In the most recent presidential election, held on 13–22 December 2000, Lt-Gen. al-Bashir was re-elected to office. Al-Bashir had first taken office as chairman of the RCC on 30 June 1989. On 16 October 1993 he was appointed President of the RCC, and in March 1996 he was elected as President of Sudan for the first time.

Following an election held on 13–22 December 2000, the distribution of seats in the National Assembly was as follows: **National Congress** 355; Others 5.

History

From 1820 until 1881 Sudan was formally part of the Ottoman Empire and of the Empire's autonomous *pashalik* in Egypt. From 1881 until 1898 it was ruled by the Mahdi. From 1899 until 1955 it was subject in theory to an Anglo-Egyptian condominium, in practice to Britain. It was under Britain that geographical and cultural divisions between the north and the South were exacerbated by administrative and political divisions established by the colonial power. On the eve of

independence in 1956 there was considerable unrest. In 1956 Sudan became an independent state and, subsequently, a member of the **Arab League** and the United Nations.

Sudan is the location of Africa's longest conflict, that between the north and the south, the latest period of which has lasted 20 years, resulting in more than 1.5m. deaths, hundreds of thousands of **refugees** and widespread **famine**. It is a complex conflict. Much of the fighting is factional. Both northern and southern opinion is divided. Some of the rebels are seeking greater autonomy for the south; others full independence. Neither government nor rebel forces have been able to win a military victory. The south comprises three provinces of Bahr al-Ghazal, Upper Nile and Equatoria, with a population of more than 3m. These three provinces border on five African states: Central African Republic, the DRC, Uganda, Kenya and Ethiopia. The inhabitants, although they constitute 40% of Muslim Africans, are predominantly black and non-Muslim. The south is—and always has been—significantly less developed and generally poorer than the north. Eventually, in 2003–04, a peace agreement was reached, although this was threatened in August 2005, when the leader of the rebel movement in the south (the Sudan People's Liberation Movement), **John Garang**, was killed in a helicopter crash.

The overthrow of President **Nimeri** in 1985 was followed by a short period of civilian rule. On 30 June 1989, however, the army overthrew the democratically-elected government of **Sadiq al-Mahdi** and installed an RCC, chaired by Brig. (later Lt-Gen.) al-Bashir. Bashir ruled by decree at the head of the RCC and banned all political parties except the **National Islamic Front** (NIF—renamed the National Congress in 1998). In 1996 Bashir was elected as President and a National Assembly was elected in a poll that was boycotted by the opposition. On 12 December 1999 President Bashir announced a state of emergency (largely as a result of an internal power struggle between himself and Hassan at-Turabi, the speaker of the National Assembly) and dissolved the National Assembly. Bashir claimed that Turabi had been trying to influence the National Assembly to introduce constitutional change, which would have strengthened his authority. After December 1999 Turabi's supporters made only weak attempts to retaliate, while Bashir consolidated his position by introducing more decrees designed to reduce Turabi's influence in the National Congress. Turabi then established the Popular National Congress (PNC). In 2000 Turabi unexpectedly signed a memorandum of understanding with John Garang. This prompted the government to detain Turabi, who remains under house arrest. Elections held in December 2000 were boycotted by a number of key opposition parties, which claimed that they were flawed and unfair. The **European Union** declined a request by the Sudanese government to monitor the elections, for which it felt that the necessary conditions were not in place. Bashir was re-elected, receiving 86% of the votes in the absence of significant opposition.

As regards the north–south conflict, there have been a number of attempts to find a peaceful resolution to the civil war in Sudan. In September 1993 the governments of Kenya, Uganda, Ethiopia, Eritrea and Djibouti (members of the

Inter-governmental Authority on Development—IGAD) decided to make a further effort to initiate negotiations between the government and the SPLA. Four rounds of talks were held in Nairobi during 1994, but ended in stalemate over the key issues of self-determination and secularization. These same issues had wrecked previous peace initiatives. Peace talks resumed in October 1997 under the sponsorship of IGAD, and resulted in agreement that the Declaration of Principles, a basis for a settlement drafted in 1994, should be the basis for settlement talks. Eventually, in September 2003, the government and the SPLA signed a security agreement allowing for the integration of troops in certain disputed areas. Elsewhere, the two sides retained separate armed forces. Negotiations continued on political and economic issues. However, this process was to lead over the next two years to a peace agreement.

Meanwhile, another conflict has developed into a major crisis in the **Darfur** region in western Sudan. Rebel militias and government forces and militias had been involved for some time in clashes in this region, but during 2003–05 the situation rapidly worsened and the conflict widened to involve larger and larger numbers of civilians. Government-supported 'Arab' militias, known locally as ***janjaweed***, began increasingly to attack villages and settlements, massacring whole communities of black Africans. Throughout this period, despite growing pressure from the international community and the threat of sanctions, the government of Sudan continued to support a campaign of what amounted to 'ethnic cleansing' of black Africans in Darfur. Large movements of people have resulted from this conflict, and the internally displaced persons and refugees fleeing into Sudan are thought to number more than 1m. Many have described the conflict in terms of **genocide**, although the UN is officially hesitant to label it thus.

Sudan, economy

In 2003, according to estimates by the **World Bank**, Sudan's gross national income (GNI), measured at average 2001–03 prices, was US $16,372m., equivalent to $460 per head (or $1,880 on an international purchasing-power parity basis). During 1990–2003, it was estimated, the population increased at an average annual rate of 2.3%, while gross domestic product (GDP) per head increased, in real terms, by an average of 3.4% per year. Overall GDP increased, in real terms, at an average annual rate of 5.8% in 1990–2003; growth in 2003 was 6.0%. In 1992–2000 the average annual rate of inflation was 64.8%. Consumer prices increased by an annual average of 18.1% in 1999 and 7.4% in 2000. Production of **oil** and petroleum products and **agriculture**, in particular the production of **cotton**, sesame, groundnuts, gum arabic and sugar, and the rearing of livestock, are important sectors of the economy. Japan, the People's Republic of China and Saudi Arabia are Sudan's major trading partners. The national currency is the Sudanese dinar. In 2003 the average exchange rate was US $1 = 260.98 dinars.

Economic progress has been constrained by the **civil war**, military expenditure, social dislocation, the deterioration of basic infrastructure and lack of access to aid and foreign investment. Sudan is also vulnerable to external shocks, including floods and **drought**. As a result, **poverty** levels have risen in spite of growth. In recent years the economic situation has improved thanks to revenue from oil exports and weather that has favoured agriculture. A lasting and sustainable peace is needed for continued improvement. If the peace agreement recently concluded endures, then Sudan's economic prospects are good. The death, in August 2005, of **John Garang**, the leader of the rebel SPLM movement in the south, however, has cast doubt on the prospects for a lasting peace settlement.

None the less, in the 1990s Sudan achieved its strongest economic growth since **independence** in 1956. Sudan began implementing **International Monetary Fund** macroeconomic reforms that have successfully stabilized inflation. Agriculture remains an important sector and expanded at the rate of 8.5% annually over the last decade. More recently, Sudan has benefited from investment in oil production, which is expected to reduce the country's import bill and improve the availability of foreign exchange for development financing. Oil has in fact emerged as the major source of economic growth and revenue for Sudan since 1999. In the summer of 2003 oil production stood at 264,000 barrels per day. Sudan reported in April 2005 that further substantial quantities of oil had been discovered in the western region of **Darfur**.

Sudan-Egyptian relations

In 1952 in Egypt a coup by army officers, led by **Gen. Muhammad Neguib** (and including **Gamal Abdel Nasser**, Abdul al-Hakim and other Free Officers) overthrew **King Farouk** and established a new government. Neguib became Commander-in-Chief of the armed forces, Prime Minister and President of the republic while Nasser held the post of Minister of the Interior. Neguib, who was of partial Sudanese descent, accepted a self-government statute for Sudan which provided for the creation of a council of ministers, a house of representatives and a senate, and reserved to the governor only external affairs and ultimate emergency authority in domestic affairs. The new Egyptian government, under Neguib, even improved this statute (from the Sudanese point of view) and persuaded all of the principal Sudanese political parties to issue a pro-Egypt declaration. The statute was embodied in an Anglo-Egyptian agreement in February 1953 and was intended to lead to **independence** for Sudan not later than January 1961. Nebuib was effectively ousted by Nasser, whose political vision was far more narrowly (Egyptian) nationalist than had been that of Neguib. Sudan now shook off both Britain and Egypt and declared independence; in August 1955, the south revolted and was then subjected to extreme repression by the north before independence was formally declared on the first day of 1956.

Suez Canal

The Suez Canal forms a 163 km ship canal in Egypt between Port Said on the **Mediterranean** and Suez on the Red Sea. The canal allows water **transport** from Europe to Asia without circumnavigating Africa. Before its construction some transport was conducted by offloading ships and carrying the goods overland between the Mediterranean and the Red Sea. It was built between 1859 and 1869 by a French company led by Ferdinand de Lesseps and the Canal was owned by the Egyptian government and France. External debts forced Egypt to sell its share in the Canal to Great Britain, and British troops moved in to protect it in 1882.

In 1956 **Gamal Abdel Nasser** and the Egyptian state nationalized the Canal which caused Britain, France and Israel to invade in the week-long Suez War.

Sukuma

The major ethno-linguistic group in Tanzania. Others include the **Masai**, the Haya, the Gogo, the Nyamwezi, the Ha and the **Chagga**.

Sunni(s)

The great majority of Muslims are followers of the Sunni path (sunna – the way, course, rule or manner of conduct). The remainder are mainly followers of the Shi'a tradition and are Shi'a or Shi'ites. The Sunna is based on the Qur'an and six books of traditions (hadith), and the Sunnis are organised into four orthodox schools or rites – Hanafi, Hanbali, Shafi'i and Maliki – each with their own specific religious/legal code. The Sunnis, unlike the Shi'a or Shi'ites, recognise the authority of the fourth and succeeding caliphs (successors to the Prophet Mohammed).

Swahili

The lingua franca of East Africa. Swahili is widely spoken and understood in most East African countries and inland as far as the Democratic Republic of the Congo. A combination of **Arabic** and local Bantu languages, it is the official language in Kenya, Uganda and Tanzania.

Swaziland, Kingdom of

The Kingdom of Swaziland is a land-locked country in southern Africa, bordered by South Africa to the north, west, south and south-east, and by Mozambique to the east. Swaziland is 17,363 sq km in area. At mid-2003 the population was estimated at 1,077,000. Most of the people (95%) are Swazi (African), and there is a small minority (5%) of Europeans. English and siSwati are the official languages. About 60% of the population profess Christianity, while most of the remainder adhere to traditional beliefs. The capital is Mbabane, whose population was estimated at 100,833 at mid-2003.

Political profile

The Constitution of 13 October 1978 vests supreme executive and legislative power in the hereditary King, who is the Head of State, and provides for a bicameral legislature, comprising a House of Assembly and a Senate. The functions of the legislature are confined to debating government proposals and advising the King. Executive power is exercised through the Cabinet (later redesignated the Council of Ministers), which is appointed by the King. The Swaziland National Council (Libandla), which comprises members of the royal family and is headed by the King and the constitutional dual monarch, the Queen Mother, provides advice on matters regulated by traditional law and custom.

Following a number of amendments to the electoral system, which were approved by the King in October 1992, the House of Assembly was redesignated as the National Assembly and expanded to 65 deputies (of whom 55 are directly elected from candidates nominated by traditional local councils, known as Tinkhundla, and 10 appointed by the King), and the Senate to 30 members (of whom 20 are appointed by the King and 10 elected by the National Assembly). Elections to the National Assembly are conducted by secret ballot, in two rounds of voting; the second round of the elections is contested by the three candidates from each of the Tinkhundla who secure the highest number of votes in the first poll. Swaziland is divided into 273 regional tribal areas, comprising 55 elected Tinkhundla. In November 2003 the King accepted a new draft constitution, which had yet to be ratified in March 2005.

Political activity was banned by royal proclamation in 1973, and formally prohibited under the 1978 Constitution. Since 1991, following indications that the Constitution was to be revised, a number of political associations have re-emerged. They include the Imbokodvo National Movement (INM), the Ngwane National Liberatory Congress (NNLC), the People's United Democratic Movement (PUDEMO), the Swaziland National Front (SWANAFRO), the Swaziland Progressive Party (SPP) and the Swaziland United Front (SUF).

The Head of State of Swaziland is HM King Mswati III, who succeeded to the throne on 25 April 1986.

Elections to the National Assembly were held most recently on 18 October 2003.

History

The Swazi people have been led by a monarch since about the mid-17th century. Swaziland remained independent until around 1890 when it came under the protection and administration of the British Governor of the Transvaal. Britain established a protectorate over Swaziland in 1903. It was assumed that, in time, the three High Commission Territories of **Bechuanaland** (Botswana), **Basutoland** (Lesotho) and Swaziland would eventually be incorporated into South Africa. However, in 1909, when the South Africa Bill was before Parliament in the United Kingdom, pledges were made that Parliament would have the fullest opportunity of discussing the transfer issue, and, more importantly, that no such transfer would take place against the wishes of the inhabitants. In 1910, when the Transvaal became a province of the **Union of South Africa**, Swaziland came under the direct control of the United Kingdom. The question of the transfer was raised frequently by the Union government, but when the National Party came to power in South Africa in 1948, incorporation of the protectorate into an **apartheid** system was unacceptable to both British and world opinion. In 1964 a Legislative Council was formed. The British government indicated that it was willing to give Swaziland some measure of self-government, and in 1966 a new constitution was drawn up which made provision for Swaziland to become a protected Kingdom. Under the new Constitution, the King was to be known as the King of Swaziland instead of Paramount Chief and was to be recognized as Head of State. Elections were held in April 1967 and full **independence** was granted on 6 September 1968.

In April 1973 King Sobhuza II repealed the Westminster-type Independence Constitution by proclamation and assumed supreme power. In 1978 the King instituted an electoral system whereby royal nominees were selected to fill an electoral college that, in turn, selected 40 members of the House of Assembly. King Sobhuza II died on 21 August 1982, having reigned for 61 years, and within a few days a caucus of Princes and Chiefs had chosen one of Sobhuza's many sons, Prince Makhosetive, and his mother as heir and Queen Mother respectively. After a four-year regency, the Prince was crowned (at the age of 18) as King Mswati III on 25 April 1986. King Mswati III introduced some political reform: following three Review Commissions, members of the House of Assembly were directly elected in 1993 by secret ballot for the first time in 20 years; also, a Constitutional Review Commission (CRC) was established in 1996 and given two years to examine the remnants of the original Constitution (suspended by King Sobhuza II in 1973), and to draft a new one, taking into account all aspects of governance in Swaziland. Following several extensions to its term, the CRC report was eventually presented to King Mswati III in August 2001. The CRC recommended that there should be little or no change to the current political system. In December 2001 the Minister of Justice and Constitutional Affairs announced the formation of a new committee whose role would be to draft the new Constitution, taking the CRC's report as its guide. The composition of the committee did not allow the banned political parties to contribute, though individuals were welcome to do so.

In 2002 the traditional Swazi system of governance found itself at odds with modern expectations over an increasing number of issues. One example was the decision to proceed with a down-payment for the purchase of a private jet for use by the royal family, without consulting parliament, at a time when more and more families were affected by food shortages and **HIV/AIDs**. In another, the mother of a girl selected to be one of the King's new wives took legal action against the King's emissaries for taking the girl without her permission. (The girl is now officially a fiancée of the King, and the mother has abandoned legal action.) There were continued concerns about royal extravagance in 2003, when it was revealed that

US $15.5m. of public funds had been spent on luxury cars and palaces, at a time when two-thirds of Swazis are living in chronic **poverty** and one-quarter of the population depend on emergency food aid from the international community. The Swaziland Coalition of Concerned Civil Organizations (SCCCO), formed in early 2003, has been attempting to put pressure on the government to resolve issues concerning the rule of law and the Constitution through dialogue. The Coalition comprises several elements of civil society, including the trade unions, the employers' federation, the business community and the Church. Deputies in the National Assembly are selected on the basis of a local power base from within the 55 Tinkhundla constituencies. The Prime Minister is appointed by the King, as are the majority of the members of the Cabinet. Elections took place most recently in 2003. The Commonwealth Observer Group (COG) rejected the credibility of the electoral process entirely. It was also critical of the draft constitution, which failed to stipulate how and when the King would transfer his power. King Mswati dissolved the Cabinet before the second round of the elections held in 2003, removing the Prime Minister and appointing an interim head of government, Paul Shabangu. After the elections the King appointed a new Cabinet and a new Prime Minister, Absolom Themba Dlamini, who had managed the royal conglomerate Tibiyo TakaNgwane for 10 years. The King reopened parliament in March.

International relations

Swaziland's economy depends heavily on receipts from the **Southern African Development Community** customs union, and on close integration with South Africa. In 1995 South Africa criticized Swaziland's governance and monarchy, straining relations. In that year the South African government also rejected a long-standing claim still maintained by Mswati to a region in Mpumalanga province, formerly part of the Transvaal. Relations with the wider international community have become increasingly strained because of the perceived excesses of King Mswati III and the slow progress of reform.

Swaziland, economy

In 2003, according to estimates by the **World Bank**, Swaziland's gross national income (GNI), measured at average 2001–03 prices, was US $1,895m., equivalent to $1,350 per head (or $4,850 per head on an international purchasing-power parity basis). During 1990–2003, it was estimated, the population increased at an average annual rate of 2.8%, while gross domestic product (GDP) per head increased, in real terms, by an average of 0.1% per year. Overall GDP increased, in real terms, at an average annual rate of 2.9% in 1990–2003; growth in 2003 was 2.2%. In 1990–2002 annual inflation averaged 9.5%; consumer prices increased by an average of 11.7% in 2002. Swaziland's major industries include coal-mining and the production of wood pulp, sugar, and soft drink concentrate. In 2004 the main destinations for Swaziland's exports were South Africa, the **European Union (EU)**, the USA and Mozambique. The main suppliers of imports in 2004 were South Africa, the EU, Japan and Singapore. The national currency is the lilangeni (plural: emalangeni). In 2004 the average exchange rate was US $1 = 6.4597 emalangeni.

Swaziland is a small, land-locked country whose economy is largely based on **agriculture** and agro-industry. Despite being the second smallest African nation, it has one of the continent's highest incomes per head, ranking as a 'middle income country'. Subsistence agriculture, practised mainly in the Middleveld and Lubombo plateau, employs about 60% of the population. Citrus fruit and wood pulp are the major sectors, and asbestos and coal are the major minerals. Despite its relatively prosperous economy, there are substantial problems facing the government and the King.

The Swazi economy depends heavily on South Africa, from which it receives 95.6% of its imports and to which it sends 59.7% of its exports, and is therefore vulnerable to any set-back in its neighbour's economy. Political change in South Africa has eroded some of Swaziland's advantage in attracting foreign capital, on which much growth has depended in the past. Following disastrous harvests in 2004 and a worsening of the **HIV/AIDS** epidemic, the European Commission approved funds totalling 2m. euros for humanitarian aid for Lesotho and Swaziland. A better harvest was expected in 2005, but no matter what the outcome Swaziland's dependence on aid will continue, following three years of **drought** combined with the world's highest HIV infection rate. Swaziland's ability to deal with the epidemic and to initiate political reform will be the key factor in establishing the domestic and international confidence needed for economic growth and development.

T

At-Tajdid Movement

Tunisian political party.

Et-Takaful (Solidarity)

Egyptian political party, established in 1995. It advocates the imposition of a solidarity tax on the rich in order to provide for the needs of the poor. Its chairman is Dr Usama Muhammad Shaltout.

Takfir wal Hijra

An international Islamist group whose name is variously translated as 'Penance and Flight' or 'Penance and Exodus'. It operates mainly in Egypt, but there are other groups with the same name and some links to groups in Jordan and Algeria.

Tambo, Oliver

Former President of the **African National Congress (ANC)**. Tambo led the ANC movement from exile in Lusaka, Zambia, during the 1980s.

Tandja, Col (retd) Mamadou

Elected as President of Niger in 2004. Born in 1938, Tandja participated in the coup which overthrew Diori Hamani, Niger's first elected President in 1974, and subsequently served as interior minister. He contested the presidential election of 1993, but was defeated by Mahamane Ousmane. In 1996 he again contested the presidency, but was defeated on this occasion by Ibrahim Mainassara.

Tanganyika

Formerly a German colony in **East Africa**, Britain acquired Tanganyika as a mandated territory in 1919 after Germany's defeat in the First World War. Previously, the territory was part of **German East Africa**, which included Tanganyika, Burundi and Rwanda. Pressure for change and for **independence** began to grow after the Second World War. In 1954 the Tanganyika African National Union (TANU) was formed by **Julius Nyerere**. Britain established a constitution in 1955 which espoused the 'equality of races', giving the opportunity for elections in which electors in each constituency should all elect one member of each of the three 'races' (European, Asian and African), but the party formed to apply this, the United Tanganyika Party, never secured much support and was eclipsed by TANU. In 1957 Nyerere, who had been seeking independence in 25 years' time, was appointed as a member of the legislative council, together with Rashid Kawawa, but he soon resigned in order to press for independence by 1969. In elections spread over a period in 1958–59, TANU won all of the seats it contested and in 1960 extended its success throughout the country. The multiracial experiment was abandoned, after a change of governor and colonial secretary in 1959, and Tanganyika achieved independence in December 1961. It chose to be a republic and a member of the British **Commonwealth**.

Tanzania, United Republic of

The United Republic of Tanzania consists of **Tanganyika**, on the African mainland, and the nearby islands of **Zanzibar** and **Pemba**. Tanganyika lies on the east coast of Africa, bordered by Uganda and Kenya to the north, by Rwanda, Burundi and the Democratic Republic of the Congo (DRC, formerly **Zaire**) to the west, and by Zambia, Malawi and Mozambique to the south. Zanzibar and Pemba are in the Indian Ocean, about 40 km off the coast of Tanganyika, north of Dar es Salaam. Tanzania is 945,087 sq km in area. At the census of 2002 the population was enumerated at 34,569,232. Most of the people are of Bantu origin. There are some 120 **ethnic groups** on the mainland, none of whose number exceeds 10% of the total population. The biggest group is the Sukuma; others include the **Masai**, the Haya, the Gogo, the Nyamwezi, the Ha and the **Chagga**. The official languages are **Swahili** and English, and there are numerous tribal languages. There are Muslim, Christian and Hindu communities. Many Africans follow traditional beliefs. The capital is Dar es Salaam, whose population was estimated at 1,360,850 at mid-1988.

Political profile

Under the provisions of the 1977 Constitution, with subsequent amendments, legislative power is held by the unicameral National Assembly, whose members serve for a term of five years. There is constitutional provision for both directly elected members (chosen by universal suffrage) and nominated members (including five members elected by and from the Zanzibar House of Representatives). The number of directly elected members exceeds the number of nominated members. The Electoral Commission may review and, if necessary, increase the number of constituencies before every general election. Executive power lies with the President, elected by popular vote for five years. The President must be at least 40 years of age and his mandate is limited to a maximum of two five-year terms.

The President appoints a Vice-President, to assist him in carrying out his functions, and presides over the Cabinet, which is composed of a Prime Minister and other ministers who are appointed from among the members of the National Assembly.

Zanzibar has its own administration for internal affairs, and the amended Zanzibar Constitution, which came into force in January 1985, provides for the President, elected by universal adult suffrage, to hold office for a maximum of two five-year terms, and for the House of Representatives, of 45–55 members, to be directly elected by universal adult suffrage. The President of Zanzibar appoints the Chief Minister, and the two co-operate in choosing the other members of the Supreme Revolutionary Council, which has a maximum of 20 members.

In May 1992 the United Republic's Constitution was amended to legalize a multi-party political system.

In a presidential election held on 29 October 2000, Benjamin William Mkapa received 71.7% of the votes and was duly re-elected as President. (Mkapa was elected as President for the first time in 1995.) In an election for the Zanzibar President, likewise held on 29 October 2000, Amani Abeid Karume was the successful candidate, receiving 67% of the votes.

Following an election held on 29 October 2000, the distribution of seats in the National Assembly was as follows: Chama Cha Mapinduzi (CCM—Revolutionary Party of Tanzania) 244; Civic United Front (CUF) 15; **Chama Cha Demokrasia na Maendeleo (Chadema—Party for Democracy and Progress)** 4; Tanzania Labour Party (TLP) 3; United Democratic Party (UDP) 2. (In addition to the 231 elective seats, 10 seats are reserved for presidential nominees and 27 seats for **women** (included in the figures above), five for members of the Zanzibar House of Representatives and one for the Attorney-General.

Following an election held on 29 October 2000, the distribution of seats in the Zanzibar House of Representatives was as follows: CCM 34; CUF 16. (In addition to the 50 elective seats, five seats are reserved for regional commissioners, 10 for presidential nominees and 10 for women.)

History

The modern Tanzanian state is formed from the former colony of Tanganyika, on the mainland, and the former Protectorate of Zanzibar. After the First World War, control of Tanganyika passed from Germany to Britain under a League of Nations mandate. After the Second World War, Tanganyika became a UN trust territory under British control. During the 1940s there were growing demands for self-determination. In 1954 **Julius Nyerere** founded the Tanganyikan African National Union (TANU), which became the focus of African **nationalism**. The colonial authorities responded with constitutional changes that increased the representation of the African population and elections were held in 1958–59 and again in 1960. The result was overwhelming victory for TANU. The new government and Britain agreed at a constitutional conference to full **independence** for Tanganyika in 1961.

Tanganyika became a republic in December 1962 and Nyerere was directly elected as President. In 1965 the Constitution was changed to establish a one-party system. Zanzibar became independent from Britain in 1963. In 1964 a revolution by the majority black African population overthrew the government. The Constitution was annulled. The Sultan (whose family had governed Zanzibar since the 18th century) was expelled and many of Zanzibar's Arab population fled the country. Zanzibar was proclaimed a people's republic. The union of Tanganyika and Zanzibar took place in April 1964. The union was formally named the United Republic of Tanzania in October 1964. On 5 February 1977 the ruling parties of the two countries merged to form the CCM.

Nyerere relinquished the presidency in 1985 and was succeeded by Ali Hassan Mwinyi. During Mwinyi's presidency Tanzania began to experiment with economic liberalization and democratic reform. President Mkapa was first elected in 1995 and re-elected in 2000.

International relations

Concern over increasing Islamic militancy in Zanzibar and **East Africa** generally caused international flights to be suspended in 2003. The USA claimed in January that it, together with the Tanzanian security forces, had uncovered a plot by the al-Haramain Islamic Foundation to attack tourist hotels in late 2003. The US administration has recently urged the Tanzanian government to suppress potential terrorist groups within its borders.

Tanzania has enjoyed cordial relations with its neighbours, and faces few serious threats to its security. In 1995 Tanzania, Uganda and Kenya revitalized the **East African Community (EAC)**, which is intended to boost trade links between the three countries. A secretariat, based in Arusha, has produced ambitious plans for further co-operation on development, including lowering customs tariffs and a single currency for the region. The EAC treaty was signed on 30 November 1999.

Tanzania's main security concern is instability generated by the crisis in the Great Lakes region on its north-west border. After the Rwandan **genocide** in 1994, some 500,000 **Hutu** refugees fled from Rwanda to the Kagera district of Tanzania. The **UN High Commission for Refugees (UNHCR)** and aid agencies met the cost of housing the **refugees** but their presence caused extensive environmental damage to the region. In November 1996 the Tanzanian and Rwandan governments agreed a repatriation programme with UNHCR, which resulted in the return of most of the Rwandan refugees. Tanzania continues to play a key role in the Burundi peace process and, together with South Africa, has been instrumental in placing pressure on the transitional government of Burundi and the four main rebel groups to negotiate. President Mkapa is the co-facilitator of the peace process and Tanzania has hosted some of the key meetings. In 2000 the Arusha Accord—the basis of the Transitional National Government in Burundi—was signed. Tanzania's primary motivation has been to avoid the spread of instability across its borders. There are currently about 500,000 Burundian refugees in camps in Tanzania, plus a number who have lived in settlements since the early 1970s. Voluntary returns to northern Burundi began in January 2002. However, in June UNHCR decided to stop assisting voluntary repatriations to southern and eastern Burundi owing to concerns about the security situation in those areas.

Tanzania, economy

In 2003, according to estimates by the **World Bank**, mainland Tanzania's gross national income (GNI), measured at average 2001–03 prices, was US $9,817m., equivalent to $290 per head (or $610 per head on an international purchasing-power parity basis). During 1990–2003, it was estimated, the population of the country as a whole increased at an average annual rate of 2.7%, while gross domestic product (GDP) per head increased, in real terms, by an average of 1.2% per year. Overall GDP increased, in real terms, at an average annual rate of 3.7% in 1990–2003; growth was 5.6% in 2003. The annual rate of inflation averaged 14.9% in 1990–2003; consumer prices increased by 4.9% in 2003. Tanzania's major industries include textiles, agribusiness, mining, light manufacturing and **oil**-refining. In 2004 the main markets for Tanzania's exports were India, the Netherlands, Japan, the United Kingdom, the People's Republic of China (PRC), Kenya and Germany. The main suppliers of imports in that year were South Africa, the PRC, India, Zambia, the United Arab Emirates, the USA, the United Kingdom and Kenya. The national currency is the Tanzanian shilling. In 2003 the average exchange rate was US $1 = 1,089.33 shillings.

Tanzania is one of the world's poorest countries. More than one-half of national income is derived from **agriculture**. Since the late 1980s Tanzania has been committed to structural adjustment programmes. In November 1996 Tanzania agreed an Enhanced Structural Adjustment Facility (ESAF) with the **International Monetary Fund (IMF)**. This allowed lending on generous terms, to fund retrenchment and reform of the public sector. The priority of President Mkapa's government has been economic reform, in accordance with IMF guide-lines. Measures taken have included budgetary retrenchment in all sectors of public spending, further privatization of parastatal companies, and initiatives to increase tax revenue. These are intended to ensure balanced budgets and avoid public-sector borrowing. The government has also attempted to promote foreign investment by reforming the complex Investment Code and taxation system. President Mkapa has also initiated a campaign against **corruption**. The Tanzanian government is now focused on meeting the targets of the IMF programme. Steps to improve revenue collection, expenditure control and to implement civil service reform (including retrenchment) are being taken. Tanzania reached **Heavily Indebted Poor Countries (HIPC)** initiative completion point on 27 November 2001. As part of the HIPC initiative, the United Kingdom has cancelled £118m. of Tanzania's **debt**. The IMF noted that Tanzania had 'continued to maintain macroeconomic stability and to make substantial progress'.

Tanzim al-Jihad

Egyptian grouping formed after splitting from **al-Gama'a al-Islamiyya (Islamic Group)** in Egypt and then joining the somewhat dormant Jihad group in Egypt. It is barely active.

Ould Taya, Col Maaouiya Ould Sidi Ahmed

Head of State of Mauritania from December 1984, when he overthrew **Lt-Col Mohamed Khouna Ould Haidalla**, until August 2005. He was elected as President in the first multi-party elections in Mauritania in January 1992. He was deposed in a military coup in August 2005 by Col Ely Ould Mohamed Vall.

Taylor, Charles

Former President of Liberia. Charles Taylor was born in Liberia in 1948 to a Liberian mother and an American father. He was educated in the USA, where he took part in protests against the regime in Liberia of President William Tolbert. When President Tolbert was ousted in 1980, Taylor joined Samuel Doe's government, but was soon charged with fraud and fled to the USA, where he was arrested. He escaped custody, returning to Liberia to lead the National Patriotic Front. In 1997 he was elected as President. Liberia's political system under Taylor lacked pluralism and freedom of expression. Taylor was intolerant of criticism and virtually eliminated the opposition. Leading opposition figures, including Ellen Johnson Sirleaf, runner up to Taylor in the 1997 elections, and Charles Brumskine, were accused of treason and forced to flee the country because of harassment and threats to their families.

In June 2003 Taylor was indicted by a UN-backed war crimes tribunal for his alleged support for rebels during a brutal **civil war** in neighbouring Sierra Leone. The indictment and an arrest warrant were issued as Taylor attended talks in Ghana aimed at ending the ongoing rebellion in Liberia, during which he unexpectedly offered not to stand for re-election, should this be stipulated in a peace plan. The arrest order was not heeded and Taylor returned to Liberia where he claimed that a coup attempt had been foiled. Intense fighting followed as rebel forces advanced towards Monrovia. In August 2003 Taylor remained President of Liberia but was besieged in Monrovia by two separate rebel armies. Several opposition parties returned for the planned elections in October 2003, but operated in a climate of fear.

Fighting intensified in Liberia as rebels battled for control of Monrovia. The UN Secretary-General recommended to the Security Council that a multinational peace-keeping force be deployed in Liberia in response to the critical humanitarian situation, and urged US military intervention—which was denied, although US President George W. Bush urged Taylor to resign. In response to calls for intervention, the **Economic Community of West African States** agreed to provide peace-keepers. Facing increasing pressure from the international community, and from rebel forces, Taylor announced in July 2003 that he had accepted an offer from the Nigerian Head of State, **Olusegun Obasanjo**, of political asylum and relinquished power. Taylor's departure satisfied the rebel forces and allowed for delegates of the incumbent government, rebel factions, political opposition and civil organizations, under the aegis of the UN, to reach a comprehensive peace agreement. The agreement provided for the establishment of a transitional power-sharing government and legislature involving all parties. Under the agreement, Vice-President Moses Zeh Blah transferred power to the new administration on 14 October 2003. Gyude Bryant was elected President of the transitional government.

Temne

A major ethno-linguistic grouping in West Africa, particularly in Sierra Leone.

Terre'Blanche, Eugene

Leader of the right-wing extremist **Afrikaanse Weerstandsbeweging** (Afrikaner Resistance Movement). Sentenced to two terms of imprisonment for assault with intent to do grievous bodily harm and attempted murder.

Terrorism

Terrorism could be said to involve 'the use of violence or the threat of violence against specific or non-specific targets to create terror in order to induce a change in policy'. Like war, it is an extension of politics by other means. Although generally used of non-state groups, terrorism can be used by the state to crush opposition. There is a long history of the use of terror in the region, starting during the colonial period and continuing into the present. It has been said that one-man's terrorist is another man's freedom fighter, and the history of Africa in the colonial and post-colonial period has demonstrated time and again that the distinctions are a matter of political outlook as much as of the distinctive methods used to advance or suppress a cause.

The current 'war against terrorism' declared by US President George W. Bush, following attacks on Washington, DC, and New York in September 2001 by members of the Islamist organization or network al-Qa'ida, is directed mainly against Islamist groups, but is, in effect, an internationally orchestrated effort to suppress a wide range of groups across the world, supporting and defending a variety of causes by means of armed struggle or other forms of violence, and identified as 'terrorists'.

Third World

Term formerly commonly used to refer to the developing countries of Africa, Asia and Latin America. In a Cold War context, in which the global struggle between capitalism (First World) and communism (Second World) dominated international relations, many newly independent countries sought an independent path—a third way—and a way of defining this **independence**. The term Third World became fashionable during the period from the mid-1950s to the mid-1970s. Other terms equally popular at the same period related to the idea of 'non-alignment' in the Cold War—hence the **Non-aligned Movement**, which began in effect at Bandung in 1955. By the 1980s the 'end of the Third World' was being discussed, following the **oil** price increases of the mid- and late 1970s (orchestrated by the **Organization of Petroleum Exporting Countries**) and the emergence of the Newly Industrializing Countries—both of which challenged the idea and the reality of a single more-or-less homogenous Third World. During the 1980s, as **structural adjustment** involving far-reaching economic liberalization was imposed or adopted to an ever-increasing extent by governments of developing countries in Africa and elsewhere, there was greater emphasis on inter-dependence and integration in 'one world'—a concept which crystallized in the 1990s in the term '**globalization**'.

Tigray

Region of Ethiopia, home of the Tigrayans, who spearheaded the revolt against the Ethiopian **Dergue**, the Marxist-Leninist junta that ruled the country from 1974 until 1991, and who dominate the ruling party, the Ethiopian People's Revolutionary Democratic Front.

Tigrayans

People of Tigray, a major region in Ethiopia. They spearheaded the revolt against the Marxist-Leninist junta (the **Dergue**) which ruled Ethiopia from 1974 until 1991.

Togo (Togolese Republic)

The Togolese Republic lies in West Africa, forming a narrow strip stretching north from a coastline of about 50 km on the Gulf of Guinea. It is bordered by Ghana to the west, by Benin to the east, and by Burkina Faso to the north. Togo is 56,785 sq km in area. At mid-2003 the population was estimated at 4,909,000. The Kabré, the **Ewe** and the Kabiyé are the main ethnic groups. The official languages are French, Kabiyé and Ewe. About one-half of the population follows animist beliefs, while about 35% are Christians and 15% Muslims. The capital is Lomé, whose population was estimated at 799,122 at mid-2003.

Political profile

Under the terms of the Constitution that was approved in a national referendum on 27 September 1993, and subsequently modified, executive power is vested in the President of the Republic, who is directly elected, by universal adult suffrage, for a period of five years. The legislature is the unicameral Assemblée nationale, whose 81 members are also elected, by universal suffrage, for a five-year period. All elections take place in the context of a multi-party political system. The Prime Minister is appointed by the President from among the majority in the legislature, and the Prime Minister, in consultation with the President, nominates other ministers.

In a presidential election held on 24 April 2005, Faure Gnassingbé, the candidate of the **Rassemblement du peuple togolais (RPT—Rally of the Togolese People)** received 60.16% of the votes and was duly elected as President.

Following a general election held on 27 October 2002, the distribution of seats in the Assemblée nationale was as follows: RPT 72; Rassemblement pour le soutien de la démocratie et du développement (RSDD—Rally for the Support of Democracy and Development) 3; Union pour la démocratie et le progrès social (UDPS—Union for Democracy and Social Progress) 2; Juvento—Mouvement de la jeunesse togolaise (Juvento—Movement of Togolese Youth) 2; Mouvement des croyants pour l'égalité et la paix (MOCEP—Movement of Believers for Equality and Peace) 1; Independents 1.

History

Togoland, of which modern Togo was formerly a part, was colonized by Germany in 1894. The German administration was overthrown by a joint Anglo-French force early in the First World War. Togoland was then divided into a French-controlled eastern part and a British-controlled Western sector, each of which was governed under a League of Nations mandate. After a UN-sponsored referendum in 1956, the British sector merged with the neighbouring colony of **Gold Coast** to form Ghana, while the French part chose to become an autonomous republic. Togo was granted full **independence** in 1960. Since independence, Togo has been divided along north-south ethnic lines, with the first President, **Sylvanus Olympio**, representing southern interests. He was murdered in a coup in 1963, and replaced by Nicolas Grunitzky. Lt-Col Etienne Eyadema seized power in a military coup in 1967. He subsequently founded the RPT, the only political party at the time. For more than 30 years thereafter Togo was ruled by President Eyadema and the RPT. However, the regime was not entirely unchallenged. In the 1980s Eyadema survived a number of coup attempts, most notably in 1986, when he was assisted by the intervention of French paratroopers.

Pro-**democracy** demonstrations within Togo were often brutally suppressed. During the early 1990s this led some 250,000 Togolese to flee to neighbouring countries. Eventually, Eyadema agreed to recognize opposition parties. However, the military-backed RPT continued to dominate politics and during this period one opposition leader was murdered and attempts were made on the lives of others. In 1993, following international pressure, and with the co-operation of France and Burkina Faso, presidential elections were held for the first time. However, they were boycotted by opposition candidates, following the exclusion of the President's main rival, Gilchrist Olympio. Voter turn-out was low and Eyadema was returned with a comfortable majority. In legislative elections held in 1994 opposition parties won

42 of the 81 seats. Eyadema ignored the result, however, and appointed a Prime Minister (Edem Kodjo) from the RPT. This failure to implement democratic principles led the **European Union (EU)** to suspend aid to Togo. Presidential elections held in 1998 were associated with large-scale electoral fraud: when the vote count indicated victory for Gilchrist Olympio, the authorities suspended the electoral process and the army seized the ballot boxes. The head of the National Electoral Commission resigned in protest, only to be replaced by the Minister of the Interior, who proclaimed Eyadema the winner. An EU observer team condemned the conduct of the elections and was forced to leave the country following harassment by the Togolese authorities. In response, the EU reaffirmed its suspension of technical co-operation and assistance. An offer by Eyadema to enter into a dialogue with opposition leaders led to the signing, in 1999, of the Lomé Framework Agreement. The Agreement included a pledge by Eyadema not to contest presidential elections scheduled for 2003, and a promise to dissolve the RPT-dominated National Assembly in 2000.

President Eyadema did not honour his pledge to dissolve the RPT-dominated National Assembly, however. Under pressure to set up an electoral timetable, arrangements were made for legislative elections to take place in October 2001. Both the EU and the UN offered financial and technical assistance to the Togolese authorities. Nevertheless, the elections had to be postponed owing to lack of preparation. A new date was set for March 2002. Meanwhile, Yawovi Agboyibo of the Comité d'action pour le renouveau (Action Committee for Renewal) was imprisoned for criticizing the Prime Minister. Harassment of opposition supporters and the media continued unabated. In the run-up to the March elections the authorities refused to accept three of the EU's four technical assistants and also refused to finance the Independent National Electoral Commission. Problems also arose over the issue of voter registration cards. Agboyibo was forced to remain in prison despite winning an appeal against his sentence. The opposition parties, united in their support for his release, threatened to boycott the elections if he could not participate. The EU, which had repeatedly called for Agboyibo's release, and frustrated by the lack of progress, withdrew financial support for the electoral process. Agboyibo was finally released on 14 March 2002. However, a controversial move by the government had meanwhile undermined the prospects for successful parliamentary elections. The electoral code was amended in February 2002, without consultation with the opposition, an act that contravened the spirit of the Lomé Framework Agreement. The amended code marginalized candidates and voters residing outside of Togo and Togolese citizens with dual nationality. It also abolished the National Electoral Commission. All dialogue with the opposition broke down. Meanwhile, fissures appeared within the RPT. On 27 June 2002 the Prime Minister, Agbeyome Kodjo, was dismissed. He was expelled from the RPT and replaced as Prime Minister by **Koffi Sama**, who announced the formation of a new government in July. Kodjo subsequently fled the country. This followed his public support for a former president of the parliament, Dahuku Pere, who had openly criticized the party leadership for allowing the country to fall into decline. At the end of December 2002 the National Assembly approved changes to the Togolese Constitution, which directly contravened assurances given by Eyadema in the Lomé Framework Agreement by permitting him to stand for a third term as President. Eyadema remained as President thereafter until his death in February 2005.

Eyadema's death was followed by the closure of the country's borders by the **military** (thus preventing the constitutional successor, Fambarée Natchaba, from returning from abroad), the hurried amendment of the Constitution by the National Assembly, and the announcement by four army generals that Eyadama's son, Faure Gnassingbé, had replaced his father as Head of State. The **African Union (AU)** denounced this move as a military coup, while the **Economic Community of West African States** imposed sanctions in response. There was also widespread protest inside the country in the immediate aftermath of the new President's appointment at this violation of the Constitution. In the face of such domestic and external protest, Faure Gnassingbé relinquished the presidency three weeks after taking power, and agreed to hold elections within 60 days, as the Constitution required, in late April 2005. The main opposition parties agreed to support a single presidential candidate. Their first choice would have been Gilchrist Olympio, but he was disqualified from participating in the election as he no longer lived in Togo. His deputy in the Union des forces de changement (UFC—Union of Forces for Change), Emmanuel Bob Akitani, was chosen instead. Gnassingbé's victory in the ensuing election prompted violent unrest in Togo. Akitani's response was to claim that he had won the election and to declare himself President. However, the army, composed almost entirely of northerners from the same ethnic group as the late President Eyadema and loyal to his son, was unwilling to concede this claim. The French government (which has long backed the Eyadama family) announced itself broadly satisfied with the elections, incurring the anger of many Togolese—and the French opposition. On the day after the presidential election was held, President **Olusegun Obasanjo** of Nigeria invited both candidates to Abuja (Nigeria), where, after negotiations had taken place, he announced that the winning side would bring the losers into a government of national reconciliation. Gnassingbé subsequently confirmed this statement. A new Cabinet—comprising 30 ministers, of whom only five had served in the previous government—was announced in early June, but the opposition alliance refused to participate in it, despite being urged to do so by the AU. The opposition stated that they would only co-operate with the ruling RPT if new elections were held, claiming that the April polls had been fraudulently conducted.

International relations

Togo enjoys good relations with France and the USA. However, the failure of the government to institute a democratic system, together with its poor human rights record, has damaged Togo's relations with the EU. Although partially reinstated in

2004 in recognition of partial steps towards democratization, the EU's full financial co-operation has been suspended since 1993.

Togo, economy

In 2003, according to estimates by the **World Bank**, Togo's gross national income (GNI), measured at average 2001–03 prices, was US $1,722m., equivalent to $310 per head (or $1,500 on an international purchasing-power parity basis). During 1990–2003, it was estimated, the population increased at an average annual rate of 2.7%, while gross domestic product (GDP) per head declined by an average of 1.2% per year. Overall GDP increased, in real terms, at an average annual rate of 1.4% in 1990–2003. Real GDP increased by 3.1% in 2003. Annual inflation averaged 2.6% in 1990–93. Following the devaluation of the CFA franc in January 1994, inflation in that year averaged 39.2%. Consumer prices increased by an annual average of 3.2% in 1995–2002. Consumer prices increased by 3.0% in 2002. In 2004 the main markets for Togo's exports were Burkina Faso, Ghana, Benin, the People's Republic of China (PRC), Mali, the Netherlands and Taiwan. Togo's main suppliers of imports in 2004 were the PRC, France, Malaysia, Italy, Germany, the United Kingdom, the Netherlands, Thailand and Belgium. The national currency is the CFA franc (see the **Franc Zone**). In 2004 the average exchange rate was US $1 = 528.29 francs CFA. **Agriculture** is the mainstay of the Togolese economy, employing 65% of the labour force. Togo is also a major producer of phosphates, the mining of which is the most important industrial activity. After a boom in phosphate prices in 1975, Togo embarked on an ambitious investment programme, creating numerous public enterprises, many of which subsequently became a severe drain on the economy. Output of phosphates declined by an estimated 22% in 2002 owing to power shortages and the cost of developing new deposits. Like most small African nations, Togo relies heavily on subsistence agriculture, which contributes about 40% of GDP. **Cotton**, **coffee** and **cocoa** are the main agricultural exports, generating about 35% of total export earnings. Economic progress was severely obstructed by the unrest of 1992–93. The modern sector collapsed, the tax base shrank, transit trade shifted to other countries, external aid virtually disappeared, and GDP fell by 22% over two years.

Output by the mining sector is expected to increase thanks to new private management at Togo's International Fertilizer Group. The building of a container terminal at Lomé port will help boost construction activity. However, the continued suspension of full external development assistance, particularly by the EU, will continue to constrain Togo's economic performance for the foreseeable future. In 2005 the country's long-term economic prospects remain dependent on the restoration of political stability, which, it is hoped, will encourage the inward investment necessary to re-establish Togo as a centre for regional trade and financial services.

Togoland

A German protectorate during the late 19th century. Later Togo.

Tolbert

The history of Liberia, virtually an American preserve in Africa, was disrupted in 1980 by the violent removal of the dominant Tolbert family and ruling Truly Whig Party by the radical sergeant, later general, Samuel Doe. Doe alienated the USA and his own compatriots, turning for protection to the Israeli secret service, but survived the increasing hazard of a series of coups in the 1980s.

Tombalbaye, François

First President of Chad, from 1960. A representative of the educated southern élite, largely unsympathetic to the needs and demands of the Muslims in the north, whose opposition to his government he insisted on regarding as simple banditry. In 1966 Tombalbaye was challenged by the **Front de libération nationale du Tchad (FROLINAT—National Liberation Front of Chad)**, a northern liberation movement headquartered in Libya. He turned for help to France, with which Chad had a military agreement. Help was provided with supplies initially, but soon this came, in 1968–70, to include direct intervention with paratroops and aircraft, which secured Tombalbaye's position until 1975, when he was assassinated. He was succeeded by **Félix Malloum**.

Todd, Garfield

Prime Minister of Southern **Rhodesia** after Godfrey Huggins became Prime Minister of the **Central African Federation** in 1953.

Touré, Ahmed Sekou

President of Guinea from **independence** in 1958 until his death in 1984, Sekou Touré disrupted France's plans for a French-controlled West African community when he opted for total independence. As a result of his rejection of the idea of a French West African community, France broke off relations with Guinea and the breach was not healed until the 1970s. An influential figure on the left in African politics, Sekou Touré turned first for assistance to the USSR, but by 1961 had opted for a policy of non-alignment.

Touré, Gen. Amadou Toumani

An army general, Touré first came to power in Mali in 1991, having overthrown military ruler Moussa Traoré after his security forces killed more than 100 pro-**democracy** demonstrators. He gained widespread respect, and political credit, for not only rescuing Mali from dictatorship but also for handing power back to elected civilians in the following year. He was elected as President in May 2002.

Tristan da Cunha

Tristan da Cunha lies in the South Atlantic Ocean, 2,800 km west of Cape Town and 2,300 km south-west of **Saint Helena**. It is part of a group of islands that includes Inaccessible Island and the three Nightingale Islands (both within 40 km of Tristan da Cunha) and Gough Island, or Diego Alvarez, (425 km south). The British navy took possession of the island in 1815 when Napoléon Bonaparte was exiled to Saint Helena and a small garrison was stationed there. After the garrison was withdrawn a small colony remained. The United Society for the Propagation of the Gospel has maintained an interest in the island since 1922 and in 1932 one of its missionary teachers was recognized as Honorary Commissioner and magistrate. In 1938 Tristan da Cunha and the other uninhabited islands in the group were made dependencies of Saint Helena and in 1950 the office of Administrator was created. An Island Council (of eight elected members, one of which must be a woman, and three appointed members) was established in 1952. On 10 October 1961 a volcanic cone, thought long extinct, erupted close to the main settlement of Edinburgh of the Seven Seas, and it was necessary to evacuate the island. The majority of islanders returned in 1963. The island's main source of revenue derives from a royalty for crayfish fishing and income from the sale of postage stamps and handicrafts. The fishing industry and the administration employ all of the population. Development aid from the British government ended in 1980 and the island is largely self-sufficient. In 1969 electricity was extended to all homes and a radio-telephone service installed. A satellite system, which provides direct dialling for telephone and fax facilities, was installed in 1992. The island is remote and regular communications are restricted to about six calls a year by fishing vessels from Cape Town, an annual visit by a British vessel from Cape Town and an annual call by a South African vessel with supplies. There is, however, a wireless station in daily contact with Cape Town. The population in December 2000 was 290, including 11 expatriates. In June 2001 a hurricane destroyed the hospital, community centre and numerous homes in Edinburgh. The British Department for International Development granted a £75,000 emergency aid package in response to the disaster. Tristan da Cunha expects to be represented in 2005, for the first time, at the Annual Overseas Territories Consultative Council in London, by Chief Islander, Anne Green.

Trovoada, Miguel

Prime Minister of São Tomé and Príncipe following the elections held immediately after **independence** in July 1975. The Constitution promulgated in November 1975 effectively vested absolute authority in the hands of the President. In April 1979 Trovoada was dismissed as Prime Minister. In September he was arrested, charged with complicity in a coup attempted in 1978 and detained until 1981, when he was permitted to leave the islands. Another alleged coup attempt was forestalled in November 1980. In December 1981 rioting broke out on Príncipe, where food shortages had led to agitation for the island's autonomy. In 1989, the **Movimento de Libertação de São Tomé e Príncipe (MLSTP—Liberation Movement of São Tomé and Príncipe)**, now known as the **MLSTP—Partido Social Democrata (MLSTP—Social Democrat Party)**, after an extraordinary meeting of its central committee, embarked on a transition to full multi-party **democracy**. In the presidential election held in March 1991, Miguel Trovoada, having returned from exile to contest the election as an independent, but with the support of the Partido da Convergência Democrática—Grupo de Reflexão (Party of Democratic Convergence—Reflection Group), was elected unopposed, succeeding **Dr Manuel Pinto da Costa**, President since 1975. He then served two five-year terms as President, the maximum permitted by the Constitution. In July 2001 he was succeeded by **Fradique de Menezes**.

Truth and Reconciliation Commission (TRC)

Established in South Africa in December 1995. Chaired by Archbishop Desmond Tutu, the role of the Truth and Reconciliation Commission (TRC), as set out in an Act of the new parliament, was to compile as complete a picture as possible of human rights violations that had taken place between 1 March 1990 and 5 December 1993. One part of its work would be to accumulate testimony, and another to consider applications for amnesty which separate units, each headed by a judge, would then hear and adjudicate. There was also a reparations committee. The hearings began in April 1996, in East London. The TRC brought about an extraordinary process of confessions by those employed by and involved with the previous **apartheid** state of the crimes they had committed during the final years of the **National Party** regime. Among the 8,000 applicants for amnesty were the killers of **Steve Biko** and the Cradock Four, and after 24 and 16 years, respectively, of systematic cover-up and official perversion of the legal process, South Africans finally learned who had committed some of the most notorious of the state's many murders of its citizens. Regarded by some as a necessary and valuable catharsis, and by others as an opportunity for criminals to escape justice by confession of their crimes, the TRC—whose work was open to the public—was viewed by the international community as a significant and laudable attempt to close the divisions that had opened up in South African society and to deal with the legacy of a century of repression and violence.

Tshombe, Moïse

Leader of the political party called **Conakat**, which operated in the latter years of the Belgian Congo, and through which the Balunda aimed to exercise power in **Katanga**, either within a federal state or independently.

Tsvangirai, Morgan

President of the main opposition party, the **Movement for Democratic Change (MDC)**, in Zimbabwe. Morgan Tsvangirai emerged from a trade union background to become the most effective opposition leader in Zimbabwe. As a miner, he became involved in trade union activities and rose rapidly to become leader of the mining union. In the late 1980s Tsvangirai became head of the Zimbabwe Congress of Trade Unions, which had been established on the country's **independence**. However, it was not until some 10 years later that he emerged as a political force. In December 1997 and early 1998, Tsvangirai led a series of strikes against tax increases, which brought the country to a standstill. These forced the government of President **Mugabe** to cancel two tax increases. In 1999 Tsvangirai helped to create the MDC out of the radical trade union organization he was involved with. Within months, the new party had defeated the government over its referendum on constitutional reform, which included clauses allowing the seizure of white-owned farms without compensation. It was the most dramatic political set-back for President Mugabe since independence. But even this was eclipsed by the MDC's electoral performance. In June 2000 the MDC, headed by Tsvangarai, challenged the power of Mugabe's **Zimbabwe African National Union—Patriotic Front (ZANU—PF)**. In the general election, in spite of harassment, the MDC won 57 of the constituency-based seats, compared with 62 won by ZANU—PF, a result without precedent in Zimbabwe, where opposition parties had never held more than a handful of seats. Tsvangirai himself was not elected. Declining the opportunity of a seat in one of the cities, where the MDC's support is strongest, the MDC leader chose instead to contest the election in his home district which, like most rural constituencies, was won by Zanu—PF. His role as the first real credible alternative to Mugabe's government has been fraught with danger. Since his emergence as MDC leader he has been assaulted by supporters of ZANU—PF, and has been charged with treason three times, once for his alleged role in plotting the assassination of Mugabe and planning a coup with former Israeli security forces, a charge he has denied.

Since 2000 Tsvangirai has been undertaking a delicate political operation—attempting to maintain popularity and political momentum while holding together the very disparate interest groups gathered under the MDC umbrella, and at the same time resisting the threats and pressure directed against him and his supporters by the Mugabe regime. He draws most of his support from urban areas, but industrialists and white farmers have also rallied to his cause. Tsvangirai is regarded as representing a younger generation of Zimbabweans, who are less interested in Mugabe's historical role as Zimbabwe's founding father than in his recent record of economic mismanagement and suppression. Tsvangarai has continued to be the visible face of the MDC despite the repression and attempts to marginalize the movement by the Mugabe government. In the March 2005 elections, ZANU—PF regained overall control, although the MDC gained some seats and, supported by the United Kingdom and the USA, has claimed that the poll was characterized by widespread fraud.

Tswana

Ba-Tswana constitute 95% of the population of Botswana, Kalanga, Basarwa and Kgalagadi 4%, and whites 1%. The main languages are English and Se-Tswana.

Tubman, William

President of Liberia in 1944–71. Responsible for the **Sanniquellie Declaration** and for early attempts to create a West African customs union.

Tunisia, Republic of

Tunisia is situated in **North Africa**, bordering the Mediterranean Sea, between Algeria and Libya. The capital is Tunis. At July 2002 the population was estimated at 9,815,644, of which Arabs and **Berbers** together comprised 98%, Europeans 1% and Jews and 'others' a further 1%. The state religion is **Islam**. Ninety-eight per cent of the population are Muslims and 1% Christians. Jews and 'others' account for the remaining 1%. **Arabic** and French are the two official languages.

Political profile

The Constitution of the Republic of Tunisia was promulgated on 1 June 1959 and amended on 12 July 1988. Both the National Assembly and the President of the Republic are elected every five years by universal suffrage. Every citizen who has had Tunisian nationality for at least five years and who has attained 20 years of age has the right to vote. The Head of State and President of the Republic is **Zine el-Abidine Ben Ali** (took office on 7 November 1987; re-elected 2 April 1989, 20 March 1994, 24 October 1999 and 24 October 2004). The head of government and Prime Minister is Muhammad Ghannouchi. The Council of Ministers is appointed by the President. The legislative branch is the unicameral Chamber of Deputies or Majlis an-Nuwaab (182 seats). The most recent legislative elections, won by the **Rassemblement constitutionnel démocratique (RCD—Constitutional Democratic Rally)**, were held on 24 October 2004. In the resulting Majlis the RCD occupied 152 seats, the **Mouvement des démocrates socialistes (MDS—Movement of Socialist Democrats)** 14, the Parti de l'unité populaire (PUP—Party of Popular Unity) 11, the Union démocratique unioniste (UDU—Democratic Unionist Union) seven, **At-Tajdid**/Ettajdid Movement (Renewal) three and the Parti social libéral (PSL—Liberal Social Party) two. Reforms enabled opposition parties to win up to 20% of the total number of seats, and the number they occupied rose, accordingly, from 19 to 37. The legal system is based on the French civil law system and Islamic Law. There is some judicial review of legislative acts in the Supreme Court in joint session. There is also a Court of Cassation.

Tunisia became a multi-party **democracy** in 1988. In order to gain legal recognition, political parties must uphold the aims of and work within the Constitution, and are not permitted to pursue purely religious, racial, regional or linguistic objectives. Political parties can only be formed with the approval of the Minister of the Interior.

History

In the 19th century the heavy debts that the beys had contracted provided the European powers with a pretext for intervention in Tunisia. France, Great Britain, and Italy took control of Tunisia's finances in 1869. In 1881 France dispatched 30,000 troops to Tunisia ostensibly to counter border raids into French-occupied Algeria. They quickly occupied Tunis and forced the ruling bey to sign over his power to France, through the treaties of Bardo (1881) and Mersa (1883), which provided for the discreet transformation of Tunisia into a protectorate under a French resident general.

A nationalist movement developed relatively quickly in Tunisia. In 1920 the **Destour Party** (Constitutional Party) was organized. In 1934 a more radical faction, led by **Habib Bourguiba**, formed the **Neo-Destour Party**. During the Second World War Tunisia came under Vichy rule after the fall of France (June 1940), and Tunisian nationalists took advantage of this to intensify their campaign for **independence**. After the war nationalist agitation intensified further, and Bourguiba set about bringing Tunisia's position to international attention. By the early 1950s France was ready to make concessions and granted Tunisia a large degree of autonomy. The French settler (***colon***) population, however, opposed further reforms and negotiations quickly broke down. Bourguiba was arrested in 1952 and his subsequent imprisonment precipitated a wave of civil unrest and violence.

In 1954 Bourguiba was released in order to negotiate the agreement that led, in 1955, to Tunisian internal self-government and, in 1956, to full independence. Habib Bourguiba became Prime Minister. The country became a republic in 1957 when the bey, Sidi Lamine, was deposed by a vote of the constituent assembly, which then made Bourguiba President. He instituted sweeping political and social changes. He established Tunisia as a strict one-party state and implemented rights for **women** that were unmatched by any other Arab nation. Regarding **Islam** as a force that was holding the country back, Bourguiba set about reducing its role in society by removing religious leaders from their traditional areas of influence, especially in areas such as **education** and law. The **Shari'a** courts were also abolished, and lands that had financed mosques and religious institutions were confiscated.

Bourguiba followed a generally pro-Western foreign policy, but relations with France were strained over Algerian independence, which Tunisia supported, and the evacuation of French troops from Tunisia. The French naval installations at Bizerte were the scene of violent confrontation in 1961; France finally agreed to evacuate them in 1963. Relations between Tunisia and Algeria deteriorated after the latter gained its independence from France in 1962, and border disputes between the two countries were not settled until 1970. Bourguiba's support for a negotiated settlement with Israel in the Arab–Israeli conflict caused strains in its relations with other

Arab countries. Domestically, Bourguiba's policies emphasized modernization and planned economic growth. An agrarian reform plan, involving the formation of co-operatives, was begun in 1962, but it was halted in 1969 owing to harsh implementation and **corruption**. In the 1970s there was increasing conflict within the ruling Destour Party between liberals and conservatives, as well as public demonstrations (**'bread riots'**) against the government. In 1981 Bourguiba authorized the legal formation of opposition political parties, indicating a possible shift in the direction of **democracy**, and multi-party legislative elections were held for the first time in 1981. By 1986 six opposition parties had legal status. None the less the 1980s were largely characterized by popular unrest and labour difficulties, as well as by the search for a successor to the aged Bourguiba.

In 1987 Bourguiba was ousted by Gen. **Zine el-Abidine Ben Ali**, who had served as Minister for the Interior. Ben Ali quickly moved to appease the Islamic opposition, making a pilgrimage to Mecca and ordering that the Ramadan fast be observed. Since he took power the domination of the government by the RCD has held fast. The new regime restored diplomatic relations with Libya and signed a treaty of economic co-operation with Libya, Algeria, Mauritania and Morocco. Ben Ali initially moved towards liberal reforms, but after elections in 1989 in which Islamic activists performed strongly, he instituted repressive measures against them. During the 1994 election campaign the government arrested political dissidents and barred the Islamic party **an-Nahda** from participating. Running uncontested and endorsed by all of the legal opposition parties, Ben Ali received almost 100% of the vote. In 1999 Ben Ali was again re-elected, once more with almost 100% of the vote, although on this occasion he had faced a token challenge from two opposition candidates. Bourguiba's death in April 2000 inspired widespread and open dissent against Ben Ali's regime, and there are continuing signs of unrest.

International relations

Tunisia is attempting to strengthen its contacts with the West, relations with which have generally been good owing to Tunisia's liberal economic and social policies and its suppression of **Islamic fundamentalism**. Tunisia was host to the Palestine Liberation Organization after it was expelled from Lebanon. Relations with other Arab states, particularly those with Kuwait and Saudi Arabia, deteriorated as a result of Tunisia's support for Iraq during the Gulf War (1991). The government regards the political impact of Islamic fundamentalism (in the form of the **Groupe islamique armé (GIA—Armed Islamic Group)** in neighbouring Algeria with concern. Relations with Libya are improving, not least owing to the fact that the government ignores the activities on its territory of those seeking to circumvent sanctions in force against Libya.

Tunisia, economy

Tunisia has a diverse economy, with important agricultural, mining, **energy**, tourism, and manufacturing sectors. Governmental control of economic affairs, while still substantial, has gradually lessened over the past decade with increasing privatization, simplification of the tax structure, and a prudent approach to **debt**. Real growth averaged 5.4% in the past five years, and inflation is slowing. Growth in tourism and increased trade have been key elements in this steady growth, although tourism revenues have slowed since 11 September 2001 and may take another year or longer to fully recover. Tunisia's association agreement with the **European Union (EU)** entered into force on 1 March 1998, the first such accord between the EU and a Mediterranean country. Under the agreement Tunisia will gradually remove barriers to trade with the EU over the next decade. Broader privatization, further liberalization of the investment code to increase foreign investment, and improvements in government efficiency are among the challenges for the future. Tunisia was ranked as the most competitive African economy in the World Economic Forum's 2000–01 report.

Tunisian Combatant Group (TCG)

Also referred to as the Tunisian Islamic Fighting group, the Tunisian Combatant Group's goals reportedly include establishing an Islamic state in Tunisia and targeting Tunisian and Western corporate interests. Founded probably in 2000, by Tarek Maaroufi and Saifallah Ben Hassine, the group has come to be associated with al-Qa'ida and with other Islamist groups in Europe since 2001. In December 2001, the Belgian authorities arrested Maaroufi, charging him with passport and visa fraud and linking him to the assassination of Ahmed Shah Masoud in Afghanistan. According to the Italian authorities, the TCG members see themselves as part of the *salafist* movement and are in contact with the Algerian **Groupe salafiste pour la predication et le combat (GSPC—Salafist Group for Call and Combat)**.

Tutsi(s)

Traditionally defined as a group that is ethnically distinct from the **Hutu(s)**, with whom they have lived in close proximity for centuries mainly in Burundi and Rwanda. In fact, social and economic rather than genetic distinctions may provide a better explanation of the Tutsis' ability politically to dominate the Hutu and **Twa** peoples with whom they intermingle. Relations between the Tutsi and the Hutu were generally peaceful until the late 20th century, when they became increasingly characterized by eruptions of violent conflict in which large numbers of both Tutsis and Hutus were killed. More than 900,000 Tutsis and so-called 'moderate' Hutus are estimated to have died in the **Rwandan genocide** of 1994.

Twa

A people living mainly in the areas of rainforest in Rwanda, Burundi and the Democratic Republic of the Congo. Historically hunters and gatherers, and probably the aboriginal population of much of Central Africa, many Twa and other similar groups—often referred to collectively by Europeans (English) as '**pygmies**'—have adapted to **agriculture**, but most have been effectively marginalized socially and economically over the centuries by the expansion and intervention of Bantu-speaking peoples and others, including Europeans.

U

Uê-Kédadji

Political grouping in São Tomé and Príncipe. A coalition movement which won eight seats in the Assembléia Nacional in elections held in 2002.

Uganda, Republic of

The Republic of Uganda is a land-locked equatorial country in East Africa, bordered by Sudan to the north, the Democratic Republic of the Congo (DRC) to the west, Kenya to the east and Rwanda, Tanzania and Lake Victoria to the south. Uganda is 241,038 sq km in area (including inland water). At mid-2004 the population was estimated at 26,302,000. There are more than 20 ethnic groups, of which the largest are the Baganda, the Banyankole, the Basoga, the Iteso, the Acholi and the Langi. The official language is English and there are many local languages, the most important of which is Luganda. About 75% of the population follow Christian beliefs, while some 15% are Muslims. The capital is Kampala, whose population at the census of 2002 was provisionally enumerated at 1,208,544.

Political profile

Following the January 1986 coup, power was vested in a broad-based interim government, headed by an executive President. A National Resistance Council (NRC) was formed to legislate by decree. In addition, resistance committees were formed at local and district level. Political activity was suspended, although political parties were not banned. National elections were held in February 1989. Representatives were elected directly to local-level resistance committees; these elected representatives to district-level resistance committees, and these, in turn, elected representatives to the NRC. The NRC was expanded from 98 members, all nominated by the President, to 278 members, of whom 68 were nominated by the President and 210 were elected. In October 1989 the NRC approved legislation prolonging the Government's term of office by five years from January 1990, when its mandate had been due to expire. A new Constitution was enacted by an elected Constituent Assembly in September 1995 and came into force in the following month. The first direct presidential election was held in May 1996, and national legislative elections took place in the following month to a 276-member Parliament, as the NRC became—comprising 214 directly elected and 62 nominated members. Voting also took place in June for local councils (which replaced the resistance committees). Further local elections were held in November 1997 and January 2002. Under the terms of the new Constitution, a national referendum on the future introduction of a multi-party political system took place in June 2000, at which voters overwhelmingly endorsed the retention of the existing 'no-party' system (this was nullified by the Constitutional Court in 2004). Following legislative elections in June 2001, the number of seats in Parliament stood at 292, comprising 214 directly elected representatives and 78 nominated members.

At a presidential election held on 12 March 2001 **Gen. Yoweri Kaguta Museveni** received 69.3% of the votes and was re-elected as President. Museveni first became President in January 1986 after he had overthrown the regime of Basilio Okello. He was elected as President for the first time in 1996.

Political parties were ordered to suspend active operations, although not formally banned, in March 1986. As noted above, at a referendum on the future restoration of a plural political system, which took place on 29 June 2000, the retention of the existing 'no-party' system was overwhelmingly endorsed by voters. However, the result was nullified by the Constitutional Court in mid-2004. Following a successful challenge to the Political Parties and Organisations Act 2002, political parties were permitted to resume their activities nationally from March 2003. Discussions on a proposed transition to multi-party politics commenced in 2004. By April of that year some 60 new political parties had emerged, but only 13 had sought registration. In mid-2005 legislation was passed allowing for a return to full multi-party **democracy**; the legislation was approved by 92.5% of voters in a national referendum on 28 July 2005.

Registered political parties in Uganda include the Conservative Party (CP), the Democratic Party (DP), the Forum for Democratic Change, the Forum for Multi-Party Democracy, the Movement for New Democracy in Uganda, the National Resistance Movement Organisation (NRM-O), the Nationalist Liberal Party, the Uganda Freedom Movement, the Uganda People's Congress (UPC) and the Uganda People's Democratic Movement (UPDM). New parties seeking registration in 2004 included the Movement for Democratic Change (MDC), the National Progressive Movement (NPM) and the People's Independent Party (PIP).

History

Britain acquired Uganda at the end of the 19th century. In 1894 Uganda was declared a British protectorate, but it was never fully colonized. It included a number of kingdoms, of which the most important was Buganda, based along the northern shore of Lake Victoria, and under the rule of the Kabaka, Frederick Mutesa II. Others included Bunyoro, Toro, Ankole and Busogo. According to the 1900 Uganda agreement, the Kabaka was obliged to accept British advice on certain matters.

Constitutional change in Uganda had begun in 1950 when the legislative council was given an equal number of official and unofficial members. In 1954 the size of the legislative council was doubled. In 1953 an ill-timed remark by a British minister about an East African Federation was interpreted by the Kabaka to presage a British plan to create a new framework for the preservation of white rule and led to a quarrel between the Kabaka and the Governor, Sir Andrew Cohen. The Kabaka was dispatched into exile until 1955. A new Constitution was elaborated, which the Kabaka accepted under the Namirembe agreement, by which he agreed to transform Buganda into a constitutional monarchy and recognize that it constituted an integral part of Uganda as a whole. The Buganda *lukiko* (parliament) was to send representatives to sit in the Uganda parliament. The Kabaka was thus restored, but the principality to which he returned was a nascent democracy, within a larger democracy, and the British aim to create an independent Uganda as a unitary parliamentary democracy (not a federation) was well advanced. Britain failed to resolve the territorial dispute between Buganda and Bunyoro, which dated back to 1893, but in 1961 appointed the Molson Commission to try to resolve the issue. In 1961 Uganda was granted self-government and Benedikto Kiwanuka became the first Prime Minister. Bugandan separatism delayed full **independence**. The UPC, which had been formed by **Milton Obote** to fight for independence, entered into an alliance with the Bugandan home-rule party, Kabaka Yekka, to win a parliamentary majority and Obote replaced Kiwanuka.

Growing self-government, through a legislative and an executive council, led to full independence in October 1962. Obote, the leader of the UPC, was elected as Prime Minister. In the following year Uganda became a republic in the British **Commonwealth** and the Kabaka accepted the symbolic office of President. In 1964 the government of Uganda conducted a plebiscite, which conclusively restored certain disputed territories to Bunyoro. Early in 1966 Obote assumed emergency powers, dismissed and arrested a number of his ministers and dismissed the President. Two months later he introduced a new constitution, which precipitated renewed conflict with the *lukiko*, and appointed himself President. The Kabaka's palace was sacked and the Kabaka himself driven into exile. Obote was overthrown in 1971 by a former paratroop sergeant, **Idi Amin**, who established a brutal dictatorship. The Asian community was expelled in 1972, and intellectuals were persecuted. In 1979 border tension prompted an invasion by Tanzania (which had become increasingly concerned with the political instability of Uganda under Amin), with the support of exiled members of the Ugandan National Liberation Front (UNLF). Amin was overthrown and fled into exile. Ill-organized elections in 1980 returned Obote's UPC to power. Obote's government relied on the support of the army and soon became entangled in a savage guerrilla war against the National Resistance Army (NRA), led by Lt-Gen. Yoweri Museveni, who disputed Obote's mandate. Growing dissent between the Acholi and the Langi factions within the army resulted in 1985 in Obote's overthrow by the Acholi, who were led by Brig. (later Lt-Gen.) Basilio Okello. Okello established a Military Council, but, after a bitter battle in January 1986, the NRA occupied Kampala and Museveni was installed as President. A National Resistance Council was established as a quasi-parliament under an amended version of the 1967 Constitution. In 1989 a nation-wide system of Village Resistance Councils was created. Party political activity was suspended, though party structures remained legal.

In 1986 President Museveni took control of a country in which 1m. had been killed by war, 2m. had been uprooted as **refugees**, 500,000 had been seriously injured and the economy was in ruins. Considerable progress has been made in restoring peace across Uganda and in rebuilding infrastructure shattered by **civil war**. A characteristic of President Museveni's approach has been the 'no party' system whereby Uganda is governed. In 1985–95 Museveni governed through a system of 'Resistance Councils', based at grassroots level, which collectively formed the National Resistance Movement (NRM). Activity by political parties, mainly the UPC and the DP was banned; there were no elections. In 1995 Uganda adopted a new constitution, agreed by a Constituent Assembly elected in 1994, which consisted mostly of NRM supporters. The Constitution provided for presidential, parliamentary and local elections over the next two years, to be held under the existing restrictions on activity by political parties. Presidential and legislative elections took place, respectively, in May and June 1996. These were generally free and fair, notwithstanding the ban on party activity. In the presidential election President Museveni was the successful candidate, receiving 74.2% of the votes. NRM sympathizers won a majority of seats in the Parliament.

In June 2000 a referendum was held to decide whether Uganda should return to multi-party politics or retain the prevailing system of government. In a poor turn-out, voters overwhelmingly endorsed retention of the prevailing system. Presidential elections were held on 12 March 2001. Violence and intimidation, including by government forces, marked the later stages of the campaigning. After Museveni, who received 69% of the votes, had been declared the winner, his main rival, Dr Kiiza Besigye, challenged the result in the Ugandan Supreme Court. However, although the Court criticized the Electoral Commission's performance, it did not challenge Museveni's victory. In parliamentary elections held on 26 June 2001, 876 candidates contested 214 constituency seats. The resultant Parliament was again dominated by NRM loyalists.

In July 2005 the Parliament voted to amend the Constitution to allow President Museveni a third presidential term. In August Ugandans voted in favour of the restoration of multi-party politics after almost 20 years of 'no party' government under Museveni.

International relations

Uganda entered the conflict in the DRC in August 1998 in support of anti-government rebels and Rwanda. Uganda claimed its involvement in the conflict was necessary to secure the western border against attack from Ugandan rebel groups based in the DRC. On 10 July 1999 Uganda and the five other countries involved in the conflict signed the Lusaka Cease-fire Agreement. The Agreement provided for a cessation of hostilities, the establishment of a commission to investigate cease-fire violations, the elaboration of mechanisms to disarm militias and the monitoring of the withdrawal of foreign troops according to an agreed schedule. The Agreement also specified the deployment of a UN observer mission and the initiation of an inter-Congolese dialogue. In 2001 President Museveni initiated the withdrawal of the Uganda People's Defence Forces (UPDF), announcing his intention to abandon the peace process. Subsequently, however, Uganda agreed to abide by the Lusaka Agreement. In September the Presidents of Uganda and the DRC signed an agreement (facilitated by Angola) which covered the withdrawal of Ugandan troops from the DRC and a range of bilateral measures, including the establishment of diplomatic relations and commercial and cultural links.

The Ugandan and Rwandan leaderships developed close relations during the 1980s and early 1990s. However, tensions arose in 1998 as a result of their diverging agendas *vis-à-vis* the DRC. These subsequently escalated into clashes between their respective armies at Kisangani, DRC, in 1999 and 2000. Tensions were heightened by mutual accusations of interference in each other's domestic affairs (including supporting dissidents), prompting Museveni to refer to Rwanda as a 'hostile nation' during the approach to presidential election in Uganda in 2001.

Uganda, economy

In 2003, according to estimates by the **World Bank**, Uganda's gross national income (GNI), measured at average 2001–03 prices, was US $6,063m., equivalent to $240 per head (or $1,440 per head on an international purchasing-power parity basis). During 1990–2003, it was estimated, the population increased at an average annual rate of 2.9%, while gross domestic product (GDP) per head increased, in real terms, by an average of 2.9% per year. Overall GDP increased, in real terms, at an average annual rate of 6.5% in 1990–2003; growth was 4.9% in 2003. The annual average rate of inflation was 9.2% in 1990–2003; consumer prices decreased by 0.3% in 2002 and increased by 8.8% in 2003. Mining, manufacturing and textiles are important sectors of the economy. The United Kingdom, South Africa and India are Uganda's major trading partners. The national currency is the new Uganda shilling. In 2004 the average exchange rate was US $1 = 1,810.3 new shillings.

Uganda has substantial natural resources, including fertile soils, regular rainfall, and sizeable deposits of **copper** and **cobalt**. **Agriculture** is the most important sector of the economy, employing more than 80% of the labour force. **Coffee** is the major export crop, accounting for more than one-half of export revenues. Impressive progress has been made with economic reforms since 1986, albeit from a very low base. The government has consistently promoted a free-market approach and many institutional barriers to profitable business have been removed. However, **corruption** remains endemic and legal redress is difficult to obtain. Public expenditure is under control and well allocated, although donors continue closely to monitor defence spending patterns.

Uganda remains heavily burdened by international **debt**, most of it to financial institutions. With UK support, Uganda became the first country to benefit from debt cancellation ($347m.) under the **Heavily Indebted Poor Countries (HIPC) initiative**. In January 2000 additional relief of $656m. was granted under HIPC II and the United Kingdom cancelled bilateral debt of $23m. In September Uganda became the first country to benefit under the Enhanced HIPC scheme.

In 2002 economic growth was less than expected, owing to poor rainfall, lower agricultural growth, lower prices for coffee and lower-than-expected customs receipts. These problems reduced the value of the new Uganda shilling and increased inflation, although Uganda's record in controlling inflation remained one of the best in Africa.

Umkhonto we Sizwe (Spear of the Nation)

The military wing of the **African National Congress** in South Africa.

Umma Party (UP)

The Umma Party (UP) was formed in Sudan in the 1940s as a direct response to the formation by **Ismail al-Azhari** of the **Ashigga Party**, which aimed at the union of Sudan with Egypt. The UP, by contrast, was created to work for the **independence** of Sudan under the leadership of Sayyid Abd ar-Rahman al-Mahdi, a major religious figure and posthumous son of the famous Mahdi of the 1880s. The UP was accused, or at least suspected, by its opponents of aspiring to a revival of the Mahdist monarchy, with British help. Throughout the late 1940s and early 1950s, al-Azhari's party, renamed the National Unionist Party, was dominant, and in 1954 al-Azhari became Prime Minister after his party had achieved an overwhelming victory at the polls. However, after the replacement of al-Azhari by Abdullah Khalil in 1956 and the military coup of **Gen. Ibrahim Abboud**, which ousted Khalil in 1958, the UP began to advance. In 1965 the military regime of Gen. Abboud was itself replaced by a coalition in which the UP was dominant. In 1969, however, a coup led by **Gen. Nimeri** established a more left-wing and pro-Egyptian government.

União Caboverdiana Independente e Democrática—Partido Democrata Cristão (UCID—PDC, Independent and Democratic Union of Cape Verde—Christian Democrat Party)

Political party in Cape Verde. Established in 1974 by emigrants opposed to the **Partido Africano da Independência de Cabo Verde (African Party of Independence of Cape Verde)**. Obtained legal recognition in 1991. Member of the **Aliança para a Mudança (Alliance for Change)**, a coalition formed in October 2000 with the **Partido de Convergência Democrática (Party of Democratic**

Convergence) and the **Partido de Trabalho e Solidariedade (Party of Labour and Solidarity)**.

União Nacional para a Independência Total de Angola (UNITA—National Union for the Total Independence of Angola)

Established in 1966 to secure **independence** from Portugal. Later received Portuguese support to oppose the **Movimento de Libertação de Angola (MPLA—Liberation Movement of Angola)**. UNITA and the **Frente Nacional de Libertação de Angola (National Liberation Front of Angola)** conducted guerrilla campaigns against the MPLA government with aid from some Western countries in 1975–76. UNITA was supported by South Africa until 1984 and again in 1987–88, and by the USA after 1986. Its long-time leader, **Dr Jonas Savimbi**, opposed **José Eduardo dos Santos** in the first round of the 1992 presidential elections, but a resumption of hostilities between UNITA and government forces prevented a second round from taking place. Provision in the **Lusaka Protocol** of November 1994 for the second round of presidential elections was not pursued. UNITA obtained legal status in March 1998. Its interim leader is Gen. Paulo Lukumba.

União Nacional para a Independência Total de Angola—Renovada (UNITA—R, National Union for the Total Independence of Angola—Renewed)

Founded in 1998, this splinter group claimed to be the legitimate leadership of the **União Nacional para a Independência Total de Angola (UNITA—National Union for the Total Independence of Angola)** and was recognized as such, even though it commanded only minority support among UNITA members.

Unilateral Declaration of Independence

In 1965 the white government of Southern **Rhodesia** declared its **independence** of Britain in an attempt to deflect pressure for a transition to majority black rule. The action was condemned by Britain and the UN as illegal. The Rhodesian government and the economy was subject to international sanctions as a result, which had significant effects on the structure and performance of the Rhodesian economy, including, ironically, making it substantially more independent and self-reliant.

Union of African States

In November 1958 Ghana and Guinea (later joined by Mali) drafted a charter that was to form the basis of a Union of African States. In January 1961 at a meeting in Casablanca, Morocco, a group of countries (which came to be known as the **Casablanca Group**) adopted an African Charter and decided to establish an African Military Command and an African Common Market. Meetings of French-speaking countries during 1960 and 1961 gave rise to a charter establishing the Union Africaine et Malgache, which later became the Organisation commune Africaine et Mauricienne. In May 1961 a meeting at Monrovia, Liberia, gave rise to the **Monrovia Group** which agreed a charter for an organization of Inter-African and Malagasy States. Eventually, in 1963, at a conference of 32 African states held in Addis Ababa, Ethiopia, the creation of an organization of African states led to the Charter of the **Organization of African Unity (OAU)**, which represented a compromise between the loose association preferred by the Monrovia Group and the federal structure espoused by the Casablanca Group. The OAU, which came into being as an organization bringing together, in principle, all African states (including **North Africa** as well as Africa south of the Sahara), was replaced in 2001–02 by the **African Union**—in effect a Union of African States.

Union pour le Bénin du future (UBF—Union for Benin of the Future)

A coalition of political parties known as the 'presidential movement' in Benin.

Union congolaise des républicains (UCR—Congolese Union of Republicans)

Political party in the Republic of the Congo, led by Côme Mankassa.

Union constitutionelle (UC—Constitutional Union)

Moroccan political party, founded in 1983. Has a 25-member politbureau. Leadership is currently vacant.

Union pour la démocratie et les libertés (UDL—Union for Democracy and Freedoms)

Algerian political grouping, founded in 1997 and led by Abdelkrim Seddiki.

Union pour la démocratie et le progrès social (UDPS—Union for Democracy and Social Progress)

Major political party in the Democratic Republic of the Congo, established in 1982. The UDPS is led by Etienne Tshisekedi Wa Mulumba.

Union pour la démocratie et la République (UDR—Union for Democracy and the Republic)

Political party in Chad, established in 1992. Supports liberal economic policies and a secular, decentralized republic. It boycotted the legislative elections held in 2002. The UDR is led by Dr Jean Bawoyeu Alingué.

Union pour la démocratie et la République—Mwinda (UDR—Mwinda, Union for Democracy and the Republic—Mwinda)

Political party in the Republic of the Congo, founded in 1992. The UDR—Mwinda is led by André Milongo.

Union democratique (UD—Democratic Union)

Moroccan political party, founded in 2001. The UD's president is Bouazza Ikken.

Union démocratique du Cameroun (UDC—Democratic Union of Cameroon)

Political party in Cameroon, established in 1991. The UDC is led by Adamou Ndam Njoya.

Union des démocrates et progressistes indépendantes (UDPI—Union of Independent Democrats and Progressives)

Political party in Burkina Faso. Expelled from the Groupe du 14 février in mid-2000. The UDPI is led by Longo Dongo.

Union douanière et économique de l'Afrique centrale (UDEAC—Customs and Economic Union of Central Africa)

The Union douanière et économique de l'Afrique centrale (UDEAC) was established at Brazzaville, Congo, in 1964. In 1968 the Central African Republic and Chad withdrew to join the Congo (Léopoldville), or **Zaire**, in another union—the Union économique de l'Afrique centrale. Then, in December 1968, the Central African Republic rejoined the UDEAC. At a summit meeting in December 1981 UDEAC leaders agreed in principle to form an economic community of Central African states—the **Communauté économique des états d'Afrique centrale (CEEAC—Economic Community of Central African States)**, to include UDEAC members (six countries) and also Burundi, Rwanda, São Tomé and Príncipe and Zaire (now the Democratic Republic of the Congo). CEEAC became active in 1985.

Union économique et monétaire ouest-africaine (UEMOA—West African Economic and Monetary Union)

Founded in 1994, the Union économique et monétaire ouest-africaine (UEMOA) replaced the **Communauté économique de l'Afrique de l'ouest (CEAO—Economic Community of West Africa)**. Its members are Benin, Burkina Faso, Côte d'Ivoire, Guinea-Bissau, Mali, Niger, Senegal and Togo. Its objective is to promote regional monetary and economic convergence. It envisages the eventual creation of a sub-regional common market. A preferential tariff scheme, eliminating duties on most local products and reducing import duties on many Union-produced industrial goods by 30%, became operational in July 1996. In addition, a community solidarity tax, of 0.5%, was imposed on all goods from third countries sold within the Union in order to strengthen UEMOA's capacity to promote economic integration; this was increased to 1% in December 1999. In 1997 UEMOA Heads of State and Government agreed to reduce import duties on industrial products originating in the Union by a further 30%. An inter-parliamentary committee, viewed as the predecessor of a UEMOA legislature, was inaugurated in Mali in March 1998. In September, Côte d'Ivoire's stock exchange was transformed into the regional stock exchange to further integration. In August 1999 an inter-parliamentary committee adopted a draft treaty on the establishment of a UEMOA parliament. In January 2000, internal tariffs were eliminated on all local products, including industrial goods, and a joint external tariff was imposed on goods originating from outside the new customs union. Guinea-Bissau was excluded from this arrangement owing to its unstable political situation. The UEMOA countries also belong to the **Economic Community of West African States (ECOWAS)** and, in accordance with a plan adopted by the two organizations in February 2000, aim to harmonize UEMOA's economic programme with that of a planned second West African monetary union. A merger was then envisaged to make possible the subsequent creation of a West African Monetary Zone and the replacement of the **Communauté financière africaine (CFA)** by a new single West African currency.

Union des forces acquises à la paix (UFAP—Union of Forces Acquired for Peace)

Political grouping in the Central African Republic, established in 1998. An opposition alliance, including political parties, trade unions and human rights organizations. Weakened by withdrawals in 1999. The UFAP's president is Paul Bellét.

Union des forces démocratiques (UFD—Union of Democratic Forces)

A political-military group in Chad, led by Dr Mahamat Nahour.

Union des forces démocratiques (UFD—Union of Democratic Forces)

A political party in the Republic of the Congo. Supports the government. The UFD's president is David Charles Ganou.

Union générale tunisienne du travail (UGTT—General Tunisian Labour Union)

Major Tunisian trade union federation.

Union nationale des forces populaires (UNFP—National Union of Popular Forces)

Moroccan political party, established in 1959, after a split within the nationalist **Istiqlal**. Leadership dominated by the charismatic Mehdi Ben Barka. Ben Barka claimed that, in breaking away from the Istiqlal, the founders of the UNFP had introduced to Morocco 'a more modern conception of political parties. Whereas before parties saw themselves much more as an assemblage or in relation to a leader than in relation to a programme—that is, somewhat like the Middle East in the 1930s—one can now say that, increasingly, clientele parties will be clearly differentiated from parties based on a programme and an ideology'. Critics would argue that the UNFP largely failed to make a decisive break from clientelist politics and that Ben Barka himself was built into a charismatic leader and began to act like a *zaim* (or grand patron). Ben Barka was murdered in France in 1965, after having been kidnapped by Moroccan secret agents, aided by the French. In 1972, a split occurred between the Casablanca and Rabat sections of the party. Since the split, in 1974, which led to the establishment of the **Union socialiste des forces populaires (Socialist Union of Popular Forces)**, the UNFP has been led by Moulay Abdallah Ibrahim. It maintains close links with the trade union federation UMT and favours radical change as the basis for the construction of **socialism** in Morocco. It boycotted the 1977 parliamentary elections, and also refused to participate in the 1983–84 elections.

Union nationale pour la démocratie et le progrès (UNDP—National Union for Democracy and Progress)

Political party in Cameroon. Founded in 1991, split in 1995. The UNDP's chairman is Bello Bouba Maigari.

Union nationale démocratique du peuple centrafricain (UNDPC—National Democratic Union of the Central African People)

Political party in the Central African Republic, established in 1998. Based in the south east, the party has an Islamist philosophy. The UNDPC is led by Mahamat Saleh.

Union nationale pour le développement et le renouveau (UNDR—National Union for Development and Renewal)

Political party in Chad, which supports greater decentralization and increased limitations on the power of the state. The UNDR's leader is Saleh Kebzaboh.

Union nationale pour la solidarité et le développement (UNSD—National Union for Solidarity and Development)

Political party in Benin, founded in 1995. Merged with the Rassemblement pour la République (RPR—Rally for the Republic) in 1999.

Union pan-africaine pour la démocratie sociale (UPADS—Pan-African Union for Social Democracy)

Political party in the Republic of the Congo. The president of UPADS (in exile) is Pascal Lissouba.

Union patriotique pour la démocratie et le progrès (UPDP—Patriotic Union for Democracy and Progress)

Political party in the Republic of the Congo. Member of the **Forces démocratiques unies (FDU—United Democratic Forces)**. The president of the UPDP is Auguste-Célestin Gongarad-Nkoua.

Union des populations camerounaises (UPC—Union of the Cameroon Peoples)

Political party in Cameroon, established in 1948. The party split into two main factions in 1996—the UPC (N), led by Ndeh Ntumazah and the UPC (K), led by Augustin Frédéric Kodock.

Union pour le progrès (UP—Union for Progress)

Political party in the Republic of the Congo. Member of the **Forces démocratiques unies (FDU—United Democratic Forces)**. The UP's president is Jean-Martin Mbemba.

Union pour le progrès national (UPRONA—Union for National Progress)

Political party in Burundi, established in 1958. After the 1961 elections the numerous small parties that had been defeated merged with UPRONA, which became the sole legal political party in 1966. Party activities were suspended following the coup of September 1987 but resumed in 1989. UPRONA's original chairman was Charles Mukasi, but in October 1999 moderate members of the central committee who opposed Mukasi's rejection of the Arusha talks elected Dr Luc Rukingama as a rival chairman.

Union pour le redressement national (URN—Union for National Recovery)

Political party in the Republic of the Congo. Member of the **Forces démocratiques unies (FDU—United Democratic Forces)**. Founded in 1999. The URN's president is Gabriel Bokilo.

Union pour la République (UPR—Union for the Republic)

Political party in the Central African Republic. Established in 1997 by former members of the Mouvement populaire de la révolution (MPR—Popular Movement of the Revolution).

Union pour la renaissance—Mouvement sankariste (UNIR—MS, Union for Rebirth—Sankarist Movement)

Political party in Burkina Faso, founded in 2000. UNIR—MS's president is Benewende Stanislas Sankara.

Union sacrée de l'opposition radicale (USOR—Sacred Union of the Radical Opposition)

Political grouping in the Democratic Republic of the Congo, founded in 1991. Comprised around 130 movements and factions opposed to President Mobutu, in which the **Union pour la démocratie et le progrès social (UDPS—Union for Democracy and Social Progress)** was the dominant party. A radical faction, known as the **Union sacrée de l'opposition radicale et ses alliés (USORAL—Sacred Union of the Radical Opposition and its Allies)** emerged in 1994.

Union sacrée de l'opposition radicale et ses alliés (USORAL—Sacred Union of the Radical Opposition and its Allies)

A political party in the Democratic Republic of the Congo opposed to President **Mobutu**, which emerged in 1994 from within the **Union sacrée de l'opposition radicale (USOR)**.

Union sacrée renovée (USR—Sacred Union Renewed)

Political party in Democratic Republic of the Congo, established in 1993 by several former ministers in the government of national salvation.

Union socialiste des forces populaires (USFP—Socialist Union of Popular Forces)

Moroccan socialist party, founded in 1959 as the **Union socialiste des forces populaires (USFP—Socialist Union of Popular Forces)**, but emerged as the USFP after the UNFP split in 1972. One faction of the UNFP, led by Abderrahman Bouabid, was briefly banned in 1973 and 1974, but re-legalized as a result of a limited political liberalization initiated by the king in 1974. It changed its name to the USFP in the same year. A left-wing progressive party with a considerable (100,000) following, it remained in opposition to the government throughout the rest of the decade, accusing it of election rigging in 1977. It was severely suppressed after the riots in Casablanca in 1981, in which it was considered an instigator. Its newspapers were banned for a year and some leading cadres, including Bouabid, as well as leaders of the allied Democratic Labour Confederation (CDT) were arrested and jailed. Some of these were pardoned in 1983, and the USFP decided to participate, for the first time, in local and national elections. In November 1983, Bouabid was included in the government. After the 'bread riots' of January 1984, large numbers of USFP militants were arrested. Generally, the USFP gains its support in the urban areas among the organized working class and the trades unions, particularly those affiliated to the CDT, and among students and intellectuals. It is broadly a social democratic party with leanings towards democratic **socialism**. It has a youth wing, known as the United Youth, which tends to be more radical than the main party, and also contains a minority revolutionary socialist tendency, known by the name of its clandestine newspaper *Revolutionary Option (al-Ikhtier al-Haouri)*. It is, however, nationalist rather than internationalist in outlook, and supports the government on the issue of **Western Sahara**. Its First Secretary is Abd ar-Rahman el-Youssoufi.

Union of South Africa

The Union of South Africa was established following the **Boer War** (1899–1902) and then, in 1910, granted virtual **independence**. The **Afrikaners**, or **Boers**, vied for effective political control with the predominantly British white minority, who maintained a strong presence, particularly in the Cape and in Natal. Britain retained formal control of **Bechuanaland**, **Basutoland** and Swaziland, which were known as the high commission territories. South African ambitions to annex these territories were thwarted and they eventually proceeded to gain independence from both Britain and the Union of South Africa in the 1960s.

UNITAF

A US-led coalition force, which began operations in Somalia in December 1992. The objectives were primarily humanitarian. The main relief centres in the starvation area were secured by January 1993. Following the success of this exercise, UN

Security Council Resolution 814 was adopted, providing for the deployment of 28,000 UN troops and 2,800 civilians, to take over from UNITAF for six months from 1 May. This operation was called **United Nations Operation in Somalia (UNOSOM)** II. In June 1993 UN forces were attacked by militia belonging to the **United Somali Congress/Somali National Alliance** (USC/SNA), led by **Gen. Aideed**. Subsequently UN Security Council Resolution 837 was adopted, authorizing all necessary measures against those responsible, including their arrest and detention for trial. The UN Secretary-General's Special Representative, Adm. Howe, ordered the arrest of Gen. Aideed. Between June and October 1993, 70 UN troops were killed in total. UN Security Council Resolution 865 was passed on 22 September, supporting UNOSOM's efforts, but calling for greater emphasis on the political front. However, Somali deaths totalled several hundreds in clashes that occurred as UN troops hunted unsuccessfully for Aideed in Mogadishu. Following the deaths of 12 US troops in early October, US President Clinton announced that all US forces would be withdrawn by March 1994. Subsequently, UN Security Council Resolution 885 was adopted, suspending the arrest actions against Gen. Aideed.

United Arab Republic

The United Arab Republic resulted from the political union (in 1958) of Egypt and Syria. The capital was Cairo. **Gamal Abdel Nasser** was President. As an initial step toward creating a pan-Arab union, the republic abolished Syrian and Egyptian citizenship, termed its inhabitants Arabs, and called the country 'Arab territory'. It considered 'the Arab homeland' to be the entire area between the Persian Gulf and the Atlantic coast. With Yemen (North Yemen), it formed (1958) a loose federation called the **United Arab States**. In 1961, Syria withdrew from the union after a military coup, and Yemen soon followed, thus ending the union. Egypt continued to use the name until 1971.

United Arab States

A loose federation of Egypt, Syria and Yemen formed in 1958. At the time, Egypt and Syria had also constituted the **United Arab Republic**. It was dissolved in 1961.

United Democratic Front

The internal front of the **African National Congress** in South Africa while it was still outlawed in the 1980s.

United Nations

In all, 54 states in Africa are members of the United Nations and maintain permanent missions to the UN. Several African inter-governmental organizations also maintain permanent missions at the UN, including the **African Union** and the Asian-African

Legal Consultative Organization. In return, the United Nations is widely represented in Africa, through its various offices, institutions and organizations.

United Nations Angola Verification Mission(s) (UNAVEM)

The UN Security Council authorized the creation of a special mission to monitor the redeployment and withdrawal of Cuban troops from Angola. UNAVEM I began operations in January 1989. In 1993 the UN established UNAVEM II, to monitor compliance with peace measures agreed by the government of Angola and the **União Nacional para a Independência Total de Angola (UNITA—National Union for the Total Independence of Angola)**. A lack of co-operation by either of the two parties, however, severely limited the effectiveness of UNAVEM II. In early 1995 the UN Security Council established UNAVEM III, which was to comprise a military peace-keeping force of some 7,000 troops. Its deployment, however, was conditional on the cessation of hostilities and the disengagement of the government and UNITA forces. As a result of mediation by the UN's special representative in Angola, **Jonas Savimbi** (the leader of UNITA) and **José Eduardo dos Santos** (for the government) met in early May 1995 in Lusaka for direct talks and achieved a significant degree of agreement in the Lusaka Accord. Subsequent protracted negotiations led eventually to the inauguration of a government of national unity and reconciliation in April 1997. In June the UN Security Council voted unanimously to disband UNAVEM III and replace it with a smaller operation, the UN Observer Mission in Angola (MONUA), to oversee the implementation of the remaining provisions of the Lusaka Accord.

United Nations High Commissioner for Refugees (UNHCR)

The Office of the High Commissioner was established in 1951 to provide international protection for **refugees** and to seek durable solutions to their problems. The High Commissioner is elected by the UN General Assembly and is responsible to the UN Economic and Social Council (ECOSOC). The Executive Committee, established by ECOSOC, gives the High Commissioner policy directives in respect of material assistance programmes and advice in the field of international protection. It oversees the UNHCR's general polices and use of funds. UNHCR headquarters are in Geneva, Switzerland, but there are three regional offices for Africa, one each for West Africa (Dakar, Senegal), Central Africa (Kinshasa, Democratic Republic of the Congo) and Southern Africa (Pretoria, South Africa). The original mandate was with respect to refugees, defined as those forced to flee for refuge outside their own country. In recent years, there has been a significant shift in UNHCR's focus of activities. Increasingly it has been called upon to support people who have been displaced within their own countries—internally displaced persons (IDPs)—or threatened with displacement as a result of armed conflict. In addition, greater support has been given to refugees who have returned to their country of origin, to assist their reintegration and to enable local communities to support returnees through Quick Impact Projects. The UNHCR is thus concerned with refugees, internally displaced persons, asylum-seekers and recently returned refugees.

United Nations Missions in Angola

Peace talks between the two main warring factions in Angola—the **Movimento Popular de Libertação de Angola (MPLA—Popular Movement for the Liberation of Angola)** and the **União Nacional para a Independência Total de Angola (UNITA—National Union for the Total Independence of Angola)**—took place between April 1990 and May 1991, leading to a cease-fire and the signing of a Peace Agreement known as the Bicesse Accords in May 1991. The cease-fire was monitored by a UN mission, known as the **United Nations Angola Verification Mission (UNAVEM)**. There were three successive UNAVEMs in all. Then, in July 1997, **UN Security Council Resolution 1118** reconfigured UNAVEM to the UN Observer Mission in Angola (MONUA). As well as deploying military and police observers, MONUA also focused on human rights issues. On 26 February 1999 the UN adopted **UN Security Council Resolution 1229**, which terminated MONUA's mandate but allowed the human rights element to continue functioning. The chairman of the UN Angola Sanctions Committee visited Angola and the region in May 1999 and produced a list of recommendations on ways to tighten up the implementation of sanctions against UNITA. These were examined by two expert panels. The Security Council adopted **UN Security Council Resolution 1295** which focused on the panels' key recommendations, and proposed a monitoring mechanism to follow on from the work of the panels. In August 2002 a mandate was agreed in the UN Security Council for the establishment of a new United Nations Mission in Angola (UNMA), headed by Dr Gambari as special representative of the Secretary-General. In this capacity he reconstituted the Joint Commission charged with completing the remaining tasks under the **Lusaka Protocol**. On 21 November 2002, a ceremony in the Angolan National Assembly declared the Lusaka Process, and with it the role of the Joint Commission, to have ended.

United Nations Mission in the Democratic Republic of the Congo

In August 1999 the UN Security Council authorized the deployment of up to 90 military liaison personnel to support the implementation of a cease-fire agreement which had been signed in July in Lusaka, Zambia, by the Heads of State of the Democratic Republic of the Congo (DRC), Angola, Namibia, Rwanda, Uganda and Zimbabwe. The Council approved the establishment of MONUC (the UN Mission to the Congo) in late November 1999. With an initial mandate until 1 March 2000, the mission was to oversee the implementation of the agreement, including monitoring the cease-fire and the disengagement of forces. It was also mandated to facilitate the delivery of humanitarian assistance and to develop a mine action plan and undertake emergency demining activities. In February 2000 the Security Council approved the expansion of the mission to comprise up to 5,537 military personnel, including up to 500 observers. In April a plan was agreed in Kampala, Uganda, by the parties to the conflict, and in December a revised plan adopted in Harare, Zimbabwe. However, by early 2001 the Lusaka accord and Kampala and Harare plans remained to be implemented and only a small contingent of MONUC observers had been deployed in the DRC. In February 2001 the Security Council adopted a resolution increasing the capacity and scope of MONUC. Small contingents of MONUC were deployed from March onwards, in the rebel-occupied area of Kisangani, among other areas. By February 2002, 55 teams of military observers were stationed in the DRC. Some progress towards the implementation of the Lusaka accord was made at the Inter-Congolese Dialogue held in Sun City, South Africa, between February and April 2002, when a bilateral power-sharing agreement was concluded between the DRC government and the Mouvement pour la libération du Congo (MLC—Movement for the Liberation of the Congo) which was supported by the Ugandan government. Attempts by the Rwandan-backed Rassemblement congolais pour la démocratie—Goma (RCD—Goma, Congolese Rally for Democracy—Goma) controlling Kisangani to discredit the MONOC as 'pro-government' were effectively halted by a Security Council resolution in June demanding that the RCD—Goma rebels cease their obstruction of the mission's activities in Kisangani immediately. MONUC's mandate was successively extended into 2003.

United Nations Mission in Ethiopia and Eritrea (UNMEE)

At the end of July 2000 the UN Security Council authorized the establishment of the UN Mission in Ethiopia and Eritrea (UNMEE) to facilitate compliance with and verify a cease-fire agreement signed by the governments of Ethiopia and Eritrea in mid-June with a view to settling a two-year border conflict. In mid-September the Security Council authorized the deployment of 4,200 military personnel to the operation, which was given an initial six-month mandate. This mandate was extended subsequently on several occasions. A security zone was declared in April 2001 and UNMEE continued to monitor the withdrawal of the forces of both countries from this zone. The UN Security Council adopted a resolution in September 2001 extending the UNMEE's mandate for six months. In March 2002 the UN Security Council approved a further six-month extension of UNMEE's mandate. In mid-April the Eritrea-Ethiopia Boundary Commission published its decision on the delimitation of the common border. UNMEE was to remain to supervise the physical demarcation of the border. Difficulties associated with gaining full access to the border regions ensured the continuation of UNMEE's work throughout 2002.

United Nations Mission in Sierra Leone (UNAMSIL)

In July 1998 the UN Security Council established a **UN Observer Mission in Sierra Leone (UNOMSIL)** to monitor the military and security situation in the country following the restoration of a democratically-elected government. UNOMSIL was authorized to oversee the disarmament and demobilization of former combatants (including civilian militias) and assist in monitoring respect for international humanitarian law. The Special Representative, with the civilian component of the mission, was authorized to advise the Sierra Leonean authorities on police practice, training and reform, and to help address the country's human rights needs. In January 1999, following a sudden escalation of hostilities, UNOMSIL's mandate was extended for a further two months. In March the Security Council condemned the ongoing violation of human rights in Sierra Leone and extended the mandate of UNOMSIL first until June and then until December 1999. A peace agreement was signed in July in Lomé, Togo, between the parties to the conflict, and in October the Security Council established UNAMSIL, comprising up to 6,000 military personnel, to help consolidate peace in the country. This mission was to assume responsibility for all aspects of UNOMSIL, the mandate of which was terminated at that point.

During early 2000, in contravention of the Lomé accord, Sierra Leone rebels repeatedly obstructed the implementation of the disarmament and demobilization programme. In May, following an attack on a contingent of UNAMSIL troops in the previous month, rebels killed several mission personnel and captured and detained around 500 others. In response to the resumption of hostilities, the United Kingdom deployed a force in Sierra Leone with a mandate to evacuate British nationals. This had the effect of restricting rebel activities until a further increase in UNAMSIL's military personnel was approved—providing for a total of 13,000 troops—and deployed. In July the Security Council adopted a resolution banning the direct and indirect importation of rough **diamonds** from rebel-controlled areas, following mounting concern at the role played by illicit diamond exploitation in support of the rebel movement. A new cease-fire agreement was reached in early November, but fighting continued, and in March 2001 the Security Council expanded the mission's authorized personnel to 17,500 troops and approved a revised concept of operations that envisaged the deployment of UNAMSIL personnel into rebel-held territory. Progress was slow and the mission's mandate was extended in March 2002 for a further six months. In support of legislative and presidential elections held in Sierra Leone in May 2002, UNAMSIL temporarily redeployed some 11,000 troops to high-risk areas of the country and provided practical assistance to the electoral process. UNAMSIL continued to support the government of Sierra Leone in restoring the nation-wide authority of the state, consolidating peace, security and national reconciliation, promoting the rehabilitation of the judicial system and respect for human rights, and by addressing outstanding issues such as the reintegration of former combatants. UNAMSIL external personnel amounted to 17,275 troops and 258 military observers as of mid-2002.

United Nations Operation in Somalia (UNOSOM)

UN involvement in Somalia began in January 1992, starting with a small Cease-fire Observer Force and building to a peace-keeping operation, UNOSOM I. The impetus was humanitarian with the primary aim of ensuring the safety of relief operations to help the **famine**-stricken population in the south of the country. However, factional opposition to UNOSOM I led to the adoption of UN Security Council Resolution 794, which provided for the use of all necessary measures to establish a secure environment for relief operations. A US-led coalition force (**UNITAF**) began operations in December 1992. The main relief centres in the starvation area had been secured by January 1993. Following the success of this exercise, UN Security Council Resolution 814 was adopted, providing for the deployment of 28,000 UN troops and 2,800 civilians, to take over from UNITAF for six months from 1 May. This operation was called UNOSOM II. In June 1993 UN forces were attacked by militia belonging to the **United Somali Congress/Somali National Alliance** (USC/SNA), led by **Gen. Aideed**. Subsequently UN Security Council Resolution 837 was adopted, authorizing all necessary measures against those responsible, including their arrest and detention for trial. The UN Secretary-General's Special Representative, Adm. Howe, ordered the arrest of Gen. Aideed. Between June and October 1993, 70 UN troops were killed in total. UN Security Council Resolution 865 was passed on 22 September supporting UNOSOM's efforts, but calling for greater emphasis on the political front. However, Somali deaths totalled several hundreds in clashes, as UN troops hunted unsuccessfully for Aideed in Mogadishu. Following the deaths of 12 US troops in early October, US President Clinton announced that all US forces would be withdrawn by March 1994. Subsequently, UN Security Council Resolution 885 was adopted, suspending the arrest actions against Gen. Aideed. UN Security Council Resolution 886 extended UNOSOM's mandate until 31 May 1994, but made it clear that it was the prime responsibility of the **Somalis** themselves to find a solution to the Somali crisis. UN Security Council Resolution 897 called for a reduced force of up to 22,000 troops mainly to protect airports and ports, keep open supply routes for humanitarian aid and assist with the repatriation of **refugees**. The Resolution also made it clear that the Somalis would bear the ultimate responsibility for setting up viable national political institutions and for reconstructing their country.

In view of the very limited progress achieved in political reconciliation, the UN had to consider whether it was necessary to prepare options for UNOSOM's mandate and future operations. The Security Council therefore dispatched a mission to Somalia to explain that the future of UNOSOM was in doubt. The Secretary-General subsequently issued a report recommending the withdrawal of UNOSOM forces. The last troops left Mogadishu on 3 March 1995. Since the withdrawal of UNOSOM, the UN has maintained a political office in Nairobi, Kenya, from where it monitors internal political developments.

United Party (UP)

The predominantly English United Party (UP) was the main political opposition to the **National Party (NP)** in South African politics through the post-war period up to the rise of the **African National Congress** and the Pan-Africanist Congress in the 1950s and 1960s. Although itself an almost entirely white party of a relatively conservative outlook, it was regarded during this period as 'the enemy' in the Afrikaner 'nationalist' vision of the NP government, as was the English-language press. Only the small **Progressive Party** provided a more 'progressive' outlook.

United Somali Congress (USC)

A US-led coalition force (**UNITAF**) began humanitarian relief operations in Somalia in December 1992. The main relief centres in the starvation area had been secured by January 1993. Following the success of this exercise, UN Security Council Resolution 814 was adopted, providing for the deployment of 28,000 UN troops and 2,800 civilians, to take over from UNITAF for six months from 1 May. This operation was called **UNOSOM** II. In June 1993 UN forces were attacked by militia belonging to the United Somali Congress (USC)/**Somali National Alliance** (USC/SNA), led by **Gen. Aideed**. Subsequently UN Security Council Resolution 837 was adopted, authorizing all necessary measures against those responsible, including their arrest and detention for trial. The Secretary-General's Special Representative, Adm. Howe, ordered the arrest of Gen. Aideed. Between June and October 1993, 70 UN troops were killed in total. UN Security Council Resolution 865 was passed on 22 September supporting UNOSOM's efforts, but calling for greater emphasis on the political front. However, Somali deaths totalled several hundreds in clashes, as UN troops hunted unsuccessfully for Aideed in Mogadishu. Following the deaths of 12 US troops in early October, US President Clinton announced that all US forces would be withdrawn by March 1994. Subsequently, UN Security Council Resolution 885 was adopted, suspending the arrest actions against Gen. Aideed.

UN Observer Mission in Sierra Leone (UNOMSIL)

In July 1998, the UN Security Council established an Observer Mission in Sierra Leone (UNOMSIL) to monitor the military and security situation in the country following the restoration of a democratically-elected government. UNOMSIL was authorized to oversee disarmament and demobilization of former combatants (including civilian militias) and assist in monitoring respect for international humanitarian law. The Special Representative, with the civilian component of the mission, was authorized to advise the Sierra Leonean authorities on police practice, training and reform, and to help address the country's human rights needs. In January 1999, following a sudden escalation of hostilities, UNOMSIL's mandate was extended for a further two months. In March the Security Council condemned the ongoing violation of human rights in Sierra Leone and extended the mandate of UNOMSIL first until June, and then until December 1999. A peace agreement was signed in July in Lomé, Togo, between the parties to the conflict, and in October, the Security Council established the **UN Mission in Sierra Leone (UNAMSIL)**, comprising up to 6,000 military personnel, to help consolidate peace in the country.

This mission was to assume responsibility for all aspects of UNOMSIL, the mandate of which was terminated at that point.

UN Security Council Resolution 242

Resolution 242, adopted in November 1967, six months after the Arab–Israeli 'Six Day' War, acknowledged the existence and security of the State of Israel but also made the withdrawal of Israeli armed forces from the Occupied Territories the condition of a lasting peace. Various UN resolutions between 1967 and October 1973 reaffirmed this key resolution.

UN Security Council Resolution 338

Resolution 338 of 22 October 1973, after the Arab-Israeli 'Yom Kippur' War, called on the parties to the conflict to begin immediately, after a cease-fire, to apply **UN Security Council Resolution 242** in all its provisions.

UN Security Council Resolution 864

Resolution 864 (1993) imposed an arms and **oil** embargo in relation to Angola, with limited exceptions. UN Security Council Resolution 1127 also required member states to deny permission to any aircraft to take off from, land in, or over-fly their territories if it had taken off from or was destined to land at a place in the territory of Angola with limited exceptions, and banned the sale or supply of aircraft and aircraft components, the provision of engineering and maintenance servicing, the certification of airworthiness, the payment of new claims against existing insurance contracts, or the provision or renewal of direct insurance with respect to any aircraft registered in Angola or with respect to any aircraft which had entered the territory of Angola with limited exceptions.

UN Security Council Resolution 976

Resolution 976 of 8 February 1995 authorized the deployment of a 7,000-strong peace-keeping force particularly to oversee the demobilization of troops on both sides in the Angolan **civil war**. The United Kingdom provided a 600-strong logistics battalion for a three-month period. The UN declared that all military tasks were officially completed on 13 December 1996. This cleared the way for deputies of the **União Nacional para a Independência Total de Angola (UNITA—National Union for the Total Independence of Angola)** to the National Assembly (elected in 1992) to take their seats in Luanda. A government of national unity and reconciliation, including four UNITA ministers and seven vice-ministers, was inaugurated on 11 April 1997.

UN Security Council Resolution 1118

On 1 July 1997 UN Security Council Resolution 1118 reconfigured the **United Nations Angola Verification Mission (UNAVEM)** to the UN Observer Mission in Angola (MONUA). As well as deploying military and police observers, MONUA also focused on human rights issues. Although both sides were publicly committed to the peace process, progress in implementing the provisions of the **Lusaka Protocol** was slow.

UN Security Council Resolution 1127

UN Security Council Resolution 1127 (1997) imposed travel restrictions on named senior officials of the **União Nacional para a Independência Total de Angola (UNITA—National Union for the Total Independence of Angola)** in Angola and adult members of their immediate families with limited exceptions, including measures in respect of travel documents, visas or residence permits; and required the closure of all UNITA offices.

UN Security Council Resolution 1173

UN Security Council Resolution 1173 (1998) imposed a ban on contacts with the leadership of the **União Nacional para a Independência Total de Angola (UNITA—National Union for the Total Independence of Angola)** in Angola with limited exceptions. It also imposed a freeze on funds of UNITA, named senior officials of UNITA and adult members of their families, restrictions on the direct or indirect import from Angola of all **diamonds**, and banned the sale or supply of specified mining equipment, mining services, specified motorized vehicles or water-craft and spare parts, and ground or water-borne transportation services with limited exceptions.

UN Security Council Resolution 1229

On 26 February 1999 the UN Security Council adopted Resolution 1229, which terminated MONUA's mandate in Angola, but allowed the human rights element to continue functioning. The chairman of the UN Angola Sanctions Committee visited Angola and the region in May 1999 and produced a list of recommendations on ways to tighten up the implementation of sanctions against the **União Nacional para a Independência Total de Angola (UNITA—National Union for the Total Independence of Angola)**. These were examined by two expert panels. The Security Council adopted **Resolution 1295** which focused on the panels' key recommendations. It also proposed a monitoring mechanism to follow on from the work of the Expert Panels.

UN Security Council Resolution 1295

In May–June 1999 the UN Security Council adopted Resolution 1295 which focused on the key recommendations of the Expert Panels it had set up under **UN Security Council Resolution 1229.** It also proposed a monitoring mechanism to follow on from the work of the Expert Panels.

United Socialist Party (USP)

Political party in Botswana, founded in 1994. The USP's leader is N. Modubule.

Upper Volta

Formerly part of the colonial territory of **Afrique occidentale française (French West Africa)**. Now Burkina Faso.

Urabi movement (Egypt)

First nationalist movement in Egypt, in the 19th century.

Urbanization

The process of urban growth or the growing influence of the towns on the countryside. The most urbanized countries in Africa, ironically, are two desert states, one of which is Libya, where 88% of the population lives in towns, 33% in the capital, Tripoli; and the other is Mauritania, where more than one-third of the population live in the capital, Nouakchott. Other countries with large urban populations include Egypt, South Africa and Nigeria.

Uruguay Round

Final 'round' of discussion, within the framework of the **General Agreement on Tariffs and Trade (GATT)**, of international trade issues and questions of protection and liberalization. The GATT has been effectively replaced since the mid-1990s by the **World Trade Organization**, which regulates and supervises international trade arrangements and agreements and is charged with reducing barriers to international trade and promoting economic liberalization on a regional and global scale.

Uteem, Cassam

Former President of Mauritius. Uteem resigned in mid-February 2002 in protest at anti-**terrorism** legislation approved by the National Assembly. He was succeeded by Vice-President **Angidi Varriah Chettiar**, who then also resigned over the controversial legislation. **Karl Offman** was elected President towards the end of February 2002.

V

Vanguards of Conquest

Militant Egyptian Islamist grouping. Breakaway group from **Islamic Jihad**. Its leader is Yasir as-Sirri.

Veiga, Carlos

Together with **Pedro de Verona Rodrigues Pires**, Veiga has been one of Cape Verde's dominant political personalities since **independence** in 1975. Both men are former Prime Ministers.

Verwoerd, Hendrick

Prime Minister of South Africa during the early 1960s. Trained in Germany during the 1930s, Vervoerd had been a professor of applied psychology and brought a certain intellectualism to the crude racism that had brought the Afrikaner **National Party** to power in 1948. He was largely responsible for the elaboration of the **apartheid** system of 'separate development'. Verwoerd was assassinated in 1966.

Viljoen, Abraham

Former theology professor turned farmer. One of the first **Afrikaners** to meet with the exiled **African National Congress**. Brother of **Constand Viljoen**, one-time chief of the South African Defence Force and leader of a broad alliance of right-wing groups called the Afrikaner Volksfront (Afrikaner People's Front).

Viljoen, Constand

One-time chief of the South African Defence Force and leader of a broad alliance of right-wing groups called the Afrikaner Volksfront (Afrikaner People's Front). The possibility of a right-wing coup by thc Afrikaner Volksfront together with the South African Defence Force evaporated when an attempt by Viljoen to lead a group of 5,000 Volksfront combatants into the nominally independent tribal 'homeland' of Bophuthatswana to support its dictator, Lucas Mangope, ended ignominiously. The simultaneous intervention of a bunch of extremists from **Eugene Terre'Blanche**'s

Afrikaanse Weerstandsbeweging (AWB—Afrikaner Resistance Movement) wrecked Viljoen's plans: the Bophuthatswana army, which was supposed to supply Viljoen's men with weapons, mutinied and the invaders withdrew. Viljoen, appalled at the fiasco, left the Volksfront and registered a party of his own, the **Freedom Front**, to contest elections and campaign by constitutional means. He duly won seven seats in the first election and took his place in a parliamentary front bench as a political leader. **Nelson Mandela** even appointed one of the Freedom Front hard-liners to the position of ambassador to the Czech Republic.

VIVA—Rassemblement national pour la démocratie et le progrès (VIVA—RNDP, VIVA—National Rally for Democracy and Progress)

Political party in Chad, established in 1992. Supports a unitary, democratic republic. The president of VIVA—RNDP is Kassire Delwa Koumakoye.

Vorster, Balthazar Johannes

Minister of Justice and Police in the South African government under President **Hendrick Vervoerd**, he succeeded Vervoerd after his assassination to become Prime Minister. Presided over a hardening of repression and authoritarian rule, while white South Africa enjoyed a period of economic buoyancy as the price of **gold** rose in international markets.

W

Wade, Abdoulaye

President of Senegal. Born in 1927, Wade is a lawyer and veteran politician. He has been exiled and imprisoned several times. He founded the Parti démocratique sénégalais (PDS—Senegalese Democratic Party) and has contested five presidential elections. He found himself in a political impasse when he was voted into office in March 2000. The presidential polls were not held at the same time as legislative elections, and his coalition government was in a minority in parliament. However, elections in April 2001 consolidated Wade's power base by giving his supporters control of the Assemblée nationale. The PDS won 89 of the 120 parliamentary seats.

WAFA—Wafa wa al-Adl

Algerian political grouping. WAFA's leader, Ahmed Taleb Ibrahimi, was a former Algerian foreign minister and, in 1999, presidential candidate. Founded in 1999, WAFA was refused government recognition as a political party in 2000 on the grounds that it contained a large number of supporters of the **Front islamique du salut**.

Wafd Party (Egypt)

In **Arabic** *wafd* means 'delegation'. The Wafd was formed in 1919 under the leadership of Saad Zaghlul, a lawyer. Two days after the end of the Second World War Zaghlul demanded that a delegation be permitted to travel to London, United Kingdom, to present the case for Egyptian **independence**. Refusal by the British High Commissioner was followed by three years of organized protests. In November 1922 Britain declared nominal independence for Egypt, while retaining various major powers for itself. This arrangement was underwritten by the Egyptian Constitution of 1923. The Wafd won the first general election and Zaghlul became Prime Minister. After his death in 1927 the Wafd was led by Mustafa Nahas Pasha. In 1931 Prime Minister Nahas Pasha was dismissed by King **Fuad** (reigned 1922–36), who also suspended the Constitution. Just before his death in 1936 the king reinstated the Constitution and the Wafd was returned to power with a large majority in elections held in April of that year. In August the Anglo-Egyptian Treaty, which retained key British responsibilities regarding foreign affairs, was signed. The Regency Council, headed by Nahas Pasha, ruled, however, on behalf of the 16-year-old King **Farouk**. When Farouk achieved his majority in 1938, he dismissed Nahas Pasha, resisting British pressure to retain him. Farouk's pro-Italian stance led the British ambassador, in 1942 (as German troops advanced on Egypt from Libya), to compel the king, on pain of deposition, to reappoint Nahas Pasha. The latter remained in office until October 1944 and ensured Egypt's affiliation to the **Arab League**. After the débâcle of the 1948–49 Palestine War and the establishment of Israel, Farouk agreed to a reconciliation with the Wafd leadership. A general election held in January 1950 placed the Wafd firmly in power. The government now pressed Britain to withdraw its troops from Egypt. When Britain refused, in October 1951, the Egyptian government unilaterally abrogated the 1936 Anglo-Egyptian Treaty (which was valid until 1956) and demanded Britain's immediate and unconditional withdrawal from the **Suez Canal** zone. Guerrilla action against British forces by militant Wafdists ensued. Following riots in Cairo in 1951 the king dismissed the Wafd Government. A military coup by the **Free Officers** in July 1952 led to the banning of the Wafd along with other political parties. It was not until June 1977, a quarter of a century later, following the promulgation of the Law of the System of Political Parties, that Fuad Serag ad-Din, a veteran of the pre-1952 Wafd Party, obtained a licence to establish the **New Wafd Party**.

The Wall (Morocco and Western Sahara)

After the initial success of the armed forces of the **POLISARIO Front** in their guerrilla war against Morocco, which had invaded the **Western Sahara** in 1976, the Moroccan army constructed a wall in the desert during the 1980s in order to protect the occupied territory of the Western Sahara from POLISARIO incursions. The wall was built in six stages from August 1980 until April 1987. It eventually enclosed the whole of the Moroccan-occupied territory, extending for 2,400 km (a greater length than that of the Great Wall of China), with 20,000 km of barbed wire, deep trenches, sand banks and walls of stones 2 m high and 1.8 m wide. It is 'defended' by 160,000 Moroccan soldiers, 240 heavy artillery batteries, more than 1,000 armoured vehicles, 10m. anti-personnel mines (banned by international conventions) and fully equipped with electronic surveillance devices and systems provided by the USA and by Westinghouse, an American electronics corporation involved in the production of military equipment.

Washington Consensus

A term used to refer to the broad agreement on a strongly interventionist approach to macroeconomic reform and liberalization as the appropriate development strategy for Africa, Asia and Latin America, on the part of the major multilateral and bilateral lending agencies—led by the **International Monetary Fund** and the

World Bank (hence the 'Washington' consensus)—developed during the 1980s and continuing well into the 1990s. Challenged increasingly from the latter part of the 1980s onwards, by a range of other agencies and institutions, including the UN Development Programme, it remained the dominant or hegemonic framework for development assistance until the late 1990s, when a broader approach, giving greater priority to creating the conditions for human development within national strategies for development, began to gain ground. Despite talk of a 'post-Washington Consensus' in the early years of the 21st century, many consider that the global development framework of **Poverty Reduction Strategy Papers** and other mechanisms, as adopted by the major government and multilateral agencies from 2000 onwards, still reflects a Washington consensus underpinned by a commitment to enforced **globalization** for the former '**Third World**'.

Water

A major source of global economic and, increasingly, political concern. Water availability is a major issue in many parts of Africa. While the countries of Central and West Africa are largely relatively water-rich, with some countries such as the Democratic Republic of the Congo and the Republic of the Congo having a superabundance of supplies as a result of high rainfall and extensive riverine resources (including the Congo River itself), large areas of **North Africa** and the Horn, East Africa and **Southern Africa** are vulnerable or water-stressed. Libya, Tunisia, Algeria, Western Sahara and Mauritania all have an average annual rainfall of well below 500 mm. Most of the countries of the Sahel and Horn of Africa (e.g. Senegal, Burkina Faso, Mali, Niger, Chad, Sudan, Somalia) experience constant uncertainty with respect to intra-annual and inter-annual rainfall and have in recent decades experienced periodic **drought**, ranging from severe to very severe. Periodic drought has also been experienced in Southern Africa in recent decades. Paradoxically, one of the driest areas with low and sporadic rainfall, the Sahara, may have the largest underground water supplies in the form of aquifers of fossil water reserves. Already, these are being exploited in Libya by the Great Artificial River (GAR) project, paid for out of **oil** revenues (at a cost of some US $32,000m.), which taps into the north-eastern edge of the Northern Sahara Basin which runs under Tunisia and Algeria, the northern sector of the Marzuk Basin, which lies largely within Libya's boundaries, and the northern sectors of the Nubian Basin, which runs down the eastern part of Libya. Other major underground basins in the Sahara include the Illumeden Basin, which runs from southern Algeria across into north-western Niger and north eastern Mali, and the Taodeni Basin, which stretches from south-western Algeria, across northern Mali into eastern Mauritania. The development of major dams on the Senegal River, under the auspices of the **Organisation pour la mise en valeur du fleuve Sénégal (OMVS—Organization for the Exploitation of the Senegal River)**, which co-ordinates the development of the Senegal River basin by Senegal, Mauritania and Mali, should afford the member states an adequate water supply. But political difficulties between Mauritania and Senegal have tended to reduce co-operation and the effective development of water use. At present the two countries use only a small proportion (Senegal 20% and Mauritania less than 5%) of the volume that the OMVS proposes to allocate them under the scheme. A plan exists, to be funded by the **African Development Fund**, Kuwait and Saudi Arabia, to bring water from the Senegal River north west to Nouakchott by 170 km of canal, to feed a storage facility for pretreated water of 150,000 cu m and a half-underground water reservoir of 5,000 cu m, which would triple the city's water supply by 2020 and feed a purification plant. Egypt and Sudan have for many decades negotiated with difficulty over the waters of the Nile and other countries also have vested interests, including Ethiopia and Uganda. Difficulties are likely to arise in future as demand increases and supply diminishes.

Weapons of Mass Destruction (Libya)

Britain had raised the issue of weapons of mass destruction in August 2002, when the foreign office minister, Mike O'Brien met **Col Qaddafi** in Sirte, the first ministerial contact for 20 years. In December 2003, in a surprise move, the government of Libya announced that it would halt its major weapons development programmes (including programmes to develop nuclear as well as chemical and biological weapons). The Libyans admitted to the International Atomic Energy Agency (IAEA) that they had been secretly importing raw uranium and other sophisticated equipment for the development of a nuclear weapons capability for more than a decade. Libya agreed to let UN nuclear experts conduct 'snap' inspections of its sites, and plans were agreed to enable inspectors to travel to Libya, before the end of the year, to begin dismantling its nuclear facilities in the first stage of a long-term regime of supervising the process.

Western Sahara – *see also* Sahrawi Arab Democratic Republic

The Western Sahara lies to the south of Morocco and to the north of Mauritania, and borders the Atlantic Ocean. It was formerly (until 1976) a Spanish colony, known as the **Spanish Sahara**. The Western Sahara covers an area of some 266,000 sq km. The main towns are in the northwest of the territory; the largest of these is El Ayoune. At July 2002 the total population was estimated as 256,177, of which the vast majority are Arabs and Muslims, speaking either Moroccan **Arabic** or Hassaniya Arabic.

The legal status of the territory and the issue of its sovereignty remain unresolved. The Western Sahara is currently a disputed territory, subject to a UN 'peace process' that has itself been extremely prolonged (it has been under way since 1991), following a long war (1976–91) between Morocco and the **POLISARIO Front** (the Popular Front for the Liberation of the Saguia el Hamra and Río de Oro)—the political movement representing the **Sahrawis**, or people of the Western Sahara. Morocco invaded the territory in 1976 as the Spanish left and effectively occupied the north-western areas, pushing the Sahrawis eastwards into Algeria, where many have remained, in refugee camps, since that time. The POLISARIO Front fought back, initiating a bitter guerrilla war, and 'liberated' the eastern and southern areas nearest, respectively, to Algeria and Mauritania. In February 1976 the Front formally proclaimed a government-in-exile of the Sahrawi Arab Democratic Republic (SADR) and elected **Muhammad Abdel Aziz** as President. The SADR was recognized by 54 nations and was eventually (in 1984) admitted to the **Organization of African Unity**. Mauritania initially joined Morocco in fighting the POLISARIO Front in the south, but between 1978 and 1979 broke off its military involvement and renounced any claim to the territory. Morocco gradually extended the area under its control, building a '**wall**' in the desert to exclude the POLISARIO fighters. Guerrilla activities continued, however, until a UN-monitored cease-fire was implemented on 6 September 1991. The UN established a peace-keeping force (**MINURSO**), which was deployed in the Moroccan-occupied part of the territory to supervise a UN-sponsored referendum. More than a decade passed as the parties to the conflict failed to agree on precisely who would be eligible to vote in this referendum. The matter remained unresolved at the end of 2003, despite the fact that the right to self-determination of the Sahrawi people was recognized by the International Court of Justice as long ago as 1975.

Western Sahara, economy

The area of the Western Sahara under Moroccan occupation depends on rain-fed farming and livestock production, maritime and coastal fishing, phosphate mining and trade as the principal sources of income for the population. The territory generally lacks sufficient rainfall for sustainable agricultural production, and much of the food for the rapidly expanding (largely Moroccan immigrant) urban population must be imported. All trade and other economic activities are controlled by the Moroccan government. There has been increasing interest from both Moroccan and foreign companies in the exploitation of **oil**, gas and mineral resources. Despite the efforts of the UN to resolve the continuing conflict, Moroccan administration, combined with a programme to encourage settlement by Moroccans in the territory, is establishing an effective Moroccan presence which many **Sahrawis** are concerned will create a *fait accompli* and undermine any possibility of self-determination and **independence** for the Sahrawi people in their own state. The 'liberated' areas in the east and south of the territory, outside the Moroccan-occupied areas, are generally inhospitable, although free movement allows the Sahrawis based in the refugee camps to undertake limited trade in livestock and other (often imported) goods with Mauritania. The Sahrawis in the refugee camps have depended heavily for nearly three decades on basic goods provided by the **UNHCR** and other agencies, including 'northern' NGOs, but have also made substantial efforts to achieve as much self-sufficiency and social independence as possible in their desert enclave. Their efforts to construct a dignified and self-reliant economy and society, within the severe constraints they face, have been much admired by sympathizers world-wide.

Wolof

A major ethno-linguistic group in West Africa. Found in Mauritania and Senegal.

Women

The position of women in the region as a whole is still very disadvantaged, as compared with that of men (and girls as compared with boys, particularly as regards access to **education** and qualifications). Gender inequality in the region is high, although not as severe as in the Middle East and South Asia. There are signs of significant improvements in some areas, mainly social, cultural and, in some countries, also political. The region's maternal mortality rate is high, however, and basic welfare for women is poor.

Women's rights (Morocco)

Women's rights in Morocco were boosted after King **Mohammed VI** announced a reform of the country's strict laws (*mudawana*) that govern women's and family rights. Changes in the law would make polygamy more difficult; they would also raise the legal age for marriage from 15 to 18, simplify divorce procedures for women and give divorced women greater protection. Women activists had feared that the reforms, first promised when King Mohammed came to the throne in 1999, would never take place, after large-scale public protests from Islamist conservatives. In 2000 some 300,000 demonstrators took to the streets of Casablanca to object to any change in the *mudawana*. The 'modernizers' could only muster some 100,000 for a march on the same day in Rabat. In 2003, however, an agreement among the political parties paved the way for the election of 35 women to the Moroccan parliament.

Women's rights (Rwanda)

Rwanda tops the international league table for the number of women in parliament, ahead of Sweden and Norway. Under the post-**genocide** Constitution, one-third of seats were set aside for women, while the remainder were open to both sexes. Women hold six out of 20 seats in the senate and 39 out of 80 in the chamber of deputies. The women in parliament review all laws before they are passed to ensure they are 'female-friendly'. One notable success was a law which strengthened women's rights to inherit land—since 1999 a woman has had equal rights to her own family's land after she is married. Rwanda's female parliamentary deputies are not the only women in public life. The president of the supreme court is a woman, and there are several female ministers. In Rwanda's pre-colonial monarchy, queen mothers could exercise a powerful role, but always from behind the scenes. More recently, Rwanda had a woman Prime Minister before the genocide, Agathe

Uwilingiyamana, though she was a caretaker leader who headed a transitional government for less than a year before she was assassinated in April 1994. But for all the progress, Rwanda remains a male-dominated society, despite the fact that the population has still not returned to parity nearly 11 years after the genocide. It also remains the case that few laws originate from within parliament, which mostly acts as a rubber stamp rather than a genuine counterweight to the powerful presidency.

Workers' and Soldiers' Defence Committees

Organizations established by **Jerry Rawlings** in Ghana to support his regime after the coup of 31 December 1981. Although supposed to be complementary to and supportive of other similar 'committees' formed in the rural areas (see **Peasants' and Workers' Defence Committees**), the Workers' and Soldiers' Defence Committees were reported by Zaya Yeebo, once a minister in the Rawlings government, to have seized food products and even seed grain from peasants, believing them to be overcharging, and sold these at low prices in the cities.

World Bank

The International Bank for Reconstruction and Development (IBRD), better known as the World Bank, has played a significant role in the economies of Africa. As a major lending agency, it has been able to apply increasing pressure, from the late 1970s onwards, for economic reform and liberalization against a backdrop of growing **debt**. Conditionality (which allows loans to be made only under specified preconditions) has increased the ability of the Bank to persuade and even oblige governments to adopt painful reform measures, usually involving cuts in public expenditure, reductions in subsidies and increased prices for basic goods, which have often resulted in outbursts of popular protest. Together with the **International Monetary Fund**, the Bank has been one of the most powerful and influential of the **international financial institutions** operating in the region.

World Food Programme (WFP)

The principal food agency of the United Nations. It aims to alleviate acute hunger by providing food relief. Priority is given to vulnerable groups, such as children and pregnant women. WFP programmes are in operation in many countries in Africa, particularly in those countries where **drought** and **famine** occur relatively frequently.

World Islamic Front for the Jihad against the Jews and the Crusaders

The result of a merger between the Egyptian **Islamic Jihad** group and **Osama bin Laden**'s al-Qa'ida, the World Islamic Front for the Jihad against the Jews and

Crusaders was formed in early 1998. The focus of the new group was to internationalize *jihad*. The proliferation of armed Islamist groups across the Middle East and outside the region during the 1980s and 1990s, made possible by the expansion of an international network of financial institutions and banking, facilitated the birth of a new phenomenon, the Islamist international.

World Trade Organization (WTO)

International trade organization regulating trading conditions on a global basis and promoting 'free trade', established by accord in December 1993 to replace the framework of the **General Agreement on Trade and Tariffs (GATT)**. In the accord it is stated that the parties to the agreement recognize that 'their relations in the field of trade and economic endeavour should be conducted with a view to raising standards of living, ensuring full employment and a large and steady growing volume of real income and effective demand and expanding the production and trade in goods and services, while allowing for the optimal use of the world's resources in accordance with the objective of sustainable development, seeking both to protect and to preserve the environment and enhance the means for doing so in a manner consistent with their respective needs and concerns at different levels of economic development'. In Africa many countries, including Egypt, Tunisia and Morocco, were already members by the end of the 1990s. Despite the rhetoric of **globalization** and 'free markets', it is not at all clear that the World Trade Organization has the power and influence to oblige the major developed economies to reduce the formal and informal protection they provide for key sectors of their economies, although it undoubtedly has contributed significantly in recent years, since its establishment, following on from the GATT, to the 'opening up' of many economies in the developing world. It is also far from clear whether the benefits of global or even inter-regional free trade will outweigh the costs for most of the countries of Africa, which have few comparative advantages in world markets. On the other hand, considerable benefits could be realized from a greater degree of intra-regional trade.

X

Xhosa

Major ethnic group or people of South Africa. African 'click' language spoken by Xhosa people.

Y

Yalá, Kumba

Former President of Guinea-Bissau. Presidential elections were held in December 1999 and were generally considered to have been free and fair. Kumba Yalá, the leader of the opposition, was elected in the second round with 72% of the vote and was inaugurated in February 2000. Yalá pledged to promote national reconciliation, balance the economy, restore production and give priority to **agriculture**. He also committed himself to reducing public spending and to cancelling ministerial perquisites. He favoured good relations with Senegal, Guinea, Portugal and France. However, relations between the former military junta of Ansumane Mané and Yalá's government were uneasy, with Mané regularly trying to usurp the President's powers. Matters finally came to a culmination in November 2000 when Mané (who was officially retired) tried to revoke the military promotions Yalá had instigated and proclaimed himself head of the armed forces. There was brief fighting in Bissau before loyalist troops prevailed. Mané escaped with a small number of followers. His body was later displayed on national television—it is highly likely that he was assassinated by government troops. In December 2001 the government announced that it had prevented a military coup. President Kumba Yalá dismissed the Prime Minister, Faustino Fudut Imbali, appointing Almara Nhassé as his replacement, and a new government was formed. Representatives of the government, political parties and civil organizations participated in a national reconciliation forum in April 2002. Yalá was ousted by the army in September 2003, in a bloodless coup. He was accused of undermining the political and economic stability of the country and on 17 September officially resigned the presidency. On 28 September **Henrique Pereira Rosa**, a business executive, and Artur Sanhá, were sworn in as interim President and Prime Minister, respectively.

Yaoundé Conventions

A series of agreements relating to the European Community's (EC) relationship with the **African, Caribbean and Pacific (ACP) countries**. The First Yaoundé Convention (1963) proceeded for bilateral negotiations between the members of the two groups. It was to run for five years and dealt with preferential access (mainly for primary products) to the European Economic Community (EEC) and the provision of aid. The Second Convention (1969) continued the same policy but by 1969 **Commonwealth** African countries were beginning to explore the possibility of a special relationship with the EEC. In 1973 Britain, Ireland and Denmark joined the EEC and lengthy negotiations commenced to enable Commonwealth countries also to become associates of the EEC. Forty-three ACP countries determined to negotiate as a bloc. The result was the first **Lomé Convention**.

Yassine, Sheikh Abdessalam

Morocco's main Islamic political leader. Under house arrest for some years, he was released in May 2000 but warned to be cautious when making any public statements.

Yoruba

Major ethnic group/people of south-west Nigeria. Also an ethnic and linguistic group in some other West African countries. In Benin, for example, the Yoruba constitute some 12% of the total population and Yoruba is one of the main languages.

Youlou, Abbé Fulbert

President of Congo-Brazzaville, who was overthrown in a popular revolution. Alphonse Massemba-Débat and then Marien Ngouabi took the country to the left, but the latter was assassinated in 1977 and the former shortly afterwards executed. President **Denis Sassou-Nguesso** of the **Parti congolais du travail (PCT—Congolese Labour Party)** kept both the pro-Russian and pro-Chinese parties under strict control, but his own ill-planned use of public funds and extravagant spending on grandiose projects debilitated the economy, increasing imports and foreign **debt** and exacerbating ethnic tensions.

Z

Zaire – *see also* Congo (Democratic Republic of the Congo)

Zaire is the country that was previously the Belgian Congo and then, after **independence** in 1960, the Democratic Republic of the Congo, until November 1965, when Col. Joseph-Désiré Mobutu assumed full executive powers and declared himself head of the 'Second Republic'. By 1970 Mobutu had eliminated almost all possible opposition, and in October 1971 the country was renamed the Republic of Zaire. The fall of Mobutu and his replacement by the leader of the rebel forces, Laurent-Désiré Kabila, who renamed the country the Democratic Republic of the Congo (DRC, as it had been in 1961–71), took place in May 1997. Since then the country has been known as the DRC.

Zambia, Republic of

The Republic of Zambia is a land-locked state in southern central Africa, bordered to the north by Tanzania and the Democratic Republic of the Congo (DRC), to the east by Malawi and Mozambique, to the south by Zimbabwe, Botswana and Namibia, and to the west by Angola. Zambia is 752,614 sq km in area. At mid-2003 the population was estimated at 10,812,000. There are more than 70 different ethnic groups in Zambia, of which the largest are the Bemba of the north east and the Copperbelt, the Nyanga of the east and Lusaka, the Tonga of the south and the Lozi in the west. The official language is English. The principal African languages are Nyanja, Bemba, Tonga, Lozi, Lunda and Luvale. Christians comprise an estimated 50% of the population and are roughly divided between Protestants and Roman Catholics. A sizeable proportion of the population follow traditional animist beliefs. Most Asians are Muslims, although some are Hindus. The capital is Lusaka, whose population was estimated at 1,394,315 in mid-2003.

Political profile

Under the provisions of the Constitution, which was formally adopted in May 1996, Zambia is a multi-party state. Executive power is vested in the President, who is the constitutional Head of State. Legislative power is vested in a National Assembly, which comprises 158 members, of whom 150 are elected by universal adult suffrage, and eight nominated by the President. The President and the National Assembly are elected simultaneously by universal adult suffrage for a five-year term. The maximum duration of the President's tenure of office is limited to two five-year terms. The President governs with the assistance of a Vice-President and a Cabinet, whom he appoints from members of the National Assembly. The Constitution also provides for a 27-member House of Chiefs, which represents traditional tribal authorities. Each of Zambia's nine provinces has a minister, who is appointed by the President.

In a presidential election held on 27 December 2001 **Levy Patrick Mwanawasa**, the candidate of the Movement for Multi-party Democracy (MMD), received 29.15% of the votes and was elected as President.

Following a legislative election held on 27 December 2001, the distribution of seats in the National Assembly was as follows: MMD 69; United Party for National Development (UPND) 49; Forum for Democracy and Development (FDD) 12; United National Independence Party (UNIP) 13; Heritage Party (HP) 4; Zambia Republican Party (ZRP) 1; Independents 1; Patriotic Front (PF) 1.

History

The Republic of Zambia gained **independence** from the United Kingdom on 24 October 1964. The UNIP, led by Dr **Kenneth Kaunda**, won elections held in 1964 and 1973. At the end of 1972 Zambia was declared a one-party state. In 1991 the National Council accepted Dr Kaunda's recommendation that multi-party elections be held. The elections were won by the MMD, led by former trade union leader **Frederick Chiluba**, who was elected as President. The UNIP became the main opposition party. The incoming government undertook to move towards more open government and greater **democracy**. One of its first actions was to lift the state of emergency, which had been in place for 27 years. Dr Kaunda, who had retired, returned to active politics in 1994. He regained the leadership of the UNIP at a party convention in June 1995. During the approach to the presidential and parliamentary elections held in November 1996, the government became increasingly intolerant of opposition. Two editors of the main independent newspaper were detained for writing articles critical of the government. In May 1996 the National Assembly enacted legislation that required presidential candidates to be of Zambian parentage (Kaunda's parents were Malawian) and limited Presidents to a maximum of two terms. Kaunda urged his followers to mount a campaign of civil disobedience. There were violent clashes with police at UNIP rallies. UNIP and a number of other smaller opposition parties boycotted the elections. Chiluba and the MMD won an emphatic victory, occupying 139 of the 158 seats in the National Assembly. In August 1997 Kaunda and an opposition ally were wounded at a UNIP rally on which police opened fire.

In October 1997 a small group of middle-ranking army officers, led by 'Capt. Solo', took over the media centre at the headquarters of the Zambia National Broadcasting Corporation. The Zambian army quickly restored order and detained the ringleaders of this attempted coup. President Chiluba declared a state of emergency (later extended by the National Assembly to May 1998), granting the police extraordinary powers. More than 100 people, including Kaunda and the leader of one of the other main opposition parties, were detained. Kaunda was charged with having had prior knowledge of the coup. The trial of all those charged began in June 1998. However, Kaunda and his security chief were discharged and immediately released. At the conclusion of the trial in September 1999, 58 soldiers were found guilty of treason and received mandatory sentences of life imprisonment. In early 2001 President Chiluba indicated that he might seek a third presidential term. However, a constitutional amendment would have been required to enable him to do so. In May 67 so-called anti-third term deputies in the National Assembly signed a motion to impeach Chiluba. On the following day Chiluba addressed the nation and declared that he would relinquish office at the end of his second term. In August he announced that the former Vice-President, Levy Patrick Mwanawasa, had been selected as the MMD's presidential candidate. Chiluba's third-term ambitions and the irregular nature of Mwanawasa's selection led to rifts within the MMD. Breakaway deputies formed new political parties, among them the HP, the FDD and the PF. Presidential and parliamentary elections were held in December 2001. Levy Mwanawasa of the MMD was declared the winner in early January 2002. The MMD emerged as the single largest party in the National Assembly, but, overall, the opposition parties occupied the largest number of seats. Observers of the election from the **European Union (EU)** and other monitoring groups were critical of the way the elections had been conducted. A rift between Mwanawasa and Chiluba, who remained president of the MMD until his resignation in March 2002, became evident soon after Mwanawasa assumed office. Mwanawasa instigated extensive reform and restructuring, removing many Chiluba loyalists from their positions. In August 2003 the immunity from prosecution of former President Chiluba was lifted and he was immediately charged with the theft of US $30m. while in office, as well as 200 other offences. In the same month several members of the opposition in the National Assembly initiated a motion to impeach President Mwanawasa. The attempt was unsuccessful, however, and those who organized the attempted impeachment were later ejected by Mwanawasa.

International relations

In June 2005, in recognition of Mwanawasa's pursuit of reforms, the EU resumed dialogue with and aid to Zambia. Zambia's relations with Zimbabwe under **Robert Mugabe** have been good. Chiluba often demonstrated solidarity with Mugabe, calling on other African leaders to oppose his 'persecution' by the international community. Mwanawasa has encouraged policies (e.g. the encouragement of commercial farming) at odds with those pursued by Mugabe, while, at the same time, offering him rhetorical support. The Zambian government was involved in efforts to resolve the ongoing conflict in the DRC—President Chiluba was appointed to co-ordinate peace initiatives by the **Southern African Development**

Community and the **Organization of African Unity**. Zambia was instrumental in formulating the 1999 Lusaka Accord. Zambia has remained host to tens of thousands of Congolese refugees who fled the DRC during the conflict there.

Zambia, economy

In 2003, according to estimates by the **World Bank**, Zambia's gross national income (GNI), measured at average 2001–03 prices, was US $4,124m., equivalent to $380 per head (or $850 per head on an international purchasing-power parity basis). During 1990–2003, it was estimated, the population increased at an average annual rate of 2.3%, while gross domestic product (GDP) per head decreased, in real terms, by an average of 0.7% per year. Overall GDP increased, in real terms, at an average annual rate of 1.5% in 1990–2003; growth in 2003 was 5.1%. In 1990–2003 the average annual rate of inflation was 50.3%. Consumer prices increased by an average of 21.4% in 2003. Mining, service industries, tourism, and **agriculture** are all important sectors of the economy. In 2004 the main markets for Zambia's exports were Tanzania, South Africa, the People's Republic of China, Japan, Thailand, Switzerland, Belgium and Malaysia. The main suppliers of imports in 2004 were South Africa, Zimbabwe and the United Arab Emirates. The national currency is the Zambian kwacha. In 2004 the average exchange rate was US $1 = 4,778.88 kwacha.

Zambia is a poor country, despite its mineral wealth. The economy is heavily dependent on **copper**, **cobalt**, and zinc mining. Copper and other metal exports account for about 75% of the country's foreign exchange earnings. A collapse in copper prices, **oil** price shocks, and misguided economic policies in the early 1970s had an extremely negative effect on the economy. These were compounded by the ongoing contraction of food production since **independence**. The resulting economic decline has been severe, with income per head declining by almost 5% annually in 1974–90. Eighty-five per cent of the population lives on less than $1 a day. Inequality is substantial.

On assuming power in 1991 the MMD government of **Frederick Chiluba** moved swiftly to liberalize the economy, setting in place an extensive programme of privatization and structural reform. In 1995 the economy was badly affected by the collapse of three banks, but Zambia nevertheless successfully completed an **International Monetary Fund (IMF)** Rights Accumulation Programme by December 1995 and qualified for an Enhanced Structural Adjustment Facility (ESAF) loan of $1,300m. The Paris Club, meeting in February 1996, agreed a rescheduling (on 'Naples terms') of Zambia's medium-term official bilateral **debt**. The pace of reform slowed in the second half of the 1990s and a number of issues, including weak governance and **corruption**, emerged to concern Zambia's creditors. A major issue was the delay in privatizing Zambia Consolidated Copper Mines (ZCCM), whose losses were huge owing to mismanagement, over-staffing, corruption and low world price of copper. Privatization was finally implemented in

March 2000, with the sale of most of ZCCM's assets. The UK government agreed a grant of $81m., designed to make the remaining nationalized asset, the Nkana smelter and refinery, commercially viable. Despite concern about the slow pace of reform, the IMF approved a three-year, $320m. **Poverty Reduction and Growth Facility** in the first quarter of 1999 and, at the same time, the World Bank approved a $173m. Public Sector Reform and Export Promotion credit. A $28m. Public Sector Capacity Building Programme credit, designed to improve public service delivery, was approved in 2000.

Zambia reached decision point under the enhanced **Heavily Indebted Poor Countries (HIPC) initiative** at the end of 2000, thereby qualifying for a two-thirds' reduction in its stock of debt. The UK government has confirmed its policy of full flow of **debt relief**. The Zambian government has produced a **Poverty Reduction Strategy Paper (PRSP)**, which was endorsed by the boards of the IMF and the World Bank in May 2002. The PRSP is intended to become the framework strategy by which government, donors and civil society will seek to achieve progress in reducing **poverty**. Successful implementation of the PRSP was a key condition for reaching completion point under HIPC and for continued assistance from the **Bretton Woods institutions** and the donor community. **Mwanawasa**'s pursuit of 'economic reform', the achievement of macroeconomic stability and a general pattern of economic growth of 3.5%–5.5% annually since 2000 have won him the support of foreign donors. In 2004 Zambia experienced its strongest period of economic growth as well as its lowest rate of inflation for 20 years, obliging the IMF to revise its economic forecasts for the country. An IMF mission in 2004 concluded that 'boosted by increased production in the mining, agriculture, construction and service sectors, real GDP is estimated to have increased by 5 percent in 2004, significantly above the budget target of 3.5%'. Following this upturn, the Paris Club agreed in May 2005 to annul $1,800m. of Zambia's debt in line with its successful implementation of the HIPC initiatives. Zambia's recent economic performance has been more promising after many years of stagnation and decline, and the government has maintained the PRGF on schedule. GDP growth in 2005 was more than 5.5% and export earnings apparently rose to $870m. in the second half of 2004. Debts have been cancelled—a total of $3,900m. under the IMF's HIPC initiative, as well as those owing to Paris Club creditors. The USA has chosen Zambia as one of 15 countries eligible for special emergency AIDS relief.

az-Zanati, Muhammad

Secretary of the General People's Congress in Libya.

Zanzibar

Islands (Zanzibar and **Pemba**) off the east coast of Africa, now part of the Union of Tanzania. The Sultan of Zanzibar was an Arab who was also Sultan of Muscat in Arabia, but had moved his capital to Zanzibar in 1840. Zanzibar and Muscat were separated in 1861, with the two sons of the Sultan setting up separate states and dynasties. Zanzibar became a British territory in 1890, in exchange for giving Heligoland to Germany, which maintained its presence on the mainland in Tanganyika as part of **German East Africa**, apart from a coastal strip some 10 miles in length, which included Mombasa and which Britain leased from the Sultan of Zanzibar in 1887. Elections held in 1961 had given control to a coalition of the Zanzibar National Party and the Zanzibar People's Party, but in 1963 the British transferred power to the Sultan and the Arab minority, with the result that Zanzibar carried into **independence** an inbuilt racial conflict in which the scales had been tipped in favour of a minority. In January 1964, the Afro-Shirazi Union seized power in a coup. This party, which represented the bulk of the African population of around 200,000 (the Arabs in Zanzibar numbering around 44,000), had suffered a set-back in the 1961 elections, but was not prepared to allow the islands to be governed by an unrepresentative minority. The Afro-Shirazi Union wanted neither the sultan nor any kind of Arab overlordship. Its leaders—Abeid Karume, Abdullah Hanga and Othman Sherif—led what was essentially an African, anti-Arab revolt and proclaimed a republic, with the first two as President and Vice-President respectively. Their allies in this reversal of power included a minor Arab party, the Umma Party, led by Abdul Rahman Muhammed Babu, the local correspondent of the New China News Agency, and a soldier-of-fortune, self-styled Field-Marshall John Okello. The Afro-Shirazis and their allies were soon branded as the tools of the People's Republic of China. **Julius Nyerere** sent his home minister and some armed police to take control of the situation and the British left one week after their arrival. In April 1964 Tanganyika and Zanzibar were joined together to constitute a new unified state, with Nyerere as President and Karume as senior Vice-President. In October the Union was named Tanzania. A new Constitution provided for a one-party state, and in September 1965 Nyerere was returned to power as President in the first one-party election. However, Nyerere was denied all influence in Zanzibar and Karume established an autocratic regime on the islands. In 1969 he secured the return to Zanzibar from the mainland of a number of political exiles and opponents, who were thereby condemned to death. Karume was, however, assassinated in 1972 and his successor, Aboud Jumbe, reorganized the islands' government, retaining a separate administration from that of the mainland and ruthlessly suppressing all opposition. In April 1977 the national assembly adopted a permanent Constitution for Tanzania, providing for the election of 10 Zanzibari representatives to the assembly; but in October 1979, the Supreme Revolutionary Council of Zanzibar adopted a separate Constitution, governing Zanzibar's internal administration. In early 1984 a political crisis developed in Zanzibar as a result of growing dissatisfaction with the Union, with demands for greater autonomy for the islands. Jumbe and three of his ministers resigned and in April, Ali Hassan Mwinyi was elected as President of Zanzibar and as a supporter of the Union made extensive changes to the Supreme Revolutionary Council. In January 1985 a new, more liberal constitution for the islands was introduced, providing for the House of Representatives to be directly elected by universal suffrage. When Julius Nyerere retired from office in 1985, Mwinyi took over as his successor, establishing a pattern of alternating mainland and Zanzibari Presidents of the United Republic of Tanzania. In Zanzibar Idris Abdul Wakil, former Speaker of the Zanzibari House of Representatives), was elected as President of Zanzibar to replace Mwinyi.

Mwinyi adopted a policy of economic liberalization—described by Nyerere as 'unplanned retreats from socialism'—with support from the **International Monetary Fund**. He held firm to this, despite considerable opposition and was vindicated when appointed chairman in 1990 of the **Chama Cha Mapinduzi (CCM—Revolutionary Party)**—which had been formed in 1977 through a merger of the Tanganyika African National Union (TANU) and the Afro-Shirazi Party (ASP). In October 1990 parliamentary and presidential elections were held in Zanzibar and the sole candidate for the presidency, Dr Salmin Amour was elected with 97.7% of the votes. National elections took place in the same month, and Mwinyi was re-elected for a second term, with 95.5% of the votes. At the beginning of 1993 it emerged that the Zanzibar government had unilaterally arranged for the islands to join the Organization of the Islamic Conference (OIC)—an action that infringed both the 1964 Articles of Union and the 1977 Union Constitution. In an atmosphere of worsening inter-communal tension, predominantly Christian mainlanders demanded the resignation of Mwinyi (a Muslim and a Zanzibari). In August Zanzibar withdrew from membership of the OIC but significant damage had been done to relations between the mainland and the islands. A motion put to the national assembly, providing for a separate administration for the mainland and Zanzibar, was passed but later rescinded. In order to provide for a more open expression of different political views, between 1993 and 1995, increasing numbers of opposition movements were officially recognized. Multi-party elections for the national assembly were held for the first time in October 1995, both in Zanzibar and throughout the Union. The CCM won 186 out of 232 seats, despite the growth of opposition parties and shortly afterwards, Benjamin Mkapa of the CCM, a candidate favoured by Nyerere (who continued to play an important political role behind the scenes) was elected President of the Union, with 62% of the votes. Omar Ali Juma, previously Chief Minister of Zanzibar, was appointed Vice-President.

In Zanzibar itself the CCM secured only 26 of the 50 seats in the House of Representatives, with the Civic United Front (CUF)—a party favouring Zanzibari autonomy—winning 24, including every constituency on Pemba. Dr Salmin Amour of the CCM narrowly won the presidential election (with 50.2% of the vote) against a CUF candidate (who polled 49.8% of the vote) and initiated a period of political repression in which the main target was the CUF. During December 1997 and January 1998, 18 members of the CUF were arrested on suspicion of conspiring to overthrow the Amour government. Tension remained high, despite mediation by representatives from the mainland and from the UN and the withholding of aid by international donors. In 2000 Amour indicated that he would seek re-election when his term of office as President came to an end later in the year, but attempts to alter the Constitution of Zanzibar to enable him to serve a third term of office were rejected by the CCM leadership. Tension increased, and in August the army deployed troops in Zanzibar, ostensibly to maintain security but, in the view of many—particularly the opposition—to control the CUF. Presidential and legislative elections were held in October but were widely condemned as fraudulent. Throughout late 2000 and early 2001 there were numerous demonstrations organized by the opposition, with serious clashes between the protestors and the armed police. At the end of January, in two days of violence, 40 people were killed, 100 injured and more than 400 arrested. In April 2001 an estimated 60,000 supporters of 12 opposition parties gathered peacefully in Dar es Salaam to demand new elections in Zanzibar, a new constitution for the United republic and independent electoral commissions. A 'peace accord' was signed between the CCM and CUF in Zanzibar in October 2001 and, despite some difficulties in the ensuing period, a number of proposed changes to the Zanzibari Constitution, increasing its clarity and transparency in regard to electoral matters, were approved by the House of Representatives in April 2002.

az-Zawahiri, Ayman

Leader of the Egyptian **Islamic Jihad**, also a founding member of al-Qa'ida. Zawahiri has reportedly had a huge impact on **Osama bin Laden**'s thinking—politically, militarily and religiously. At about this time, the terror war essentially turned into a religious war: the fundamental Islamic militants versus the world, with the USA, Saudi Arabia and Egypt being the prime targets. In essence, Zawahiri became bin Laden's political thinker, religious leader, organizer and planner. Because Zawahiri could not reverse the trend toward his main target, Egypt, he managed to convince bin Laden that the principal target for disruption was the USA because of its interference in the Middle East—particularly in Egypt and Saudi Arabia. Both Zawahiri and bin Laden sought to bring about a world dominated by their brand of **Islam**. The seeds were planted in Saudi Arabia, Egypt, Somalia, Yemen, Afghanistan, and, because of its geographic location and religious bent, Pakistan. Bin Laden had access to the necessary funding for the group's activities, while Zawahiri had the knowledge, experience, and organizational abilities to carry out those activities. Over the years the Egyptian Jihad groups had gained experience in secret work, cell building and organization. Their ranks were populated with well-trained scientists, engineers, medical personnel and seasoned fighters. Because of their talent and experience, these Egyptian Jihad groups took control of al-Qa'ida Egyptian Jihad. It is important to note that Zawahiri places a high premium on recruiting well-educated individuals. Those interested in joining al-Qa'ida Egyptian Jihad were subjected to a battery of tests, which were basically intelligence tests. Those who scored well were chosen and trained in special camps, while those who performed poorly were sent to more basic boot camps.

Zenawi, Meles

Prime Minister of Ethiopia, who toppled the **Dergue** in 1991 and established a more open, albeit still effectively one-party state under the ruling Ethiopian People's Revolutionary Party (EPRDF). Born in 1954, Meles joined the fight against the Mengistu regime in the 1970s. Upon Mengistu's overthrow, he was chosen as transitional Head of State and was one of the architects of the 1994 Constitution, which provided for a federal republic with ethnically-based regions. In 1995 he became Prime Minister. Initially a Marxist-Leninist, by the 1990s he had become ostensibly a proponent of the free market and parliamentary **democracy**, but at the same time managed to retain a high degree of authority and control, making use of repressive methods to maintain the dominance of the EPRDF over Ethiopian politics.

Ki-Zerbo, Gen. Saye

Seized power in **Upper Volta** in 1980 to become Head of State. Ki-Zerbo was replaced by a civilian government, which was itself ousted in 1983 by **Thomas Sankara**, who changed the country's name to Burkina Faso.

Zéroual, Liamine

A former general who was brought out of retirement to serve as President of Algeria from January 1994, after the assassination of **Mohammed Boudiaf**. Zéroual was elected as President in November 1995 and remained in office until April 1999. He presided over the period of most intense conflict in Algeria since the declaration of a state of emergency in 1992. He fielded a succession of governments of varying political complexions, all of which implemented **International Monetary Fund** programmes agreed in May 1995 out of necessity, but without any vision of comprehensive reform, much less of political institutions to sustain it. While macroeconomic indicators showed improvements, the state of the real economy deteriorated and the country remained gripped by political conflict. In 1999 Zéroual was replaced by **Abdelaziz Bouteflika** after all six of his rivals in the presidential election withdrew, alleging electoral fraud.

Zimbabwe, Republic of

The Republic of Zimbabwe is a land-locked state in southern Africa, with Mozambique to the east, Zambia to the north-west, Botswana to the south-west and South Africa to the south. Zimbabwe is 390,757 sq km in area. At mid-2003 the population was estimated at 12,891,000. The majority of the population (70%) belong to the **Shona** ethnic group, and about one-fifth to the **Ndebele**. The official languages are English, Chishona and Sindebele. About 55% of the population are Christians. A large number of the African population follow traditional beliefs, while the Asian minority comprises both Muslims and Hindus. The capital is Harare, whose population was estimated at 1,469,149 at mid-2003.

Political profile

Under the terms of the 1980 Constitution (as subsequently amended), legislative power is vested in a unicameral Parliament, consisting of a House of Assembly, which comprises 150 members, of whom 120 are directly elected by universal adult suffrage, 20 are nominated by the President, 10 are traditional Chiefs and eight are provincial governors. Members of the House of Assembly serve for five years. Executive authority is vested in the President, elected by Parliament for six years. The President appoints, and acts on the advice of, a Cabinet, which comprises two Vice-Presidents and other Ministers and Deputy Ministers. The Cabinet must have the confidence of Parliament, to which it is responsible.

In a presidential election held on 9–11 March 2002 **Robert Gabriel Mugabe** received 56.2% of the votes and was re-elected as President. Mugabe was first inaugurated as Zimbabwe's (executive) President in 1987, on the retirement of **Rev. Canaan Banana**. He was re-elected in 1990, 1996 and 2002.

Following an election held on 31 March 2005, the (provisional) distribution of seats in the House of Assembly was as follows: **Zimbabwe African National Union—Patriotic Front (ZANU—PF)** 78; **Movement for Democratic Change (MDC)** 41; Independent 1.

History

The 1965 **Unilateral Declaration of Independence (UDI)** by Ian Smith's Rhodesian Front government led to international economic sanctions and a long guerrilla war. After the failure of the 1978 'internal settlement' nominally headed by Bishop Muzorewa, the British government organized a constitutional conference at Lancaster House in 1979. The conference resulted in an agreement to grant **independence** to **Rhodesia**. In December an interim UK administration was formed to supervise the cease-fire and parliamentary elections. Mugabe's ZANU—PF won 57 of the 80 seats reserved for black candidates under the new Constitution. This brought the guerrilla war and 15 years of international isolation to an end. In April 1980 Zimbabwe achieved independence, the last of Britain's African colonies to do so. The Zimbabwe government later changed the original 'Westminster-style' Constitution that came into effect at independence. The most significant changes were the abolition of the Senate to create a single chamber House of Assembly, and the replacement of the non-executive Head of State by an executive President (to which position President Mugabe was first elected in 1987). The early 1980s were marked by tension between the government and supporters of **Joshua Nkomo**'s Patriotic Front—Zimbabwe African People's Union (PF—ZAPU), which was based around the Ndebele people of Matabeleland. Thousands of Ndebele were killed in a government crack-down, creating serious antagonisms which remain to this day. In 1986 moves began to effect a reconciliation between PF—ZAPU and the governing ZANU—PF. This culminated in the unification of the two parties in 1987, when PF—ZAPU was effectively absorbed by ZANU—PF.

At least five opposition parties boycotted the parliamentary elections held in 1995, claiming that they would not be free and fair. Only ZANU—Ndonga and the Forum Party presented more than one candidate to challenge ZANU—PF. Fifty-five ZANU—PF candidates were unopposed and subsequently declared to have been elected. ZANU—PF won 118 of the 120 contested seats and ZANU—Ndonga won two seats in Manicaland. A turn-out of 57% was recorded. There were no reports of violence or intimidation during voting. However Margaret Dongo, a former ZANU—PF candidate who contested the election as an independent, successfully applied to the High Court for the election to be re-run in Harare South constituency owing to an irregularity. In November she successfully contested a by-election there to become the third opposition deputy. The presidential election held on 16–17 March 1996 was contested by President Mugabe unopposed after Bishop Abel Muzorewa and Rev. Ndabaningi Sithole withdrew from the poll. Official results indicated that Mugabe received 93% of the votes cast in a turn-out of 32%.

In June 1999 President Mugabe appointed a constitutional commission to draw up a new constitution to replace the one agreed at Lancaster House. The commission consulted widely and people were encouraged to make their views known. Commission members contested parts of the draft constitution. Without a formal vote, the commission presented the draft to the President. The government amended the draft to include a provision that the 'former colonial power' should compensate farmers for land acquired as part of its proposed land resettlement programme. The new draft constitution was submitted to a referendum in February 2000. More than one-half (53%) of those who participated in the referendum voted against the draft constitution. Nevertheless, the ruling party pushed an amendment to the Constitution through the parliament on 6 April 2000, attempting to place an obligation on the former colonial power to pay compensation for any land acquired by the government for resettlement.

In 1980 the government of Zimbabwe established the goal of acquiring 8.3m. ha of land from the white commercial farming sector and resettling 162,000 households by 1990. In this period, with financial support from the UK government, the Zimbabwe government resettled 66,000 households—mainly **refugees**, displaced people and the landless poor—on approximately 3m. ha of land. Some beneficiaries received small plots of land, while others were grouped together as small co-operatives.

In 1990, when constitutional restrictions on land acquisition lapsed, the government formulated a new land policy. It enacted the Land Acquisition Act in 1992, which enabled it to limit the size of farms and compulsorily acquire land by paying 'fair compensation'. The government also reoriented its land policy to favour 'more capable' farmers at the expense of the landless poor. Additionally, the policy aimed to establish a strategic black commercial farming sector through distribution of large plots to blacks. The scheme lacked transparency and was perceived in some quarters to be a mechanism for rewarding party officials and their associates. Ultimately, very little resettlement of poor Zimbabweans took place in the 1990s. Academic studies have found that the government's performance on land reform was inconsistent, ineffective and inegalitarian. The government failed to make land reform a national priority and lacked the vision and the technical capacity to appreciably advance the needs of the landless poor. It also failed to grant small black farmers secure tenure or freehold title.

In July 2000 the government launched a 'fast track' land reform programme. This aimed to resettle 162,000 families on 5m. ha of white-owned farm land within four years. The programme was widely perceived as a politically-motivated attack on those whom the ruling party judged to support the opposition MDC, and as a mechanism to improve President Mugabe's prospects of successfully contesting the presidential election scheduled for 2002.

The 'fast track' programme lacked transparency and fairness, and without the required infrastructural inputs (seed, water, fertilizer) has proved unsustainable. In addition, the programme apparently gave little consideration to the effects of resettlement on farm workers and their families, who were made homeless. Furthermore, the 'fast track' programme has been associated with state-sponsored violent occupations of land by 'war veterans', the slaughter of livestock, the destruction of seed-beds, the spread of bovine diseases and the destruction of wildlife sanctuaries. A state of lawlessness still prevails in many rural areas. The consequences for Zimbabwe's food production and tourism industry have been devastating. In 2004, none the less, the government announced its intention to nationalize all farmland.

In October 2000 a UN Development Programme Experts Report confirmed donors' concerns that people were being 'dumped' on land without support and without important infrastructural and tilling inputs. The report found that there was no land reform plan as such and that the 'fast track' approach was not feasible. For these reasons, the international community has been unable to offer support. In late 2000 the UN Development Programme (UNDP) proposed to the Zimbabwe government that it should adjust the 'fast track' resettlement programme in accordance with the country's capacity to implement it. The UNDP also proposed independent monitoring of the situation in commercial farming areas; the promotion of internal dialogue; and the possible resumption of UNDP technical assistance. UNDP stressed the importance of transparent, just and fair land reform that respects the rule of law and is in accordance with the principles agreed at the 1998 Land Conference and the laws of Zimbabwe. The government's reply suggested that it was not willing to compromise on the major issues obstructing re-engagement by the international community.

A grouping of **Commonwealth** foreign ministers met in Abuja, Nigeria, on 6 September 2001 to discuss the situation in Zimbabwe. On land reform, they agreed that reform must be implemented in a fair, just and sustainable manner, in the interest of all the people of Zimbabwe, and that any land reform programme should be on the basis of the UNDP proposals of December 2000. The government agreed to honour the principles enshrined in the Harare Commonwealth Declaration, to prevent further occupation of farmland, to restore the rule of law, to take firm action against violence and intimidation and to honour the freedom of expression. At that meeting the United Kingdom reaffirmed its commitment to a significant financial contribution to such a land reform programme and gave an undertaking to encourage other international donors to do the same.

In November 2001 the government amended its Land Acquisition Act to allow it to allocate land without giving owners the right to contest seizures. This contravened the letter and spirit of what had been agreed at Abuja. The wider credibility of Abuja has been damaged by Zimbabwe's scant regard for its commitments since the agreement was signed. In the run-up to the presidential election held in March 2002, the ruling party intensified its campaign of violence and intimidation against the opposition and introduced draconian legislation to suppress freedom of expression. The human rights organization Amnesty International reported that more than 100 politically motivated killings had occurred in 2001, the vast majority of them of opposition supporters. The violence and killings continued after the election. The **European Union (EU)**, the Commonwealth and the USA have all imposed sanctions on Zimbabwe.

The MDC, which is the main opposition party in Zimbabwe, was formed in 1999. It has its roots mainly in Zimbabwe's trade union movement, civil society and professional groups, although it is a broad coalition of all those advocating political change. Its leader is **Morgan Tsvangirai**. The MDC contested the legislative elections held in June 2000. The pre-election period was marred by politically-motivated violence and intimidation, and the vote itself by allegations of malpractice by the ruling party. The MDC won all of the urban areas and most of Matabeleland and Manicaland. Of the 120 contested seats, ZANU—PF won 62, the MDC 57 and ZANU—Ndonga one. The MDC mounted legal challenges to the official results in 37 constituencies, alleging vote-rigging and systematic pre-election violence by the ruling party. It subsequently won a number of its petitions, and others are still being considered. About 400 international observers monitored the election. Almost one-half of these were from the EU. Their report concluded that ZANU—PF had been responsible for the bulk of the pre-election violence, and that although the polling day itself was mostly orderly, the use of violence by ZANU—PF had created serious doubts about the fairness of Zimbabwe's electoral process. None the less, for the first time Zimbabwe had a sizeable parliamentary opposition that was able to block constitutional amendments.

Morgan Tsvangirai also contested the presidential election held in March 2002. The pre-election period was again marred by political violence. Thirty members of the opposition were killed in the first quarter of 2002 and there were many reported cases of members of the opposition having been attacked and tortured. The election was deemed neither free nor fair by a broad swathe of international opinion, including the **Southern African Development Community** Parliamentary Forum and the Commonwealth. The reaction to the election among African countries was mixed. Some, including Senegal and Ghana, were critical. Others, such as Tanzania and Namibia, judged the election to have been free and fair. The election period was characterized by a campaign of violence waged against the opposition by the ruling party; manipulation of both the electoral administration and the count; and draconian restrictions on freedom of speech, movement, association and assembly. ZANU—PF attacked the judiciary and harassed the independent media. It also prevented EU observers from being able to observe the election and the EU withdrew its team. The EU and USA imposed targeted sanctions on the regime before the election. New Zealand, Australia, Canada, Switzerland, Norway and Liechtenstein have also applied sanctions. The Commonwealth suspended Zimbabwe from its Councils on 19 March 2002. In April South African and Nigerian facilitators were appointed to facilitate inter-party talks in Zimbabwe. A meeting between the two parties was scheduled for 13 May 2002, but ZANU—PF withdrew shortly before then and has refused to re-engage in dialogue.

Three crucial pieces of legislation were enacted prior to the presidential election of March 2002: The Public Order and Security Act replaced the Law and Order (Maintenance) Act, originally introduced by the Rhodesian authorities. The new Act makes it difficult for the opposition to campaign and effectively destroys freedom of expression. An Electoral Act has prevented opponents of the ruling party from campaigning or demonstrating and has undermined the electoral process. The third piece of legislation—the Access to Information Act—targeted the independent media through the establishment of a state-appointed Media and Information Commission. The Act made it difficult for foreign journalists to gain press accreditation and forced all Zimbabwean journalists to obtain annual 'licences'. Among other draconian provisions, it became an offence to defame the President.

In June 2003 the leader of the MDC, Morgan Tsvangirai, was arrested twice during a week of opposition protests. He was charged with treason, adding to an existing treason charge from 2002 arising from an alleged plot to kill President Mugabe. In July 2004 the High Court postponed judgment on his trial indefinitely.

In the most recent legislative election, held in March 2005, ZANU—PF regained some of the ground it had lost to the MDC in 2000.

International relations

At the end of August 1998 Zimbabwe deployed troops to the Democratic Republic of the Congo (DRC). These were withdrawn in late 2002 following the signing of a peace agreement in the DRC.

Zimbabwe was suspended from the Councils of the Commonwealth in March 2002, following a Commonwealth election observers' report, which stated that 'the conditions in Zimbabwe did not adequately allow for a free expression of will by the electors'.

Zimbabwe, economy

In 2001, according to the **World Bank**, Zimbabwe's gross national income (GNI), measured at average 1999–2001 prices, was US $8,811m., equivalent to

$480 per head (or $2,180 per head on an international purchasing-power parity basis). During 1990–2003, it was estimated, the population increased at an average annual rate of 1.9%, while gross domestic product (GDP) per head decreased, in real terms, by an average of 1.9% per year during 1990–2002. Overall GDP increased, in real terms, at an average annual rate of 0.1% in 1990–2002; GDP declined by 8.4% in 2001 and by 5.6% in 2002. The rate of inflation averaged 98.8% annually in 1995–2003. Consumer prices increased by an average of 598.7% in 2003. In 2004 the main markets for Zimbabwe's exports were South Africa, Zambia and the People's Republic of China (PRC). The main suppliers of imports in that year were South Africa, the Democratic Republic of the Congo and the PRC. The national currency is the Zimbabwe dollar (Z.$). In 2003 the average exchange rate was US $1 = Z.$697.4240.

Zimbabwe has traditionally been the second most industrialized country in the southern African region. Well-developed infrastructure and financial systems were inherited at **independence**. For many years Zimbabwe's income per caput was significantly higher than that of most sub-Saharan African countries. At its peak in 1992, manufacturing accounted for 27% of GDP (it has now fallen below 15%). Commercial farming (producing tobacco, meat, **cotton**, maize, sugar and plants) has been export-oriented, accounting for around 19% of GDP, and earning 40% of the country's foreign exchange. Mining (of **gold**, ferrous alloys, asbestos and nickel) accounts for about 33% of exports.

With the support of the **International Monetary Fund (IMF)**, Zimbabwe launched an Economic Structural Adjustment Programme (ESAP) in 1991 after a decade of pursuing socialist economic policies. The IMF considered a new programme of support in 1997, but following the announcement of extraordinary compensation for so-called 'war veterans', amounting to some 3% of GDP, disbursement of new IMF funds was placed on hold. The government agreed a Standby Arrangement (SBA) with the IMF in both June 1998 and August 1999, but on both occasions failed to meet agreed targets, resulting in a halt to disbursements. In 2000 Zimbabwe went into arrears to the World Bank, and in February 2001 to the IMF. Until the arrears position is cleared, neither institution can disburse any funds to Zimbabwe. In June 2002 the IMF declared Zimbabwe to be in 'non-co-operation'. In September 2002 it took steps to revoke Zimbabwe's voting rights and withdrew completely from Zimbabwe in 2003. In February 2005 the IMF attempted to achieve a reconciliation with the Harare authorities, in order to avert Zimbabwe's expulsion from the Fund. This conciliatory move followed efforts made by Zimbabwe during the previous year to comply with the IMF's demands, including down-payments of $16.5m.

Zimbabwe's economy is now in crisis. For the past two years the country's economic performance has been the worst in Africa. The economy has contracted for three years and appears likely to weaken further in 2005. The rate of inflation is about 133%, interest rates are unsustainably low, and the rate of unemployment is higher than 70%. The economic decline has been caused largely by years of government **corruption** and mismanagement. This has been compounded by disruption to the crucial agricultural sector, where the government has sanctioned invasions of commercial farms by its supporters who often have no farming expertise, precipitating a collapse in investor confidence and capital flight.

Mugabe has described the land seizures as one of the greatest achievements since independence. However, such an assessment leaves out of account food shortages and the state of the economy as a whole, which has almost halved since 2000. In March 2005 it was reported that 44% of the land seized was no longer being cultivated. Seventy per cent of the people are now unemployed and live in **poverty**. After the recent elections, **Morgan Tsvangirai**, the leader of the opposition **Movement for Democratic Change**, described the country's experience since independence and the years under Mugabe (since 1965) as 'a period of sustained economic decline'.

The tobacco crop, once the core of the Zimbabwean export economy, was 70% smaller in 2005 than it was in 2000, when the government's 'fast track' seizures of 5,000 farms began. The quality of the tobacco is reported to have declined and international buyers are offering lower prices. There is also a chronic shortage of foreign exchange, which has led to shortages of fuel and other key inputs including power (Zimbabwe imports 35% of its electricity from Mozambique and South Africa, but is heavily indebted to both countries and cannot afford to pay for further supplies). At the beginning of May 2005 the critical shortage of foreign exchange was evident, when the state offered only \$11m. at its weekly auction. The requirement of fuel importers alone was \$230m. In mid-2005 the Zimbabwe dollar was significantly overvalued on the official market and most foreign exchange is now traded on the parallel market. Tourism, once a major source of foreign exchange, had declined by 80% compared with 1999. The IMF will reassess Zimbabwe in late 2005 and proceed with withdrawal if the government has not taken steps to comply with its conditions. Zimbabwe also has one of the highest **HIV/AIDS** prevalence rates in the world—24% of the adult population. This is having a severe economic impact.

Food shortages have reached a dangerous level. In January 2005 President Mugabe ordered the UN to halt its survey of crops and to dramatically reduce its food distribution programme. Consequently, the **World Food Programme (WFP)** cut its provision of food from 5m. people to 1m., concentrating on children orphaned by AIDS, older people and other vulnerable groups. In June, however, Mugabe agreed to allow the UN to increase its food aid to Zimbabwe, but under tight restrictions. The WFP would not be allowed to distribute food directly to the general population, but would be limited to school feeding programmes, home-based AIDS care and food-for-work schemes. Mugabe stated that Zimbabwe would welcome imports of 1.2m. tons of food, but stopped short of formally requesting assistance. Zimbabwe has been badly affected by shortages of vital supplies, including fuel and even its staple, maize. In May 1.2m. tons of maize was being bought from abroad, although it was unclear how this would be paid for in view of the lack of foreign exchange. Aid agencies estimated that about 4m. people, one-third of the population, would need food aid. In July President Mugabe, who had previously indicated that Zimbabwe did not need assistance, requested a loan of hundreds of millions of dollars from South Africa for food, fuel and electricity purchases. In August it was reported that efforts to secure a $1,000m. from the PRC to relieve Zimbabwe's shortfall of fuel, food and power, had failed, causing the value of the Zimbabwean dollar to fall to its lowest level ever.

Zimbabwe African National Union (ZANU)

In 1972 the forces of the Zimbabwe African national Union (ZANU) began a sustained guerrilla attack on the existing regime in **Rhodesia**. The ZANU was led by **Robert Mugabe**. In 1976 ZANU joined with the Zimbabwe African People's Union (ZAPU), led by **Joshua Nkomo**, to form the Patriotic Front (PF). In 1978 the white government of Ian Smith in Rhodesia arranged an 'internal settlement', but the PF vowed to continue the struggle. In the following year Britain convened a constitutional conference in London and a settlement was finally reached. In 1980 Zimbabwe became independent and Robert Mugabe of ZANU became Prime Minister.

Zimbabwe African National Union—Patriotic Front) (ZANU—PF)

The Zimbabwe African Patriotic Front (ZAPU) was a political movement, led by **Joshua Nkomo**, which, like the **Zimbabwe African National Union (ZANU)**, embarked on an armed struggle to overthrow the white regime in **Rhodesia**. In 1976 it joined with its rival organization, the ZANU, to form the Patriotic Front. After Zimbabwe's **independence**, and **Robert Mugabe**'s appointment as Prime Minister, Joshua Nkomo and the ZAPU began to be sidelined and eventually effectively merged with ZANU to become ZANU—PF.

Zulu

People of **southern Africa**. Well known for their resistance to British intervention in southern Africa—in the Zulu Wars—and for their leader, Chaka. One of the most famous encounters between the Zulu and British forces was the battle that took place at Rourke's Drift. The Zulu retained their specific identity in part through territorial specificity—there continued to be an identifiable **Zululand**, Kwa-Zulu—throughout the colonial period and under the **apartheid** regime to emerge as a coherent political force in the struggle against white rule.

Zululand

The homeland of the Zulu people—Kwa-Zulu—in the south-eastern part of South Africa.

Zuma, Jacob

Deputy President of South Africa until June 2005. A **Zulu** with little formal education, Zuma rose to become head of intelligence of the **African National Congress (ANC)** after having been imprisoned for 10 years during the struggle against **apartheid**. He gained recognition for helping to achieve a reconciliation between the ANC and the Zulu-dominated **Inkatha Freedom Party**. In June 2005 he faced calls for his resignation after his former financial adviser, Schabir Shaik, was found guilty of **corruption** and was sentenced to 15 years' imprisonment. The National Prosecuting Authority subsequently announced that it was considering pressing charges against Zuma. On 14 June 2005 President **Thabo Mbeki** informed the National Assembly that he had decided to dismiss his deputy and potential successor for corruption, even though Zuma had not been charged with any crime.